DATE DUE

DEMCO 38-297

FIFTH EDITION

JUVENILE JUSTICE

KÄREN M. HESS, Ph.D.
Normandale Community College

With contributions by **Christine Hess Orthmann, M.S.**
Orthmann Writing and Research, Inc.

Miller-Motte College
Fayetteville Campus

WADSWORTH
CENGAGE Learning™

Australia • Brazil • Japan • Korea • Mexico • Singapore • Spain • United Kingdom • United States

WADSWORTH
CENGAGE Learning™

Juvenile Justice, Fifth Edition
Kären M. Hess

Publisher: Linda Schreiber

Senior Acquisitions Editor:
    Carolyn Henderson Meier

Assistant Editor: Erin Abney

Editorial Assistant: John Chell

Media Editor: Ting Jian Yap

Marketing Manager: Michelle Williams

Marketing Assistant: Jillian Myers

Senior Marketing Communications
    Manager: Tami Strang

Content Project Manager: Christy Krueger

Creative Director: Rob Hugel

Senior Art Director: Maria Epes

Print Buyer: Judy Inouye

Rights Acquisitions Account
    Manager, Text: Bob Kauser

Rights Acquisitions Account
    Manager, Images: Robyn Young

Production Service: Sara Dovre Wudali,
    Buuji, Inc.

Photo Researcher: Terri Wright

Copy Editor: Linda Ireland

Cover Designer: RHDG/Tim Heraldo

Cover Image: Duane A. Laverty/AP Images

Compositor: Pre-PressPMG

For product information and technology assistance, contact us at
Cengage Learning Customer & Sales Support, 1-800-354-9706

For permission to use material from this text or product,
submit all requests online at **www.cengage.com/permissions.**
Further permissions questions can be e-mailed to
permissionrequest@cengage.com

Library of Congress Control Number: 2009925248

ISBN-13: 978-0-495-50438-5

ISBN-10: 0-495-50437-8

Wadsworth
10 Davis Drive
Belmont, CA 94002-3098
USA

Cengage Learning is a leading provider of customized learning solutions with office locations around the globe, including Singapore, the United Kingdom, Australia, Mexico, Brazil, and Japan. Locate your local office at **www.cengage.com/global**

Cengage Learning products are represented in Canada by Nelson Education, Ltd.

To learn more about Wadsworth, visit **www.cengage.com/wadsworth**

Purchase any of our products at your local college store or at our preferred online store **www.ichapters.com**

Printed in the United States of America
1 2 3 4 5 6 7 13 12 11 10 09

Brief Contents

Contents

PART II:

 OUR NATION'S YOUTHS

**Chapter 4: Youth in Society: Developmental Risks and
               Protective Factors 90**

PART III:

 THE CONTEMPORARY JUVENILE
JUSTICE SYSTEM

Chapter 8: The Police and Juveniles   233

Foreword

The juvenile justice system—and there are those who would put quotation marks around "system"—has several specialized components. Each component has long been used to autonomy. Each too often has only superficial knowledge of the other components. And the components seldom work together, even though each may be managing the same problem.

The system should be more than this. Our children are entitled to more. Their lives and their parents' lives are greatly affected by the agencies' responses to their problems. Unfortunately the responses often are unintentionally inconsistent and noncomplementary.

For the system to improve it must know itself. And that means that each professional within each component must know the functions and functioning of all other professionals in the system as they relate to the delinquency, misconduct and neglect of children. At the least the classic function of each component must be recognized.

- *The police*—must protect the safety of children and the public and investigate the behavioral facts.
- *Welfare and probation services*—must investigate the social facts and provide inpatient and outpatient counseling and supervision of children and their parents.
- *Schools*—must educate children academically and, to a great extent, socially and must ensure peace within their walls.
- *Lawyers*—must stand for their clients, advocating the views of each, whatever they may be.
- *Service providers*—must have treatments that can reunite families and prevent a recurrence of the misconduct that initiated the public's intervention.
- *The court*—must arbitrate and insist on rehabilitative and protective dispositions, and must use force and power within the confines of statutes and the Constitution to ensure due execution of these dispositions.

Each should perform its function knowledgeable of what the others are or may do and of the impact each may have on the others. There needs to be a coordination, a flow, a focus on the child and the family.

Beyond this primary interagency knowledge and respect, there must exist within families—whether the children's own or ones found for them or provided by the streets—solid values, caring and stability. Youths will reflect the values and stability of their families. Therefore the system cannot focus only on the child. It must look at the affective family for its influence on both the causes and the rehabilitation of misconduct, whether it be delinquency, status offenses or inadequate parental care.

Each component must look at the family as it affects its own particular function but, more, it must share its investigation and consider the investigations of others, moving toward a collaborative disposition involving the family that will be the most effective for the children.

And even this is not enough. Each professional working with children must understand children, their behavioral patterns and psychological development, and their changing emotional needs as they mature, seek independence and acquire sexual appetites. They must understand that boys don't become truant just because they don't like school, and that they join gangs because gangs can better satisfy emotional needs that their families have not. Children are not small adults. Legally, they lack the maturity to make important judgments under the stress of changing bodies and with the insistent need for independence.

The juvenile justice system must understand itself and become a system in the true sense of the word, working together toward the common goal of assisting children in trouble and protecting them and the public. The juvenile justice system must know itself. This book can be its primer.

Judge Emeritus Lindsay G. Arthur

Preface

*J*uvenile Justice, Fifth Edition, is a practical, applied text designed to introduce students to the juvenile justice system as it exists today, including the tremendous heterogeneity found among jurisdictions throughout the country. This completely revised edition provides students with an understanding of the complex amalgam of programs, policies, practices and philosophies that, together, comprise "the juvenile justice system" and the myriad challenges the system faces at this critical point in time. Budgets and resources are stretched thin, caseloads and court dockets in jurisdictions across the country are overwhelmed, and many families are struggling to hold themselves together. Juvenile crime, which had steadily tracked downward from 1994 to 2004, has shown a slight increase in recent years. There is tremendous demand from all sides to make the juvenile justice system more efficient and effective. But in the midst of all of these pressures are new revelations regarding adolescent brain development, new data regarding which interventions are effective, new assessment tools to help practitioners better meet the needs of youth who come in contact with the system—new reasons to hope that juvenile justice can, indeed, accomplish the multiple goals of serving youth in need and those who become delinquent, while protecting society and helping restore victims and communities. But a new direction is needed.

The Approach of This Text

A sea change is occurring in juvenile justice. Interestingly, it has less to do with charting new territory than it does returning to its roots. More than a century ago, a separate justice system for juveniles was established, based on the belief that children were developmentally distinct from adults and deserved to be treated as such by the state. Over the past 30 years, however, this system has progressively eroded to become increasingly more similar to the adult criminal justice system. Today, it can be said the juvenile justice system is in the midst of an identity crisis. But there is reason for optimism.

When the first edition of this text was published in 1990, violent juvenile crime was on an upward trend and the "get tough" movement was taking hold. Across the country, legislators and policymakers, spurred by a fearful public's demands to crack down on juvenile crime, implemented increasingly punitive sanctions for youthful offenders and allowed the relatively well-defined boundaries between the juvenile and criminal justice systems to become progressively more porous. Today, 15 years beyond the mid-1990s peak in violent juvenile crime and armed with decades of research about the effects of "get tough" measures, the juvenile justice system is beginning to realize that this response has not achieved what it was set in place to do.

One of the overriding themes of this text, paralleling a fundamental trend in the field, is the need to refocus on treating juveniles as juveniles. Without question, there are youths who are violent, dangerous predators and who need to be, based on the gravity of their offenses and the priority of public safety, processed in the criminal justice system. However, for many youths who encounter the system, such a response is inappropriate. Research in developmental neurology provides compelling evidence that adolescence is a period of profound brain growth and cognitive maturing, as neural wiring related to impulsivity, risk-and-consequence assessment, and decision-making skills is not completed until the average person is in his or her mid-20s. These findings have led many researchers and policymakers to push for system reforms that will reflect recent research in adolescent development.

Another basic theme of this text is the need to take a systemic approach to juvenile justice issues. Problems with children do not occur in isolation; they occur within an environment of many interactive parts. The family, the school, peers and the community as a whole—all influence how a child develops and grows into an adult. Educators, counselors, social workers, law enforcement officers, attorneys, judges, probation officers and correctional service providers—each makes an important contribution in working to achieve the common goals of preventing or reducing juvenile crime and victimization.

Juvenile justice today stands at a critical crossroads. The failures of the past have caused some to declare the system ineffective and obsolete, broken beyond repair and better off dismantled. Others, however, see a system full of potential but in desperate need of reform and a return to its rehabilitative roots. Very few believe juvenile justice should stay "as is," operating to maintain the status quo. The time is ripe for change in this field.

Organization of the Text

Part I of this text provides an overview of juvenile justice from its origins, to its philosophical and theoretical bases. It begins with definitions of juvenile justice, how delinquency is measured and the juvenile justice process itself (Chapter 1). Next, the history and philosophy behind the juvenile justice evolution is explained (Chapter 2). The section concludes with theories of what causes delinquency and juvenile offending (Chapter 3).

Part II describes the nation's youths in society and the developmental risk and protective factors they may encounter (Chapter 4). This is followed by a discussion of juvenile victims, including those who are neglected, abused and missing (Chapter 5); juvenile offenders (Chapter 6) and youth gangs (Chapter 7).

Part III takes an up-close look at the contemporary juvenile justice system and its three major components: law enforcement, the juvenile court and juvenile corrections. The first area of discussion focuses on the law enforcement response to abused/neglected children and to offenders (Chapter 8). This is followed by a look at alternatives between arrest and appearing in juvenile court, a stage referred to as pretrial services and diversion (Chapter 9). Next the juvenile court process is discussed from intake to disposition (Chapter 10), followed by a look at juvenile corrections (Chapter 11).

Part IV discusses practices and programs being conducted and proposed in the juvenile justice system. Of utmost importance in these turbulent times is finding effective ways to prevent delinquency and recidivism (Chapter 12). Finally is a discussion of the need to rethink current juvenile justice policies and practices and how the juvenile justice system might be retooled in the twenty-first century (Chapter 13).

New to This Edition

The fifth edition of *Juvenile Justice* has been completely updated; the vast majority of sources, save for "classics," were published after 2005, and all statistics are the most recently available at press time. The text has also been reorganized, now beginning with an overview of the juvenile justice system rather than with its history, to better draw the students into the subject and give them needed background. Specific changes within each chapter are as follows.

Chapter 1 Juvenile Justice: Definitions, Measurement and Process

- New material on official statistics versus self-reports
- The media's impact on public perception of juveniles
- The organization/structure of juvenile justice
- The juvenile justice *process*
- Confidentiality versus openness
- Expanded material on disproportionate minority contact (DMC)

Chapter 2 The History and Philosophy behind the Juvenile Justice System

- Trimmed coverage of historical material
- Added *Shioutakon v. District of Columbia* (1956)
- Tightened the discussion of the Juvenile Justice and Delinquency Prevention (JJDP) Act
- Added brief mention of two 1970s cases dealing with juvenile cases and the media

Chapter 3 Theories of Delinquency and Juvenile Offending

- Expanded discussion of conflict theory
- Added material on the Gluecks' studies of male delinquency to sociological theories
- Expanded Shaw and McKay's social disorganization theory, Agnew's strain theory, learning theory, social control theory and labeling theory
- New section on victimization theories and on Agnew's general theory on crime

Chapter 4 Youths in Society: Developmental Risk and Protective Factors

- Changed term *fetal alcohol syndrome* (FAS) to *fetal alcohol spectrum disorder* (FASD) to account for a broadening of the disorder in recent years
- Significantly expanded the child development discussion, including brain development (ages 4–13)
- Summarized cognitive and moral development in Kohlberg's moral reasoning

- Expanded corporal punishment discussion, and added controversy on spanking
- Increased coverage of effects of violent media on delinquency (TV, video games)
- New material on prenatal exposure to cigarette smoke; parent criminality/incarceration, foster care and low family attachment as risk factors; school, peer and community risk factors; and early work experiences

Chapter 5 Juvenile Victims

- Deleted section on Historical Roots of Abuse and section on Ritualistic Abuse by Satanic Cults
- Added coverage of the Adam Walsh Act (SORNA)
- Expanded discussion of institutional abuse to cover youths in the juvenile justice system
- New coverage on Child Abduction Response Teams (CART), AMBER Alert, and exemplary programs to prevent or reduce child victimization: Nurse-Family Partnerships, Building Peaceful Families, Safe Kids/Safe Streets
- New section on the Juvenile Victim Justice System

Chapter 6 Juvenile Offenders

- Added data on violence by adolescent girls
- Added section on juvenile co-offending, juvenile firesetting and juvenile sex offenders
- Moved content on conduct disorder/antisocial personality disorder to Chapter 4, under Individual Risk Factors
- Deleted several tables from previous edition and summarized the content in narrative text
- Added a table (more global) encapsulating relevant statistics

Chapter 7 Youth Gangs

- An entirely new chapter devoted to youth gangs (content was scattered throughout several chapters in previous edition)
- Updated and expanded material on MS-13
- Added material from *Highlights of the 2006 National Youth Gang Survey* (NYGS) throughout
- Added 3 Rs of gang culture as well as new content on gang membership and violent victimization
- Deleted many tables and figures, and cast relevant data as narrative

Chapter 8 The Police and Juveniles

- Merged and streamlined Chapters 7 and 8
- Added increasing harshness within the juvenile justice system during the 1980s and 1990s, with many states treating more juvenile offenders as criminals in need of punishment rather than rehabilitation
- Updated information on youth gun violence and violence in schools, including recent data from the 2007 *Indicators of School Crime and Safety*

- New material from the NCJJ—role of law enforcement in safe schools
- New and expanded material on bullying, with a feature on cyber-bullying and recent MySpace suicide case
- The new police response to school shooters (how it differs from original Columbine response)

Chapter 9 Pretrial Services and Diversion

- New content on the juvenile prosecutor
- Expanded discussion on assessment and its importance, including coverage of assessment tools and instruments
- New material on teen courts, mental health courts and traffic court
- Updated/expanded material on drug courts and gun courts
- New material on respite care

Chapter 10 The Juvenile Court

- Streamlined to combine two previous chapters (old Chapters 9 and 10)
- Updated jurisdictional age changes
- New material on *Roper v. Simmons* (2005)—juvenile death penalty case
- Expanded and revised content on case processing of neglected and abused youth
- New content/section on juvenile court personnel
- New content on blended sentencing
- New content: The National Council of Juvenile and Family Court Judges (NCJFCJ) *Juvenile Delinquency Guidelines: Improving Court Practice in Juvenile Delinquency Cases*
- New content and perspective on transferring juveniles to criminal court, including recent research findings, distinction between culpability and competency

Chapter 11 Juvenile Corrections

- New content on juvenile boot camps and coverage (box feature) of boot camp death
- New content on sexual assault in juvenile facilities including Prison Rape Elimination Act (PREA)
- Updated/expanded material on girls in correctional facilities
- New material on mandated education for youths in secure confinement facilities
- New content on confinement education programs
- New coverage of re-entry/aftercare and its importance, including principles of Intensive Aftercare Programs (IAPs) and promising aftercare programs

Chapter 12 Preventing Delinquency and Recidivism

- Consolidated material that was scattered throughout the previous edition (in Chapters 3, 6, 7, 8, 12 and 13) regarding prevention efforts in schools, communities and other venues

- Deleted laundry list of examples of programs (e.g., Gould-Wysinger Award winners), as they were severely outdated; replaced with descriptions of *Blueprint* programs (empirically supported/evidence for effectiveness)
- Newest available data on violence prevention, including gang prevention
- New data from the Federal Advisory Committee on Juvenile Justice (FACJJ)

Chapter 13 Juvenile Justice at a Crossroads: The Accelerating Call for Reform (previously called Epilogue)

- Discusses trends in juvenile justice; cutting-edge policies, programs and practices
- Content from the most recent reports available from work groups and partnerships actively involved in juvenile justice reform

How to Use This Book

Juvenile Justice is more than a textbook; it is a planned learning experience. The more actively you participate in it, the better your learning will be. You will learn and remember more if you first familiarize yourself with the total scope of the subject. Read and think about the Contents; it outlines the many facets of juvenile justice. Then follow these steps for *triple-strength learning* as you study each chapter:

1. Read the objectives at the beginning of the chapter. These are stated as "Do You Know" questions. Assess your current knowledge of each question. Examine any preconceptions you may hold. Glance through the terms presented to see if you can currently define them. Watch for them as you read—they are in bold print the first time they are defined in the text. Then skim the outline to get a sense of the flow of the chapter.
2. Read the chapter, underlining, highlighting or taking notes, whichever is your preferred style.

    a. Pay special attention to all information that is graphically highlighted.

    For example:

       Juvenile justice currently consists of a "one-pot" jurisdictional approach.

    The key concepts of the chapter are presented this way.

    b. Look up unfamiliar words in the Glossary at the back of the book.

3. When you have finished reading a chapter, reread the "Do You Know" questions at the beginning of the chapter to make sure you can give an educated response to each question. If you find yourself stumped by one, find the appropriate section in the chapter and review it. Do the same thing for the "Can You Define" terms.
4. Finally read the discussion questions and be prepared to contribute to a class discussion of the ideas presented in the chapter.

By following these steps, you will learn more information, understand it more fully and remember it longer. It's up to you.

Note: The material selected to highlight using the triple-strength learning instructional design includes only the chapter's key concepts. While this information is certainly important in that it provides a structural foundation for understanding the topic(s) discussed, do not simply glance over the "Do You Know" questions, highlighted boxes and summaries and expect to master the chapter. You are also responsible for reading and understanding the material that surrounds these basics—the "meat" around the bones, so to speak.
Good learning!

Supplements

The Instructor's Resource Manual for this edition has been revised and updated. It includes learning objectives, key terms, a detailed chapter outline, a chapter summary, discussion topics, InfoTrac® College Edition exercises, topically relevant Internet sites with accompanying activities and an updated test bank. Each chapter's test bank contains questions in multiple-choice, true-false, fill-in-the-blank and essay formats, with a full answer key. The test bank is coded to the learning objectives that appear in the main text, and includes the page numbers in the main text where the answers can be found. Finally, each question in the test bank has been carefully reviewed by experienced criminal justice instructors for quality, accuracy and content coverage. Our Instructor Approved seal, which appears on the front cover, is our assurance that you are working with an assessment and grading resource of the highest caliber.

Lesson Plans have been developed and are new to this edition. For each chapter, the lesson plans contain learning objectives, a chapter outline, a chapter summary, lectures notes and tips, class discussion topics and activities, and suggestions for class assignments.

Acknowledgments

First we would like to acknowledge the original lead author, **Robert W. Drowns** (1931–1996). Mr. Drowns was a retired police officer and an instructor at Metropolitan State University (Minnesota). In addition to conducting seminars and workshops on various aspects of juvenile justice, he was a consultant to the Office of Juvenile Justice and Delinquency Prevention (OJJDP).

We would like to thank the reviewers of previous editions of *Juvenile Justice* for their constructive suggestions: Jennifer Allen, Western Illinois University; Kelly J. Asmussen, Peru State College; Steve W. Atchley, Delaware Technical Community College; Jerald C. Burns; Colleen Clark, Minnesota State University–Mankato; Dorinda Dowis, Colorado State University; Patrick Dunworth; J. Price Foster, University of Louisville; Burt C. Hagerman; Patricia M. Harris; Frederick F. Hawley; James Paul Heuser; Robert Ives; James Jengeleski, Shippensburg University; Peter Kratcoski; Matthew C. Leone; Clarence Augustus Martin; Richard H. Martin, Elgin Community College; Roger McNally, SUNY Brockport; David Olson, Loyola University, Chicago; and Paul Steele, University of New Mexico.

A heartfelt thank you to Christine Hess Orthmann for her hours of research and writing, without whose efforts this text would not have been possible.

Additional thank you's go to Bobbi Peacock, our photo development editor, and Terri Wright, our photo researcher, for their excellent work on selecting images for this text. And thank you to Denny Daniels for his careful checking of the manuscript for accuracy. Finally, a round of thanks goes to Carolyn Henderson-Meier, executive editor at Wadsworth Publishing; Christy Krueger, project manager at Wadsworth Publishing; and Sara Dovre Wudali, production editor at Buuji, Inc. I am truly appreciative of these editors for their attention to detail and their support throughout the revision process.

About the Author

Kären Matison Hess, PhD. Dr. Hess has written extensively in law enforcement and criminal justice, including these texts for Cengage Publishing: *Constitutional Law for the Criminal Justice Professional*, 4th ed.; *Corrections for the 21st Century: Criminal Investigation*, 9th ed.; *Criminal Procedure*; *Introduction to Law Enforcement and Criminal Justice*, 9th ed.; *Introduction to Private Security*, 5th ed.; *Management and Supervision in Law Enforcement*, 4th ed.; *The Police and the Community: Strategies for the 21st Century*, 4th ed.; *Police Operations*, 3rd ed.; and *Seeking Employment in Criminal Justice and Related Fields*, 6th ed.

She has been a frequent instructor for report writing workshops and seminars for law enforcement agencies, a member of the English department at Normandale Community College and President of the Institute for Professional Development. Dr. Hess is a member of the Academy of Criminal Justice Sciences (ACJS), the International Association of Chiefs of Police (IACP), the National Criminal Justice Association (NCJA), the National Council of Teachers of English (NCTE), the Police Executive Research Forum (PERF) and the Textbook and Academic Author's Association (TAA), of which she is a fellow and a board member of the TAA Foundation.

CHAPTER 1

Juvenile Justice
Definitions, Measurements and Process

THE WAY IN WHICH A SOCIETY TREATS ITS CHILDREN—ITS YOUNG PEOPLE—SAYS SOMETHING ABOUT THE FUTURE OF THAT SOCIETY, ITS BELIEFS, AND THE VIABILITY OF THOSE BELIEFS. THE WAY IN WHICH A SOCIETY TREATS THOSE OF ITS CHILDREN WHO BREAK ITS LAWS SAYS SOMETHING ABOUT ITS HUMANITY, ITS MORALITY, ITS RESILIENCE, AND ITS CAPACITY FOR SELF-CORRECTION.

—NATIONAL CENTER FOR JUVENILE JUSTICE

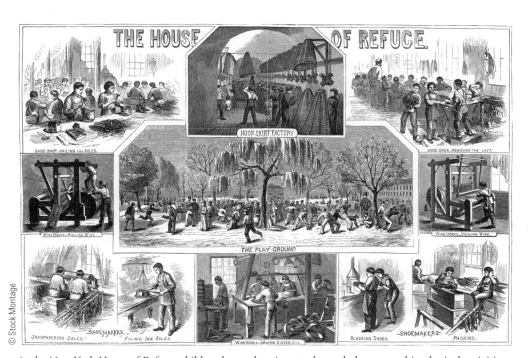

At the New York House of Refuge, children learned various trades and also engaged in physical activities.

© Stock Montage

Do You Know?

- What *parens patriae* is and why it is important in juvenile justice?
- What the most common oldest age for juvenile court jurisdiction is?
- What types of justice exist?
- How researchers measure the nature and extent of youthful offenses?
- What the Federal Bureau of Investigation's Uniform Crime Reports measures?
- How prevalent delinquency is according to self-reports?
- What the terminology of the contemporary juvenile justice system emphasizes?
- What the three components of the juvenile justice system are?
- What issues the contemporary juvenile justice system faces?
- What primary lesson is learned from the funnel effect?
- How the contemporary conservative and liberal approaches to juvenile justice differ?

Can You Define?

adjudicated	distributive justice	*parens patriae*	social justice
dark figure of crime	diversion	particular justice	status offense
delinquent	funnel effect	petitioned	Uniform Crime
discrimination	juvenile justice	restorative justice	Reports
disparity	one-pot approach	retributive justice	universal justice

Chapter Outline

Introduction

The Scope of the Juvenile Justice System

Who Is a Juvenile?

What Is Justice?

Measuring the Number of Juvenile Victimizations and Offenses

The FBI's Uniform Crime Reports (UCR)

The National Incident-Based Reporting System (NIBRS)

The Bureau of Justice Statistics National Crime Victimization Survey (NCVS)

The UCR and NCVS Compared

Self-Reports

The Media's Effect on Public Perception of Juveniles

Terminology

Organization and Structure of Juvenile Justice

The Components of the Juvenile Justice System

The Juvenile Justice Process

Arrest

Referral

Intake

Diversion

Detention

Petitioning/Charges Filed

Adjudication Hearing/ Delinquency Finding

Dispositional Hearing

Probation

Confinement in a Secure Correctional Facility

Transfer to Adult Court

The Juvenile Justice System and Criminal Justice System Compared

Issues in Juvenile Justice

To Divert or Not?

Which Is More Just: A Conservative or a Liberal Approach to Delinquency?

Confidentiality versus Openness

Disproportionate Minority Contact (DMC)

Introduction

Juvenile justice is a system that provides a legal setting in which youth can account for their wrongs or receive official protection. It is also a term that necessarily implies distinct and separate treatment between youth and adults in dispensing justice. If justice is fairness in treatment by the law, why is this separation needed? Is justice not "one size fits all"? The separate juvenile justice system began over 100 years ago with the establishment of the first juvenile court in 1899.

 The underlying premise of the first juvenile court was that of *parens patriae*, the responsibility of the state to protect its children and youth.

Making the states responsible for its children and youth resulted in not one, but 51 juvenile justice systems in the United States, each with its own history and set of laws and policies to deliver services in its own way (King, 2006, p.1). Even within a single state, the mandates conceived in each state's capitol building must be interpreted and implemented by various local officials, under widely varying conditions, and with widely varying effects. Add to these 51 separate systems the federal juvenile justice system and the challenge of understanding what juvenile justice is becomes even greater.

The Scope of the Juvenile Justice System

An extreme challenge facing the juvenile justice system is the one-pot approach to children and youth evident throughout history. The **one-pot approach** places those who are abused and neglected, those who commit status offenses, and those who are delinquents into the same judicial system. A **status offense** is an act that would not be considered a crime if committed by an adult, for example, smoking cigarettes or skipping school. A juvenile **delinquent** is a youth who commits an act that would be a crime were it to be committed by an adult. The term is intended to avoid stigmatizing youth as criminals. Chapter 5 focuses on youth who have been victimized: battered, neglected, missing, exploited. Chapter 6 focuses on juveniles who break the law, both status offenders and delinquents. Throughout this text keep in mind that the juvenile justice system must accommodate both children and youth who have serious problems and those who are problems, some of whom commit violent offenses. In addition to this challenge the states must establish just who falls into the *juvenile* classification.

Who Is a Juvenile?

The age at which a child comes under the juvenile court's jurisdiction is established by each state. Most states have upper age limits of juvenile jurisdiction in abuse, neglect and dependency cases and in status offenses—typically through age 20. Many states exclude married or otherwise emancipated juveniles from juvenile court jurisdiction.

In most states the juvenile court has jurisdiction over all youth charged with violating the law who were younger than age 18 at the time of the offense. The youngest age for juvenile court jurisdiction in delinquency matters ranges from age 6 to age 10. The oldest age for juvenile court jurisdiction in delinquency matters ranges from 15 to 17, with 17 being the most common age, as summarized in Table 1.1.

Table 1.1   Oldest Age for Juvenile Court Jurisdiction in Delinquency Matters

Age	State
15	Connecticut, New York, North Carolina
16	Georgia, Illinois, Louisiana, Massachusetts, Michigan, Missouri, New Hampshire, South Carolina, Texas, Wisconsin
17	Alabama, Alaska, Arizona, Arkansas, California, Colorado, Delaware, District of Columbia, Florida, Hawaii, Idaho, Indiana, Iowa, Kansas, Kentucky, Maine, Maryland, Minnesota, Mississippi, Montana, Nebraska, Nevada, New Jersey, New Mexico, North Dakota, Ohio, Oklahoma, Oregon, Pennsylvania, Rhode Island, South Dakota, Tennessee, Utah, Vermont, Virginia, Washington, West Virginia, Wyoming

SOURCE: Howard N. Snyder and Melissa Sickmund. *Juvenile Offenders and Victims: 2006 National Report.* Washington, DC: U.S. Department of Justice, Office of Justice Programs, Office of Juvenile Justice and Delinquency Prevention, March 2006, p.103. Reprinted by permission.

In previous editions of this text the age range was from 16 to 19, with the most common age being 18. This lowering of the oldest age reflects the nationwide trend that took hold during the 1980s and 1990s to "get tough" on youth in trouble with the law. Some states, however, are beginning to reconsider this upper age of juvenile court jurisdiction, as discussed later in the chapter.

 Seventeen is most commonly recognized as the oldest age for juvenile court jurisdiction in delinquency matters.

State legislatures can extend the duration of time the juvenile court has jurisdiction over youth for disposition purposes, if doing so is in the best interests of the juveniles and the state. Currently statutes in 35 states extend certain juvenile court jurisdiction in delinquency cases until age 25. These differences in state statutes regarding who falls under juvenile court jurisdiction make it imperative that juvenile justice practitioners and researchers become familiar with their state's statutes.

Another basic difference among the various juvenile justice systems is just how they view justice itself.

What Is Justice?

Centuries ago Aristotle warned that no government could stand that is not founded on justice. As a nation, America is firmly committed to "liberty and justice for all." But is this the reality? And exactly what is justice?

Aristotle wrote that the *just* is that which is lawful (**universal justice**) and that which is fair and equal (**particular justice**):

> Of particular justice and that which is just in the corresponding sense, one kind is that which is manifested in distributions of honour or money or the other things that fall to be divided among those who have a share in the constitution. . . .
>
> This, then, is what the just is—the proportional; the unjust is what violates the proportion. Hence one term becomes too great, the other too small, as indeed happens in practice; for the man who acts unjustly has too much, and the man who is unjustly treated too little, of what is good (Ross, 1952, pp.378–379).

Distributive or **social justice** provides an equal share of what is valued in a society to each member of that society. This includes power, prestige and possessions. **Retributive justice** seeks revenge for unlawful behavior.

Distributive justice or social justice is frequently ignored but certainly must be considered in any discussion of justice. Usually, however, the focus is on retributive justice, harkening back to the ancient concept of an eye for an eye (*lex talionis*). When distributive and retributive justice are not differentiated, critics may claim that retributive justice has failed when, in effect, it has no power over the failure. In discussing justice for juveniles, Springer (1986, p.76) suggests:

> It is beyond the scope of this paper to discuss social justice, what Aristotle called "distributive justice," but it is within its scope to make mention of the sad consequences of our inability to provide a decent social environment for what would appear to be a growing segment of our youthful society.
>
> This is not the place to engage in discourse on the dire ends of poverty, class divisions, urbanization, industrialization, urban blight, unemployment, breakdown of religion, breakdown of the family, and all of the other established criminogenic factors. It is the place, however, to recognize, at least, that the criminal justice system is the least effective means of crime prevention and social control. If we are interested in a relatively crime-free society, we must look elsewhere than the courts.

Another type of justice, restorative justice, has gained momentum and support throughout juvenile justice in recent years. Restorative justice, which can be traced back to the Code of Hammurabi in 2000 B.C., holds offenders accountable to the victim and the victim's community, rather than to the state. Rather than seeking retribution (punishment), it seeks restitution—to repair the damages as much as possible and to restore the victim, the community and the offender: "Restorative justice suggests that the response to youth crime must strike a balance among the needs of victims, offenders and communities and that each should be actively involved in the justice process to the greatest extent possible" (Bazemore and Umbreit, 2001, p.1).

 Restorative justice focuses on repairing the harm done to victims and to the community and stresses that offenders must contribute to the repair.

Table 1.2 summarizes the differences between the traditional retributive approach to justice and restorative justice. Figure 1.1 illustrates the restorative justice approach. The renewed interest in and focus on restorative justice and using restorative conferencing as a correctional alternative are discussed in Chapter 9.

Throughout the text, the most current information available about who is actually being served by the juvenile justice system will be provided. The following discussion provides background on just how this information is obtained.

Measuring the Number of Juvenile Victimizations and Offenses

Just how serious is the problem of youthful victims and offenders in the United States? Researchers use a variety of tools to address this question. This overview is intended to help familiarize students with how such statistics

Table 1.2   Paradigms of Justice—Old and New

Old Paradigm/Retributive Justice	New Paradigm/Restorative Justice
1. Crime defined as violation of the state	1. Crime defined as violation of one person by another
2. Focus on establishing blame, on guilt, on past (did he/she do it?)	2. Focus on problem solving, on liabilities and obligations, on future (what should be done?)
3. Adversarial relationships and process normative	3. Dialogue and negotiation normative
4. Imposition of pain to punish and deter/prevent	4. Restitution as a means of restoring both parties; reconciliation/restoration as goal
5. Justice defined by intent and by process: right rules	5. Justice defined as right relationships; judged by the outcome
6. Interpersonal, conflictual nature of crime obscured, repressed; conflict seen as individual vs. state	6. Crime recognized as interpersonal conflict; value of conflict recognized
7. One social injury replaced by another	7. Focus on repair of social injury
8. Community on sidelines, represented abstractly by state	8. Community as facilitator in restorative process
9. Encouragement of competitive, individualistic values	9. Encouragement of mutuality
10. Action directed from state to offender: • victim ignored • offender passive	10. Victim's and offender's roles recognized in both problem and solution: • victim rights/needs recognized • offender encouraged to take responsibility
11. Offender accountability defined as taking punishment	11. Offender accountability defined as understanding impact of action and helping decide how to make things right
12. Offense defined in purely legal terms, devoid of moral, social, economic, political dimensions	12. Offense understood in whole context—moral, social, economic, political
13. "Debt" owed to state and society in the abstract	13. Debt/liability to victim recognized
14. Response focused on offender's past behavior	14. Response focused on harmful consequences of offender's behavior
15. Stigma of crime unremovable	15. Stigma of crime removable through restorative action
16. No encouragement for repentance and forgiveness	16. Possibilities for repentance and forgiveness
17. Dependence on proxy professionals	17. Direct involvement by participants

SOURCE: Howard Zehr. *IARCA Journal*, March 1991, p.7.

and other information about youth who are victimized and those who victimize are obtained.

 Researchers commonly use three methods to measure the nature and extent of unlawful acts by juveniles: official data, self-report data and victim surveys.

Official data is information and statistics collected by the police, courts and corrections agencies on the local, regional and national levels. Two of the most frequently consulted official sources of crime data are those compiled by the Federal Bureau of Investigation (FBI) and the Bureau of Justice Statistics (BJS). Other sources of official statistics are the Office of Juvenile Justice and Delinquency Prevention (OJJDP) and the National Institute of Justice (NIJ).

The FBI's Uniform Crime Reports (UCR)

Information about crime comes from statistics gathered from around the country. In 1930 Congress assigned the FBI to serve as a national clearinghouse for crime statistics. The FBI's National Crime Information Center (NCIC) instituted the **Uniform Crime Reports** (UCR) program to collect offense information for the Part I offenses of murder and nonnegligent manslaughter, forcible

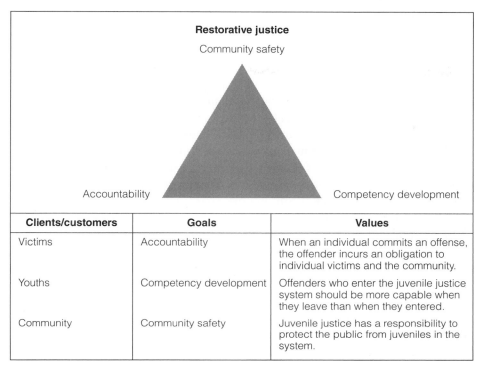

Restorative justice

Community safety

Accountability   Competency development

Clients/customers	Goals	Values
Victims	Accountability	When an individual commits an offense, the offender incurs an obligation to individual victims and the community.
Youths	Competency development	Offenders who enter the juvenile justice system should be more capable when they leave than when they entered.
Community	Community safety	Juvenile justice has a responsibility to protect the public from juveniles in the system.

Figure 1.1   Restorative Justice Approach

Adapted from D. Maloney, D. Romig and T. Armstrong. 1998. *Juvenile Probation: The Balanced Approach*. Reno, NV: National Council of Juvenile and Family Court Judges.

SOURCE: Shay Bilchik. *Guide for Implementing the Balanced and Restorative Justice Model*. Washington, DC: Office of Juvenile Justice and Delinquency Prevention, December 1998, p.6.

rape, robbery, aggravated assault, burglary, larceny-theft and motor vehicle theft. In 1978, arson was added to the list as a Part I reportable offense.

 The FBI's Uniform Crime Reports contain statistics on violent crimes (murder, aggravated assault causing serious bodily harm, forcible rape, robbery) and property crimes (burglary, larceny/theft, motor vehicle theft and arson).

The UCR program also collects arrest data on Part I offenses and 21 other crimes, such as driving under the influence, that comprise the Part II offenses. The annual publication of this program, *Crime in the United States*, reports that in 2006, more than 17,500 law enforcement agencies, serving 94.2 percent of the nation's population, contributed data to the FBI either directly or through state UCR programs.

Over the years the UCR developed into a broad utility for summary-based reporting of crime. The Part I crimes were considered by experts of the time to be the most serious and most commonly reported crimes occurring in the United States, as well as the most likely to occur with sufficient frequency to provide an adequate basis for comparison. Therefore, from 1960 to 2004, the eight Part I crimes served as a collective Crime Index, a general snapshot of offenses occurring throughout the country that was used to gauge fluctuations in the volume and rate of crime reported to law enforcement.

However, by the late 1970s the law enforcement community saw a need for a more detailed crime reporting program to meet the needs of law enforcement in the twenty-first century. One of the primary criticisms of the UCR Index program was that it used a hierarchy system in which only the most serious offense in an incident was recorded. For example, if an individual was assaulted and robbed, UCR would record only one offense—the assault. The robbery would go unaccounted. Also, in recent years, the Crime Index has not been a true indicator of the degree of criminality of a locality. For example, larceny-thefts currently account for almost 60 percent of the total crimes reported. Consequently, the volume of larcenies overshadows more serious but less frequently committed crimes.

Because of these numerous shortcomings, in June 2004 the FBI's Criminal Justice Information Services (CJIS) Division, Advisory Policy Board (APB), approved discontinuing the use of the Crime Index in the UCR program and its publications. The CJIS APB recommended that the FBI publish a violent crime total and a property crime total until a more viable index is developed.

A summary of the figures for crimes committed in 2006 is depicted in the Crime Clock (Figure 1.2). The Crime Clock should be viewed with care. This graphic does not imply a regularity in the commission of the Part I offenses; rather it represents the annual ratio of crime to fixed time intervals. The most recent UCR figures are available online at http://www.fbi.gov/ucr/ucr.htm.

The UCR's statistics on number of crimes reported and number of arrests illustrate the extent of the delinquency problem. The statistics must be interpreted cautiously, however. The data represent only youth who have been arrested. Many are never caught. It has been estimated that 80 to 90 percent of children in the United States younger than 18 commit some offense for which they could be arrested, but only about 3 percent are. In addition, multiple arrests of the same youth for different crimes are counted separately. The total

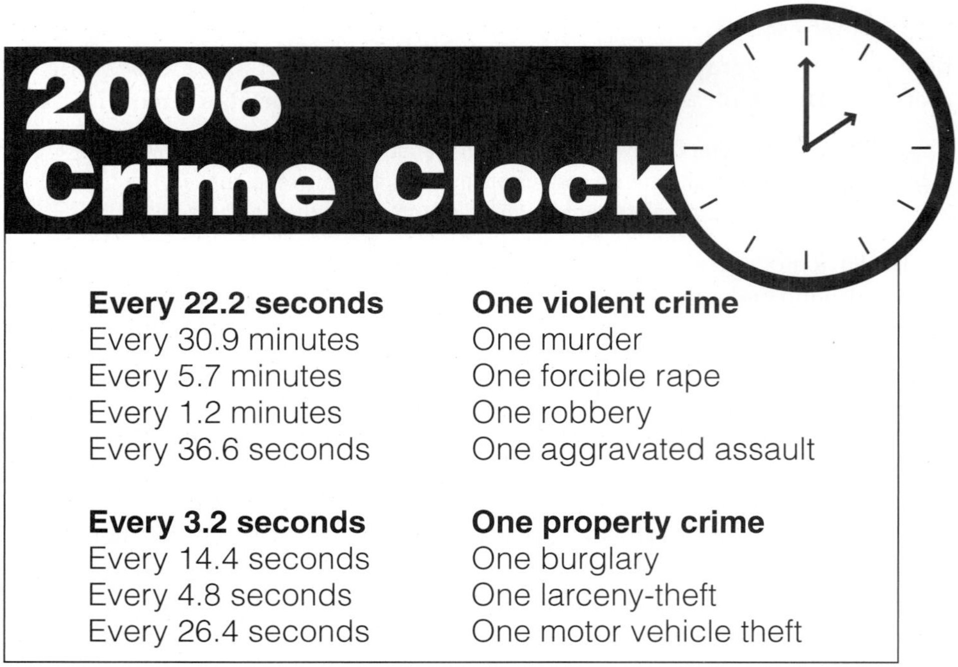

Every 22.2 seconds	**One violent crime**
Every 30.9 minutes	One murder
Every 5.7 minutes	One forcible rape
Every 1.2 minutes	One robbery
Every 36.6 seconds	One aggravated assault
Every 3.2 seconds	**One property crime**
Every 14.4 seconds	One burglary
Every 4.8 seconds	One larceny-theft
Every 26.4 seconds	One motor vehicle theft

Figure 1.2 2006 Crime Clock

SOURCE: Federal Bureau of Investigation, *Crime in the United States, 2006*. Online: http://www.fbi.gov/ucr/cius2006/about/crime_clock.html. Accessed July 9, 2008.

number of arrests does not equal the number of youth who have been arrested because chronic offenders have multiple arrests.

The National Incident-Based Reporting System (NIBRS)

Efforts to redesign and modernize the UCR program resulted in the development of the National Incident-Based Reporting System (NIBRS) in 1988. Intended to supplement or replace the summary data of the UCR, the NIBRS collects detailed incident information on 46 offenses representing 22 categories of crimes. A complete list of the crime categories included in NIBRS is available on the FBI Web site at http://www.fbi.gov/hq/cjisd/nibrsfaq.pdf. According to McEwen (2003, p.402):

> Compared with the summary UCR statistics, NIBRS provides more detailed data. Crime analysis is enhanced by having details on individual crimes that can then be analyzed and summarized in a variety of different ways. NIBRS also expanded the number of reportable offenses in 22 categories, known as Group A offenses, to 46. The expansion to 46 crime classifications provides a means for police departments to analyze virtually every problem that might arise, including offenses related to domestic violence, use of guns, hate crimes and terrorism.
>
> Even though the NIBRS program offers expanded capabilities, it has been slow to be accepted at the state and local levels. Cost is a major consideration.

Implementing the National Incident-Based Reporting System (Roberts 1997, p.1) begins with the basic difference between the UCR and the NIBRS: "The way we count crime in the United States is changing in fundamental respects. We are shifting from monthly aggregate reporting of summary crime and arrest statistics to detailed reporting of crimes and arrest activities at the local level." In 2004, the most recent year for which data are available, 5,271 agencies submitted NIBRS data, representing 20 percent of the U.S. population and 16 percent of crime statistics collected by the FBI. At that time 26 programs were certified by the FBI, and 12 states were in various stages of testing their NIBRS solutions.

One reason departments may be reluctant to switch to NIBRS is that they will doubtless see a significant increase in crime statistics, while actual crime may, in fact, be decreasing.

The other most commonly referred to official data is that compiled by the Bureau of Justice Statistics.

The Bureau of Justice Statistics National Crime Victimization Survey (NCVS)

The Bureau of Justice Statistics (BJS) National Crime Victimization Survey (NCVS) began in 1973 and, as previously described, gathers information on personal crime experience through interviews with approximately 160,000 people age 12 years and older in 86,000 households nationwide. The survey collects data on crimes against individuals and households, regardless of whether they were reported to law enforcement. The data from this representative sample are then extrapolated to estimate the proportion of each crime type reported to law enforcement and detail reasons given for reporting or not reporting.

The NCVS collects detailed information on the frequency and nature of the crimes of rape, personal robbery, aggravated and simple assault, household burglary, personal and household theft, and motor vehicle theft. The survey provides information about victims' age, sex, race, ethnicity, marital status, income and educational level; their offenders' sex, race, approximate age and victim-offender relationship; and the crimes: time and place of occurrence, use of weapons, nature of injury and economic consequences. Questions also cover the victims' experiences with the criminal justice system, self-protective measures used and possible substance abuse by offenders.

The UCR and NCVS Compared

The UCR and NCVS differ significantly. The UCR focuses on criminology whereas the NCVS focuses on victimology: "Academically and organizationally, victimology is best conceived of as an area of specialization within criminology. . . . Criminologists ask why certain individuals become involved in lawbreaking while others do not. . . . Victimologists ask why some individuals, households and entities (such as businesses) are targeted while others are not" (Karmen, 2007, p.13). As noted, the NCVS projects crime levels from a selected source of information and reports a substantially higher number of crimes than those reported in the UCR. Some analysts believe neither report is accurate and that crime is two to five times higher than either source reports.

The UCR captures crimes reported to law enforcement but excludes simple assaults. The NCVS includes crimes both reported and not reported to law enforcement but excludes homicide, arson, commercial crimes and crimes against children under age 12 (all included in the UCR program). Even when the same crimes are included in the UCR and NCVS, the definitions vary.

Another difference is how rate measures are presented. The UCR crime rates are largely per capita (number of crimes per 100,000 persons), whereas the NCVS rates are per household (number of crimes per 1,000 households). Because the number of households may not grow at the same rate as the total population, trend data for rates measured by the two programs may not be compatible. As might be expected, given the differences in how the data are collected, the rates per 100,000 victims can differ significantly between the two reporting systems. In fact, in every instance when comparisons are made between the FBI's 2004 UCR data and the BJS's 2004 NCVS data, the NCVS shows a much higher incident rate per 100,000 than the UCR. Despite these differences, these two official sources are helpful in understanding the extent of crime and victimization.

Self-Reports

Self-report studies let youth personally reveal information about their violations of the law. Self-report formats include one-to-one interviews, surveys and anonymous questionnaires. If truancy, alcohol consumption, smoking marijuana or cigarettes and petty theft are included in self-report scales, delinquency appears almost universal.

 According to self-report studies, delinquency is almost universal.

When the prevalence and frequency of offending according to court records and self-reports are compared, it is obvious that self-report data reveal a greater prevalence and frequency of offending than do court records, as shown

Table 1.3 Prevalence and Frequency of Offending: Court Records versus Self-Reports

	Prevalence		Frequency	
	Court	*Self-Report*	*Court*	*Self-Report*
Age				
11	1.7	28.4	1.1	2.9
12	2.1	27.9	2.1	4.6
13	8.0	41.5	2.8	11.6
14	10.6	46.4	2.8	13.5
15	13.1	47.6	3.1	16.8
16	13.6	51.3	2.2	18.3
17	12.7	61.1	2.4	21.8
Total	34.0	85.9	4.6	49.2
Offense Type				
Burglary	4.7	22.3	1.6	3.2
Vehicle theft	23.8	33.1	1.8	5.9
Larceny	25.6	66.1	2.0	11.6
Robbery	3.3	8.6	1.2	5.6
Assault	12.7	61.3	2.4	11.4
Vandalism	8.4	47.9	1.9	8.2
Marijuana use	1.8	49.1	1.2	29.9
Drug selling	3.9	21.7	1.6	28.8
Property	27.5	71.8	3.6	14.3
Aggressive	17.4	70.4	2.9	16.1
Drug	4.5	50.8	1.8	41.1

Notes: Prevalence = % offending.

Frequency = Average offenses per offender.

SOURCE: David P. Farrington; Darrick Jolliffe; J. David Hawkins; Richard F. Catalano; Karl G. Hill; and Rick Kosterman. "Comparing Delinquency Careers in Court Records and Self-Reports." *Criminology*, August 2003, p.941. Reprinted by permission.

in Table 1.3. In comparing self-reports to official crime data, Kirk (2006) found a sizable number of youth self-reported being arrested without having a corresponding official arrest record. In addition, a substantial proportion of youth with an official arrest record failed to self-report they had been arrested.

The University of Michigan's Institute for Social Research (ISR) routinely surveys thousands of high school seniors regarding delinquent activities, the results of which are published in *Monitoring the Future*. Anonymous, self-report data are also compiled by PRIDE Surveys, a private organization that works with schools and school districts throughout the country to administer questionnaires designed to elicit information on youth behaviors and other crucial factors that affect learning, such as family issues, discipline, safety, gangs and substance abuse.

Another resource for data on self-reported delinquent and risk-related behaviors is the Centers for Disease Control and Prevention (CDC) Youth Risk Behavior Surveillance System (YRBSS), a national program that monitors six categories of priority health-risk behaviors among youth and young adults: (1) behaviors that contribute to unintentional injuries and violence; (2) tobacco use; (3) alcohol and other drug use; (4) sexual behaviors that contribute to unintended pregnancy and sexually transmitted diseases, including HIV infection; (5) unhealthy dietary behaviors; and (6) physical inactivity. YRBSS synthesizes and summarizes results from national school-based surveys conducted by the CDC and state and local school-based surveys conducted by state and local education and health agencies. Select results from the national survey, 39 state surveys and 22 local surveys conducted among students in grades 9 through 12 during 2007 are given in Table 1.4.

Official Statistics versus Self-Reports Just as the findings from the UCR and the NCVJ differ significantly, so do those between official statistics and self-reports. The debate about the relative ability of self-report studies and official statistics to describe juvenile crime and victims is ongoing. Self-report studies can capture information on activities that never come to juvenile justice agencies' attention. These self-report studies show a much higher proportion of

Table 1.4 High School Students Reporting Involvement in Delinquent and Risk-Related Behavior, Including Drug, Alcohol and Cigarette Use, 2007

Delinquent/Risk-Related Behavior	Grade 9	Grade 10	Grade 11	Grade 12	Total
Were involved in a physical fight[1]	40.9%	36.2%	34.8%	28.0%	35.5%
Were injured in a physical fight[1]	5.6	3.7	3.5	3.3	4.2
Carried a weapon on school property[2]	6.0	5.8	5.5	6.0	5.9
Were threatened or injured with a weapon on school property[2]	9.2	8.4	6.8	6.3	7.8
Did not go to school because they felt unsafe at or going to/from school[3]	6.6	5.4	4.7	4.8	5.5
Were offered, sold or given an illegal drug by someone on school property[4]	21.2	25.3	22.8	19.6	22.3
Experienced dating violence[5]	8.5	8.9	10.6	12.1	9.9
Were forced to have sexual intercourse[5]	6.6	8.2	8.5	8.3	7.8
Seriously considered attempting suicide[6]	14.8	15.6	13.5	13.5	14.5
Attempted suicide[7]	7.9	8.0	5.8	5.4	6.9
Rode with a driver who had been drinking alcohol[8]	27.6	28.7	29.2	31.5	29.1
Drove while drinking alcohol[8]	5.5	8.7	11.5	18.3	10.5
Lifetime alcohol use[9]	65.5	74.7	79.4	82.8	75.0
Current alcohol use[9]	35.7	41.8	49.0	54.9	44.7
Episodic heavy drinking (binge drinking = 5+ alcoholic drinks in a row)[10]	17.0	23.7	29.9	36.5	26.0
Currently smoke more than 10 cigarettes/day[11]	10.1	9.0	9.0	13.6	10.7
Current marijuana use[12]	14.7	19.3	21.4	25.1	19.7
Current cocaine use[13]	2.7	3.2	2.9	4.4	3.3
Lifetime inhalant use[14]	15.0	14.6	12.5	10.2	13.3
Lifetime illegal steroid use[15]	4.8	3.7	3.1	3.8	3.9
Lifetime hallucinogen use[15]	5.1	8.0	8.1	10.4	7.8
Lifetime methamphetamine use[16] (T47)	3.6	4.1	5.4	4.5	4.4
Lifetime Ecstasy use[17] (T49)	4.6	5.3	5.6	7.6	5.8

SOURCE: Adapted from Danice K. Eaton, Laura Kann, Steve Kinchen, Shari Shanklin, James Ross, Joseph Hawkins, William A. Harris, Richard Lowry, Tim McManus, David Chyen, Connie Lim, Nancy D. Brener and Howell Wechsler. *Youth Risk Behavior Surveillance—United States, 2007*. Atlanta, GA: Centers for Disease Control and Prevention, Surveillance Summaries, *Morbidity and Mortality Weekly Report*, Vol. 57, No. SS-4, June 6, 2008.

[1]Table 9, p.45; [2]Table 13, p.49; [3]Table 17, p.53; [4]Table 59, p.95; [5]Table 11, p.47; [6]Table 21, p.57; [7]Table 23, p.59; [8]Table 5, p.41; [9]Table 35, p.71; [10]Table 37, p.73; [11]Table 29, p.65; [12]Table 39, p.75; [13]Table 41, p.77; [14]Table 43, p.79; [15]Table 45, p.81; [16]Table 47, p.83; [17]Table 49, p.85.

the juvenile population involved in delinquent behavior. However, such studies also have limitations in that youth may not remember incidents or they may choose not to report them.

Both self-report and official statistics, when properly and carefully used, provide insight into crime and victimization. Delbert Elliott, Director of the Center for the Study and Prevention of Violence, argues that to focus solely on either self-reports or official statistics while abandoning the other is "radically shortsighted; to systematically ignore the findings of either is dangerous, particularly when the two measures provide apparently contradictory findings" (Snyder and Sickmund, 2006, p.64). Elliott stresses that a full understanding of the etiology and development of delinquent behavior is enhanced by using and integrating self-reports and official data.

A Caution on Using Statistics   Statistics help constitute what can be called the "big picture" of what is really happening in the United States: "Accurate statistics about crimes and victims are vital because they can shed light on a number of important matters":

- Statistics can provide realistic assessments of the threat posed to individuals by criminal activity.
- Statistics reveal patterns of criminal activity.
- Trends reveal how situations change as time goes by.
- Statistics reveal the costs and losses imposed by criminal behavior.
- Statistics can be used to project a rough or "ballpark figure" of how many people are likely to need assistance.
- Statistics also are required to evaluate the effectiveness of recovery efforts and preventive strategies.
- Profiles are statistical portraits that yield an impression of what is usual or typical about the average victim. (Karmen, 2007, pp.43–45)

Karmen (p.45) stresses: "As useful and necessary as statistics are, they should always be viewed with a healthy dose of scientific skepticism." He notes: "Cynics joke that statistics can be used by special interest groups just like a lamppost is used by a drunkard—for support rather than for illumination."

Be mindful of several limitations present when interpreting crime data. Official statistics reflect only reported crimes, and these reports are voluntary and vary in accuracy and completeness. In addition not all police departments submit crime reports, and federal crimes are not included. Furthermore it is estimated that less than half the crimes committed are reported to the police. The true number of crimes, called the **dark figure of crime**, is unknown and may be substantially greater than official data indicate. Official statistics also do not provide information about the personality, attitudes and behavior of delinquents. This comes from self-reports.

Another caution: Any large-scale data collection program has many possible sources of error. For example, in the UCR program, a police officer may classify a crime incorrectly; and in the NCVS, a Census Bureau interviewer may incorrectly record a victim's response. Crime data are also affected by how victims perceive and recall events. In addition clerical errors may occur at any stage. Both programs have extensive accuracy checks to minimize errors. Despite these difficulties, police departments make frequent use of the information from the UCR program.

In addition to using official data and self-reports, juvenile justice practitioners and the general public may rely on media accounts to understand juveniles and their activities.

The Media's Effect on Public Perception of Juveniles

Much of what the public knows about juvenile crime comes from the media, which may overdramatize and distort the true extent and seriousness of the problem. Study after study shows that the media focuses on crime and violence to the neglect of other aspects of law enforcement: "Americans love crime coverage, which accounts for 50 percent of news on television. Race, sex and class matter" (Wexler, 2006, p.6). Researchers Weitzer and Kubrin (2004, p.497) found: "Many Americans report that they are fearful of crime. One frequently cited source of this fear is the mass media. The media, and local television news in particular, often report on incidents of crime, and do so in a selective and sometimes sensational manner." Naturally, violent crimes committed by young people are often considered more shocking and, thus, "newsworthy" than those perpetrated by adults. Consequently, this bias in reporting juvenile crime may lead the public to a distorted perception or generalization that our nation's youth are, as a group, more violent than previous generations.

In commenting on the media's coverage of crime, Karmen (2007, p.31) points out: "It appears that incidents receive intensive and sustained [media] coverage only if some aspect of the victim-offender relationship stands out as an attention-grabber. . . . Editors and journalists sift through an overwhelming number of real-life tragedies that come to their attention . . . and select the cases that are most likely to shock people out of their complacency or arouse the public's social conscience." He (p.32) suggests: "In the quest for higher ratings, coverage can sink to an 'If it bleeds, it leads' orientation characterizing commercially driven 'infotainment.'"

Having looked at who is served by the juvenile justice system, the various ages established by state statutes and the various sources of information about children and youth, the focus now is on the terminology, organization and structure of the juvenile justice system.

Terminology

As the juvenile justice system evolved into one separate from the adult system, the terms used were tailored to fit the juvenile system.

 The terminology of the juvenile justice system underscores its emphasis on protecting youth from harmful labels and their stigmatizing effects.

Youth are not *arrested;* they are *taken into custody.* If the allegations against a youth are true, the youth is called a *delinquent* rather than a *criminal.* Youth sentenced to custodial care upon release receive *aftercare* rather than *parole.* Table 1.5 shows other differences between terminology used in the juvenile and criminal justice systems. These differences in terminology will be evident throughout the next section, which examines the organization and structure of the juvenile justice system.

Table 1.5   The Language of the Juvenile and the Criminal Justice Systems

Juvenile Court Term	Adult Court Term
Adjudication: decision by the judge that a child has committed delinquent acts.	*Conviction of guilt*
Adjudicatory hearing: a hearing to determine whether the allegations of a petition are supported by the evidence beyond a reasonable doubt.	*Trial*
Adjustment: the settling of a matter so that parties agree without official intervention by the court.	*Plea bargaining*
Aftercare: the supervision given to a child for a limited period of time after he or she is released from training school but while he or she is still under the control of the juvenile court.	*Parole*
Commitment: a decision by the judge to send a child to training school.	*Sentence to imprisonment*
Delinquent act: an act that if committed by an adult would be called a crime. The term does not include such ambiguities and noncrimes as being ungovernable, truancy, incorrigibility and disobedience.	*Crime*
Delinquent child: a child who is found to have committed an act that would be considered a crime if committed by an adult.	*Criminal*
Detention: temporary care of an allegedly delinquent child who requires secure custody in physically restricting facilities pending court disposition or execution of a court order.	*Holding in jail*
Dispositional hearing: a hearing held subsequent to the adjudicatory hearing to determine what order of disposition should be made for a child adjudicated as delinquent.	*Sentencing hearing*
Hearing: the presentation of evidence to the juvenile court judge, his or her consideration of it and his or her decision on disposition of the case.	*Trial*
Juvenile court: the court that has jurisdiction over children who are alleged to be or found to be delinquent. Juvenile delinquency procedures should not be used for neglected children or for those who need supervision.	*Court of record*
Petition: an application for a court order or some other judicial action. Hence, a delinquency petition is an application for the court to act in a matter involving a juvenile apprehended for a delinquent act.	*Accusation or indictment*
Probation: the supervision of a delinquent child after the court hearing but without commitment to training school.	*Probation* (with the same meaning as the juvenile court term)
Residential child care facility: a dwelling other than a detention or shelter care facility that is licensed to provide living accommodations, care, treatment and maintenance for children and youth. Such facilities include foster homes, group homes and halfway houses.	*Halfway house*
Shelter: temporary care of a child in physically unrestricting facilities pending court disposition or execution of a court order for placement. Shelter care is used for dependent and neglected children and minors in need of supervision. Separate shelter care facilities are also used for children apprehended for delinquency who need temporary shelter but not secure detention.	*Jail*
Take into custody: the act of the police in securing the physical custody of a child engaged in delinquency. The term is used to avoid the stigma of the word "arrest."	*Arrest*

SOURCE: Harold J. Vetter and Leonard Territo. *Crime and Justice in America. A Human Perspective.* Copyright © 1984 by West Publishing Co. Reprinted by permission of Wadsworth Publishing Co.

Organization and Structure of Juvenile Justice

Although the following discussion is focused on the organization, administration and structure of juvenile *delinquency* services, it applies equally to juveniles who are abused, neglected and dependent, and those who are status offenders. The organization and administration of these services may be centralized (12 states), decentralized (18 states) or a combination (21 states), as shown in Figure 1.3 (King, 2006, p.5).

Centralized states are characterized by a state executive agency having across-the-board state control of services. *Decentralized states* are characterized, at minimum, by local control of services. Often local authorities run detention centers and some share responsibility for aftercare services with state agencies.

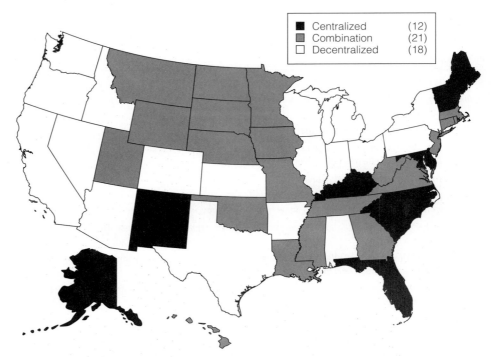

Figure 1.3 Organization of Juvenile Delinquency Services

SOURCE: Patrick Griffin and Melanie King. "National Overviews." *State Juvenile Justice Profiles*. Pittsburgh, PA: National Center for Juvenile Justice, 2006. Online: http://www.ncjj.org/stateprofiles/.

Combination states, as the name implies, have a mix of state-controlled and locally operated delinquency services. In some instances the state divides responsibility for services between the executive and judicial branches. Regardless of how the states choose to organize their services, each state has three basic components in their juvenile justice system.

The Components of the Juvenile Justice System

 The juvenile justice system is a complex amalgamation of three major components: law enforcement, courts and corrections.

Each component acts independently and interdependently as the total system functions.

Law enforcement is often the gatekeeper to the system, although juveniles may enter the system by other routes. Within the law enforcement component, juveniles may be assigned to a separate division or may be handled by all officers. In addition, as noted, states vary in the age establishing juvenile status. In many instances, older juveniles may be transferred into the adult system.

What happens in one component directly affects the other two components. If law enforcement arrests and elects to process thousands of juveniles, this could create a problem with overcrowded dockets in the courts. Likewise, if the courts sentence thousands of juveniles, the correctional system can become overcrowded, resulting in early release of prisoners and a potential problem for law enforcement.

The Juvenile Justice Process

Case processing of juvenile offenders varies from state to state. Even within a state, juvenile case processing can vary from community to community, reflecting local practice and tradition (Snyder and Sickmund, 2006, p.104). Any description of juvenile justice processing in the United States must, therefore, be general, outlining a common series of decision points as illustrated in Figure 1.4. The descriptions of each stage are adapted from the *Disproportionate Minority Contact Technical Assistance Manual*, 3rd edition (2007, pp.1–7 to 1–8).

Arrest

Youth are considered arrested when law enforcement agencies apprehend, stop or otherwise contact them and suspect them of having committed a delinquent act, an act that, if an adult committed it, would be criminal, including crimes against persons, crimes against property, drug offenses and crimes against the public order.

Referral

Referral occurs when a potentially delinquent youth is sent forward for legal processing and is received by a juvenile or family court or juvenile intake

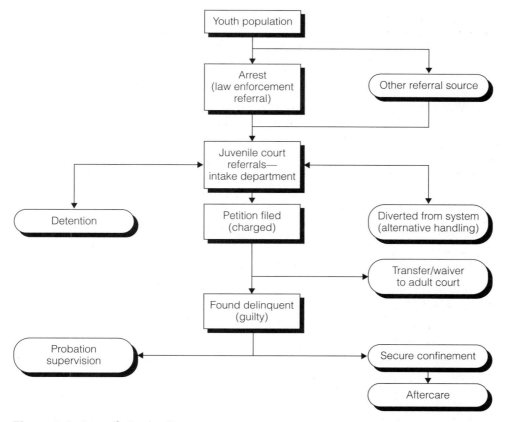

Figure 1.4   Juvenile Justice Process

SOURCE: Adapted from William Feyerherm, Howard N. Snyder, and Francisco Villarruel. "Chapter 1: Identification and Monitoring." In *DMC Technical Assistance Manual*, 3rd Edition, August 2006, p.1–5.

agency, either as a result of law enforcement action or a complaint by a citizen or school.

Intake

Youth referred to juvenile court for delinquent acts are often screened by an intake department (within or outside the court). The intake department may dismiss the case for lack of legal sufficiency, resolve the matter informally (without filing charges) or resolve it formally (filing charges).

Diversion

Diversion refers to removing a youth from the juvenile court's jurisdiction, either by dismissing the case, referring the case to an alternative treatment or transferring the case to the criminal justice system. The diversion population includes all youth referred for legal processing but handled without filing formal charges. Diversion is a focus of Chapter 10.

Detention

Detention refers to the secure placement of a youth into a facility at some point during court processing of their case (i.e., before disposition). In some jurisdictions, this population also includes youth held in secure detention while awaiting placement following a court disposition. It may also include youth held in jails and lockups but not those held in shelters, group homes or other nonsecure facilities.

Petitioning/Charges Filed

Formally charged (**petitioned**) delinquency cases appear on a court calendar in response to the filing of a petition, complaint or other legal document requesting the court to adjudicate a youth as a delinquent or status offender or to waive jurisdiction and transfer a youth to criminal court. Petitioning occurs when a juvenile court intake officer, prosecutor or other official determines a case should be handled formally. In contrast, informal handling is voluntary and does not include filing charges.

Adjudication Hearing/Delinquency Finding

At the *adjudication hearing* (comparable to the preliminary hearing in the adult system) the youth is questioned about the alleged offense. If the evidence is insufficient, the petition may be dismissed. If enough evidence exists that the child is delinquent, a court date is set for the disposition hearing (comparable to the trial in the adult system). Being **adjudicated** delinquent is roughly equivalent to being convicted in criminal court. It is a formal legal finding of responsibility.

Dispositional Hearing

If found to be delinquent, a youth normally proceeds to a disposition hearing, where the judge has several alternatives. Based on the findings of the investigation, the judge may place the youth on probation or in a foster home, release the child to the parents, commit the child to an institution or make the child a ward of the court. Serious juvenile offenders may be committed to mental institutions, reformatories, prisons, and county and state schools for delinquents. Some cities, such as New York and Chicago, have set up youth courts that are adult courts using the philosophy of juvenile courts. These youth courts usually confine their hearings to misdemeanors and are described in Chapter 11.

Probation

In probation cases youth are placed on formal or court-ordered supervision following a juvenile court disposition. Probation is discussed in detail in Chapter 12.

Confinement in a Secure Correctional Facility

In confinement cases youth are placed in secure residential or correctional facilities for delinquent offenders. The confinement population does not

Arrest and referral are two critical stages in the processing of a juvenile and can lead to diversion and informal handling of the youth (in essence, giving them a "second chance") or to formal processing and a juvenile record.

include youth placed in any form of out-of-home placement. Group homes, shelter homes and mental health treatment facilities, for example, would usually not be considered confinement. Correctional alternatives are described in Chapter 12.

Transfer to Adult Court

Waived cases are those in which a youth is transferred to criminal court as a result of a judicial finding in juvenile court. During a waiver hearing, the juvenile court usually files a petition asking the juvenile court judge to waive jurisdiction over the case. The juvenile court judge decides whether the case merits criminal prosecution. When a waiver request is denied, the matter is usually scheduled for an adjudicatory hearing in the juvenile court. If the request is granted, the juvenile is judicially waived to criminal court for further action. Juveniles may be transferred to criminal court through a variety of other methods as discussed in Chapter 10. Although the juvenile systems parallels the adult criminal justice system, important differences exist.

The Juvenile Justice System and the Criminal Justice System Compared

Historically the juvenile justice system strives to be an informal, private, non-adversarial system that stresses rehabilitation rather than punishment of youth. This is in direct contrast to the criminal justice systems of most states. Table 1.6 shows the juvenile court process compared to the adult process. In considering the comparing and contrasting of the juvenile and criminal justice systems, the difference in terminology should also be observed.

Note the common ground in operating assumptions, the role of law enforcement and intake/prosecution and other critical stages of the juvenile and criminal justice process. Also bear in mind that youth may move between the juvenile and criminal justice systems, as illustrated in Figure 1.5 (see p.23).

Diversion may occur at numerous points during the processing of a case. Whether such diversion is of benefit is one of several important issues in juvenile justice.

Issues in Juvenile Justice

 Issues in juvenile justice include whether to divert or not, whether to take a conservative or liberal approach to delinquency, whether to keep a juvenile's records confidential or to share information and whether minorities are over-represented in the juvenile justice system.

To Divert or Not?

No problem is more troublesome than the delicate balance between protecting children in a free society and protecting society from criminal behavior. Concern over this issue was evident during the conception and birth of juvenile justice centuries ago. Indeed, throughout the evolution of the juvenile justice system, society's values and attitudes toward crime and those who commit it

Table 1.6   Comparison of the Juvenile and the Criminal Systems

Although the juvenile and criminal justice systems are more alike in some jurisdictions than in others, generalizations can be made about the distinctions between the two systems and about their common ground.

Juvenile Justice System	*Common Ground*	*Criminal Justice System*
Operating Assumptions		
▪ Youth behavior is malleable.	▪ Community protection is a primary goal.	▪ Sanctions should be proportionate to the offense.
▪ Rehabilitation is usually a viable goal.	▪ Law violators must be held accountable.	▪ General deterrence works.
▪ Youth are in families and not independent.	▪ Constitutional rights apply.	▪ Rehabilitation is not a primary goal.
Prevention		
▪ Many specific delinquency prevention activities (e.g., school, church, recreation) are used.	▪ Educational approaches are taken to specific behaviors (drunken driving, drug use).	▪ Prevention activities are generalized and are aimed at deterrence (e.g., Crime Watch).
▪ Prevention is intended to change individual behavior and is often focused on reducing risk factors and increasing protective factors in the individual, family and community.		
Law Enforcement		
▪ Specialized juvenile units are used.	▪ Jurisdiction involves the full range of criminal behavior.	▪ Open public access to all information is required.
▪ Some additional behaviors are prohibited (truancy, running away, curfew violations).	▪ Constitutional and procedural safeguards exist.	▪ Law enforcement exercises discretion to divert offenders out of the criminal justice system.
▪ Some limitations are placed on public access to information.	▪ Both reactive and proactive approaches (targeted at offense types, neighborhoods, etc.) are used.	
▪ A significant number of youth are diverted from the juvenile justice system, often into alternative programs.	▪ Community policing strategies are employed.	
Intake—Prosecution		
▪ In many instances, juvenile court intake, not the prosecutor, decides which cases to file.	▪ Probable cause must be established.	▪ Plea bargaining is common.
▪ The decision to file a petition for court action is based on both social and legal factors.	▪ The prosecutor acts on behalf of the state.	▪ The prosecution decision is based largely on legal facts.
▪ A significant portion of cases are diverted from formal case processing.	▪ Prosecution is valuable in building history for subsequent offenses.	
▪ Intake or the prosecutor diverts cases from formal processing to services operated by the juvenile court prosecutor's office or outside agencies.	▪ Prosecution exercises discretion to withhold charges or divert offenders out of the criminal justice system.	
Detention—Jail/Lockup		
▪ Juveniles may be detained for their own protection or the community's protection.	▪ Accused offenders may be held in custody to ensure their appearance in court.	▪ Accused individuals have the right to apply for bond/bail release.
▪ Juveniles may not be confined with adults unless there is "sight and sound separation."	▪ Detention alternatives of home or electronic detention are used.	

(continued)

Table 1.6   *(Continued)*

Juvenile Justice System	Common Ground	Criminal Justice System
Adjudication—Conviction		
▪ Juvenile court proceedings are "quasi-civil" (not criminal) and may be confidential.	▪ Standard of "proof beyond a reasonable doubt" is required.	▪ Defendants have a constitutional right to a jury trial.
▪ If guilt is established the youth is adjudicated delinquent regardless of offense.	▪ Rights to be represented by an attorney, to confront witnesses and to remain silent are afforded.	▪ Guilt must be established on individual offenses charged to conviction.
▪ Right to jury trial is not afforded in all states.	▪ Appeals to a higher court are allowed.	▪ All proceedings are open.
▪ Experimentation with specialized courts (e.g., drug courts, gun courts) is under way.		
Disposition—Sentencing		
▪ Disposition decisions are based on individual and social factors, offense severity and youth's offense history.	▪ Decisions are influenced by current offense, offending history and social factors.	▪ Sentencing decisions are bound primarily by the severity of the current offense and by the offender's criminal history.
▪ Dispositional philosophy includes a significant rehabilitation component.	▪ Decisions hold offenders accountable.	▪ Sentencing philosophy is based largely on proportionality and punishment.
▪ Many dispositional alternatives are operated by the juvenile court.	▪ Decisions may give consideration to victims (e.g., restitution and "no contact" orders).	▪ Sentence is often determinate, based on offense.
▪ Dispositions cover a wide range of community-based and residential services.	▪ Decisions may not be cruel or unusual.	
▪ Disposition orders may be directed to people other than the offender (e.g., parents).		
▪ Disposition may be indeterminate, based on progress demonstrated by the youth.		
Aftercare—Parole		
▪ Function combines surveillance and reintegration activities (e.g., family, school, work).	▪ The behavior of individuals released from correctional settings is monitored.	▪ Function is primarily surveillance and reporting to monitor illicit behavior.
	▪ Violation of conditions can result in reincarceration.	

SOURCE: *Juvenile Justice: A Century of Change.* Washington, DC: National Report Series. *Juvenile Justice Bulletin,* December 1999, pp.10–12.

have swung back and forth, constantly adjusting to suit how society perceives delinquency, as discussed in the next chapter. The decision to divert youth from the juvenile justice process at numerous points along the way results in what is often called the funnel effect.

The Funnel Effect   The **funnel effect** describes how at each point in the system fewer and fewer youth pass through. This phenomenon, as it pertains to the entire criminal justice system, is described by Sickmund (2002): "For every 1,000 violent crimes committed, 604 are reported to the police; 286 arrests are made of which 46 involve suspects younger than 18. Twenty-three juvenile court adjudications result. Of these 8 residential placements are ordered and 14 other sanctions imposed, for example, probation, community service,

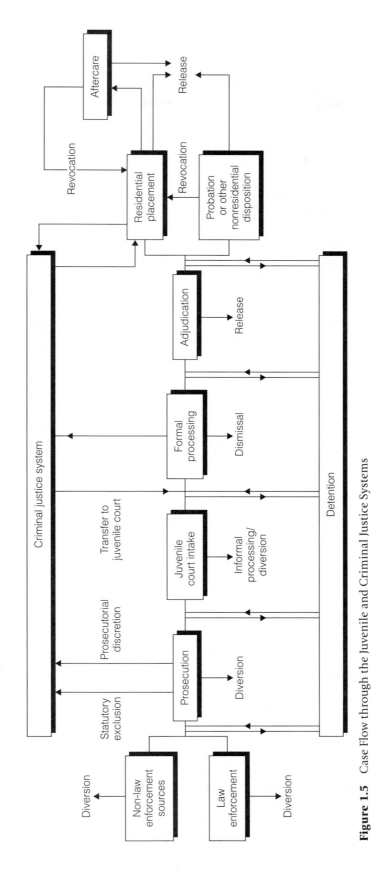

Figure 1.5 Case Flow through the Juvenile and Criminal Justice Systems

SOURCE: Howard N. Snyder and Melissa Sickmund. *Juvenile Offenders and Victims 2006 National Report*. Washington, DC: U.S. Department of Justice, Office of Justice Programs, Office of Juvenile Justice and Delinquency Prevention, March 2006, p.105.

fines and the like." This same funnel effect in delinquency case processing is illustrated in Figure 1.6.

According to Crowe's classic work in the Serious Habitual Offender Comprehensive Action Program (SHOCAP) (1991, pp.36–37), the funnel effect teaches a number of crucial lessons:

- Schools and police are fundamental to the community control of delinquency.
- School and police officials have more contact with our children than does anyone else, except parents.
- The juvenile justice system is irrelevant to the prevention and diversion of delinquency because the schools and the police are not a significant part of the system. They are at the opening of the "funnel" and have been mistakenly excluded from the concept of the community's responsibility for controlling delinquency.

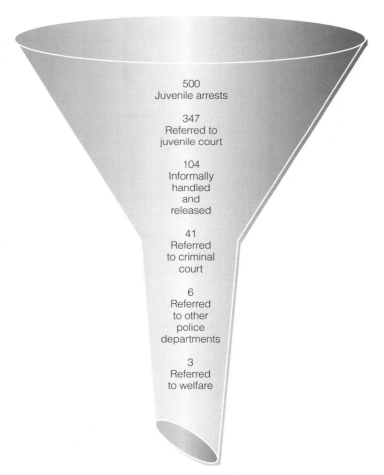

Figure 1.6   Police Response to Juvenile Crime

To understand how police deal with juvenile crime, picture a funnel, with the result shown here. For every 500 juveniles taken into custody, approximately 70 percent are sent to juvenile court, and a little more than 20 percent are released.

SOURCE: Adapted from FBI, *Crime in the United States, 2006.* Washington, DC: U.S. Government Printing Office, 2006, table 68.

- The contact and information that *could* be shared between parents, schools and police are *key* to the effective functioning of the juvenile justice system. They are the filter to the end of the funnel that feeds the legal system that has only one purpose—effective control of individuals whom the community is unable to control.

 The funnel effect illustrates the crucial role of law enforcement, schools and parents in the juvenile justice system and process.

Closely related to the issues of whether youth should be diverted from the system is the issue of whether society should take a conservative or liberal approach to delinquency.

Which Is More Just: A Conservative or a Liberal Approach to Delinquency?

When viewed against the backdrop of prevailing social sentiment and philosophy regarding crime and punishment, citizens' current attitudes remain pivotal in defining the structure and process of the juvenile justice system. Today's justice professionals and, in fact, society as a whole have differing attitudes and opinions regarding how the juvenile justice system *should* address the issues of delinquency. These philosophies are often categorized as either conservative or liberal. The *conservative* attitude is to "get tough," "stop babying these kids" and "get them off the streets."

 The conservative approach to juvenile justice is "get tough on juveniles"—to punish and imprison them.

The conservative philosophy accepts retribution as a purpose of punishment. The conservative view also supports the use of imprisonment to control crime and antisocial behavior. Rehabilitative programs may be provided during incarceration, but it is imprisonment itself, with its attendant deprivations, that must be primarily relied on to prevent crime, delinquency and recidivism. Correctional treatment is not necessary.

In contrast, the *liberal* attitude toward juvenile justice is "treatment, not punishment" for youth who are antisocial and wayward.

 The liberal approach to juvenile justice stresses treatment and rehabilitation, including community-based programs.

Another issue facing the juvenile justice system is whether juvenile justice proceedings and records should be confidential or open.

Confidentiality versus Openness

In addition to having their own distinct juvenile justice systems, states have begun to de-emphasize traditional confidentiality concerns while emphasizing information sharing. During the early 1990s, states made significant changes in how the juvenile justice system treats information about juvenile offenders, particularly violent juvenile offenders. As juvenile crime became more serious, community protection, the public's right to know and service providers' need to share information displaced the desire to protect minors from the stigma of youthful indiscretions. Legislatures throughout the country have increasingly called for a presumption of open hearings and records, at least for some juvenile offenders: "Once a mainstay of juvenile court, confidentiality, has given way to substantial openness in many states" (Snyder and Sickmund, 2006, p.108). Delinquency hearings are open in 14 states and are open with limits depending on the type of cases as shown in Figure 1.7.

The *Juvenile Offenders and Victims: 2006 National Report* notes:

> Formerly confidential records are now being made available to a wide variety of individuals. Many states open records to schools and youth-serving agencies as well as individuals and agencies within the justice system.... As of the end of the 2004 legislative session, juvenile codes in all states allow information contained in juvenile court records to be specifically released to one or more of the following parties: the prosecutor, law enforcement, social service agencies, schools, the victim or the public. ... In addition the media can access juvenile offenders' identities in most states. (Snyder and Sickmund, p.109)

Yet another issue is whether disproportionate minority contact is the result of racism in the juvenile justice system.

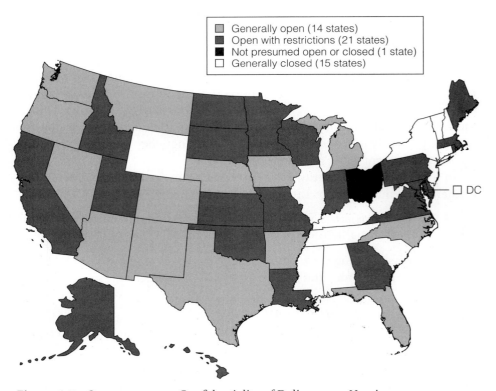

Figure 1.7   Openness versus Confidentiality of Delinquency Hearings

SOURCE: Howard N. Snyder and Melissa Sickmund. *Juvenile Offenders and Victims: 2006 National Report.* Washington, DC: U.S. Department of Justice, Office of Justice Programs, Office of Juvenile Justice and Delinquency Prevention, March 2006, p.108.

Disproportionate Minority Contact (DMC)

The most recent study of disproportionate minority contact in the juvenile justice system looked at longitudinal community studies of delinquency in Pittsburgh, Pennsylvania; Rochester, New York; and Seattle, Washington and found a distinguishable level of disproportionate minority contact (DMC) in the juvenile justice system. Minorities, especially African American and Hispanic youth, are, on the whole, more likely to come into contact with the criminal justice system whether it be at the arrest stage or further along at the stage of confinement (Huizinga et al., 2007). This study found that minority youth continue to be greatly over-represented in the juvenile justice system, with minority youth constituting 34 percent of the juvenile population nationwide, but representing 62 percent of juveniles detained and 67 percent of those committed to secure juvenile facilities, with black youth over-represented more than any other group.

The *Disproportionate Minority Contact Technical Assistance Manual* describes the Relative Rate Index (RRI) as a way to measure differences in respect to populations related to the specific occurrence of an event. The baseline of every RRI is the occurrence of an event by a white person. For example, if the RRI of blacks or African American youth is 2.96 in regard to arrests, this means that a black or African American juvenile is 2.96 times more likely to be arrested than a white juvenile in the population. Table 1.7 summarizes the RRI for black/African American youth at various points in the juvenile justice process.

DMC will be explored further in later discussions of arrests, diversion, confinement and transfer to criminal court. Although it is clear that minorities are over-represented in the juvenile justice system, the more basic question is whether this represents racial discrimination. Many discussions of racial discrimination are muddied as the result of failure to differentiate between *discrimination* and *disparity* (Walker et al., 2007, p.18). **Discrimination** refers to unfair, differential treatment of a particular group of youth, for example, Hispanics. **Disparity** refers to a difference, but not necessarily involving discrimination.

Table 1.7 RRI for Black/African American Youth in the Juvenile Justice System

Data Items	White Rate of Occurrence	Minority Rate of Occurrence	Relative Rate Index
Population at Risk			
Arrest	63.58	188.50	2.96
Referral	31.79	36.49	1.15
Diversion	16.18	8.84	0.55
Detention	29.50	44.13	1.50
Petitioned/Charge Filing	67.21	73.12	1.09
Delinquent Findings	69.60	62.31	0.90
Probation	50.51	48.32	0.96
Confinement in Secure Correctional Facilities	1.43	2.65	1.85
Transferred to Adult Court	0.61	0.91	1.49

SOURCE: William Feyerherm, Howard N. Snyder, and Francisco Villarruel. "Chapter 1: Identification and Monitoring." In *DMC Technical Assistance Manual*, 3rd Edition, 2007, p.1–12.

Consider, for example, the fact that most college classes have primarily relatively young students, but this does not indicate age discrimination (Walker et al.). In criminal justice the critical distinction is between legal and extralegal factors: *"Legal factors* include the seriousness of the offense, aggravating or mitigating circumstance, or an offender's prior criminal record. These are considered legitimate bases for decisions by most criminal justice officials because they relate to an individual's criminal behavior. *Extralegal factors* include race, ethnicity, gender, social class and lifestyle" (Walker et al.). Walker et al. (p.412) conclude:

> Methodologically sophisticated research reveals that racial and ethnic differences in juvenile victimization and offending rate can be attributed in large part to family and community characteristics. African American and Hispanic youth are more likely than white youth to be the victims of violent crime because they spend more time away from home, and are more likely to live in single-parent households and disadvantaged communities. Similarly, the higher rates of violent offending found among minority youth than white youth reflect the fact that minority youth are more likely to live in disadvantaged neighborhoods, to be members of gangs, and to have weak bonds to social institutions such as schools. The sources of risk of victimization and offending are similar for all teenagers, but the likelihood of experiencing these risk factors is higher for youth of color than for white youth.
>
> The results of studies examining the effect of race/ethnicity on juvenile justice processing decisions suggest that the juvenile justice system, like the criminal justice system for adults, is not free of racial bias. There is compelling evidence that racial minorities are treated more harshly than whites at various points in the juvenile justice process. Most importantly, minority youth are substantially more likely than white youth to be detained pending disposition, adjudicated delinquent, and waived to adult court. They also are sentenced more harshly than their white counterparts, at least in part because of the tendency of criminal justice officials to attribute their crimes to internal (personality) rather than external (environmental) causes.

The preceding issues are not new; they have their roots in the evolution of the juvenile justice system itself, as discussed in the next chapter.

 SUMMARY

- The underlying premise of the first juvenile court is *parens patriae,* the responsibility of the state to protect its children and youth.
- Seventeen is most commonly recognized as the oldest age for juvenile court jurisdiction in delinquency matters.
- Distributive or social justice provides an equal share of what is valued in a society to each member of that society. This includes power, prestige and possessions. Retributive justice seeks revenge for unlawful behavior. Restorative justice focuses on repairing the harm done to victims and to the community and stresses that offenders must contribute to the repair.
- Researchers commonly use three methods to measure the nature and extent of unlawful acts by juveniles: official data, self-report data and victim surveys.

- The FBI's Uniform Crime Reports contain statistics on violent crimes (murder, aggravated assault causing serious bodily harm, forcible rape, robbery) and property crimes (burglary, larceny-theft, motor vehicle theft and arson).
- According to self-report studies, delinquency is almost universal.
- The terminology of the juvenile justice system underscores its emphasis on protecting youth from harmful labels and their stigmatizing effects.
- The juvenile justice system is a complex amalgamation of three major components: law enforcement, courts and corrections.
- Issues in juvenile justice include whether to divert or not, whether to take a conservative or liberal approach to delinquency, whether to keep juveniles' records confidential or to share information and whether minorities are over-represented in the juvenile justice system.
- The funnel effect illustrates the crucial role of law enforcement, schools and parents in the juvenile justice system and process.
- The conservative approach to juvenile justice is "get tough on juveniles"—to punish and imprison them. The liberal approach to juvenile justice stresses treatment and rehabilitation, including community-based programs.

DISCUSSION QUESTIONS

1. At what age do people become adults in your state?
2. Do you support a separate justice system for juveniles? Why or why not?
3. Which view of justice do you support?
4. What are some problems with the Uniform Crime Reports? The National Incident-Based Reporting System?
5. How influential is the media in shaping the public's attitudes toward juveniles?
6. How do the components of the juvenile justice system interact?
7. What do you consider the most important issue facing juvenile justice?
8. What are the major differences between the criminal justice system and the juvenile justice system?
9. Do you tend to favor a liberal or a conservative approach to delinquency?
10. Given that minorities are over-represented in the juvenile justice system, do you believe this is the result of discrimination?

REFERENCES

Bazemore, Gordon and Umbreit, Mark. *A Comparison of Four Restorative Conferencing Models.* Washington, DC: OJJDP Juvenile Justice Bulletin, February 2001. (NCJ 184738)

Crime in the United States, 2006. Uniform Crime Reports. Washington, DC: Federal Bureau of Investigation, 2006. http://www.fbi.gov/ucr/cius2006/about/crime_summary.html. Accessed July 8, 2008.

Crowe, Timothy D. *Habitual Juvenile Offenders: Guidelines for Citizen Action and Public Response.* Serious Habitual Offender Comprehensive Action Program (SHOCAP). Washington, DC: Office of Juvenile Justice and Delinquency Prevention, October 1991.

Disproportionate Minority Contact Technical Assistance Manual, 3rd edition. Washington, DC: Office of Juvenile Justice Delinquency Prevention, 2007.

Huizinga, David; Thornberry, Terrence; Knight, Kelly; and Lovegrove, Peter. *Disproportionate Minority Contact in the Juvenile Justice System: A Study of Differential Minority Arrest/Referral to Court in Three Cities.* Washington, DC: Department of Justice, September 2007.

Karmen, Andrew. *Crime Victims: An Introduction to Victimology,* 6th ed. Belmont, CA: Wadsworth Publishing Company, 2007.

King, Melanie. *Guide to the State Juvenile Justice Profiles.* Washington, DC: Technical Assistance to the Juvenile Court Bulletin, April 2006.

Kirk, David S. "Examining the Divergence across Self-Report and Official Data Sources on Inferences about the Adolescent Life-Course of Crime." *Journal of Quantitative Criminal Criminology,* June 2006, pp.107–129.

McEwen, Tom. "Information Management." In *Local Government Police Management*, 4th ed., edited by William A. Geller and Carrel W. Stephens. Washington, DC: International City/County Management Association, 2003, pp.391–421.

Roberts, David J. Implementing the National Incident-Based Reporting System: A Project Status Report. Washington, DC: U.S. Department of Justice, Bureau of Justice Statistics, July 1997. (NCJ 165581).

Ross, W. D., trans. "Nicomachean Ethics." *Aristotle: II.* Chicago: Encyclopedia Britannica, 1952.

Sickmund, Melissa. *Crime Funnels: U.S. Response to Crime.* Pittsburgh, PA: National Center for Juvenile Justice, 2002.

Snyder, Howard N. and Sickmund, Melissa. *Juvenile Offenders and Victims 2006 National Report.*

Washington, DC: U.S. Department of Justice, Office of Justice Programs, Office of Juvenile Justice and Delinquency Prevention, March 2006.

Springer, Charles E. *Justice for Juveniles.* Washington, DC: U.S. Department of Justice, Office of Juvenile Justice and Delinquency Prevention, 1986.

Walker, Samuel; Spohn, Cassia; and DeLone, Miriam. *The Color of Justice: Race, Ethnicity, and Crime in America,* 4th ed. Belmont, CA: Wadsworth Publishing Company, 2007.

Weitzer, Ronald and Kubrin, Charis E. "Breaking News: How Local TV News and Real-World Conditions Affect Fear of Crime." *Justice Quarterly,* September 2004, pp.497–520.

Wexler, Chuck. "How Issues of Race and Murder Play Out in the Media." *Subject to Debate,* May 2006, p.6.

HELPFUL RESOURCE

A Primer on Crime and Delinquency Theory, 2nd ed. by Robert M. Bohm. Belmont, CA: Wadsworth Publishing Company, 2001.

CHAPTER 2

The History and Philosophy behind the Juvenile Justice System

CHILDREN ARE OUR MOST VALUABLE NATURAL RESOURCE.

—HERBERT C. HOOVER

London's Bridewell was similar to a debtor's prison. It confined both children and adult "vagrants."

DO YOU KNOW?

■ When and where the first house of refuge (reformatory) was opened in the United States?

■ Who the child savers were and what their philosophy was?

■ When and where the first juvenile court was established?

■ How the first juvenile courts functioned?

■ What functions probation was to serve within the juvenile court system?

■ How Progressive Era proponents viewed crime? What model they refined?

■ What resulted from the 1909 White House Conference on Youth?

■ What act funded federal programs to aid children and families?

■ What the Four Ds of juvenile justice refer to?

■ What was established by the following key cases: *Kent v. United States, In re Gault, In re Winship, McKeiver v. Pennsylvania, Breed v. Jones, Schall v. Martin*?

■ What effect isolating offenders from their normal environment might have?

■ What the Uniform Juvenile Court Act provided?

■ What the major impact of the 1970 White House Conference on Youth was?

■ What the two main goals of the JJDP Act of 1974 were?

■ What juvenile delinquency liability should be limited to according to the American Bar Association?

CAN YOU DEFINE?

Bridewell	deserts	justice model	preventive detention
child savers	deterrence	medical model	youthful offenders
corporal punishment	double jeopardy	net widening	
decriminalization	due process	poor laws	

CHAPTER OUTLINE

Introduction

Social Control in Early Societies

Developments in England:
A Brief Overview

The Development of Juvenile
Justice in the United States

The Puritan Period
(1646–1824)

The Refuge Period (1824–1899)

Houses of Refuge

Reform Schools

Foster Homes

The Child Savers

*Other Developments during the
Refuge Period*

The Juvenile Court Period
(1899–1960)

The 1899 Juvenile Court Act

*Early Efforts at Diversion:
The Chicago Boy's Court
and Youth Counsel Bureau*

*Federal Government Concern
and Involvement*

The Juvenile Rights Period
(1960–1980)

The Four Ds of Juvenile Justice

The Kent Decision

The Gault Decision

*The President's Commission
on Law Enforcement and
Administration of Justice*

Youth Service Bureaus

*The Uniform Juvenile
Court Act*

*The White House Conference on
Youth*

*The Office of Juvenile Justice
and Delinquency Prevention
and the Juvenile Justice and
Delinquency Prevention Act*

*A Return to Due Process Issues:
Other Landmark Cases*

The Issue of Right to Treatment

Decriminalization of Status Offenses

*Development of Standards for
Juvenile Justice*

The Crime Control Period
(1980–Present)

*Schall v. Martin (1984) and
Preventive Detention*

Still Evolving

Introduction

A separate justice system for **youthful offenders** (usually under age 18) is, historically speaking, relatively recent. An understanding of how this system evolved is central to understanding the system as it currently exists and the challenges it faces (see Figure 2.1).

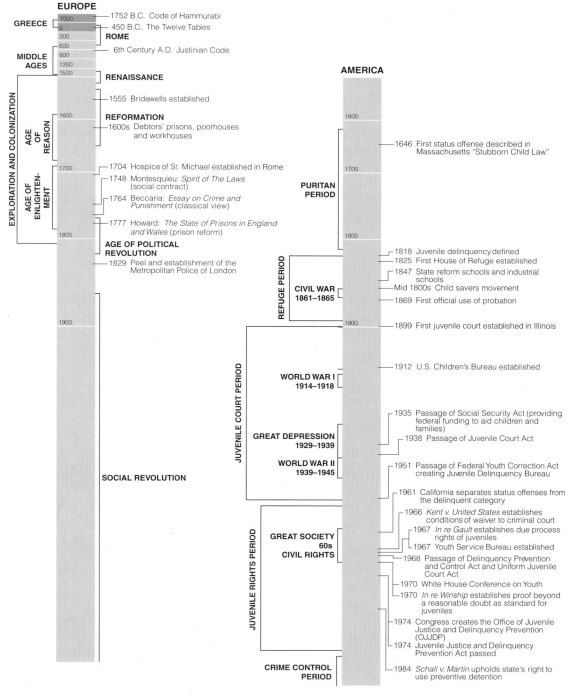

Figure 2.1   Timeline of Significant Dates in Juvenile Justice

It has been said that the historian is a prophet looking backward. History reveals patterns and changes in attitudes toward youths and how they are treated. The emphasis has changed from punishment to protection and back. As one philosophy achieves prominence, problems persist and critics clamor for change. History also reveals mistakes that can be avoided in the future as well as hopes and promises that remain unfulfilled.

Social Control in Early Societies

People have banded together for companionship and protection for tens of thousands of years. As early societies developed, they established rules to maintain social order and protect their members' safety. Everyone was to conform to society's expectations. Those who broke the rules were severely punished. Most early societies treated all wrongdoings and criminal offenses alike. Children and adults were subject to the same rules and laws, were tried under the same legal process and, when convicted, suffered the same penalties.

In early societies men were the heads of their families. In such patriarchal societies rebellion against a father, even by adult sons, was not tolerated. Punishment was swift and severe. The father in ancient Roman culture also exercised unlimited authority over his family, being allowed to administer **corporal punishment** (inflict bodily pain) and even sell his children into slavery. One important concept from the Roman civilization that influenced the development of juvenile justice was *patria postestas*—referring to the absolute control fathers had over their children and the children's absolute responsibility to obey. This concept evolved into the doctrine of *parens patriae*, a basic tenet in our juvenile justice system.

Developments in England: A Brief Overview

Events in England had a great influence on the juvenile justice system that developed in the United States. The earliest legal document written in English contained the laws of King Aethelbert (around A.D. 600). These laws made no special allowance for an offender's age. In fact several cases document children as young as 6 being hanged or burned at the stake.

Early in English history, the Church of Rome greatly influenced how children were viewed. Church doctrine stated that children younger than 7 had not yet reached the age of reason and, thus, could not be held liable for sins. English law adopted the same perspective. Under 7 years of age, children were not considered legally able to have the required intent to commit a crime. From ages 7 to 14, it was presumed they did not have such intent, but if evidence proved differently, children could be found guilty of committing crimes. After age 14, individuals were considered adults.

In thirteenth-century England, common law (law of custom and usage) gave kings power of being the "father of his country." The king was perceived as guardian over the person and property of minors, who were considered wards of the state and, as such, received special protection. The Latin phrase meaning "father of the country" is *parens patriae* giving the king the right and responsibility to care for children. *Parens patriae* was used to justify the state's intervention in the lives of its feudal lords and their children, and it placed juveniles between the civil and the criminal systems. The chancery courts heard issues involving guardianship but did *not* have jurisdiction over children who committed crimes. Such youths were handled within the criminal court system.

The sixteenth and seventeenth centuries in Europe—a period called the Renaissance—marked the transition from medieval to modern times and were characterized by an emphasis on art and the humanities, as well as a more humanistic approach to criminal justice. In 1555, London's **Bridewell** Prison became the first institution to control youthful beggars and vagrants. Based on an underlying theme of achieving discipline, deterrence and rehabilitation through work and severe punishment, Bridewell's goals were "to make [wayward youths] earn their keep, to reform them by compulsory work and discipline, and to deter others from vagrancy and idleness" (Grunhut, 1948, p.15). Parliament passed a law in 1576 calling for construction of Bridewell-type institutions in every county to confine both children and adults who were considered idle and disorderly. Some parents voluntarily committed their children to Bridewells believing the emphasis on hard work would benefit the youth.

During Elizabeth I's reign (1558–1603), England passed **poor laws** that established the appointment of overseers to *indenture* poor and neglected children into servitude. Such children were forced to work for wealthy families who, in turn, trained them in a trade, domestic service or farming. Such involuntary apprenticeships were served until the youths were 21 or older. These Elizabethan poor laws were the model for dealing with poor children for the next 200 years.

In 1601 England proposed establishing large workhouses for children who could not be supported by their parents. The children would be placed there and "bred up to labor, principles of virtue implanted in them at an early age, and laziness be discouraged . . . and, settled in a way serviceable to the public's good and not bred up in all manners of vice" (Webb and Webb, 1927, p.52). This proposal was finally implemented with the passage of the Gilbert Act of 1782 decreeing that all poor, aged, sick and infirm be placed in *poorhouses* (almshouses). Under the act, poor infants and children who could not go with their mothers were not placed in the poorhouse but with a "proper person" (de Scheveinitz, 1943, pp.20–21).

Another important milestone in the development of juvenile justice was the founding of the London Philanthropic Society in 1817, one purpose of which was to reform juvenile offenders. The Society opened the first English house of refuge for children, a major shift from family-oriented discipline to institutional treatment.

The Development of Juvenile Justice in the United States

While the English justice system served as the basis for juvenile justice in America, a distinctively American system evolved in response to conditions unique to this country. Juvenile justice in the United States is generally recognized as having progressed through five distinct stages, beginning with the first European settlers to land in the New World, whose philosophies defined and shaped what is now referred to as the Puritan Period.

The Puritan Period (1646–1824)

The American colonists brought with them much of the English criminal justice system, including poor laws and the forced apprenticeship system for poor and neglected children. They also continued the centuries-old philosophy of *patria postestas*, giving fathers absolute authority over all family matters and justifying harsh consequences for children who misbehaved. In fact, early laws prescribed the death penalty for children who disobeyed their parents. The colonial Puritan philosophy regarding juvenile behavior was enacted into law in 1646 when Massachusetts passed the Stubborn Child Law, creating the first status offense, an act considered illegal for minors only. The law stood unrevised for more than 300 years.

Even then, age was a consideration in juvenile justice, as Blackstone (1776, p.23) summarized the law regarding youths' responsibility: "Under seven years of age indeed an infant cannot be guilty of a felony; for then a felonious discretion is almost an impossibility in nature; but at eight years old he may be guilty of a felony." Furthermore, according to the common law, although a youth under age 14 may be adjudged incapable of discerning right from wrong, it appeared to the court and the jury that he *could* discern between good and evil (Blackstone). Thus, if accused of a major criminal act, the juvenile would proceed through the justice system as an adult. Trials and punishment were based on age, and anyone older than 7 was subject to the courts. Jails, the only form of incarceration, were primarily used for detention pending trial.

During this period, the fundamental mode of juvenile control was the family, with the church and other social institutions also expected to handle juvenile delinquents. Until the end of the eighteenth century, the family was also the main economic unit, with family members working together farming or in home-based trades. Children were important contributors to these family-based industries. The privileged classes found apprenticeships for their children so they could learn marketable skills. The children of the poor, in contrast, often were bound out as indentured servants.

The end of the eighteenth century brought the Industrial Revolution, which forever changed the face of America. Families left the fields and farms and flocked to the cities to work in factories. Child labor in these factories replaced the apprenticeship system. Increasing industrialization, urbanization and immigration had created severe problems for families and their children. The social control once exerted by the family weakened—children in the workforce had to obey their bosses' demands, often in conflict with their parents' demands. In addition, poverty was increasing for many families. This combination of poverty and diminished family control set an "ominous stage," with some Americans fearing a growing "dangerous class" and seeking ways to "control the wayward youth who epitomized this threat to social stability" (Krisberg and Austin, 1993, p.15).

To counteract the continued breakdown of traditional forms of social control, communities created institutions for children where they could learn good work and study habits, live in a disciplined and healthy environment, and develop character. Five distinct, yet interrelated, institutions evolved to handle poor, abused, neglected, dependent and delinquent children brought before a court: (1) indenture and apprenticeship, (2) mixed almshouses (poorhouses), (3) private orphanages, (4) public facilities for dependent children and (5) jails.

Another significant development during this period was an 1818 committee report linking pauperism, or poverty, with juvenile delinquency—the first public recognition of the term *juvenile delinquency*. This correlation remained an object of focus in juvenile justice throughout the 1800s and 1900s.

The rising concern and social reform that marked the turn of the nineteenth century saw reformers seeking to change laws and public policy as they affected children. During 1820 and 1821, the Society for the Prevention of Pauperism surveyed U.S. prisons and found a prevailing spirit of revenge in prisoner treatment. Their report criticized imprisoning individuals regardless of age or the severity of crime. In 1824 the Society reorganized to become the Society for the Reformation of Juvenile Delinquents in the City of New York, whose purpose was to establish a reformatory. This development signaled a fundamental shift in the underlying philosophy concerning youths and the justice system and moved American juvenile justice into its next evolutionary stage—the Refuge Period.

The Refuge Period (1824–1899)

During the Refuge Period reformers created separate institutions for youths such as houses of refuge, reform schools and foster homes. However, from the onset, these special institutions for juveniles still housed together delinquent, dependent and neglected children, a practice that, unfortunately, persists in many juvenile detention facilities today (Krisberg and Austin, 1993, p.17).

Houses of Refuge

 In 1824 the New York House of Refuge, the first U.S. reformatory, opened to house juvenile delinquents, defined in its charter as "youths convicted of criminal offenses or found in vagrancy."

The House of Refuge was the predecessor of today's training schools. Children were placed there by court order and usually stayed until they reached the age of maturity. Children who misbehaved lost certain rewarded positions or were whipped. The labor of the House was contracted out to local businesses. Youths were given apprenticeships and training in practical occupations.

HIGHLIGHTS OF PURITAN PERIOD REFORM

Philosophy Children were inherently sinful and in need of strict control and/or punishment when necessary. Most nonconforming children were of lower-class parentage.

Treatment Misbehaving children were generally controlled by familial punishment. External, community punishment and control were necessary only when the parents failed.

Policies Communal legal sanctions were guided by the British tradition of common law, allowing children older than 7 to receive public punishment. Children could be punished publicly for several status offenses such as rebelliousness, disobedience and sledding on the Sabbath. Thus, separate systems of justice were set up for children and adults. Institutions created to care for orphaned and neglected children included almshouses and orphanages.

SOURCE: Adapted from materials of the Center for the Assessment of the Juvenile Justice System (Hawkins et al., 1980).

The states' authority to send children to such houses of refuge under the doctrine of *parens patriae* was upheld in 1838 in Pennsylvania in *Ex parte Crouse*. In this case a mother claimed that her daughter was incorrigible and had her committed to the Philadelphia House of Refuge. The girl's father sought her release but was denied by the court, which stated:

> The object of the charity is reformation, by training its inhabitants to industry; by imbuing their minds with principles of morality and religion; by furnishing them with means to earn a living; and above all, by separating them from the corrupting influence of improper associates. To this end, may not the natural parents, when unequal to the task of education, or unworthy of it, be superseded by the *parens patriae*, or common guardian of the community?

However, many houses of refuge were prisons with harsh discipline, including severe whippings and solitary confinement. Despite public disapproval of the harsh discipline and health hazards, 20 such institutions had opened in the United States by 1860.

Krisberg and Austin (1993, p.16) suggest: "Although early 19th-century philanthropists relied on religion to justify their good works, their primary motivation was protection of their class privileges. Fear of social unrest and chaos dominated their thinking. The rapid growth of a visible impoverished class, coupled with apparent increases in crime, disease and immorality, worried those in power."

From 1859 to 1890 many houses of refuge were replaced by reform schools, which often were indistinguishable from the houses of refuge.

Reform Schools

By the middle of the nineteenth century, the more progressive states began to develop new institutions—*reform schools*—intended to provide discipline in a "homelike" atmosphere where education was emphasized. Although reform schools emphasized formal schooling, they also retained large workshops and the contract system of labor.

Foster Homes

While many states were building reform schools, New York in 1853 emphasized placing neglected and delinquent children in private *foster homes*, frequently located in rural areas. At the time, the city was viewed as a place of crime and bad influences, in contrast with the clean, healthy, crime-free country.

The foster home was to be the family surrogate used in all stages of the juvenile justice process. For a variety of reasons this concept faltered. Personality conflicts between foster parents and juvenile clients often caused disruption. In addition, accrediting and monitoring foster home licenses was inadequate and sometimes ignored completely.

The Child Savers

Many reforms swept through the United States during the nineteenth century, including the child-saving movement, which began around the middle of the 1800s. The **child savers** believed that children's environments could make them "bad." These wealthy, civic-minded citizens tried to "save" unfortunate children by placing them in houses of refuge and reform schools.

These reformers were shocked that children could be tried in a criminal court like adults and be sentenced to jail with hardened criminals. The reformers believed that society owed more to its children.

 The child savers were reformers whose philosophy was that the child was basically good and was to be treated by the state as a young person with a problem.

The reformers thought that children's contact with the justice system should not be a process of arrest and trial, but should seek answers to what the children are, how they have become what they are, and what society should do in the children's, as well as society's, best interests to save them from wasted lives. The child savers' motivating principles were (Task Force Report, 1976, p.6):

- Children should not be held as accountable as adult transgressors.
- The objective of juvenile justice is to help youngsters, to treat and rehabilitate them rather than punish.
- Dispositions should be predicated on an analysis of the youth's special circumstances and needs.
- The system should avoid the punitive adversary role and formalized trappings of the adult criminal process.

The child savers were not entirely humanitarian, however. They viewed poor children as a threat to society and who needed to be reformed to conform, to value hard work and to become contributing members of society (Platt, 1968).

Other Developments during the Refuge Period

Organizations such as the Young Men's Christian Association (YMCA, 1851) and the Young Women's Christian Association (YWCA, 1861) provided recreation and counseling services to youths, thereby preventing delinquency.

The Civil War (1861–1865) was followed by reconstruction and massive industrialization. Many children were left fatherless by the war, and many families moved to urban areas seeking work. Often children were exploited in sweatshops or roamed the streets in gangs while their parents worked in factories.

In 1866 the first specialized institution for male juveniles was authorized in Washington, DC. This House of Corrections consisted of several cottages containing 60 or more beds. At this time state reformatories also came into existence, including the New York State Reformatory at Elmira, which opened in 1877.

By the end of the 1800s, reform schools introduced vocational education, military drill and calisthenics into the institutions' regimens. At the same time, some reform schools changed their names to "industrial schools" and later to "training schools," to emphasize the "treatment" aspect of corrections. For example, the Ohio Reform Farm School opened in 1857, later became the Boy's Industrial School, and was renamed again to the Fairfield School for Boys.

© The Bettmann Archive/CORBIS

In this engraving from an American newspaper of 1868, a 6-year-old sentenced for vagrancy to the House of Refuge on Blackwell's Island, New York City, pleads unavailingly for mercy for his first offense.

Several other significant events occurred during the 1800s that altered the administration of juvenile justice (Griffin and Griffin, 1978, p.20):

1870—First use of separate trials for juveniles (Massachusetts)
1877—Separate dockets and records established for juveniles (Massachusetts)
1880—First probation system applicable to juveniles instituted
1898—Segregation of children under 16 awaiting trial (Rhode Island)
1899—First juvenile court established (Illinois)

A juvenile court movement began during the 1890s which provided citizen participation in community-based corrections. This citizen participation through the Parent Teacher Association (PTA), founded in 1897, induced the Cook County (Illinois) Bar Association to write the law establishing a juvenile court in Chicago (Hunt, 1973), the first of its kind, propelling juvenile justice into its third evolutionary phase—the Juvenile Court Period.

The Juvenile Court Period (1899–1960)

The Juvenile Court Period was born at the beginning of what is often referred to as the Progressive Era or the Age of Reform—the first quarter of the twentieth century. According to reformers, children were not inherently bad but were made so by society and their environment. Progressives believed that the family was especially influential and that parents were responsible for bringing their children up to be obedient and to work hard. When parents were unable to fulfill such responsibilities, reformers believed in state intervention. Their vision materialized in the shape of the 1899 Juvenile Court Act, titled an "Act to Regulate the Treatment and Control of Dependent, Neglected and Delinquent Children."

The 1899 Juvenile Court Act

Passed in Illinois, this act represented the U.S. criminal justice system's first formal recognition that it owed a different duty to children than to adults and that impressionable, presumably salvageable youths should not be mixed in prisons with hardened criminals. The law created a public policy based on the **medical model**—that is, a treatment model—to retard the social and moral decay of the environment, family and youths. An underlying philosophy of the medical model was that delinquency was a preventable condition, and in cases where prevention failed and delinquent behavior occurred, the condition could be treated and cured.

The act created the first juvenile court in the United States and provided social reform and a structured way to restore and control children in trouble. It also provided a way to care for children who needed official protection.

 In 1899 the Illinois legislature passed a law establishing a juvenile court that became the cornerstone for juvenile justice throughout the United States.

Key features of this act included:

- Defining a delinquent as any detainee younger than 16.
- Separating children from adults in institutions.
- Setting special, informal procedural rules for juvenile court.
- Providing for use of probation officers.
- Prohibiting detention of children younger than 12 in a jail or police station.

HIGHLIGHTS OF REFUGE PERIOD REFORM

Children were protected from confinement in jails, prisons and institutions by the opening of houses of refuge. Responsibilities shifted back and forth between the private and public sectors. Between 1878 and 1898 Massachusetts established a state-wide system of probation to aid the court in juvenile matters, a method of corrections currently used in every state.

Child labor was regulated, special services for handicapped children were developed and public education grew. Public responsibility for protecting and caring for children became accepted. However, no legal machinery existed to handle juveniles who needed special care, protection and treatment as wards of the state rather than as criminals.

Philosophy Poverty was a crime that could be eliminated by removing children from offending environments and reforming their unacceptable conduct. Youth problems increased as by-products of rapid urbanization: poverty, immigration and unhealthy environments.

Treatment Nonconforming children were controlled by external institutions, such as houses of refuge and reformatories created by paternalistic child savers. Public education was used to "Americanize" foreign and lower-class children. Several private organizations were created to assimilate foreign and lower-class youths into American culture. Private groups were organized to rescue children from poor and unfit environments. Locked facilities were built across the nation. Orphan asylums became popular ways to house and mold the conduct of children left homeless by the Civil War and/or neglected by unfit parents.

Policies Local and state governments became providers of care and treatment for neglected and delinquent children. The *parens patriae* tradition, correctional policies that separated adult and youthful offenders, and indeterminate sentencing for juvenile inmates were adopted. Statutory definitions of juvenile delinquency were expanded to include new status offenses, such as begging, cheating and gambling.

The Juvenile Court Act gave "original jurisdiction in *all* cases coming within the terms of this act," removing those younger than 16 from the criminal court's jurisdiction and placing them in a paternalistic system that viewed juvenile delinquents as victims of their environments not responsible for their offenses. Rehabilitation and the child's welfare were of prime concern. The adjudicative process within the juvenile court was to be special; it was *not* to function as an adult criminal court but more like a social welfare agency. The Juvenile Court Act equated poor and abused children with delinquent and criminal children and provided that they be treated in essentially the same way, establishing the one-pot approach described in Chapter 1.

 The first juvenile courts were administrative agencies of circuit or district courts. They served a social welfare function, embracing the rehabilitative ideal of reforming children rather than punishing them.

Passage of the Illinois Juvenile Court Act marked the first time that probation and probation officers were formally made *specifically* applicable to juveniles. The act stipulated:

The court shall have authority to appoint or designate one or more discreet persons of good character to serve as probation officers during the pleasure of the court . . . it shall be the duty of the said probation officer to make such investigation as may be required by the court; to be present in court in order to represent the interests of the child when the case is heard; to furnish to the court such information and assistance as the judge may require; and to take such charge of any child before and after trial as may be directed by the court.

 Probation, according to the 1899 Illinois Juvenile Court Act, was to have both an investigative and a rehabilitative function.

Social workers served the juvenile court as probation officers and held this same philosophy. They collected facts about youths' misbehavior, including the history of their families, school performance, church attendance and neighborhood. They made recommendations for disposition to the judges and provided community supervision and casework services to the vast majority of children adjudicated by the juvenile courts.

Besides providing for probation officers, the Juvenile Court Act also stipulated that juvenile courts were to have separate records and informal procedures. The adversary function of the criminal court was deemed incompatible with the procedural safeguards of the juvenile court, reflecting the basic doctrine of *parens patriae*. Because children were legally wards of the state, they were perceived to be without constitutional rights. The act was construed liberally so that the care, custody and discipline of children would approximate as nearly as possible that given by individual parents. Custody or guardianship was a legal status created by court order giving an adult the right and duty to protect, provide food and shelter, train and discipline a child. To that end, several important parts of a criminal trial, such as the indictment, pleadings and jury, were eliminated. Despite this, juvenile court was initially regarded as far more humane than criminal court.

Some scholars assert the system was set up to take advantage of children. Disputing the benevolent motives of the juvenile court founders, scholars have suggested that the civil liberties and privacy rights of juveniles diminished in the process. Although reformers of the time were optimistic, college-educated people who believed that individualized treatment based on a juvenile's history was critical, they were also concerned with their own futures: "During the Progressive Era, those in positions of economic power feared that the urban masses would destroy the world they had built. . . . From all sectors came demands that new action be taken to preserve social order, and to protect private property and racial privilege" (Krisberg and Austin, 1993, p.27).

 The progressives further developed the medical model, viewing crime as a disease to treat and cure by social intervention.

Interestingly, an early critique by two prominent progressives of the first juvenile courts in Cook County, Illinois, noted: "Children who do wrong can be found in every social stratum, but those who become wards of the court are the children of the poor" (Breckenridge and Abbott, 1912, pp.42–43). Their findings, which were based on an evaluation of court records dating from 1899 to 1909, confirmed that the juvenile court constituted a powerful means of social control by the dominant class.

Commonwealth v. Fisher (1905) defended the juvenile court ideal, reminiscent of the holding of the court in the *Crouse* case of 1838:

> To save a child from becoming a criminal, or continuing in a career of crime, to end in maturer years in public punishment and disgrace, the legislatures surely may provide for the salvation of such a child, if its parents or guardians be unwilling or unable to do so, by bringing it into one of the courts of the state without any process at all, for the purpose of subjecting it to the state's guardianship and protection.

Early Efforts at Diversion: The Chicago Boy's Court and Youth Counsel Bureau

Diversion is the official halting of formal juvenile proceedings against a youthful offender and, instead, treating or caring for the youth outside the formal juvenile justice system. In 1914 diversion from juvenile court began in the Chicago Boy's Court, an extralegal form of probation to process and treat young offenders without labeling them as criminals.

The Boy's Court version of diversion used four community service agencies: a Catholic church agency, a predominantly Protestant agency, a Jewish Social Service Bureau and the Colored Big Brothers. The court released juveniles to the supervision and authority of these agencies. After a sufficient time to evaluate each youth's behavior, the agencies reported back to the court. The court took the evaluation and, if satisfactory, the judge officially discharged the individual. No record was made.

Toward the end of the Juvenile Court Period, in the early 1950s, developments in youth diversionary programs included New York City's Youth Counsel Bureau, established to handle delinquents not deemed sufficiently advanced in misbehavior to direct to court. Referrals were made to the bureau from police, parents, schools, courts and other agencies. The bureau provided a counseling service and discharged those whose adjustments appeared promising. No record was kept to label the youths delinquent.

Federal Government Concern and Involvement

The earliest federal interest in delinquency and child dependency was demonstrated by the 1909 White House Conference on Children and Youth, the theme of which centered on the institutionalization of dependent and neglected children:

> Following the 1909 White House Conference on Dependent Children, in which family preservationists won the debate with the children's rights defenders of the charitable private agencies, the foster care population, ironically, increased. Child welfare's policies supported family preservation, but the practice of child removal advanced by the charity workers continued— to the present day (Golden, 1997, pp.120–121).

 The 1909 White House Conference on Dependent Children established the U.S. Children's Bureau in 1912.

In addition, in 1912 Congress passed the first child labor laws.

The aftermath of World War I, the Great Depression and World War II occupied much of the federal government's attention from 1920 to 1960 as it sought to help citizens cope with the pressures of the times. Nonetheless, by 1925 all but two states had juvenile court systems, and the U.S. Children's Bureau and the National Probation Association issued a recommendation for *A Standard Juvenile Court Act* in 1925.

 Passage of the Social Security Act in 1935 began major federal funding for programs to aid children and families.

In 1936, the Children's Bureau began administering the first federal subsidy program, providing child welfare grants to states for the care of dependent, neglected, exploited, abused and delinquent youths.

Recognizing the considerable power and influence the juvenile court held over children's lives and the formulation of youth policy, a group of concerned juvenile court judges came together in 1937 to found the National Council of Juvenile and Family Court Judges (NCJFCJ), an assembly that, over the years, has "established itself as an influential and respected organization" (Schwartz, 1989, p.91).

The federal government passed the Juvenile Court Act in 1938, adopting many features of the original Illinois act. Within 10 years every state had enacted special laws for handling juveniles.

In the 1940s a number of conferences on children and youths were held, but most public support was directed toward the war and reconstructing families after the war. In 1951 Congress passed the Federal Youth Corrections Act and created a Juvenile Delinquency Bureau (JDB), positioned within the Department of Health, Education and Welfare, which reflected the prevalence of the medical model at that time as well as the emphasis on prevention.

Courtesy, Colorado Historical Society (Scan 10027289)

Judge Benjamin Lindsay presided in juvenile court in Denver, Colorado, from 1900 to 1927. These first juvenile courts were informal proceedings focusing on rehabilitation rather than punishment.

By the end of the Juvenile Court Period, social work and the juvenile justice system movement were flourishing with their combined focus on youths and their families. The movement gradually became more concerned with professionalism in the intake process and correctional supervision. This went unnoticed by outsiders until the early 1960s.

By the end of the Juvenile Court Period, the U.S. Supreme Court had begun to seriously question the use of *parens patriae* as the sole reason for denying children many constitutional rights extended to adults charged with a crime. In 1956 in *Shioutakon v. District of Columbia*, the courts established the role of legal counsel in juvenile court. If juveniles were to have their liberty taken away, such juveniles had the right to a lawyer in court.

The end of this period also marked the beginning of radical societal changes in the United States that would last the next two decades and extend throughout the fourth developmental phase of our juvenile justice system—the Juvenile Rights Period.

The Juvenile Rights Period (1960–1980)

In the 1960s the American family was undergoing significant changes that directly affected social work and its liaison between the juvenile, the family and the court. Divorces increased, with the result that more children lived in single-parent households. Births to unmarried women increased, and more women entered the labor force.

Juvenile crime received increased attention when, in 1960, the U.S. attorney general reported that delinquency and crime were costing the American public more than $20 million per year. In addition, poor, lower-class delinquents were now joined by youths with middle- and upper-class backgrounds and rural youths.

HIGHLIGHTS OF JUVENILE COURT PERIOD REFORM

Policymakers and practitioners differed over the most effective treatment for unacceptable behavior and over who should be responsible for organizing and regulating juvenile justice. Specialized rules of juvenile procedure were being set forth by a growing number of judicial bodies. The juvenile court was perceived to be a means for attaining certain social ends. However, a growing concern was that the juvenile system carried its own stigma harmful to juveniles by procedures that denied due process of law. By the late 1940s, the gap between the theoretical assistance and actual punitive practices became obvious. Legal challenges to the system's informality and lack of safeguards were brought.

Philosophies Adolescence was accepted as a unique period of biological and emotional transition from child to adult requiring careful control and guidance. Misbehavior by middle-class youths was to be expected and controlled by concerned families, but lower-class youths were to be reformed via public efforts. Controlling and improving societal rather than individual conditions might decrease the incidence of youthful crime. Children were to be gently led back to conformity, not harshly punished.

Treatment Children were primarily treated by public efforts guided by new public policies and research. Children in need were handled primarily by juvenile courts.

Policies The juvenile court system was adopted by every state to adjudicate youths separately from adults, expanding the *parens patriae* precedent. The federal government broadened its role and began providing direction for youth services, sponsoring conferences, passing legislation to improve conditions for families and youths during the Depression, passing child-labor legislation, supporting the protection of children's basic constitutional rights and creating the Children's Bureau as the first national child welfare agency.

President Lyndon Johnson's Great Society initiative of the 1960s, known for its "War on Poverty," advanced causes for families and children, providing federal money to attack poverty, crime and delinquency. Further, the 1960s saw racial tensions at an all-time high with leaders such as Malcolm X and groups such as the Black Muslims and the Black Panthers demanding "power to the people." As noted by Krisberg and Austin (1993, p.44): "The riots of the mid-1960s dramatized the growing gap between people of color in the United States and their more affluent 'benefactors.'"

Civil rights efforts during the 1960s helped broaden concerns for all children, especially those coming under the jurisdiction of juvenile courts: "Juvenile law, perhaps more than any other aspect of law, reflects the stumbling and confused nature of our society as its values and goals evolve. So it was in the 1960s, when American society put itself through an extraordinary period of self-examination, that a great many problems were identified in the way we handle juvenile crime" (Rieffel, 1983, p.3).

The Four Ds of Juvenile Justice

To deal with problems identified within the juvenile justice system, new policies were established regarding four key concepts—deinstitutionalization, diversion, due process and decriminalization. Although it was not until the end of this period when sociologist LaMar Empey (1978) formally described these as "the Four Ds of juvenile justice," their implementation in and impact on the juvenile justice system began early in the 1960s.

 The Four Ds of juvenile justice are deinstitutionalization, diversion, due process and decriminalization.

Throughout this period, the major developments in juvenile justice focused on one or a combination of these key concepts. For example,

decriminalization—referring to legislation that makes status offenses non-criminal acts—was first witnessed in 1961, when California became the first state to separate status offenses from the delinquent category. New York followed suit in 1962, when the revised New York Family Court Act created a new classification for noncriminal misconduct—**PINS**, Person in Need of Supervision. Other states followed as well, adopting such labels as CINS, CHINS (Children in Need of Supervision), MINS (Minors in Need of Supervision), JINS (Juveniles in Need of Supervision) and FINS (Families in Need of Supervision). These new labels were intended to reduce the stigma of being labeled a delinquent. Throughout the juvenile rights period, a broad range of status offenses were decriminalized.

Other policy changes involved the applicability of due process rights to juveniles. Legal challenges to the notion that the juvenile justice system—and the juvenile court in particular—truly was a benign parent, went as far as the U.S. Supreme Court in the 1960s. Society began to demand that children brought before the juvenile court for matters that exposed them to the equivalent of criminal sanctions receive **due process** protection. The due process clause of the U.S. Constitution requires that no person be deprived of life, liberty or property without due process of law. The Supreme Court began protecting juveniles from the court's paternalism. Due process became a clear concern in *Kent v. United States* (1966).

The Kent *Decision*

Morris Kent, a 16-year-old with a police record, was arrested and charged with housebreaking, robbery and rape. Kent admitted the charges and was held at a juvenile detention facility for almost a week. The judge then transferred jurisdiction of the case to an adult criminal court. Kent received no hearing of any kind.

 The procedural requirements for waiver to criminal court were articulated by the Supreme Court in *Kent v. United States.*

In reviewing the case, the Supreme Court decreed: "As a condition to a valid waiver order, petitioner [Kent] was entitled to a hearing, including access by his counsel to the social records and probation or similar reports which are presumably considered by the court, and to a statement of the reasons for the Juvenile Court's decision."

An appendix to the *Kent* decision contained the following criteria established by the Supreme Court for states to use in deciding whether to transfer juveniles to adult criminal court for trial. The juvenile court was to consider:

- The seriousness of the alleged offense and whether community protection requires waiver.
- Whether the alleged offense was committed in an aggressive, violent, premeditated or willful manner.
- Whether the alleged offense was against persons or property, greater weight being given to offenses against persons, especially if personal injury resulted.
- The prospective merit of the complaint.

- The desirability of trial and disposition of the offense in one court when the juvenile's associates in the alleged offense are adults who will be charged with crimes in the adult court.
- The sophistication and maturity of the juvenile as determined by considering his or her home, environmental situation, emotional attitude and pattern of living.
- The juvenile's record and previous history.

The *Kent* decision warned that the juvenile court's traditional lack of concern for procedural and evidentiary standards would no longer be tolerated.

The Gault *Decision*

In re Gault (1967) elevated the juvenile court process to a national issue: "The *Gault* decision is, by far, the single most important event in the history of juvenile justice" (Schwartz, 1989, p.99). This case changed the adjudication process almost completely into a deliberately adversarial process. *In re Gault* concerned a 15-year-old Arizona boy, already on probation, who was taken into custody at 10:00 A.M. for allegedly making an obscene phone call to a neighbor. No steps were taken to notify his parents. When Mrs. Gault arrived home at about 6:00 P.M. and found her son missing, she went to the detention home and was told that he was there and that a hearing would be held the next day. At the hearing, a petition was filed with the juvenile court charging general allegations of "delinquency." No particular facts were stated; the complaining neighbor was not present; no one was sworn in; no attorney was present; and no record of the proceedings was made. Gault admitted to making part of the phone call in question. At the end of the hearing, the judge said he would consider the matter.

Gault was held in detention for 2 more days and then released. Another hearing was held 4 days later which also had no complaining witnesses, sworn testimony, counsel or transcript. The probation officer's referral report charging lewd phone calls was filed with the court. The report was not made available to Gault or his parents. The judge committed him to the state industrial school until age 21. Gault received a 6-year sentence for an action for which an adult would have received a fine or a 2-month imprisonment. The U.S. Supreme Court overruled Gault's conviction on the grounds that he was deprived of his due process rights.

 The *Gault* decision requires that the due process clause of the Fourteenth Amendment apply to proceedings in state juvenile courts, including the right of notice, the right to counsel, the right against self-incrimination and the right to confront witnesses.

In delivering the Court's opinion, Justice Fortas stated:

> Where a person, infant or adult, can be seized by the State, charged and convicted for violating a state criminal law, and then ordered by the State to be confined for six years, I think the Constitution requires that he be tried in accordance with the guarantees of all provisions of the Bill of Rights made applicable to the States by the Fourteenth Amendment. Undoubtedly this would be true of an adult defendant, and it would be a plain denial of equal

protection of the laws—an invidious discrimination—to hold that others subject to heavier punishments could, because they are children, be denied these same constitutional safeguards. I consequently agree with the Court that the Arizona law as applied here denied to the parents and their son the right of notice, right to counsel, right against self-incrimination, and right to confront the witnesses against young Gault. Appellants are entitled to these rights, not because "fairness, impartiality and orderliness—in short the essentials of due process"—require them and not because they are "the procedural rules which have been fashioned from the generality of due process," but because they are specifically and unequivocally granted by provisions of the Fifth and Sixth Amendments which the Fourteenth Amendment makes applicable to the States.

Thus, the Gault decision provided the standard of due process for juveniles.

The remaining two Ds—deinstitutionalization and diversion—surfaced as focal points for policy change following a harsh examination of the juvenile justice system by the 1967 President's Commission on Law Enforcement and Administration of Justice.

The President's Commission on Law Enforcement and Administration of Justice

In 1967, the President's Commission gave evidence of "disenchantment with the experience of the juvenile court" (President's Commission, 1967, p.17). It criticized lack of due process, law enforcement's poor relationship to youths and the handling of juveniles and the corrections process of confining status offenders and children "in need" to locked facilities.

According to the President's Commission (p.69): "Institutions tend to isolate offenders from society, both physically and psychologically, cutting them off from schools, jobs, families and other supportive influences and increasing the probability that the label of criminal will be indelibly impressed upon them." The commission, therefore, recommended that community-based correctional alternatives to institutionalization, or deinstitutionalization, should be considered seriously for juvenile offenders.

At the same time, the U.S. Department of Justice published *The Challenge of Crime in a Free Society* (1967), also questioning the policy of incarceration for nonviolent juvenile offenders. In this document, Harvard professor and criminologist James Q. Wilson expressed his views on two competing philosophies of juvenile crime deterrence—whether harsh policies deter juvenile delinquency or if arresting youthful offenders, particularly first-time offenders, might actually steer juveniles toward a lifetime of delinquent behavior. Wilson also theorized that juvenile offenders who have endured arrest may actually enjoy greater status among their peers, and that the typically light sentences of juvenile offenders might breed contempt for the system.

 Isolating offenders from their normal social environment may encourage the development of a delinquent orientation and, thus, further delinquent behavior.

The issues raised by the President's Commission, Wilson and others studying juvenile justice policy and practice indicated a need to integrate rather than isolate offenders. The resulting community-based correctional programs, such as probation, foster care and group homes, represented attempts to respond to these issues by normalizing social contacts, reducing the stigma attached to being institutionalized and providing opportunities for jobs and schooling.

The President's Commission also strongly endorsed diversion for status offenders and minor delinquent offenses. In addition, the commission recommended establishing a national youth service bureau and local or community youth service bureaus to assist the police and courts in diverting youths from the juvenile justice system.

Youth Service Bureaus

In 1967 the President's Commission established a federal youth service bureau to coordinate community-centered referral programs. Local youth service bureaus were to divert minor offenders whose behavior was rooted in problems at home, in school or in the community. While a broad range of services and certain mandatory functions were suggested for youth service bureaus, individually tailored work with troublemaking youngsters was a primary goal.

As envisioned by the commission, youth service bureaus were not part of the juvenile justice system. The bureaus would provide necessary services to youths as a substitute for putting them through the juvenile justice process, thus avoiding the stigma of formal court involvement. The three main functions of local youth service bureaus were diversion, resource development and system modification.

Diversion included accepting referrals from the police, courts, schools, parents and other sources, and working with the youths in a voluntary, noncoercive manner through neighborhood-oriented services. *Resource development* included offering leadership at the neighborhood level to provide and develop a variety of youth assistance programs, as well as seeking funding for new projects. *System modification* included seeking to change attitudes and practices that discriminate against troublesome youths and, thereby, contribute to their antisocial behavior. Finally, the President's Commission advocated *prevention* as the most promising and important method of dealing with crime, a philosophy embodied in the Uniform Juvenile Court Act of 1968.

The Uniform Juvenile Court Act

In 1968 the historic Delinquency Prevention and Control Act was passed. One provision of this act was to reform the juvenile justice system nationally. Although titled a "court" act, the legislation included provisions that affected law enforcement and corrections, illustrating the interconnectedness of the components of the system.

 The Uniform Juvenile Court Act provided for the care, protection and development of youths, without the stigma of a criminal label, by a program of treatment, training and rehabilitation in a family environment when possible. It also provided simple judicial and interstate procedures.

The act described probation services, referees, venue and transfer, custody and detention, petitions and summons, hearings, children's rights, disposition, court files and records, and procedures for fingerprinting and photographing children. These areas are described in detail in the chapters dealing with law enforcement and the courts.

Despite the best intentions of this act, a growing body of empirical evidence had cast serious doubt upon the ability of social casework, the linchpin of correctional treatment along with probation and parole, to help rehabilitate youths (Hellum, 1979). And although rehabilitation remained the major premise on which the juvenile justice system rested, research had found that correctional "treatment," especially in institutions, was often unnecessarily punitive and sometimes sadistic. Modern reformers became appalled that noncriminal youths and status offenders could so easily find their way into the same institutions as seriously delinquent youths. This spawned a rapid growth in community-based alternatives to institutionalization, as well as renewed national interest in juvenile justice.

The White House Conference on Youth

The 1970 White House Conference on Youth warned: "Our families and children are in deep trouble. A society that neglects its children and fears its youth cannot care about its future" (*The White House Conference on Youth*, 1972, p.346). The message from the conference was interpreted as a call for special federal assistance to identify the needs of families.

 The major impact of the 1970 White House Conference on Youth was that it hit hard at the foundation of the U.S. system for handling youths, including unnecessarily punitive institutions.

Beginning in 1971 a series of federal cases tried to specify minimum environmental conditions for juvenile institutions. By 1972 a cooperative effort among federal administrations focused on programs for *preventing* delinquency and rehabilitating delinquents outside the traditional criminal justice system, prompting adoption of the Juvenile Justice and Delinquency Prevention Act of 1974.

The Office of Juvenile Justice and Delinquency Prevention and the Juvenile Justice and Delinquency Prevention Act

In 1974 Congress created the Office of Juvenile Justice and Delinquency Prevention (OJJDP) and placed it in the Department of Justice. Congress also passed the Juvenile Justice and Delinquency Prevention (JJDP) Act by a vote of 329 to 20 in the House and with only one dissenting vote in the Senate. The landmark JJDP Act required that for states to receive federal funds, incarceration and even temporary detention should be used for young people only as a last resort.

 The Juvenile Justice and Delinquency Prevention Act of 1974 had two key goals: deinstitutionalization of status offenders and separation or removal of juveniles from adult facilities.

The JJDP Act made funds available to states that removed status offenders from prisons and jails and created alternative voluntary services to which status offenders could be diverted. The act was amended in 1976, 1977, 1980, 1992 and 2002. It was due for renewal in 2007 and, as of July 1, 2008, was still being reviewed by Congress for reauthorization.

The 1980 amendment called for the removal of juveniles from adult jails. In 1992, Congress added a disproportionate minority confinement (DMC) mandate requiring that states receiving JJDP Act formula grants provide assurances that they will develop and implement plans to reduce overrepresentation of minorities.

While the JJDP Act promoted developing diversionary tactics for juvenile offenders through monetary incentives, claiming such practices would benefit both the system and the youths it handled, the policy of diversion soon revealed weaknesses and was met with some criticism.

A Brief Note about Diversion and Net Widening   The juvenile due process requirements from *Kent* and *Gault*, combined with the rising costs of courts and correctional facilities at the end of the 1960s and throughout the 1970s, resulted in wider use of community-based alternatives to treat youths before and after adjudication. Young offenders were diverted into remedial education, drug abuse programs, foster homes and out-patient health care and counseling facilities.

However, diversion does not necessarily mean less state social control over juveniles. It has had the negative effect of transferring state power from juvenile courts to police and probation departments. Many youngsters who earlier would have been simply released were instead referred to the new diversionary programs. This phenomenon, called **net widening**, was the opposite of diversion's original purpose, which was to lessen the states' power to control juveniles.

Not only does diversion widen the net, it also increases the risk of violating rights of due process and fundamental fairness because referrals usually occur *before* adjudication. Thus, it is often never established that referred youngsters are actually guilty of any offense that might make them properly the subjects of conditional placement. Diversion is discussed in greater depth in Chapter 10.

A Return to Due Process Issues: Other Landmark Cases

As in the first half of the Juvenile Rights Period, the 1970s saw a continuation of cases addressing juveniles' rights and juvenile court becoming more like adult court in several important ways. Three landmark cases during the 1970s addressed juvenile rights regarding the standard of proof, jury trials and double jeopardy. Whether dealing with status offenders, youths who had committed violent crimes or protecting abused or neglected children, the court no longer had free reign.

The *Winship* Decision: Standard of Proof in Juvenile Proceedings   *In re Winship* (1970) concerned a 12-year-old New York boy charged with taking $112 from a woman's purse. He was adjudicated a delinquent based on a *preponderance of the evidence* submitted at the juvenile hearing. He was committed to a training school for 18 months, with extension possible until he was 18 years old, a total possible sentence of 6 years. The question raised was whether New York's statute allowing juvenile cases to be decided on the basis of a preponderance of evidence was constitutional.

Gault had already established that due process required fair treatment for juveniles. The Court held that: "The Due Process Clause protects the accused against conviction except upon *proof beyond a reasonable doubt* of every fact necessary to constitute the crime with which he is charged" (italics in original). New York argued that its juvenile proceedings were civil, not criminal; but the Supreme Court said the standard of proof beyond a reasonable doubt not only played a vital role in the criminal justice system, but it also ensured a greater degree of safety for the presumption of innocence of those accused of crimes.

 In re Winship established proof beyond a reasonable doubt as the standard for juvenile adjudication proceedings, eliminating lesser standards such as a preponderance of the evidence, clear and convincing proof and reasonable proof.

The *McKeiver* Decision: No Right to a Jury Trial   The move toward expanding juveniles' civil rights was slowed by the ruling in *McKeiver v. Pennsylvania* (1971), in which the Court ruled that juveniles do not have the right to a jury trial. This case involved a 16-year-old Pennsylvania boy charged with robbery, larceny and receiving stolen goods, all felonies in Pennsylvania. He was adjudicated a delinquent. The question for the Court to decide was whether the due process clause of the Fourteenth Amendment guaranteeing the right to a jury trial applied to adjudication of a juvenile court case.

In *McKeiver* the Court held that *Gault* and *Winship* demonstrated concern for the fundamental principle of fairness in justice, with the fact-finding elements of due process necessary and present for this fairness. The Court emphasized in *McKeiver*: "One cannot say that in our legal system the jury is a necessary component of accurate fact finding. There is much to be said for it, to be sure, but we have been content to pursue other ways for determining facts."

 McKeiver established that a jury trial is not a required part of due process in adjudicating a youth as delinquent by a juvenile court.

The Court advocated the presence of an interactive juvenile court judge and concluded that juvenile courts should not become fully adversarial like criminal courts. Requiring a jury might put an end to "what has been the idealistic prospect of an intimate informal protective proceeding." Requiring jury trials for juvenile courts could also result in delays, as well as in the possibility of public trials.

The *Breed* Decision: Double Jeopardy   **Double jeopardy** was the issue in *Breed v. Jones* (1975). The Supreme Court ruled that defendants may not be tried twice for the same offense. Breed was 17 when apprehended for committing acts with a deadly weapon. A California juvenile court found the allegation true. A dispositional hearing determined there were not sufficient facilities "amenable to the care, treatment and training programs available through the facilities of the juvenile court," as required by the statute. Breed was transferred to the criminal court where he was again found guilty. Breed argued he had been tried twice for the same offense, constituting double jeopardy. The Supreme Court agreed and reversed the conviction.

 A juvenile cannot be adjudicated in juvenile court and then tried for the same offense in an adult criminal court (*Breed v. Jones,* 1975).

Beginning in 1976 the majority of states enacted legislation that made it easier to transfer youths to adult courts, signaling a change in philosophy that would eventually lead juvenile justice into its next (and current) phase—the Crime Control Period—to be discussed shortly.

Two other Supreme Court decisions in the 1970s dealt with the media's right to publish information regarding juvenile cases. In *Oklahoma Publishing Company v. District Court in and for Oklahoma City* (1977) a court order prohibited the press from publishing the name and photo of a youth involved in a juvenile court proceeding, although the material was obtained legally from a source outside the court. The Supreme Court found the court order to be an unconstitutional infringement on freedom of the press.

In a similar case, *Smith v. Daily Mail Publishing Company* (1979), the Court also held that if information regarding a juvenile case is lawfully obtained by the media, the First Amendment interest in a free press takes precedence over the interests in preserving the anonymity of juvenile defendants.

The Issue of Right to Treatment

Also in the 1970s, two conflicting types of cases emerged: one type tried to establish a "right to treatment," the other to establish the "least restrictive alternative." *Martarella v. Kelley* (1972) established that if juveniles judged to be in need of supervision are not provided with adequate treatment, they are deprived of their rights under the Eighth and Fourteenth Amendments. *Morales v. Turman* (1973) ruled that juveniles in a Texas training school have a statutory right to treatment. And, in *Nelson v. Heyne* (1974), the Seventh U.S. Court of Appeals also confirmed juveniles' right to treatment:

> When a state assumes the place of a juvenile's parents, it assumes as well the parental duties, and its treatment of its juveniles should, so far as can be reasonably required, be what proper parental care would provide. . . . Without a program of individual treatment, the result may be that the juvenile will not be rehabilitated, but warehoused.

Although many state courts have established a right to treatment, including minimum standards, the U.S. Supreme Court has not yet declared that juveniles have a constitutional right to treatment.

Decriminalization of Status Offenses

In line with efforts to deinstitutionalize status offenders, the American Bar Association (ABA) Joint Commission on Juvenile Justice Standards voted in 1977 for the elimination of uniquely juvenile offenses, that is, status offenses, such as cigarette smoking or consuming alcohol.

 According to the American Bar Association, juvenile delinquency liability should include only such conduct as would be designated a crime if committed by an adult.

The referral of status offenses to juvenile court has been viewed by many as a waste of court resources. These critics believe that court resources are best used for serious recidivist delinquents.

Development of Standards for Juvenile Justice

In 1977 a tentative draft of the Institute of Judicial Administration/American Bar Association *Juvenile Justice Standards* was published in 23 volumes. In 1978 the state of Washington began extensive legislative revision of its juvenile justice system based, in part, on these standards. Following implementation of the new legislation it was found that:

- Sentences were considerably more uniform, consistent and proportionate to the seriousness of the offense and the prior criminal record of the youth.
- While the overall severity level of sanctions was reduced during the first two years, there was an increase in the certainty that a sanction of some kind would be imposed.
- There was a marked increase in the use of incarcerative sanctions for the violent and serious/chronic offender, but nonviolent offenders and chronic minor property offenders were less likely to be incarcerated and more apt to be required to pay restitution, do community service or be on probation.
- Compliance with the sentencing guidelines was extremely high; nevertheless, differential handling of minorities and females still existed.
- There was a better record of holding juveniles accountable for their offenses.
- While the new legislation completely eliminated the referral of *status offenses*, it did not eliminate the referral of *status offenders*. Runaways were more likely to be contacted for delinquent acts, for example. (Rieffel, 1983, pp.36–37, italics in original)

In the 1970s the rising fear of youth crime and rebelliousness coincided with a growing disillusionment with the effectiveness of the juvenile justice system. Citizens and lawmakers, amid mounting skepticism of the principles of rehabilitation established by the JJDP Act, began calling for more punitive measures against juvenile offenders, especially those who committed serious or violent felonies. The result was a much harsher attitude toward youth crime and a call to "get tough" with youthful lawbreakers, philosophies characteristic of the current crime control period.

HIGHLIGHTS OF JUVENILE RIGHTS PERIOD REFORM

The combination of serious, stigmatizing results achieved without due process safeguards led the Supreme Court in the 1960s to impose new requirements in determining when a juvenile could be made a ward of the state.

Since its inception, the juvenile court was guided by a welfare concept. When the Supreme Court took issue with its procedures, the juvenile court environment moved from a simple family atmosphere to a more adversarial system. Treating juveniles changed to a criminal approach, dispensing punishment and placing youths in locked facilities.

Philosophies Dissent arose among professional child welfare workers and policymakers about the causes of and treatment for juvenile delinquency. Consensus arose among the public and policymakers that the traditional agents of control—family, police, schools and courts—could not curb the rise of delinquency.

Treatment The juvenile court system was revised to include due process, deinstitutionalization, decriminalization and diversion programs. Community-based therapy, rather than institutionalization, became the preferred method of treatment.

Policies Large-scale federal financial and programmatic grants-in-aid were made available to states and localities for delinquency prevention and control programs. The juvenile court came under severe criticism because its philosophy of helping all juveniles rather than punishing delinquents led to an indiscriminate mixing of neglected or abused children, status offenders and violent offenders.

The Crime Control Period (1980–Present)

As mainstream attitudes about the response to and treatment of juvenile offenders swung to more punitive measures, the formerly prevailing medical
model of viewing unlawful behavior began to shift to what is often called a
justice model. The issues involved and how they are viewed in each model are
summarized in Table 2.1.

The Carter administration (presidential term 1977–1981) was deeply committed to removing juveniles from adult jails, and the Department of Justice recommended a 34 percent increase in funding for fiscal 1981–82 for the OJJDP, to
be targeted at juvenile jail removal. However, when Ronald Reagan took office
in 1981, his administration significantly reduced this funding level, claiming
that the goal of removing children from adult jails had been largely accomplished and that, even if it had not, it was a state and local problem (Schwartz,
1989, pp.83–84).

Table 2.1 Comparison of the Medical and Justice Models

Issue	Medical Model 1930–1974	Justice Model 1974–Present
Cause of crime	Disease of society or of the individual.	Form of rational adaptation to societal conditions.
Image of offender	Sick; product of socioeconomic or psychological forces beyond control.	Capable of exercising free will, of surviving without resorting to crime.
Object of correction	To cure offender and society; to return both to health; rehabilitation.	Humanely control offender under terms of sentence; offer voluntary treatment.
Agency/institution responsibility	Change offender; reintegrate back into society.	Legally and humanely control offender; adequate care and custody; voluntary treatment; protect society.
Role of treatment and punishment	Voluntary or involuntary treatment as means to change offender. Treatment is mandatory; punishment used to coerce treatment; punishment and treatment viewed as same thing.	Voluntary treatment only; punishment and treatment not the same thing. Punishment is for society's good, treatment is for offender's good.
Object of legal sanctions (sentence)	Determine conditions that are most conducive to rehabilitation of offender.	Determine conditions that are just considering wrong done, best protection for society and deter offender from future crime.
Type of sentence	Indeterminate, flexible; adjust as offender changes.	Fixed sentence (less good time).
Who determines release time?	"Experts" (parole board for adults, institutional staff for juveniles).	Conditions of sentence as interpreted by Presumptive Release Date (PRD) formula.

SOURCE: D. F. Pace, *Community Relations Concepts*, 3rd ed. Copyright © 1993, p.127. Placerville,
CA: Copperhouse. Reprinted by permission.

By the 1980s the "best interests" of society had gained ascendency over those of youths. In the 1980s the OJJDP became increasingly conservative, with the emphasis shifting to dealing with hard-core, chronic offenders. Also in the 1980s, state and federal concerns tended to center on the problems created by procedural informality and the juvenile court's broad discretion. The adversary system of legal process replaced the sedate environment and process of the "family" court that was directed to consider the "best" interest of the child's health, safety and welfare. The courts returned to a focus on what was right according to the law.

In addition, the conservative swing added two more Ds to our juvenile justice system: deterrence and deserts (Krisberg, 1992). **Deterrence** involves using punishment to prevent future lawbreaking. It does so in several ways, the most obvious being locking offenders up so they cannot harm society further. Incarceration may result in further deterrence by (1) serving as a direct lesson to the incarcerated person that crime does not pay and (2) sending the same message to others in the public.

Deserts, or *just deserts* as it is often called, is a concept of punishment as a kind of justified revenge—the offending individual gets what is coming. This is the concept of *lex talionis*, or an eye for an eye, expressed in the Code of Hammurabi centuries ago.

In 1982, 214 long-term public institutions in the United States were designated either "strict" or "medium" custody training schools. Most schools involved agricultural training, thought to be reformative and requiring location in rural areas. An unanticipated effect of this was to remove the corrections problem from community awareness—out of sight, out of mind.

Throughout the 1980s and 1990s, public support increased for tougher policies directed at juvenile offenders, and state legislatures responded by passing laws that cracked down on juvenile crime, signaling a reversal of the juvenile due process trend of the previous two decades (Snyder and Sickmund, 2006, p.96). Breen (2001, p.50) observes:

> This policy shift is evidenced by 49 states that now allow juvenile court prosecutors to waive jurisdiction and transfer cases to adult court. In the opinion of some experts, this authority was given to prosecutors because they traditionally did not have the "soft on crime" attitudes of juvenile court judges. In 26 states, the jurisdictions of juvenile courts now exclude certain violent crimes such as murder, rape and armed robbery. A retreat from the due process revolution of the 1960s is also apparent in *Schall v. Martin.* . . . Here the U.S. Supreme Court, citing the doctrine of *parens patriae*, upheld the constitutionality of New York's law allowing the preventive detention of juveniles.

Schall v. Martin *(1984) and Preventive Detention*

At 11:30 P.M. on December 13, 1977, juvenile Gregory Martin was arrested on charges of robbery, assault and criminal possession of a weapon. Because of the late hour and because he lied about his address, Martin was kept in detention overnight. The next day he was brought before the family court accompanied by his grandmother. The family court judge noted that he had lied to the police about his address, that he was in possession of a loaded weapon and that he appeared to lack supervision at night. In view of these circumstances, the judge ordered Martin detained until trial. New York law authorized such pretrial or **preventive detention** of accused juvenile delinquents if "there is a substantial probability that they will not appear in court on the return date or there is a serious risk that they may before the return date commit an act which if committed by an adult would constitute a crime."

While Martin was in preventive detention, his attorneys filed a habeas corpus petition demanding his release. The petition charged that his detention denied him due process rights under the Fifth and Fourteenth Amendments. The suit was a class action suit on behalf of all youths held in preventive detention in New York. The New York appellate courts upheld Martin's claim, stating that most delinquents are released or placed on probation; therefore, it was unfair to confine them before trial. Indeed, later at trial, Martin was adjudicated a delinquent and sentenced to 2 years probation.

The prosecution appealed the decision disallowing pretrial detention to the Supreme Court for final judgment. The Supreme Court reversed the decision, establishing the right of juvenile court judges to deny youths pretrial release if they perceived them to be dangerous.

 In *Schall v. Martin* (1984) the Supreme Court upheld the state's right to place juveniles in preventive detention, fulfilling a legitimate state interest of protecting society and juveniles by detaining those who might be dangerous to society or to themselves.

Pretrial detention need not be considered punishment merely because the juvenile is eventually released or put on probation. In *Schall* the Court reiterated its belief in the fundamental fairness doctrine and the doctrine of *parens patriae*, trying to strike a balance between the juvenile's right to freedom pending trial and the right of society to be protected. All 50 states have similar language allowing preventive detention in their juvenile codes.

Schall also established a due process standard for detention hearings. This standard included procedural safeguards, such as a notice, a hearing and a statement of facts given to juveniles before being placed in detention. The Court further stated that detention based on prediction of future behavior did not violate due process. Many decisions made in the justice system, such as the decision to sentence or grant parole, are based partly on predicting future behavior. These decisions have all been accepted by the Court as legitimate exercises of state power.

Still Evolving

Developments with the evolving juvenile justice system in the United States had a direct effect on the relationships between children and their parents, children and the state and parents and the state. The major developments and influences on these relationships are summarized in Table 2.2. Bear in mind, however, the developments described and neatly categorized in the table are actually fluid, overlapping and ongoing.

Table 2.2   Juvenile Justice Developments and Their Impact

Periods	Major Developments	Precipitating Influences	Child/State	Parent/State	Parent/Child
Puritan 1646–1824	Massachusetts Stubborn Child Law (1646)	A. Christian view of child as evil B. Economically marginal agrarian society	Law provides: A. Symbolic standard of maturity B. Support for family as economic unit	Parents considered responsible and capable of controlling child	Child considered both property and spiritual responsibility of parents
Refuge 1824–1899	Institutionalization of deviants; New York House of Refuge established (1824) for delinquent and dependent children	A. Enlightenment B. Immigration and industrialization	Child seen as helpless, in need of state intervention	Parents supplanted as state assumes responsibility for correcting deviant socialization	Family considered to be a major cause of juvenile delinquency
Juvenile Court 1899–1960	Establishment of separate legal system for juveniles— Illinois Juvenile Court Act (1899)	A. Reformism and rehabilitative ideology B. Increased immigration, urbanization and large-scale industrialization	Juvenile court institutionalizes legal irresponsibility of child	*Parens patriae* doctrine gives legal foundation for state intervention in family	Further abrogation of parents' rights and responsibilities
Juvenile Rights 1960–1980	Increased "legalization" of juvenile law— *Gault* decision (1966); Juvenile Justice and Delinquency Prevention Act (1974) calls for deinstitutionalization of status offenders	A. Criticism of juvenile justice system on humane grounds B. Civil rights movements by disadvantaged groups	Movement to define and protect rights as well as provide services to children	Reassertion of responsibility of parents and community for welfare and behavior of children	Attention given to children's claims against parents; earlier emancipation of children
Crime Control (1980–present)	Shift from medical (treatment) model to justice model and "get tough" attitude; "best interests" of society gained ascendancy over those of youths; Supreme Court approves of preventive detention for youths—*Schall* decision (1984); emphasis on deterrence and just deserts	A. Increase in violent juvenile crime B. Proliferation of gangs C. Spread of drug use	Adversary system of legal process replaces sedate "family" court process; courts return to a focus on what is right according to the law	Parents in some states are held liable for their child's criminal conduct	Unknown

SOURCE: J. David Hawkins; Paul A. Pastor, Jr.; Michelle Bell; and Sheila Morrison. *Reports of the National Juvenile Justice Assessment Center: A Topology of Cause-Focused Strategies of Delinquency Prevention.* Washington, DC: U.S. Government Printing Office, 1980. Updated by author.

In examining the development of juvenile justice, it is clear that the system today is considerably different in philosophy and form than that which existed several centuries ago. This history paved the way for current "innovations" in policy and practice, such as Balanced and Restorative Justice (BARJ) clauses, Juvenile Accountability Incentive Block Grants (JAIBG), peer juries, community

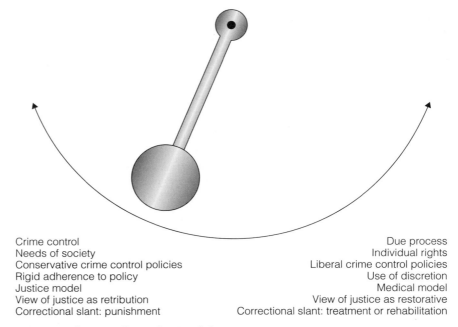

Crime control	Due process
Needs of society	Individual rights
Conservative crime control policies	Liberal crime control policies
Rigid adherence to policy	Use of discretion
Justice model	Medical model
View of justice as retribution	View of justice as restorative
Correctional slant: punishment	Correctional slant: treatment or rehabilitation

Figure 2.2   The Juvenile Justice Pendulum

mediation, the Blueprints for Violence Prevention program, Targeting Community Action Planning (TCAP) and many other programs—initiatives explored in later chapters.

Also keep in mind that the philosophies, policies, practices and programs that dominate the field today and are the focus of the remainder of this text, will likely pass, at some point, into the history chapters for future juvenile justice practitioners, as the juvenile justice system continues to evolve in response to our ever-changing society and its needs. This fluctuation has been graphically illustrated by the swinging of a pendulum from side to side, often falling somewhere between the two extremes, as illustrated in Figure 2.2. Which direction the juvenile justice system will take in the twenty-first century is unclear.

Krisberg (1992, p.157) observes: "Although the conservative revolution in juvenile justice was motivated by the concepts of deterrence and deserts, the emergence of a 'get tough' philosophy also produced another 'D' in the world of juvenile justice—disarray." One reason for this observation may be the conflicting views on the causes of delinquency as discussed in the next chapter.

 SUMMARY

- In 1824 the New York House of Refuge, the first U.S. reformatory, opened to house juvenile delinquents, defined in its charter as "youths convicted of criminal offenses or found in vagrancy."
- The child savers were reformers whose philosophy was that the child was basically good and was to be treated by the state as a young person with a problem.

- In 1899 the Illinois legislature passed a law establishing a juvenile court that became the cornerstone for juvenile justice throughout the United States.
- The first juvenile courts were administrative agencies of circuit or district courts and served a social service function with the rehabilitative ideal of reforming children rather than punishing them.
- Probation, according to the 1899 Illinois Juvenile Court Act, was to have both an investigative and a rehabilitative function.
- The progressives further developed the medical model, viewing crime as a disease to treat and cure by social intervention.
- The 1909 White House Conference on Youth established the U.S. Children's Bureau in 1912.
- Passage of the Social Security Act in 1935 was the beginning of major federal funding for programs to aid children and families.
- The Four Ds of juvenile justice are deinstitutionalization, diversion, due process and decriminalization.
- The procedural requirements for waiver to criminal court were articulated by the Supreme Court in *Kent v. United States*.
- The *Gault* decision required that the due process clause of the Fourteenth Amendment be applied to proceedings in state juvenile courts, including the right of notice, the right to counsel, the right against self-incrimination and the right to confront witnesses.
- *In re Winship* established proof beyond a reasonable doubt as the standard for juvenile adjudication proceedings, eliminating lesser standards such as a preponderance of the evidence, clear and convincing proof and reasonable proof.
- *McKeiver v. Pennsylvania* established that a jury trial is not a required part of due process in the adjudication of a youth as a delinquent by a juvenile court.
- *Breed v. Jones* established that a juvenile cannot be adjudicated in juvenile court and then tried for the same offense in an adult criminal court (double jeopardy).
- In *Schall v. Martin* (1984) the Supreme Court upheld the state's right to place juveniles in preventive detention. Preventive detention was perceived as fulfilling a legitimate state interest of protecting society and juveniles by detaining those who might be dangerous to society or to themselves.
- Isolating offenders from their normal social environment may encourage the development of a delinquent orientation and, thus, further delinquent behavior.
- The Uniform Juvenile Court Act (1968) provided for the care, protection and development of youths, without the stigma of a criminal label, by a program of treatment, training and rehabilitation in a family environment when possible. It also provided simple judicial and interstate procedures.
- The major impact of the White House Conference on Youth was that it hit hard at the foundation of our system for handling youths, including unnecessarily punitive institutions.
- The Juvenile Justice and Delinquency Prevention (JJDP) Act of 1974 had two key goals: deinstitutionalization of status offenders and separation or removal of juveniles from adult facilities.
- According to the American Bar Association, juvenile delinquency liability should include only such conduct as would be designated a crime if committed by an adult.

DISCUSSION QUESTIONS

1. The juvenile justice system has been defined as "justice that applies to children and adolescents with concern for their health, safety and welfare under sociolegal standards and procedures." Is this definition adequate? Why or why not?

2. Under the principle of *parens patriae*, how does the state (or the court) accept the role of "parent"? Are all households administered and managed alike?

3. Who are the present "child savers"? What states, associations and individuals have contributed to the present child-saver philosophy?

4. What do you consider the major milestones in the evolution of juvenile justice?

5. Is it possible for one system to effectively and fairly serve both children who need correction and those who need protection?

6. How may diversion result in "widening the net" of juvenile justice processing?

7. What are the rationales on which police diversion of juveniles is based in your community and state?

8. What are the major types of police diversion programs in your area and state?

9. What evidence suggests that diversion programs are effective in reducing juvenile recidivism? What findings, if any, contradict this evidence? Do you know of a diversion program that is working or one that has failed? Why did it succeed or fail?

10. What are the advantages and disadvantages of diversion?

REFERENCES

American Bar Association Joint Commission on Juvenile Justice Standards. Juvenile Justice Section. Washington, DC, no date.

Blackstone, William. *Commentaries on the Laws of England*, Vol. 4. Oxford: Clarendon, 1776.

Breckenridge, Sophoniska P. and Abbott, Edith. *The Delinquent Child and the Home.* New York: Random House, 1912.

Breen, Michael D. "A Renewed Commitment to Juvenile Justice." *The Police Chief*, March 2001, pp.47–52.

The Challenge of Crime in a Free Society. Washington, DC: U.S. Department of Justice, U.S. Government Printing Office, 1967.

de Scheveinitz, Karl. *England's Road to Social Security.* Philadelphia: University of Pennsylvania, 1943.

Empey, LaMar. *American Delinquency: Its Meaning and Construction.* Homewood, IL: Dorsey, 1978.

Golden, Renny. *Disposable Children: America's Child Welfare System.* Belmont, CA: Wadsworth Publishing Company, 1997.

Griffin, Brenda S. and Griffin, Charles T. *Juvenile Delinquency in Perspective.* New York: Harper & Row, 1978.

Grunhut, Max. *Penal Reform.* New York: Clarendon, 1948.

Hawkins, J. David; Pastor, Paul A., Jr.; Bell, Michelle; and Morrison, Sheila. *Reports of the National Juvenile Justice Assessment Center: A Topology of Cause-Focused Strategies of Delinquency Prevention.* Washington, DC: National Institute for Juvenile Justice and Delinquency Prevention, U.S. Government Printing Office, 1980.

Hellum, F. "Juvenile Justice: The Second Revolution." *Crime and Delinquency*, Vol. 3, No. 25, 1979, pp.299–317.

Hunt, G. Bowdon. "Foreword." In *A Handbook for Volunteers in Juvenile Court*, by Vernon Fox. Special issue of *Juvenile Justice.* February 1973.

Krisberg, Barry. "The Evolution of the Juvenile Justice System." Appeared in *The World & I*, April 1990, pp.487–503. Reprinted in *Criminal Justice 92/93*, 16th ed., edited by John J. Sullivan and Joseph L. Victor. Guilford, CT: Dushkin Publishing Group, Inc., 1992, pp.152–159.

Krisberg, Barry and Austin, James F. *Reinventing Juvenile Justice.* Newbury Park, CA: Sage Publications, 1993.

Platt, Anthony M. *The Child Savers: The Invention of Delinquency.* Chicago: University of Chicago Press, 1968.

The President's Commission on Law Enforcement and Administration of Justice. *The Task Force Report: Juvenile Delinquency and Youth Crime.* Washington, DC: U.S. Government Printing Office, 1967.

Rieffel, Alaire Bretz. *The Juvenile Justice Standards Handbook.* Washington, DC: American Bar Association, 1983.

Schwartz, Ira M. In *Justice for Juveniles: Rethinking the Best Interests of the Child.* Lexington, MA: D.C. Heath and Company, 1989.

Snyder, Howard N. and Sickmund, Melissa. *Juvenile Offenders and Victims 2006 National Report.* Washington, DC: U.S. Department of Justice, Office of Justice Programs, Office of Juvenile Justice and Delinquency Prevention, March 2006.

Task Force Report on Juvenile Justice and Delinquency Prevention. *Juvenile Justice and Delinquency Prevention.* Washington, DC: U.S. Government Printing Office, 1976.

Webb, Sidney and Webb, Beatrice. *English Local Government: English Poor Law History*, Part I. New York: Longmans, Green, 1927.

The White House Conference on Youth. Washington, DC: U.S. Government Printing Office, 1972.

CASES CITED

Breed v. Jones, 421 U.S. 519 (1975)

Commonwealth v. Fisher, 213 Pa. 48, 62 A. 198, 199, 200 (1905)

Ex parte Crouse, 4 Whart. 9 (Pa. 1838)

In re Gault, 387 U.S. 1 (1967)

Kent v. United States, 383 U.S. 541 (1966)

Martarella v. Kelley, 349 F. Supp. 575 (S.D.N.Y. 1972)

McKeiver v. Pennsylvania, 403 U.S. 528 (1971)

Morales v. Turman, 364 F. Supp. 166 (E.D. Tex. 1973)

Nelson v. Heyne, 491 F.2d 352 (7th Cir. 1974)

Oklahoma Publishing Company v. District Court in and for Oklahoma City, 480 U.S. 308 (1977)

Schall v. Martin, 467 U.S. 253 (1984)

Shioutakon v. District of Columbia, 236 F.2d 666 (1956)

Smith v. Daily Mail Publishing Company, 443 U.S. 97, 99 (1979)

In re Winship, 397 U.S. 358 (1970)

CHAPTER 3

Theories of Delinquency and Juvenile Offending

THERE ARE TWO GREAT INJUSTICES THAT CAN BEFALL A CHILD. ONE IS TO PUNISH HIM FOR SOMETHING HE DIDN'T DO. THE OTHER IS TO LET HIM GET AWAY WITH DOING SOMETHING HE KNOWS IS WRONG.

—ROBERT GARDNER

© REUTERS/Lucas Jackson

Difficult economic times are often associated with upturns in crime committed by both adults and juveniles. While some youth may try legitimate means to earn income, others are tempted by the faster results and commonly greater amounts available through illegal methods, despite the risk of legal sanctions. Here are 13-year-old boy sells apples while dressed in period costume outside the New York Stock Exchange in September 2008.

Do You Know?

- How crimes were originally differentiated?
- What two theories exist to explain the purpose of the law?
- What function is served by punishment according to the Durkheimian perspective? The Marxist perspective?
- What two competing worldviews have existed over the centuries and the concepts important to each view?
- What proponents of the classical view and those of the positivist view advocate for offenders?
- What theories have been developed to explain the cause of crime and delinquency and the major premises of each?
- Whether any single theory provides a complete explanation?

Can You Define?

anomie	critical theory	labeling theory	secondary deviance
anomie theory	determinism	natural law	social contract
classical view of criminality	deterrence	positivist view of criminality	social disorganization theory
concordance	differential association theory	primary deviance	social ecology theory
conflict theory	ecological model	radical theory	strain theory
consensus theory	incapacitation	routine activity theory	

Chapter Outline

Introduction
Justice and the Law
Purposes of Law
Consensus Theory
Conflict Theory
Two Competing Worldviews
The Classical Worldview

The Positivist Worldview
Causes of Crime and Delinquency: An Overview
Biological Theories
Psychological Theories
Sociological Theories
Critical Theories

Victimization Theories
A Summary of Theories on the Causes of Crime and Delinquency
A General Theory of Crime

Introduction

Philosophy, theory and history are intertwined—they simultaneously affect and, in turn, are affected by each other. The separation of discussions involving these elements into various chapters is artificial. Therefore, be mindful of information already presented in Chapter 2 while proceeding through this chapter, as these concepts wrap around and support those already covered. It may, at times, appear as if this chapter is backtracking. Indeed, in many cases, the theories discussed will have coincided with particular historical events or philosophical eras that prevailed at various times during the evolution of juvenile justice. In other instances, no such specific correlation exists. In either case, the material presented is intended to fill in some of the "why" and "how" gaps left from the preceding chapter.

As seen in Chapter 2, the juvenile justice system has evolved slowly, influenced by many circumstances. In addition to its historical evolution, the system has deep roots in theories about justice, delinquency, crime and punishment. While the previous chapter focused on historical events with specific relevance to juveniles, this chapter takes a step back to look at broader issues that apply to both youths and adults, such as justice, law and theories of criminality, in an effort to better understand why the paths of juvenile and adult justice diverged.

Justice and the Law

Every society has norms, that is, rules or laws governing the actions and interactions of its people. These are usually of two types: folkways and mores. Folkways describe how people are expected to dress, eat and show respect for one another. They encourage certain behaviors. Mores, in contrast, are the *critical* norms vital to a society's safety and survival. Mores are often referred to as **natural law**—the rules of conduct that are the same everywhere because they are basic to human behavior.

Some behaviors, such as murder and rape, are deemed by any reasonable person to be inherently bad. Natural law states that certain acts are wrong by their very nature, and behavior that disregards the common decency one human owes to another is morally and legally wrong. Each society has a general idea of what constitutes natural law. Our founding fathers identified such principles when they wrote of the "inalienable rights to life, liberty and the pursuit of happiness" and of "truths held to be self-evident."

Acts considered immoral or wrong in themselves, such as murder and rape, are called *mala in se*. Acts that are prohibited because they infringe on others' rights, not because they are necessarily considered evil by nature, such as having more than one wife, are called *mala prohibita*.

 Crimes were originally differentiated as:

mala in se	mala prohibita
wrong in and of itself	a prohibited wrong
origin in mores	origin in folkways
natural law	man-made law
common law	statutory law
stable over time	changes over time

Natural laws may be declared to be criminal acts by man-made laws. Natural laws have remained relatively unchanged over the years, while man-made laws are altered nearly every legislative session.

Purposes of Law

According to sociologist Max Weber, the primary purpose of law is to regulate human interactions—that is, to support social order. Throughout history, law has served many other purposes, including to protect the interests of society, govern behavior, deter antisocial behavior, enforce moral beliefs, support those in power, regulate human interactions, uphold individual rights, identify lawbreakers, punish lawbreakers and seek retribution for wrongdoing.

Two prominent theories about the underlying purpose of law are consensus theory and conflict theory.

Consensus Theory

 Consensus theory holds that individuals within a society agree on basic values—on what is inherently right and wrong. Laws express these values.

This theory dates back at least as far as Plato and Aristotle. Deviant acts are deviant because society, in general, feels they are abnormal and unacceptable behavior. Consensus theory was expanded upon by the French historian and philosopher Charles de Montesquieu (1689–1755), a founder of political science. Montesquieu's philosophy centered around the **social contract** theory developed by the seventeenth-century English philosopher Thomas Hobbes, whereby free, independent individuals agree to form a community and give up a portion of their individual freedom to benefit the security of the group.

This social contract applied to minors as well as adults. Youths were expected to obey the rules established by society and to suffer the consequences if they did not. A century later the concept of the social contract was expanded upon by Emile Durkheim.

Punishment and Social Solidarity—The Durkheimian Perspective

Emile Durkheim (1858–1917), a pioneer in sociology, argued that punishment is a moral process to preserve the shared values of a society, that is, its collective conscience. When individuals deviate from this collective conscience, society is outraged and seeks revenge to restore the moral order: "Punishment thus transforms a threat to social order into a triumph of social solidarity" (Garland, 1991, p.123). Punishment also reinforces the notions that "authorities are in control, that crime is an aberration, and that the conventions that govern social life retain their force and vitality" (Garland, p.127).

 The Durkheimian perspective sees punishment as revenge and as a way to restore and solidify the social order.

Two key elements of Durkheim's perspective are (1) that the general population is involved in the act of punishing, giving it legitimacy, and (2) it is marked by deeply emotional, passionate reactions to crime. Durkheim (1933, pp.73–80) believed:

- Crime is conduct "universally disapproved of by members of each society."
- "An act is criminal when it offends strong and defined states of the collective conscience."

According to Durkheim, criminal law synthesizes society's essential morality and establishes boundaries that cannot be crossed without threatening the society's very existence. Durkheim (1951 [1897], p.252) developed a concept known as **anomie**, meaning normlessness, the breakdown of societal norms as a result of society's failure to distinguish between right and wrong.

Emile Durkheim (1858–1917) was a French sociologist and author who established the method and theoretical framework of social science.

Although laws usually reflect the majority values of a society, which is important in a democracy, they rarely represent the views of everyone. This may result in conflict.

Conflict Theory

 Conflict theory suggests that laws are established to keep the dominant class in power.

Conflict theory shifts the focus from lawbreaking to lawmaking and law enforcing and how laws protect the interests and values of the dominant groups within a society. Under this theory, crime will be more likely to flourish in heterogeneous societies where consensus over society's values is lacking: "Conflict theory holds that the administration of criminal justice reflects the unequal distribution of power in society. The more powerful groups use the criminal justice system to maintain their dominant position and to repress groups or social movements that threaten it" (Walker et al., 2007, p.95). Examples of conflict theory include the segregation laws prevalent throughout the South from the 1890s through the 1960s and vagrancy laws today, which apply to the poor and other populations that "threaten" the social order (Walker et al.). Conflict theory, as manifested in criminal laws aimed at behavior engaged in primarily by the socioeconomically disadvantaged, also explains disproportionate minority contact (DMC) and the over-representation of racial and ethnic minorities throughout the criminal justice system (Walker et al., p.96). For example, local law enforcement generally focuses more effort and resources on, and receives greater public demand and support for, combating "street crimes," which are committed predominantly by racial and ethnic minorities, while white-collar crimes tend to not be as vigorously targeted.

The roots of this theory can be found in the writings of Marx and Engels who wrote in the *Manifesto of the Communist Party* (1848):

> The history of all hitherto existing society is the history of class struggles.
> Freeman and slave, patrician and plebeian, lord and serf, guild-master
> and journeyman, in a word, oppressor and oppressed stood in constant

opposition to one another, carried on an interrupted, now hidden, now open fight, a fight that each time ended in either a revolutionary reconstruction of society at large, or in the common ruin of the contending classes.

Punishment and Class Power—The Marxist Perspective   Rather than viewing punishment as a means of providing social solidarity, Marx (1818–1883) saw punishment as a way to enhance the power of the upper class and an inevitable result of capitalism. Marx referred to the lower class as a "slum proletariat" made up of vagrants, prostitutes and criminals. "In effect, penal policy is taken to be one element within a wider strategy of controlling the poor; punishment should be understood not as a social response to the criminality of individuals but as a mechanism operating in the struggle between social classes" (Garland, 1991, p.128).

 The Marxist perspective sees punishment as a way to control the lower class and preserve the power of the upper class.

This rationale was doubtless operating throughout the Middle Ages, the Renaissance, the Reformation and into the nineteenth century. Society was divided into a small ruling class, a somewhat larger class of artisans and a vastly larger class of peasants. Intimidation through brutal criminal law was an important form of social control. Flicker (1990, p.38) sees this rationale operating in the development of our juvenile justice system:

> The unfortunate historical fact is that the juvenile justice system . . . began with the right observation and the wrong conclusion. Manifestly, poor people are more likely to beg, steal, and commit certain other crimes related to their social and economic status than affluent people. Although socially unacceptable, crime could be seen as a response to poverty. It was a way to get money. The preferred solutions—jobs, vocational training, financial assistance for the unemployable—required a constructive community attitude toward the disadvantaged. But a combination of Calvinism, prejudice, and social Darwinism confused cause and effect—idleness, inferiority, and criminality were seen as causing poverty, rather than the reverse. Therefore progressive elements in the community, the social reformers, felt justified in saving impoverished children from the inexorable path of crime by investigating their homes and families, attempting to imbue them with principles of Christian morality, and, if unsuccessful, removing them to a better environment.

The theoretical roots of these two perspectives on crime and punishment can be found in centuries-old competing worldviews.

Two Competing Worldviews

Two distinct and opposing views exist as to who or what is responsible for crime—the classical view and the positivist view.

The Classical Worldview

In the eighteenth century, criminologists began to apply the scientific method to explore the causes of crime. A leader of the classical school was Cesare Beccaria (1738–1794), whose *On Crimes and Punishment* was published in 1764.

 The classical worldview holds that humans have free will and are responsible for their own actions.

Other important principles of the classical theory, also called the **classical view of criminality**, include:

- Individuals have free will. Some choose to commit crime.
- Laws should bring the greatest measure of happiness to the largest number of people.
- Those who break the law should be punished according to penalties established in the law.
- The focus is on crime.

Like Durkheim, Beccaria believed that society functions under a social contract, with individuals giving up certain freedoms to live peacefully together. Classical theorists believed that delinquency was the result of free will. Consequently, they advocated harsh and immediate punishment so offenders would be "unwilling" to commit future crimes.

 Proponents of the classical view advocate punishment for offenders.

Several aspects of the classical view are found in the juvenile justice system. Classical theory suggests that the threat of punishment will lower youths' tendency toward delinquency. If the punishment is severe enough, youths will avoid delinquent activity, a process known as **deterrence**. However, the effectiveness of deterrence is uncertain. Many law violators believe they will never be caught, and if they are, they believe they can "beat the rap." Those who violate the law under the influence of drugs may think they are invincible. Punishment is no threat to them. Juveniles may also resist the threat of punishment because of peer pressure.

Being rejected by the gang would be worse than getting caught by the police. Indeed, being arrested and serving time are often seen as rites of passage, endowing a sort of higher status on those who make the journey. Also, many juveniles know the differences between juvenile and adult court and believe they will receive less severe punishment because of their age.

Classical theory also advocates **incapacitation** as a consequence for criminal activity. Institutionalization is intended not to rehabilitate offenders, but to keep them away from law-abiding society. Classical theory holds that criminal offenders should be sanctioned merely because they deserve punishment, and that punishment should be founded on what the offender deserves. Critics say this "just-deserts" approach is actually a desire for revenge. Since the first juvenile court in 1899, the juvenile justice system has opposed deserts-based punishment. Incarcerated juveniles were usually given short sentences (1 to 3 years at most) and sent to a nonpunitive, rehabilitation-oriented institution.

Classical-view theorists suggest that deterrence, incapacitation and, in some cases, just-deserts punishment is the way to deal with delinquency.

Classical theorists' views conflict with those adhering to the *parens patriae* philosophy, which advocates reform as a more appropriate way to deal with delinquency. During the nineteenth century another view of criminality was developed in reaction to the classical theory.

The Positivist Worldview

A leader of the positivist worldview was Cesare Lombroso (1835–1909), an Italian physician who studied the brains of criminals. Lombroso maintained that criminals were born with a predisposition to crime and needed exceptionally favorable conditions in life to avoid criminal behavior. As the originator of the positivist view of criminality—that is, transferring emphasis from the crime itself to the criminal behavior—Lombroso has been called the father of modern criminology. He firmly believed that criminals were literally born, not made—that the primary cause of crime was biological. He was writing at the same time that Charles Darwin's theory of evolution was becoming widely circulated and was probably greatly influenced by Darwin's ideas. Although some of Lombroso's work was later found to be flawed, he had started people thinking about causes for criminal behavior other than free will.

 The positivist worldview holds that humans are shaped by their society and are the product of environmental and cultural influences.

Other important principles of the positivist theory, also called the **positivist view of criminality**, include:

- Individuals' actions are determined not by free will but by biological and cultural factors.
- The purpose of law is to avert revolution and convince the masses to accept the social order.
- The focus is on the criminal.

The positivist-view theorists, who believe delinquent behavior is the result of a youth's biological makeup and life experiences, think treatment should include altering one or more of the factors that contributed to the unlawful behavior.

 Proponents of the positivist view advocate rehabilitation for offenders.

Positivist theorists stress community treatment and rehabilitation rather than incapacitation. For years the *parens patriae* attitude prevailed, with youths shielded from being labeled and punished as criminals.

Building on Lombroso's idea that environmental influences affect criminal behavior, some scholars developed the positivist view of criminality based on the concept of determinism. **Determinism** views human behavior as the product of multiple environmental and cultural influences rather than a single factor.

Throughout the ages societies have embraced one view or the other, with many people taking a middle position but tending toward one view. And these two worldviews have profoundly affected the various theories about the causes of crime and delinquency that have been set forth over the years.

Causes of Crime and Delinquency: An Overview

Delinquency is a focal point for the juvenile justice system. More energy and effort are spent by those within the system on delinquency than on any other responsibility. The United States generates more aftercare programs than any other country. But delinquency, its causes and effects are usually examined *after the fact*, with research on preventing delinquency getting relatively little attention, which leaves the question: What leads youths to become delinquent?

Do children often grow up to be like their parents because they have inherited something from them or because of the way their parents have raised them? This question is especially relevant for children who become delinquents. Many researchers have tried to answer this question, and the vast array of theories that have resulted range from the very conservative to what some may consider outlandish.

The various theories that have developed over time are of two basic kinds: those that attempt to explain why people fail to obey society's laws—why do they become criminals?—and those that approach the issue from the other side and try to explain why people obey the laws—why do they *not* become criminals? As you explore the following theories, keep these two approaches in mind.

During the first half of the twentieth century, several interpretations of the cause of delinquency gained prominence. The earliest theories explored biological and psychological factors. In fact, physical and psychological examinations of children who were brought before the court were standard orders in the juvenile court process. Judicial disposition often included individual counseling and psychological therapy. In the 1950s, under the influence of therapists such as Carl Rogers, group counseling became common in most juvenile institutions.

Slowly, this approach was replaced with social milieu and environmental explanations for delinquency. Delinquency prevention attempts focused on reorganizing the social environment—both physically, through housing renewal, and socioeconomically, through social welfare. There was a significant philosophical shift of the blame for delinquency from personal to social factors. Consequently, the federal government was increasingly drawn into the process of juvenile delinquency prevention.

 Early efforts to explain crime and delinquency were set forth in the classical theory and the positivist theory. Later theories focused on biological, psychological or sociological causes of crime and delinquency. Most recently, critical theories of the causes of crime and delinquency have been developed.

Biological Theories

Biological theorists contend that criminals are born, not made. The classic studies of Lombroso (1913) and Garofalo (1915) support a hereditary, genetic causation for deviant behavior. Some researchers believe that a genetic mishap may cause one member of a family to deviate from the norm. For example, Richard Speck, who murdered eight Chicago nurses, showed an unusual genetic structure—he had one extra male chromosome. Speck is not the only convicted criminal to display such a genetic abnormality.

Modern biological theorists possess scientific rigor, and they look to bio-chemical relationships, endocrine imbalances, chromosomal complements, brain wave activity and other biological determinants of behavior. Violence and aggression have been associated with the presence or absence of certain chemicals in the brain. The fact that biological explanations are supported by research cannot be ignored when looking at the causes of delinquent and anti-social behavior.

 Biological theories include physiognomy, phrenology, body type and heredity studies, including studies of twins and adoptees.

Physiognomy Studies   Physiognomy assigns character traits to physical features, especially facial features. In the Middle Ages the law specified that if "two people were suspected of having committed the same crime, the uglier one should be regarded as more likely the guilty party" (Curran and Renzetti, 1994, p.39). Indeed, people tend to have a mental picture of criminals. Some researchers have pointed out that criminals tend toward large, prominent or crooked noses, abnormal ears, lantern jaws, high cheek bones, higher sex drives, lower intelligence, larger body types, longer arms, larger lips or abnormal amounts of body hair. Researchers search for predominant factors among criminals and compare these factors with their presence or absence in the general population.

Phrenology   Phrenology studies the shape of the skull to predict intelligence and character. This was the approach used by Cesare Lombroso, who believed that at birth criminals are recognizable by certain anomalies. Such anomalies do not cause crime, but they indicate a predisposition to criminal behavior. Techniques used in phrenology are sometimes demonstrated at fairs or shopping malls.

Body Type Theories   Going beyond the study of the skull to predict predisposition to criminality, William Sheldon (1898–1977) theorized that humans can be divided into three distinct body types, or somatotypes, corresponding to three distinct personalities: (1) the endomorphic—soft, fat, easygoing; (2) the mesomorphic—athletic, muscular, aggressive; and (3) the ectomorphic—thin, delicate, shy, introverted.

Heredity Studies   Results of several studies of twins and of adopted boys lend support for a biological basis for predisposition to crime (Bohm, 2001, p.36). In twin studies, the hypothesis is that heredity is the same for identical twins because they come from a single egg (and, thus, share identical genetic material), and that heredity is different for fraternal twins because they come from two eggs. In either instance, environment is assumed to be very similar. More than a half-century of using this methodology revealed that identical twins were more likely to demonstrate **concordance** (where both twins have criminal records) than were fraternal twins, a finding that supports the heredity link. A problem with the twin studies, however, at least for those children reared together, is the potential confounding of genetic and environmental influences.

The findings from adoption studies revealed that the percentage of adoptees who were criminal was greater when the biological father had a criminal record than when the adoptive father had one. Thus, like the twin studies, the adoption studies presumably demonstrated the influence of heredity but could not adequately separate it from the influences of the environment.

Other Approaches Supporting Biological Causation Theories   An expanding body of biological research has indicated that chromosomal factors may be responsible for criminal behavior. If this is true, certain people are victims of their own heritage. For example, high testosterone has been associated with aggressive physical and sexual behavior. Testosterone injected into female rats causes them to adopt the male characteristics of aggressive physical and sexual behavior. Evidence also indicates that self-control and IQ, two highly heritable traits, have defined correlation to antisocial and criminal behavior as well (Beaver et al., 2009).

For several decades, brain research has been illuminating the way specific chemicals or elements in the body, as well as allergic reactors, contribute to aggression and perhaps criminality. For example, abnormal levels of manganese, zinc, copper or chromium may cause or contribute to antisocial behavior. Serotonin, a neurotransmitter that helps regulate emotions, has been found to play a role in violent behavior: "Since serotonin deficits have been tied to both genetic defects and environmental factors, serotonin studies may help sociologists and scientists find a common ground in the debate on how to reduce violent crime" (Donohue, 1995, p.1).

Current studies using functional magnetic resonance imaging (fMRI) allow researchers to actively view brain activity while a subject is exposed to specific stimuli, such as violent video games or people experiencing pain. One highly progressive group of researchers at the University of Chicago's Center for Cognitive and Social Neuroscience is exploring the biological underpinnings of, among other things, adolescents' perception of and desire to inflict pain. In a study group of conduct disordered (CD) juveniles (conduct disorder is discussed in greater detail in Chapter 4), Decety et al. (2009) found evidence that youth with highly aggressive CD show an atypical neural response pattern when viewing others in pain. Such results suggest the brains of asocial youth may be hardwired differently than those of youth considered to develop "normally." While such revolutionary research is still in its infancy, preliminary findings of studies such as this indicate a complex but undeniably biological basis to aggressive behavior in adolescents.

The relationship between genetics and crime causation remains highly controversial. And while many researchers dismiss the existence of a "crime gene," the nature vs. nurture debate remains a focal point among those searching for a biological basis for deviant behavior.

Psychological Theories

Many delinquent youths have to deal with poor home lives and destructive relationships, environments that can lead to a disturbed personality structure marked by negative, antisocial behavior. While many delinquents do not show significant psychological disturbances, enough do suffer from problems to allow psychological factors to be considered in the theory of delinquency.

Adolescence is normally a time of inner tensions, excessive energy and ambiguity. It is a time when the individual is neither child nor adult. Youths still have childish needs and a desire for dependency, though they have adult expectations imposed by themselves or others. If the emotional foundation is weak, the result can be catastrophic.

A major characteristic of juvenile delinquents is that they act out their inner conflicts. In acting out, youths freely express their impulses, particularly hostile ones. Acting out is the free, deliberate, often malicious indulgence of impulse, which often leads to aggression as well as other manifestations of delinquency, such as vandalism and cruelty to animals. Acting out essentially reflects an absence of self-control and a desire for immediate gratification.

Such a lack of self-control may result from an early history of severe parental rejection or deprivation, or from witnessing or being the victim of severe physical abuse and violence: "Being abused or neglected as a child increased the likelihood of arrest as a juvenile by 59 percent, as an adult by 28 percent, and for a violent crime by 30 percent" (Widom and Maxfield, 2001, p.1). Children strike back against a world they perceive as hostile. Acting out may also give adolescents a sense of importance, a way to overcome feelings of inadequacy and inferiority. The acting out may be a form of defense against feelings of anxiety produced by an awareness of guilt.

Adolescents who act out come from all socioeconomic levels and are not psychopathic according to conventional classifications. They may have a clear sense of conscience and be capable of strong feelings of loyalty to a gang. But their impulses are stronger than their self-control. Exploring psychological causes of crime has produced a number of explanations, including:

- Criminals are morally insane; what they do criminally they do not perceive as wrong.
- Personality is developed in early childhood. Future behavior is determined in early childhood. Subsequent sociological and environmental associations do not change this early behavior development.
- Certain people have personalities so deviant that they have little or no control over their impulses.
- There are criminal families in which succeeding generations gravitate toward criminality.
- Mental and moral degeneration cause crime.

 Psychological theories about crime focus on intelligence and psychoanalysis.

Intelligence and Crime   H. H. Goddard (1866–1957) was one of the earliest psychologists to link intelligence and criminality. Goddard believed that criminals are not necessarily biologically inferior, although they might be intellectually inferior. This correlation was again brought to public attention by Hernstein and Murray (1994), who used the bell-shaped normal curve from statistical studies to promote the idea that individuals' intelligence falls within this curve and may also account for criminality.

Psychoanalysis   The psychoanalytic theory of Sigmund Freud (1859–1939) was a popular explanation for human behavior. It stated that personality imbalances had their roots in abnormal emotional and mental development. A person might become fixed at a certain developmental stage or regress to an earlier stage.

Of most importance to the study of criminality is Freud's explanation of problems that arise from fixation at or regression to the phallic stage (3 to 6 years of age). Fixation or regression to this stage may result in sexual assault, rape or prostitution. It may also result in unresolved Oedipal or Electra conflicts:

> Individuals who do not successfully resolve the oedipal or electra complex, and thus do not develop a strong superego capable of controlling the id, were called psychopaths by Freud. (Sociologists call them sociopaths.) Many criminal offenders are presumed to be psychopaths, sociopaths, or antisocial personalities and are characterized by no sense of guilt, no subjective conscience, and no sense of right and wrong (Bohm, 2001, p.53).

Sociological Theories

Sociology is the study of human social structures and human relationships. Most people start life as members of families and later learn to live with other work and social groups. Some sociologists believe that criminals are molded by social conditions and the environment in which they develop. This position runs counter to biological theory in contending that criminals are made, not born. Behavioral theorists argue that people become who they are because of their life experiences.

As children grow and develop, they learn from their families the rules that govern their conduct. Any wrongdoing or mischief reflects what was learned and manipulated for whatever gain might be desired, without taking into account the risk or punishment that might result. If children who misbehave are

© Katherine McGlynn/The Image Works

Youths in Brooklyn, New York, play with toy guns as a prelude to becoming gang members when real guns will replace these toys.

corrected by their parents, they are likely to conform to society's expectations; if they are not corrected, they are likely to ignore society's rules.

Not everyone has the same goals or ways to achieve them. Some people choose to reach goals of financial success and power through illegal acts. During the socialization process, children may learn antisocial values, if such values are important in their social and cultural environments. In such instances socialization actually contributes to delinquent behavior. To what extent social conditions cause criminal behavior is a subject of much debate.

Although delinquency may begin when children first enter school, its most serious manifestations usually occur in adolescence. Most youths at one time or another test the limits—for example, shoplift, steal from their mother's purse or engage in similar petty thefts. Such behavior is usually outgrown without intervention from the juvenile justice system if the parents administer appropriate discipline. Unfortunately not all youths outgrow these tendencies to misbehave.

Pioneering research by Sheldon and Eleanor Glueck (1896–1980 and 1898–1872 respectively) supports a sociological causation for delinquency. The husband-wife team at Harvard University studied former inmates from the Massachusetts Reformatory and published their initial findings in *500 Criminal Careers* (1930). Results from two follow-up studies were reported in *Later Career Criminals* (1937) and *Career Criminals in Retrospect* (1943). These extensive studies of delinquent boys enabled the Gluecks to create a controversial social *predictive index*. The accuracy of this index was tested in the 1950s, and of 220 predictions, 209 were accurate. The social factors in their index included how children were disciplined and supervised, how much affection was shown in the home and family cohesiveness. In their classic work, *Unraveling Juvenile Delinquency*, the Gluecks (1950) reported that 85 percent of the delinquents released from a Massachusetts correctional institution were from families in which other members were delinquent. In 45 percent of the delinquent cases, the mother of the offender had a criminal record; in 66 percent the father had a criminal record.

There are several opinions about the relationship of sociological theories and crime occurrence, including:

- Lack of education, poverty-level income, poor housing, slum conditions and conflict within home and family probably increase crime commission. Achievement expectations are low. If all these conditions disappeared, crime would decrease.
- Continual lawbreaking causes an individual to become part of a subculture that advocates crime and violence as a way to achieve goals or solve problems. It operates outside society's rules. Crimes committed within the subculture are rarely reported to police.
- Behavior is learned. There is good and bad, right and wrong behavior. Identical pressures affect criminals and noncriminals alike.

 Sociological theories include ecological models, social disorganization, functionalism, anomie or strain theory, learning theories and social control theories.

The Ecological Model   Ecology is the study of the relationships between organisms and their environment. Findings from ecology were the basis for the **ecological model**, first described by sociologist Robert Park, University of Chicago (1964–1966). Park et al. (1928) compared the growth of a city and its attendant crime problems with growth in nature. They found that cities were environments like those found in nature, governed by the same forces that affect natural ecosystems.

Ecologists explain that the plant life in an area of land goes through several stages of growth. First is an invasion period when a new species of plant attempts to gain a foothold. Next the new plant may take over the area or dominate it. Finally the environment stabilizes, accepting the presence of its new dominant organism. A *biotic balance* occurs when the relationships between the different species of plants and their necessary conditions for survival maintain equilibrium. All of the organisms are then able to survive and prosper. Ecologists also describe how two different organisms can live together in a mutually *beneficial* relationship known as *symbiosis*.

Park encouraged his colleagues and students to study the dynamics of urban life using this ecological model to explain many of the conditions that existed and the problems that plagued cities. Communities could be studied in part by analyzing the invasion, domination and succession of different ethnic and racial groups. Problems within the community could perhaps be alleviated by studying the presence or absence of a biotic balance and symbiosis in a neighborhood.

In addition, according to Park et al., researchers can demarcate a city based on its outwardly moving growth pattern of concentric zones, with each zone representing a particular form of development and community life, as illustrated in Figure 3.1. The ecological model stressed that any explanation of criminal behavior cannot be taken out of its social context.

Social Disorganization Theory   Two other Chicago sociologists, Shaw and McKay (1942), applied the ecological model to a study of delinquency. Their **social ecology theory** suggested that ecological conditions predicted delinquency and that gang membership is a normal response to social conditions.

Their area studies involved 25,000 delinquents from the Juvenile Court of Cook County from 1900 to 1933. They, too, found concentric zones within an area, with transitional inner-city zones (zone 2) having the highest crime rates. This higher rate of delinquency occurred despite an almost complete turnover in ethnic composition. They also found that even in the worst neighborhoods in zone 2, only about 20 percent of the youths had police or court records.

Shaw and McKay's **social disorganization theory** contended that urban areas produced delinquency directly by weakening community controls and generating a subculture of delinquency passed from one generation to the next. They defined social disorganization as a condition lacking the usual controls over delinquents, with delinquent behavior often approved of by parents and neighbors, having many opportunities available for delinquent behavior and little opportunity or encouragement for legitimate employment. Shaw and McKay used five indicators of social disorganization: (1) residents of low economic status, (2) many different ethnic groups, (3) high residential turnover, (4) dysfunctional families and (5) urbanization. Their social disorganization

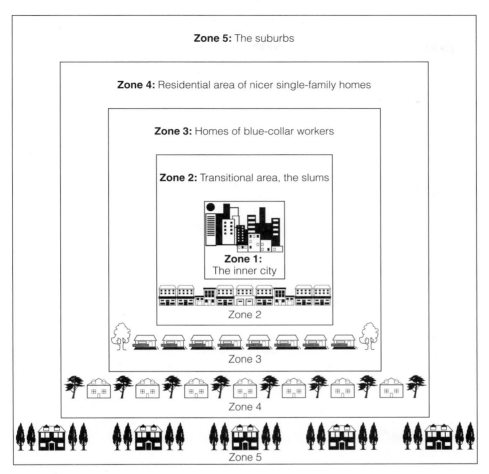

Figure 3.1   The Ecological Model

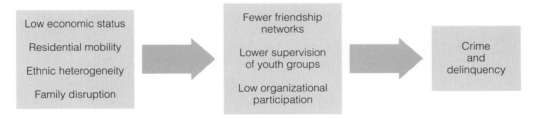

Figure 3.2   Social Disorganization Model

SOURCE: Constructed by R. J. Sampson and W. B. Groves. "Community Structure and Crime: Testing Social-Disorganization Theory." *American Journal of Sociology*, 94, 1989, p.783. Printed in S. Giora Shoham and John Hoffman, *A Primer in the Sociology of Crime*. New York: Harrow and Heston Publishers, 1991, p.51. Reprinted by permission.

theory was built upon by other sociologists, including Sampson and Groves (1989), who developed the social disorganization model shown in Figure 3.2.

Functionalism   Functionalism, sometimes called structural functionalism, is one of two grand sociological paradigms (the other being conflict theory). Durkheim, discussed previously under consensus theory, theorized that large, modern, heterogeneous societies are held together by a functional interdependence—every element in society serves a purpose and function. One of the primary assumptions of this theory is that social structure is based on an agreement by the majority of society's members regarding what is important and valued (hence the "consensus of values" referred to in consensus theory). But if the majority of society values adherence to the law, what purpose is served by crime? According to the functionalist perspective, crime and deviance serve several "greater" purposes for society including:

- Promoting social solidarity—when someone breaks the law, society comes together to reject the deviant and impose punishment, thereby increasing the sense of cohesion and shared values among the law abiding.
- Clarifying and maintaining social boundaries—crime and the ensuing punishment serves as a reminder to people of where the acceptable boundaries lie for behavior.

Anomie or Strain Theory Merton (1910–2003) saw a basic conflict between cultural goals in the United States and our social structure. Merton (1938) adopted Durkheim's concept of anomie—the breakdown of social norms, individuals dissociating themselves from the collective conscience of the group—as the basis for his theory. Merton (1957) viewed crime as being caused by the frustration of people in the lower socioeconomic levels within an affluent society that denies them legal access to social status and material goods. He views this denial as not only unjust but also as a root of many social ills, including crime. Merton further suggests that this is especially true of our "underprivileged youth" who need not only groceries in the literal sense, but also "groceries for growing."

Because most people believe in the American Dream (that is, through hard work anyone can become rich), strive for it and fall short, they experience a strain (Merton, 1938). **Anomie** or **strain theory** is explored by Messner and Rosenfeld in *Crime and the American Dream* (2007, p.11):

> Our analysis is grounded in the variant of anomie theory associated with the work of the American sociologist Robert K. Merton. Merton combines strategic ideas from Durkheim with insights borrowed from Karl Marx, another founding figure in the social sciences, to produce a provocative and compelling account of the social forces underlying deviant behavior in American society. . . .
>
> Most importantly, we accept Merton's underlying premise that motivations for crime do not result simply from the flaws, failures, or free choices of individuals. A complete explanation of crime ultimately must consider the sociocultural environments in which people are located.

The views of Messner and Rosenfeld are presented in the preface of their text (pp.x–xi):

> The essence of our argument is that the distinctive patterns and levels of crime in the United States are produced by the cultural and structural organizations of American society. American culture is characterized by a strong emphasis on the goal of monetary success and a weak emphasis on the importance of the legitimate means for the pursuit of success. This combination of strong pressures to succeed monetarily and weak restraints on the

selection of means is intrinsic to the dominant cultural ethos: the American Dream. The American Dream contributes to crime directly by encouraging people to employ illegal means to achieve goals that are culturally approved. It also exerts an indirect effect on crime through its interconnections with the institutional balance of power in society.

The American Dream promotes and sustains an institutional structure in which one institution—the economy—assumes dominance over all others. The resulting imbalance in the institutional structure diminishes the capacity of other institutions, such as the family, education, and the political system, to curb crime-causing cultural pressures and to impose controls over and provide support for the members of society. In these ways, the distinctive cultural commitments of the American Dream and its companion institutional arrangements contribute to high levels of crime.

Cohen (1955) also built upon Merton's work, adapting his anomie/strain theory in an attempt to explain gang delinquency. Cohen replaced Merton's social goals of wealth with acceptance and status. Youths abandoned the middle-class values for their own values—attaining status among their peers. Cohen's study of delinquent subculture, set forth in *Delinquent Boys* (1955), found that delinquency was caused by social and economic limitations, inadequate family support, developmental handicaps and status frustration. The result: short-run hedonism and group autonomy.

Closely related to strain theorists are those who look at the correlation between unemployment and crime. For example, Carlson and Michalowski (1997, pp.210–211) note:

> The proposition that increases in unemployment will generate increases in crime has long been accepted as a basic tenet of the macro sociology of crime and delinquency. A number of otherwise competing models of crime causation such as conflict theory, Marxian theories, social disorganization theories, and strain theory share the assumption that economic distress generated by rises in unemployment will increase crimes against both persons and property.

Another strain theorist is Robert Agnew (1992) who believed that instead of pursuing specific goals such as the American Dream, most people are more interested in being treated fairly in whatever goals they pursue. He identified three sources of strain: (1) failure to achieve positively valued goals, (2) the removal of positively valued stimuli and (3) the presentation of negative stimuli. Agnew suggested that a major goal of many adolescents is autonomy from adults. He contends that denial of autonomy may lead to delinquency as a way of asserting autonomy—for example, disorderly conduct, obtaining money (stealing) to gain financial independence from parents or venting frustration against those who deny them autonomy (e.g., by imposing curfews). Agnew also points out that strainful events and conditions may cause youths to feel bad, creating pressure to take action that will correct the situation or to take revenge.

Learning Theories   In the 1930s and 1940s, Sutherland (1883–1950) set forth the proposition that criminal behavior is learned through imitation or modeling. In *Principles of Criminology* (1939) with Cressey, he set forth the principles of differential association. Among their propositions are the follow-ing (Sutherland and Cressey, 1974, pp.75–77):

- Criminal behavior is learned in interaction with other persons in a process of communication.
- The principal part of the learning of criminal behavior occurs within inti-mate personal groups.
- The process of learning criminal behavior by association with criminal and anticriminal patterns involves all the mechanisms involved in any other type of learning.
- A person becomes delinquent because of an excess of definitions favorable to the violation of law over definitions unfavorable to the violation of law. This is the principle of differential association.

Sutherland's **differential association theory** is still an important theory of crime causation: "Learning theory explains criminal behavior and its pre-vention with the concepts of positive reinforcement, negative reinforcement, extinction, punishment, and modeling or imitation. In learning theory crime is committed because it is positively reinforced, negatively reinforced or imitated" (Bohm, 2001, p.86). Bohm (pp.86–87) explains these terms:

- Positive reinforcement presents a stimulus that increases or maintains a re-sponse. The stimulus (reward) may be material or psychological.
- Negative reinforcement removes or reduces a stimulus that increases or maintains a response (often referred to as aversion stimulus such as fear of pain or poverty).
- Extinction is a procedure in which behavior that was positively reinforced is no longer reinforced.
- Punishment presents an aversive stimulus to reduce a response.

According to learning theory, criminal behavior is reduced through extinction or punishment.

Many of these factors were explored thoroughly during the 1960s and 1970s based on the behavior modification studies initiated by B. F. Skinner.

Social Control Theories   Social control theorists, instead of focusing on why people commit crime, ask why people do *not* act unlawfully. An influen-tial contemporary social control theorist is Travis Hirschi, whose text *Causes of Delinquency* (1969) greatly influenced current thinking. Hirschi's social control theory traces delinquency to the bond that individuals maintain with society. Social controls rather than moral values are what maintain law and order. A lack of attachment to parents and school can result in delinquency. Hirschi believed that delinquency resulted from a lack of proper socialization and par-ticularly ineffective child-rearing practices: "For Hirschi, proper socialization involves the establishment of a strong moral bond between the juvenile and society. This *bond to society* consists of (1) *attachment* to others, (2) *commitment* to conventional lines of action, (3) *involvement* in conventional activities, and (4) *belief* in the moral order and law" (Bohm, 2001, p.90). Attachment to oth-ers includes respect for significant others as well as an internalization of their norms and values. Commitment involves not only a commitment to conformity but an understanding of the potential results of nonconformity. Involvement includes using time and energy wisely in school, work and outside activities.

Critical Theories

As the name suggests, some theorists became disenchanted with the failure of existing theories to satisfactorily explain the causes of crime. **Critical theory** combines the classical free-will and positivist determinism views of crime, suggesting that humans are both self-determined and society-determined: "Critical theories assume that human beings are the creators of the institutions and structures that ultimately dominate and constrain them" (Bohm, 2001, p.104).

 Critical theories include labeling theory, conflict theory and radical theory.

Labeling Theory   **Labeling theory** has its roots in the work of George Herbert Mead (1863–1931), whose ideas can be summarized in three propositions (Bohm, 2001, pp.105–106):

- Humans act toward things on the basis of the meanings the things have for them.
- The meaning of things arises out of social interaction.
- These meanings are handled in, and modified through, an interpretative process people use to deal with things they encounter.

Messner and Rosenfeld (2007, p.50) suggest: "Labeling theory makes its principal contribution by calling attention to the interplay between social control and personal identity." Ironically, labeling theory suggests that official efforts to control crime may actually increase it. When individuals are labeled as delinquents, others may treat them as such. This increases the likelihood of those so-identified individuals having difficulty associating with "nondelinquents," which may steer them toward associations with others labeled as delinquents in order to "fit in" and feel like they belong.

Research on the social processes that might translate labeling into subsequent deviance found that formally labeled juvenile offenders may become aware of stereotypical beliefs existing in their schools and communities and, fearing rejection, may withdraw from conventional peers (Bernburg et al., 2006). After observing a sample of 1,000 students, Bernburg et al. noted that the labeled and nonlabeled adolescents often avoided one another to reduce uncomfortable interactions, a process that may result in labeled youths seeking out deviant peer groups to be with those in a similarly disadvantaged social position. The researchers concluded: "Juvenile justice intervention [resulting in labeling a youth as delinquent] increased the likelihood of gang membership more than fivefold . . . and was also significantly related to an increased likelihood of subsequent delinquency."

In labeling theory, it is important to differentiate between primary deviance and secondary deviance. **Primary deviance** is the initial criminal act. **Secondary deviance** is accepting the criminal label and consequently committing other crimes. A youth labeled as delinquent may come to believe this—a self-fulfilling prophecy—and begin to take on the role. The influence of labeling theory was especially strong in the 1960s and 1970s and was obvious in the creation of separate terminology for juvenile and adult court, as seen in Chapter 1. Even the term *delinquent* was an attempt to avoid labeling a youthful offender as a criminal.

Conflict Theory   Conflict theory was explained at the beginning of the chapter, but to briefly review: "Conflict theories emphasize the political nature of crime production, posing the question of how the norms of particular groups are encoded into law and how, in turn, law is used as a means by which certain groups dominate others" (Messner and Rosenfeld, 2007, p.50). More specifically: "For conflict theorists, the amount of crime in a society is a function of the extent of conflict generated by *stratification, hierarchical relationships, power differentials,* or the ability of some groups to dominate other groups in that society. Crime, in short, is caused by *relative powerlessness*" (Bohm, 2001, p.111). Closely related to conflict theory is radical theory.

Radical Theory   Radical theory has its roots in the writing of Karl Marx and the conflict between those in power and the powerless. Bohm (2001, pp.114–115) describes **radical theory** as a way to explain crime:

> Radical criminologists focus their attention on the social arrangements of society, especially on political and economic structures and institutions (the "political economy") of *capitalism.* . . .
>
> Crime is a product of the political economy that, in capitalist societies, encourages an individualistic competition among wealthy people and among poor people and between rich and poor people (the intra- and inter*class* struggle) and the practice of taking advantage of other people (*exploitation*).

Many of the preceding theories related to the causes of crime and delinquency have similarities. One approach to the causes of crime and delinquency that differs substantially from the preceding theories is to include the victim as a potential cause.

Victimization Theories

Victimization theories have been used to defend delinquent acts by "blaming the victim." For example, a rape victim may be accused of dressing provocatively or of being in a neighborhood known for gang violence. The most widely cited victimization theory is perhaps Cohen and Felson's (1979) **routine activity theory**, which identifies three elements as critical contributors to crime: (1) a motivated offender, (2) a suitable target and (3) lack of a capable guardian. This theory, which is an extension of the human ecology analysis, posits that changes in everyday routine activities can influence crime through any one of these factors. As such, it also suggests that victims make themselves targets by placing themselves in positions that include motivated offenders and lack of guardians.

A Summary of Theories on the Causes of Crime and Delinquency

As noted by Ohlin (1998, p.143):

> One of the most striking developments in juvenile justice over the past 20 years has been the increasing rapidity and the widening scope of change in theories, goals, and knowledge about delinquency and its prevention or control. Many competing biological, psychological, social, and cultural theories of delinquency have emerged in the past two decades, yet none is sufficient to account for the rate and forms of delinquency today.

 No single theory is sufficient to explain why delinquency exists. A reasonable combination of theories must be considered.

Table 3.1 presents a summary of the most prominent theories on the causation of crime and delinquency. Appendix A provides a more detailed summary of the philosophical influences on delinquency.

Table 3.1   Review of the Major Theories of the Causes of Crime

Theory	*Major Premise*
Choice Theory	People commit crimes when they perceive that the benefits of law violation outweigh the threat and pain of punishment.
Biosocial Theories	
Biochemical	Crime, especially violence, is a function of diet, vitamin intake, hormonal imbalance or food allergies.
Neurological	Criminals and delinquents offer suffer brain impairment. Attention deficit disorder and minimum brain dysfunction are related to antisocial behavior.
Genetic	Delinquent traits and predispositions are inherited. The criminality of parents can predict the delinquency of children.
Psychological Theories	
Psychoanalytic	The development of personality early in childhood influences behavior for the rest of a person's life. Criminals have weak egos and damaged personalities.
Social learning	People commit crimes when they model their behavior after others they see being rewarded for the same acts. Behavior is enforced by rewards and extinguished by punishment.
Cognitive	Individual reasoning processes influence behavior. Reasoning is influenced by the way people perceive their environment and by their moral and intellectual development.
Social Structure Theories	
Social disorganization	The conflicts and problems of urban social life and communities control the crime rate. Crime is a product of transitional neighborhoods that manifest social disorganization and value conflict.
Strain	People who adopt society's goals but lack the means to attain them seek alternatives, such as crime.
Social Process Theories	
Learning	People learn to commit crimes from exposure to antisocial behaviors. Criminal behavior depends on the person's experiences with rewards for conventional behaviors and punishments for deviant ones. Being rewarded for deviance leads to crime.
Social control	A person's bond to society prevents him or her from violating social rules. If the bond weakens, the person is free to commit crimes.
Conflict Theories	
Conflict	People commit crimes when the law, controlled by the rich and powerful, defines their behavior as illegal. The immoral actions of the powerful go unpunished.
Left realism	Crime is a function of relative deprivation; criminals prey on the poor.
Radical feminism	The capital system creates patriarchy, which oppresses women. Male dominance explains gender bias, violence against women and repression.
Peacemaking	Peace and humanism can reduce crime; conflict resolution strategies can work.
Integrated Theories	
Latent trait: general theory of crime	Crime and criminality are separate concepts. People choose to commit crime when they lack self-control. People lacking in self-control will seize criminal opportunities.
Developmental	Criminals go through lifestyle changes during their offending career. As people mature, the factors that influence their propensity to commit crime change. In childhood, family factors are critical; in adulthood, marital and job factors are key.
Victimization Theories	
Victim precipitation	Victims trigger criminal acts by their provocative behavior. Active precipitation involves fighting words or gestures. Passive precipitation occurs when victims unknowingly threaten their attackers.
Lifestyle	Victimization risk is increased when people have a high-risk lifestyle. Placing oneself at risk by going out to dangerous places results in increased victimization.
Routine activities	Crime rates can be explained by the availability of suitable targets, the absence of capable guardians and the presence of motivated offenders.

SOURCE: Joseph J. Senna and Larry J. Siegel. *Introduction to Criminal Justice*, 9th ed. Belmont, CA: Wadsworth Publishing Company, 2002, pp.102–103. Reprinted by permission.

A General Theory of Crime

Criminologist Agnew (2005, pp.11–12) draws on the writings and research of numerous individuals who have studied the causes of crime and integrates them into a general theory of crime: "The general theory focuses on the major, direct causes of crime and groups these causes into a few well-defined clusters, organized by life domain (self, family, school, peer group and work)." His integration of theories and research into why people commit crime consists of eight basic propositions:[1]

1. Crime is most likely when the constraints against crime are low and the motivations for crime are high, as illustrated in Figure 3.3.
2. Several individual traits and features of the individual's immediate social environment directly influence the constraints against and the motivations for crime. Many of these traits and environmental variables are strongly associated with one another and can be grouped into the clusters organized by life domain. These life domains include the self (comprised of personality traits of irritability and low self-control), the family (poor parenting practices, no/bad marriages), the school (negative school experiences, limited education), peers (peer delinquency) and work (unemployment, bad jobs).
3. The life domains have reciprocal effects on one another, although some effects are stronger than others.
4. Crime sometimes affects the life domains in ways that increase the likelihood of subsequent crime. For example, crime sometimes contributes to irritability and to poor parenting practices, negative school experiences and association with delinquent peers. Further, prior crime sometimes directly increases the likelihood of subsequent crime. These effects are most likely when individuals already possess traits conducive to crime and are in environments conducive to crime.
5. The life domains interact with one another in affecting crime. Each life domain has a greater effect on crime when the other life domains are conducive to crime (e.g., the individual is already at risk for crime). For example, traits like irritability and low self-control have a larger effect on crime among individuals in "negative" family, school, peer and work environments.

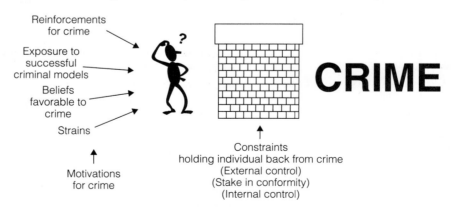

Figure 3.3   The Constraints against and Motivations for Crime

Robert Agnew. *Why Do Criminals Offend? A General Theory of Crime and Delinquency.* Los Angeles, CA: Roxbury Publishing Co., 2005, p.14.

---

[1]From "FOUNDATION FOR A GENERAL STRAIN THEORY OF CRIME AND DELINQUENCY" by Robert Agnew. Reprinted by permission of the American Society of Criminology.

6. The life domains have largely contemporaneous effects on one another and on crime, although each life domain has a large lagged (delayed) effect on itself. For example, *current* levels of crime are largely a function of *current* personality traits and family, school, peer and work experiences, rather than *prior* traits and family, school, peer and work experiences.

7. The life domains have nonlinear effects on crime, such that as a life domain increases in size it has an increasingly large effect on crime. For example, the effect of negative school experiences on crime becomes progressively larger as school experiences become progressively worse.

8. Certain biological factors and features of the larger social environment affect the level and operation of the life domains. The key factors affecting the life domains are age, sex, race/ethnicity, socioeconomic status and the characteristics of the community in which the individual lives—especially the socioeconomic status of the community.

Having examined the primary theories and philosophies that have prevailed throughout the evolution of the juvenile justice system, you should better understand the ideologies that led juvenile justice to diverge from the path of adult criminal justice. You should also be able to better understand the population the juvenile justice system is responsible for and why some youths become delinquent and others do not.

 ## SUMMARY

- Unlawful behaviors or crimes were originally differentiated in two ways: (1) *mala in se*, an act considered wrong in and of itself based on mores, natural law and common law, and stable over time, or (2) *mala prohibita*, a prohibited wrong, originating in folkways and man-made statutory law and changeable over time.

- Two prominent theories as to the underlying purpose of law are consensus theory and conflict theory.

- Consensus theory contends that individuals within a society agree on basic values, on what is inherently right and wrong. Laws express these values. Consensus theory includes the Durkheimian perspective, which sees punishment as revenge and a way to restore and solidify the social order.

- Conflict theory suggests that laws are established to keep the dominant class in power. It includes the Marxist perspective, which sees punishment as a way to control the lower class and preserve the power of the upper class.

- The classical worldview holds that humans have free will and are responsible for their own actions. Proponents of the classical view advocate punishment for offenders. They suggest that deterrence, incapacitation and, in some cases, "just-deserts" punishment is the way to deal with delinquency.

- The positivist worldview holds that humans are shaped by their societies and are the products of environmental and cultural influences. Proponents of the positivist view advocate rehabilitation for offenders.

- Early efforts to explain crime and delinquency according to these theories were expanded upon and refined. Later theories focused on biological, psychological or sociological causes of crime and delinquency. Most recently, critical theories of the causes of crime and delinquency have been developed.

■ Biological theories include physiognomy, phrenology, body type and heredity studies, including studies of twins and adoptees.

■ Psychological theories explaining crime focus on intelligence and psychoanalysis.

■ Sociological theories include ecological models, social disorganization, functionalism, anomie or strain theory, learning theories and social control theories.

■ Critical theories include labeling theory, conflict theory and radical theory.

■ No single theory is sufficient to explain why delinquency exists. A reasonable combination of theories must be considered.

DISCUSSION QUESTIONS

1. Do you take the position of those who hold a classical view or those who hold a positivist view? Do you hold the same view for children as you do for adults?

2. What instances of the Durkheimian or Marxist perspective of punishment can you cite from the historical overview of juvenile justice?

3. Which of the theories of the causation of crime and delinquency seem most logical?

4. Diagram the ecological model as it might look for a major city.

5. How is labeling theory of importance to parents? Teachers? You?

6. Have you ever been labeled? Was it a positive or negative label, and how did you feel about it?

7. Do you believe you can make the American Dream a reality for yourself? Why or why not?

8. Do you support a separate justice system for juveniles? Why or why not?

9. What sources of strain (stress) are there in your life? Might they lead you into a criminal act?

10. Why is it important to know how the juvenile justice system evolved and the theories that have been set forth for the causes of crime and delinquency?

REFERENCES

Agnew, Robert. "Foundation for a General Strain Theory of Crime and Delinquency." *Criminology*, Vol. 30, 1992, pp.47–87.

Agnew, Robert. *Why Do Criminals Offend? A General Theory of Crime and Delinquency.* Los Angeles, CA: Roxbury Publishing Company, 2005.

Beaver, Kevin M.; Schutt, J. Eagle; Boutwell, Brian B.; Ratchford, Marie; Roberts, Kathleen; and Barnes, J. C. "Genetic and Environmental Influences on Levels of Self-Control and Delinquent Peer Affiliation." *Criminal Justice and Behavior*, Vol. 36, No. 1, 2009, pp.41–60.

Bernburg, Jon Gunnar; Krohn, Marvin D.; and Rivera, Craig. "Official Labeling, Criminal Embeddedness and Subsequent Delinquency: A Longitudinal Test of Labeling Theory." *Journal of Research in Crime and Delinquency*, Vol. 67, 2006, p.431.

Bohm, Robert M. *A Primer on Crime and Delinquency.* 2nd ed. Belmont, CA: Wadsworth Publishing Company, 2001.

Carlson, Susan M. and Michalowski, Raymond J. "Crime, Unemployment, and Social Structures of Accumulation: An Inquiry into Historical Contingency." *Justice Quarterly*, June 1997, pp.210–241.

Cohen, Albert K. *Delinquent Boys: The Culture of the Gang.* New York: Free Press, 1955.

Cohen, Lawrence E. and Felson, Marcus. "Social Change and Crime Rate Trends: A Routine Activity Approach." *American Sociological Review*, Vol. 44, 1979, pp.588–608.

Curran, Daniel J. and Renzetti, Claire M. *Theories of Crime.* Boston: Allyn & Bacon, 1994.

Decety, Jean; Michalska, Kalina J.; Akitsuki, Yuko; and Lahey, Benjamin B. "Atypical Empathic Responses in Adolescents with Aggressive Conduct Disorder: A Functional MRI Investigation." *Biological Psychology*, Vol. 80, 2009, pp.203–211.

Donohue, Stephen. "A Crime-Causation Hornet's Nest." *Law Enforcement News*, December 15, 1995, pp.1, 12.

Durkheim, Emile. *The Division of Labor in Society.* New York: Free Press, 1933.

Durkheim, Emile. *Suicide* (1897). Glencoe, IL: Free Press, 1951.

Flicker, Barbara Danziger. *Standards for Juvenile Justice: A Summary and Analysis,* 2nd ed. New York: Institute for Judicial Administration, 1990.

Garland, David. "Sociological Perspectives on Punishment." In *Crime and Justice: A Review of Research*, Vol. 14, edited by Michael Tonry. Chicago: University of Chicago Press, 1991, pp.115–165.

Glueck, Sheldon and Glueck, Elenor. *Unraveling Juvenile Delinquency*, Cambridge, MA: Harvard University Press, 1950.

Hernstein, Richard J. and Murray, Charles. *The Bell Curve: Intelligence and Class Structure in American Life*. New York: Free Press, 1994.

Hirschi, Travis. *Causes of Delinquency*. Berkeley: University of California Press, 1969.

Lombroso, Cesare. *Crime: Its Causes and Remedies*. Montclair, NJ: Patterson Smith, 1968. Originally published in 1911.

Marx, Karl and Engels, Friedrich. *Manifesto of the Communist Party*. Chicago: Encyclopedia Britannica, Inc., 1848, p.419.

Merton, Robert K. "Social Structure and Anomie." *American Sociological Review*, Vol. 3, 1938, pp.672–682.

Merton, Robert K. *Social Theory and Social Structure*, rev. ed. New York: Free Press, 1957.

Messner, Steven F. and Rosenfeld, Richard. *Crime and the American Dream*, 4th ed. Belmont, CA: Wadsworth Publishing Company, 2007.

Ohlin, Lloyd E. "The Future of Juvenile Justice Policy and Research." *Crime & Delinquency*, Vol. 44, No. 1, January 1998, pp.143–153.

Park, Robert E.; Burgess, Ernest W.; and McKenzie, Roderick D. *The City*. Chicago: University of Chicago Press, 1928.

Sampson, R. J. and Groves, W. B. "Community Structure and Crime: Testing Social-Disorganization Theory." *American Journal of Sociology*, Vol. 94, 1989, pp.774–802.

Shaw, Clifford and McKay, H. D. *Juvenile Delinquency and Urban Areas*. Chicago: University of Chicago Press, 1942.

Sutherland, Edwin H. and Cressey, Donald R. *Principles of Criminology*. Philadelphia: J.B. Lippincott, 1939.

Sutherland, Edwin H. and Cressey, Donald R. *Criminology*, 9th ed. Philadelphia: Lippincott, 1974.

Walker, Samuel; Spohn, Cassia; and DeLone, Miriam. *The Color of Justice: Race, Ethnicity, and Crime in America*, 4th ed. Belmont, CA: Wadsworth Publishing Company, 2007.

Widom, Cathy S. and Maxfield, Michael G. *An Update on the "Cycle of Violence."* Washington, DC: National Institute of Justice Research in Brief, February 2001. (NCJ 184894)

HELPFUL RESOURCE

A Primer on Crime and Delinquency Theory, 2nd ed. by Robert M. Bohm. Belmont, CA: Wadsworth Publishing Company, 2001.

CHAPTER 4

Youth in Society: Developmental Risks and Protective Factors

LIFE AFFORDS NO GREATER RESPONSIBILITY, NO GREATER PRIVILEGE, THAN THE RAISING OF THE NEXT GENERATION.

—C. EVERETT KOOP,
FORMER U.S. SURGEON GENERAL

© Michael Weisbrot/Stock Boston

Children playing in an unsafe, abandoned tenement building in New York City's lower east side.

DO YOU KNOW?

- What ages are most critical in child development?
- What characteristics of a healthy family are?
- What common values might be passed on to children by their parents?
- What the most significant individual risk factor is for predicting later delinquency?
- What three developmental pathways to delinquency have been identified and the behaviors associated with each?
- How most youths with conduct disorder should be viewed by the juvenile justice system?
- What the hazards of labeling a youth a psychopath are?
- In what areas risk factors have been identified? Protective factors?
- What two of the most serious consequences for children who live in poverty are?
- What two major peer influences can lead adolescents to delinquency?

CAN YOU DEFINE?

adult supremacy

antisocial personality disorder

attention deficit hyperactivity disorder (ADHD)

conduct disorder (CD)

developmental pathway

emotional/behavioral disorder (EBD)

fetal alcohol spectrum disorder (FASD)

Norman Rockwell family

parental efficacy

protective factor

psychopath

radial concept

risk factor

truancy

CHAPTER OUTLINE

Introduction

Normal Child Development— A Brief Overview

The Critical First Three Years

The Next Ten Years

Adolescence

A Summary of Social Cognition and Moral Development

The Influence of the Family

Socialization and Values

American Child-Rearing Rights and Parenting Practices

The Path to Victimization and Delinquency: At-Risk Behaviors and Circumstances

Individual Risk Factors

Early Antisocial Behavior and Aggression

Conduct Disorder

Developmental and Cognitive Disabilities

Prenatal Exposure to Cigarette Smoking, Drugs, Alcohol and HIV

Substance Abuse

Early Sexual Activity and Teen Pregnancy

Exposure to Violence on Television, in Films and in Video Games

Race

Family Risk Factors

Divorce and Broken Homes

Poverty

Parent Criminality and Incarceration

Separation from Parents and Foster Care

Poor Family Attachment or Bonding

School Risk Factors

Truancy and Frequent Absences

Dropping Out of School

Peer Risk Factors

Community Risk Factors

Protective Factors

Individual Protective Factors

Family Protective Factors

School Protective Factors

Peer Protective Factors

Community Protective Factors

Early Work Experiences: A Risk or Protective Factor?

Prevention and Early Intervention Efforts

Helping America's Youth (HAY)

Introduction

Before examining our contemporary juvenile justice system, it is important to understand those served by this system—our youths—and the environments from which they come. According to *America's Children* (2007, p.vii), in 2006 there were 73.7 million children under age 18 in the United States, or 25 percent of the population. This was down from a peak of 36 percent at the end of the "baby boom" in 1964. The report also notes that racial and ethnic diversity continues to increase. In 2006, 58 percent of children under age 18 were White, non-Hispanic; 20 percent were Hispanic; 15 percent were Black; 4 percent were Asian; and 4 percent were all other races. The number of Hispanic children has increased faster than that of any other racial and ethnic group, growing from 9 percent of the child population in 1980 to 20 percent in 2007.

The National Center for Juvenile Justice (*Annual Report 2003*, p.4) stresses: "No aspect of national interest is more significant than what happens to young people when they are troubled, particularly those we label as 'abused children,' 'dependent children,' 'neglected children,' 'status offenders' and 'juvenile delinquents.' No problem is more troublesome than the delicate balance between protecting children in a free society and protecting society from criminal behavior." Preventing our children and youths from becoming "problems" of the justice system is a logical first step.

This chapter takes a broad look at the pool of American citizens from which the juvenile justice system draws its clients and focuses on normal patterns of growth and development and special challenges to anticipate. Understanding the general process of child development is important because it is during this time that the seeds of juvenile delinquency and later adult criminality can germinate. Thus, this background is critical to those working in juvenile justice because, for every child who enters the juvenile justice system, something in these early stages of child development and family interaction has "gone wrong."

Normal Child Development—A Brief Overview

The study of child development usually deals with children from birth to adolescence and concerns their physical, intellectual, emotional and social growth as they adjust to the demands of society. Although the prenatal period is certainly an important stage, the following discussion on child development will focus on the postnatal period through the late teen years, with various prenatal risk factors mentioned later in the chapter.

Growth and development do not occur in isolation. They involve a complex interaction of family, school and community, with the family being the first and most vital influence. As children grow, the school becomes an important influence, be it preschool, kindergarten, public or private school. As youths approach adolescence, the influence of parents and teachers wanes and that of peers becomes stronger. All of this occurs within the broader community in which children live. This **radial concept** of the influences on growth and development is illustrated in Figure 4.1.

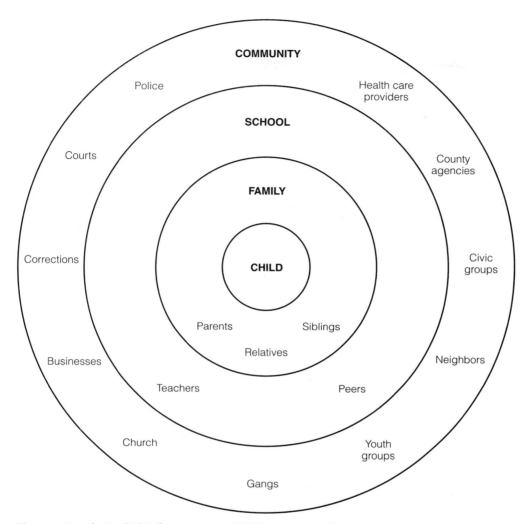

Figure 4.1   The Radial Influences on a Child's Growth and Development

The Critical First Three Years

Child development experts state that the first three years of life lay the foundation for all that follows.

 The period from birth to age 3 is the most formative time of a child's life.

Human brain development occurs at a phenomenal rate in the first three years of life, with neural connections being formed, broken down and reformed faster than at any other time in a person's life. Children who are nurtured, spoken to and touched in caring, positive ways during these formative years respond with increased brain development, whereas children who experience abuse or neglect suffer diminished brain growth. Dr. Frank Putnam, an expert on the biological and psychological effects of stress and trauma on child development and former researcher at the National Institute of Mental Health (NIMH), reports: "The abused kids we studied at NIMH had smaller brains, even when you control for body size, because they don't have rich connections among the nerve cells. . . . [That is why] intervention from ages zero to three is so crucial" (Cass and Curry, 2007, p.100).

It is during this time, with attentive parents or older siblings, that children learn the concept of consequences—rewards and punishments. They also begin to distinguish right from wrong and to develop what is commonly called a *conscience*. This stage is fundamentally important with regard to later delinquency and criminality.

Between the ages of 1 and 3, normal conflicts arise between parents and their children: toilet training, eating certain vegetables, going to bed at a set time, staying within prescribed boundaries and the like. Social conflicts are also common between children at this age in the form of sharing issues and, occasionally, dominance and authority issues (who gets to decide what we play), although the latter typically becomes more prominent at slightly older ages. How these conflicts are resolved will establish the pattern for how the child will deal with conflict later in life. Research suggests that the most aggressive age in humans is 2 years old. Unfortunately, many parents, relatives and friends attribute hitting, biting and throwing tantrums to the "terrible twos." But ignoring such behavior or reacting in kind with violence such as spanking or otherwise striking a child can have dire consequences.

The Next Ten Years

Building on the foundation of the first three critical years, children continue to grow and develop physically, mentally and emotionally over the next decade of their lives. During this time they are continuously learning, and brain development is still occurring rapidly. In fact: "Every researcher of early childhood emphasizes the importance of early childhood nurturing and stimulation for putting a child on a positive path toward adulthood because they literally help the brain grow, especially between birth and age seven" (Cass and Curry, 2007, p.100). Brain growth begins to taper off around age 9 or 10, a period sometimes linked to a phenomenon known as "the fourth grade plunge," when schools begin identifying significant academic deficits and failures among students (p.100).

Most youths get through this phase fairly well, without being unduly influenced by peers. Family influence still usually prevails at this stage. However, it is during this 10-year or so period of preadolescence that those youth who start to push limits and commit offenses turn into the harder-core delinquents. These youngsters are considered to have experienced an "early age of onset" of delinquency, as discussed later in the chapter.

Adolescence

Adolescence generally refers to the teen years, the period from age 12 or 13 to age 18 or 19: "Adolescence is a period of transition from childhood to adulthood, with adolescents preparing for adult family and work roles. Reflecting this fact, adolescents are given *some, but not all* of the privileges and responsibilities of adulthood. They are also expected to assume greater responsibility for their behavior, devote more effort to their schoolwork and expand their social relationships, including romantic relationships" (Agnew, 2005, pp.158–159).

Adolescence is often characterized by rapid growth and sexual maturity, self-consciousness, peer pressure and the shift of the primary support system from parents to friends, mood swings, experimentation, re-evaluation of values and a search for identity. Adolescents seek increasing levels of independence but can also be very much influenced by their peers. Each generation produces a distinct adolescent subculture with a common language, clothing, music and standards. The result is what is often referred to as a *generation gap*. Table 4.1 summarizes some of the key changes that occur as adolescents develop. Such information can help guide adult expectations regarding "typical" adolescent behavior and attitudes.

Table 4.1   Key Aspects of Adolescent Development

Development Domain	Early Adolescence (10–12 years)	Middle Adolescence (13–15 years)	Late Adolescence (16+ years)
Physical Development	■ Puberty starts (usually 2 years earlier for girls than boys)—period of rapid growth ■ Fidget, squirm, have trouble sitting still ■ Bodily changes begin to show	■ Puberty continues ■ Clumsiness due to rapid physical development ■ Extremely aware of and sensitive to own development and that of peers ■ At-risk habits start (smoking, drinking, drugs)	■ Boys' growth has doubled since age 12—they are taller and heavier (on average) than girls ■ Eating disorders may appear (bulimia, anorexia)
Cognitive Development	■ Inconsistent thoughts ■ Shift from immature to mature thinking ■ Logic and reasoning discovered ■ Able to imagine beyond immediate environment ■ Is important to feel that their opinions count ■ Thoughts lead to feelings of self-consciousness ■ Girls are more communicative than boys	■ Abstract thinking begins ■ Problem solving, analytical thinking and writing may be deficient ■ Greater separation in school between those who succeed and those who fail ■ Parents have less influence ■ Decreased evidence of creativity and flexibility ■ Peer conformity critically important ("belongingness")	■ Critical-thinking and reasoning skills begin ■ Want to think out their own decisions ■ Concerned about the purpose and meaning of life ■ Develop beliefs, values, career choices, and identity ■ Increased peer conformity ■ New challenges and experiences are required
Emotional Development	■ Seek independence, establish individuality ■ Want some control in decisions affecting life ■ Propensity toward awkwardness, self-consciousness and bouts with low self-esteem ■ Need praise and approval from adults to demonstrate concern and care about their welfare	■ Crave freedom ■ Adept at masking true feelings and state of mind ■ Intense desire and need for privacy ■ Rapid hormonal and body changes often lead to low self-esteem and lack of confidence ■ Seek independence from, but still need structure and limits from, parents and adults ■ Increased sexual desires and experimentation ■ Need praise and approval from adults to demonstrate concern and care about their welfare	■ Develop sense of personal identity ■ Self-esteem continues to develop and improve ■ Competencies such as decision making, stress management and coping with problems develop ■ Friendships are based on mature intimacy, and sharing thoughts and feelings—rather than just hanging out and doing things together ■ Strong sexual feelings are experienced ■ Generally, strong ties with the family are maintained with increased need for parental love, care and respect

(continued)

Table 4.1   *(Continued)*

Development Domain	Early Adolescence (10–12 years)	Middle Adolescence (13–15 years)	Late Adolescence (16+ years)
Social Development	■ Have a desire to "fit in," to be well-liked is important ■ Cliques are formed with others ■ Want to be with friends without adult supervision ■ Feel that peer pressure is constantly present ■ Begin experimenting with smoking, alcohol and sex ■ Appreciate conversations that lead to an exchange of ideas to better understand other people's points of view	■ Friendship and romance become increasingly important ■ Realize that others have different points of view ■ Begin to define themselves and develop more concrete self-concept ■ Show increased communication and negotiation skills ■ Explore rights and responsibilities ■ Want to hang out with older teens ■ Parents start to have less influence	■ Independence developed and demonstrated ■ Susceptibility to peer pressure declines ■ Parent-teen conflicts decrease ■ Cooperation and communication increase ■ Identity formation experienced through exploration and experimentation ■ Want to distinguish themselves from the crowd ■ Have large circle of acquaintances and small circle of friends ■ After-school work prevalent

SOURCE: Adapted from Barry Glick. "Kids in Adult Correctional Systems." *Corrections Today*, August 1998, p.97. Reprinted by permission.

Juveniles often pretend to be adults in various ways, but becoming emotionally mature, socially accepted adults requires a struggle. From a social standpoint, many never succeed. Adolescents may try to look like adults, talk like adults or take on what they believe to be adult ways, but in general they remain quite immature. At the same time that they imitate adult behavior, juveniles also strive for individuality, independence and freedom, which they believe they can achieve by disassociating themselves from society and their parents. Such a position between imitation and disassociation can generate a great deal of internal conflict and psychological stress.

A Summary of Social Cognition and Moral Development

Understanding the typical progression of cognitive and moral development in youth is, without doubt, highly germane to those working in juvenile justice because children's behavior is a direct result of these processes. These developmental stages provide a basis for numerous legislation and policy initiatives dealing with crime and delinquency by setting forth scientifically determined age ranges at which a person typically knows right from wrong and at what age offenders are deemed reasonably capable of understanding the consequence of their actions. These stages also play a role in determining suitable sanctions or treatment options for delinquent youth.

The development of social cognition, based on the theory of cognitive development set forth by Swiss philosopher Jean Piaget, is outlined in Table 4.2. Piaget theorized that children progress through four main periods as they attempt to make sense of the world around them and understand their place within it. These four periods, or cognitive schemes, are roughly correlated with age and become increasingly sophisticated with maturity: the sensorimotor period (ages 0–2), the preoperational period (ages 2–7), the concrete operational period (ages 7–11) and the formal operational period (age 11 and up). It is important to be aware of

Table 4.2 Development of Social Cognition

	Understanding Self	*Understanding Others*	*Understanding Friends*	*Understanding Social Roles*	*Understanding Society*
Preoperational Period (About ages 2–7)	Understands concrete attributes. Understands major emotions, but relies on situation.	Understands concrete attributes, including stability of behavior.	One-way assistance (ages 4–9).	Can generalize role (age 4). Understands person can change role and remain same person.	Feels no need to explain system (ages 5–6).
Concrete Operational Period (About ages 7–12)	Understands personal qualities. Relies on inner feelings as guide to emotions. Understands shame and pride.	Understands personal qualities.	Fairweather cooperation (ages 6–12).	Understands that people can occupy two roles simultaneously.	Understands social functions observed or experienced (ages 7–8). Provides fanciful explanations of distant functions (ages 9–10). Has acquired concrete knowledge of society.
Formal Operational Period (After about age 12)	Capable of complex, flexible, precise description. Understands abstract traits. Establishes identity.	Capable of complex, flexible, precise description.	Intimate sharing (ages 9–15).	Can deal with abstract conception of society, government, and politics (by age 15).	

SOURCE: Elizabeth Hall, Michael E. Lamb and Marion Perlmutter. *Child Psychology Today,* 2nd ed. New York: Random House, 1986, p.562. Reprinted with permission of the McGraw-Hill Companies.

MORAL REASONING AND DILEMMAS

Inspired by the work of Piaget, psychologist Lawrence Kohlberg sought to understand how children react to moral dilemmas and subsequently devised a six-stage theory of moral development. His study into moral reasoning led to the conclusion that the process of moral development, which continues to evolve throughout one's life, is principally concerned with justice (Kohlberg, 1981). In brief, Kohlberg's six stages were organized into three levels:

- Level 1 (*Pre-Conventional*)
    Stage 1—Obedience and punishment orientation (*How can I avoid punishment?*)
    Stage 2—Self-interest orientation (*What's in it for me?*)

- Level 2 (*Conventional*)
    Stage 3—Interpersonal accord and conformity (*The good boy/good girl attitude*)
    Stage 4—Authority and social-order maintaining orientation (*Law and order morality*)

- Level 3 (*Post-Conventional*)
    Stage 5—Social contract orientation
    Stage 6—Universal ethical principles (*Principled conscience*)

The classic example of a Kohlberg dilemma is the Heinz dilemma: A woman was near death from a special kind of cancer. There was only one drug that doctors thought might save her—a form of radium that a druggist in the same town had recently discovered. The drug was expensive to make, but the druggist was charging ten times what the drug cost him to produce. He paid $200 for the radium and charged $2,000 for a small dose of the drug. The sick woman's husband, Heinz, went to everyone he knew to borrow the money, but he could only get together about $1,000. He told the druggist that his wife was dying and begged him to either sell it cheaper or let him pay the balance later. But the druggist said, "No. I discovered the drug, and I'm going to make money from it." So Heinz got desperate and broke into the man's store to steal the drug for his wife.

Should Heinz have broken into the laboratory to steal the drug for his wife? Why or why not?

individual differences that may occur and to recognize that development may not always progress in a smooth, continuous manner.

A large part of the responsibility for ensuring that our children successfully navigate the growing-up process, develop a moral conscience and avoid offending behaviors rests with the family.

The Influence of the Family

The family is the foundation for the protection, care and training of our children. It is the first institution to affect children's behavior and to provide knowledge of and access to society's goals, values and expectations. Because the family is usually the first teacher and model for behavior and misbehavior, the structure and interaction patterns of the home greatly influence whether children learn social or delinquent behavior. In general, the family can have a positive impact on insulating children from antisocial and criminal patterns, providing it can control rewards and effectively maintain positive relationships within itself. Delinquency is highest when family interaction and controls are weak.

 In healthy families, self-esteem is high, communication is direct and honest, rules are flexible and reasonable and members' attitudes toward the outside world are trusting and optimistic.

Children develop their sense of being worthwhile, capable, important and unique from the attention and love given to them by their parents. They can develop a sense of worthlessness, incapability, unimportance and facelessness from a lack of attention and love, or from physical or sexual abuse.

In November 1989, the General Assembly of the United Nations adopted several articles outlining the "rights of the child" (United Nations, 1989). The importance of the family was stressed in the preamble to this declaration of rights. The United Nations recognized that:

- The family, as the fundamental group of society and the natural environment for the growth and well-being of all its members and particularly children, should receive the protection and assistance that it needs to fully assume its responsibilities within the community.
- The child, for the full and harmonious development of his or her personality, should grow up in a family environment, in an atmosphere of happiness, love and understanding.
- The child should be fully prepared to live an individual life in society, and be brought up in the spirit of the ideals proclaimed in the Charter of the United Nations, and in particular in the spirit of peace, dignity, tolerance, freedom, equality and solidarity.

These powerful statements convey not only the importance of the family, but also the values the family is to instill in children as it nurtures them and teaches them to be individuals as well as contributing members of society.

Socialization and Values

Children should learn in the home that others have rights that they must respect. They should learn about social and moral values; to be considerate of

The family is, for most children, the strongest socializing force in their lives. To thrive, children need the love and support of their parents.

others' property, possessions and individual selves; to manage their own affairs and to take responsibility for their actions.

Values are extremely important in any society. Values reflect the nature of the society, indicate what is most important and describe how people are expected to behave. Throughout the ages societies have embraced certain values, taught these values to their children and punished those who did not adhere to them. When youths do not accept the values of society, conflict is inevitable.

 Common values that should be passed on to children include fairness, honesty, promise-keeping, respect, responsibility and self-control.

Unfortunately, in many families, no values or negative values, such as the use of violence to resolve disputes, are passed on.

American Child-Rearing Rights and Parenting Practices

Historically, physical punishment of misbehaving children has received general support in the United States. The familiar adage, "Spare the rod, and spoil the child," attests to the traditional American view that it is parents' responsibility to teach their children right from wrong.

Force and violence toward children, including physical punishment, has been characterized as **adult supremacy**, which has its roots in a common law concept of status derived from a feudal order that denied children legal identity and treated them as objects. In the United States until about 1900, the only person in the family who had any legal rights was the father. Adult supremacy subordinates children to the absolute and arbitrary authority of parents, a relationship whereby power is sanctioned by legal rules. Indeed, courts today give parents wide latitude in disciplining their children so they learn to respect authority.

Parental efficacy examines how parental support and control of youth are associated with delinquency. One area of parental control which has received increasing scrutiny is the use of corporal punishment.

The Debate: To Spank or Not to Spank?   "Spanking and harsher forms of physical discipline have been part of American culture for centuries. The debate over whether adults should have the right to strike a child has created tension between those who firmly believe in the benefits and those who consider it abuse" (Glanton, 2001). Currently, spanking of children is expressly permitted by law in 49 states (Minnesota being the exception). Nearly half of all states still allow the use of corporal punishment in schools.

Before children can reason, physical measures are commonly relied on. The question often becomes not so much whether such physical coercion is appropriate, but rather what *degree* of physical coercion is appropriate. When does punishment become abuse? Is a slap on the hand the same as a slap to the face? Is a "paddling" through clothing with a bare hand the same as a beating with a belt on a bare bottom?

A meta-analysis of 88 studies conducted over six decades on parental use of corporal punishment led to the conclusion that parents who spank their children risk causing long-term harm that outweighs the short-term benefit of instant obedience: "Parental corporal punishment is associated significantly with a range of child behaviors and experiences, including both short- and long-term, individual- and relationship-level, and direct (physical abuse) and indirect (e.g., delinquency and antisocial behavior) constructs" (Gershoff, 2002, p.549).

Several major national organizations, including the American Academy of Pediatrics (AAP), have taken an official stand against parental use of corporal punishment. An AAP policy statement, originally issued in 1998 and reaffirmed in 2004, asserts: "The more children are spanked, the more anger they report as adults, the more likely they are to spank their own children, the more likely they are to approve of hitting a spouse, and the more marital conflict they experience as adults. Spanking has been associated with higher rates of physical aggression, more substance abuse, and increased risk of crime and violence when used with older children and adolescents" ("Policy Statement: Guidelines for Effective Discipline," 1998, p.726).

Other experts have taken a slightly different position. Robert Larzelere, a psychology professor at the Nebraska Medical Center, contends that mild, nonabusive spanking can be an effective reinforcement of nonphysical disciplinary methods, especially in dealing with defiant 2- to 6-year-olds. Larzelere, concerned with the global trend to adopt increasingly extreme antispanking bans which lack scientific basis, stresses the need to balance advocacy with science. Larzelere and Kuhn (2005, p.1) reviewed 50 years of research on child discipline and selected 26 qualifying studies for meta-analysis in what has become the first scientific review comparing child outcomes of physical punishment versus alternative tactics parents could use instead. Their results indicated effect sizes that significantly favored conditional spanking over 10 of 13 alternative disciplinary tactics for reducing child noncompliance or antisocial behavior. Their analysis demonstrated that the following alternative disciplinary measures had significantly *worse* outcomes than conditional spanking for either noncompliance (N) or antisocial aggression (A) or both: reasoning (N & A), threats or verbal power assertion (N), privilege removal (N), time out or isolation (A), ignoring (N), love withdrawal (A), restraint or physical power assertion (N), child-determined end to time out (N), scolding (A) and diverting (A). These researchers stress: "Spanking should only be used when children respond defiantly to milder disciplinary tactics, such as time out, or to stop harmful misbehavior (e.g., running into the street)." They also recommend that conditional spanking should always be used in a way that reduces the need to use it in the future and should never be used in a child's first 12 months.

For children to grow and thrive, certain basic needs must be met. These include choices and challenges, healthy and safe surroundings, love, respect and recognition, encouragement, nurturing, direction and independence. Unfortunately, for many of our nation's children, this is *not* the reality. Their healthy development is hindered by inadequate medical care, poverty, violence and disintegrating families, factors that place youth at risk for numerous problems throughout life. Having considered the "normal" pathway a person takes as they develop from child to adolescent to adult, consider next some of the characteristics, behaviors and circumstances that increase the chances a child may veer off the law-abiding course and onto the track for delinquency.

AT ISSUE: PARENT RIGHTS VS. CHILD RIGHTS

Adults have a legally protected right to bodily integrity, free from assault, but children do not, except in extreme circumstances. Parents are authorized to use force against their children because society believes adults are older and presumably wiser, and because the right to rear one's child as one chooses is held to be fundamental.

The USA and Somalia are the only countries that have not ratified the UN's 1989 Convention on the Rights of the Child (CRC), mentioned earlier in this chapter. Critics contend the CRC intrudes too much into the parent-child relationship and usurps parents' role and authority in determining how to raise their own child:

"The Convention on the Rights of the Child may be a positive tool for promoting child welfare for those countries that have adopted it. But we believe the text goes too far when it asserts entitlements based on economic, social and cultural rights. . . . The human rights-based approach . . . poses significant problems as used in this text."—President George W. Bush, 2001

"Americans need to re-evaluate why we believe it is reasonable to hit young, vulnerable children when it is against the law to hit other adults, prisoners, and even animals."—Elizabeth Thompson Gershoff, psychologist, Columbia University.

Should the freedom to spank one's child be dictated by legislation? At what level should this issue be addressed: local, state, federal or international?

The Path to Victimization and Delinquency: At-Risk Behaviors and Circumstances

Despite the numerous theories on why children become delinquent, researchers are able to agree on one point: there is no single path to delinquency. The presence of multiple risk factors and how they interact to increase a youth's chance of offending create countless ways for a child to go from obedient to delinquent. Conversely, the existence of certain protective factors can work to offset the risk factors and keep a child headed toward a law-abiding adulthood (Shader, 2002, p.1).

Various definitions of risk factors exist, but in the context of juvenile justice, a working definition of a **risk factor** is a condition, characteristic or variable that increases the likelihood that a child will become delinquent. Exposure to multiple risk factors can have a cumulative effect, and the relative impact any risk factor has on a child may be either augmented or diminished by the developmental state of that child (Shader, 2002, p.2).

 Researchers have identified dozens of risk factors related to delinquency and have grouped them into five basic domains: individual, family, school, peers and community.

A caution on risk factors: Keep in mind that this chapter deals with the general youth population—before they become either victims or offenders—and the circumstances that increase the likelihood that such children will enter the juvenile justice system, either as victims or offenders: "Although researchers use risk factors to detect the likelihood of later offending, many youth with multiple risk factors never commit delinquent or violent acts. A risk factor may increase the probability of offending, but it does not make offending a certainty" (Shader, 2002, p.2).

Individual Risk Factors

Numerous individual risk factors have been identified as increasing the likelihood that a youth will come in contact with the juvenile justice system, either as a victim or an offender. The following list of risk factors was compiled from several sources, including Shader (2002), Wasserman et al. (2003) and Helping America's Youth (2007):

- Early antisocial behavior
- Early onset of aggression
- Conduct disorders, mental illness, other mental health issues
- Developmental disabilities and disorders
- Emotional factors (such as high behavioral activation and low behavioral inhibition)
- Poor refusal skills
- Hyperactivity (ADHD)
- Cognitive and neurological deficits and disorders
- Low intelligence (low IQ), mental retardation
- Lack of guilt and empathy
- Chronic medical and/or physical conditions
- Prenatal exposure to cigarette smoking, drugs, alcohol or HIV
- Favorable attitudes toward drug use

- Early onset of alcohol and/or drug use
- Gun possession/illegal gun ownership
- Early sexual involvement
- Teen parenthood
- Exposure to television or media violence
- Victimization (abuse, neglect)
- Gender: Being male
- Race: Being African American or Hispanic

Although space limitations preclude an in-depth discussion of every listed risk factor, certain select factors will be examined in greater detail. (Victimization is the topic of Chapter 5 and, thus, will not be covered more here.) Be aware that many of these risk factors also tend to co-occur, such as hyperactivity, emotional factors and poor refusal skills.

Early Antisocial Behavior and Aggression

Wasserman et al. (2003, p.2) assert: "Early antisocial behavior may be the best predictor of later delinquency. Antisocial behaviors generally include various forms of oppositional rule violation and aggression, such as theft, physical fighting, and vandalism. In fact, early aggression appears to be the most significant social behavior characteristic to predict delinquent behavior before age 13."

 The most significant individual risk factor for predicting later delinquency is early antisocial behavior, specifically aggression.

Developmental Pathways   Longitudinal research has revealed that the development of disruptive and delinquent behavior in boys typically occurs in an orderly, progressive manner known as a **developmental pathway**: "A pathway is identified when a group of individuals experience a behavioral development that is distinct from the behavioral development of other groups of individuals. In a developmental pathway, stages of behavior unfold over time in an orderly fashion" (Kelley et al., 1997, p.2). Figure 4.2 illustrates a common sequence of

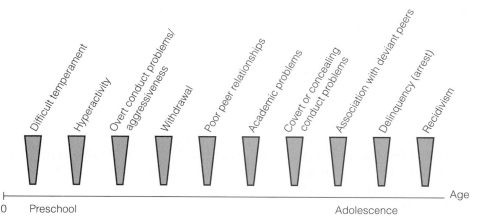

Figure 4.2   Approximate Ordering of the Different Manifestations of Disruptive and Antisocial Behaviors in Childhood and Adolescence

SOURCE: Barbara Tatem Kelley et al. *Developmental Pathways in Boys' Disruptive and Delinquent Behavior.* Washington, DC: OJJDP Juvenile Justice Bulletin, December 1997, p.4. (NCJ 165692)

the manifestations of disruptive and antisocial behaviors as a child gets older. As indicated, a difficult temperament is generally the earliest problem noted in infants, with hyperactivity becoming more apparent once a child begins to walk, and so on.

Kelley et al. (1997, p.4) explain that this figure "highlights the fact that a child can exhibit considerable continuity in disruptive and antisocial behaviors, even though the behaviors are manifested differently with increasing age. Children's development toward serious deviant behavior can be thought of as leading to diversification of behaviors, rather than replacement of one problem behavior with another. Few children progress to the most serious behaviors or accumulate the largest variety of such problems. It is more common for children to penetrate the deviancy continuum to a lesser degree, reach a plateau, or reverse to a less serious level."

Disruptive and delinquent behavior typically manifests in a predictable sequence, although the age of onset can show great variation among individuals (see Figure 4.3):

> [Conduct such as stubborn behavior] tended to occur earliest at median age 9, with a wide range of onset—the 25th percentile at age 3 and the 75th percentile at age 13. This was followed by minor covert acts, such as lying and shoplifting, at median age 10. Defiance, which involves doing tasks in one's own way, refusing to follow directions and disobeying, emerged next at median age 11. Aggressive behaviors, such as bullying and annoying others, followed at age 12, along with property damage, such as vandalism and fire setting. More seriously aggressive acts, such as physical fighting and violence, came last at median age of 13. (Kelley et al., 1997, p.6)

Figure 4.4 shows how these problem behaviors can be sequenced into three distinct developmental pathways to delinquency, each with progressively more serious problem behaviors.

- The *authority conflict path* includes stubbornness, doing things one's own way, refusing to do things and disobedience. It may culminate in authority avoidance by staying out late, truancy and/or running away.
- The *covert behavior path* includes lying, shoplifting, setting fires, damaging property, joyriding, pickpocketing, stealing from cars, fencing stolen goods, writing illegal checks and using illegal credit cards. It may culminate in serious delinquency such as stealing a car, selling drugs and/or breaking and entering.
- The *overt behavior path* includes annoying others, bullying and fighting. It may culminate in violence, including attacking someone, strong-arming and/or forcing sex.

Kelley et al. (1997, p.4) see "children's failures to master developmental tasks and to acquire other prosocial skills reflected in these tasks as breeding grounds for the development of disruptive and delinquent behavior. Therefore, many youths who eventually become seriously and chronically delinquent somewhere during childhood and adolescence probably missed opportunities to learn one or more key prosocial behaviors."

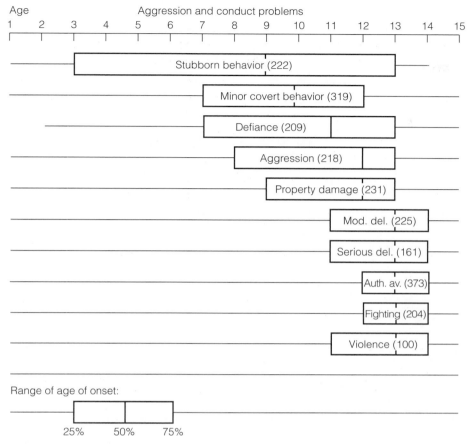

Figure 4.3 Sequence of Age of Onset of Disruptive and Delinquent Child Behavior

SOURCE: Barbara Tatem Kelley et al. *Developmental Pathways in Boys' Disruptive and Delinquent Behavior.* Washington, DC: OJJDP Juvenile Justice Bulletin, December 1997, p.8. (NCJ 165692)

Conduct Disorder

A **conduct disorder (CD)** is a serious childhood psychiatric condition that manifests itself in aggression, lying, stealing and other chronic breaches of socially acceptable behavior. Children with conduct disorder are often seen by others as "bad" or labeled delinquent when they should be treated, instead, as mentally ill.

 Most youths with conduct disorder should be treated as mentally ill rather than as delinquent.

Conduct disorder is not to be confused with oppositional defiant disorder (ODD), which is a separate diagnosis given to youth who demonstrate persistent

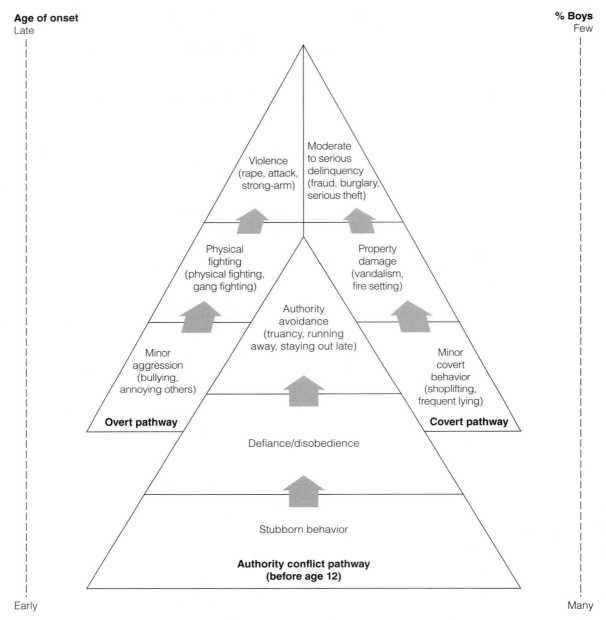

Figure 4.4 Three Pathways to Boys' Disruptive Behavior and Delinquency

SOURCE: Barbara Tatem Kelley et al. *Developmental Pathways in Boys' Disruptive and Delinquent Behavior.* Washington, DC: OJJDP Juvenile Justice Bulletin, December 1997, p.9. (NCJ 165692)

negativity, disobedience and hostility toward authority. While youth with ODD are likely to be in trouble with their parents, they are not engaged in behavior that brings them into trouble with the law (if they are, this becomes conduct disorder). Youths with conduct disorder are likely to have ongoing problems if they and their families do not receive early and comprehensive treatment.

Antisocial Personality Disorder   If a conduct disorder is allowed to persist, it may develop into **antisocial personality disorder**, which the American

Psychiatric Association (APA) defines as a disorder that exists in individuals age 18 or older who show evidence of a conduct disorder before age 15 as well as a pattern of irresponsible and antisocial behavior since age 15 (*Diagnostic and Statistical Manual of Mental Disorders*, 2000). It occurs in about 3 percent of American males and fewer than 1 percent of American females. Table 4.3 lists the behaviors indicative of conduct disorders and irresponsible, antisocial behavior.

Although antisocial personality disorder is a diagnosis reserved for adults, you will notice in looking through the indicators in Table 4.3 that many of these behaviors will be presented over the next several pages as risk factors for delinquency and criminality.

People with antisocial personality disorder are often referred to as socio-paths or psychopaths, labels that, again, are valid only for those over age 18; yet the behaviors have their beginnings in childhood and adolescence. Psychopathic or sociopathic behavior refers to chronic asocial behavior rooted in severe deficiencies in developing a conscience during childhood. Failure to develop feelings of guilt is usually attributed to the absence or neglect of a strong identification with stable parental figures or to having parents who have problems with social values. Failure to develop a conscience often begins with the use or exploitation of children by parents. The children are encouraged to carry out the parents' own forbidden impulses and wishes. This encourages children in their own antisocial behavior. Such patterns of behavior usually originate with an overly dominant mother and a child who believes in acting out maternal wishes.

A **psychopath** is regarded as virtually lacking in conscience, displaying remarkable emotional blandness, particularly about actions that profoundly shock "normal" people. A psychopath cares not between right and wrong. They may claim to recognize, and even speak smoothly about, devotion to accepted values and societal norms, and they can be charming in casual personal contacts. Meanwhile, they may be stealing from someone they call a "friend," or harboring malicious intentions toward someone they profess to care about. Psychopaths often make glib promises and resolutions. They are profoundly egocentric and never see their own responsibility for anything that goes wrong. Although most psychopaths have normal intelligence, their thinking is essentially superficial. Despite an ability to learn, they do not profit by the lessons of their own experience, so their behavior is out of step with what they abstractly know. In fact, not only do they seem indifferent to the consequences for other people of what they do, but they seem unconcerned about the almost certain negative consequences for themselves.

It is important to note that the APA prohibits psychiatrists from rendering a diagnosis of antisocial personality disorder, or psychopathy, in someone younger than 18, recognizing that many youths display callous or detached behavior during adolescence: "Sometimes persistent traits and tendencies of this sort and inadequate emotional responses indicate the picture of the psychopath early in his career. Sometimes, however, the child or the adolescent will for a while behave in a way that would seem scarcely possible to anyone but the true psychopath and later change, becoming a normal and useful member of society" (Cleckley, 1988, p.270).

Table 4.3   Antisocial Personality Disorder

A. Current age at least 18.

B. Evidence of conduct disorder with onset before age 15, as indicated by a history of *three* or more of the following:

   (1) was often truant

   (2) ran away from home overnight at least twice while living in parental or parental surrogate home (or once without returning)

   (3) often initiated physical fights

   (4) used a weapon in more than one fight

   (5) forced someone into sexual activity with him or her

   (6) was physically cruel to animals

   (7) was physically cruel to other people

   (8) deliberately destroyed others' property (other than by firesetting)

   (9) deliberately engaged in firesetting

   (10) often lied (other than to avoid physical or sexual abuse)

   (11) has stolen without confrontation of a victim on more than one occasion (including forgery)

   (12) has stolen with confrontation of a victim (e.g., mugging, purse-snatching, extortion, armed robbery)

C. A pattern of irresponsible and antisocial behavior since the age of 15, as indicated by at least *four* of the following:

   (1) is unable to sustain consistent work behavior, as indicated by any of the following (including similar behavior in academic setting if the person is a student):

     (a) significant unemployment for six months or more within five years

     (b) repeated absences from work unexplained by illness in self or family

     (c) abandonment of several jobs without realistic plans for others

   (2) fails to conform to social norms with respect to lawful behavior, as indicated by repeatedly performing antisocial acts that are grounds for arrest (whether arrested or not), e.g., destroying property, harassing others, stealing, pursuing an illegal occupation

   (3) is irritable and aggressive, as indicated by repeated physical fights or assaults (not required by one's job or to defend someone or oneself), including spouse- or child-beating

   (4) repeatedly fails to honor financial obligations, as indicated by defaulting on debts or failing to provide child support or support for other dependents on a regular basis

   (5) fails to plan ahead, or is impulsive, as indicated by one or both of the following:

     (a) traveling from place to place without a prearranged job or clear goal for the period of travel or clear idea about when the travel will terminate

     (b) lack of a fixed address for a month or more

   (6) has no regard for the truth, as indicated by repeated lying, use of aliases, or conning others for personal profit or pleasure

   (7) is reckless regarding his or her own or others' personal safety, as indicated by driving while intoxicated or recurrent speeding

   (8) if a parent or guardian lacks ability to function as a responsible parent, as indicated by one or more of the following:

     (a) malnutrition of child

     (b) child's illness resulting from lack of minimal hygiene

     (c) failure to obtain medical care for a seriously ill child

     (d) child's dependence on neighbors or nonresident relatives for food or shelter

     (e) failure to arrange for a caretaker for young child when parent is away from home

     (f) repeated squandering, on personal items, of money required for household necessities

   (9) has never sustained a totally monogamous relationship for more than one year

   (10) lacks remorse (feels justified in having hurt, mistreated or stolen from another)

D. Occurrence of antisocial behavior not exclusively during the course of schizophrenia or manic episodes

SOURCE: American Psychiatric Association. *Diagnostic and Statistical Manual of Mental Disorders*, 4th ed, Text Revision (DSM-IV-TR). (Copyright 2000 American Psychiatric Association), pp.344–346. Reprinted with permission.

Aside from being proscribed by the APA, there is an inherent danger of labeling a youth as psychopathic.

 Labeling a youth as a psychopath reduces the youth's likelihood of receiving treatment and increases the youth's likelihood of being transferred to the criminal justice system and treated as an adult.

The salient point to be made here is that many youths who have valid mental illness concerns early in life are not diagnosed and treated as such but rather are viewed as troublemakers who should be dealt with, often harshly, through the justice system. This is an unfortunate missed opportunity to intervene with these youths while their personalities are still rather pliable, *before* their distorted thinking patterns become entrenched and their actions turn criminal.

Developmental and Cognitive Disabilities

A broad spectrum of developmental, behavioral, intellectual/cognitive and learning disabilities place youth at increased risk for delinquent behavior. Compounding the problem for youth and those tasked with helping them, many of these disabilities and disorders commonly co-occur.

Emotional and Behavioral Disorders (EBD)   One challenging segment of youths are those labeled as having an **emotional/behavioral disorder (EBD)**. These youths usually have one or more of the following behavior patterns: severely aggressive or impulsive behavior; severely withdrawn or anxious behaviors, pervasive unhappiness, depression or wide mood swings; severely disordered thought processes that show up in unusual behavior patterns, atypical communication styles and distorted interpersonal relationships. EBD is a broad category that often co-occurs with autism, Asperger syndrome and ADHD.

Hyperactivity and ADHD   As seen in Figure 4.2, hyperactivity is a frequently observed predelinquent behavior in young children. **Attention deficit hyperactivity disorder (ADHD)** is a common childhood disruptive behavior disorder characterized by heightened motor activity (fidgeting and squirming), a short attention span, distractibility, impulsiveness and lack of self-control. ADHD is often accompanied by a learning disability.

Learning Disabilities   Five to 10 million children in the United States experience some form of learning disability: "A learning disabled person is an individual who has one or more significant deficits in the essential learning

---

REALITY CHECK

An unfortunate truth for many youths in this population is that, even absent any actual delinquent behavior, they may still be funneled into the juvenile justice system:

"Increasingly, it is not so much the criminality of the behavior but the lack of alternatives for children with severe emotional and behavior problems, children who have been expelled from school, and children whose families cannot provide adequate care that brings them into the juvenile justice system."—American Bar Association 2003 report on juvenile justice in Ohio

processes" (Association for Children with Learning Disabilities [ACLD], p.4). The most commonly observed symptoms are short attention span; poor memory; difficulty following directions; hand-eye coordination problems; inadequate ability to discriminate between and among letters, numerals, or sounds; poor reading ability; difficulties with sequencing; and disorganization (ACLD, p.3). Not surprisingly, such children often have discipline problems, are labeled underachievers and are at great risk of becoming dropouts.

Although usually associated with education, the consequences of learning disabilities go well beyond school. Behaviors that may be problematic include responding inappropriately, saying one thing but meaning another, forgetting easily, acting impulsively, demanding immediate gratification and becoming easily frustrated and then engaging in disruptive behavior. Youths with learning disabilities often have experienced failure after failure and lack self-esteem.

Increasing amounts of evidence indicate that a potential cause of developmental disorders and deficiencies in children can be traced to prenatal exposure to various toxins, such as cigarette smoke and alcohol. Prenatal exposure to HIV can also have devastating consequences to children.

Prenatal Exposure to Cigarette Smoking, Drugs, Alcohol and HIV

Research from a variety of disciplines indicates that maternal cigarette smoking (MCS) during pregnancy is related to an array of problematic outcomes, including various measures of criminal offending (McGloin et al., 2006, p.412). Although MCS is a significant precursor to neuropsychological deficit, and such deficit significantly predicts life-course persistent (LCP) offending, McGloin et al. contend that this is not the mediating mechanism at work in the relationship between MCS and LCP offending. Instead, these researchers suggest two potential mediators that might explain the relationship between MCS and offending. First, a mother who smokes cigarettes during pregnancy may reflect her hedonistic tendencies to put her needs ahead of her child's health. The second potential mediator is that MCS is a known risk for temperamental and conduct problems in childhood, making these children more likely to be subjected to poor parenting. These two mediating factors could also be at work in situations where a pregnant woman abuses drugs.

Children exposed to cocaine while in the womb, so-called crack children, may exhibit social, emotional and cognitive problems. Some research suggests the risk is greatly exaggerated, as the crack baby scare peaked between 1988 and 1991: "It turns out that 'crack baby' may be a creature of the imagination as much as medicine. According to one physician, drugs remain a serious health problem, and cocaine specifically contributes to premature birth and small head size" (Goodman, 1992, p.69). Other studies, however, conclude the risk is worth noting, particularly in light of its co-occurring tendencies with other risk-producing factors. Research by Bendersky et al. (2006) found evidence that prenatal exposure to cocaine constituted a risk factor for aggressive behavior problems in school-age children and that the group at greatest risk appeared to be exposed boys living in difficult environmental circumstances.

Another serious problem is **fetal alcohol spectrum disorder (FASD)**, which includes but is not limited to fetal alcohol syndrome (FAS), now the leading known preventable cause of mental retardation in the western world. When a pregnant woman drinks alcohol (beer, wine, liquor), she risks giving birth to a child who may pay a price in mental and physical deficiencies for his or her entire life. Among the characteristics of the syndrome are low birth weight, failure to thrive, developmental delay, organ dysfunction, facial abnormalities, epilepsy and poor coordination ("Fetal Alcohol Syndrome," 2007a.). According to the Mayo Clinic, as many as 40,000 babies are born with some type of alcohol-related damage each year in the United States, affecting one to two out of every 1,000 births ("Fetal Alcohol Syndrome," 2007b).

Another group of children that may suffer increased risk of delinquency or other problem behaviors are those prenatally exposed to HIV. Such children may experience deficits in both gross and fine motor skills; reduced flexibility and muscle strength; cognitive impairment including decreased intellectual levels, specific learning disabilities, mental retardation, visual/spatial deficits, and decreased alertness; and language delays.

Substance Abuse

During adolescence teens try new things, including experimenting with alcohol and other drugs. This may be out of curiosity, because it feels good, to feel grown up or to fit in. Most teens only experiment, but some develop serious alcohol and drug problems. Those at greatest risk are those with a family history of substance abuse or who are depressed, have low self-esteem or feel like they don't fit in ("Teens: Alcohol and Other Drugs," 2004).

Child Health USA 2006 reported that in 2004, 10.6 percent of adolescents aged 12 to 17 years reported using illicit drugs in the past month, with use increasing with age. Alcohol was the most commonly used drug, with 17.6 percent reporting past-month use. Marijuana was the most commonly used illicit drug (7.6 percent). *Monitoring the Future*, a study conducted by the University of Michigan Institute for Social Research of 50,000 students in grades 8, 10 and 12 from 400 schools, was begun in 1975 and has released reports since that time. In 2006 the report stated that teen drug use continued a decade-long downward trend, particularly among older teens, but use of prescription-type drugs remained high (Johnston et al., 2006).

Hunter Hurst, Director of the National Center for Juvenile Justice, offers a caution on the offender–drug use link and to not assume a cause-effect relationship, noting that while many offenders do use drugs, drugs do not reciprocally cause crime: "Everyone from federal judges on down will tell you they do, but from a research standpoint, it's more true that if you are an offender, you will be a drug user" (Cass and Curry, 2007, p.144). The relationship does not necessarily work in the reverse: that if you are a drug user, you will also be an offender. In fact, while approximately 80 percent of juvenile offenders have substance abuse disorders, only 20 percent of drug users commit crimes (p.144).

Nonetheless, youths who persistently abuse illegal substances often experience an array of problems including academic difficulties, health-related problems, poor peer relationships and involvement with the juvenile justice system.

Early Sexual Activity and Teen Pregnancy

Early sexual involvement and teen parenthood have also been identified as risk factors for victimization and delinquency. In 2005, 46.8 percent of high school students reported ever having had sexual intercourse, a slight increase since 2003. Among 9th-grade students, more males were sexually active than females, but by grade 12 females were more likely to be sexually active than males (*Child Health USA 2006*, p.41). Early sexual activity is an obvious precursor to teen pregnancy, another risk factor for youths.

The 2006 teen birth rate increased for the first time in 15 years, and although it is only a single-year increase, many health experts believe it bears watching (Centers for Disease Control and Prevention, 2008). Teen mothers are less likely to complete high school and more likely to end up on welfare. Children of teen mothers are at increased risk of low birth weight and prematurity, mental retardation, poverty, poor school performance, inadequate health care, inadequate parenting and abuse and neglect.

Exposure to Violence on Television, in Films and in Video Games

Violence has been an integral part of American society since its inception, when the country won its independence through a violent war. Hollywood and the general media industry have continued to glamorize the violence that persists in American culture.

Few would argue that our youth are exposed to much violence in movies and on television. The question, which has been debated for decades, is whether such viewing is detrimental to those who are growing up. According to a report by the American Academy of Pediatrics: "Research has associated exposure to media violence with a variety of physical and mental health problems for children and adolescents, including aggressive behavior, desensitization to violence, fear, depression, nightmares, and sleep disturbances. More than 3500 research studies have examined the association between media violence and violent behavior; all but 18 have shown a positive relationship" ("Policy Statement: Media Violence," 2001). Similarly, results from a 15-year longitudinal study by psychologists at the University of Michigan found that children, both males and females, who are exposed to media violence, who identify with aggressive television characters and who perceive the violence to be realistic are most at risk for later aggression.

Similar arguments and concerns surround the impact on children who play violent video games. Some researchers argue that playing violent video games may actually be more harmful than watching violent television or movies because of the interactive nature of the games. Research has found strong links between violent games, aggressive behavior and delinquency, as constantly improving technology makes virtual gore more realistic than ever (Anderson and Dill, 2000, p.772). Anderson (2003) presents several myths about violent video games and facts debunking them:

- **Myth**—Violent video game research has yielded very mixed results. **Fact**: Some studies have yielded nonsignificant video game effects, just as some smoking studies failed to find a significant link to lung cancer. But when combining all relevant empirical studies using meta-analytic techniques, five separate effects emerge with considerable consistency. Violent video games are significantly associated with: increased aggressive behavior, thoughts, and affect; increased physiological arousal; and decreased prosocial (helping) behavior.

- **Myth**—No studies link violent video game play to serious aggression. **Fact**: High levels of violent video game exposure have been linked to delinquency, fighting at school and during free play periods, and violent criminal behavior (e.g., self-reported assault, robbery).
- **Myth**—The effects of violent video games are trivially small. **Fact**: Meta-analyses reveal that violent video game effect sizes are larger than the effects of secondhand tobacco smoke on lung cancer, of lead exposure on IQ scores in children and of calcium intake on bone mass. Furthermore, the fact that so many youths are exposed to such high levels of video game violence further increases the societal costs of this risk factor.

Race

Disproportionate minority contact (DMC) was first introduced in Chapter 1. Considering the fact that minority youth are greatly over-represented in the juvenile justice system, it is fairly apparent that race presents a significant risk factor. The Children's Defense Fund (*America's Cradle to Prison Pipeline*, 2007, p.34) stresses: "Racial disparity runs through every major system impacting children's life chance: limited access to health care; lack of early Head Start and quality preschool experiences; children waiting in foster care for permanent families; and failing schools with harsh discipline policies that suspend, expel and discourage children who drop out and don't graduate and push more children into juvenile detention and adult prison." This report notes that a Black boy faces a 1-in-3 chance of going to prison in his lifetime; a Latino boy, a 1-in-6 chance; and a White boy, a 1-in-17 chance (p.37).

The race risk factor is compounded by many other co-occurring risk factors found throughout the other major domains of family, community, school and peers: unstable families, poverty, poor health care, lack of early education and enrichment opportunities, incarcerated parents, unsafe neighborhoods, substance abuse and availability of guns and drugs.

Family Risk Factors

Unquestionably, the American family has undergone great changes over the years. What began as an extended family, with two or three generations of a family living together, gradually became a nuclear family consisting of parents and their children. When the children grew up, they moved out and started their own families. Changes that have occurred in contemporary American society have been more complex and problematic, including more single-parent families, blended families, adoptive families and dysfunctional families. The **Norman Rockwell family**—a working father, a housewife mother and two children of school age—is no longer the norm.

In many American families, the traditional bonds of discipline and respect between parent and child have loosened considerably, if not unraveled completely. If the integration process between parents and children is deficient, the children may fail to learn appropriate behaviors: "Ask a guidance counselor, teacher or law enforcement officer the greatest problem they face when it comes to juvenile crime, and the answer is unanimous—parents" (Garrett, 2005, p.6).

Because of the family's central role in child development and socialization, a constellation of risk factors are present for those youths whose families are fragmented, dysfunctional or otherwise unable to provide adequately for the child's needs. Following are some of the most commonly recognized family risk factors for victimization and delinquency:

- Divorce/broken home
- Transitions/moving frequently/unstable residential patterns
- Poverty/low socioeconomic status
- Parent criminality
- Incarceration of a parent
- Separation from parents
- Poor parent-child relationships/poor family attachment or bonding
- Family management problems/poor parental supervision and lack of monitoring
- Harsh, lax or inconsistent discipline
- Parental psychopathology
- Familial antisocial behaviors
- Sibling antisocial behavior
- Maternal depression
- Low parent education/illiteracy
- Having a young mother
- Family violence
- Domestic abuse
- Child victimization, maltreatment and neglect

As with individual risk factors, many of these family risk factors tend to co-occur, such as family violence, divorce and unstable residential patterns, which effectively multiply the negative impacts these factors have on the children involved.

Divorce and Broken Homes

Family structure is often cited as a significant risk factor for delinquency and other antisocial problem behaviors. According to *America's Children* (2008), in 2007 just over two-thirds (68 percent) of children ages 0–17 lived with two married parents, down from 77 percent in 1980. A study of single-father and single-mother families found: "Mean levels of delinquency are highest among adolescents residing in single-father families and lowest among adolescents in two-biological-parent married families. Adolescents in single-mother and step-families fall in the middle" (Demuth and Brown, 2004, p.77). However, their research also found that parental absence is not a statistically significant predictor of adolescent delinquency.

While clear that divorce has a shattering effect on families with young children, what is less apparent is how much of the stress derives directly from the dissolution of a marriage and how much results from the myriad co-occurring circumstances: "As with many family factors, establishing the exact effects of divorce on children is difficult because of other co-occurring risks, such as the loss of a parent, other related negative life events (e.g., predivorce child behavior problems, family conflict, decrease in family income), and a parent's subsequent remarriage" (Wasserman et al., 2003, p.5).

While the complex dynamics of divorce would require a greater depth of discussion than this text allows, certain basic points can be made. Rarely does divorce happen quickly and quietly. Often there are months or years of conflict, tension and fighting—verbal and physical—that precede the split. Children may witness hurtful behavior and hear hurtful statements, made by and directed at people who are supposed to love and care for each other. Children may also be used as leverage or weapons by one parent against another, and may perceive the manipulation as an acceptable way to get what you want from someone else.

Once a divorce happens, children frequently are made to go live with one of the parents, either on a full-time or part-time basis. In cases of full custody, the loss of access to the other parent can have devastating consequences for youth. In cases of joint custody, youth commonly face a future of shuffling between residences and may feeling like neither place seems like "home." Such transient residential status has also been identified as a risk factor for delinquency.

Poverty

In 2006, 13 million children under 18 years of age—17.4 percent of all children in this country—lived in households with incomes below the federal poverty threshold (*America's Cradle to Prison Pipeline*, 2007, p.26). While children represent over one-third of people in poverty, they comprise only one-quarter of the population. *Child Health USA 2006* (p.14) notes: "Poverty affects many aspects of a child's life, including living conditions, access to health care and adequate nutrition, all of which contribute to health status."

Black and Hispanic children are particularly vulnerable to poverty. Indeed, "[t]he most dangerous place for a child to try to grow up in America is at the intersection of poverty and race" (*America's Cradle to Prison Pipeline*, p.4). While there are more poor White children in this country, in terms of raw numbers, minority youth are disproportionately poor: 35.3 percent of Black children and 28.0 percent of Latino children live in poverty, compared to 10.8 percent of White, non-Latino children (*America's Cradle to Prison Pipeline*, p.30). In addition, children living in single-parent families are at higher risk of poverty: "Single mother households are almost six times as likely to be poor as two parent households" (*America's Cradle to Prison Pipeline*, p.41).

Home conditions of economic deprivation or uncertainty can expose children to ills ranging from malnutrition to extreme psychopathology. This country has pockets of squalor found on tenant farms, in migrant camps and in the tenements of large cities.

However, it takes more than economic relief to lift families from a pattern of irresponsibility or depravity. Social agencies in every community know certain families that can be counted on to produce more than their share of school failures, truancy, sexual deviation, alcoholism, disorderliness and disease. They are also all too familiar with the inadequate personalities who become parents of other inadequate personalities in a recurring sequence that led early geneticists to talk about heredity and social incompetence. It must be remembered,

© Ariel Skelley/CORBIS

Children who experience success in school are likely to experience success in life; those who experience failure in school are likely to experience failure in life. Here children enjoy learning while using a computer.

however, that poverty alone cannot be blamed for delinquency. Many children raised in extreme poverty grow up just fine.

 Two of the most serious consequences of poverty for children are homelessness and increased risk of lead poisoning.

Homelessness The National Law Center on Homelessness and Poverty estimates that approximately 3.5 million people, 1.35 million of them children, are likely to experience homelessness in a given year ("Homelessness in the United States," 2004). The National Alliance to End Homelessness reported 744,313 homeless people in January 2005.

The National Coalition for the Homeless notes the problem of varying definitions used to measure the extent of homelessness, but most include the circumstance of living in a shelter or on the street ("NCH Fact Sheet #2," 2007). The coalition estimates that of the total homeless population, 51 percent are single men, 30 percent are families with children, 17 percent are women and 2 percent are unaccompanied youths. The coalition suggests two trends responsible for the rise in homelessness over the past 20 to 25 years: a growing shortage of affordable rental housing and a simultaneous increase in poverty ("NCH Fact Sheet #1, 2007). This increase is the result of eroding work opportunities and a decline in public assistance.

According to the Institute for Children and Poverty, available housing and shelter for homeless families is decreasing ("Facts on Family Homelessness," 2005). In 2005, one-third of requests for shelter by homeless families were denied. Homeless children have less chance of succeeding in school, with one-half of homeless children attending three different schools in one year and 75 percent of homeless children performing below grade level in reading. In addition, one-half of homeless women and children fled domestic violence and 47 percent of homeless children have anxiety, depression or withdrawal problems.

Some homeless youths are entirely on their own, including runaways and thrownaways (their families have kicked them out). Difficulties facing such youths are discussed in Chapter 5.

Lead Exposure   A new study spanning more than 20 years has added fresh evidence to what many researchers have known for decades: "Prenatal and postnatal blood lead concentrations are associated with higher rates of total arrests and/or arrests for offenses involving violence" (Wright et al., 2008, p.101). Lead exposure has detrimental neurodevelopmental consequences and has been linked to lower IQ, diminished tolerance for frustration and attention deficit and hyperactivity, all of which are known individual risk factors for delinquent and criminal behaviors. According to the principal investigator for the study: "We need to be thinking about lead as a drug and a fairly strong one. . . . These kids have been exposed to this drug, chronically, since before birth."

Children who live in poverty are also much more likely than others to be exposed to lead from old paint and old plumbing fixtures and from the lead in household dust. Other sources of lead are old water systems, lead crystal and some imported cans and ceramics. Babies exposed to low doses of lead before birth often are born underweight and underdeveloped. Even if they overcome these handicaps, when they go to school they face more obstacles such as behavioral problems, low IQ and deficiencies in speech and language. In 2001–2004 about 1 percent of children ages 1–5 had elevated blood lead levels (*America's Children*, 2008, p.10).

Parent Criminality and Incarceration

Not surprisingly, parents who espouse a lawbreaking way of life will likely pass on their antisocial values and attitudes to their children. An estimated 1.5 million children have a parent in prison, a number that does not include those youths whose parent is in jail ("Adolescents with Incarcerated Parents," 2006). Another 3.5 million children have parents on probation or parole (Rowland and Watts, 2007, p.34). The number of children who have mothers in prison has doubled since 1990 (Rowland and Watts, p.35). Typically incarcerated mothers are unmarried and the sole support of their children, who may end up with "reluctant relatives" or in foster care.

The cohort of children whose parents are incarcerated is often considered to be one of the country's largest at-risk populations (Miller, 2006; Whitaker and Buell, 2007). Research has shown that children of incarcerated parents are five to six times more likely to become involved in criminal activity than the average child and usually possess most, if not all, of the known factors thwarting normal childhood development: "trauma from witnessing a parent's arrest and distrust of law enforcement; the potential of multiple housing changes; dealing with parental abandonment and related guilt and anger; high probability of change in schools; living in poverty conditions of caregivers; witnessing or learning criminal behavior from a parent prior to arrest; and the experience of stigma, which may create a 'conspiracy of silence' or shunning by schoolmates" (Rowland and Watts, 2007, p.35).

A co-occurring risk for children with incarcerated parents is the potential to be removed from the home and placed in foster care. Some research has shown that nearly 75 percent of the children who were placed in foster care were actually removed from the home prior to their mother's first incarceration, not as a direct result of their parents' incarceration (Moses, 2006).

Separation from Parents and Foster Care

Separation from parents is a family risk factor for delinquency. This risk factor is present for any children in abusive or neglectful home environments who may, at some point, become clients of the child welfare system. Many juvenile justice experts contend that entry into the child welfare system is often a precursor to involvement with the juvenile justice system: "'In my experience, foster care is just one of those preparatory steps before the kid commits a crime,' one juvenile court judge asserts. 'The vast majority of kids in foster care will do something—trespass, shoplift, assault, smoke marijuana, whatever. If you get in foster care, the risk factors go up, and you'll probably see the kid in the delinquency system'" (Morris, 2004, p.1).

An added complication is that once a child enters the juvenile justice system, it becomes increasingly more difficult to divert that child back out of the system. According to University of Illinois professor Joseph Ryan: "We know once child-welfare youth are in the juvenile-justice system, they're less likely to get probation and more likely to get pushed deeper into the juvenile-justice system" (Chamberlain, 2008). Researchers have found that youth with at least one foster care placement are significantly more likely to receive a delinquency petition at some point, compared with children who have never entered foster care (Morris, p.1).

Poor Family Attachment or Bonding

Lack of parent-child attachment and bonding has long been recognized as a source of long-term social problems in youths as they age. Emotionally detached parents, with tenuous bonds to their children, are raising a generation of maladjusted children, and the problems extend well beyond the family into the schools and community. The quality and quantity of supervision provided to youth by these parents is low, affording such children more opportunities to find trouble and lessening the probability that any type of corrective discipline or consequences will befall wayward youth.

A survey of educators found that "emotionally immature" parents were reported as being the most crucial problem schools faced: "Discipline and violence problems in schools can be directly traced back to parenting problems in our society" (Yeager et al., 2006). Such parents detach from their children academically and developmentally and defend their children's bad behavior. What begins as a family problem becomes a school and community problem as these children become older.

School Risk Factors

The preschool, kindergarten and elementary school years are extremely important windows in the socialization and development of young children.

In fact, many children spend more waking hours each day in the school setting, under the care and supervision of their teachers, than with any other adult, including parents. Unfortunately many children enter school undersocialized and ill-equipped to handle the demands of this new environment. Life course criminologist Wright states: "Think about what school requires: discipline, the ability to acquire and process information and regurgitate it, self-control, the ability to move from one social clique to another, and follow directions from an authority figure. These are complex skills" (Cass and Curry, 2007, p.99).

The following circumstances have been identified as possible school risk factors for juvenile victimization and delinquency:

- Truancy/frequent absences
- Dropping out of school
- Negative attitude toward school/low bonding and school attachment
- Low academic aspirations or commitment to school
- Low academic achievement
- Identified as learning disabled
- Negative labeling by teachers
- Inadequate school climate (poorly organized and functioning schools)
- Low parent college expectations for child
- Frequent school transitions
- School suspensions

Truancy and Frequent Absences

Perhaps one of the greatest risk factors in regard to school is truancy. **Truancy**, which is loosely defined as habitual unexcused absence from school, is considered a status offense because, while compulsory attendance laws vary somewhat from state to state, every state requires children between certain ages to be in school during the academic year absent a valid excuse. If a child is not in school, they are not learning or gaining the knowledge and problem-solving skills required to move successfully into the adult world of employment and self-sufficiency. At the same time, if they are not in school, youth are very likely to be engaged in proscribed activities such as drug use, property crimes or even more serious offenses: "In several jurisdictions, law enforcement officials have linked high rates of truancy to daytime burglary and vandalism" (Baker et al., 2001, p.2). Research has clearly identified truancy as a precursor to myriad negative outcomes: "A lack of commitment to school has been established by several studies as a risk factor for substance abuse, delinquency, teen pregnancy, and school dropout" (Gonzales et al., 2002, p.3).

Dropping Out of School

A school *dropout* is a 16- to 24-year-old not enrolled in school and not having earned high school credentials (diploma or equivalent). In 2004 there were approximately 3,766,000 high school dropouts in the United States. The rate has usually declined over the past several decades, but 2004 saw the first increase since 1998. Hispanic students have the highest dropout rates, with 23.8 percent of this group dropping out in 2004 (*Child Health USA 2006*, p.15).

According to the U.S. Department of Commerce, high school dropouts are more likely to be unemployed and, if employed, to earn less than those who complete high school. The cost to society of dropping out is not insignificant, with the average high school dropout costing society more than $200,000 (Heilbrunn, 2005, p.3).

Peer risk factors commonly come into play at the same time as school risk factors, as the school environment is the most likely place for youth to be in contact with their peers.

Peer Risk Factors

As children age, the influence of parents wanes while that of peers increases. To many youths, how they are perceived by their peers is of paramount importance. Peer risk factors commonly associated with delinquency include:

- Peer rejection
- Peer alcohol, tobacco and/or other drug use
- Association with delinquent and/or aggressive peers
- Gang involvement or membership

Gangs are discussed in depth in Chapter 7.

Figure 4.5 illustrates the development of early offending behavior and peer influences in the context of the school environment.

Note in Figure 4.5 the boxes identifying aggressive and disruptive behaviors and peer rejection. An element linking aggressive or disruptive behavior and peer rejection is a child's degree of self-control, which, according to John Wright, a developmental criminologist at the University of Cincinnati, is the key development factor with regard to a child's risks for later delinquency and incarceration. Wright asserts that a child who lacks basic self-control "will be ostracized because children are very perceptive about whom they like and don't like, and this may make him more aggressive. . . . Most kids have this skill [of self-control] at a fairly early age; those who don't—name the problems. Failure

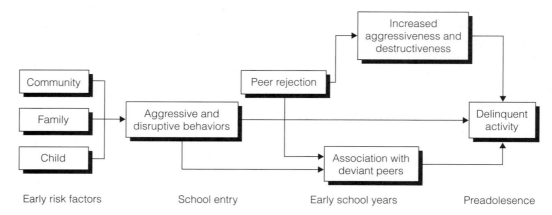

Figure 4.5 Development of Early Offending Behavior and Peer Influences

SOURCE: J. D. Coie and S. Miller-Johnson. "Peer Factors and Interventions." In *Serious and Violent Juvenile Offenders: Risk Factors and Successful Interventions*, edited by R. Loeber and D. P. Farrington. Thousand Oaks, CA: Sage Publications, Inc., 2001, pp.191–209. Reprinted by permission of Sage Publications, Inc.

to navigate the social landscape in elementary school places a kid at really high risk of bad outcomes later in life—chronic unemployment, relationship problems, incarceration" (Cass and Curry, 2007, p.100). In studying the "cause" of low self-control in children, some research has offered evidence that maternal self-control, through its influence on how a mother both punishes and supervises her child, influences the development of self-control in children (Nofziger, 2008, p.218).

 A strong case can be made that during adolescence deviant peers or peer rejection can influence nondelinquent juveniles to become delinquent.

Community Risk Factors

Of course, children do not exist in bubbles. As they age and gain independence, they venture more into the broader community, where numerous other risk factors present themselves:

- Availability of alcohol and other drugs
- Availability of firearms
- High-crime neighborhood
- Community instability and disorganization
- Social and physical discord
- Living in an economically disadvantaged neighborhood with high poverty
- Safety concerns and feeling unsafe in the neighborhood
- Low community attachment
- Neighborhood youth in trouble

Guns and drugs are discussed in greater detail in Chapter 7. The role of the broader community in juvenile justice and delinquency prevention is the focus of Chapter 8.

Protective Factors

Numerous behaviors and circumstances related to individual characteristics, family, school, peers and the community have been identified that may protect youths from becoming victims or offenders. Oftentimes a **protective factor** is the opposite of an identified risk factor. For example, if poor parental supervision is a risk factor, then a high degree of parental monitoring is a protective factor. Low IQ is a risk factor; high IQ, a protective factor.

 Protective factors also relate to individual characteristics, family, school, peers and community.

Individual Protective Factors
- Healthy, conventional beliefs and clear standards
- High expectations for self
- High IQ
- Perception of social support from adults and peers
- Positive, resilient temperament

THE CRADLE TO PRISON PIPELINE[1]: A LIFE COURSE PERSPECTIVE

Many children are born into certain life circumstances with the odds already stacked against them. The Children's Defense Fund has issued a compelling report examining how accumulated and convergent risks form a Cradle to Prison Pipeline that traps these children "in a trajectory that leads to marginalized lives, imprisonment and often premature death" (p.16). According to this report:

> The United States of America is not a level playing field for all children and our nation does not value and protect all children's lives equally. . . . Countless children, especially poor children of color . . ., "are already in the Pipeline to Prison before taking a single step or uttering a word," and many youths in juvenile justice facilities never were in the pipeline to college or success. "They were not derailed from the right track; they never got on it." (p.3)

While the report presents an abundance of sobering facts and bleak scenarios, it also offers hope that, with a firm resolve and true commitment, there can be positive change made in the lives of our nation's youth:

> The Pipeline is not an act of God or inevitable; it is a series of human choices at each stage of our children's development. We created it, we can change it. We know what to do. We can predict need. We can identify risk. We can prevent damage. We can target interventions. We can monitor progress. In doing so, we can guarantee returns on public investments and control costs to children and society. (p.4)

To effect permanent change, it is necessary to change our response to this issue from reactive to proactive: "Education costs less than ignorance, preventive health care far less than emergency rooms, preventive family services less than out-of-home care, and Head Start much less than prisons" (p.20). This mind-set is perhaps our greatest challenge, for as a society, we seem content to spend our efforts and dollars on the back end of the pipeline instead of the front end, with states currently spending, on average, nearly three times more per prisoner as per public school student (p.20).

[1] From: *America's Cradle to Prison Pipeline.* Washington, DC: Children's Defense Fund, October 2007. © October 2007 corrected printing by the Children's Defense Fund. All rights reserved. Reprinted by permission.

- Positive expectations and optimism for the future
- Religiosity and involvement in organized religious activities
- Self-efficacy
- Social competencies and problem-solving skills
- Intolerant attitude toward deviance
- Gender: Being female

Family Protective Factors

- Effective parenting
- Good relationships with parents and attachment/bonding to family
- Having a stable family
- Having parents who set high expectations
- Opportunities for prosocial family involvement
- Rewards for prosocial family involvement

School Protective Factors

- Above-average academic achievement
- Strong school motivation and positive attitude toward school
- Sufficient reading and math skills
- High expectations of students

- High-quality schools
- Clear standards and rules
- Opportunities for prosocial school involvement
- Rewards for prosocial school involvement
- Presence and involvement of caring, supportive adults
- Student bonding (attachment to teacher, belief, commitment)

Peer Protective Factors

- Good relationships with peers
- Involvement with positive peer group activities

Community Protective Factors

- Clear social norms
- High expectations
- Nondisadvantaged neighborhood
- Safe environment
- Low neighborhood crime
- Presence and involvement of caring, supportive adults
- Prosocial opportunities for participation
- Rewards for prosocial community involvement
- Availability of neighborhood resources

Early Work Experiences: A Risk or Protective Factor?

As youths attain legal working age and go into the community to find employment, the question becomes: Is work a positive or negative influence in these young people's lives? Results of numerous studies are contradictory.

According to Apel et al. (2006): "Research has repeatedly found various negative consequences associated with youth employment, including detachment from parents, poor school performance and dropout, and an increased risk of delinquency and substance use."

A study by Wu et al. (2003) found that adolescent employment is positively associated with drug and alcohol use among both males and females. These researchers contend that the mere fact that a youth has a job does not appear to be sufficient in deterring drug or alcohol use; instead, stable employment that reflects a strong commitment or stake in conformity seems to be required.

Other research has examined how job quality might be a detrimental influence on behavior: "Our findings suggest that low-wage, service sector employment opportunity directly increases the likelihood of violent delinquency" (Bellair et al., 2003, p.6). Brame et al. (2004) came to similar conclusions, with their research identifying adolescent employment as a risk factor based on its association with increased involvement in criminal activity.

Opposite conclusions, however, have been reached by other researchers regarding the effects of early employment on youth. Studies by Wright and Cullen

(2004) found that employment can build social capital that then bonds young people to social institutions: "The results demonstrate that prosocial coworkers disrupt previously established delinquent peer networks and are associated with reductions in adult criminal behavior" (p.183). They contend: "Stable employment appears to be a key transition in the life course that is associated with reductions in criminal behavior and drug use" (p.198).

Prevention and Early Intervention Efforts

Prevention is often heralded as the preferred approach to the problems of victimization and delinquency. Ignoring prevention efforts has been likened to "providing expensive ambulances at the bottom of a cliff to pick up the youngsters who fall off, rather than building a fence at the top of the cliff to keep them from falling in the first place" (Hawkins and Catalano, 1993).

Early intervention that focuses on the most at-risk youth has been shown, through myriad studies, to be a valid prevention tool. For example, the *Chicago Longitudinal Study* (2000) examined 1,539 children enrolled in the Chicago Public Schools who received services from one or more of 20 Child-Parent Centers (CPCs) while in preschool from 1983–1985 and/or during kindergarten from 1985–1986. Ninety-three percent of the children in the sample group were African American. The study followed these children through their years in the public education system and also gathered comparable data for a control group of youths who did not receive CPC services. Data from the study showed that the children who participated in the CPC preschool program significantly academically outperformed those who did not, were retained less often and had lower rates of special education placement (p.6). The results of this study are not unique in terms of substantiating the benefits of early intervention: "Minority preschoolers from low-income families who participated in school-based intervention programs fared better decades later educationally, socially and economically than peers who did not have the benefit of such programs" (Scott, 2007, p.13).

Numerous cost-benefit analyses have been done to show how much (or, rather, how little) *preventing* crime and delinquency costs compared to dealing with the law enforcement, court and correctional costs associated with offenders, not to mention the much larger cost to society in terms of lost work productivity, collateral family impacts, medical and counseling treatment for addictions, and so on. For example, the CPC study showed that for every dollar invested in the preschool program, $4.71 is saved in reduced costs of remedial education and justice system expenditures and in increased earning capacity and tax revenues (p.14). A separate study in Minnesota examined how investing in youth can benefit the entire community when children are prepared for kindergarten, when intervention programs keep teens uninvolved in crime and when drug courts can turn an addict into a clean, productive member of society: "Taxpayers can expect future savings of $2.75 to $5 for every dollar invested in effective mentoring and youth-intervention programs. . . . At-risk kids with a caring adult in their lives are far less likely to drop out of high school, get pregnant or commit crimes" (St. Anthony, 2008, p.D2).

Helping America's Youth (HAY)

Helping America's Youth (HAY) is a nationwide effort to raise awareness about the challenges facing our youths, especially youth boys, and to motivate caring adults to connect with youths in three areas: family, school and community. This initiative brought together a comprehensive array of 10 collaborating federal agencies to produce a guide to make these connections: the U.S. Departments of Health and Human Services, Justice, Agriculture, Education, Labor, Housing and Urban Development, the Interior and Commerce; the Office of National Drug Control Policy; and the Corporation for National and Community Services.

The *Community Guide to Helping America's Youth* includes suggestions for forming community partnerships, developing youth-adult partnerships and making the partnerships work. It also includes information on assessing a community and connecting its resources as well as an extensive listing of proven programs for youths that can be searched by risk factor, protective factor or keyword and by age.

In addition HAY has held regional conferences throughout the country to increase public awareness and encourage adults to connect with youths in their communities.

 SUMMARY

- The period from birth to age 3 is the most formative time of a child's life.

- In healthy families, self-esteem is high, communication is direct and honest, rules are flexible and reasonable and members' attitudes toward the outside world are trusting and optimistic.

- Common values that might be passed on to youths include equality, honesty, promise-keeping, respect, responsibility and self-control.

- The most significant individual risk factor for predicting later delinquency is early antisocial behavior, specifically aggression.

- The *authority conflict path* includes stubbornness, doing things one's own way, refusing to do things and disobedience. It may culminate in authority avoidance by staying out late, truancy and/or running away. The *covert behavior path* includes lying, shoplifting, setting fires, damaging property, joyriding, pickpocketing, stealing from cars, fencing stolen goods, writing illegal checks and using illegal credit cards. It may culminate in serious delinquency such as stealing a car, selling drugs and/or breaking and entering. The *overt behavior path* includes annoying others, bullying and fighting. It may culminate in violence, including attacking someone, strong-arming and/or forcing sex.

- Most youths with conduct disorders should be treated as mentally ill rather than as delinquent.

- Labeling a youth as a psychopath reduces the youth's likelihood of receiving treatment and increases the youth's likelihood of being transferred to the criminal justice system and treated as an adult.

- Two of the most serious consequences of poverty for children are homelessness and an increased risk of lead poisoning.

- A strong case can be made that during adolescence deviant peers or peer rejection can influence nondelinquent juveniles to become delinquent.

- It is important to understand the risk and protective factors that may be related to individual characteristics, family, school, peers and the community.

DISCUSSION QUESTIONS

1. The adult world stresses material and financial gain, social status and winning at any cost. Can children adjust to or understand this attitude? What values should adults communicate to children about these attitudes?

2. Does your community have any ghettos or areas where poverty exists? What are some visible signs of such conditions?

3. How does your community handle homeless people, particularly youths? Are there special programs for homeless families with children?

4. Is controlled spanking in certain cases justified? Were you spanked as a child?

5. What values should be passed to the next generation?

6. Do you believe adolescents should be employed?

7. How much of an impact do you think violence on television and in the movies (fictional violence) has on aggressive behavior in youths?

8. How do you think the news industry (reporting on factual or real-world violence) affects the way our society in general, and children in particular, view crime and delinquency?

9. Which of the risk factors are most significant in terms of victimization and delinquency? Least significant?

10. Which of the protective factors are most significant? Least significant?

REFERENCES

"Adolescents with Incarcerated Parents." *The Prevention Researcher*, 2006.

Agnew, Robert. *Why Do Criminals Offend? A General Theory of Crime and Delinquency*. Los Angeles, CA: Roxbury Publishing Company, 2005.

American Bar Association. *Justice Cut Short: An Assessment of Access to Counsel and Quality of Representation in Delinquency Proceedings in Ohio*. Juvenile Justice Center, National Juvenile Defender Center, March 2003, p.1. Online: http://www.njdc.info/pdf/Ohio_Assessment.pdf

America's Children: Key National Indicators of Well-Being 2008. Federal Interagency Forum on Child and Family Statistics, 2008.

America's Cradle to Prison Pipeline. Washington, DC: Children's Defense Fund, October 2007.

Anderson, Craig. "Violent Video Games: Myths, Facts, and Unanswered Questions." *Psychological Science Agenda*, American Psychological Association Online, October 2003, Vol. 16, No. 5. Online: http://www.apa.org/science/psa/sb-anderson.html. Accessed July 23, 2008.

Anderson, Craig A. and Dill, Karen E. "Video Games and Aggressive Thoughts, Feelings, and Behavior in the Laboratory and in Life." *Journal of Personality and Social Psychology*, 2000, Vol. 78, No. 4, pp.772–790.

Annual Report 2003. Pittsburg, PA: National Center for Juvenile Justice, 2003.

Apel, Robert; Paternoster, Raymond; Bushway, Shawn D.; and Brame, Robert. "A Job Isn't Just a Job: The Differential Impact of Formal versus Informal Work on Adolescent Problem Behavior. *Crime and Delinquency*, Vol. 52, No. 2, 2006, pp.333–369.

Association for Children with Learning Disabilities (ACLD). "Taking the First Step to Solving Learning Problems." Pittsburgh, PA: Association for Children with Learning Disabilities, pamphlet, no date.

Baker, Myriam L.; Sigmon, Jane Nady; and Nugent, M. Elaine. *Truancy Reduction: Keeping Students in School*. Washington, DC: Office of Juvenile Justice and Delinquency Prevention, Juvenile Justice Bulletin, September 2001. (NCJ 188947)

Bellair, Paul E.; Roscigno, Vincent J.; and McNulty, Thomas L. "Linking Local Labor Market Opportunity to Violent Adolescent Delinquency." *Journal of Research in Crime and Delinquency*, February 2003, pp.6–33.

Bendersky, Margaret; Bennett, David; and Lewis, Michael. "Aggression at Age 5 as a Function of Prenatal Exposure to Cocaine, Gender, and Environmental Risk." *Journal of Pediatric Psychology*, 2006, Vol. 31, No. 1, pp.71–84.

Brame, Robert; Bushway, Shawn D.; Paternoster, Raymond; and Apel, Robert. "Assessing the Effect of Adolescent Employment on Involvement in Criminal Activity." *Journal of Contemporary Criminal Justice*, August 2004, pp.236–256.

Cass, Julia and Curry, Connie. "Part II: Case Studies of Children in or at Risk of the Pipeline in Ohio and Mississippi." In *America's Cradle to Prison Pipeline*. Washington, DC: Children's Defense Fund, October 2007.

Centers for Disease Control and Prevention. "Teen Pregnancy and Birth Rates: Birth Rates in Teen Girls Ages 15–19, 2006." Online: http://www.cdc.gov/features/dsTeenPregnancy/. Page reviewed and updated May 7, 2008. Accessed July 23, 2008.

Chamberlain, Craig. "Group Homes Appear to Double Delinquency Risk for Foster Kids, Study Says." News Bureau, University of Illinois at Urbana–Champaign, February 28, 2008. Online: http://www.news.uiuc.edu/news/08/0228grouphomes.html. Accessed July 23, 2008.

Chicago Longitudinal Study. Madison, WI: University of Wisconsin–Madison, August 2000.

Child Health USA 2006. Washington, DC: Health Resources and Services Administration, 2006.

Cleckley, Hervey. *The Mask of Sanity*, 5th ed. Augusta, GA: Emily S. Cleckley, private printing, 1988.

Demuth, Stephen and Brown, Susan L. "Family Structure, Family Processes, Adolescent Delinquency: The Significance of Parental Absence versus Parental Gender." *Journal of Research in Crime and Delinquency*, February 2004, pp.58–81.

Diagnostic and Statistical Manual of Mental Disorders, 4th ed., Text Revision (DSM-IV-TR). Arlington, VA: American Psychiatric Association, 2000.

"Facts on Family Homelessness." The Institute for Children and Poverty, 2005.

"Fetal Alcohol Syndrome." Kids Health, 2007a.

"Fetal Alcohol Syndrome." Rochester, MN: Mayo Clinic, 2007b.

Garrett, Ronnie. "Kids Today . . ." *Law Enforcement Technology*, May 2005, p.6

Gershoff, Elizabeth Thompson. "Corporal Punishment by Parents and Associated Child Behaviors and Experiences: A Meta-Analytic and Theoretical Review." *Psychological Bulletin*, Vol. 128, No. 4, 2002, pp.539–579.

Glanton, Dahleen "Discipline or Abuse?" *Chicago Tribune*, April 1, 2001.

Gonzales, Ramona; Richards, Kinette; and Seeley, Ken. *Youth Out of School: Linking Absence to Delinquency*, 2nd ed. Denver, CO: Colorado Foundation for Families and Children, 2002.

Goodman, Ellen. "The Myth of the Crack Babies." *Boston Sunday Globe*, January 12, 1992, p.69.

Hawkins, J. David and Catalano, Richard. *Communities That Care: Risk-Focused Prevention Using the Social Development Strategy*. Seattle, WA: Developmental Research and Programs, Inc., 1993.

Heilbrunn, Joanna Zorn. *The Legal and Economic Implications of Truancy: Executive Summary*. Denver, CO: National Center for School Engagement, September 2005.

Helping America's Youth. *The Community Guide to Helping America's Youth*. Washington, DC: The White House. Online: http://guide.helpingamericasyouth.gov/programtool-factors.cfm, last referenced January 19, 2007. Accessed July 23, 2008.

"Homelessness in the United States and the Human Right to Housing." National Law Center on Homelessness and Poverty, January 2004.

Johnston, Lloyd D.; O'Malley, Patrick M.; Bachman, Jerald G.; and Schulenberg, John E. *Monitoring the Future: National Results on Adolescent Drug Use*. Ann Arbor, MI: The University of Michigan Institute for Social Research, 2006.

Kelley, Barbara Tatem; Loeber, Rolf; Keenan, Kate; and DeLamatre, Mary. *Developmental Pathways in Boys' Disruptive and Delinquent Behavior*. Washington, DC: OJJDP Juvenile Justice Bulletin, December 1997. (NCJ 165692)

Kohlberg, Lawrence. *The Philosophy of Moral Development: Moral Stages and the Idea of Justice* (*Essays on Moral Development, Volume I*). New York: Harper & Row, 1981.

Larzelere, Robert E. and Kuhn, Brett R. "Comparing Child Outcomes of Physical Punishment and Alternative Discipline Tactics: A Meta-Analysis." *Clinical Child and Family Psychology Review*, March 2005, pp.1–37.

McGloin, Jean Marie; Pratt, Travis C.; and Piquero, Alex R. "A Life-Course Analysis of the Criminogenic Effects of Maternal Cigarette Smoking During Pregnancy: A Research Note on the Mediating Impact of Neuropsychological Deficit." *Journal of Research in Crime and Delinquency*, November 2006, pp.412–426.

Miller, Keva M. "The Impact of Parental Incarceration on Children: An Emerging Need for Effective Intervention." *Child and Adolescent Social Work Journal*, August 2006, pp.472–486.

Morris, Leslee. "Youth in Foster Care Who Commit Delinquent Acts: Study Findings and Recommendations." *The Link*. Child Welfare League of America, Summer/Fall 2004, pp.1, 4.

Moses, Marilyn C. "Does Parental Incarceration Increase a Child's Risk for Foster Care Placement?" *NIJ Journal*, November 2006.

"NCH Fact Sheet #1." Washington, DC: National Coalition for the Homeless, June 2007.

"NCH Fact Sheet #2." Washington, DC: National Coalition for the Homeless, August 2007.

Nofziger, Stacey. "The 'Cause' of Low Self-Control." *Journal of Research in Crime and Delinquency*, May 2008, pp.191–224.

"Policy Statement: Guidance for Effective Discipline." *Pediatrics*, April 1998, pp.723–728.

"Policy Statement: Media Violence." *Pediatrics*, November 2001, pp.1222–1226.

Rowland, Melissa and Watts, Alice. "Washington State's Effort to Reduce the Generational Impact on Crime." *Corrections Today*, August 2007, pp.34–42.

St. Anthony, Neal. "Investing in Youth Has a Measurable Economic Payoff." (Minneapolis/St. Paul) *Star Tribune*, July 15, 2008, pp. D1–D2.

Scott, Cynthia. "Preschool Programs Pay Off." *Minnesota*, November/December 2007, p.13.

Shader, Michael. *Risk Factors for Delinquency: An Overview*. Washington, DC: Office of Juvenile Justice and Delinquency Prevention, 2002. Online: http://ojjdp.ncjrs.org/ccd/ pubsrfd.html

"Teens: Alcohol and Other Drugs." American Academy of Child and Adolescent Psychiatry, July 2004.

United Nations. *Convention on the Rights of the Child*. Adopted by the General Assembly of the United Nations, November 20, 1989.

U.S. Congress, House Committee on Education and Labor. *Hearing Before Subcommittee on Elementary, Secondary, and Vocational Education on H.R. 123*. 96th Congress, 1st Session, April 24, 1979.

Wasserman, Gail A.; Keenan, Kate; Tremblay, Richard E.; Coie, John D.; Herrenkohl, Todd I.; Loeber, Rolf; and Petechuk, David. *Risk and Protective Factors of Child Delinquency*. Washington, DC: Office of Juvenile Justice and Delinquency Prevention, Child Delinquency Bulletin Series, April 2003. (NCJ 193409)

Whitaker, Mary Scully and Buell, Maureen. "Children with Incarcerated Parents: Everyone Has a Role." *Corrections Today*, August 2007, p.91.

Wright, John Paul and Cullen, Francis T. "Employment, Peers and Life-Course Transitions." *Justice Quarterly*, March 2004, pp.183–202.

Wright, John Paul; Dietrich, Kim N.; Ris, M. Douglas; Hornung, Richard W.; Wessel, Stephanie D.; Lanphear, Bruce P.; Ho, Mona; and Rae, Mary N. "Association of Prenatal and Childhood Blood Lead Concentrations with Criminal Arrests in Early Adulthood." *Public Library of Science Medicine*, May 27, 2008, Vol. 5, No. 5, p.101 (doi:10.1371/journal. pmed.0050101). Received: August 14, 2007; Accepted: March 18, 2008; Published: May 27, 2008. Accessed July 23, 2008.

Wu, Li-Tzy; Schlenger, Williem E.; and Galvin, Deborah. "The Relationship between Employment and Substance Use among Students Aged 12 to 17." *Journal of Adolescent Health*, Vol. 32, No. 1, 2003, p.5.

Yeager, Dale; Sulliman, Sam; Demidont, Andreas; and Brandenberger, Dane. *The State of School Safety in American Schools 2004–2006*. Southeastern, PA: SERAPH Research Team, publically released version of a report prepared for Congress, 2006.

CHAPTER 5

Juvenile Victims

THE CYCLE OF ABUSED AND NEGLECTED CHILDREN WHO HAVE BECOME ABUSING AND NEGLECTING PARENTS WITH THEIR CHILDREN IN TURN BEING ABUSED, NEGLECTED, RUNNING AWAY, ACTING OUT AND OFTEN ENDING UP BEFORE THE COURTS HAS NOT BEEN BROKEN.

—METROPOLITAN COURT JUDGES COMMITTEE

© John Sturrock / Alamy

Living in poverty is one of two leading causes of child abuse. Extreme poverty can lead to homelessness, as seen with this family of 5, who is living in their car.

Do You Know?

- What risks maltreated children and youths face?
- What the major cause of death of young children is?
- What the three levels of child maltreatment are?
- What the most common form of child maltreatment is and how serious it is?
- What often characterizes the homes of neglected children?
- What the three components of child abuse and neglect laws typically are?
- What are thought to be the two leading causes of child abuse?
- What the likely result of violence is for children?
- Whether child abuse is directly linked to delinquency?
- Which age group has the highest victimization rate?
- What six episode types of missing children are identified in the NISMART–2 study?
- What two federal agencies have concurrent jurisdiction for missing and exploited children? What approach each takes toward missing children?
- What the leading cause of youth suicide is?
- What common warning signs of potential youth suicide are?

Can You Define?

anticipated strain

collective maltreatment

dependency

extrafamilial sexual abuse

individual maltreatment

institutional maltreatment

intrafamilial sexual abuse

maltreatment

maximalist alarmist perspective

minimalist skeptical perspective

neglect

osteogenesis imperfecta (OI)

runaway

stereotypical kidnapping

thrownaway

vicarious strain

Chapter Outline

Introduction

Defining Child Maltreatment and Rating Its Severity

Three Levels of Child Maltreatment

Child Victimization: The Seriousness of the Problem

Child Neglect

Indicators of Neglect

Physical or Emotional Child Abuse

Child Abuse and Neglect Laws

Indicators of Physical Abuse

Indicators of Emotional Abuse

Causes of Abuse

Domestic and Family Violence

Child Abuse and the Link with Delinquency

Child Sexual Harassment and Abuse

Child Sexual Abuse and the Internet

Indicators of Sexual Abuse

Consequences of Being Sexually Abused

Cultural Values and Sexual Abuse

The Issue of Credibility

Children and Youths as Victims of Crime and Violence

Missing and Exploited Children

Missing Benign Explanation

Missing Involuntary, Lost or Injured

Runaway/Thrownaway

Nonfamily Abduction

Stereotypical Kidnapping

Family Abduction

A Child Abduction Response Team (CART)

AMBER Alert

Introduction

Since 1986 the number of children who are abused, neglected and endangered every year has nearly doubled—to about 1 million today. Emotional and behavior disorders, teen pregnancy, prostitution, substance abuse, and delinquency and criminality are some of the immediate and long-term consequences a child may face because of maltreatment.

Most maltreatment cases enter the child welfare system through child protective services (CPS) agencies. These are generally agencies authorized to act on behalf of a child when parents are unable or unwilling to do so. All states require these agencies to assess or investigate reports of child abuse and neglect and to offer rehabilitative services to families where maltreatment has or is likely to occur.

In 2005, state CPS agencies received an estimated 3.3 million referrals alleging child abuse or neglect. Approximately 6 million children were included in these referrals (*Child Health USA 2007*, 2008, p.35). Investigations concluded that an estimated 899,000 children were abused or neglected during 2005, a rate of about 12.1 per 1,000 children under age 18. Neglect was the most common type of maltreatment. Other types of abuse included physical abuse, sexual abuse, psychological maltreatment, medical neglect and categories of abuse based on specific state laws as shown in Figure 5.1. Victimization rates were highest among young children, from birth to age 3 (p.35).

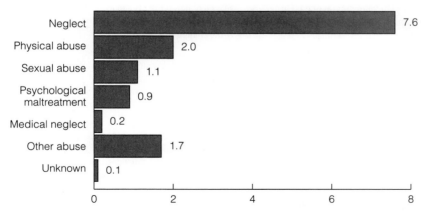

Figure 5.1   Child Abuse and Neglect among Children under Age 18 by Type of Maltreatment: 2005

SOURCE: U.S. Department of Health and Human Services, Health Resources and Services Administration, Maternal and Child Health Bureau. *Child Health USA 2007*. Rockville, MD: U.S. Department of Health and Human Services, 2008.

Defining Child Maltreatment and Rating Its Severity

Maltreatment refers to an act or omission by a parent or other caregiver that results in harm or serious risk of harm to a child. It includes neglect, medical neglect, physical abuse, sexual abuse and psychological maltreatment

 Maltreated youths are at an increased risk for performing poorly in school; displaying symptoms of mental illness; for girls, becoming pregnant; using drugs; and engaging in serious and violent delinquency.

Maltreatment exists in many forms. Definitions of the various types of maltreatment vary from state to state and even locality to locality. The most common subtypes of child maltreatment and their severity are described in Table 5.1.

Table 5. 1   Defining Child Maltreatment and Rating Its Severity

Subtype of Maltreatment	Brief Definition	Examples of Least and Most Severe Cases
Physical Abuse	A caregiver inflicts a physical injury upon a child by other than accidental means.	*Least*—Spanking results in minor bruises on arm. *Most*—Injuries require hospitalization, cause permanent disfigurement or lead to a fatality.
Sexual Abuse	Any sexual contact or attempt at sexual contact that occurs between a caretaker or responsible adult and a child for the purposes of the caretaker's sexual gratification or financial benefit.	*Least*—A child is exposed to pornographic materials. *Most*—A caretaker uses force to make a child engage adult and a child for the purposes of the in sexual relations or prostitution.
Physical Neglect	A caretaker fails to exercise a minimum degree of care in meeting a child's physical needs.	*Least*—Food is not available for regular meals, clothing is too small, child is not kept clean. *Most*—A child suffers from severe malnutrition or severe dehydration due to gross inattention to his or her medical needs.
Lack of Supervision	A caretaker does not take adequate precautions (given a child's particular emotional and developmental needs) to ensure his or her safety in and out of the home.	*Least*—An 8-year-old is left alone for short periods of time (i.e., less than 3 hours) with no immediate source of danger in the environment. *Most*—A child is placed in a life-threatening situation without adequate supervision.
Emotional Maltreatment	Persistent or extreme thwarting of a child's basic emotional needs (such as the need to feel safe and accepted).	*Least*—A caretaker often belittles or ridicules a child. *Most*—A caretaker uses extremely restrictive methods to bind a child or places a child in close confinement such as a closet or trunk for 2 or more hours.
Educational Maltreatment	A caretaker fails to ensure that a child receives adequate education.	*Least*—A caretaker allows a child to miss school up to 15 percent of the time (when he or she is not ill and there is no family emergency). *Most*—A caretaker does not enroll a child in school or provide any educational instruction.
Moral-Legal Maltreatment	A caretaker exposes or involves a child in illegal or other activities that may foster delinquency or antisocial behavior.	*Least*—A child is permitted to be present for adult activities, such as drunken parties. *Most*—A caretaker causes a child to participate in felonies such as armed robbery.

SOURCE: Adapted from Douglas Barnett, Jody Todd Manly and Dante Cicchetti. "Defining Child Maltreatment: The Interface between Policy and Research." In D. Cicchetti and S.L. Toth (eds.), *Child Abuse, Child Development and Social Policy*, pp.7–73. Norwood, NJ: Ablex Publishing, 1993.

REALITY CHECK: THE DARK UNDERBELLY OF COHABITATION

Several studies support the concern over maltreatment of children in "nontraditional" living situations:

- A study published in 2005 in the journal of the American Academy of Pediatrics found that children living in households with unrelated adults are nearly 50 times as likely to die of inflicted injuries as children living with two biological parents.
- Several studies co-authored by David Finkelhor, director of the University of New Hampshire's Crimes Against Children Research Center, concluded that children living

in stepfamilies or with single parents are at higher risk of physical or sexual assault than children living with two biological or adoptive parents.

- Research by Robin Wilson, a family law professor at Washington and Lee University, revealed that girls whose parents divorce face significantly higher risk of sexual assault, whether they live with their mother or father.

SOURCE: "Children at Higher Risk in Nontraditional Homes," 2007.

Rates of child maltreatment vary across demographic groups. Girls' victimization rate is typically higher than the rate for boys. More than half of all maltreatment victims are White, followed by Black (26 percent) and Hispanic (12 percent). The victimization rate is inversely related to age, with the youngest children having the highest rate.

The vast majority of perpetrators of maltreatment (80 percent) are parents—birth parents, adoptive parents and stepparents. Women are over-represented among both caregivers and maltreatment perpetrators. Nonparental relatives, unmarried partners of parents and daycare providers each made up small proportions of child maltreatment perpetrators. Foster parents, residential facility staff and legal guardians each made up less than 1 percent of maltreatment perpetrators (Snyder and Sickmund, 2006, p.55).

An *Associated Press* article ("Children at Higher Risk in Nontraditional Homes," 2007) reports: "Many scholars and social workers who monitor America's families see the abusive-boyfriend syndrome as part of a broader, deeply worrisome trend" that many refer to as "the dark underbelly of cohabitation."

Harris (2004, p.8) points out the large number of children negatively affected by physical and emotional abuse as well as neglect by parents and other adults who expose them to toxic meth lab operations, firearms, pornographic material, domestic violence and unlawful activity. He notes that methamphetamine abuse and production have become major factors in the increase of child neglect and abuse cases handled by the child welfare system.

The most serious consequence of maltreatment is death. According to Snyder and Sickmund (2006, p.56), the youngest children are the most vulnerable child maltreatment victims. In 2003 children younger than 1 year old accounted for 44 percent of maltreatment fatalities. Children younger than 4 years were 79 percent of maltreatment fatalities. Mothers were the most common perpetrators in child maltreatment fatalities (59 percent); fathers were involved in 39 percent of maltreatment fatalities. Nearly 4 in 10 maltreatment fatalities resulted from neglect alone. Physical abuse accounted for 3 in 10 fatalities, and about the same percent resulted from multiple forms of maltreatment in combination (p.56).

Child abuse has been identified as the biggest single cause of death of young children.

Fatal child abuse may involve repeated abuse over a period of time (e.g., battered child syndrome) or may involve a single, impulsive incident such as shaking a baby. Fatal neglect cases usually result not from anything a caregiver *does* but from what a caregiver *does not* do—their *failure to act*. The neglect may be chronic (e.g., extended malnourishment) or acute (e.g., an infant who drowns because of being left unsupervised in a bathtub) (Child Welfare Information Gateway, 2008).

Before looking more closely at the various forms of maltreatment, consider the big picture, the stages of child maltreatment case processing through child protective services and the juvenile/family court system as illustrated in Figure 5.2. Notice that CPS may provide protective custody of a child outside the home or provide protective supervision of the child within the family unit at any point that a case is closed or dismissed. The specific options once a case enters formal court processing are the focus of Chapter 11.

Three Levels of Child Maltreatment

Child maltreatment is often discussed primarily as an act between individuals. In reality, however, three separate levels of maltreatment exist.

 The three levels of maltreatment are collective, institutional and individual.

Collective Maltreatment   **Collective maltreatment** is seen in the effects that poverty, exploitation and other forms of social injustice have on child welfare. Millions of children who live in poverty in the United States eat and drink contaminated food and water, are exposed to dangerous environmental chemicals and lack the benefits of the network of adult support and supervision available to parents in higher socioeconomic brackets. Many youth, of all socioeconomic levels, are exploited through child pornography. Constant violence blares forth from television sets across the country. Child care is often grossly inadequate, and the physical punishment of children is widely sanctioned. The collective attitude in America ignores the natural and legal rights of children.

Another form of collective child maltreatment is that of illegal child labor. One common form of child labor in both industrialized and developing countries is use of children in agriculture. Investigations by Human Rights Watch in Egypt, Ecuador, India and the United States found that the children working in agriculture are endangered and exploited on a daily basis. Despite the vast differences among these four countries, many of the risks and abuses faced by child agricultural workers are strikingly similar ("Child Labor," 2006). In the United States, the more than 300,000 children working as hired laborers on commercial farms risk pesticide poisoning, heat illnesses, injuries and life-long disabilities from the daily exposure to dangerous and grueling work conditions.

Institutional Maltreatment   **Institutional maltreatment** of children, sometimes called administrative abuse, includes the approved use of force and

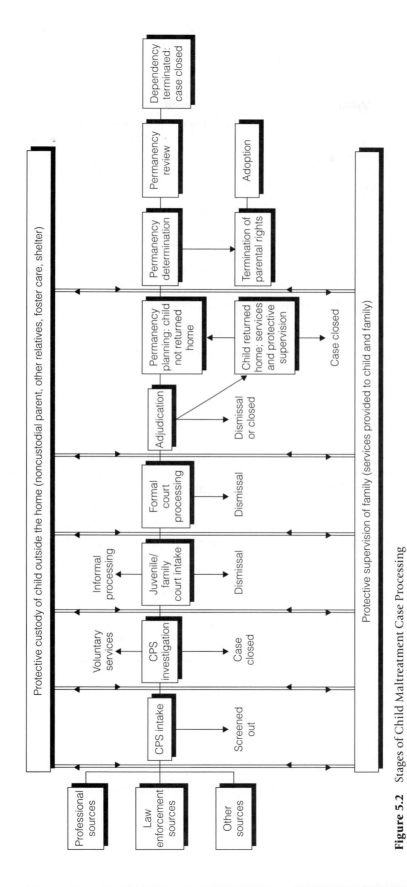

Figure 5.2   Stages of Child Maltreatment Case Processing

SOURCE: Howard N. Snyder and Melissa Sickmund. *Juvenile Offenders and Victims: 2006 National Report.* Washington, DC: Office of Juvenile Justice Delinquency Prevention, March 2006, p.48.

violence against children in the schools and the neglect and denial of children's due process rights in government institutions, including child welfare and correctional institutions. The use of corporal punishment in schools has been declining; "paddling" has decreased since the early 1980s and has been banned in many states. New legal restrictions in school districts throughout the country prevent teachers from even touching a student in a "disciplinary" manner, let alone striking one. Like illegal child labor, corporal punishment of children is a worldwide concern as attested to by the launch in April 2001 of the Global Initiative to End All Corporal Punishment of Children.

Of special concern is the maltreatment that youths may encounter while in contact with the justice system. Children involved with the juvenile justice system experience more trauma than youths in the general population: "Studies report varying rates of post-traumatic stress disorder (PSTSD) among youths in the juvenile justice system, with estimates ranging from a low of 3 percent to a high of 50 percent" (Ford et al., 2007).

Another group of youths who may experience institutional abuse are the approximately 5,000 unaccompanied minors detained by the U.S. Immigration and Naturalization Service: "Bewildered and frightened, these children often are kept in jail-like settings while their cases are pending. . . . Such children frequently and systematically are denied fundamental human rights" (Becker, 2000).

Individual Maltreatment   Individual maltreatment is what is normally thought of when child abuse is discussed and describes what occurs when one or more people emotionally or physically abuse a child. Individual abuse includes child sexual abuse. A graphic example of such abuse was demonstrated by a Chicago couple who allegedly raped, drugged and fed fried rats and boiled cockroaches to their four children for at least four years.

Child Victimization: The Seriousness of the Problem

Child abuse and neglect is, without doubt, a tragic and unfortunate reality. But disagreement exists over how prevalent the problem of child victimization is truly.

A DEBATE

Experts disagree on just how serious the problem of child abuse is. Karmen (2007, p.180) describes two conflicting views: the maximalist alarmist and minimalist skeptical perspectives. The **maximalist alarmist perspective** contends that the problem of child and sexual abuse is reaching epidemic proportions: "Dire consequences will follow unless drastic steps are taken. . . . Maximalists try to mobilize people and resources to combat what they believe is a growing crisis."

These claims have resulted in a predictable opposite position—that of the **minimalist skeptical perspective** (p.180): "Minimalists consider maximalist estimates to be grossly inflated for either a well-intentioned reason or perhaps for a self-serving purpose." Karmen notes that the most heated debates concern the actual fate of missing children, the true extent of physical child abuse and the true prevalence of incest and child molestation.

Which side of the debate do you tend to favor?
As you read through the chapter, see if your views change. For a better informed perspective consult *Crime Victims: An Introduction to Victimology*, 5th edition, by Andrew Karmen. Belmont, CA: Wadsworth Publishing Company, 2007.

Child Neglect

 Neglect is the most common form of child maltreatment and may be fatal.

Broadly defined, child **neglect** is inattention to the basic needs of a child, including appropriate supervision, adequate clothing and proper nutrition. Often the families from which neglected children come are poor and disorganized. They have no set routine for family activity. The children roam the streets at all hours. They are continually petitioned to juvenile court for loitering and curfew violations. The family unit is often fragmented by death, divorce or the incarceration or desertion of parents.

Broken homes often deprive children of affection, recognition and a sense of belonging unless a strong parent can overcome these responses and provide direction. If a child's protective shield is shattered, the child may lose respect for moral and ethical standards. The broken home, in and of itself, does not cause delinquency. But it can nullify or even destroy the resources youths need to handle emotional problems constructively. Children from broken homes may suffer serious damage to their personalities. They may develop aggressive attitudes and strike out. They may think that punishment is better than no recognition. Even when marriages are intact, both parents often work. Consequently, many parents spend little time in the home interacting with their children.

Some children are stunted in their emotional growth by being raised in a moral vacuum in which parents ignore them. Even more problematic are parents who do not adhere to moral and ethical standards or who have different values than the dominant moral order; they set poor examples for their children. Such parents cannot ignore the probability that their children may model their actions.

 The homes of neglected children often are disorganized, with parents who ignore the children or who set bad examples for them.

Some parents deliberately refrain from discipline in the mistaken belief that authoritative restrictions inhibit children's self-expression or unbalance their delicate emotional systems. At the other extreme are parents who discipline their children injudiciously, excessively and often, weighing neither transgression nor punishment. Parents' warped ideas, selfish attitudes and twisted values can lead to their children becoming delinquents. Family policies that are inconsistent or that emphasize too much leniency or excessive punishment may result in retaliation directed at society in general.

Children's behavior develops from what they see and understand to be happening around them. If children are exposed to excessive drinking, the use of drugs, illicit sex, gambling and related vices by parents or adult role models, they may copy these behaviors.

Neglected children often lack the food, clothing, shelter, medical care, supervision, education, protection or emotional support they need to develop appropriate physical, mental and emotional health. They also may suffer emotional harm through disrespect and denial of self-worth, unreasonable or chronic rejection and failure to receive necessary affection, protection and a sense of family belonging. They may suffer ill health because they are not vaccinated against common childhood illness or are exposed to secondhand smoke or lead. They may even die from preventable accidents.

Another large contributor to neglect is crack cocaine. Even more devastating, however, are the traumatic accidents that maim or kill children. Some of these mishaps result from safety hazards in the home. Many permanent childhood injuries could have been prevented by adequate supervision, often the result of a parent being high on drugs or alcohol.

Certainly not all neglect is intentional. It may be the result of parental immaturity or a lack of parenting skills. It may also be the result of a parent's physical, psychological or mental deficiencies. Other parents who neglect their children may do so because they cannot tolerate stress, they cannot adequately express anger or they have no sense of responsibility.

Indicators of Neglect

Among the *physical indicators* of child neglect are frequent hunger, poor hygiene, inappropriate dress, consistent lack of supervision (especially in dangerous activities or for long time periods), unattended physical problems or medical needs and abandonment. The *behavioral indicators* of neglect may include begging, stealing food, extending school days by arriving early or leaving late, constant fatigue, listlessness or falling asleep in school, alcohol or drug abuse, delinquency, stealing and reporting that no one is at home to care for them (Bennett and Hess, 2007, p.327).

Physical or Emotional Child Abuse

The problem of child abuse is serious. Such abuse may be physical or emotional. Abuse can also be indirect or "secondhand," as in cases where children are allowed to witness domestic violence between partners. Many states now consider such exposure to violence to be a form of child abuse.

Physical child abuse covers a wide spectrum of behavior. Sometimes the abuse is discipline carried too far. Controversy exists among child development scholars and parents about where the line between discipline and abuse should be drawn, and many parents who cause physical harm to their children while administering disciplinary measures claim they never *intended* to injure their children. The definition of physical abuse, however, leaves less room for interpretation and addresses the issue of intent, stating it is the *nonaccidental*, or intentional, physical injury of a child caused by the child's caretaker.

Injury to a child need not be limited to physical attacks and external wounds. Children may also be damaged through emotional abuse, the chronic failure of a child's caretaker to provide affection and support. Emotional abuse includes any treatment that seriously damages a child's emotional development. For example, Charles Manson was raised by an uncle who constantly called him derogatory names and sent him to school dressed in girl's clothing.

Unfortunately the physical and emotional abuse of children is nothing new in this country or elsewhere throughout the world. In fact, many times throughout history such abuse was widely and openly practiced.

Child Abuse and Neglect Laws

Before the creation of the first juvenile court in the United States, the Society for the Prevention of Cruelty to Children was formed in 1871 after church workers removed a severely beaten and neglected child from her home under a law that protected *animals*. The first Child Protection Service was founded in 1875. Fifty years later the Social Security Act authorized public funds for child welfare.

During the 1940s advances in diagnostic X-ray technology allowed physicians to detect patterns of healed fractures in their young patients. In 1946 Dr. John Caffey, a pediatric radiologist, suggested that multiple fractures in the long bones of infants had "traumatic origin," perhaps willfully inflicted by parents. Two decades later Dr. C. H. Kempe and his associates coined the phrase *battered child syndrome* based on clinical evidence of maltreatment. Karmen (2007, p.190) notes: "In the typical case, the victim was younger than 3 years old and suffered traumatic injuries to the head and to limbs; and the caretakers claimed that the wounds were caused by an accident and not a beating." In 1964 individual states began enacting mandatory child abuse laws using Dr. Kempe's definition of a battered child, and by 1966 all 50 states had enacted such legislation.

Laws regarding child abuse and neglect have been passed at both federal and state levels.

 Typically child abuse/neglect laws have three components: (1) criminal definitions and penalties, (2) a mandate to report suspected cases and (3) a civil process for removing the child from the abusive or neglectful environment.

Federal Legislation   In 1974 the federal government passed Public Law (PL) 93–247, the Federal Child Abuse Prevention and Treatment Act. It was amended in 1978 under PL 95–266. The law states in part that any of the following elements constitutes a crime:

> The physical or mental injury, sexual abuse or exploitation, negligent treatment, or maltreatment of a child under the age of 18, by a person who is responsible for the child's welfare under circumstances that indicate the child's health or welfare is harmed or threatened.

Nonetheless federal courts have also ruled that parents are free to strike children because "the custody, care and nurture of the child resides first in the parents" (*Prince v. Massachusetts*, 1944). This fundamental right to "nurture" has been supplanted by the Supreme Court with the "care, custody and management" of one's child (*Santosky v. Kramer*, 1982). This shift from "nurture" to "management" could herald a return to older laws, such as the one expressed in *People v. Green* (1909): "The parent is the sole judge of the necessity for the exercise of disciplinary right and of the nature of the correction to be given." The court need only determine whether "the punishment inflicted went beyond the legitimate exercise of parental authority."

Up to the present, the courts' role has been to decide what, when and to what degree physical punishment steps beyond "the legitimate exercise of parental authority" or what is "excessive punishment." The courts always begin with the presumption that parents have a legal right to use force and violence against their own children. In *Green*, 70 marks from a whipping were held to be excessive and unreasonable, even though the parent claimed he was not criminally liable because there was no permanent injury and he had acted in good faith. But the assumption remained that the parent had an unquestionable right "to administer such reasonable and timely punishment as may be necessary to correct growing faults in young children."

Current laws often protect parents, and convictions for child abuse are difficult to obtain because of circumstantial evidence, the lack of witnesses, the husband-wife privilege and the fact that an adult's testimony often is enough to establish reasonable doubt. All too often the court determines punishment to be reasonable, never re-examining the age-old presumption that hitting children is permissible.

A determination of "reasonableness" was made in *Ingram v. Wright* (1977) regarding the use of physical punishment of children by teachers. The Florida statute specified that the punishment was not to be "degrading or unduly severe." One student was beaten by 20 strokes with a wooden paddle; another was beaten by 50 strokes.

In 2000 Congress passed the Child Abuse Prevention and Enforcement Act, making more funds available for child abuse and neglect enforcement and prevention initiatives. In 2006 the Adam Walsh Child Protection and Safety Act, named for the 6-year-old son of John and Reve Walsh who was abducted and murdered in Florida in 1981, was signed into law and was aimed at tracking sex crime offenders and subjecting them to stiff, mandatory minimum sentences ("Adam Walsh Act Signed into Law," 2006, p.5). The act expands previous sex registry requirements, setting forth strict guidelines for states, territories and tribal nations to develop and maintain a jurisdiction-wide sex offender registry. Failure to comply with the guidelines can result in a 10 percent reduction in federal Byrne grant funding. Title I of the act is the Sex Offender Registration and Notification Act (SORNA), which details a comprehensive set of minimum standards for sex offender registration and notification in the United States and seeks to close the loopholes that existed under prior laws. The act also established the Office of Sex Offender Sentencing, Monitoring, Apprehending, Registering and Tracking (the SMART Office), housed in the Office of Justice Programs at the U.S. Department of Justice. This office is responsible for directing the sex offender registration and notification program, administering grant programs and providing technical assistance, coordination and support to other entities ("A Closer Look," 2006, p.3).

State Laws   Since the 1960s every state has enacted child abuse and neglect laws. On the whole, states offer a bit more protection to children by statute than does the federal government. Legal definitions vary from state to state. California, for example, declares it illegal for anyone to willfully cause or permit any child to suffer or for any person to inflict unjustifiable physical or mental suffering on a child or to cause the child to "be placed in such situations that its person or health is endangered" (California Penal Codes section 273A).

Alaska defines abuse broadly: "The infliction, by other than accidental means, of physical harm upon the body of a child." Other state statutes are much less broad. For example, Maryland's statute states that a person is not guilty of child abuse if the defendant's intentions were good, but his or her judgment was bad. The defendant in *Worthen v. State* (1979) admitted he had punished his 2-year-old stepdaughter because she was throwing a temper tantrum, "but sought to explain it as not having exceeded the bounds of parental propriety."

The jury found him guilty of assault and battery for the multiple contusions about the girl's face, ribs, buttocks and legs, but the appellate court ordered a new trial because the trial court in its jury instructions had omitted the defense of good intentions and also the defense that the stepfather had not exceeded the bounds of parental authority. What is "reasonable" varies from state to state, from one judge or court to another and from jury to jury.

Indicators of Physical Abuse

Among the *physical indicators* of physical abuse to a child are unexplained bruises or welts, burns, fractures, lacerations and abrasions. Such physical injuries may be in various stages of healing. Among the *behavioral indicators* of physical abuse are children who are wary of adults, apprehensive when other children cry, show extreme aggressiveness or extreme withdrawal, are frightened of parents or are afraid to go home (Bennett and Hess, 2007, pp.327–328).

Some common physical conditions have been mistaken for physical abuse; for example, hemophiliacs bruise easily, and inflammation of the nose's mucous membrane can cause black eyes. The condition of **osteogenesis imperfecta (OI)**, which is characterized by bones that break easily, can also be mistaken for child abuse. According to the Osteogenesis Imperfecta Foundation: "A minor accident may result in a fracture; some fractures may occur while a child is being diapered, lifted or dressed."

Parents' behavior can also provide clues to physical abuse. This can include contradictory explanations for a child's injury; attempts to conceal a child's injury or to protect the identity of the person responsible; the routine use of harsh, unreasonable discipline inappropriate to the child's age or behavior; and poor impulse control (Bennett and Hess, 2007, p.328).

Indicators of Emotional Abuse

Physical indicators of emotional abuse may include speech disorders, lags in physical development and a general failure to thrive. *Behavioral indicators* of emotional abuse may include such habit disorders as sucking, biting and rocking back and forth, as well as conduct disorders such as antisocial or destructive behavior. Other possible indicators are sleep disorders, inhibitions in play, obsessions, compulsions, phobias, hypochondria, behavioral extremes and attempted suicide (Bennett and Hess, 2007, p.327).

Causes of Abuse

Parents or caretakers commit most emotional and physical child abuse. The causes of such abuse often center on a cycle of abuse passed from one generation to the next. Other characteristics that correlate to child abuse include low income, social isolation and parental expectations that exceed a child's abilities.

 The two leading causes of child abuse are thought to be violence between husbands and wives and poverty.

The American Medical Association (1985, p.797) has identified characteristics of children that increase their risk of being abused: premature birth; birth of a child to adolescent parents; colic, which makes infants difficult to soothe; congenital deficiencies or abnormalities; hospitalization of the newborn resulting in a lack of parental contact; and presence of any condition that interferes with parent-child bonding. Additional causes of child abuse include racial discrimination and the desensitization to violence by frequently viewing brutality on television and in the movies.

Domestic and Family Violence

One of the most frequently experienced or observed types of violence is domestic violence. According to published studies, there is a 30 percent to 60 percent overlap between violence against children and violence against women in the same families (Kelleher et al., 2006, p.4). Although the studies on which these ranges are based employ different methods and different populations, they consistently report a significant level of co-occurrence.

Family violence, abuse and neglect can be found in families of all social and economic backgrounds. Children are lied to and lied about, mutilated, shot, stabbed, burned, beaten, bitten, sodomized, raped and hanged. Figure 5.3 illustrates a model of intrafamily violence, the variables affecting it, individual characteristics of family members, precipitating factors, social variables and the consequences for the child, the family and society.

As Figure 5.3 shows, many familial variables and family member characteristics affect intrafamily violence. Furthermore, conditions in the society within which the family lives also affect familial violence. Such violence may have a multitude of consequences, not only for the child but also for the family and society at large.

Witnessing Violence—Secondary Victimization   Violence does not have to be directed specifically at an individual for it to impact that individual. Witnessing actual violence or fearing its potential occurrence can strain and, thus victimize, a person. **Vicarious strain** refers to real-life strains experienced by others around the individual; **anticipated strain** refers to the individual's expectation that current strains will continue into the future or that new strains will be experienced. Agnew (2002) studied the relationship between vicarious and anticipated strain and concluded: "Delinquency is related not only to experienced victimization, but also to certain types of anticipated and vicarious physical victimization" (p.603).

McGee and Baker (2002) studied the impact of violence on problem behavior among adolescents and found a strong association between youths exposed to violence through direct victimization, witnessing violence, and association with delinquent peers and adjustment outcomes, including internalizing (self-rejection, depression) and externalizing (offenses) problem behavior. They also found a link between victimization and avoidance as a coping strategy. Furthermore, their research revealed a greater influence of victimization on offenses, self-rejection and avoidance among men and a stronger influence of victimization on depression among women in the sample (p.74).

The Cycle of Violence   Violence is learned behavior that often is self-perpetuating. When adults teach children by example that those who are bigger and stronger can use violence to force their wishes on others who are smaller, the lesson is remembered. Children who witness domestic abuse learn that it is okay to hurt the people you care about and it is acceptable to use violence to get what

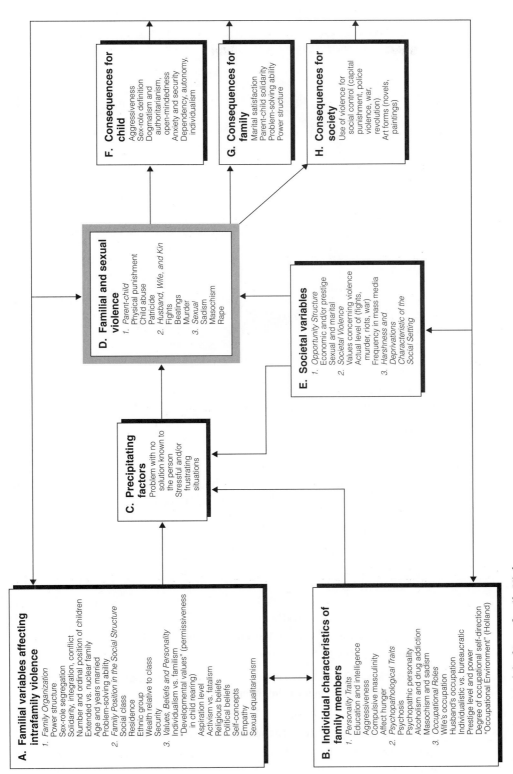

Figure 5.3 Model of Intrafamily Violence

SOURCE: Suzanne K. Steinmetz and Murray A. Straus. *Violence in the Family.* New York: Dodd, Mead, 1974, pp.18–19.

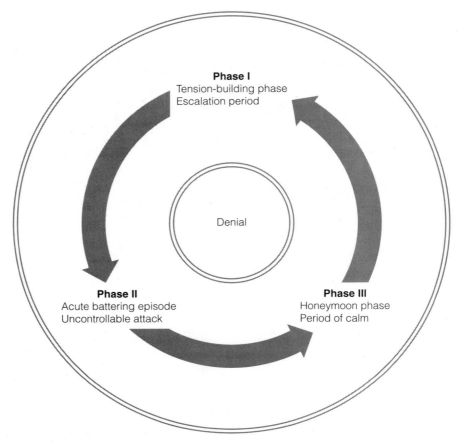

Figure 5.4   The Cycle of Violence

you want. In addition, family violence has been directly linked with delinquency, especially violent offenses. This cycle of violence is illustrated in Figure 5.4.

Karmen (2007, p.6) describes a cycle of violence in which victims are transformed into victimizers over time: "A group of picked-upon students may band together to ambush their bullying tormentors; a battered wife may launch a vengeful attack against her brutal husband; or a child subjected to periodic beatings might grow up to parent his sons in the same excessively punitive way he was raised. A study that tracked the fortunes of boys and girls known to have been physically and sexually abused over a follow-up period of several decades concluded that being harmed at an early age substantially increased the odds of future delinquency and criminality."

 Violence often leads to more violence. Children who are abused are more likely to be delinquents and violent themselves.

Child Abuse and the Link with Delinquency

The connection between children's histories of neglect or abuse and subsequent delinquency, crime and other problems has been largely ignored by our juvenile justice and social service systems. This is difficult to understand, given the growing body of evidence that shows that those who experience violent, abusive childhoods are more likely to become child or spouse abusers than those who do not.

Research by English et al. (2002, p.1) reveals strong support for the relationship between child abuse and neglect and delinquency, adult criminality and violent criminal behavior: "Abused and neglected children are 4.8 times more likely to be arrested as juveniles, 2 times more likely to be arrested as an adult and 3.1 times more likely to be arrested for a violent crime than matched controls." These findings replicate results of earlier studies and underscore the devastation that can be caused by maltreatment of children and youths. Cohen et al. (2004, pp.II-1–5) also found that victims of officially identified abuse were more likely to be arrested as adults and more likely to be arrested for a variety of crimes.

Lemmon (2006, p.5) studied the relationship between childhood maltreatment recurrence and various dimensions of delinquency and found that repeated child maltreatment significantly predicted the initiation, continuation and severity of delinquency, controlling for other risk factors. Rebellion and Van Gundy (2005, p.247) also found that longitudinal studies suggest that abuse experienced in childhood contributed to violent offending as well as property offending, and that neither self-control theory nor social bonding theory appears capable of explaining the relationship.

 Child abuse has been directly linked with delinquency.

Loeber et al. (2001, p.1) assert: "Delinquency and victimization are often intertwined and mutually stimulate each other." They note that many victims are prone to engage in illegal activities, associate with delinquents, victimize other delinquents and avoid legal recourse to resolve conflicts. When delinquent behavior occurs, it may bring about further abuse, resulting in a vicious cycle and ever-worsening behavior.

Children and adolescents who have patterns of delinquency that emanate from the home are imitating the behavior of parents or other family members. In extreme cases, children have been taught how to commit crimes.

PERSPECTIVES FROM THE NATIONAL CONFERENCE ON JUVENILE JUSTICE (NCJJ)

The question of how child abuse and neglect factor into delinquency and later criminality is a recurring topic of discussion in national forums where juvenile justice issues are addressed.

At the 34th Annual NCJJ, Dr. Michael Lindsey presented a session titled "The Link between Child Abuse, Neglect, and Delinquency" (March 6, 2007). In this session he noted that cases often progress from abuse and neglect cases handled by child protective services (CPS) to delinquency cases handled by the juvenile justice (court) system, but often the resources available to the child and family at the welfare level are diminished once the case "moves up" to the delinquency/justice level. He asserts that systematic reform is required to make individual successes more pervasive.

At the 35th Annual NCJJ, child abuse and neglect and juvenile delinquency were presented as "Two Sides of the Same Coin" by Judge Michael Nash (March 10, 2008). During the session, it was emphasized that communication, coordination and cooperation are crucial elements needed between child protective services and those in the juvenile justice system because their clients are often the same youths at different stages in life.

It is crucial that people going into the juvenile or criminal justice fields recognize the influence that child maltreatment has on juvenile delinquency and adult criminality.

Many studies have amplified the link between child abuse and criminal behavior, and many criminal justice professionals on the front lines with juvenile delinquents believe the war on crime will be won only when the focus shifts from building more prison cells to investing more in children—through early childhood programs such as health care for children and pregnant women, Head Start for infants and toddlers, parenting training for high-risk families, programs aimed at preventing child abuse, recreational programs, after-school programs and mentoring programs.

Child Sexual Harassment and Abuse

"Sexual harassment of students is a real and serious problem in education at all levels, including elementary and secondary schools, colleges and universities. It can affect any student, regardless of sex, race or age. It threatens a student's physical or emotional well-being, influences school achievement and makes it difficult for students to achieve their career goals" (*Sexual Harassment: It's Not Academic*, 2005). Sexual harassment was declared illegal in Title IX of the Education Amendments of 1972 (Title IX), which prohibits sex discrimination, including sexual harassment. Schools must make concerted efforts to prevent and remedy sexual harassment in order to ensure safe environments where students can learn. Harassment, if ignored or not reported, rarely stops on its own and is likely to continue and worsen.

Sexual harassment is not the only problem some youths experience. Every year roughly 100,000 cases of child sexual abuse are reported. Couple this with experts' estimates that more than 90 percent of child molestations are *not* reported to the criminal justice system and the magnitude of the problem becomes apparent. Some experts believe that as many as 50 percent of young women have been sexually abused before their eighteenth birthday.

Sexual abuse can be classified as intrafamilial or extrafamilial. **Intrafamilial sexual abuse** is sexual abuse by a parent or other family member. **Extrafamilial sexual abuse** involves a friend or stranger. Babysitters are responsible for a relatively small portion of the reported criminal offenses against children: 4.2 percent of all offenses for children under age 6. Among the reported offenses that babysitters commit, sex crimes outnumber physical assaults nearly two to one.

Child Sexual Abuse and the Internet

Another identified source of child sexual abuse is the Internet. An estimated 30 million youths go online each year to do homework or explore cyberspace. Geraghty (2007, p.30) cautions: "The Internet provides a child predator with access to children on a scale that makes the world his local playground. It is a medium through which digital images and movies documenting the most horrific crimes against children are distributed to a worldwide audience." He notes that all the services the Internet provides—e-mail, the World Wide Web, instant messaging—can be used to facilitate crimes against children. Examples of how this occurs are provided by Collins (2007, p.40):

A fourth-grade student was frequently pulled out of lunch by her teacher, who sexually abused her in the class coatroom and took explicit photographs to memorialize the moment. He demanded her silence by threatening to

IN THE HEADLINES

Senator Biden (D-DE), noting that law enforcement is aware of more than 400,000 people trafficking in child pornography on the Internet, contends: "The bottom line is that the Internet has facilitated an exploding, multi-billion dollar market for child pornography, with 20,000 new images posted every week. This is a market that can only be supplied by the continued sexual assault and exploitation of more children, and the research shows that victims are getting younger and younger and they are being exposed to sadistic abuse."

SOURCE: "Internet Child Pornography Targeted by Senate Measure." Criminal Justice Newsletter, July 2, 2007, p.7.

flunk her and post the pictures on the Internet if she told anyone. Another child, a prepubescent boy, was violently sexually assaulted for several years by a man who acted as his live-in babysitter. While the boy never disclosed his abuse to anyone, thousands of photographs depicting his horrific abuse were circulated around the globe. In another location, a man with no previous criminal record filmed himself sodomizing his 10-month-old granddaughter. He did not need to convince the child to keep the secret; in fact, he said he selected that particular victim because she was preverbal.

The Child Protection and Sexual Predator Punishment Act, passed in 1998, imposes tougher penalties for sex crimes against children, particularly those facilitated by the use of the Internet. The act prohibits contacting a minor via the Internet to engage in illegal sexual activity and punishes those who knowingly send obscenity to children.

In addition to child pornography, the Internet facilitates child sexual abuse in other ways, such as:

- Allowing networking among child abuse perpetrators.
- Enabling perpetrators to seek out and groom victims.
- Facilitating cyber-stalking.
- Promoting child sexual tourism.
- Assisting in the trafficking of children. (Wortley and Smallbone, 2006, p.21)

Human trafficking can involve young children, particularly those not living with their parents, as these youth are vulnerable to coerced labor exploitation, domestic servitude or commercial sexual exploitation. Sex traffickers target children because the youths are gullible and there is a market demand for young victims. The average age of entry into prostitution through human trafficking is 12 to 14 years old (*Human Trafficking of Children in the United States*, 2007).

Numerous challenges exist in controlling Internet child pornography: the decentralized structure of the Internet (a network of networks), uncertainties surrounding jurisdiction, the lack of Internet regulation, differences in legislation among jurisdictions throughout the world, the expertise of offenders, the sophistication and adaptation of Internet technology and the sheer and growing volume of Internet activity (Wortley and Smallbone, 2006, pp.26–27).

Several initiatives are aimed at protecting children in cyberspace. The OJJDP funds the Internet Crimes against Children (ICAC) Task Force, which seeks to protect children online. This program helps state and local law enforcement agencies develop effective responses to online enticement and child pornography cases, including community education, forensic, investigative and victim service components. The National Center for Missing and Exploited Children (NCMEC) has a congressionally mandated Cyberline, a reporting mechanism for child sexual exploitation, which has handled more than 440,000 leads and serves as the national clearinghouse for child pornography cases across the country (Collins, 2007, p.40).

Project Safe Childhood (PSC) is designed and sponsored by the U.S. Department of Justice to empower federal, state and local law enforcement officers with tools needed to investigate cybercrimes against children. Forty-six federally funded ICAC task forces, consisting of more than 1,000 affiliated state and local organizations, have been created across the country since 1998 (McNulty, 2007, p.36). Since 2000, these task forces have completed investigations that have resulted in 7,328 arrests. In addition, the FBI made 1,648 arrests in 2005 as part of its Innocent Images National Initiative (IINI).

Indicators of Sexual Abuse

Rarely are the *physical indicators* of sexual abuse seen. Two possible indicators, especially in preteens, are venereal disease and pregnancy.

Among the possible *behavioral indicators* of sexual abuse are being unwilling to change clothes for or to participate in physical education classes; withdrawal, fantasy or infantile behavior; bizarre sexual behavior; sexual sophistication beyond one's age or unusual behavior or knowledge of sex; poor peer relationships; delinquent or runaway behavior; and reports of being sexually assaulted (Bennett and Hess, 2007, p.328).

As with physical abuse, the parents' behavior may also provide indicators of sexual abuse. Such behaviors may include jealousy and being overprotective of a child. A parent may hesitate to report a spouse who is sexually abusing their child for fear of destroying the marriage or for fear of retaliation. Intrafamilial sex may be preferred to extramarital sex (Bennett and Hess, 2007, p.328).

Consequences of Being Sexually Abused

Sexual abuse can have many adverse effects on its young victims, including guilt, shame, anxiety, fear, depression, anger, low self-esteem, concerns about secrecy, feelings of helplessness and an inordinate need to please others (Karmen, 2007, p.192). In addition, victims of sexual abuse have higher levels of school absenteeism, less participation in extracurricular activities and lower grades.

Research by Siegel and Williams (2003, p.84) found: "Sexual abuse victims were significantly more likely to have been arrested as adults than their matched counterparts even controlling for a childhood history characterized by family problems serious enough to have resulted in a dependency hearing." In this case **dependency** refers to the legal status of children over whom a juvenile court has assumed jurisdiction because the court has found their care to fall short of legal standards of proper care by parents, guardians or custodians.

Cultural Values and Sexual Abuse

Cultural values play a role in determining what constitutes abuse. Some practices regarded as normal and acceptable within one culture may be considered sexual abuse by mainstream society or by those from other cultures. For example, in Somalia and other parts of Africa, female circumcision or female genital mutilation (FGM) is a rite of passage performed on infants and young girls. In the United States, however, this practice is considered abuse and is illegal, a situation that causes significant conflict for Somali women who have immigrated to this country.

According to the U.S. Department of Health and Human Resources, an estimated 160,000 girls and women in the U.S. immigrant community have submitted to FGM. Some contend it is hypocritical of the United States to censure another culture for doing to its young girls what America routinely does to its boys.

Another example of how different cultures regard the issue of sexual abuse is seen in the practice of polygamy involving juvenile girls. Within certain areas of the United States, most notably in Utah, polygamy was an acceptable Mormon practice, accompanied by the cultural value that very young girls, some as young as 10, may be forced into arranged marriages. Although the church disavowed polygamy in 1890 in exchange for statehood, an estimated 300,000 families are headed by men with more than one spouse.

Polygamist Tom Green made headlines when he was charged with child rape for having sex with a 13-year-old girl he had married in 1986. Green had 5 wives and 30 children. In 2002 the high-profile case of teenager Elizabeth Smart, allegedly kidnapped by Brian David Mitchell, a self-styled prophet, brought the practice of polygamy back to national attention. Mitchell supposedly kidnapped Smart to make her his second wife. Mitchell remains institutionalized, deemed incompetent to stand trial.

© Reuters NewMedia Inc./CORBIS

Elizabeth Smart (center) and her father (left) applaud as President George W. Bush speaks in the Rose Garden of the White House, April 30, 2003, surrounded by the Smart family and families of other kidnapped children.

The Issue of Credibility

Because physical indicators of sexual abuse are often not present, allegations of sexual abuse can be difficult to prove. Investigators must also weed out false accusations.

Sometimes allegations of child sexual abuse are made in the context of divorce and custody cases. Unfortunately, the warlike atmosphere inherent in divorce often discredits valid claims. Though rare, false allegations of abuse do occur. Karmen (2007, p.196) notes: "When allegations surface during the height of a divorce and tug-of-war over a child, two camps quickly emerge. One side argues that since there are no outsiders who witness violations of the incest taboo within the home, these 'family secrets' usually are not exposed unless the parents break up. The other side contends that baseless allegations are being taken too seriously, and the resulting investigations ruin the lives of innocent parents, usually fathers."

Coercing a child to lie about abuse that never occurred is a form of abuse all its own. Unfortunately, many youths become victims of this type of abuse when they are caught in the middle of custody battles. As parents fight to prove they are better equipped to raise the children, they unwittingly inflict a great deal of emotional and psychological damage on the very people they say they are trying to protect.

Children and Youths as Victims of Crime and Violence

One of the most obvious ways youths are victimized is by becoming a victim of crime. This may occur under the umbrella of ongoing abuse, as already discussed, or it may be an isolated episode by a nonfamily member, as in the case of robbery. Make no mistake; child abuse is violent crime. But the official crime statistics collected by government agencies often lump child abuse events into the general category of violent crime. Thus, keep in mind as you consider such data that an unknown, perhaps considerable, portion of these victimizations are the result of child abuse and not simply single-episode acts of violent crime. According to Snyder and Sickmund (2006), of all offenses reported to law enforcement:

- One of every four violent crime victims is a juvenile, and most are female (p.31).
- More than one-third of juvenile victims of violent crime are under age 12 (p.32).
- About two-thirds of violent crimes with juvenile victims occur in a residence (p.36).
- Few statutory rapes involve both juvenile victims and juvenile offenders, with the majority of victims being females (95 percent), most of whom were ages 14 or 15. Male offenders were generally much older than their female victims (p.37).
- In the 10 years from 1993 to 2002, the number of juveniles murdered in the United States fell 44 percent, to the lowest level since the mid-1980s (p.20).
- On an average day in 2002, about four juveniles were murdered, roughly two White and two Black youth. Adjusting for the differences in their numbers

in the general population, this means that in 2002 the risk of a Black youth being murdered was four times that of a White youth (p.22).

 Youths are victims of crime twice as often as those over age 25.

Baum (2005) reports that from 1993 to 2003 juveniles ages 12 to 14 and juveniles ages 15 to 17 experienced average annual rates of nonfatal violence about two and a half times higher than the rate for adults (83 and 84 per 1,000, respectively, versus 32 per 1,000). Four in five victims of nonfatal violent crime, ages 12 to 14, perceived the offender to be a juvenile. Juveniles experienced declines for all nonfatal crimes measured—rape/sexual assault, robbery, aggravated assault and simple assault. Victimization rates for overall violence declined more for younger teens than for older teens.

Teplin et al. (2005, p.1586) studied mortality rates among 1,829 delinquent youths and compared them to the mortality rates of the general population of Cook County, Illinois. They found the overall mortality rate for the delinquents was more than four times greater than that of the general population and nearly eight times as high among female offenders.

Schreck et al. (2007, p.381) researched the validity of the social interactionist (SI) perspective as an explanation of violent victimization. They theorized that early puberty creates unusually high levels of distress for adolescents, causing them to behave in ways that annoy others and provoke victimization. They found that such measures of distress significantly increased violent victimization among youths in the sample and concluded: "Adolescents who experienced emotional distress, performed poorly in school and violated minor rules were more likely to become victims of violent crime" (p.397).

Missing and Exploited Children

Another category of victimized youths is children who are missing and exploited. Oftentimes, these children are "missing" by choice because of intolerable conditions in the home, including abuse and violence. The National Center for Missing and Exploited Children (NCMEC) is a private, nonprofit organization established in 1984 to spearhead national efforts to locate and recover missing children and raise public awareness about ways to prevent child abduction, molestation and sexual exploitation. Since its creation through March 2008, NCMEC has helped law enforcement with more than 141,200 missing child cases, played a role in the recovery of more than 125,000 children, handled more than 2.2 million phone calls through its nationwide hotline and received more than 576,000 reports of child sexual exploitation on its CyberTipline ("General Information and Publications," 2008).

According to the NCMEC, approximately 2,100 children across the country are reported as missing every day (*2006 Annual Report*, p.13). FBI figures indicate 63,711 active juvenile missing person cases in the NCIC database (Mills-Senn, 2006, p.10). Snyder and Sickmund (2006) report:

- Annually about 19 in 1,000 children below the age of 18 are missing from caretakers. Only a small fraction of missing children were abducted (about

10 in 100), most by family members (8 in 10). Runaway youth account for nearly half of all missing children (p.43).

- Teens ages 15 to 17 accounted for 68 percent of the estimated 1.7 million youths who were gone from their homes either because they had run away or because their caretakers threw them out. Fewer than 4 in 10 of all runaway/thrownaway youths were truly missing—their parents knew where they were staying. Most youths who ran away or were thrown out of their homes were gone less than a week (77 percent) (p.45).

The Missing Children's Act was passed in 1982 and the Missing Children's Assistance Act in 1984. The Missing Children's Assistance Act of 1984 defines a *missing child* as:

> Any individual, less than 18 years of age, whose whereabouts are unknown to such individual's legal custodian—if the circumstances surrounding the disappearance indicate that (the child) may possibly have been removed by another person from the control of his/her legal custodian without the custodian's consent; or the circumstances of the case strongly indicate that (the child) is likely to be abused or sexually exploited.

This act requires the Office of Juvenile Justice and Delinquency Prevention (OJJDP) to conduct periodic national incidence studies to determine the actual number of children reported missing and the number of missing children recovered for a given year. This requirement is being met through the National Incidence Studies of Missing, Abducted, Runaway, and Thrownaway Children in America (NISMART). NISMART has completed its second in-depth study of this population and has identified six episode types of missing children.

 The six episode types of missing children included in the NISMART-2 study are missing benign explanation; missing involuntary, lost or injured; runaway/thrownaway; nonfamily abduction; stereotypical kidnapping; and family abduction.

The latest available data from NISMART is from 2002. Comparisons of NISMART-1 and NISMART-2 find no evidence of an increase in the incidence of missing children (Snyder and Sickmund, 2006, p.46). This report also states that one-third of all kidnap victims were younger than 18. The kidnappings of children younger than 12 were most likely to be committed by a family member, primarily a parent. Among female victims ages 15 to 17, about two-thirds were kidnapped by an acquaintance and one-quarter were kidnapped by a stranger (p.40). Frequently the greatest challenge with missing children cases is determining the cause.

NISMART-2 defines a missing child in two ways: those who are missing from their caretakers (caretaker missing) and those who are missing from their caretakers and reported to an agency for help in locating them (reported missing) (Sedlak et al., 2002, p.3). According to NISMART-2 an estimated 1,315,600 were caretaker missing children; 797,500 were reported missing children. Table 5.2 summarizes statistics for these two types of missing children and the episode type involved.

Table 5.2   Reasons Children Became Missing

Episode Type	Estimated Total*	95% Confidence Interval[†]	Percent*	Rate per 1,000 Children in U.S. Population (N = 70,172,700)
Caretaker Missing Children (n = 1,315,600)				
Nonfamily abduction	33,000[§]	(2,000–64,000)	3[§]	0.47[§]
Family abduction	117,200	(79,000–155,400)	9	1.67
Runaway/thrown away	628,900	(48,000–776,900)	48	8.96
Missing involuntary, lost or injured	198,300	(124,800–271,800)	15	2.83
Missing benign explanation	374,700	(289,900–459,500)	28	5.34
Reported Missing Children (n = 797,500)				
Nonfamily abduction	12,100[§]	(< 100–31,000)	2[§]	0.17[§]
Family abduction	56,500	(22,600–90,400)	7	0.81
Runaway/thrown away	357,600	(238,000–477,200)	45	5.10
Missing involuntary, lost or injured	61,900	(19,700–104,100)	8	0.88
Missing benign explanation	340,500	(256,000–425,000)	43	4.85

NOTE: All estimates are rounded to the nearest 100.
*Estimates total more than 1,135,600, and percents total more than 100 because children who had multiple episodes are included in every row that applies to them.
[†]The 95 percent confidence interval indicates that if the study were repeated 100 times, 95 of the replications would produce estimates within the ranges noted.
*Nonfamily abduction includes stereotypical kidnapping.
[§]Estimate is based on an extremely small sample of cases; therefore, its precision and confidence interval are unreliable.
SOURCE: Andrea J. Sedlak, David Finkelhor, Healther Hammer and Dana J. Schultz. *National Estimates of Missing Children: An Overview.* Washington, DC: OJJDP, National Incidence Studies of Missing, Abducted, Runaway and Thrownaway Children (NISMART), October 2002, p.6.

Missing Benign Explanation

A missing benign explanation episode occurs when a child's whereabouts are unknown to the child's caretaker and this causes the caretaker to (1) be alarmed, (2) try to locate the child and (3) contact the police about the episode for any reason, as long as the child was not lost, injured, abducted, victimized or classified as runaway/thrownaway (Sedlak et al., 2002, p.4).

Missing Involuntary, Lost or Injured

A one-year count revealed an estimated 198,300 children were involuntarily missing, lost or injured (Sedlak et al., 2002, p.10). A missing involuntary, lost or injured episode occurs when a child's whereabouts are unknown to the child's caretaker and this causes the caretaker to be alarmed for at least one hour and tries to locate the child under one of two conditions: (1) the child was trying to get home or make contact with the caretaker but was unable to do so because the child was lost, stranded or injured; or (2) the child was too young to know how to return home or make contact with the caretaker (Sedlak et al., p.4).

Running away from home is seen by many youths as a solution to problems at home or school.

Runaway/Thrownaway

A one-year count indicated an estimated 1,682,900 children either ran away or were thrown away (Sedlak et al., 2002, p.10). "A **runaway** incident occurs when a child leaves home without permission and stays away overnight, or a child 14 years old or younger (or older and mentally incompetent) who is away from home chooses not to return when supposed to and stays away overnight; or a child 15 years old or older who is away from home chooses not to return and stays away two nights" (Sedlak et al., p.4).

When adolescents cannot cope with a relationship in a family, they may perceive their only recourse to be running away. Historically, running away has been considered a behavioral manifestation of psychopathology. In fact, the American Psychiatric Association has classified the "runaway reaction" as a specific disorder.

Many runaways are insecure, depressed, unhappy and impulsive with low self-esteem. Typical runaways report conflict with parents, alienation from them, rejection and hostile control, and lack of warmth, affection and parental support. Running away may compound their problems. Many become street-wise and turn to drugs, crime, prostitution or other illegal activities.

Problems reported by youths seeking services from runaway and homeless youth centers included such family problems as emotional conflict at home, parents who were too strict and physical abuse and neglect. The National Council of Juvenile and Family Court Judges has stated: "We know that many [youths] who are on the streets are there as a result of sound rational choices they have made for their own safety and welfare, such as avoiding physical abuse, sexual abuse, or extreme neglect at home." For 21 percent of the 1.7 million runaway/thrownaway youths, their episode involved physical or sexual abuse at home prior to leaving or fear of such abuse upon their return (Snyder and Sickmund, 2006, p.45). Other problems reported included parental drug and/or alcohol abuse, mental health problems within the family and domestic violence between the parents.

The two most frequently mentioned personal problems were a poor self-image and depression. Other problems included issues at school such as truancy, poor grades and not getting along with teachers; drug and/or alcohol abuse; and being in trouble with the justice system.

A **thrownaway** incident occurs when a child is asked or told to leave home by a parent or other household adult, no adequate alternative care is arranged for the child by a household adult and the child is out of the household overnight; or a child who is away from home is prevented from returning home by a parent or other household adult, no adequate alternative care is arranged for the child by a household adult and the child is out of the household overnight (Sedlak et al., 2002, p.4).

Very few runaways are homeless and living on the street, and most do not go far: "Survival and safety issues are fairly minimal for the large majority of juveniles who stay with friends or relatives. However a minority face serious risks, such as exploitation by predatory adults, involvement in criminal activity, drug abuse or unsafe sex; health problems stemming from exposure to the elements, poor nutrition and other effects of living on the street and a higher risk of depression and suicide" (Dedel, 2006, p.3).

Nonfamily Abduction

A one-year estimate shows approximately 58,200 children were abducted by nonfamily members (Sedlak et al., 2002, p.10). A nonfamily abduction occurs when a nonfamily perpetrator takes a child by physical force or threat of bodily harm or detains a child for at least one hour in an isolated place by physical force or threat of bodily harm without lawful authority or parental permission; or when a child who is younger than 15 years old or is mentally incompetent, without lawful authority or parental permission, is taken or detained by or voluntarily accompanies a nonfamily perpetrator who conceals the child's whereabouts, demands ransom or expresses the intention to keep the child permanently (Sedlak et al., p.4).

Stereotypical Kidnapping

A **stereotypical kidnapping** occurs when a stranger or slight acquaintance perpetrates a nonfamily abduction in which the child is detained overnight, transported at least 50 miles, held for ransom, abducted with intent to keep the child permanently or killed (Sedlak et al., 2002, p.4). One-third of all kidnap victims known to law enforcement are under age 18, and the risk of kidnapping increases substantially for female juveniles after age 9 (Snyder and Sickmund, 2006, p.40).

Family Abduction

One-year estimates from NISMART-2 indicate that approximately 203,900 children are abducted by family members. A family abduction occurs when, in violation of a custody order, a decree or other legitimate custodial rights, a member of the child's family, or someone acting on behalf of a family member, takes or fails to return a child, and the child is concealed or transported out of state with the intent to prevent contact or deprive the caretaker of custodial rights indefinitely or permanently. For a child 15 or older, unless mentally incompetent, there must be evidence that the perpetrator used physical force or threat of bodily harm to take or detain the child (Sedlak et al., 2002, p.4).

Sedlak et al. (p.10) note: "Contrary to the common assumption that abduction is a principal reason why children become missing, the NISMART-2 findings indicate that only a small minority of missing children were abducted, and most of these children were abducted by family members (9 percent of all caretaker missing children)."

International Parental Kidnapping   If a child is abducted from this country to another, the laws, policies and procedures of the foreign country determine whether and how the child will be returned (*A Family Resource Guide on International Parental Kidnapping*, 2007, p.4). The following warning signs may indicate the threat of an international kidnapping: previously abducted or threatened to abduct the child, citizenship in another country and strong emotional or cultural ties to that country, friends or family living in another country, no strong ties to the child's home state, a strong support network and no financial reason to stay in the country.

All 50 states and the District of Columbia have laws that treat parental kidnapping as a felony under specified circumstances: "Generally, abductions and retentions that involve crossing state lines or leaving the country are felonies" (*A Family Resource Guide*, p.77). Friends, relatives and others who assist the abduction or who retain or conceal the child can often be criminally charged as accomplices or co-conspirators. In addition, two federal criminal statutes apply in international family abduction cases: the Fugitive Felon Act and the International Parental Kidnapping Crime Act (*A Family Resource Guide*, p.78).

A Child Abduction Response Team (CART)

Several compelling reasons exist for having a Child Abduction Response Team (CART): "Most abductions are short term and involve sexual assault; 44 percent of abducted children who are killed are killed in less than one hour of being abducted; 75 percent are killed within 3 hours of being abducted; 91 percent are killed within 24 hours of being abducted; 99 percent of those murdered are killed within 7 days of being abducted" (Swager, 2007, p.137). Because of the time-sensitive nature of child abductions, the mission of a CART is to bring expert resources to child abduction cases quickly. Such a team typically consists of seasoned, experienced officers from around the region, each with a preplanned response related to that officer's field of expertise, and may also include mounted patrol, ATVs, helicopters, and K9s—whatever resources are readily available. A CART might also include a family coordinator, a media coordinator, a crime scene coordinator, a street patrol coordinator, an interview team coordinator, a research coordinator, a search coordinator and a coordinator of other agencies involved (Moore, 2006, p.130).

AMBER Alert

Another approach to a missing child report is the AMBER Alert. The AMBER (America's Missing: Broadcast Emergency Response) Alert network was established in 1996 in response to the death of Amber Hagerman, who was abducted while riding her bicycle in Arlington, Texas, and then brutally murdered. AMBER Alerts are emergency messages broadcast when a law enforcement agency determines that a child has been abducted and is in imminent danger. The broadcasts include information that could assist in the child's recovery including a physical description about the child and abductor. All 50 states now have statewide AMBER Alert plans ("Department of Justice Marks 11th Anniversary of AMBER Alert," 2007, p.1). These alerts may be put on television and radio stations, electronic message systems on highways and other media. In most departments, the public information officer (PIO) is the communication cornerstone of this network: "The public information officer (PIO) should be the primary point of contact for the media. This means that the PIO should be responsible for conveying all information from the law enforcement agency to the public via the media and for fielding inquiries from journalists and the public" (*Amber Alert: Best Practices Guide for Public Information Officers*, 2006).

According to AMBER Alert's home page (http://www.amberalert.gov/faqs. htm), the program is a proven success and has helped rescue more than 426 children nationwide. In several jurisdictions throughout the country, the AMBER Alert system is being expanded to cell phone customers, with subscribers able to register through their participating carriers' Web sites to receive text messages (Kallestad, 2005). The program is also being expanded to include tribal law enforcement agencies.

Responsibility for Investigating Missing and Exploited Children

The primary responsibility for investigating missing and exploited children falls at the local and state levels, but the federal government is also involved. Two federal agencies in particular have responsibilities in the area but approach the problem from very different perspectives.

 The Department of Health and Human Services through its Administration for Children and Families (ACF) and the Justice Department through its Office of Juvenile Justice and Delinquency Prevention (OJJDP) have concurrent jurisdiction for missing and exploited children.

Both agencies' authority comes from the 1974 Juvenile Justice and Delinquency Prevention (JJDP) Act, amended in 1978 by the Runaway and Homeless Youth (RHY) Act. The RHY Act took a "social welfare, emergency care" approach to the problem of runaways, playing down law enforcement solutions. This approach is the focus of the ACF, which emphasizes facilitating counseling and communication efforts between the runaway and the family.

The OJJDP approach is very different, focusing on the challenges that runaways present to law enforcement and the juvenile justice system. This approach acknowledges that secure custodial care is often the only practical response to runaway juveniles and the dangers they pose, not only to themselves but also to the community.

 The ACF takes a social welfare, emergency care approach to missing children; the OJJDP focuses on the challenges that missing children present to law enforcement and the juvenile justice system.

Clearly, these two approaches are often at odds with each other. Therefore, coordination between the two agencies is vital if the runaway problem is to be effectively addressed.

Before leaving the discussion of children and youths as victims, consider another devastating way in which youths become victims by taking their own lives.

Youths and Suicide

Youths ages 7 to 17 are about as likely to be victims of suicide as they are to be victims of homicide (Snyder and Sickmund, 2006, p.25). In most states, juvenile suicides are more common than juvenile homicides (p.26).

 The leading cause of youth suicide is untreated depression.

About 5 percent of children and adolescents in the general population suffer from depression at any given point in time. Major signs of depression in adolescents include frequent sadness, tearfulness or crying; hopelessness; decreased interest in activities or inability to enjoy previously favorite activities; persistent boredom; low energy; social isolation and poor communication; low self-esteem and guilt; extreme sensitivity to rejection or failure; increased irritability, anger or hostility; difficulty with relationships; frequent complaints of physical illnesses such as headaches and stomachaches; frequent absences from school or poor performance in school; poor concentration; a major change in eating and/or sleeping patterns; talk of or efforts to run away from home; and thoughts or expressions of suicide or self-destruction (*The Depressed Child*, 2004, p.1).

Sometimes depression may not be readily apparent. The person may try to cover it up with overactivity, preoccupation with trivia or acting-out behavior such as delinquency, the use of drugs or sexual promiscuity. With or without overt signs of depressions, the possibility of suicide must be considered.

Adolescent suicide is the third leading cause of death among 14- to 24-year-olds and the sixth leading cause of death for 5- to 14-year-olds in the United States (*Teen Suicide*, 2004, p.1). It is estimated that 500,000 teens attempt suicide every year with 5,000 succeeding. These are epidemic proportions. According to the *Sourcebook of Criminal Justice Statistics 2003* (p.239), the number of juveniles attempting to commit suicide has risen from 7.3 percent in 1991 to 8.4 percent in 2005. However, the number of juveniles who have seriously considered suicide has declined from 29.0 percent in 1991 to 16.9 percent in 2005.

Warning signs of suicide include threatening to kill oneself; preparing for death by giving away favorite possessions, writing good-bye letters or making a will; expressing hopelessness for the future and giving up on oneself; and talking as if no one else cares.

Given the dire consequences that might result from child maltreatment, efforts to prevent or reduce victimization of children and youth are critical.

Exemplary Programs to Prevent or Reduce Child Victimization

Numerous programs are aimed at preventing or reducing victimization of the nation's children and youths. Project Safe Childhood, the program to safeguard the nation's children and youths from exploitation via the Internet, was discussed earlier in the chapter. One extremely successful early intervention program is the Nurse-Family Partnership.

Nurse-Family Partnership

The Nurse-Family Partnership (NFP) is a program that targets low-income, unmarried, first-time mothers. It connects specially trained nurse practitioners with expectant mothers before their babies are born in an effort to achieve healthy pregnancies and, consequently, healthy babies, with the expectation that this intervention will help achieve long-term improvements in the lives of at-risk families. The intervention process is effective because it concentrates on developing therapeutic relationships within the family and works across five broad domains of family functioning: parental roles, family and friend support, health (physical and mental), home and neighborhood environment, and major life events (e.g., pregnancy planning, education, employment).

The program, founded by Dr. David Olds, seeks to help new mothers become better parents, build a strong network of support for mother and child, make homes safe places for babies to live and play, get referrals for health care and child care, find ways to continue their education and develop job skills and set family goals for both mother and baby. Although the primary client is the first-time mother, ultimately her baby and all the members of her support system (e.g., friends, parents, boyfriend, child's father) become involved in the program. Nurses begin visiting first-time mothers during pregnancy and continue with weekly or biweekly visits until the child is 2 years old. During home visits, nurses promote the physical, cognitive and social-emotional development of the children and provide general support and instruction in parenting skills.

The NFP currently serves 20,000 families annually and is expanding. The program has undergone extensive testing and evaluation through nearly 30 years of ongoing, longitudinal, randomized trials. Meta-analysis of these scientifically controlled studies has found consistent, dramatic benefits for first-time, low-income mothers and their children, including improved prenatal health, fewer childhood injuries, fewer subsequent pregnancies, increased intervals between births, increased maternal employment and improved school readiness. NFP has been nationally recognized by the Prevention Research

Center for the Promotion of Human Development, the Brookings Institute, the Partnership for America's Economic Success, the RAND Corporation, Helping America's Youth (HAY), Blueprints for Violence Prevention, the Coalition for Evidence-Based Policy and the Office of Juvenile Justice and Delinquency Prevention.

Specific program effects when the child reaches age 15 include benefits to mothers (61 percent fewer arrests, 72 percent fewer convictions and 978 fewer days in jail), benefits to children (48 percent reduction in child abuse and neglect, 59 percent reduction in arrests and 90 percent reduction in adjudication as a person in need of supervision for incorrigible behavior) and benefits to society ($17,180 lifetime cost savings for every NFP mother and child and $5.70 saved for every $1 invested in high-risk families) (Lee et al., 2008).

Building Peaceful Families

Building Peaceful Families (BPF) is a Silicon Valley organization devoted to helping families build violence-free homes through training and through events celebrating the value of responsible, positive parenting, with a focus on fathers: "BPF operates from the philosophy that while the desire to be a father may be innate, what a responsible father does is learned; key to this learning is understanding that a responsible father is not abusive to his children or to the mother of his children" ("Building Peaceful Families," 2007, p.13). A key initiative of BPF is the Bay Area Fatherhood Conference, designed both for fathers who are parenting or attempting to parent their children and for fathers who have little or no contact with their children. The 2006 conference brought together nearly 650 people for a day-long celebration of the importance of fatherhood. Participants included fathers on probation or parole; fathers with cases in family court, dependency court and juvenile court; and fathers in special programs run by the Department of Corrections.

Safe Kids/Safe Streets

Safe Kids/Safe Streets (SK/SS) is an initiative funded by the Office of Juvenile Justice and Delinquency Prevention (OJJDP) within the Department of Justice to help communities reduce child abuse and neglect and the aftereffects of such treatment through collaborative, communitywide efforts. These strategies are grounded in research about the causes and correlates of juvenile delinquency in addition to principles of effective prevention and intervention techniques (Cronin et al., 2006, p.1). This foundation allows SK/SS to effectively pursue the goals of broadening access to available resources, strengthening primary prevention efforts, improving services for families through empowerment and maintaining accountability for actions. Advisory committees identify and prioritize needs in the planning stages. They then restructure and strengthen the existing system, as SK/SS desires communities to build on their existing resources. SK/SS promotes community ownership and responsibility.

SK/SS encourages a proactive rather than reactive strategy. By establishing an integrated system with an emphasis on prevention efforts, the community should improve its response to the abuse and neglect of children and adolescents with the goal of breaking the cycle of childhood victimization and subsequent delinquent and criminal behavior.

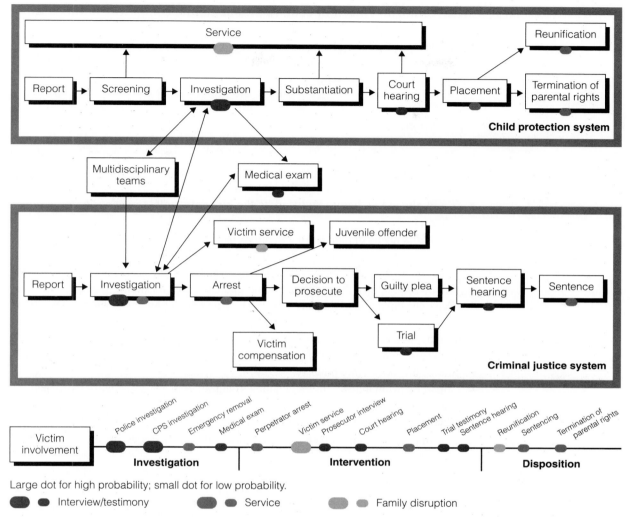

Figure 5.5 The Juvenile Victim Justice System

SOURCE: David Finkelhor, Theodore P. Cross and Elise N. Cantor. *How the Justice System Responds to Juvenile Victims: A Comprehensive Model.* Washington, DC: OJJDP Juvenile Justice Bulletin, December 2005, p.3. (NCJ 210951)

In addition to programs to help prevent or reduce the victimization of the country's children and youths, the justice system has responded to juvenile victims by developing a comprehensive Juvenile Victim Justice System

The Juvenile Victim Justice System

Finkelhor et al. (2005) describe the juvenile victim justice system as a complex set of agencies and institutions that include police, prosecutors, criminal and civil courts, child protection agencies, children's advocacy centers, and victim services and mental health agencies. The system has a structure and sequence, but its operation, despite the thousands of cases it handles every year, is not as widely recognized and understood as the operation of the more familiar juvenile offender justice system. Figure 5.5 depicts the Juvenile Victim Justice System.

According to Finkelhor et al. (p.2), one central complexity of the juvenile victim justice system is it encompasses two distinct subsystems, the criminal justice system and the child protection system. These systems are typically considered separate, but the interaction between cases involving juvenile victims is considerable and increasing.

 ## SUMMARY

- Maltreated youths are at an increased risk for performing poorly in school; displaying symptoms of mental illness; for girls, becoming pregnant; using drugs; and engaging in serious and violent delinquency.
- Child abuse has been identified as the biggest single cause of death of young children.
- The three levels of abuse are collective, institutional and individual.
- Neglect is the most common form of child maltreatment and may be fatal.
- The homes of neglected children are often disorganized and broken, and neglecting parents ignore their children or set bad examples for them.
- Typically child abuse/neglect laws have three components: (1) criminal definitions and penalties, (2) a mandate to report suspected cases and (3) a civil process for removing a child from the abusive or neglectful environment.
- The two leading causes of child abuse are thought to be violence between husbands and wives and poverty.
- Violence often leads to more violence. Children who are abused are more likely to be delinquent and violent themselves.
- Child abuse has been directly linked with delinquency.
- Youths are also victimized by crime and violence twice as often as those over age 25.
- The six episode types of missing children included in the NISMART-2 study are missing benign explanation; missing involuntary, lost or injured; runaway/thrownaway; nonfamily abduction; stereotypical kidnapping; and family abduction.
- The Department of Health and Human Services through ACYF and the Justice Department through OJJDP have concurrent jurisdiction for missing and exploited children. The ACYF takes a social welfare, emergency care approach to missing children; the OJJDP focuses on the challenges that missing children present to law enforcement and the juvenile justice system.
- The leading cause of youth suicide is untreated depression.
- Warning signs of suicide include threatening to kill oneself; preparing for death by giving away favorite possessions, writing good-bye letters or making a will; expressing hopelessness for the future and giving up on oneself; and talking as if no one else cares.

DISCUSSION QUESTIONS

1. What causes parents or caretakers of children to abuse them?
2. Do your state laws against child abuse and neglect contain two or more of these components: nonaccidental physical injury, physical neglect, emotional abuse or neglect, sexual abuse, abandonment?
3. Of all abuses, which has the most lasting effect? Why?
4. How can a society cope with child abuse and strive to control it?
5. What protection does a child have against abuse? Should the courts rescind parental rights in abuse cases?
6. Do courts act in the best interests of children when they allow abused children to remain with the family?
7. What are the strongest predictors of future delinquent or violent behavior?
8. Are the definitions of *child abuse* and *child neglect* the key elements in determining the volume of child abuse cases in various jurisdictions? How is the volume of cases determined?
9. In your area, how are children protected from abuse? Can the system be improved? How?
10. Are the six episode types of missing children identified by NISMART-2 helpful?

REFERENCES

"Adam Walsh Act Signed into Law." *The JRSA Forum*, December 2006, p.5.

Agnew, Robert. "Experienced, Vicarious, and Anticipated Strain: An Exploratory Study on Physical Victimization and Delinquency." *Justice Quarterly*, December 2002, pp.603–632.

Amber Alert: Best Practices Guide for Public Information Officers. Washington, DC: Department of Justice, July 2006. (NCJ 212703)

American Medical Association. "AMA Diagnostic and Treatment Guidelines Concerning Child Abuse and Neglect." *Journal of the American Medical Association*, Vol. 254, No. 6, 1985, pp.796–800.

Baum, Katrina. *Juvenile Victimization and Offending, 1993–2003*. Washington, DC: Bureau of Justice Statistics Special Report, August 2005. (NCJ 209468)

Becker, Jo. "The Other Immigrant Children." Human Rights Watch. Published in the *Miami Herald*, July 1, 2000. Online: http://hrw.org/english/docs/2000/01/07/usdom12803.htm. Accessed October 23, 2008.

Bennett, Wayne M. and Hess, Karen M. *Criminal Investigation*, 8th ed. Belmont, CA: Wadsworth Publishing Company, 2007.

"Building Peaceful Families." *Synergy*, Winter 2007, pp.13–14.

Child Health USA 2006. Rockville, MD: U.S. Department of Health and Human Services, 2006.

"Child Labor." New York: Human Rights Watch, 2006. Online: http://www.hrw.org/children/labor.htm. Accessed October 23, 2008.

Child Maltreatment 2006. U.S. Department of Health and Human Services, 2008.

Child Welfare Information Gateway. *Child Abuse and Neglect Fatalities: Statistics and Interventions*. Washington, DC: U.S. Department of Health and Human Services, Administration on Children, Youth and Families, 2008. Online: http://www.childwelfare.gov/pubs/factsheets/fatality.cfm. Accessed October 21, 2008.

"Children at Higher Risk in Nontraditional Homes." *Associated Press*, November 18, 2007. Online: http://www.msnbc.msn.com/id/21838575/. Accessed October 21, 2008.

"A Closer Look at the Adam Walsh Child Protection and Safety Act." *NCJA Justice Bulletin*, October 2006, p.3.

Cohen, Patricia; Smailes, Elizabeth; and Brown, Jocelyn. *Effects of Childhood Maltreatment on Adult Arrests in a General Population Sample*. Washington, DC: Department of Justice, 2004. (NCJ 199707)

Collins, Michelle K. "Child Pornography: A Closer Look." *The Police Chief*, March 2007, pp.40–47.

Cronin, Roberta; Gragg, Francis; Schultz, Dana; and Eisen, Karla. *Lessons Learned from Safe Kids/Safe Streets*. Washington, DC: U.S. Department of Justice, Office of Juvenile Justice and Delinquency Prevention, November 2006. (NCJ 213682)

Dedel, Kelly. *Juvenile Runaways*. Washington, DC: Office of Community Oriented Policing Services, February 2006.

"Department of Justice Marks 11th Anniversary of AMBER Alert." *OJJDP News @ a Glance, January/February 2007*, p.1.

The Depressed Child. American Academy of Child and Adolescent Psychiatry, July 2004.

English, Diana J.; Widom, Cathy Spatz; and Brandford, Carol. *Childhood Victimization and Delinquency, Adult Criminality, and Violent Criminal Behavior: A Replication and Extension*. Washington, DC: National Institute of Justice, February 1, 2002. (NCJ 192291)

A Family Resource Guide on International Parental Kidnapping. Washington, DC: Office of Juvenile Justice and Delinquency Prevention, January 2007. (NCJ 215476)

Finkelhor, David; Cross, Theodore P.; and Cantor, Elise N. *How the Justice System Responds to Juvenile Victims: A Comprehensive Model.* Washington, DC: OJJDP Juvenile Justice Bulletin, December 2005.

Ford, Julian D.; Chapman, John F.; Hawke, Josephine; and Albert, David. *Trauma among Youth in the Juvenile Justice System: Critical Issues and New Directions.* Delmar, NY: National Center for Mental Health and Juvenile Justice, June 2007.

Geraghty, Michael. "The Technical Aspects of Computer-Facilitated Crimes against Children." *The Police Chief*, March 2007, pp.30–33.

Harris, Jerry. "Drug-Endangered Children." *FBI Law Enforcement Bulletin*, February 2004, pp.8–11.

Hotakainen, Rob; Johns, Emily; and Allen, Martha Sawyer. "Bishops Failed to Protect Children, Report Says." (Minneapolis/St. Paul) *Star Tribune*, February 28, 2004, pp.A1, A15.

Human Rights Watch. *World Report 2008.* Online: http://hrw.org/wr2k8/pdfs/wr2k8_web.pdf. Accessed October 23, 2008.

Human Trafficking of Children in the United States. Washington, DC: Office of Safe and Drug-Free Schools. August 6, 2007. Online: http://www.ed.gov/about/offices/list/osdfs/factsheet.html. Accessed October 23, 2008.

"Internet Child Pornography Targeted by Senate Measure." *Criminal Justice Newsletter*, July 2, 2007, p.7.

Kallestad, Brent. "Cellphone Users to Get Amber Alert." *The Miami Health Herald*, August 5, 2005.

Karmen, Andrew. *Crime Victims: An Introduction to Victimology*, 5th ed. Belmont, CA: Wadsworth Publishing Company, 2007.

Kelleher, Kelly; Gardner, William; Coben, Jeff; Barth, Rick; Edleson, Jeff; and Hazen, Andrea. *Co-Occurring Intimate Partner Violence and Child Maltreatment: Local Policies/Practices and Relationships to Child Placement, Family Services and Residence.* Washington, DC: U.S. Department of Justice, unpublished report, March 2006, Document No. 213503, Award No. 2002-WG-BX-0014.

Lee, Stephanie; Aos, Steve; and Miller, Marna. *Evidence-Based Programs to Prevent Children from Entering and Remaining in the Child Welfare System: Benefits and Costs for Washington.* Olympia: Washington State Institute for Public Policy, July 2008, Document No. 08-07-3901.

Lemmon, John H. "The Effects of Maltreatment Recurrence and Child Welfare Services on Dimensions of Delinquency." *Criminal Justice Review*, March 2006, pp.5–32.

Loeber, Rolf; Kalb, Larry; and Huizinga, David. *Juvenile Delinquency and Serious Injury Victimization.* Washington, DC: OJJDP Juvenile Justice Bulletin, August 2001. (NCJ 188676)

McGee, Zina T. and Baker, Spencer R. "Impact of Violence on Problem Behavior among Adolescents." *Journal of Contemporary Criminal Justice*, February 2002, pp.74–93.

McNulty, Paul J. "Project Safe Childhood." *The Police Chief*, March 2007, pp.36–39.

Mertens, Jennifer. "Lost and Found." *Law Enforcement Technology*, February 2006, pp.8–16.

Mills-Senn, Pamela. "Making the ID." *Law Enforcement Technology*, June 2006, pp.10–20.

Moore, Carole. "Missing Children Coordination." *Law Enforcement Technology*, July 2006, p.130.

National Center for Missing and Exploited Children. "General Information and Publications." Online: http://www.ncmec.org/en_US/publications/NC21.pdf. Accessed October 24, 2008.

National Center for Missing and Exploited Children. *2006 Annual Report.* Online: http://www.ncmec.org/en_US/publications/NC171.pdf. Accessed October 24, 2008.

National Child Abuse and Neglect Data System (NCANDS). *Summary of Key Findings from Calendar Year 2000*, April 2002.

Nurse-Family Partnerships: Helping First-Time Parents. Denver, CO: Nurse-Family Partnership National Service Office Information Packet. Online: http://www.nursefamilypartnership.org/. Accessed October 24, 2008.

Osteogenesis Imperfecta Foundation. *OI Issues: Child Abuse.* Online: http://www.oif.org/tier2/childabuse.htm

Rebellion, Cesar J. and Van Gundy, Karen. "Can Control Theory Explain the Link between Parental Physical Abuse and Delinquency? A Longitudinal Analysis." *Journal of Research in Crime and Delinquency*, August 2005, pp.247–274.

Schreck, Christopher; Burek, Melissa W.; Stewart, Eric A.; and Miller, J. Mitchell. "Distress and Violent Victimization among Young Adolescents: Early Puberty and the Social Interactionist Explanation." *Journal of Research in Crime and Delinquency*, November 2007, pp.381–405.

Sedlak, Andrea J.; Finkelhor, David; Hammer, Heather; and Schultz, Dana J. *National Estimates of Missing Children: An Overview.* Washington, DC: Office of Juvenile Justice and Delinquency Prevention, October 2002. (NCJ 196465)

Sexual Harassment: It's Not Academic. Washington, DC: U.S. Office of Education, pamphlet, March 14, 2005. Online: http://www.ed.gov/about/offices/list/ocr/docs/ocrshpam.html. Accessed October 24, 2008.

Siegel, Jane A. and Williams, Linda M. "The Relationship between Child Sexual Abuse and Female Delinquency and Crime: A Prospective Study." *Journal of Research in Crime and Delinquency*, February 2003, pp.71–94.

Snyder, Howard N. and Sickmund, Melissa. *Juvenile Offenders and Victims: 2006 National Report.* Washington,

DC: Office of Juvenile Justice Delinquency Prevention, March 2006.

Sourcebook of Criminal Justice Statistics 2003. Ann L. Pastore and Kathleen Maguire, eds. Washington, DC: Bureau of Justice Statistics. Online: http://www.albany.edu/sourcebook. Accessed October 24, 2008.

Swager, Brent. "Tampa's Child Abduction Response Team." *Law and Order*, September 2007, pp.134–138.

Teen Suicide. American Academy of Child and Adolescent Psychiatry, July 2004.

Teplin, Linda A.; McClelland, Gary M.; Abram, Karen M.; and Mileusnic, Darinka. "Early Violent Death among Delinquent Youth: A Prospective Longitudinal Study." *Pediatrics*, Vol. 115, No. 6, 2005, p.1586.

Wortley, Richard and Smallbone, Stephen. *Child Pornography on the Internet.* Washington, DC: Office of Community Oriented Policing Services, May 2006.

CASES CITED

Ingram v. Wright, 430 U.S. 651 (1977)

People v. Green, 155 Mich. 524, 532, 119 N.W. 1087 (1909)

Prince v. Massachusetts, 321 U.S. 158 (1944)

Santosky v. Kramer, 455 U.S. 745 (1982)

Worthen v. State, 42 Md. App. 20, 399 A.2d 272 (1979)

CHAPTER 6

Juvenile Offenders

THE GREATEST FUTURE PREDICTOR OF VIOLENT BEHAVIOR IS A PREVIOUS
HISTORY OF VIOLENCE. WITHOUT SYSTEMATIC AND EFFECTIVE INTERVENTION,
EARLY AGGRESSION COMMONLY WILL ESCALATE INTO LATER VIOLENCE AND
BROADEN INTO OTHER ANTISOCIAL BEHAVIOR.

—AMERICAN PSYCHOLOGICAL ASSOCIATION
COMMISSION ON VIOLENCE AND YOUTH

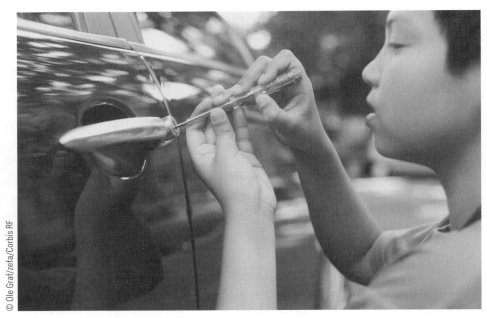

© Ole Graf/zefa/Corbis RF

Property crimes are the most common types of delinquency offenses, with data indicating that more than 25 percent of all arrests for property crimes are of juveniles.

DO YOU KNOW?

■ What acts are classified as status offenses in most states?

■ Whether arrests for status offenses have generally increased or decreased in recent years?

■ Which delinquency offenses result in the highest number of juvenile arrests?

■ Whether juvenile arrests for property crimes have increased or decreased?

■ Whether violent juvenile crime is increasing or decreasing?

■ What two general trajectories for youth violence are identified by the surgeon general?

■ When most youth violence begins and ends?

■ How public health and juvenile justice view violence?

CAN YOU DEFINE?

binge drinking	delinquent	rave	serious juvenile offender
chronic juvenile offender	deviance	recidivism	
	expressive violence	serious child delinquent	violent juvenile offender
contagion	instrumental violence		

CHAPTER OUTLINE

Introduction

An Overview of Juvenile Offenses

Status Offenders and Offenses

Running Away

Truancy

Curfew Violations

Early Substance Use

Other Problem Behaviors

Juvenile Delinquents and Delinquency

Property Offenses Committed by Juveniles

Violent Crime Committed by Juveniles

Profile of Delinquency

Age Trends

Female Delinquents

Minority Offenders

Co-Offending

Serious, Chronic and Violent Juvenile Offenders

Serious Child Delinquents

Chronic Juvenile Offenders and Recidivism

Violent Juvenile Offenders

Predictors of Youth Violence

Myths about Youth Violence

System Response to Violent Juvenile Offenders

A Comprehensive Approach

The Public Health Model and the Juvenile Justice Perspective

Are Delinquency and Youth Violence Inevitable?

Introduction

The juvenile justice system is charged with handling a broad spectrum of youths labeled as "offenders," from those who smoke cigarettes and stay out too late at night (status offenses), to those who vandalize and steal others' property, to those who commit violent crimes against others but are too young to transfer to adult criminal court. An unfortunate reality is that many of these offenders first had contact with "the system" as victims, as discussed in the previous chapter. In some cases, the prevalence of risk factors (Chapter 4) simply proved too great for these kids to escape the likelihood of becoming ensnared in the system as a juvenile offender.

An Overview of Juvenile Offenses

Juvenile "offenders" is a broad category that encompasses youth engaged in a wide range of activities, from status offenses, such as liquor laws and curfew violations, to property crimes, to serious violent offenses. These three general offense types provide a natural division in which to discuss juvenile misbehavior. And, as will be seen, the number of youths engaged in the various types of offending varies considerably.

An estimated 2.2 million arrests involving juveniles were made in 2006. Snyder (2008, p.1) reports: "Juveniles accounted for 17% of all violent crime arrests and 26% of all property crime arrests in 2006. The substantial growth in juvenile violent crime arrests that began in the late 1980s and peaked in 1994 was followed by 10 consecutive years of decline. . . . However, this long-term downward trend was broken in 2005 with a 2% annual increase in Violent Crime Index arrests followed by a 4% increase in 2006." Table 6.1 shows the total number of juvenile arrests in 2006 compared with previous years. Property crimes continue to head the list.

Note, however, in Table 6.1 that arrests are often made for conduct that falls outside the parameters of *delinquency*; that is, status offenses are often included in juvenile arrest data.

Status Offenders and Offenses

Status offenses are based solely on the offender's age and are unique to juveniles. The upper age limit for status offenses ranges from 16 to 19, but in most states it is 17. Anyone above the legal age who engages in the same behaviors would not be committing an offense. Historically, girls have been disproportionately

Table 6.1   Number of Juvenile Arrests in 2006—2.2 Million

The 2.2 million arrests of juveniles in 2006 was 24% fewer than the number of arrests in 1997

Most Serious Offense	2006 Estimated Number of Juvenile Arrests	Percent of Total Juvenile Arrests		Percent Change		
		Female	Under Age 15	1997–2006	2002–2006	2005–2006
Total	2,219,600	29%	29%	−24%	−3%	1%
Violent Crime Index	**100,700**	**17**	**29**	**−20**	**8**	**4**
Murder and nonnegligent manslaughter	1,310	5	8	−42	18	3
Forcible rape	3,610	2	36	−31	−20	−10
Robbery	35,040	9	23	−16	34	19
Aggravated assault	60,770	23	32	−21	−1	−2
Property Crime Index	**404,700**	**32**	**33**	**−44**	**−17**	**−5**
Burglary	83,900	11	32	−37	−6	5
Larceny-theft	278,100	41	34	−45	−19	−8

Table 6.1 *(Continued)*

Most Serious Offense	2006 Estimated Number of Juvenile Arrests	Percent of Total Juvenile Arrests		Percent Change		
		Female	Under Age 15	1997–2006	2002–2006	2005–2006
Property Crime Index *(continued)*						
Motor vehicle theft	34,600	17	23	−53	−28	−8
Arson	8,100	14	58	−22	−5	0
Nonindex						
Other assaults	249,400	34	39	2	5	−1
Forgery and counterfeiting	3,500	33	11	−59	−34	−20
Fraud	8,100	34	15	−31	−14	−5
Embezzlement	1,400	45	4	3	−3	20
Stolen property (buying, receiving, possessing)	21,300	15	25	−45	−12	1
Vandalism	117,500	13	41	−14	10	11
Weapons (carrying, possessing, etc.)	47,200	10	33	−10	31	2
Prostitution and commercialized vice	1,600	74	14	15	16	9
Sex offense (except forcible rape and prostitution)	15,900	10	47	−16	−18	−9
Drug abuse violations	196,700	16	15	−11	1	2
Gambling	2,200	3	15	−43	20	−14
Offenses against the family and children	5,200	37	31	−48	−40	−6
Driving under the influence	20,100	23	3	1	−8	9
Liquor laws	141,400	36	9	−15	−5	9
Drunkenness	16,300	25	11	−30	−7	12
Disorderly conduct	207,700	33	39	7	8	0
Vagrancy	5,000	30	33	−36	4	10
All other offenses (except traffic)	386,000	27	25	−19	−3	2
Suspicion (not included in totals)	500	22	22	−74	−72	−15
Curfew and loitering	152,900	31	27	−31	6	4
Runaways	114,200	57	33	−45	−11	−2

- In 2006, there were an estimated 60,700 juvenile arrests for aggravated assault. Between 1997 and 2006, the annual number of such arrests fell 21%.

- Between 1995 and 2004, juvenile robbery and aggravated assault arrests declined substantially (down 44% and 23%, respectively). However, in the next two years, while juvenile aggravated assault arrests continued to fall (slightly), juvenile arrests for robbery increased (11% in 2005 and 19% in 2006).

- In 2006, females accounted for 17% of juvenile Violent Crime Index arrests, 32% of juvenile Property Crime index arrests, and 16% of juvenile drug abuse arrests.

- In 2006, youth under the age of 15 accounted for about one-third of all violent (29%) and property crime (33%) arrests.

NOTE: Detail may not add to totals because of rounding.
DATA SOURCE: *Crime in the United States 2006*.Washington, DC: Federal Bureau of Investigation, 2007, tables 29, 32, 34, 36, 38 and 40. Arrest estimates were developed by the National Center for Juvenile Justice.
Snyder, Howard N. *Juvenile Arrests 2006*. Washington, DC: OJJDP Juvenile Justice Bulletin, November 2008, p.3. (NCJ 221338)

sanctioned for status offenses, meaning they tend to be brought into the juvenile justice system more readily for committing these acts than do boys (Davis, 2007, p.409).

 Status offenses include actions such as running away, habitual truancy, violating curfew and early substance use, including alcohol.

We will only briefly mention these offenses here, since many were already discussed in previous chapters.

Running Away

The runaway problem was discussed in Chapter 5. However, running away is a status offense in most communities, so the juvenile justice system has jurisdiction in the matter and can act "in the best interest of the child." In 2006 an estimated 114,200 arrests were made of youths for running away, a 2 percent decrease from 2005, and a 45 percent decrease since 1997. Fifty-seven percent of the arrests involved females, and 33 percent involved juveniles under age 15 (Snyder, 2008, p.3).

Truancy

Truancy was first discussed in Chapter 4 as a risk factor for delinquency and has been identified as one of the top ten problems in our nation's schools, with absentee rates as high as 30 percent in some cities. Truancy is the most frequent status offense for those under age 15. Although national data regarding truancy rates and numbers are limited, some data indicates that truancy peaks around grade 9 (ages 14–15), with the number of truants declining after age 16 (Heilbrunn, 2007, p.3). Since most states have set the upper age of mandatory school attendance at 15, meaning once a child turns 16 they may voluntarily withdraw from or "drop out" of school, some researchers hypothesize that the decline in truancy rates for 16–18 year olds is likely partially attributable to the fact that those students most prone to truancy are more apt to drop out completely once they reach the mandatory attendance age (Heilbrunn, p.3). Students who have withdrawn from school cannot be counted as truant.

Curfew Violations

One of the most common status offenses is curfew violation. In 2006 an estimated 152,900 juvenile arrests were made for curfew and loitering violations, a decrease of 31 percent from 1997 but an increase of 4 percent from the previous year (Snyder, 2008, p.3). Twenty-seven percent of curfew arrests involved juveniles under age 15, and 31 percent involved females.

According to Ward, Jr. (2000, p.17): "For over a century, American communities have imposed juvenile curfews to help maintain order and reduce crimes committed by youths." McDowall et al. (2000, p.76) note: "Between 1990 and 1995, 60 percent of the 200 largest American cities enacted a new curfew statute or revised an existing one."

The effectiveness of curfew laws is controversial. A press release by the National League of Cities states: "The overwhelming majority of cities with curfews say the curfews are effective in improving safety in several areas: combating juvenile crime (effectiveness reported by 97 percent of respondents), fighting truancy (96 percent of respondents), making streets safer (95 percent of respondents) and reducing gang violence (98 percent of respondents) ("Cities Say Curfews Help Reduce Gang Activity and Violent Crime," 2001, p.1).

However, McDowall et al. (2000, pp.88–89) contend: "Our analysis provides, at best, extremely weak support for the hypothesis that curfews reduce juvenile crime rates. Of the offense and victimization measures, only burglary, larceny and simple assault arrests significantly decreased after cities adopted curfew statutes. . . . Any influence of the curfews appeared only for revised statutes, however, and new laws were ineffective in reducing offending or victimization."

In addition, some parents and organizations such as the American Civil Liberties Union have taken curfew ordinances to court, claiming that they violate students' and parents' constitutional rights. It is claimed that curfews are age discrimination in its purest form and that curfews undermine parental authority, are ineffective and punish law-abiding teenagers. In October of 1998 a U.S. Fourth Circuit Court of Appeals held in *Schleifer v. City of Charlottesville* that Charlottesville, Virginia's curfew was not a violation of the child's or the parents' rights. This case was appealed all the way to the Supreme Court, which in 1999 denied the request to review the case.

Early Substance Use

Drug and alcohol use continue to be a major source of arrests of juveniles. In 2006, an estimated 196,700 juvenile arrests were made for drug abuse violations (an increase of 2 percent from 2005 levels), 141,400 arrests were made for liquor law violations (an increase of 9 percent from 2005), and 20,100 arrests were made involving juveniles driving under the influence (an increase of 9 percent from 2005) (Snyder, 2008, p.3).

The most frequent self-reported offense for those 16 and older is liquor law violations. Table 6.2 summarizes students' reported use of alcohol and drugs. Beer consumption held a slight edge over wine cooler and liquor consumption, and marijuana was clearly the most popular illicit drug. Note that reported use in 2006–07 of alcohol and drugs is down across the board from the 1996–97 levels.

One concern with underage drinking involves the growing body of evidence linking alcohol with adolescent violence. Although studies demonstrating a relationship between alcohol use by juveniles and adolescent violence are not new, recent data has confirmed that youth who often engage in underage drinking are significantly more likely to commit violence *while sober* than nondrinking youth (Felson et al., 2008, p.119).

A growing concern is **binge drinking**, which is the consumption of large quantities of alcohol within a short period of time. Such rapid ingestion of alcohol causes fast intoxication and can lead to alcohol poisoning, in which the body's breathing and gag reflexes become severely impaired. While no standard definition exists regarding how much alcohol over how long a time frame constitutes a "binge," a common amount used in the United States is five drinks for adult males and four drinks for adult females within a two- to three-hour time

Table 6.2 Students Reporting Use of Alcohol and Drugs by Grade Level of Respondent and Frequency of Use, 1996–97, 2001–02 and 2006–07

Annual Use[a]	1996–97	2001–02	2006–07
Any alcohol	58.3%	50.4%	43.5%
Grades 6 to 8	44.7	34.0	30.6
Grades 9 to 12	71.0	65.0	59.8
12th grade	76.5	72.3	68.8
Beer	46.9	37.2	34.0
Grades 6 to 8	33.2	22.5	22.8
Grades 9 to 12	59.6	50.3	48.3
12th grade	65.3	57.6	56.5
Wine coolers, breezers	43.6	37.9	32.4
Grades 6 to 8	33.6	25.7	21.1
Grades 9 to 12	52.9	48.8	46.7
12th grade	55.4	53.6	54.6
Liquor	39.9	32.7	30.1
Grades 6 to 8	23.7	15.4	16.8
Grades 9 to 12	54.9	48.1	46.9
12th grade	62.3	59.4	57.4
Any illicit drugs	30.1	22.3	19.2
Grades 6 to 8	20.7	11.9	12.0
Grades 9 to 12	38.9	31.6	28.3
12th grade	41.6	37.4	33.1
Marijuana	25.6	19.5	15.2
Grades 6 to 8	14.7	8.3	7.3
Grades 9 to 12	35.8	29.4	25.2
12th grade	39.4	35.7	30.5
Cocaine[b]	4.5	3.7	4.0
Grades 6 to 8	3.0	2.1	2.3
Grades 9 to 12	5.9	5.1	6.2
12th grade	7.0	7.1	8.2
Uppers (stimulants)	7.7	4.8	5.0
Grades 6 to 8	4.9	2.4	2.6
Grades 9 to 12	10.3	7.0	8.0
12th grade	10.7	8.5	9.1
Downers (depressants)	5.7	4.8	5.1
Grades 6 to 8	4.0	2.4	2.8
Grades 9 to 12	7.2	6.9	8.0
12th grade	7.4	8.1	9.1
Inhalants	8.0	4.8	5.5
Grades 6 to 8	8.9	4.9	5.1
Grades 9 to 12	7.1	4.6	6.0
12th grade	5.8	4.3	5.6

Table 6.2   *(Continued)*

Annual Use[a]	1996–97	2001–02	2006–07
Hallucinogens[c]	6.6	4.0	3.4
Grades 6 to 8	3.6	1.9	1.9
Grades 9 to 12	9.5	5.9	5.2
12th grade	11.7	8.3	6.4
Heroin	2.7	2.2	2.6
Grades 6 to 8	2.4	1.5	1.7
Grades 9 to 12	3.1	2.9	3.7
12th grade	3.4	3.7	4.3
Steroids	NA	2.5	2.7
Grades 6 to 8	NA	1.9	1.9
Grades 9 to 12	NA	3.0	3.6
12th grade	NA	3.4	4.1
Ecstasy	NA	NA	3.6
Grades 6 to 8	NA	NA	2.0
Grades 9 to 12	NA	NA	5.6
12th grade	NA	NA	6.8
OxyContin	NA	NA	3.9
Grades 6 to 8	NA	NA	2.1
Grades 9 to 12	NA	NA	6.2
12th grade	NA	NA	7.1
Crystal methamphetamine	NA	NA	3.0
Grades 6 to 8	NA	NA	2.1
Grades 9 to 12	NA	NA	4.1
12th grade	NA	NA	4.8

[a]Used one or more times in the past year.
[b]Includes crack.
[c]Includes LSD and PCP.
SOURCE: PRIDE Surveys. *2006–2007 PRIDE Surveys National Summary, Grades 6 through 12.* Bowling Green, KY: PRIDE Surveys, 2008, pp.288, 289. Table adapted by SOURCEBOOK staff.

span. These amounts can be particularly dangerous to younger people, as blood alcohol content (BAC) is influenced by body mass. A binge can quickly raise a person's BAC to 0.20, which can prove fatal for first-time drinkers. According to the Centers for Disease Control and Prevention (2008), approximately 90 percent of all alcohol consumed by Americans under the legal drinking age of 21 is in the form of binge drinks, with some reports of children as young as 13 engaged in binge drinking.

One problem associated with alcohol and drugs is the **rave**, an all-night party generally with loud techno music, dancing, drinking and doing drugs. Ecstasy or MDMA is the drug of choice at raves, but LSD is making a comeback and is often used in combination with Ecstasy. Johnson (2001, p.186) reports: "The number one cause of deaths for persons attending raves is not drug overdoses, but DUI related traffic crashes."

The National Center for Juvenile Justice (Griffin and Torbet, 2002, p.109) cautions: "Drug users between the ages of 12 and 17 are more than 5 times as likely to shoplift, steal or vandalize property as non-users in that age range, 9 times as likely to steal cars or commit armed robbery, and 19 times as likely to break and enter or burglarize." White et al. (2002, p.131) also studied the proximal effects of alcohol and drug use on adolescent illegal activity. Analysis of four years of longitudinal data involving 506 adolescent males from the Pittsburgh Youth Study revealed that participants reported committing offenses against persons more often than general theft under the influence of alcohol or drugs: "Aggressive acts were more often related to self-reported acute alcohol use than to marijuana use. Those who reported committing illegal acts under the influence reported committing offenses with other people and being arrested more often than those who did not. Offenses under the influence were more prevalent among heavier alcohol and drug users, more serious offenders, more impulsive youth, and youth with more deviant peers."

 Arrests for the status offenses of running away, violating curfew and underage drinking have all declined since 1997, but arrests for liquor law and curfew violations have shown a one-year increase from 2005 to 2006.

Other Problem Behaviors

Two areas also of concern to the juvenile justice system are disorderly youths in public places and computer delinquents.

Disorderly Youths in Public Places   Disorderly youths may be engaged in status offenses as just discussed. Scott (2001, pp.1–2) cites these additional disorder and youth-related problems: graffiti, intimidation by youth gangs,

© Michael Newman/PhotoEdit

The American Bar Association supports decriminalizing status offenses such as smoking cigarettes.

loud car stereos, open-air drug dealing, panhandling, rave parties, reckless bicycle riding and skateboarding, shoplifting, street cruising, truancy, under-age drinking and vandalism. He (p.5) notes that such problem behaviors most commonly occur at shopping malls, at plazas in business districts, at video arcades, in public parks, on school grounds, in apartment complex common areas, at public libraries and at convenience stores and fast-food restaurants. Scott (p.3) suggests: "Whether the conduct is deemed disorderly depends on many factors, including the youths' specific objectionable behavior, the youths' ages, the complainants' tolerance levels, the community norms, and the specific times and places where the problem occurs."

A strikingly different problem is posed by youths who sit alone and use their computers to commit offenses.

The Computer Delinquent   Bowker (2000, p.7) cites several examples of juveniles pleading guilty to using computers to trespass by hacking into others' computer systems, to counterfeit money on a home computer, to traffic in child pornography on the Internet and to steal passwords from Internet providers. He estimates that during 2002, 45 million youths used the Internet. Juveniles can easily commit a five-figure high-tech embezzlement. They can disrupt traffic signals, floodgates and power grids. They can also cause expensive systems to crash, resulting in large capital outlays to restore them. In addition, there are jurisdictional concerns as juvenile hackers can cross state and even international borders.

Scott (2001, p.9) explains: "Persons involved in computer crimes acquire their interest and skills at an early age. They are introduced to computers in school, and their usual 'career path' starts with illegally copying computer programs. Serious offenders then get into a progression of computer crimes including telecommunications fraud (making free long distance calls), unauthorized access to other computers (hacking for fun and profit) and credit card fraud (obtaining cash advances, purchasing equipment through computers)."

Juvenile Delinquents and Delinquency

A juvenile **delinquent** is a youth who commits an act that would be a crime were it to be committed by an adult. Reflecting the rehabilitative philosophy of juvenile justice and the hope that many, if not most, wayward youth can be

---

A KEY ISSUE

Disagreement exists regarding how much emphasis should be placed on the formal handling of status offenders. The Juvenile Justice and Delinquency Prevention (JJDP) Act of 1974 officially decriminalized status offenses and mandated the deinstitutionalization of status offenders (DSO), requiring the removal from correctional or other detention facilities of youths being held for status offenses. One argument behind this stance was that the labeling effect on such youths, by being identified and treated as "offenders," was so stigmatizing that the end result of the system's response did more harm than good to these juveniles.

The other side of the issue, however, is that these status offenses are, technically and legally, violations of the law and that a formal response by the system is warranted and justified, particularly in light of evidence that such behaviors have been found to be precursors for more serious offending.

How much discretion should be allowed when dealing with status offenders? Should status offenders be handled within the juvenile justice system? What should be done with chronic status offenders?

redirected away from a life of offending, the term *delinquent* is intended to avoid stigmatizing youths as criminals and should *not* be applied to status offenders. Thus *delinquency* is the term used in juvenile justice to replace *criminality*. Table 6.3 summarizes high school seniors' self-reported involvement in certain delinquent activities. The adult (criminal) equivalent is given in parentheses. As noted, the most frequently engaged in delinquent behavior by self-report is shoplifting.

Table 6.3 High School Seniors Reporting Involvement in Selected Delinquent Activities in Past 12 Months, United States, Selected Classes 1991–2003

Delinquent Activity	Class of 1991 (N=2,569)	Class of 1994 (N=2,645)	Class of 1997 (N=2,638)	Class of 2000 (N=2,204)	Class of 2003 (N=2,517)
Assault					
Hit an instructor or supervisor?					
Not at all	97.0	97.0	96.4	97.1	96.8
Once	1.6	1.5	1.8	1.5	1.1
Twice	0.7	0.9	0.8	0.4	0.9
3 or 4 times	0.2	0.2	0.3	0.4	0.2
5 or more times	0.6	0.4	0.8	0.6	1.0
Hurt someone badly enough to need bandages or a doctor?					
Not at all	87.1	86.6	85.4	88.1	88.0
Once	8.2	7.5	8.9	7.3	5.6
Twice	2.3	2.5	2.7	2.0	3.1
3 or 4 times	1.1	2.1	1.6	1.1	1.7
5 or more times	1.3	1.4	1.6	1.5	1.6
Used a knife or gun or some other thing (like a club) to get something from a person?					
Not at all	96.6	95.2	95.5	97.2	96.1
Once	1.6	2.4	1.5	1.1	1.5
Twice	0.6	0.9	1.2	0.6	0.9
3 or 4 times	0.3	0.7	1.0	0.4	0.8
5 or more times	0.9	0.8	0.8	0.8	0.7
Larceny-Theft					
Taken something not belonging to you worth under $50?					
Not at all	68.1	69.3	65.8	69.5	72.3
Once	13.7	13.1	12.5	12.3	13.4
Twice	7.7	6.6	9.3	7.4	5.8
3 or 4 times	4.1	5.7	5.9	5.0	4.0
5 or more times	6.5	5.3	6.4	5.8	4.4

Table 6.3   *(Continued)*

Delinquent Activity	Class of 1991 (N=2,569)	Class of 1994 (N=2,645)	Class of 1997 (N=2,638)	Class of 2000 (N=2,204)	Class of 2003 (N=2,517)
Taken something not belonging to you worth over $50?					
Not at all	89.9	89.0	87.2	87.5	90.4
Once	4.6	5.1	6.3	5.6	4.3
Twice	2.1	2.1	2.6	2.5	1.6
3 or 4 times	1.7	1.4	1.6	1.6	1.3
5 or more times	1.8	2.3	2.3	2.9	2.4
Shoplifting					
Taken something from a store without paying for it?					
Not at all	68.9	69.7	66.6	71.3	73.2
Once	11.9	11.5	11.4	11.4	12.1
Twice	7.4	6.9	7.3	6.3	5.4
3 or 4 times	5.3	5.2	7.4	3.9	4.0
5 or more times	6.5	6.7	7.2	7.0	5.2
Auto Theft					
Taken a car that didn't belong to someone in your family without permission of the owner?					
Not at all	93.8	94.1	93.9	94.8	94.7
Once	3.3	3.0	3.4	2.7	2.3
Twice	1.2	1.3	1.2	1.2	1.1
3 or 4 times	1.0	0.8	0.6	0.6	0.7
5 or more times	0.7	0.7	0.9	0.7	1.2
Taken part of a car without permission of the owner?					
Not at all	93.7	94.3	94.6	94.9	94.5
Once	3.3	2.9	2.2	3.0	2.8
Twice	1.3	1.0	1.4	1.1	1.1
3 or 4 times	0.6	0.8	0.9	0.4	0.7
5 or more times	1.0	1.0	0.9	0.6	0.8
Trespass					
Gone into some house or building when you weren't supposed to be there?					
Not at all	75.7	75.2	75.3	77.3	77.0
Once	10.8	11.2	10.5	10.3	10.5
Twice	6.7	6.5	7.0	6.7	6.8
3 or 4 times	3.4	4.1	3.8	2.9	3.2
5 or more times	3.6	3.0	3.5	2.8	2.5

(continued)

Table 6.3   *(Continued)*

Delinquent Activity	Class of 1991 (N=2,569)	Class of 1994 (N=2,645)	Class of 1997 (N=2,638)	Class of 2000 (N=2,204)	Class of 2003 (N=2,517)
Arson					
Set fire to someone's property on purpose?					
Not at all	97.9	96.8	96.9	97.2	96.2
Once	1.1	1.7	1.7	1.3	1.6
Twice	0.4	0.5	0.4	0.8	0.9
3 or 4 times	0.1	0.5	0.2	0.2	0.3
5 or more times	0.5	0.5	0.7	0.5	1.1
Vandalism					
Damaged school property on purpose?					
Not at all	87.2	86.2	84.8	86.5	86.8
Once	6.5	6.5	7.7	7.3	6.3
Twice	3.0	3.5	3.1	3.5	3.9
3 or 4 times	1.3	2.0	2.2	1.5	1.4
5 or more times	2.0	1.9	2.2	1.4	1.6
Damaged property at work on purpose?					
Not at all	93.4	94.4	93.3	92.8	93.2
Once	3.2	2.3	2.8	3.8	3.3
Twice	1.3	1.5	1.7	1.4	1.5
3 or 4 times	0.8	0.9	1.0	0.8	1.1
5 or more times	1.3	1.0	1.1	1.1	1.0
Arrest					
Been arrested and taken to a police station?					
Not at all	X	91.1	90.6	90.9	92.0
Once	X	5.5	5.6	5.3	4.5
Twice	X	1.7	1.9	1.8	1.9
3 or 4 times	X	1.0	1.1	1.2	0.7
5 or more times	X	0.8	0.9	0.8	0.9

[a]This question was omitted from schools in California beginning in 1997.
SOURCE: Lloyd D. Johnston, Jerald G. Bachman, and Patrick M. O'Malley, *Monitoring the Future 1991*, pp.106–109; *1993*, pp.107–110; *1995*, pp.107–110; *1997*, pp.105–107; *1999*, pp.106–108 (Ann Arbor, MI: Institute for Social Research, University of Michigan); Jerald G. Bachman, Lloyd D. Johnston, and Patrick M. O'Malley, *Monitoring the Future 1992*, pp.106–109; *1994*, pp.106–109; *1996*, pp.103–105; *1998*, pp.105–107; *2000*, pp.107–109 (Ann Arbor, MI: Institute for Social Research, University of Michigan); and data provided by the Monitoring the Future Project, Survey Research Center, Lloyd D. Johnston, Jerald G. Bachman, and Patrick M. O'Malley, Principal Investigators. Table adapted by SOURCEBOOK staff. Reprinted by permission.

A CAUTION ABOUT STATISTICS AND JUVENILE CO-OFFENDING

While it is tempting, almost comforting, to place a high degree of faith in statistics—indeed, this chapter presents an ample amount of them—students are well advised to be cognizant of some potential limitations of these numbers, particularly as applied to juvenile offending:

> Juveniles who commit crimes typically commit them in the company of their peers. This basic fact has been regularly reported in the literature since the late 1920s. Nevertheless, with rare exceptions, contemporary research focuses almost exclusively on juvenile delinquents as individual actors. Indeed, police records tend to undercount co-offending, and published crime rates rarely take co-offending into account. . . . Yet co-offenders provide a basis of multiple reports of single crime events. Not only are those who first offended before age 13 most likely to be co-offenders, but also the sizes of their offending groups (from 2 to 30 in the current study) tend to further exaggerate the contributions of youthful offenders to crimes. This exaggeration seems to contribute to a fear of youths that may be counterproductive. (McCord and Conway, 2005, p.1)

So what does this mean? If four youth team up to commit a single burglary and all four are taken into custody and entered into the system as "four juvenile arrests" in the category of burglary, this co-offending event has resulted in a significantly skewed statistic. Yes, four juveniles were involved, and four arrests were made, but the offense was a single event, not four separate and distinct delinquent offenses. Thus, looking solely at number of arrests, particularly when it pertains to juvenile offenders, can present a very different picture from what the true level of crime and victimization is in society. In the example just provided, one could assume (incorrectly) that crime was four times higher than it actually is, based solely on the number of arrests. In other words, when looking at the number of juvenile arrests made, consider how such co-offending can relate to the number of actual offenses committed and the likelihood that actual crime levels are different than those implied by the "single offender" arrest statistic.

Although violent juvenile crime is certainly a valid concern to society and generates sensational media headlines, by far the most common acts of delinquency are in the form of property crime.

Property Offenses Committed by Juveniles

Both official statistics and self-reports indicate juveniles are heavily involved in property offenses, with more than one-fourth of all persons arrested in 2007 for property crimes being younger than 18 (*Crime in the United States, 2007*).

 The most frequent delinquency offenses are property crimes, with larceny-theft being the most common.

Larceny-Theft   Larceny-theft is the most frequent offense for which juveniles are arrested. Shoplifting accounts for much of the larceny-theft figures. In 2006, an estimated 278,100 juvenile arrests were made for larceny-theft, a 45 percent decrease from 1997 (Snyder, 2008, p.3). Forty-one percent of those arrested were female, and 34 percent were under age 15. Time-of-day analysis shows that shoplifting incidents peak between 3 P.M. and 6 P.M., for both male and female juvenile offenders, regardless of whether it is a school or nonschool day (Snyder and Sickmund, 2006, p.89).

Burglary   Burglary is a crime of opportunity usually committed for quick financial gain, often to support a drug habit. It is the most accessible route to money for unemployed juveniles. In 2006, an estimated 83,900 juvenile arrests were made for burglary, an increase of 5 percent over 2005 arrest data (Snyder, 2008, p.3).

Steven Puetzer/Getty Images

Shoplifting is a common form of delinquent behavior. Some youths shoplift because they have no money to purchase wanted items. Others shoplift for the thrill of it.

Snyder (p.7) observes: "Unique in the set of Property Crime Index offenses, the juvenile arrest rate for burglary declined almost consistently and fell substantially between 1980 and 2006, down 69%."

Motor Vehicle Theft   In 2006 an estimated 34,600 juvenile arrests were made for motor vehicle theft, a decrease of 53 percent from 1997. Nearly one-fourth (23 percent) of those arrested were under age 15; 17 percent were female (Snyder, 2008, p.3). According to Snyder (p.7): "The juvenile arrest rate for motor vehicle theft more than doubled between 1983 and 1990, up 137%. After the peak years of 1990 and 1991, the juvenile arrest rate for motor vehicle theft declined substantially and consistently through 2006."

Vandalism   Vandalism is usually a mischievous, destructive act done to get attention, to get revenge or to vent hostility. Children sometimes send messages of personal problems by acting out through vandalism. Destructive behavior can occur because children lack ways of communicating a need for help. Graffiti and tagging are prevalent forms of vandalism in many areas and are often associated with, but not always related to, gang activity. In 2006, an estimated 117,500 juvenile arrests were made for vandalism, a 21 percent decrease since 1991.

This vandalized car in the South Bronx depicts graphically the broken window theory: "Untended property becomes fair game for people out for fun or plunder." If it appears that no one cares—if broken windows go unfixed—vandalism and crime will flourish.

Arson   Arson, like vandalism, sends a message through a delinquent act. For many children setting fires is a symbolic act, often a symptom of underlying emotional or physical stress. Data from the FBI shows that, of all persons arrested for arson in 2007, 47.4 percent were juveniles, and among those juveniles, 59 percent were under age 15 (*Crime in the United States, 2007*). However, as with many aspects of juvenile justice, terminology is different when the age of the firesetter is factored in, with "child firesetter" used to refer to persons age 12 or younger, "adolescent firesetter" used for those age 13 to the age of majority and "arsonist" for anyone older than the legal age (Putnam and Kirkpatrick, 2005, p.2).

A distinction is made in the literature between *fireplay*, the term used to describe the relatively normal curiosity and fascination young children have with fire that carries a low level of intent to inflict harm and an absence of malice, and *firesetting*, which is associated with a higher level of intent and degree of malice and in which the youths are viewed "as willful actors who consistently use fire as an instrument of purposeful action" (Putnam and Kirkpatrick, p.2). According to the U.S. Fire Administration (2006, p.1): "For fires coded as child play and not intentional, 84 percent involved firesetters under the age of 10." An estimated 13,900 such fireplay events were reported in 2002, which caused 210 deaths, 1,250 injuries and $339 million in direct damage (U.S. Fire Administration, p.1).

Children who do not abandon normal childhood experiments with fire often are crying for help, using fire as an expression of their stress, anxiety and anger. What turns these troubled youths into repeat firesetters is positive reinforcement for their incendiary activities. Firesetting provides a sense of power and control. Juvenile firesetters often take out their hostility on school property. The U.S. Fire Administration (p.1) reports that delinquent firesetters are teens who commonly have a history of truancy, gang membership, antisocial behavior or substance abuse. The National Fire Academy (NFA) conducts a Juvenile Firesetter Intervention Specialist (JFIS) training program for any practitioner who interacts with children involved in firesetting or arson behaviors. Information on the curriculum is available through the U.S. Fire Administration's Web site (http://www.usfa.dhs.gov/).

The Decline in Arrests of Juveniles for Property Crimes   As with most of the status offense categories, arrests of juveniles for property crimes have decreased over the past decade, in some cases by a significant margin.

 Arrests for larceny-theft, burglary, motor vehicle theft, vandalism and arson declined from 1997 to 2006, although data also show a one-year increase in juvenile arrests for burglary and vandalism (from 2005 to 2006).

Whether the upward trend in arrests for burglary and vandalism continue, or whether this one-year period represents an anomaly, remains to be seen. But for the moment, arrests for most types of juvenile property offenses appear to be on the decline.

Violent Crime Committed by Juveniles

The FBI's Violent Crime Index includes murder and nonnegligent manslaughter, forcible rape, robbery and aggravated assault. An estimated one in eight violent crimes in 2006 were committed by juveniles, a figure that has remained fairly constant in recent years (Snyder, 2008, p.4): "Clearance data show that the proportion of violent crimes that law enforcement attributes to juveniles has . . . [held] between 12% and 13% from 1996 through 2006." The Federal Interagency Forum on Child and Family Statistics (2008) reports: "One measure of youth violence in society is the rate of serious crimes by youth perpetrators. In 2005, the rate of serious violent crime offenses was 17 crimes per 1,000 juveniles ages 12–17, totaling 437,000 such crimes involving juveniles. While this is somewhat higher than the 2004 rate of 14 crimes per 1,000 juveniles, it is significantly lower than the rate of 52 crimes per 1,000 juveniles in 1993."

The daily pattern of juvenile violent crime varies between school and nonschool days, with violent crime by juveniles peaking between 3 P.M. and 4 P.M. on school days and then gradually tapering off to the low point at 6 A.M. (Snyder and Sickmund, 2006, p.85). Not to diminish the importance of curfew laws, but this finding has important policy implications for communities looking for ways to lower their incidents of juvenile violent crime, suggesting that afterschool programs hold a higher crime reduction potential than do juvenile curfews (p.86).

Murder   Murder is the most serious, yet least often committed, violent crime. An estimated 1,310 juvenile arrests were made in 2006 for murder and nonnegligent manslaughter, a number that accounted for 10 percent of all arrests made for murder during 2006 (Snyder, 2008, pp.3, 4). As part of the upward trend in overall violence that occurred throughout the nation during the 1980s and into the 1990s, the juvenile arrest rate for murder more than doubled from

1980 to 1993. Since the mid-1990s, murders by juveniles have mostly declined, but from 2004 to 2006 arrest rates increased slightly. Snyder (p.6) notes: "The growth in the juvenile murder arrest rate between 2004 and 2006 returned to near its 2002 level; but even with this increase, the rate in 2006 was 73% below its 1993 peak."

Forcible Rape   The juvenile forcible rape rate has continued to decline over the past decade. In 2006 an estimated 3,610 juvenile arrests were made for forcible rape, with 36 percent of those arrested under age 15 (Snyder, 2008, p.3). Only 2 percent of juveniles arrested for forcible rape were female. The 2006 juvenile arrest rate for this violent offense was 10 percent lower than the 2005 rate, 20 percent lower than the 2002 rate and 31 percent lower than the 1997 rate (p.3).

According to Snyder and Sickmund (2006, p.87): "Sexual assaults by juvenile offenders spike at 8 A.M. and 3 P.M. on both school and nonschool days and [also] at noon on nonschool days." In other words, school days show two spikes in juvenile sexual assault activity, whereas nonschool days show three. However, violent sexual assaults by juveniles are most likely to occur between 2 P.M. and 5 P.M., particularly on school days (p.87). Juvenile sex offenders will be discussed in more detail later in the chapter.

Robbery   The juvenile arrest rate for robbery declined during much of the 1980s, but then began increasing again in 1988, peaking in the years of 1994 and 1995. Although the overall juvenile robbery arrest rate dropped 16 percent between 1997 and 2006, data for recent years show the arrest rates for this violent crime by juveniles to be on the rise again. In 2006, an estimated 35,040 juvenile arrests were made for robbery, an increase of 34 percent from 2002 rates and an increase of 19 percent from 2005 rates (Snyder, 2008, p.3). The time-of-day pattern for juvenile robberies closely follows the adult robbery pattern, peaking at 9 P.M. on both school and nonschool days (Snyder and Sickmund, 2006, p.87).

Aggravated Assault   As with juvenile arrests for murder and rape, arrests of juveniles for aggravated assault increased significantly during the 1980s and into the early 1990s, peaking in 1994, at which time they began a fairly steady, consistent descent. In 2006, an estimated 60,770 juvenile arrests were made for aggravated assault, a 21 percent decrease since 1997 but a 2 percent increase over 2005 rates (Snyder, 2008, pp.3, 6). Juvenile aggravated assault peaks at 3 P.M. on school days and at 8 P.M. on nonschool days (Snyder and Sickmund, 2006, p.87).

The Uncertain Trend in Juvenile Arrests for Violent Index Crimes   While juvenile arrests for property crimes have clearly shown a decrease in recent years and certainly over the past decade, any trend in juvenile arrests for violent crime during this time period is less clear. While the overall arrest rates for juveniles involved in violent crime have dropped since peaking in the mid-1990s, juvenile arrests for violence increased in 2005 and 2006 (Snyder, 2008, p.4).

 Arrests for violent juvenile crime dropped from the mid-1990s to the mid-2000s, but showed a slight upward trend in 2005 and 2006.

Profile of Delinquency

No single type of personality is associated with delinquency. However, some characteristics are common among delinquents. Those who become delinquent are more likely to be socially assertive, defiant, ambivalent about authority, resentful, hostile, suspicious, destructive, impulsive and lacking in self-control. They typically are doing poorly in school, skip classes often or have dropped out altogether. In short, they possess many of the risk factors and few of the protective factors discussed in Chapter 4.

Age Trends

Crime is often said to be a young person's activity. Indeed, arrest statistics show most offenders eventually "age out" of crime. Delinquency rates tend to increase dramatically as age increases, peaking in the mid- to late teens. Arrest data show that the intensity of criminal behavior slackens after the teens and continues to decline with age. Table 6.4 summarizes the arrest data for 2007 by age. Note the arrest figures in the columns for 17- and 18-year-olds and how, for many offenses, these are the ages for which the greatest number of arrests were made during 2007. Also keep in mind that the ages above 25 are grouped into 5-year cohorts, so although the raw numbers exceed those of the teenage columns, these values (e.g., 25–29, 30–34, etc.) combine five distinct ages into one number. Assuming the arrests were distributed fairly evenly across the five ages in each batch (which, of course, they aren't, but consider they are for comparison purposes), if one divides those values by 5, it becomes evident that the peak arrest numbers for most offenses occur for those persons in their late teens.

Female Delinquents

The profile of delinquency has changed in the past decade to include more females. According to Snyder (2008, p.8), 29 percent of juvenile arrests in 2006 involved females. Whereas arrests of juvenile males in 2006 had declined in

---

DELINQUENCY: A PASSING PHASE OR A PATHWAY TO ADULT CRIMINALITY?

Research shows most youthful offending is best defined as "adolescent limited" (AL), meaning the participation in low levels of delinquent activity is a relatively normal behavior for teens, and society can expect these "offenders" to grow out of their delinquent behavior as they mature (Moffitt, 1993). It is hypothesized that those youth on the AL trajectory come into delinquency more as a function of the natural transitions that occur during puberty. As such, AL offenders are highly likely to desist in their delinquent behavior as they mature—hence the label "adolescent limited" (Wright et al., 2008).

The trajectory that is more concerning is the "life-course persistent" (LCP) pathway, which involves a relatively small percentage of youth who, in early childhood, show a tendency toward antisocial behavior. These youth demonstrate an extremely stable pattern of maladaptive behavior by the time they enter adolescence. Although the delinquent activity of both AL and LCP offenders may be quite similar during adolescence, the underlying causes of their behavior are notably different:

Life-course-persistent offenders show longstanding patterns of antisocial behavior that appear to be rooted, at least in part, in relatively stable psychological attributes that are present early in development and that are attributable to psychopathology, deficient socialization or neurobiological anomalies. Adolescence-limited offending, in contrast, is driven by forces that are inherent features of adolescence as a developmental period, including susceptibility to peer pressure . . ., sensation-seeking, experimentation with risk, a tendency to discount the future, and impulsivity. All of these developmentally driven forces abate as individuals mature into adulthood. (Scott and Steinberg, 2008, p.54)

Table 6.4 Arrests by Age, 2007 (11,936 agencies; 2007 estimated population 225,518,634)

Offense Charged	Total All Ages	Ages under 15	Ages under 18	Ages 18 and Over	Under 10	10–12	13–14	15	16	17	18	19	20	21
TOTAL	10,698,310	461,937	1,649,977	9,048,333	13,357	93,571	355,009	326,311	405,753	455,976	509,517	518,623	481,599	442,744
Total percent distribution[1]	100.0	4.3	15.4	84.6	0.1	0.9	3.3	3.1	3.8	4.3	4.8	4.8	4.5	4.1
Murder and nonnegligent manslaughter	10,082	103	1,011	9,071	1	6	96	131	294	483	736	687	593	583
Forcible rape	17,132	914	2,633	14,499	8	235	671	447	576	696	829	790	736	766
Robbery	96,720	5,601	26,324	70,396	72	784	4,745	5,353	7,229	8,141	8,590	7,236	5,620	4,579
Aggravated assault	327,137	13,662	43,459	283,678	460	3,320	9,882	8,146	10,231	11,420	12,448	12,564	12,253	12,949
Burglary	228,846	18,589	61,695	167,151	631	3,939	14,019	12,580	14,498	16,028	17,104	13,729	11,120	9,217
Larceny-theft	897,626	71,314	229,837	667,789	1,804	15,542	53,968	45,808	54,513	58,202	57,221	46,250	37,423	31,665
Motor vehicle theft	89,022	4,917	22,266	66,756	33	512	4,372	5,181	6,143	6,025	5,874	4,873	4,070	3,674
Arson	11,451	3,204	5,427	6,024	349	1,013	1,842	926	720	577	517	420	312	282
Violent crime[2]	451,071	20,280	73,427	377,644	541	4,345	15,394	14,077	18,330	20,740	22,603	21,277	19,202	18,877
Violent crime percent distribution[1]	100.0	4.5	16.3	83.7	0.1	1.0	3.4	3.1	4.1	4.6	5.0	4.7	4.3	4.2
Property crime[2]	1,226,945	98,024	319,225	907,720	2,817	21,006	74,201	64,495	75,874	80,832	80,716	65,272	52,925	44,838
Property crime percent distribution[1]	100.0	8.0	26.0	74.0	0.2	1.7	6.0	5.3	6.2	6.6	6.6	5.3	4.3	3.7
Other assaults	983,964	70,038	181,378	802,586	2,194	17,638	50,206	35,952	39,029	36,359	32,356	32,319	32,468	34,893
Forgery and counterfeiting	78,005	294	2,353	75,652	26	56	212	281	599	1,179	2,538	3,476	3,393	3,204
Fraud	185,229	886	5,690	179,539	56	132	698	867	1,464	2,473	4,473	5,865	6,330	6,217
Embezzlement	17,015	49	1,288	15,727	6	12	31	58	396	785	1,200	1,192	1,065	944
Stolen property; buying, receiving, possessing	92,215	4,136	16,889	75,326	79	667	3,390	3,509	4,366	4,878	5,773	5,251	4,481	3,929
Vandalism	221,040	34,342	84,744	136,296	1,668	8,647	24,027	16,723	17,187	16,492	13,852	11,560	9,127	8,739
Weapons; carrying, possessing, etc.	142,745	10,577	33,187	109,558	438	2,524	7,615	6,251	7,604	8,755	9,517	8,640	7,320	7,085
Prostitution and commercialized vice	59,390	147	1,160	58,230	16	14	117	184	315	514	1,890	2,327	2,238	2,309

(continued)

Table 6.4 *(Continued)*

Offense Charged	Total All Ages	Ages under 15	Ages under 18	Ages 18 and Over	Under 10	10–12	13–14	15	16	17	18	19	20	21
Sex offenses (except forcible rape and prostitution)	62,756	5,574	11,575	51,181	264	1,525	3,785	2,037	1,983	1,981	2,437	2,331	2,056	1,980
Drug abuse violations	1,386,394	21,506	147,382	1,239,012	273	2,207	19,026	25,053	40,562	60,261	84,597	84,102	76,405	69,504
Gambling	9,152	226	1,584	7,568	7	12	207	283	428	647	705	664	557	447
Offenses against the family and children	88,887	1,237	4,205	84,682	112	234	891	804	1,026	1,138	1,796	1,909	2,095	2,405
Driving under the influence	1,055,981	398	13,497	1,042,484	196	16	186	537	3,169	9,393	23,954	33,125	37,157	53,215
Liquor laws	478,671	9,592	106,537	372,134	115	619	8,858	16,210	30,465	50,270	80,215	84,253	69,117	12,190
Drunkenness	451,055	1,400	12,966	438,089	75	82	1,243	2,119	3,118	6,329	12,727	14,163	14,210	21,096
Disorderly conduct	540,270	57,602	153,293	386,977	1,147	13,136	43,319	31,964	33,452	30,275	24,582	21,580	19,872	24,730
Vagrancy	25,631	904	2,924	22,707	15	142	747	766	859	395	1,143	938	770	800
All other offenses (except traffic)	2,948,031	69,448	284,096	2,663,935	2,244	12,002	55,202	57,709	72,163	84,776	102,335	118,273	120,744	125,274
Suspicion	1,589	78	303	1,286	0	15	63	55	104	66	108	106	67	68
Curfew and loitering law violations	109,815	28,949	109,815	-	456	4,751	23,742	25,435	30,467	24,964	–	–	–	–
Runaways	82,459	26,250	82,459	-	612	3,789	21,849	20,942	22,793	12,474	–	–	–	–

[1]Because of rounding, the percentages may not add to 100.0.

[2]Violent crimes are offenses of murder and nonnegligent manslaughter, forcible rape, robbery, and aggravated assault. Property crimes are offenses of burglary, larceny-theft, motor vehicle theft, and arson.

SOURCE: FBI Uniform Crime Reports 2007, Table 38. http://www.fbi.gov/ucr/cius2007/data/table_38.html

every offense category from 1997 levels, female juveniles showed increased arrests in the categories of simple assault, weapons, drug abuse violations, liquor law violations, DUI and disorderly conduct. In fact, female juvenile arrests for DUI increased 39 percent between 1997 and 2006; male juvenile arrests for DUI dropped 2 percent during this same time period (p.8).

Girls have traditionally entered the juvenile justice system through their involvement in status offenses. Violence by adolescent girls often results from a combination of victimization, substance abuse, economic conditions and dysfunctional family systems. Researchers have linked the violence perpetuated against females to these girls' increased involvement in violent crime; that is, females are becoming offenders in response to their own victimization. Such research supports the theory that violence perpetuates violence.

Some researchers contend that the recent increase in arrests is not so much a reflection of an actual increase in delinquent activity by girls as it is an indication of a change in response by the system to female delinquency. Zahn et al. (2008, p.15), in studying trends in violence by teenage girls, found: "Available evidence based on arrest, victimization, and self-report data suggests that although girls are currently arrested more for simple assaults than previously, the actual incidence of their being seriously violent has not changed much over the last two decades. This suggests that increases in arrests may be attributable more to changes in enforcement policies than to changes in girls' behavior. Juvenile female involvement in violence has not increased relative to juvenile male violence. There is no burgeoning national crisis of increasing serious violence among adolescent girls."

Minority Offenders

A concern throughout the justice system—for both adults and juveniles—is the percentage of minorities involved relative to their proportions in the general population. The issue of disproportionate minority contact (DMC) was introduced in Chapter 1. Here, consider how DMC manifests itself in terms of number of youths arrested because, as in previous years, juvenile arrests in 2006 disproportionately involved racial minorities (Snyder, 2008, p.9). In 2006 17 percent of the total juvenile population in the United States was Black; however, of all juvenile arrests for violent crime, 51 percent involved Black youths. For property crime arrests, 31 percent involved Black youth.

REALITY CHECK

Despite the ostensible belief that we should strive for gender equality, our society still retains different standards and expectations regarding acceptable behavior for boys and girls. Zahn et al. (2008, p.7) note how family dynamics may play a role in the gender differences in juvenile arrests for assault: "Parents have different expectations about their sons' and daughters' obedience to parental authority, and these expectations may affect how the justice system responds to a girl's behavior when she 'acts out' within the home. Research indicates that girls fight with family members or siblings more frequently than boys, who more often fight with friends or strangers."

Thus, we can conclude that official arrest data are both a function of actual involvement in crime and how our society, through the justice system, responds to that involvement. Such disparities are observed not only between genders but also between racial and ethnic groups.

Co-Offending

Much juvenile crime involves co-offending, meaning more than one offender is engaged in a single offense event: "Offenders age 13 and under are more likely to commit crimes in pairs and groups than are 16- and 17-year-old offenders. About 40 percent of juvenile offenders commit most of their crimes with others. Co-offenders are also more likely than solo offenders to be recidivists. . . . Co-offending actually may increase the likelihood that offenders will commit violent crimes. When young offenders affiliate with offenders who have previously used violence, the result appears to be an increase in the likelihood that they will subsequently commit a violent crime" (McCord and Conway, 2005, p.ii).

Serious, Chronic and Violent Juvenile Offenders

Serious, chronic and/or violent juvenile offenders are often transferred out of the juvenile justice system to the criminal justice system. The likelihood of such transfers increase with increased frequency of offending, increased severity of offending and increased offender age. However, it is still important for those working in juvenile justice to be familiar with this population.

- A **serious juvenile offender** has been convicted of a Part I offense as defined by the FBI Uniform Crime Reports, excluding auto theft, petty theft/larceny or distribution of a controlled dangerous substance.
- A **serious child delinquent** is between the ages of 7 and 12 and has committed one or more homicides, aggravated assaults, robberies, rapes or serious arsons.
- A **chronic juvenile offender** has a record of five or more separate charges of delinquency, regardless of the offenses' gravity.
- A **violent juvenile offender** has been convicted of a violent Part I offense, one against a person rather than property, and has a prior adjudication of such an offense, or is a youth who has been convicted of murder.

Most serious offenders are also chronic or violent offenders, and some are both chronic and violent as illustrated by the Venn diagram in Figure 6.1.

Serious or chronic offenders are typically from low-income families, are rated troublesome by teachers and peers between the ages of 8 and 10, have poor school performance by age 10, are adjudicated a delinquent before age 13 and have a sibling convicted of a crime.

Youth Violence: A Report of the Surgeon General (2001, p.4) identifies two general onset trajectories for youth violence: "Youths who become violent before about age 13 generally commit more crimes, and more serious crimes, for a longer time. These young people exhibit a pattern of escalating violence through childhood, and they sometimes continue their violence into adulthood." These youth are the *serious child delinquents*.

 The two general onset trajectories for youth violence are *early*, in which violence begins before puberty, and *late*, in which violence begins in adolescence.

Serious Child Delinquents

A key finding of the Office of Juvenile Justice and Delinquency Prevention (OJJDP) Study Group on Serious and Violent Offenders—that most chronic

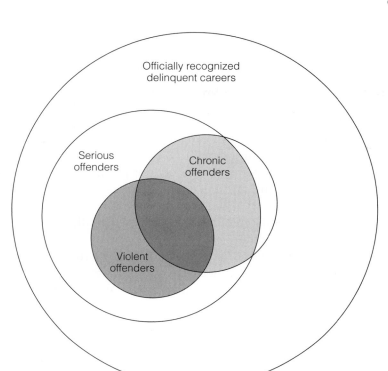

Figure 6.1   The Overlap of Serious, Chronic and Violent Offenders

SOURCE: Melissa Sickmund et al. *Juvenile Offenders and Victims: 1997 Update on Violence.* Office of Juvenile Justice and Delinquency Prevention, August 1997, p.25. (NCJ 165703)

juvenile offenders begin their delinquency careers before age 12 and some as early as age 10—led OJJDP in 1998 to establish its Study Group on Very Young Offenders. This study group found that for very young offenders, the most important risk factors are likely individual (e.g., birth complications, hyperactivity and impulsivity) or family related (e.g., parental substance abuse and poor childrearing practices).

Snyder et al. (2003) report on the most recent findings of this study group and note: "An increasing number of very young offenders, those between the ages of 7 and 12, are becoming involved with the juvenile justice system. According to the latest statistics, children younger than 13 are involved in almost 1 in 10 juvenile arrests. . . . Compared with juveniles who become delinquent in adolescence, very young delinquents are at greater risk of becoming serious, violent and chronic offenders. They are also more likely than older delinquents to continue their delinquency for extended periods of time" (p.1). The study group also suggests, however: "The good news is that prevention and intervention efforts focused on very young offenders could yield significant benefits. For these benefits to be realized, however, the unique challenges posed by these offenders must be addressed before their delinquency escalates" (Snyder at al., p.1).

Chronic Juvenile Offenders and Recidivism

Chronicity is a factor of both frequency and duration. Thus, *chronic* offenders are those who engage in numerous delinquent acts over a period of time. A review of studies of chronic offenders reveals several conclusions: "First, the proportions of chronic offenders vary considerably from study to study (from 7 percent to 25 percent). Second, the amount of crime accounted for by chronic offenders varies by ethnicity: nonwhite male chronic offenders account for a greater proportion of official serious delinquency. Third, there are large gender differences: chronic offending is lower in females than in males" (Kempf-Leonard et al., 2001, p.454).

The classic long-term study by Wolfgang et al. (1972) of delinquents in a Philadelphia birth cohort found that 6 to 8 percent of male juveniles were responsible for more than 60 percent of the serious juvenile offenses. This study also showed that by the third arrest, a delinquent was almost guaranteed a life of crime.

When analyzing chronic offending and trying to "predict" which youth are more likely to continue on a trajectory of delinquency, an important distinction to make is between the *number* of arrests and the *rate* of arrests, with rate incorporating a frequency metric. Noting that arrest *rates* are much more predictive of future arrests than are simple arrest *numbers*, Visher (1987, p.532) observes: "Juveniles in the Philadelphia study whose prior arrest rates were high were likely to continue to accumulate arrests (and by inference, to commit crime) at high rates. In other studies, high-rate adult offenders have histories of serious criminal activity, particularly violence, as juveniles."

Chronic juvenile offending is also referred to as juvenile **recidivism**. Identified risk factors for juvenile recidivism include low socioeconomic status; offense history such as earlier contact with the law, greater numbers of prior arrests and more serious prior crimes; family factors such as being physically or sexually abused, raised in a single-parent household or high number of prior out-of-home placements; and social risk factors such as associating with delinquent peers (Cottle et al., 2001, p.367). Indeed, as research by McCord and Conway (2005, p.1) found: "Analyses that consider both co-offending and age at first arrest show that youthful offenders are most at risk for subsequent crimes if they commit their crimes with accomplices." This same study revealed: "Violence appears to be learned in the company of others. Those who commit crimes with violent offenders, even if the group does not commit violent crimes, are likely to subsequently commit violent crimes" (p.1).

Violent Juvenile Offenders

A violent delinquent offender is a juvenile who commits a Part I offense against a person and who has a prior adjudication of such an offense, or a youth who has been convicted of murder. Violent youth crime increased significantly during the 1980s and early 1990s and decreased after 1994. *Youth Violence* (2001, p.1) notes: "Youth violence is a high-visibility, high-priority concern in every sector of U.S. society. No community, whether affluent or poor, urban, suburban or rural, is immune from its devastating effects. . . . Since 1993, when the epidemic peaked, youth violence has declined significantly nationwide, as signaled by downward trends in arrest records, victimization data and hospital emergency room records. But the problem has not been resolved."

Surveys consistently find about 30 to 40 percent of male youths and 15 to 30 percent of female youths report having committed a serious violent offense by age 17. Violence can be classified as instrumental or expressive. **Instrumental**

violence uses violence as a way to obtain material possessions, for example, forcefully robbing another youth to take a team jacket. **Expressive violence**, in contrast, is a way to vent emotions. Serious violence is part of a lifestyle that includes drugs, guns, precocious sex and other risky behaviors (*Youth Violence*).

 Most youth violence begins in adolescence and ends with the transition into adulthood.

Juvenile Sex Offenders A particularly challenging problem in juvenile justice concerns how to deal with juvenile sex offenders (JSOs), alternately called adolescent sex offenders (ASOs). Youthful sex offenders often begin sexual **deviance**[1] at a young age, and have committed multiple sex offenses and other delinquent acts. The victims are usually younger children the offenders know. In most cases, offenders did not resort to physical force in committing their offenses.

JSOs are differentiated in the literature from child sex offenders (CSOs) or children with sexual behavior problems, with CSOs generally 12 years old or younger. A JSO is a 13- to 18-year-old who has been charged with, convicted of or has disclosed involvement as a perpetrator of illegal sexual conduct (Harp, 2007). It is difficult to ascribe a profile to a "typical" JSO as they are a fairly diverse population. A quality that can be assigned to JSOs, however, is that most do not share the common central case characteristics of adult sex offenders. According to Harp, most JSOs, when compared to adult sex offenders, have fewer victims, fewer behaviors and a shorter duration of criminal behavior. They are less driven by sexual compulsivity, the motivation for their behavior tending instead to be curiosity and experimentation. Furthermore, no evidence has been found to suggest the majority of JSOs have a lifelong incurable sexual disorder.

A subset of JSOs is the female juvenile sex offender. According to Harp, the average age of a female JSO is 14.3 years, and the majority (78 percent) has been sexually abused, compared to 34 percent of male JSOs.

Predictors of Youth Violence

Recall from Chapter 4 the myriad risk factors for delinquency and adult criminality, such as early aggressive behavior and exposure to violence. Other predictors of violence are described by the American Psychological Association (n.d., p.6): "Social forces such as prejudice, economic inequality and attitudes toward violence in the mainstream American culture interact with the influences of early childhood to foster the expression of violence." The Association describes several developmental experiences that violent youths frequently share (p.21):

> Youths at greatest risk of becoming extremely aggressive and violent tend to share common experiences that appear to place them on a "trajectory toward violence." These youths tend to have experienced weak bonding to caretakers in infancy and ineffective parenting techniques, including lack of supervision, inconsistent discipline, highly punitive or abusive treatment, and failure to reinforce positive, pro-social behavior. These developmental deficits, in turn, appear to lead to poor peer relations and high levels of aggressiveness.

---

[1]Behavior that departs from the social norm.

Additionally, these youths have learned attitudes accepting aggressive behavior as normative and as an effective way to solve interpersonal problems. Aggressive children tend to be rejected by their more conforming peers and do poorly in school, including having a history of problems such as poor school attendance and numerous suspensions. These children often band together with others like themselves, forming deviant peer groups that reinforce antisocial behaviors. The more such children are exposed to violence in their homes, in their neighborhoods and in the media, the greater their risk for aggressive and violent behaviors.

The Influence of Neighborhood on Youth Violence   Researchers have begun to look more closely at how neighborhoods and the microsocial conditions therein influence violence levels in youth growing up in those environments. An extensive, 6-year longitudinal study of more than 6,000 children in various Chicago neighborhoods yielded some interesting results. Called the Project on Human Development in Chicago Neighborhoods (PHDCN), this study found (Liberman, 2007, p.3):

- Neighborhood conditions differ markedly for youth of different race and ethnicity, and those differing conditions in turn account for much of the racial and ethnic difference in youth violence rates.
- Youths in disadvantaged and unsafe neighborhoods are more likely to carry firearms illegally; exposure to firearms violence increases the risk that youths will themselves commit violence.
- Girls who mature early in disadvantaged neighborhoods are at greater risk for being involved in adolescent violence.

A SIGNIFICANT FINDING OF THE PHDCN

It is commonly thought that neighborhoods comprised mainly of racial or ethnic minorities experience higher levels of violence than do those that are primarily White. However, this stereotype does not always prove true, once data are collected and analyzed. The following excerpt from a report summary of the Project on Human Development in Chicago Neighborhoods (PHDCN) provides insight into youth violence in different types of neighborhoods (Liberman, 2007, pp.6–7):

Youth from different racial and ethic groups reported committing violence at different rates. African-American youth reported the most violence; Mexican-American youth reported the least, slightly below whites. Puerto Rican and "other" youths reported rates in between. Involvement in self-reported violence showed the familiar age-crime curve for all groups, peaking at about age 17. . . .

Why did youth of different ethnic groups commit more or less violence? Their neighborhood conditions, parents' marital status, and immigrant generation accounted for most of the difference. These factors accounted for more than 60 percent of the gap between African-American and white violence, and the entire gap between Mexican-Americans and whites.

Among these factors, neighborhood conditions had the strongest influence on youth violence, accounting for about 30 percent of the difference in violence between African-Americans and whites. Less violence was committed by youths living in neighborhoods with more first-generation immigrants and where more residents were employed in professional and managerial occupations.

Myths about Youth Violence

When considering youth violence, the tendency is to overgeneralize about research results. The surgeon general's report (*Youth Violence*, 2001, pp.5–6) presents and debunks several myths about youth violence:

- Most future offenders can be identified in early childhood.
- Child abuse and neglect inevitably lead to violent behavior later in life.
- African American and Hispanic youths are more likely to become involved in violence than other racial or ethnic groups.
- A new, violent breed of young superpredators threatens the United States.
- Getting tough with juvenile offenders by trying them in adult criminal courts reduces the likelihood that they will commit more crimes.
- Nothing works with respect to treating or preventing violent behavior.
- Most violent youths will end up being arrested for a violent crime.

System Response to Violent Juvenile Offenders

In response to the mounting evidence documenting how a large number of crimes are committed by a small number of repeat offenders, many of whom are also violent, the Office of Juvenile Justice and Delinquency Prevention (OJJDP), in the 1990s, instituted a Serious Habitual Offender Comprehensive Action Program (SHOCAP) aimed at youth violence. Although no longer a federally applied OJJDP program, many states have implemented their own versions of SHOCAP using recommendations of the original program, since many of the guidelines are still applicable for today's violent juvenile offenders.

The recommendations for *detention* are to establish a policy of separate and secure holding of all designated habitual offenders, to provide a special close custody classification for all designated violent offenders to protect staff and other correctional clients, and to monitor and record all activities and transactions of these offenders.

The recommendations at *intake* are mandatory holding of all identified violent offenders brought in on new charges, immediate notification of the prosecutor of the intake, and special follow-up and records preparation for the detention hearings.

The recommendations for *prosecution* of violent offenders are to file a petition (charges) with the court based on the highest provable offense, resist any pretrial release, seek a guilty plea on all offenses charged and vertically prosecute all cases (assign only one deputy district attorney to each case). Other recommendations include providing an immediate response to police and detention officials upon notification of the arrest, participating in interagency working groups and on individual case management teams, and sharing appropriate information with the crime analyst or official designated to develop and maintain profiles on violent offenders. A formal policy of seeking the maximum penalty for each conviction or adjudication should be established.

A Comprehensive Approach

All too often chronic, serious violent juvenile offenders "fall through the cracks" of the juvenile justice system because efforts are not coordinated. In response to rising numbers of habitually violent youths, the Colorado Springs Police Department instituted a Serious Habitual Offender/Directed Intervention (SHO/DI) Program aimed at this group of juvenile offenders. The program had three goals:

- To develop trust and cooperation between agencies serving juveniles
- To identify and overcome real and perceived legal obstacles to cooperative efforts
- To build a credible interagency information process to identify and track habitual juvenile offenders

The ultimate goal was to *incapacitate* repeat offenders, whether through detention, incarceration, probation or other means. One important program component was a court order signed by a juvenile judge allowing the police department to share information with other agencies in the juvenile justice system. Another important outcome of the program was a change in how the juvenile portion of the justice system was viewed. Traditionally juvenile matters received low priority. "Kiddy Court" was not taken seriously, and beginning lawyers were assigned to prosecute juveniles. This practice was changed with the institution of the SHO/DI Program.

The Public Health Model and the Juvenile Justice Perspective

One approach to youth violence is to view it not just as a problem to be dealt with by the juvenile justice system but as a threat to our national health. When violence is viewed in this way, it makes sense to adopt the approach used in our public health system. A basic principle of the public health response to problems is to focus resources on the areas of greatest need.

Another contribution from the public health model is the metaphor of **contagion** as a way to explain the spread of violence. Acts of violence tend to spread rapidly within high-risk areas or hot spots and within groups. Some criminologists find the source of high rates of violence in a subculture of violence that encourages people—young males in particular—to use physical force to command respect and settle conflicts. Others view violence as spreading through cycles of revenge and retaliation among perpetrators and victims. Research by McCord and Conway (2005, pp.10–11) illuminated some of the uncertainties surrounding a possible contagion effect among juvenile peers with respect to violent offending: "Committing a first offense with violent accomplices contributed to the likelihood that violent crimes would be committed, regardless of age at first arrest. That is, violent peers increase the likelihood that nonviolent offenders will commit violent offenses."

A barrier to implementing a public health approach is the distinct and opposing philosophical traditions of the two approaches. From the juvenile justice perspective, the most important fact about the social reality of violence in our society is that those who perpetrate violence are criminal offenders. The juvenile justice system has its roots in the adult criminal justice system, which is part of the classical tradition that conceives of human action as a product of rational and moral choice. Public health is rooted in positivist conceptions of human behavior as "caused" by external forces that, in principle, are subject to modification.

 The juvenile justice perspective on juvenile violence is that it is the result of youths' free choice and is to be punished as criminal. The public health perspective is that youths are victims of social forces and they are to be treated.

Are Delinquency and Youth Violence Inevitable?

Many people believe juvenile violence will be an unavoidable part of life in American society unless significant changes are made in how such youths are identified *before* they become seriously delinquent. Reasons for the increase in the seriousness of the offenses and the decrease in the offenders' age range from the problems of increasing gang activity and drug use in the elementary schools to the heightened level of violence in society in general and to increasing stress on families, especially in economically deprived areas. One primary reason for the rise in teen violence is the ready availability of handguns discussed in Chapter 8.

The juvenile justice system recognizes that some youthful offenders are simply criminals who happen to be young. Every experienced law enforcement officer has dealt with criminally hardened 13- or 14-year-olds. Although this group represents only a small fraction of our youths, they commit a large percentage of all violent crimes. Public safety demands that law enforcement recognize and respond to this criminal element. The challenge for the juvenile justice system is to identify this group of hard-core offenders and to treat them as adults, including providing for the use of juvenile offense records in adult sentencing. It is this group of hard-core offenders who often are responsible for the crime and violence found in the nation's schools and for the violence perpetrated by gangs. Gangs are the topic of the next chapter.

There is reason for hope, however, as the report by the surgeon general stresses: "Youth violence is not an intractable problem. We now have the knowledge and tools needed to reduce or even prevent much of the most serious youth violence" (*Youth Violence*, 2001, p.6).

 SUMMARY

- Status offenses include actions such as running away, habitual truancy, violating curfew and early substance use, including alcohol.
- Arrests for the status offenses of running away, violating curfew and underage drinking have all declined since 1997, but arrests for liquor laws and curfew violations have shown a one-year increase from 2005 to 2006.
- The most frequent delinquency offenses are property crimes, with larceny-theft being the most common.
- Arrests for larceny-theft, burglary, motor vehicle theft, vandalism and arson declined from 1997 to 2006, although data also show a one-year increase in juvenile arrests for burglary and vandalism (from 2005 to 2006).
- Arrests for violent juvenile crime dropped from the mid-1990s to the mid-2000s, but showed a slight upward trend in 2005 and 2006.

- The two general onset trajectories for youth violence are *early*, in which violence begins before puberty, and *late*, in which violence begins in adolescence.
- Most youth violence begins in adolescence and ends with the transition into adulthood.
- The juvenile justice perspective on juvenile violence is that it is the result of youths' free choice and is to be punished as criminal. The public health perspective is that youths are victims of social forces and they are to be treated.

DISCUSSION QUESTIONS

1. What are the most common status offenses in your community?
2. Do other countries have status offenses?
3. Do you believe status offenders should be treated the same as youths involved in serious, violent crimes?
4. Should the term *juvenile delinquency* encompass both those youths who commit status offenses and those who commit nonviolent crimes? Violent crimes?
5. How do you account for the decrease in arrests for status offenses? For property crimes?
6. To what do you attribute the racial disparity in youths arrested?
7. Do you think the developmental pathways have validity?
8. Have there been any instances of youths involved in serious, violent crime in your community during the past year?
9. Should parents and guardians be held legally responsible when a juvenile commits a violent crime? Why or why not?
10. For serious, violent crimes, such as armed robbery and murder, should the age of the offender be an issue?

REFERENCES

American Psychological Association. *Violence & Youth: Psychology's Response*, Vol. 1. Summary Report of the American Psychological Association Commission on Violence and Youth, no date.

Bowker, Arthur L. "The Advent of the Computer Delinquent." *FBI Law Enforcement Bulletin*, December 2000, pp.7–11.

Centers for Disease Control and Prevention. "Quick Stats: Binge Drinking." Online at http://www.cdc.gov/alcohol/quickstats/binge_drinking.htm. Page last modified August 6, 2008. Accessed November 18, 2008.

"Cities Say Curfews Help Reduce Gang Activity and Violent Crime." Washington, DC: National League of Cities News Fax, October 25, 2001.

Cottle, Cindy C.; Lee, Ria J.; and Heilbrun, Kirk. "Identifying Risk Factors for Juvenile Recidivism: A Meta-Analysis." *Criminal Justice and Behavior*, Vol. 28, No.3, 2001, p.367.

Crime in the United States, 2007. Washington, DC: U.S. Department of Justice, Federal Bureau of Investigation, September 2008.

Davis, Carla P. "At-Risk Girls and Delinquency." *Crime & Delinquency*, Vol. 53, No. 3, July 2007, pp.408–435.

Federal Interagency Forum on Child and Family Statistics. *America's Children in Brief: Key National Indicators of Well-Being, 2008.* Washington, DC: U.S. Government Printing Office, July 2008.

Felson, Richard B.; Teasdale, Brent; and Burchfield, Keri B. "The Influence of Being Under the Influence: Alcohol Effects on Adolescent Violence." *Journal of Research in Crime and Delinquency*, May 2008, pp.119–141.

Griffin, Patrick and Torbet, Patricia (eds.) *Desktop Guide to Good Juvenile Probation Practice.* Washington, DC: National Center for Juvenile Justice, June 2002.

Harp, Caren. "Tough Cases for Prosecutors: Adolescent Sex Offenders." Seminar D-4 presented at the 34th National Conference on Juvenile Justice, San Diego, CA: March 6, 2007.

Heilbrunn, Joanna Zorn. *Pieces of the Truancy Jigsaw: A Literature Review.* Denver, CO: National Center for School Engagement, January 2007.

Johnson, Matt. "Successful Rave Operations." *Law and Order*, October 2001, pp.184–188.

Kempf-Leonard, Kimberly; Tracy, Paul E.; and Howell, James C. "Serious, Violent and Chronic Juvenile Offenders: The Relationship of Delinquency Career Types to Adult Criminality." *Justice Quarterly*, September 2001, pp.449–478.

Liberman, Akiva. *Adolescents, Neighborhoods, and Violence: Recent Findings from the Project on Human Development in Chicago Neighborhoods.* Washington, DC: U.S. Department of Justice, National Institute of Justice, September 2007. (NCJ 217397)

McCord, Joan and Conway, Kevin P. *Co-Offending and Patterns of Juvenile Crime.* Washington, DC: U.S. Department of Justice, National Institute of Justice, Research in Brief, December 2005. (NCJ 210360)

McDowall, David; Loftin, Colin; and Wiersema, Brian. "The Impact of Youth Curfew Laws on Juvenile Crime Rates." *Crime & Delinquency*, January 2000, pp.76–91.

Moffitt, Terrie. "Adolescence-Limited and Life Course Persistent Antisocial Behavior: A Developmental Taxonomy." *Psychology Review*, Vol. 100, 1993, pp.674–701.

Putnam, Charles T. and Kirkpatrick, John T. *Juvenile Firesetting: A Research Overview.* Washington, DC: U.S. Department of Justice, Office of Juvenile Justice and Delinquency Prevention, May 2005. (NCJ 207606)

Scott, Elizabeth S. and Steinberg, Laurence. *Rethinking Juvenile Justice.* Cambridge, MA: Harvard University Press, 2008.

Scott, Michael S. *Disorderly Youth in Public Places.* Washington, DC: Office of Community Oriented Policing Services: Problem-Oriented Guides for Police Series, No. 6, September 2001.

Snyder, Howard N. *Juvenile Arrests 2006.* Washington, DC: OJJDP Juvenile Justice Bulletin, November 2008. (NCJ 221338)

Snyder, Howard N.; Espiritu, Rachele C.; Huizinga, David; Loeber, Rolf; and Petechuk, David. *Prevalence and Development of Child Delinquency.* Washington, DC: Office of Juvenile Justice and Delinquency Prevention, Bulletin Series, March 2003. (NCJ 193411)

Snyder, Howard N. and Sickmund, Melissa. *Juvenile Offenders and Victims 2006 National Report.* Washington,
DC: U.S. Department of Justice, Office of Justice Programs, Office of Juvenile Justice and Delinquency Prevention, March 2006.

U.S. Fire Administration. *Juvenile Firesetting: A Growing Concern.* Washington, DC: Department of Homeland Security, July 2006. (FA-307)

Visher, Christy. "Incapacitation and Crime Control: Does a 'Lock 'Em Up' Strategy Reduce Crime?" *Justice Quarterly*, December 1987, pp.513–543.

Ward, J. Richard, Jr. "Implementing Juvenile Curfew Programs." *FBI Law Enforcement Bulletin*, March 2000, pp.15–18.

White, Helene Raskin; Tice, Peter C.; Loeber, Rolf; and Strouthamer-Loeber, Magda. "Illegal Acts Committed by Adolescents under the Influence of Alcohol and Drugs." *Journal of Research in Crime and Delinquency*, May 2002, pp.131–152.

Wolfgang, Marvin; Figlio, Robert; and Sellin, Thorsten. *Delinquency in a Birth Cohort.* Chicago: University of Chicago Press, 1972.

Wright, John Paul; Tibbetts, Stephen G.; and Daigle, Leah E. *Criminals in the Making: Criminality across the Life Course.* Thousand Oaks, CA: Sage Publications, 2008.

Youth Violence: A Report of the Surgeon General. Rockville, MD: U.S. Department of Health and Human Services, Office of the Surgeon General, 2001.

Zahn, Margaret A.; Brumbaugh, Susan; Steffensmeier, Darrell; Feld, Barry C.; Morash, Merry; Chesney-Lind, Meda; Miller, Jody; Payne, Allison Ann; Gottfredson, Denise C.; and Kruttschnitt, Candace. *Violence by Teenage Girls: Trends and Context.* Washington, DC: U.S. Department of Justice, Office of Juvenile Justice and Delinquency Prevention, May 2008. (NCJ218905)

CASE CITED

Schleifer v. City of Charlottesville, 159 F.3d 843, 853 (4th Cir. 1998)

HELPFUL RESOURCE

Chesney-Lind, Meda and Shelden, Randall G. *Girls, Delinquency and Juvenile Justice*, 3rd ed. Belmont, CA: Wadsworth Publishing Company, 2003.

CHAPTER 7

Youth Gangs

THE EFFECTS OF VIOLENCE AND GANG ACTIVITY REVERBERATE BEYOND INDIVIDUALS, BEYOND A SINGLE PERPETRATOR OR A SINGLE VICTIM. WHEN A YOUNG MAN IS MURDERED, THE ENTIRE COMMUNITY FEELS THE LOSS. WHEN A YOUNG GIRL IS RAPED, THE ENTIRE NEIGHBORHOOD IS VIOLATED.

—ALBERTO R. GONZALES

© Robert Yager/Getty Images

A Los Angeles Playboy gang member flashes his hand sign while pointing a revolver loaded with hollow point bullets.

Do You Know?

■ What types of gangs exist and how they may be classified?

■ What gangs offer to youths?

■ What some causes of gangs are?

■ What membership in most gangs consists of?

■ What the three Rs of the gang culture are?

■ What other factors are important in the gang culture?

■ What activities youth gangs participate in?

■ How youth gangs acquire their power?

■ What might indicate youth gang activity?

■ What strategies to gang problems are being used? Which are most effective?

■ What a key impediment to dealing with youth gangs is?

Can You Define?

civil injunction	horizontal	socialized	turf
crew	prosecution	delinquency	vertical
gang	moniker	street gang	prosecution
graffiti	representing	tagging	youth gang

Chapter Outline

Introduction	*Peer Pressure and Ego Fulfillment*	Youth Gang Violence
Definitions	*Racism and Cultural Discord*	Youth Gangs and Drugs
Types of Gangs	*Socioeconomic Pressure*	Recognizing a Youth Gang Problem
Racial/Ethnic Gangs	*Socialized Delinquency*	*Identifying Gang Members*
Hybrid Gangs	Gang Organization—Leadership and Membership	*Gangs in Schools*
Girl Gangs	Gang Culture	Responding to an Existing Youth Gang Problem
Outlaw Motorcycle Gangs	*Gang Names*	*Suppression and Law Enforcement Efforts*
Prison Gangs	*Symbols*	*Arresting and Prosecuting Gang Members*
The Extent and Migration of Youth Gangs	*Clothing*	Youth Gang Prevention Efforts
Causes of Gangs: What Attracts Youths to Gang Membership?	*Communication Styles*	
Family Structure	*Tattoos*	
	Illegal Activities of Youth Gangs	

Introduction

Belonging to a gang is *not* illegal in this country; however, many of the activities that gangs participate in are illegal. Gangs commit shootings, assaults, robberies and other violent crimes; engage in extortion and other felonies; traffic in drugs; and generally terrorize neighborhoods. Previously loose-knit groups of juveniles and young adults who engaged in petty crimes have, over time, become powerful, organized gangs, representing a form of domestic terrorism. Gangs now exist in almost every community.

Data from the *2004 National Youth Gang Survey* (NYGS) estimate that 41 percent of youth gang members were juveniles and 59 percent were "young adults" age 18 and older (Snyder and Sickmund, 2006, p.83). Because this is a juvenile justice text, this chapter will strive to focus primarily on youth gangs comprised of members who are under age 18. Realistically, however, many gangs include both juvenile and young adult members; thus, maneuvering through this topic will necessitate traveling beyond the age boundaries set by conventional standards regarding juveniles to include some broader issues of gangs, irrespective of the age of their members.

Definitions

Everyone has a sense of what a gang is, yet no single, agreed-on definition has been developed to apply to gangs. In general, a **gang** is an ongoing group of people that have a common name or common identifying sign or symbol, form an allegiance for a common purpose and engage in unlawful or criminal activity. A **street gang** is a group of individuals who meet over time, have identifiable leadership, claim control over a specific territory in the community and engage in criminal behavior, either individually or collectively. They create an atmosphere of fear and intimidation in a community. The term **youth gang** is often used interchangeably with street gang and, in the context of juvenile justice, is preferred as it helps avoid any confusion between this type of gang and the adult criminal street gang.

A broadly applicable definition of street gangs has evolved from intense discussions among working groups of American and European gang researchers over six years in an assembly that has come to be known as the Eurogang program. The Eurogang consensus definition of a street gang is "any durable, street-oriented youth group whose own identity includes involvement in illegal activity" (Klein, 2007, p.18). The National Youth Gang Center (NYGC) defines a youth gang as "a self-formed association of peers having the following characteristics: three or more members, generally ages 12 to 24; a name and some sense of identity, generally indicated by such symbols as style of clothing, graffiti, and hand signs; some degree of permanence and organization; and an elevated level of involvement in delinquent or criminal activity" (Howell and Egley, 2008, p.1).

An important distinction must be made between youth gangs and delinquent groups. Research has shown that gang members engage in significantly more criminal behavior than members of delinquent groups; they have higher rates of police contact, more arrests and more drug-related offenses.

A KEY ISSUE: THE IMPORTANCE OF DEFINITIONS

Before a problem can be addressed and tackled, it must be defined. A key issue in combating youth gangs hinges on how they are defined. If they are broadly defined, the gang problem may appear to be gigantic. If narrowly defined, the problem may not seem significant. A uniform definition used by law enforcement, schools, parents and social workers would be of great benefit in efforts to understand the gang problem.

Types of Gangs

Contemporary gangs are more diverse, more dispersed and more dangerous than gangs of the past. Klein and colleagues have identified five types of gangs. Klein (2007, pp.54–55) notes:

> There is no *one* form of street gang. Gangs can be large or small, long term or short term, more or less territorial, more or less criminally involved, and so on. If one treats all gangs as being the same, then the treatment will often be wrong, perhaps even making things worse. . . . It is the fact of gang diversity itself that should make us cautious about generalizing too quickly about their nature. . . .
>
> "Traditional" and "nontraditional" gangs are the largest, longest-enduring, and most crime-producing gangs. They are not the most common form, but they best fit the media stereotype of large inner-city gangs with strong inter-gang rivalries and violent tendencies.
>
> "Compressed" gangs, primarily adolescent groups of 50 to 100 members and less than ten years' duration, are the most common, found in both large and small cities. Least common are "collective" gangs, rather amorphous, but large collections with little internal structure, sometimes held together by loose neighborhood ties and extensive drug dealing. The smallest in size of our five types, but the most tightly structured, is the "specialty" gang, which is not versatile like the other four types, but rather manifests a narrow pattern of criminal behavior. Drug gangs, robbery or burglary gangs, car theft gangs and skinheads are common examples.

Shelden et al. (2004, pp.42–43) offer another way of classifying gangs, describing the major types of gangs identified by various studies and different researchers nationwide:

 Gangs may be classified as hedonistic/social gangs, party gangs, predatory gangs, scavenger gangs, serious delinquent gangs, territorial gangs, organized/corporate gangs and drug gangs.

- *Hedonistic/social gangs*—only moderate drug use and offending, involved mainly in using drugs and having a good time; little involvement in crime, especially violent crime.
- *Party gangs*—commonly called "party crews"; relatively high use and sale of drugs, but their primary form of delinquency is vandalism; may contain both genders or may be one gender; many have no specific dress style, but some dress in stylized clothing worn by street gang members, such as baseball caps and oversize clothing; some have tattoos and use hand signs; their flexible turf is called the "party scene"; crews compete over who throws the biggest party, with alcohol, marijuana, nitrous oxide, sex, and music critical party elements.
- *Predatory gangs*—heavily involved in serious crimes (robberies, muggings) and the abuse of addictive drugs such as crack cocaine; may engage in selling drugs but not in organized fashion.
- *Scavenger gangs*—loosely organized groups described as "urban survivors"; prey on the weak in inner cities; engage in rather petty crimes but

sometimes violence, often just for fun; members have no greater bond than their impulsiveness and need to belong; lack goals and are low achievers; often illiterate with poor school performance.

- *Serious delinquent gangs*—heavy involvement in both serious and minor crimes, but much lower involvement in drug use and drug sales than party gangs.
- *Territorial gangs*—associated with a specific area or turf and, as a result, get involved in conflicts with other gangs over their respective turfs.
- *Organized/corporate gangs*—heavy involvement in all kinds of crime, heavy use and sale of drugs; may resemble major corporations, with separate divisions handling sales, marketing, discipline, and so on; discipline is strict, and promotion is based on merit.
- *Drug gangs*—smaller than other gangs; much more cohesive; focused on the drug business; strong, centralized leadership with market-defined roles. (The link between gangs and drugs is discussed later in the chapter.)

Criminologists have also classified gangs as cultural or instrumental. *Cultural gangs* are neighborhood centered and exist independently of criminal activity. *Instrumental gangs*, in contrast, are formed for the express purpose of criminal activity, primarily drug trafficking.

Delaney (2006, p.133) also notes that gangs can be differentiated in many ways: "Distinctions can be made based on such variables as age (e.g., a baby, posse or veteranos), race and ethnicity (Hispanic, African-American, Native American, or, in rare cases, mixed), gender composition (all males, all females, or mixed), setting (e.g., streets, prison or motorcycle), type of activity (e.g., drug sales protection, violence, turf defense, etc.), degree of criminality (e.g., minor or serious), and so on." Obviously, motorcycle and prison gangs include few, if any, juveniles. Therefore, the coverage of them will be quite cursory.

 Gangs may also be classified as racial/ethnic gangs, hybrid gangs, girl gangs, outlaw motorcycle gangs, and prison gangs.

Racial/Ethnic Gangs

Much has been written about the various racial/ethnic gangs in the United States. Among the most well known are African American gangs (Bloods, Crips, Vice Lords), Hispanic gangs (Latin Kings and Mara Salvatrucha 13), Asian gangs (Chinese, Filipino, Vietnamese, Hmong), and Indian Country gangs. An in-depth discussion of ethnic gangs is beyond the scope of this text. However, the following trends are noted in the most recently available *2005 National Gang Threat Assessment* (2008, p.v):

- Hispanic gang membership is on the rise. These gangs are migrating and expanding their jurisdictions throughout the country. Identification and differentiation of these gangs pose new obstacles for law enforcement, especially in rural communities.
- Migration of California-style gang culture remains a particular threat. The migration spreads the reach of gangs into new neighborhoods and promotes a flourishing gang subculture.

- Indian Country is increasingly reporting escalating levels of gang activity and gang-related crime and drug trafficking. The remote nature of many reservations and a thriving gang subculture make youths in these environments particularly vulnerable to gangs.

The literature on ethnic gangs is abundant, and the trends remain in evidence. However, two of the preceding trends deserve expansion.

Mara Salvatrucha (MS-13) The Mara Salvatrucha (MS-13) is considered by many gang experts to be America's most dangerous gang. *Mara* means group or "posse," and a *salvatrucha* is a "street-tough" Salvadoran. The number 13 is significant both as a common identifier for Southern California gangs and because the letter "M" is the thirteenth letter of the alphabet. The colors of MS-13 are the same as most of the Central American national flags: blue, gray, white, and black. Females are allowed to join MS-13 but must endure the same initiation ceremony as males, a violation ritual where several gang members beat the recruit to test his or her ability to take a beating. If a recruit fails the initiation rite of passage, he or she is murdered for lack of courage and spirit (Delaney, 2006).

MS-13 has migrated from El Salvador to Los Angeles and is currently spreading across the United States. The gang targets middle- and high-school students in recruiting efforts and is estimated to have 10,000 members operating in 42 states, with the largest clusters living in Los Angeles; Washington, DC; and the Mid-Atlantic region: "The gang's terrifying reputation includes a callous disregard for life and a willingness to use extreme violence with weapons ranging from machetes to semi-automatic rifles. Machetes, decapitations, and sexual violence against victims are common tools of intimidation" (McLemore, 2006). MS-13 has severed fingers of their rivals with machetes; brutally murdered suspected informants and witnesses; attacked and threatened law enforcement officers; committed rapes, assaults, break-ins, auto thefts, extortions and frauds across the United States; and been involved in drug and firearms trafficking, prostitution and money laundering.

The urgency of dealing with this gang is illustrated by the formation of the MS-13 National Gang Task Force, spearheaded by the FBI, whose goal is to decimate MS-13. The FBI has also established the Transnational Anti-Gang (TAG) initiative with partners in El Salvador's Policia Nacional Civil (PNC) to facilitate the sharing of valuable intelligence, a partnership that has already proven successful. The first joint operation conducted in late September 2007 resulted in the arrests of 10 violent MS-13 gang members, the seizure of firearms and the recovery of a 3-year-old child missing since his mother's death.

Native American Gangs Gang activity in Indian country is a relatively new phenomenon, and scant research has examined the extent and nature of such gangs. However, several studies have found that gangs are posing an increasing threat to tribal reservations.

Some reasons Native teens join gangs are similar to those of youth joining gangs in mainstream society: fragmented and dysfunctional families, poverty, substance abuse and the search to fit in and belong to a peer group. For youths in Indian Country: "Reservation gangs fill a cultural void by providing a sense of belonging and initiations similar to tribal rights of passage" (Peterson, 2008).

Other factors contributing to the proliferation and spread of Native American gangs include the frequency with which families move off and onto the reservation and a diminished connection of Indian youth to Native American culture and traditional kinship ties.

Hybrid Gangs

A new breed of increasingly violent street gangs appearing throughout the country are hybrid gangs, in which several small groups, some of them rivals, band together into one larger gang (Ortega and Calderoni, 2007). Members of hybrid gangs are generally young and particularly profit driven. They thrive in areas with relatively new gang problems and often include gangbangers who have migrated from larger cities. These gangs represent a "sea of change in gang culture" and bear little resemblance to traditional gangs. Unlike older gangs based on race or neighborhood loyalty, this new generation is singularly focused on making money from drugs, robbery and prostitution.

Girl Gangs

Although the number of female gangs is increasing, gangs are still predominately male. Three types of female gang involvement are: (1) membership in an independent gang, (2) membership in a male gang as a coed, and (3) membership in a female auxiliary of a male gang (Shelden et al., 2004, p.142). Most girls are found within the third type: "Female gangs have been around for nearly as long as male gangs. Despite the growing evidence for independent female gangs, most of them remain auxiliary to male gangs. Most researchers believe that 10 percent of all gang members are females. Female gang members are very capable of committing violent criminal acts but not in the same proportion as males" (Delaney, 2006, p.227).

The *2005 National Gang Threat Assessment* notes that young women continue to take active roles in gangs, assisting in the movement of drugs and weapons, and gathering intelligence from other gangs (p.v). A female gang may have a name affiliated with its male counterpart, such as the Vice Ladies (from the Vice Lords). These auxiliaries usually consist of sisters and girlfriends of the male gang members. The females often assist the male gang, serving as decoys for rival gang members, as lookouts during the commission of crimes or as carriers of weapons when a gang war is impending. They may also carry information in and out of prison and provide sexual favors (they are often drug dependent and physically abused).

A general consensus exists in the research literature that girls join gang life for the same reasons as their male counterparts—to meet basic human needs such as belonging/being a member of a family, self-esteem and protection (Shelden et al., p.175). "Some girls readily admit that they join because they are bored and look to gangs for a social life; they are looking for fun and excitement, and a means to find parties and boys" (Eghigian and Kirby, 2006, p.49). A review of research on girl gangs shows that some young women find themselves trapped in horrible social conditions "characterized by widespread poverty and racism" (Shelden et al., p.174).

While the most common age at which girls enter gangs is 11 or 12, with the prime age of initiation occurring between ages 13 and 14, Eghigian and Kirby (p.48) note: "It is not unheard of for girls to slide into gang involvement as early as age 8. Those who enter at this age and up to 10 years of age often have relatives who are gang members or have experienced a strong gang presence in their neighborhoods."

Delaney (p.227) points out: "The single fact that so many female gang members come from abusive and sexually exploitive environments is a strong reason for considering female gang membership a serious social problem. Most female gang members have children, and since the fathers generally refuse to take family responsibility, the fiscal burden is often shifted onto society in the form of welfare programs." Children who are born to young, unwed female gang members face an unfortunately high likelihood of growing up within the gang culture and eventually becoming gangbangers themselves (Eghigian and Kirby, p.48).

Outlaw Motorcycle Gangs

The major outlaw motorcycle gangs (OMGs) are the Hell's Angels, Bandidos, Outlaws and Pagans. These gangs' primary source of income is drug trafficking, but they are also involved in murder, assault, kidnapping, prostitution, money laundering, weapons trafficking, intimidation, extortion, arson and smuggling. The *2005 National Gang Threat Assessment* (p.v) reports that OMGs are expanding their territory and forming new clubs, as reflected in increased violence among them as they battle over territories.

Prison Gangs

Although prison gangs would seem to be more of a problem for corrections, the *2005 National Gang Threat Assessment* (2008, p.v) notes: "Prison gangs pose a unique threat to law enforcement and communities. Incarceration of gang members often does little to disrupt their activities. High-ranking gang members are often able to exert their influence on the street from within prison." In fact, prison provides a prime recruiting opportunity for some gangs. Indeed, inmates frequently report that the only way to survive the violence and victimization that persists behind bars is to join a gang for protection. Straub (2008a, p.4) contends: "A street culture has been created among young African-American men in which serving time in prison is normal and even valued."

Delaney (2006, p.27) notes: "Violence and angry confrontations directed against rivals on the street continue in prison. . . . Some prison gangs are very powerful and command respect among inmates and street gangsters alike. Prison gang leaders keep in contact with outside gangbangers in a number of ways, including through individuals who visit gang leaders in prison and receive commands; correctional officers and other staff members who have been bribed, coerced, or extorted; and direct contact with street gangsters via phone calls from prison gang leaders behind bars."

The Extent and Migration of Youth Gangs

The last quarter of the twentieth century saw significant growth in gang problems across the country. In the 1970s, less than half the states reported youth gang problems, but by the late 1990s, every state and the District of Columbia reported gang activity. During that same period, the number of cities report-ing youth gang problems mushroomed nearly tenfold. Delaney (2006, p.65) contends: "Gangs are so prevalent today that they have reached institutional status. . . . By the end of the twentieth century, gangs had proliferated in nearly all geographic areas of the United States. Gangs can be found in the suburbs, in small cities, and on Native-American reservations. Today, their numbers continue to grow, and street gangs will remain as a major social problem in American society for some time to come."

Gangs range in size from small groups of 3 to 5 up to several thousand. Nation-ally known gangs such as the Crips number around 50,000 and the Bloods num-ber about 20,000 to 30,000. Large gangs are normally broken down into smaller groups but are known collectively under one name. More than 90 percent of gangs have between 3 and 100 members, and only 4 percent have more than 100 mem-bers. The number of members in gangs in large cities ranges from 1,200 to 1,500.

From the 1970s to the mid-1990s, the number of jurisdictions reporting gang problems increased tremendously. In 1996 an estimated 846,000 youth gang mem-bers and more than 31,000 youth gangs were active throughout the United States, posing a significant problem, especially in large cities (Snyder and Sickmund, 2006, p.82). The numbers have since held fairly steady, if not receding slightly, with a current estimated 30,000 gangs, comprised of approximately 800,000 gang members, operating in communities throughout the country (Pistole, 2008).

According to the *Highlights of the 2006 National Youth Gang Survey* (NYGS), published by the Office of Juvenile Justice and Delinquency Prevention (OJJDP), the percentage of law enforcement agencies reporting gang problems in 2006 was 14.9 percent in rural counties, 32.6 percent in smaller cities, 51.0 percent in sub-urban counties and 86.4 percent in larger cities, with an overall percentage of 33.3 percent (Egley and O'Donnell, 2008). These percentages represent a decrease in reported gang problems from 2002 to 2006, for at the start of 2002, the overall percentage of law enforcement agencies reporting gang problems was 47.3 percent; 27.4 percent of rural counties reported a gang problem, smaller cities, 48.3 per-cent, suburban counties, 61.5 percent, and larger cities, 90.5 percent.

The gang problem is not restricted to metropolitan areas. As society in gen-eral has become more mobile, gangs and gang members have also increased their mobility, contributing to gang migration: "Like a cancer, gangs are spread-ing to communities across America. Gang violence has become a part of the daily lives of teachers and taxi drivers, police officers and pastors, parents and children" (Pistole). Whereas early gangs tended to exist primarily in large cities near the country's borders (Los Angeles, New York, Miami, Chicago), gangs are now sending members across the country and into the nation's heartland to take advantage of new territory, diminished competition from other gangs and law enforcement agencies with less experience in dealing with gang activity.

Causes of Gangs: What Attracts Youths to Gang Membership?

Two separate yet related questions are: (1) What causes gangs? and (2) Why do youths continue to join gangs? Myriad studies have identified causes for gangs and what attracts youths to join them.

Gangs offer their members a feeling of belonging and importance as well as protection from other youths. They may also provide financial power.

Gangs provide acceptance and protection to inner-city youth. Gangs offer a sense of belonging and importance to their members that society and family do not provide. Gang members gradually dissociate from social conformity and become responsible only to themselves and their group activities. Oft cited reasons for joining a gang are material reasons, recreation, a place of refuge and camouflage, physical protection, resistance against parents and/or society and a lack of commitment to community (Shelden et al., 2004, pp.77–78).

A pioneering work on gangs by Thrasher, *The Gang: A Study of 1,313 Gangs in Chicago* (1927), concluded that gangs resulted from a breakdown in social controls, particularly among newly arriving immigrants who settled in Chicago's ganglands. Gangs created a social order where none existed. This can be a partial explanation for why so many Asian gangs are currently forming across the country.

Using a multiple marginality framework, which introduces specific consideration of race/ethnicity in gang formation, Freng and Esbensen (2007) studied race and gang affiliation, focusing on the following variables: male, Black, Hispanic, single parent, highest parental education, ethnic identity, social isolation, parental attachment, parental monitoring, limited educational opportunities, school commitment, attitudes toward police, neutralization and street socialization. They report (pp.618–619): "The majority of multiple marginality concepts were found to be important predictors of gang membership (highest parental education, limited educational opportunities, school commitment, attitudes towards police, neutralization and street socialization). The ecological and economic factors, however, were not found to be significant except for parental education."

Table 7.1 summaries several theories as to why gangs exist.

 Similar to the risk factors for generalized delinquency, risk factors for gang involvement are grouped into five domains (Snyder and Sickmund, 2006, p.83):

- Individual—early delinquency, precocious sexual activity
- Family—single-parent households or other non-two-parent family structures, poverty, gang-involved family members, poor family management, problematic parent-child relations
- School—low academic achievement, truancy, negative labeling by teachers, feeling unsafe at school
- Peer—association with delinquent or antisocial peers
- Community—poverty, drug availability, firearm availability, gang presence in the neighborhood, low sense of attachment to the neighborhood, lack of a sense of safety

The more risk factors present, the greater the likelihood a youth will become gang involved (Snyder and Sickmund, p.84).

A longitudinal study of youth in Seattle found that those between the ages of 10 and 12 who had two or three identified risk factors were three times more

Table 7.1   Theories of Why Gangs Exist

Theory/Creator or Major Proponent	Premise
Social Disorganization Theory/Thrasher	Industrialization, urbanization and immigration break down institutional, community-based controls in certain areas. Local institutions in these areas (schools, families, churches) are too weak to give the people living there a sense of community. Consequently, within such environments, conventional values are replaced by a subculture of criminal values and traditions that persist over time, regardless of who moves into or out of the area.
Strain Theory/Merton	The lack of integration between culturally defined goals (professional success, wealth and status) and the legitimate, institutionalized means of achieving these goals imposes a strain on people, who may, as a result, react with deviant criminal behavior. Thus, people at an economic disadvantage are motivated to engage in illegitimate activities (perhaps because of the unavailability of jobs, lack of job skills, education and other factors).
Cultural-Deviance (Subcultural) Theory/Cohen	Working-class youth are ill-prepared for participation in middle-class institutions and thus become frustrated. This situation leads to reaction formation, which, in turn, fosters the development of a delinquent (gang) subculture, in which the values of middle-class society are turned upside down. These values enable youth to gain status and improved financial standing through nonutilitarian, malicious, negative behavior.
Social Learning Theory/Sutherland	Youth become delinquent through association with other delinquents and also through contact with social values, beliefs and attitudes that support criminal/delinquent behavior.
Social Bond (Control) Theory/Hirschi	Youths drift into gangs because of the limbo-like nature of adolescence—being suspended between childhood and adulthood, having greater expectations placed on them than when they were children, yet lacking the rights and privileges of adults. Proper socialization is essential at this critical juncture, which effectively "bonds" youth to society. What keeps people in check and away from deviant behavior is the social bond to society, especially the internalized norms of society.
Social Development Theory	Integrates social learning theory with control/bonding theory. The major cause of delinquency is a lack of bonding to family, school and prosocial peer groups coupled with the reinforcement of delinquent behavior. Looks at 17 risk factors (societal/cultural and individual/interpersonal) present before the onset of delinquency to determine whether and to what extent one is likely to become involved in persistent delinquent activity.
Labeling Perspective	Youths who are simply hanging out together may be referred to as a gang often enough that they come to feel as if they are a gang.
Critical/Marxist Perspectives	The capitalist political and economic system produces inequality. Those oppressed by capitalism engage in various types of crimes related to accommodation and resistance (predatory crime, personal crime) in an attempt to adapt to their disadvantaged positions and to resist the problems created by capitalist institutions.

SOURCE: Adapted from Randall G. Shelden et al. *Youth Gangs in American Society*. Belmont, CA: Wadsworth Publishing Company, 1997, pp. 28–49. Reprinted by permission.

likely to join a gang as were youths with one or no risk factors. Those with seven or more risk factors were 13 times more likely to become gang involved (Snyder and Sickmund, p.84). Furthermore, having risk factors across numerous domains increased the likelihood of gang membership more than a simple accumulation of risk factors in one area (p.84).

Gangs may result from a variety of personal, social and economic factors, including family structure and influences such as parental guidance and lack of responsibility, peer pressure and ego fulfillment, racism and cultural discord, socioeconomic factors and socialized delinquency.

Family Structure

Probably the most important factor in the formation of a gang member is family structure:

> Nearly every criminologist agrees that the family is probably the most critical factor related to crime and delinquency. In fact, for over 50 years research has shown that three or four family-related factors best distinguish the habitual delinquent from the rest of his or her peers. These factors include the affection of the parents toward the child (the lower the level of affection, the higher the rate of delinquency), the kind of discipline the parents use (those who use consistently harsh and physical discipline will produce the most habitual and violent delinquent), the prolonged absence of one or both parents (those from single parent households are more likely to become delinquent), and the degree of supervision provided by the parents (the lesser the amount of supervision, the higher the rate of delinquency). (Shelden et al., 2004, pp.203–204)

Chapter 4 discussed the importance of families in developing children's feelings of belonging and self-worth. If youths do not get this support at home or at school, they will seek it elsewhere. The largest draw a gang has for its young members is a sense of belonging, of importance, of family.

Researchers have found certain common threads running through most families that have hard-core gang members. A family containing gang members is quite often a racial minority on some form of government assistance. It often lacks a male authority figure. If a male authority figure is present, he may be a criminal or drug addict, therefore representing a negative role model. Typically, adult family members lack more than an elementary school education. Children live with minimal adult supervision. When a child from such a family first encounters law enforcement authorities, the dominant figure (usually the mother) makes excuses for the child, normally in the form of accusations against society. Thus children are taught early that they are not responsible for their actions and are shown how to transfer blame to society.

A second common type of family structure is one that may have two strong family leaders in a mother and father. Usually graduates from gangs themselves, they see little wrong with their children belonging to gangs. This attitude serves to perpetuate the traditional gang culture.

A third common family structure involves immigrant groups and parents who do not speak English. The children tend to adapt rapidly to the American way of life and, en route, lose respect for their parents and the traditions of their native culture. They quickly become experts at manipulating their parents, and the parents lose all control. This family structure is often seen with Asian gang members. It is important to recognize that many of these family structures overlap.

Peer Pressure and Ego Fulfillment

A natural part of adolescence is a shift from seeking the approval and acceptance of parents and teachers to seeking the approval and acceptance of one's peers. When a child's family has never been a true source of approval or acceptance, as is the case with many gang-members-to-be, the need for acceptance by peers is that much stronger. Consequently, the lure of the gang may be nearly irresistible, and the transition into gang life may occur more readily for these youths.

For some youths the prestige and recognition that come with gang affiliation fulfill an egotistic need that they cannot achieve through other, more mainstream, associations. They may see themselves as rebels, and the sense of danger and adventure inherent in gang activity satisfies a need to take risks. In fact biochemical research has shown that certain people thrive on the adrenaline rush that accompanies fear and risk-taking, and some researchers postulate that youths who are drawn to gangs may have a biological/chemical makeup that drives them to seek dangerous liaisons.

Racism and Cultural Discord

Racism played an early and important role in the formation of street gangs in California. Racism often results in a particular group banding together, lending support to one another and excluding all other groups, sometimes even seeking to harm members of other groups. Although racism is most often associated with White people showing prejudice against non-Whites, in reality racism refers to the belief that one's own ethnic group is superior to all others. Walker et al. (2007, p.386) contend that racial and ethnic differences exist in violent behavior among juveniles: "Data on homicide indicate that African American males have the highest offending rate, and self-reports on other types of violence reveal that Asians and whites have lower rates of offending than Native Americans, Hispanics and African Americans." A number of explanations exist for these differences, including involvement with delinquent peers and gangs (Walker et al.).

Socioeconomic Pressure

To some members, the gang is all about money and power and a chance to get out of the ghetto. Youth who do not have legitimate options for buying fancy clothes or cars may see gangs, crime and selling drugs as attractive alternatives. Such a perspective is supported by both the strain and cultural-deviance theories described previously in Table 7.1.

According to Delaney (2006, p.101): "Gang researchers and social policymakers have identified and discussed a number of traditional socioeconomic factors that impact on an individual's decision to join a gang. These factors are the shifting labor market, the development of an underclass (a nontraditional explanation, as the term *underclass* is a relatively new concept, but the conditions that led to the development of an underclass have traditional roots), poverty and the feminization of poverty, the breakdown of the nuclear family, lack of a quality education, and the gang's offering of acceptance, protection, and survival."

Socialized Delinquency

Socialized delinquency is common among lower-class children who have been frustrated or hurt by a predominantly middle-class society. To these youths socialized delinquency is not delinquency at all. It is delinquency only in terms of middle-class standards. When individuals behave in ways sanctioned by their

Table 7.2 Childhood Predictors of Joining and Remaining in a Gang

Risk Factor	Odds Ratio*	Risk Factor	Odds Ratio*
Neighborhood		Low school attachment	2.0
Availability of marijuana	3.6	Low school commitment	1.8
Neighborhood youth in trouble	3.0	Low academic aspirations	1.6
Low neighborhood attachment	1.5	**Peer group**	
Family		Association with friends who engage in problem behaviors§	2.0 (2.3)
Family structure†			
One parent only	2.4	**Individual**	
One parent plus other adults	3.0	Low religious service attendance	ns‡
Parental attitudes favoring violence	2.3	Early marijuana use	3.7
Low bonding with parents	ns‡	Early violence§	3.1 (2.4)
Low household income	2.1	Antisocial beliefs	2.0
Sibling antisocial behavior	1.9	Early drinking	1.6
Poor family management	1.7	Externalizing behaviors§	2.6 (2,6)
School		Poor refusal skills	1.8
Learning disabled	3.6		
Low academic achievement	3.1		

*Odds of joining a gang between the ages of 13 and 18 for youth who scored in the worst quartile on each factor at ages 10 to 12 (fifth and sixth grades), compared with all other youth in the sample. For example, the odds ratio for "availability of marijuana" is 3.6. This means that youth from neighborhoods where marijuana was most available were 3.6 times more likely to join a gang, compared with other youth.
†Compared with two-parent households.
‡ns = not a significant predictor.
§These factors also distinguished sustained gang membership (more than 1 year) from transient membership (1 year or less). For each factor, the number in parentheses indicates the odds of being a sustained gang member (compared with the odds of being a transient member) for youth at risk on that factor.
SOURCE: Karl G. Hill; Christina Lui; and J. David Hawkins. *Early Precursors of Gang Membership: A Study of Seattle Youth.* Washington, DC: OJJDP Juvenile Justice Bulletin, December 2001, p.4.

culture—the gang—they feel no guilt for their unlawful activities. The gang, in effect, becomes a surrogate family. Within this family, violence toward others is common. One reason for this is that gang members were often neglected or abused as children. Other factors can also help predict who might become a gang member. Table 7.2 presents childhood predictors of youths joining and remaining in a gang.

Gang Organization—Leadership and Membership

There is no such thing as a "typical" gang, and the degree of organization seen among different gangs is extremely varied. Mueller (2007) describes visualizing the overall gang problem as a pyramid: "The base is primarily made up of the unsophisticated, loosely organized gangs. In the middle of the pyramid are more structured gangs. And at the top is a relatively small number of highly sophisticated gangs that are involved in organized criminal activity." As a gang's degree of organization influences the behavior observed among its members, even low levels of organization having important implications regarding criminality: "Indeed, even incremental increases in gang organization are related to increased involvement in offending and victimization" (Decker et al., 2008, p.153).

Gang organization encompasses the structure of its leadership and subordinate members. Varying levels of member involvement can be found in most gangs.

 Most gangs contain leaders, hard-core members, regular members and fringe members or wannabes.

Gang leadership tends to be better defined and more clearly identifiable than leadership in other types of delinquent groups. The leaders are usually the oldest gang members and have extensive criminal records. They may surround themselves with hard-core members, giving orders and expecting unquestioned obedience. The hard-core members usually commit the crimes and are the most violent. Some have had to earn the right to become true gang members through some sort of initiation.

On the fringes of most gangs are youths who aspire to become gang members, frequently referred to as *wannabes*. They dress and talk like the hard-core members, but they have not yet been formally accepted into the gang. Figure 7.1 shows one common type of gang organization and illustrates how kids who start on the

Hard–Core

These youths comprise approximately 5 to 10 percent of the gang. They have been in the gang the longest and frequently are in and out of jail, unemployed and involved with drugs (distribution or use). The average age is early to mid–20s, but some hard–cores could be older or younger. Very influential in the gang.

Regular Members

Youths whose average age is 14 to 17 years, but they could be older or younger. They have already been initiated into the gang and tend to back up the hard–core members. If they stay in the gang long enough, they could become hard–core.

Claimers, Associates or "Wannabes"

Youngsters whose average age is 11 to 13 years, but age may vary. These are the youngsters who are not officially members of the gang, but they act like they are or claim to be from the gang. They may begin to dress in gang attire, hang around with the gang or write the graffiti of the gang.

Potentials or "Could Be's"

Youngsters who are getting close to an age at which they might decide to join a gang. They live in or live close to an area where there are gangs or have a family member who is involved with gangs. The potentials do not have to join gangs; they can choose alternatives and avoid gang affiliation completely. Generally, the further into a gang someone is, the harder it is to get out.

Figure 7.1 One Common Type of Gang Organization

outside of the box (potentials or "could be's") can "progress" inward to become hardened gang members.

Gangs usually adopt specific criteria for membership eligibility, and many gangs employ initiation rituals, often involving one or more criminal acts, as a prerequisite to membership.

Transforming a youth into a gang member involves slow assimilation. Once youths reach an age at which they can prove themselves to peer leaders within the gang, they may perform some sort of rite of passage or ceremony called "turning," "quoting" or "jumping in." Or they may be "courted in," simply accepted into the gang without having to prove themselves in any particular way. According to Shelden et al. (2004, p.69): "Most youth are informally socialized into the gang subculture from a very early age so that they do not so much join a gang, but rather evolve into the gang naturally. Actually turning or being jumped is little more than a rite of passage." Incidentally, some states have toughened their criminal statutes to make it a stronger felony for an adult to recruit a juvenile into a gang.

While much has been made of how difficult it is for youths to avoid the lure of gangs or to break free from them once they have joined, findings from numerous studies have failed to support these scenarios as reality. Molina (2007) notes: "It is not as difficult for adolescents to resist gang pressures as it is commonly believed. In most instances, adolescents can refuse to join gangs without reprisal. Marginal gang members can typically leave the gang without serious consequences." Snyder and Sickmund (2006, p.83) observe: "Gang membership tends to be short-lived, even among high-risk youth." Of the studies done on the typical length of gang membership, most conclude the majority of youths spend a year or less in a gang, with very few juveniles spending the bulk of their adolescent years as members of a gang.

Compared with other types of law-violating youth groups, gangs tend to have closer relational bonds and more continuous affiliation between members. Gang members also demonstrate associational patterns and bonds through certain identifying characteristics such as their names, symbols and communication styles.

Gang Culture

Shelden et al. (2004, p.69) state: "Youth gangs constitute a unique subculture in modern society. . . . They have their own unique set of values, norms, lifestyles and beliefs" which are often found in a gang code of behavior. This behavior code may include the requirement to always wear gang colors, to get a tattoo representing the gang, and, if arrested, to never reveal anything about the gang, as there is no lower life form than a "snitch."

Some gang experts talk about the three Rs of the gang culture.

 The three Rs of the gang culture are reputation, respect and revenge.

Reputation is of prime concern to gang members, both individually and collectively. A gang's reputation is its power. As gang members often have minimal financial or material assets, their most important possession becomes their reputation. In fact, a gang's reputation is often enhanced by engaging in vicious, violent crimes.

Gangs also expect, indeed demand, *respect*. And they are required to show disrespect for rival gang members, called a "diss" in gang slang: "Without question, the subcultural value that carries the highest value for all gang members is *respect*. Any sign of disrespect shown toward a gang or gang member will result in retaliation with extreme prejudice" (Delaney, 2006, p.150).

Disrespect inevitably leads to the third R—*revenge*. Every challenge must be answered, often in the form of a drive-by shooting. Even a "hard look" or minor insult directed at a gang member by a rival gang member must be avenged, an attitude that results in the bloodbaths often seen on urban streets.

Anderson's (1999) thesis is that the code of the streets is an informal system governing the use of violence, especially among young, male African Americans, that stresses maintaining respect through a violent, tough identity: "An important part of the code is not to allow others to chump you, to let them know that you are 'about serious business,' and not to be trifled with" (Anderson, p.130). Straub (2008a, p.1) states: "In many cities today, the value of maintaining 'street cred' has made senseless killing and assaults legitimized responses to the most minor snubs and slights." According to criminologist Kennedy: "The violence is much less about drugs and money than about girls, vendettas and trivial social frictions. The code of the street has reached a point in which not responding to a slight can destroy a reputation, while violence is a sure way to enhance it" (Straub, 2008b, p.60).

 Also important in the gang culture are their names, symbols, clothing, tattoos and communication styles, including hand signals and graffiti.

Gang Names

Gang names vary from colorful and imaginative to straightforward. They commonly refer to localities, rebellion, animals, royalty and religion. Localities are typically streets (e.g., the Seventeenth Streeters), cities or towns (the Center City Boys), neighborhoods (the Westsiders) and housing projects (the Tiburon Courts). Names denoting rebellion, revolution or lawlessness include the Gangsters, Outlaws, Hustlers, Savages, Warlords and Assassins. Common animal names include the Tigers, Cougars, Panthers, Cobras, Ravens and Eagles. Royal titles include the Kings, Emperors, Lords, Imperials, Knights, Dukes and even Royals. Religious names include the Popes and Disciples. Gangs may also be designated by the leader's name such as "Garcia's Boys." Often, a locality is coupled with another category, for example, the South Side Savages.

Symbols

Gangs use symbols or logos to identify themselves. Often these symbols are taken from professional or college sports teams (e.g., the Latin Kings use the L.A. Kings logo as an identifying symbol), religion and the occult (crosses and pentagrams and other universally recognized symbols, including the Playboy bunny).

Clothing

It is important for gang members to reinforce their sense of belonging by adopting a gang style of dress. Gang symbols are common. Clothing, in particular, can distinguish a particular gang. Sometimes "colors" are used to distinguish a gang. Gang members also use jerseys, T-shirts and jackets with emblems.

Representing also signifies gang allegiance. **Representing** is a manner of dressing that uses an imaginary line drawn vertically through the body. Anything to the left of the line is representing left, anything to the right is representing right: for example, a hat cocked to the right, right pant leg rolled up and a cloth or bandana tied around the right arm.

Also important may be certain hairstyles, gold jewelry in gang symbols and certain cars. The following list itemizes some identifying symbols of some better-known gangs:

- *Black Gangster Disciples* wear blue and black colors, represent to the right and have as symbols a six-point star, flaming heart and crossed pitchfork.
- *Vice Lords* wear red and black colors, represent to the left and have as symbols a five-point star, a circle surrounded by fire, a half-crescent moon, a pyramid, top hat, cane, white gloves and martini glass.
- *Latin Kings* wear gold and black colors, represent to the left and have as a symbol a three- or five-point star.
- *Asian gangs* usually wear no colors and show no representation. They are often deadly and violent.
- *Skinheads* wear black boots and leather jackets and have as a symbol the swastika. Their heads are shaved or very nearly bald.

Communication Styles

Street gangs communicate primarily through their actions. Youth gangs need and seek recognition, not only from their community, but also from rival gangs. A variety of verbal and nonverbal gang communication is ever-present. Clothing, tattoos and symbols can be powerful and effective communication tools. Other avenues of gang communication include slang, hand signals and graffiti.

Hand Signals   A common method of gang communication is that of flashing gang signs or hand signals, the purpose of which is to identify the user with a specific gang. Hand signs communicate allegiance or opposition to another group. Most hand signs duplicate or modify signing used by the deaf and hearing impaired.

Graffiti   Certainly the most observable gang communication is wall writings or **graffiti**, an important part of the Hispanic and Black gang traditions. It proclaims to the world the status of the gang, delineates the boundaries of their turf and offers a challenge to rivals. Graffiti may show opposition for a rival gang by displaying the rival gang's symbols upside down, backward or crossed out—a serious insult to the rival.

In the broken window crime model, graffiti is a foothold crime leading to a neighborhood's decay: "Neighborhoods plagued with graffiti often become breeding grounds for loitering, littering, loud music, and public urination. . . . As 'good' citizens begin to avoid 'that side of town,' the criminal element becomes more comfortable and these small public disorder crimes snowball into more serious criminal behaviors. When these more serious crimes flourish,

Five juveniles in the Grape Street gang in Los Angeles show their hand signs and colors while flashing money.

it becomes difficult to assess the true cost of the graffiti offense: expenses mount in terms of prevention, arrests, incarceration, and lost revenue" (Petrocelli, 2008, p.18). Petrocelli contends:

> Most graffiti is not ever reported to the police. Many citizens do not consider graffiti a real crime and feel there is little that police can do about it. Though it is unlikely that one incident is very costly, the cumulative public cost to clean up graffiti in the United States is more than $12 billion a year. The fear of crime and the deterioration of a neighborhood that the graffiti creates may be even more expensive. . . . The writing on the walls is a nuisance; worse, it may lead to a rise in crime. (p.18)

Many youth gangs characteristically claim identification with and control over specific domains—geographic locations, facilities or enterprises. The best-known manifestation of gang domain identification is the "turf" phenomenon. Gangs establish **turf**, or territorial boundaries, within which they operate and which they protect at all costs from invasion by rival gangs. Gang graffiti usually appears throughout the turf and defines boundaries. Such graffiti usually includes the gang name and the writer's name. It may also assert the gang's power by such words as *rifa*, meaning "to rule," or *P/V* meaning "por vida" (for life). In other words, the gang rules this neighborhood for life. The number 13 has traditionally meant that the writer used marijuana, but now it also can mean that the gang is from Southern California.

The center of a gang's turf will have the most graffiti. It may name members of the gang, often in order of authority, listed in neat rows under the gang's logo. However, with the increasing mobility of society, graffiti no longer has to necessarily remain within a gang's turf.

© Mark Richards/PhotoEdit

Graffiti has been called the "newspaper of the street" for gangs. Often abbreviations such as R.I.P. (rest in peace) are found, as in the upper left corner of this graffiti.

Hispanic graffiti is highly artistic and very detailed. It frequently refers to group or gang power. In contrast, graffiti of Black gangs shows less flair and attention to detail and often is filled with profanity as well as expressions of individual power. The symbolism is more obvious and often includes weapons.

Figure 7.2 illustrates a variety of gang communication, including hand signals and symbols used in graffiti.

Graffiti vs. Tagging **Tagging** is a type of graffiti that mimics gang graffiti, but often those doing the tagging are not members of gangs or involved in criminal activity (other than vandalism). According to Shelden et al. (2004, p.52): "Such graffiti is not done to mark turf. Rather it is a way these mostly white middle-class youths call attention to themselves." In some instances, taggers band together into a **crew**. Sometimes the tagging becomes very serious and may even turn deadly. Differences between tagging and gang graffiti are listed in Table 7.3.

Tattoos

Some gangs, particularly outlaw motorcycle gangs and Hispanic gangs, use tattoos as a method of communication and identification. The traditional Hispanic gang uses tattoos extensively, usually visible on arms, hands or shoulders. By contrast, Black gang members seldom use tattoos to identify their members. Branding, however, is becoming somewhat popular among Black and Asian gangs.

Gang tattoos are meant not only to intimidate, to show gang affiliation and to indicate rank, but they also are a gang member's permanent record, telling who he is, what he believes, what he's done, where he's been, where he did time and for how many years, and how many people he's killed. An officer trained

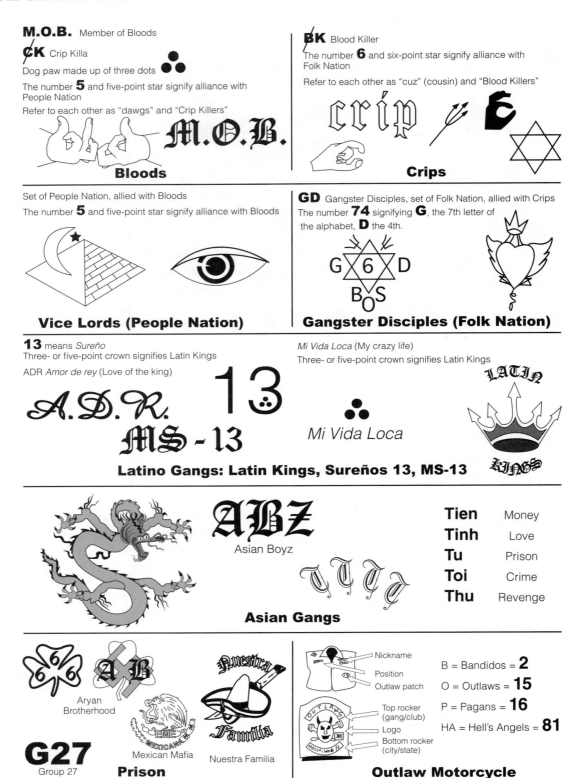

Figure 7.2 Gang Communication—Signs and Symbols

SOURCE: From Kären M. Hess and Christine Hess Orthmann. *Criminal Investigation*, 9th ed. Clifton Park, NY: Delmar Publishing Company, 2010, p.588.

Table 7.3 Differences between Tagging and Gang Graffiti

Tagger Graffiti	Gang Griffiti
Communication secondary, if present at all	Intent made to communicate
Artistic effort a major consideration	Artistic effort secondary, if present at all
Territorial claims infrequent	Territorial claims prominent
Explicit threats rare	Explicit threats made
Explicit boasts about tagger common	Explicit boasts made about gang
Pictures and symbols dominant, letters and numbers secondary	Letters, numbers and symbols dominant
Police intelligence value limited	Intelligence to police provided

SOURCE: *Addressing Community Gang Problems: A Practical Guide.* Washington, DC: Bureau of Justice Assistance, May 1998, p.37. (NCJ 164273)

to read gang tattoos can discern a suspect's history: "If gang graffiti is the newspaper of the street, then gang tattoos are the 'signposts to the soul'" (Valdemar, 2006, p.30).

Illegal Activities of Youth Gangs

The primary characteristic distinguishing gangs from lawful groups is the illegal activity of the former. Youth gang members commit a full range of street crimes, although the most distinctive form of gang offense is gang fighting, in which two or more gangs engage in violent combat. Drive-by shootings receive much media attention, particularly when stray bullets hit an innocent child or adult. Sometimes the shooters hit their mark and realize after the fact that it was a case of mistaken identity. And although noninvolved third parties are occasionally caught in the crossfire, Shelden et al. (2004, p.120) note: "The major victims of gang violence are other gang members. Innocent bystanders are rarely the victims, despite claims of law enforcement and other officials to the contrary."

 Youth gang activity ranges from property crimes to violent crimes against persons and includes graffiti painting, vandalism, arson, student extortion, teacher intimidation, drug dealing, rape, stabbings and shootings.

Tita and Ridgeway (2007, p.208) report: "Research has demonstrated that even after controlling for individual level attributes, individuals who join gangs commit more crimes than do nongang members. Furthermore, the offending level of gang members is higher when they report being active members of the gang. Therefore, gang membership clearly facilitates offending above and beyond individual level characteristics." Table 7.4 compares gang and nongang criminal behavior.

The 2006 NYGS reports that, compared to 2004 and 2005, 2006 saw an increase in two offenses: aggravated assault and drug sales followed in descending order by robbery, larceny-theft, burglary and auto theft (Egley and O'Donnell, 2008).

Table 7.4 Comparison of Gang and Nongang Criminal Behavior (Cleveland)

Crime(p[1])	Gang N = 47	Nongang N = 49
Auto Theft (***)	44.7%	4.1%
Assault Rivals (***)	72.3	16.3
Assault Own Members (*)	30.4	10.2
Assault Police (n.s.)	10.6	14.3
Assault Teachers (n.s.)	14.9	18.4
Assault Students (n.s.)	51.1	34.7
Mug People (n.s.)	10.6	4.1
Assault in Streets (*)	29.8	10.2
Theft-Other (***)	51.1	14.3
Intim/Assault Vict/Wit (***)	34.0	0.0
Intim/Assault Shoppers (*)	23.4	6.1
Drive-by Shooting (***)	40.4	2.0
Homicide (**)	15.2	0.0
Sell Stolen Goods (*)	29.8	10.2
Guns in School (***)	40.4	10.2
Knives in School (***)	38.3	4.2
Concealed Weapons (***)	78.7	22.4
Drug Use (**)	27.7	4.1
Drug Sales (School) (n.s.)	19.1	8.2
Drug Sales (Other) (***)	61.7	16.7
Drug Theft (***)	21.3	0.0
Bribe Police (n.s.)	10.6	2.0
Burglary (Unoccupied) (*)	8.5	0.0
Burglary (Occupied) (n.s.)	2.1	2.0
Shoplifting (n.s. [0.58])	30.4	14.3
Check Forgery (n.s.)	2.1	0.0
Credit Card Theft (n.s.)	6.4	0.0
Arson (*)	8.5	0.0
Kidnapping (n.s.)	4.3	0.0
Sexual Assault/Molest (n.s.)	2.1	0.0
Rape (n.s.)	2.1	0.0
Robbery (*)	17.0	2.0

[1]Level of statistical significance: *p<.05, **p<.01, ***p<.001; n.s. = no significant difference.
SOURCE: Ronald C. Huff. *Comparing the Criminal Behavior of Youth Gangs and At-Risk Youths.* National Institute of Justice Research in Brief, October 1998, p.4. (NCJ 172851)

Youth Gang Violence

Youth gang activity, when viewed from a juvenile justice perspective, is a study in violent crime. A perpetual cycle of violence by gang rivalries can date back many years. In fact, gang members often do not know why they came to be rivals with some other gangs.

Youth gangs acquire their power in the community through violent behavior.

For many gang members, violence is simply a way of life. For example, if one gang member disrespects another gang member, even within the same gang, violent retaliation may occur. Shelden et al. (2004, p.110) note that part of the violence is due to the fact that "gangs often attract young men who, frankly, enjoy violence." The ready availability of firearms in general, and semiautomatic weapons in particular, has had a profound impact on the level of violence on the streets.

One of the hazards of being involved as a perpetrator of gang violence is that the violence usually cycles back to be served upon the originator, thus forming an endless loop of offending and victimization, with youth gang members alternately being on the giving and receiving ends of the violence. Stewart et al. (2006, p.446) studied whether the code of the street reduced victimization rates and whether adopting the street code buffered the effects of harsh neighborhood conditions on victimization risk. They found: "Those adolescents who adopted the street code showed a higher chance of being victimized. Even after controlling for neighborhood characteristics, demographic correlates of victimization, and prior victimization, adopting the street code remained a significant predictor of victimization."

Research by Taylor et al. (2007, p.357) found that youth gang members were more likely to experience violent victimization, as well as greater frequency of victimization, than nongang members. Taylor (2008, p.126) also reports: "Research has consistently demonstrated the increased risk of victimization— particularly violent victimization—of gang members relative to their nongang peers." For example, 70 percent of gang-involved youths reported being the victim of general violence (assault, aggravated assault and/or robbery) compared to 46 percent of non–gang-involved youths (Taylor).

Youth Gangs and Drugs

Gangs' involvement with drugs is comprised of two dimensions: using and selling. While it is well known that many youth gang members abuse certain drugs, such as alcohol, marijuana, phencyclidine (PCP) and cocaine, what is less agreed on is the extent to which youth gangs deal in drugs. Until the early 1980s, when crack, or rock cocaine, hit the market, gangs engaged primarily in burglary, robbery, extortion and car theft. Although drug trafficking existed, it was nowhere near current levels. The reason for the spike in drug sales: enormous profit. Economic gain is often the reason youths join gangs. It is hard to convince a youth that $7.50 an hour for busing tables is preferable to making $400 for two hours' work as a drug courier. Thus many contend that gangs currently function as a primary distributor of drugs throughout the United States (*2005 National Gang Threat Assessment*, 2008, p.v).

Some caution that drug trafficking by youth gangs is not as rampant as others might claim. Shelden et al. (2004, p.123) state: "There is little question that drug usage and violent crime are closely related. What is still in doubt, however, is the relationship between drugs (both usage and sales) and gangs. Research on this issue has produced conflicting findings. . . . Gang members are

Table 7.5　Common Differences between Street Gangs and Drug Gangs

Characteristic	Street Gangs	Drug Gangs
Crime focus	Versatile ("cafeteria-style")	Drug business exclusively
Structure	Larger organizations	Smaller organizations
Level of cohesion	Less cohesive	More cohesive
Leadership	Looser	More centralized
Roles	Ill-defined	Market-defined
Nature of loyalty	Code of loyalty	Requirement of loyalty
Territories	Residential	Sales market
Degree of drug selling	Members may sell	Members do sell
Rivalries	Intergang	Competition controlled
Age of members	Younger on average, but wider age range	Older on average, but narrower age range

SOURCE: James C. Howell. *Youth Gangs Overview.* Washington, DC: Office of Juvenile Justice and Delinquency Prevention, August 1998, pp.6–7. (NCJ 167249)

about twice as likely as nongang members to use drugs and to use them more often." Aside from expert opinions that most youth gangs lack the discipline, leadership and crime skills necessary to sustain a successful drug operation, those gangs that are successful in running profitable drug businesses are serious forces to be reckoned with. Table 7.5 identifies some common differences between street gangs and drug gangs.

It is generally agreed that gangs organize along one of two basic lines: violence-oriented (expressive) gangs who exist to fight or entrepreneurially focused (instrumental) gangs structured to make money. Among those gangs for whom drug trafficking is a primary activity, however, violence may accompany their entrepreneurial activities.

Huebner et al. (2007) studied the effect of gang members' drug use on recidivism and reported that those who were affiliated with a gang or were drug dependent prior to prison had higher reconviction rates and recidivated more quickly, as compared with those who were not involved with gangs or drug use. Individuals dealing with juveniles must maintain objectivity and refrain from stereotyping gang members as drug users and pushers, keeping in mind that not all gangs deal with drugs, and not all who use drugs commit other crimes.

Gangs often purposely exploit the difference between juvenile and adult law in their drug dealing, using younger gang members whenever possible to avoid adult sanctions. Most states will not allow youths under age 15 to be certified as adults, and most have statutory restrictions on placing youths under age 18 into adult correctional facilities.

Recognizing a Youth Gang Problem

The first step in dealing with a gang problem is to recognize it. However, many communities are blind to local youth gang activity: "Most citizens, unless they are personally affected, have no idea or understanding of gang logistics.

REALITY CHECK—DISPELLING SOME MYTHS ABOUT YOUTH GANGS

Much of the image the public holds of youth gangs is stereotyped, based on a traditional notion of gangs rooted in either Hollywood's depiction of such groups or fueled by a few sensationalist stories that grab media headlines each year. While gangs certainly pose a very salient threat to communities across the country, some common misconceptions have persisted that make combating gangs in the community even more challenging. The following myths enjoy a significant degree of legitimacy among the general population:

- Most street gang members are juveniles.
- All street gangs are turf oriented.
- Street gangs stay in the big cities—there's nothing for them in the suburbs or small rural communities.
- Street gang members are "bad kids" who have few options in life other than to engage in crime because they come from broken homes where the parents are drug dealers, unemployed, in prison or otherwise unproductive members of society.
- Youth gang membership is overwhelmingly made up of minorities—mostly African Americans and Latinos.
- Youth gangs are a law enforcement problem.

Because the public tends to believe these "facts" about youth gangs, they often miss the realities of gang involvement occurring in their very own communities, making it more difficult for the problem to be effectively addressed.

Following are the counterpoint "truths" to the preceding myths:

- As has already been pointed out, numerous studies have found youths under age 18 actually comprise only about one-third of the total gang membership, although the percentage of adolescent gang members is presently larger than it has been in the past (Molina, 2007).
- Modern youth gangs are based less on territory than gangs of the past (Molina).
- More gangs are in suburban areas, small towns and rural areas than in the past (Molina).
- Many members of modern adolescent gangs are "good kids" from respectable families and college-educated parents (Molina).
- White youth comprise the largest group of teenage gang members (Greene and Pranis, 2007).
- Gangs are everyone's problem, not just law enforcement's (Decker, 2007).

The sad commentary is that most citizens do not care or refuse to acknowledge that there is a problem" (Cohn, 2006, p.6). Indeed, Decker stresses that community awareness is key to any local or state initiative to combat a gang problem. She reports that in Virginia, 75 percent of law enforcement professionals said their number one need was getting the community to be aware of the gang problem.

Youth gang activity manifests itself in a variety of ways.

 Indicators of youth gang activity include graffiti, intimidation assaults, open sale of drugs, drive-by shootings and murders.

Once a gang problem is recognized, the next step is to identify the gang members.

Identifying Gang Members

Webb et al. (2006, p.232) note that gang researchers often rely on self-reports to determine gang involvement, and although such a method is not entirely perfect, self-reports are a valid measurement technique in gang research. In addition to self-reports, other factors may indicate membership in a youth gang.

Gang members take pride in belonging to their specific gangs and will make their membership known in various ways. Many gang members have a street name, or a **moniker**. Often more than one gang member has the same moniker. The color and type of clothing can also indicate gang membership. For example, Bloods are identified by red or green colors. Crips are associated with blue or purple bandanas or scarves.

Gang affiliation might also be verified in the following ways: body tattoos of gang symbols, jewelry or apparel associated with gangs, written communications such as doodling on notebooks, hand-signing, vocabulary and use of monikers, group photos that include known gang members, known gang associates and reliable informants. Other signs that an individual may be involved in a gang include abrupt changes in personality and behavior, newly acquired and unexplained money or, conversely, requests to borrow money, and "hanging around" behavior.

Gangs in Schools

Recognizing the presence of gangs in school is a continuous challenge for administrators and juvenile justice professionals throughout the country, particularly in certain inner-city districts. Schools are a prime recruiting ground for gangs. They are also a market for illicit drugs and for extorting money from other students. Often gangs will stake out certain areas of a school as their turf. They may engage in vandalism, arson and graffiti painting, stabbings and shootings between rival gangs, as well as student extortion and teacher intimidation.

Indications that youth gangs may be operating in a school include groups of students congregating by race and naming their group to solidify their identity; an increase in the number of violent, racially based incidents; a rise in the rate of absenteeism or truancy; and a greater number of crimes in the community being committed by truants. Other indicators include graffiti and crossed-out graffiti visible on or near the school, colors worn symbolically by various groups who also use hand signals, and unique symbols on T-shirts or in jewelry. Crime and violence in our schools is discussed in Chapter 8.

Responding to an Existing Youth Gang Problem

Responding to gangs requires a systematic, comprehensive, collaborative approach that incorporates prevention, intervention and suppression strategies. The prevention component, discussed in more detail shortly, includes conflict resolution skills and peer counseling. The intervention component includes giving youth gang members the chance to finish high school or obtain a GED, to have tattoos removed, to obtain gainful employment and legal assistance. The suppression component involves collaboration among police, probation and prosecution, targeting the most active gang members and gang leaders.

The OJJDP's Comprehensive Gang Initiative model is based on five strategies: community mobilization, opportunities provision development, social intervention, suppression and organizational change and development, that is, implementing policies and procedures that result in the most effective use of available and potential resources (National Youth Gang Center, 2008, p.2). The prototype Comprehensive Gang Initiative Program is based on the following

principles: adaptability, flexibility and a multifaceted approach. The model calls
for a variety of government and private agencies to work with police and community members to simultaneously address the many factors that create and
sustain gang problems. The model has the following key components:

- A focus on harmful behaviors
- Continuous diagnosis of problems
- Coordination of groups or agencies in their response
- Monitoring performance
- Evaluating impact
- Adapting to change

 Strategies commonly used to deal with gang problems: (1) suppression or law
enforcement efforts, (2) social intervention, (3) opportunities provision,
(4) community organization and (5) organizational change and development.
The most effective approaches use a combination of these efforts.

Suppression and Law Enforcement Efforts

Suppression tactics include street sweeps, intensified surveillance, hot spot targeting, directed patrol, saturation patrol, aggressive curfew and truancy enforcement, and caravanning. Table 7.6 shows the law enforcement strategies being
used, with what frequency and with what perceived effectiveness when used.
Although in-state information exchange was the most-used strategy, it was also

Table 7.6 Law Enforcement Strategies and Perceived Effectiveness*

Strategy	Used (Percent)	Judged Effective If Used (Percent)
Some or a lot of use		
Targeting entry points	14	17
Gang laws	40	19
Selected violations	76	42
Out-of-state information exchange	53	16
In-state information exchange	90	17
In-city information exchange	55	18
Federal agency operational coordination	40	16
State agency operational coordination	50	13
Local agency operational coordination	78	16
Community collaboration	64	54
Any use		
Street sweeps	40	62
Other suppression tactics	44	63
Crime prevention activities	15	56

*Percentage of cities $n = 211$. The number of cities responding to each question varied slightly.
SOURCE: James C. Howell. *Youth Gang Programs and Strategies*. Washington, DC: OJJDP,
August 2000, p.46. (NCJ 171154)

among those judged least effective. Street sweeps and other suppression tactics were used by fewer than half the departments, but their effectiveness was judged high.

Richmond, Virginia's directed patrol program used crime statistics and crime logs to determine high-crime days and times in the target area. Additional foot, bicycle, motorcycle and walking officers were added during those times, which resulted in a significant decrease in crime. During the funded periods, Richmond dropped from being the 5th most dangerous city to the 15th. More recently, it has dropped to 25th (National Youth Gang Center, 2008, p.28).

Gang Units and Task Forces As early as the 1970s, the Los Angeles Police Department saw the need for specialized units to deal with the gang problem. Their first such program was called Community Resources Against Street Hoodlums (CRASH) and consisted of several specially trained units of patrol officers and detectives organized on a bureau or area level. CRASH put tremendous pressure on the Los Angeles gangs and resulted in many gang members being arrested. In 1988 the department instituted another program to focus specifically on the problem of narcotics and Black street gangs. This program was called Gang-Related Active Trafficker Suppression (GRATS).

Collaboration among law enforcement agencies can greatly enhance efforts to cope with the youth gang problem. Moore (2007b, p.52) points out: "Fighting gang-related crime with traditional methods is a lot like putting out a forest fire with a measuring cup—something's being done, but in the long run it's a futile gesture." She explains that task forces are formed as a coalition of differing perspectives and focus manpower and resources on a common goal. A federal initiative is the FBI's creation of more than 170 Safe Streets Task Forces (SSTFs), of which 130 are focused on violent gangs ("Fighting Gang Violence," 2007). The FBI had previously developed the National Gang Intelligence Center (NGIC) to provide a way for local, state and federal law enforcement to share gang data across jurisdictions and to identify trends related to violent gang activity and migration.

Such collaboration is also vital at the local level. In 2007, 13 California cities started a new network to identify and share effective strategies for preventing gang violence: "The network rests on the core assumption that gang violence can be reduced if participating cities develop citywide plans that mobilize the commitment of key stakeholders and that the cities share their lessons—both positive and negative—with each other" ("Thirteen California Cities Share Strategies through Gang Prevention Network," 2008). Calhoun (2008, pp.3, 6) says this initiative has several goals, including:

- Creating citywide strategies that blend enforcement, prevention and intervention.
- Creating and sustaining a vibrant network of urban leaders who will work with and learn from peers to advance their local antigang strategies.
- Identifying and documenting good practices in terms of program and policy.
- Identifying and recommending state and federal policies and practices that would support effective community-based approaches.

Civil Gang Ordinances and Injunctions   One measure being used to combat an existing gang problem is the **civil injunction**, a court order prohibiting some activity such as loitering in a specific location. Civil gang injunctions (CGIs) are a legal tool to disrupt a gang's routine activities. Obtaining a CGI varies from jurisdiction to jurisdiction but usually involves gathering evidence that gang members are a public nuisance in a specific location and applying to a civil court to require these individuals to refrain from nuisance behavior. After the injunction is issued, the targeted individuals are notified and can be arrested for violating the injunction. Figure 7.3 illustrates the gang injunction process.

Injunctions and ordinances may be challenged as unconstitutional violations of the freedom of speech, the right of association and due process rights if they do not clearly delineate how officers may apply such orders. For example, Chicago passed a gang congregation ordinance to combat the problems created by the city's street gangs. During the three years following passage of the ordinance, Chicago police officers issued over 89,000 dispersal orders and arrested more than 42,000 people. However, in *City of Chicago v. Morales* (1999), the Supreme Court struck down the ordinance as unconstitutional because its vague wording failed to provide adequate standards to guide police discretion. The lesson here is that any civil injunctions a city passes must be clear in what officers can and cannot do when they observe what they believe to be gang members congregating in public places.

Moore (2007a, p.98) gives as another example the efforts of the Sunnyside, Washington, officials passing an ordinance allowing police to aggressively

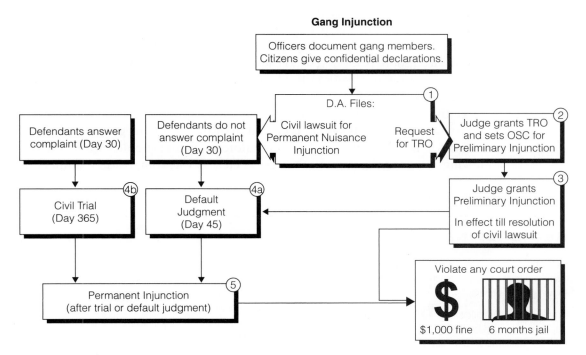

Figure 7.3   The Gang Injunction Process

SOURCE: Used by permission of San Diego Deputy District Attorney Susan Mazza.

pursue individuals who engage in peripheral gang activities. The ordinance makes joining a gang illegal and prohibits hand signals, wearing gang-related clothes and other typical gang activities. This ordinance is being opposed by the Washington ACLU, which claims that it could lead to racial profiling. Moore finds this "baffling" in light of the fact that race is paramount in gang activity.

Tougher legislation is also being used as a gang control approach. Because some gangs use their younger members to commit serious crimes, relying on the more lenient juvenile sentencing laws, some jurisdictions have allowed courts to raise the penalties for teenagers convicted of gang-related offenses.

Arresting and Prosecuting Gang Members

The justice system should view gangs as criminal organizations and capitalize on laws against organized crime; for example, money-laundering and asset forfeiture laws help in efforts to arrest and prosecute gang members and thereby weaken the street gang structure. As Lyddane (2006, p.1) points out: "It is critical to know your adversary. Understanding the gang mentality and anticipating gang behaviors will aid investigators and prosecutors in acquiring physical evidence and securing testimony that will 'connect the dots' in gang conspiracy investigations. Presenting evidence of the defendant gang affiliation through exhibits of graffiti, written gang communications, videos and photographs, and video surveillance footage of the defendants at gang events is the adhesive that joins seemingly unrelated criminal offenses into the predicate acts of a gang conspiracy."

Challenges to Investigating Gangs' Illegal Activities   It is often difficult to obtain information about a gang's illegal activities because gang members stick together and will try to intimidate the people living and working within their turf. Businesspeople and residents alike are usually fearful of telling the police anything, believing the gang will cause them great harm if they do. Morley (2008, p.52) notes: "Because of their involvement with criminal activity and those involved in illegal enterprises, gang members are likely to be witnesses to criminal acts. In a murder of a gang member, for example, very often the only witnesses will be gang members themselves."

An effective records system is critical in dealing with any gang problem. Information is an essential tool for law enforcement and should include the following: type of gang (street, motorcycle, etc.), ethnic composition, number of

IN THE HEADLINES

On December 8, 2008, Los Angeles prosecutors filed California's first lawsuit seeking to seize assets, including homes and businesses, of known gang members:

City Attorney Rocky Delgadillo said the lawsuit was filed Monday against nine leaders of the 18th Street gang to cripple their criminal enterprises. All the defendants are serving prison time. 18th Street is the largest gang in Los Angeles.

A state law passed earlier this year allows cities to sue for the financial damage gangs cause communities. Only gangs already targeted with restraining orders declaring their behavior a nuisance can be sued.

Damages gained from any lawsuits would be funneled back to the neighborhoods.

SOURCE: From the *Associated Press*, "L.A. Moves to Seize Assets of Gang Members," December 8, 2008.

active and associate members, territory, hideouts, types of crimes usually committed and method of operation, leadership and members known to be violent.

Posey (2008, p.39) suggests that departments use improving technology to combine the efforts of sworn officers and the capabilities of the information technology (IT) staff to use its computer-aid dispatch (CAD) and records management system (RMS) to deliver accurate, timely information on gang activity directly to patrol officers who need it to maximize their effectiveness when dealing with known gang members.

 A key impediment to obtaining information on youth gang members is the inability to share information, since the records of juveniles are often sealed.

Prosecuting Youth Gang Members Who Break the Law   In addition to efforts to suppress, intervene and prevent youth gang activity, the juvenile justice system needs to aggressively prosecute gang members who engage in criminal activity. However, as Shelden et al. (2004, p.263) note: "Prosecutors—key agents of the state—have a tremendous amount of discretionary power and can be quite political in dealing with gang members. As elected officials, prosecutors have a political agenda driven by a combination of public perceptions and fears (which can be and have been manipulated by a zealous media) and self-interest (getting reelected or running for higher office)."

Many prosecutors' offices have adopted vertical prosecution strategies to handle gang-related crimes. **Vertical prosecution** involves one assistant prosecutor or small group of assistant prosecutors handling one criminal complaint from start to finish through the entire court process. In contrast, **horizontal prosecution** is an organizational structure strategy whereby individual assistant prosecutors or a small group of assistant prosecutors are responsible for certain phases of the court process.

Bemburg et al. (2006), however, found that juvenile justice intervention increases subsequent gang involvement and delinquency, consistent with labeling theory. Clearly much work needs to be done regarding dealing with youth who find themselves embroiled in gang activity. A better use of resources and efforts may lie in preventing gang involvement, for only by keeping children from joining gangs in the first place will the terror and violence that gangs represent be halted.

Youth Gang Prevention Efforts

Many traditional efforts to deal with the youth gang problem have been reactive. Increasingly, however, the justice system has seen the wisdom in and benefit of youth gang prevention efforts. For example, law enforcement departments around the country have begun:

- Participating in community awareness campaigns (e.g., developing public service announcements and poster campaigns).
- Contacting parents of peripheral gang members (through the mail or during personal visits) to alert them that their children are involved with a gang.
- Sponsoring gang hotlines to gather information and facilitate a quick response to gang-related issues.
- Organizing athletic events with teams of law enforcement officers and gang members.

- Establishing working relationships with local social service agencies.
- Making presentations about gangs to schools and community groups as a combined effort at prevention and information gathering.
- Sponsoring school-based gang and drug prevention programs (e.g., DARE and GREAT).

The Gang Resistance Education and Training (GREAT) program was developed by the Bureau of Alcohol, Tobacco and Firearms, the Federal Law Enforcement Training Center and the Phoenix (Arizona) Police Department. This program, similar to the DARE program, helps students say no, but in this case to gangs. The audience is older; GREAT focuses on seventh-graders. McGloin (n.d., p.4) explains: "The program's primary objective is prevention and is intended as an immunization against delinquency, youth violence and gang membership." Students are taught to set goals, resolve conflicts nonviolently, resist peer pressures and understand the negative impact gangs can have on their lives and on their community.

 Summary

- Gangs may be classified as hedonistic/social gangs, party gangs, predatory gangs, scavenger gangs, serious delinquent gangs, territorial gangs, organized/corporate gangs and drug gangs.
- Gangs may also be classified as racial/ethnic gangs, hybrid gangs, girl gangs, outlaw motorcycle gangs and prison gangs.
- Gangs offer their members a feeling of belonging and importance as well as protection from other youths. They may also provide financial power.
- Gangs may result from a variety of personal, social and economic factors, including family structure and influences such as parental guidance and lack of responsibility, peer pressure and ego fulfillment, racism and cultural discord, socioeconomic factors and socialized delinquency.
- Most gangs contain leaders, hard-core members, regular members and fringe members or wannabes.
- The three Rs of the gang culture are reputation, respect and revenge.
- Also important in the gang culture are their names, symbols, clothing, tattoos and communication styles, including hand signals and graffiti.
- Youth gang activity ranges from property crimes to violent crimes against persons and includes graffiti painting, vandalism, arson, student extortion, teacher intimidation, drug dealing, rape, stabbings and shootings.
- Youth gangs acquire their power in the community through their violent behavior.
- Indicators of youth gang activity include graffiti, intimidation assaults, open sale of drugs, drive-by shootings and murders.
- Strategies commonly used to deal with gang problems: (1) suppression or law enforcement efforts, (2) social intervention, (3) opportunities provision, (4) community organization and (5) organizational change and development. The most effective approaches use a combination of these efforts.
- A key impediment to dealing with youth gang members is the inability to share information because the records of juveniles are often sealed.

DISCUSSION QUESTIONS

1. Are there gangs in your community? Are they youth gangs? If so, what problems do they cause?
2. Have you seen any movies or TV programs about gangs? How are gang activities depicted?
3. What do you think are the main reasons people join gangs?
4. How does a youth gang member differ from other juveniles?
5. How strong do you believe the link is between drugs, violence and gang membership?
6. Should convicted youth gang members be treated like other juvenile delinquents, including status offenders?
7. What might influence you to become a gang member? To not become a gang member?
8. Do you believe the juvenile justice system should support gang summits that claim to be working toward peaceful, lawful ways to improve the situation of gang members?
9. How much, if any, do gangs today differ from those of the 1960s and 1970s?
10. Do you think the youth gang problem will increase or decrease over the next decade?

REFERENCES

Anderson, Elijah. *The Code of the Street Decency, Violence, and the Moral Life of the Inner City.* New York: Norton, 1999.

Bemburg, Jon Gummer; Krohn, Marvin D.; and Rivera, Craig. "Official Labeling: Criminal Embeddedness and Subsequent Delinquency: A Longitudinal Test of Labeling Theory." *Journal of Research in Crime and Delinquency*, Vol. 43, No.1, 2006.

Calhoun, John A. "13 California Police Agencies Join Forces with Other Groups in a Gang Prevention Network." *Subject to Debate*, April 2008, pp.3, 6.

Cohn, Edward. "The Gang Culture Continues to Grow." *Corrections Today*, April 2006, p.6.

Decker, Marla Graff. "A Community Approach to Combating Gangs." San Diego, CA: Seminar B-13 presented at the 34th National Conference on Juvenile Justice, March 5, 2007.

Decker, Scott H.; Katz, Charles M.; and Webb, Vincent J. "Understanding the Black Box of Gang Organization." *Crime & Delinquency*, January 2008, pp.153–172.

Delaney, Tim. *American Street Gangs.* Upper Saddle River, NJ: Pearson/Prentice Hall, 2006.

Eghigian, Mars and Kirby, Katherine. "Girls in Gangs." *Corrections Today*, April 2006, pp.48–50.

Egley, Arlen, Jr. and O'Donnell, Christina E. *Highlights of the 2006 National Youth Gang Survey.* Washington, DC: Office of Juvenile Justice Delinquency Prevention, July 2008. (FS 200805)

"Fighting Gang Violence." Washington, DC: Federal Bureau of Investigation, January 11, 2007.

Freng, Adrienne and Esbensen, Finn-Aage. "Race and Gang Affiliation: An Examination of Multiple Marginality." *Justice Quarterly*, December 2007, pp.600–628.

Greene, Judith and Pranis, Kevin. *Gang Wars: The Failure of Enforcement Tactics and the Need for Effective Public Strategies.* Washington, DC: Justice Policy Institute, July 2007.

Howell, James C. and Egley, Arlen, Jr. *Frequently Asked Questions Regarding Gangs.* Tallahassee, FL: Institute for Intergovernmental Research, 2008.

Huebner, Beth M.; Varano, Sean P.; and Bynum, Timothy S. "Gangs, Guns, and Drugs: Recidivism among Serious, Young Offenders." *Criminology & Public Policy*, May 2007, pp.187–221.

Klein, Malcolm W. *Chasing after Street Gangs: A Forty-Year Journey.* Upper Saddle River, NJ: Pearson/Prentice Hall, 2007.

Lyddane, Donald. "Understanding Gangs and Gang Mentality: Acquiring Evidence of the Gang Conspiracy." *United States Attorneys' Bulletin*, May 2006, pp.1–2.

McGloin, Jean M. *Street Gangs and Interventions: Innovative Problem Solving with Network Analysis.* Washington, DC: Office of Community Oriented Policing Services, no date. (NCJ211993)

McLemore, David. "MS-13 Gang Seen as Growing Threat." Dallas/Ft. Worth Channel, October 29, 2006.

Molina, Hector J. *Gangs and Schools: Information Educators Need to Know and Share.* San Diego, CA: Seminar D-3 presented at the 34th National Conference on Juvenile Justice, March 6, 2007.

Moore, Carole. "The ACLU Plays 'Go Fish.'" *Law Enforcement Technology*, November 2007a, p.98.

Moore, Carole. "Street Gangs." *Law Enforcement Technology*, January 2007b, pp.52–57.

Morley, Patrick J. "Eyes on the Street." *Police*, October 2008, pp.52–54.

Mueller, Robert. "Inside Gang Violence: Director Outlines Changing Threat and Our Response." Washington, DC: Federal Bureau of Investigation, January 18, 2007.

National Youth Gang Center. *Best Practices to Address Community Gang Problems.* Washington, DC: Office of Juvenile Justice and Delinquency Prevention, June 2008. (NCJ 222799)

Ortega, Francisca and Calderoni, Valeria. "Gangs Unite as 'Hybrids,' Increasing Violence." *Police One*, October 1, 2007.

Peterson, Greg. "Gangs in Indian Country." *Indian Country Today*, July 1, 2008.

Petrocelli, Joseph. "Patrol Response to Graffiti." *Police*, March 2008, pp.18–19.

Pistole, John S. "Major Executive Speeches." Washington, DC: Federal Bureau of Investigation, March 3, 2008.

Posey, Ed. "Using Existing Records to Keep a Closer Eye on Sex Offenders and Gang Members in the Community." *The Police Chief*, June 2008, pp.38–47.

Shelden, Randall G.; Tracy, Sharon K.; and Brown, William B. *Youth Gangs in American Society*, 3rd ed. Belmont, CA: Wadsworth Publishing Company, 2004.

Snyder, Howard N. and Sickmund, Melissa. *Juvenile Offenders and Victims 2006 National Report*. Washington, DC: U.S. Department of Justice, Office of Justice Programs, Office of Juvenile Justice and Delinquency Prevention, March 2006.

Stewart, Eric H.; Schreck, Christopher J.; and Simons, Ronald L. "'I Ain't Gonna Let No One Disrespect Me." *Journal of Research in Crime and Delinquency*, November 2006, pp.427–458.

Straub, Frank G. "Commissioner Frank Straub Testifies on Reducing Gang and Youth Violence." *Subject to Debate*, June 2008a, pp.1, 4–5.

Straub, Frank G. "Policing Cities: Reducing Violence and Building Communities." *The Police Chief*, November 2008b, pp.60–66.

Taylor, Terrance J. "The Boulevard Ain't Safe for Your Kids . . . Youth Gang Membership and Violent Victimization." *Journal of Contemporary Criminal Justice*, May 2008, pp.125–136.

Taylor, Terrance J.; Peterson, Dana; Esbensen, Finn-Aage; and Freng, Adrienne. "Gang Membership as a Risk Factor for Adolescent Violent Victimization." *Journal of Research in Crime and Delinquency*, November 2007, pp.357–380.

"Thirteen California Cities Share Strategies through Gang Prevention Network." *Community Policing Dispatch*, July 2008.

Thrasher, Frederic M. *The Gang: A Study of 1,313 Gangs in Chicago*. Chicago: University of Chicago Press, 1927.

Tita, George and Ridgeway, Greg. "The Impact of Gang Formation on Local Patterns of Crime." *Journal of Research in Crime and Delinquency*, May 2007, pp.208–237.

2005 National Gang Threat Assessment. Washington, DC: Bureau of Justice Statistics, 2008.

Valdemar, Richard. "Murder Link." *Police*, February 2006, pp.30–42.

Walker, Samuel; Spohn, Cassia; and DeLone, Miriam. *The Color of Justice: Race, Ethnicity, and Crime in America*, 4th ed. Belmont, CA: Wadsworth Publishing Company, 2007.

Webb, Vincent J.; Katz, Charles M.; and Decker, Scott H. "Assessing the Validity of Self-Reports by Gang Members: Results from the Arrestee Drug Abuse Monitoring Program." *Crime & Delinquency*, July 2006, pp.232–252.

CASE CITED

City of Chicago v. Morales, 527 U.S. 41 (1999)

CHAPTER 8

The Police and Juveniles

CHILDREN SPEND UP TO 25 PERCENT OF THEIR WAKING HOURS IN SCHOOL. IT HAS BEEN ESTIMATED THAT 18 PERCENT OF THEIR TIME IS SPENT WITH THEIR PEERS—OTHER CHILDREN. ANOTHER 18 PERCENT OF THEIR WAKING HOURS MAY BE SPENT IN FRONT OF THE TELEVISION. POLICE ARE THE ONLY OTHER SIGNIFICANT PARENTAL TYPE, ALBEIT SURROGATE, IN CONTACT WITH OUR CHILDREN.

—TIMOTHY D. CROWE

The Drug Abuse Resistance Education (DARE) program is designed to teach elementary-age schoolchildren to say "No" to drugs. Experienced police officers teach the classroom sessions and act as facilitators. Although highly popular, the effectiveness of the program has been challenged.

DO YOU KNOW?

- What greatly influences youths' attitudes toward law and law enforcement?
- What primary responsibility officers assigned a child abuse or neglect case have?
- What challenges are involved in investigating crimes against children?
- What the majority of police dispositions involve?
- What factors affect how police officers respond to status offenders?
- Whether the police have discretionary power when dealing with juveniles?
- What action police usually take when confronting juveniles?
- What the fundamental nature of the juvenile justice system is?
- How boys who own guns for protection differ from those who do not or who own guns for sport in terms of delinquent activity?
- What four categories of threats exist?
- What the four-pronged threat assessment approach is?
- What the role of the first responder to a school shooting situation should be?
- What an effective approach to school violence should include?
- What controversial measures have been taken to make schools safer?

CAN YOU DEFINE?

beyond a reasonable
  doubt
conditional threat
detention
direct threat

indirect threat
lockdown
pulling levers
school resource officer
  (SRO)

station adjustment
street justice
taken into custody
temporary custody
  without hearing

veiled threat
window of
  opportunity

CHAPTER OUTLINE

Introduction

The Police Response to
  Neglected and Abused
  Children

Challenges to Investigation

Evidence

*A Protocol for Responding to
  Child Abuse and Neglect*

Law Enforcement's Disposition
  of Status Offenders

The Police Response to
  Delinquency

*Police Discretion and the Initial
  Contact*

Taken into Custody

The Juvenile Holdover

Detention

Prosecution

Police as Mentors to Troubled
  Youths

The Police Response to
  Juveniles with Guns

*The Boston Gun Project,
  Operation Ceasefire*

Youth Firearms Violence Initiative

Project Safe Neighborhoods

The Police Response to Youth
  Crime and Violence in Our
  Schools

*The School Resource Officer
  (SRO) Program*

Bullying

School Shootings

In Search of Safer Schools

*Other Efforts to Prevent School
  Violence*

Partnerships and Community
  Policing

Introduction

Juvenile justice, as already discussed, is basically concerned with three distinct groups of youths: those who are victims of abuse and/or neglect, those who commit status offenses and those who commit serious crimes. Law enforcement is commonly the first contact young victims and victimizers have with the juvenile justice system, serving as the gatekeeper to the rest of the system. The police are charged with protecting youths, both victims and offenders, and dealing fairly with them. A balance is sought between what is in the best interest of the youth and what is best for the community. Also, the crime-fighting philosophy must be balanced with the service ideal.

The importance of the officer on the street cannot be overlooked. Every law enforcement officer, no matter at what level, has an opportunity to be a positive influence on youths. Ultimately youths' perceptions about the law and law enforcement will be based on one-on-one interactions with law enforcement officers.

 Youths' attitudes toward law and law enforcement are tremendously influenced by personal contacts with law enforcement officers. Positive interactions are critical to delinquency prevention.

The Police Response to Neglected and Abused Children

Law enforcement agencies are charged with investigating all crimes, but their responsibility is especially great where crimes against children are involved. Children need the protection of the law to a greater degree than other members

Positive face-to-face contacts between police officers and children can help promote the idea of the police officer as a friend and helper.

of society because they are so vulnerable, particularly if the offense is committed by one or both parents. Even after the offense is committed, the child may still be in danger of further victimization.

In most states, action must be taken on a report within a specified time, frequently three days. If in the judgment of the person receiving the report it is necessary to remove the child from present custody, this is discussed with the responsible agency, such as the welfare department or the juvenile court. If the situation is deemed life-threatening, the police may temporarily remove the child.

 The primary responsibility of police officers assigned to child neglect or abuse cases is the immediate protection of the child.

Under welfare regulations and codes, an officer may take a child into temporary custody without a warrant if there is an emergency or if the officer has reason to believe that leaving the child in the present situation would subject the child to further abuse or harm. **Temporary custody without hearing** usually refers to a time period of 48 hours. Conditions that would justify placing a child in protective custody include:

- Maltreatment in the home that might cause the child permanent physical or emotional damage.
- A parent's refusal to provide needed medical or psychiatric care for a child.
- The child is physically or mentally incapable of self-protection.
- The home's physical environment poses an immediate threat.
- The parents cannot or will not provide for the child's basic needs.
- The parents abandon the child.

Among the service providers mandated to report incidents of suspected child abuse or neglect are child care providers, clergy, educators, hospital administrators, nurses, physicians, psychologists and those in the social services. No matter who receives the report or whether the child must be removed from the situation, it is the responsibility of the law enforcement agency to investigate the charge.

Challenges to Investigation

Many prosecutors at all levels of the judiciary perceive crimes against children as among the most difficult to prosecute and obtain convictions. Therefore, officers interviewing child witnesses and victims should have specialized training not only to convict the guilty but also to protect the innocent. Regardless of whether crimes against children are handled by generalists or specialists within the department, certain challenges are unique to these investigations.

 Challenges in investigating crimes against children include the need to protect the child from further harm, the possibility of parental involvement, the difficulty of interviewing children, credibility concerns and the need to collaborate with other agencies.

An innovative approach to handling child abuse and neglect cases is the Crimes against Children Mobile Unit used by the Florida Department of Law Enforcement, which brings the interview site to the child instead of the traditional reverse. A Fleetwood sleeper trailer seized from a drug dealer was gutted and equipped specifically to create a child-friendly mobile interview zone, furnished with child-sized bean bag chairs and lots of teddy bears and other toys. In addition, many hidden cameras and microphones are strategically located: "This high-tech, onsite approach achieves several things. It eases the fear that many victims feel when faced with (sometimes repeated) questioning; provides quality evidence for prosecutors; and, most importantly, is perfect for multiple victim, offender, or jurisdiction situations, cases that would overwhelm a traditional brick-and-mortar [interview room]" (Kyrik, 2007, p.76).

Consultation with local welfare authorities is sometimes needed before asking the court for a hearing to remove a child from the parents' custody or for protective custody in an authorized facility because police rarely have such facilities. As soon as possible the child should be taken to the nearest welfare facility or to a foster home, as stipulated by the juvenile court. The parents or legal guardians of the child must be notified as soon as possible.

Evidence

All the officer's observations pertaining to the physical and emotional condition of the victim must be recorded in detail. Evidence in child neglect or abuse cases includes the surroundings, the home conditions, clothing, bruises or other bodily injuries, the medical examination report and other observations. Photographs may be the best way to document child abuse and neglect where it is necessary to show injury to the child or the conditions of the home environment. Pictures should be taken immediately because children's injuries heal quickly and home conditions can be changed rapidly.

A Protocol for Responding to Child Abuse and Neglect

An effective police response to reports of child abuse and neglect should include:

- A written, agency-wide child abuse policy.
- Written interagency protocols and interagency teams to handle child abuse investigations.
- Immediate telephone notification of the police by protective service agency workers regarding all sexual abuse cases and all cases of serious physical injury or danger.
- Initial interviews conducted jointly with child protective agency workers, especially in sexual abuse cases.
- Patrol officers trained in the identification of abuse.
- Child abuse specialists, skilled as investigators and comfortable interviewing young children.
- Child-friendly interview settings.
- Limited and selective use of videotaping and anatomical dolls by properly trained individuals.

Law Enforcement's Disposition of Status Offenders

In making dispositions on juvenile matters, the police have found that the parents are often so absorbed with their own desires and problems that they have little time to consider their children's needs. Parents tend to rely on church, school or civic groups to guide their children and often pursue a policy of appeasement in the home rather than maintaining family discipline. In effect these parents want society to be their babysitters. The increasing reliance on community services and the parental emphasis on individual rights rather than responsibilities in the training and education of their children have, to a large extent, weakened the family and contributed to the growing delinquency problem, as was discussed in Chapter 4. Partly as a result of this lack of parental guidance, law enforcement agencies are faced with the constant problem of taking youths into custody on relatively minor charges such as curfew violations and loitering.

 The majority of police dispositions involve status offenses (violating curfew, truancy, loitering, underage smoking and drinking of alcoholic beverages, and running away).

Police dispositions range from taking no action to referring status offenders to social service agencies or to the juvenile court. The police alternatives are guided by the community, the local juvenile justice system and individual officer discretion. Whether the police actually arrest a juvenile usually depends on several factors, the most important being the seriousness of the offense. Other factors affecting the decision include the juvenile's character, age, gender, race, prior record, family situation and attitude. The decision may also be influenced by public opinion, the media, available referral agencies and the officer's experience.

 In the disposition of status offenders, how police resolve matters often depends on the officers' discretion, the specific incident and the resources available.

Officers' actions usually reflect community interests. For example, conflict may occur between the public's demand for order and a group of young people wanting to "hang around." How police respond to such hanging around is influenced by the officer's attitude and the standards of the neighborhood or community, rather than rules of the state. Each neighborhood or community and the officer's own feelings dictate how the police perform in such matters.

The Police Response to Delinquency

Some localities may handle a delinquent act very differently from others. For example, police investigating an auto theft in the suburbs and finding a youth responsible will often simply send the youth home for parental discipline. The youth will receive a notice of when to appear in court. In contrast, urban juveniles—especially minority youths—caught stealing an automobile are often detained in a locked facility. Sometimes, however, urban youths are at an advantage.

What rural law enforcement officers may perceive as criminal behavior is often viewed as a prank by that officer's urban counterpart. Clearly, justice for juveniles is not a neatly structured, impartial decision-making process by which the rule of law always prevails and each person is treated fairly and impartially.

Police Discretion and the Initial Contact

Between 80 and 90 percent of youths commit some offense for which they could be arrested, yet only about 3 percent of them are. This is in large part because they do not get caught. Further, those who are caught usually have engaged in some minor status offense that can be better handled by counseling and releasing in many instances. Although the "counsel and dismiss" alternative may be criticized as being soft on juveniles, this approach is often all that is needed to turn a youth around.

 Police officers have considerable discretionary power when dealing with juveniles.

Law enforcement officers have a range of alternatives to take:

- Release the child, with or without a warning, but without making an official record or taking further action.
- Release the child, but write up a brief contact or field report to juvenile authorities, describing the contact.
- Release the child, but file a more formal report referring the matter to a juvenile bureau or an intake unit for possible action.
- Turn the youth over to juvenile authorities immediately.
- Refer the case directly to the court through the district or county attorney.

In some instances youths engaging in delinquent acts are simply counseled. In other instances they are returned to their families, who are expected to deal with their child's deviant behavior. Sometimes they are referred to social services agencies for help. And sometimes they are charged and processed by the juvenile justice system.

 The most common procedure when confronting juveniles is to release the child, with or without a warning, but without making an official record or taking further action.

Parents, schools and the police are the main sources for the referral of youths into the juvenile justice system. Of these three sources, the police are, by far, the most common source of referrals.

In a few jurisdictions, if the child is not released without official record, he or she is automatically turned over to the juvenile authorities, who make all further decisions in the matter. If the child is referred to court, another decision is whether police personnel should release or detain the child. Officers try to dispose of juvenile cases in a way that considers the best interests of both the juvenile and the community.

Taken into Custody

Police contact with children may result either from a complaint received or from observing questionable behavior. In their initial contact with juveniles, the police are indirectly guided by the language of the Juvenile Court Act, which states that juveniles are **"taken into custody,"** not arrested. This is interpreted to mean the police's role is to salvage and rehabilitate youth, a role indirectly sanctioned by many judges who encourage settling disputes and complaints without referral to the court. Despite this preferred terminology, many criminal justice professionals still refer to the action as a juvenile *arrest*.

When a juvenile is taken into custody, this is technically not considered an arrest. The law enforcement process for arrest is modified in most jurisdictions when juveniles are apprehended. Police officers should be concerned about the mental health of juveniles. They should be good listeners and try to discover the problem or the reason for the juveniles' behavior. It is paramount in administering juvenile justice that youths be protected by all sociolegal requirements.

 The fundamental nature of the juvenile justice system is rehabilitative rather than punitive.

Most states' juvenile justice systems reflect this basic rehabilitative philosophy. However, during the 1980s and 1990s, an increasing number of states adopted a more punitive philosophy toward handling youthful offenders, treating juvenile offenders as criminals in need of punishment rather than treatment or rehabilitation, which was part of the broader trend within the criminal justice system as a whole to "get tough" on crime (Snyder and Sickmund, 2006, p.97). This philosophical shift will be discussed in greater detail in the chapters on pretrial services (Chapter 9) and the juvenile court (Chapter 10), but it is worth noting here because the police response to juvenile offending necessarily adjusts to keep in step with how the remainder of the justice system views delinquency.

The Supreme Court has emphasized the full constitutional rights of persons under legal age. The protection, critical to the juvenile offender, is twofold:

1. At no point in any criminal investigation may the rights of the juvenile be infringed upon.
2. A crime by a juvenile must be proven beyond a reasonable doubt, and all subsequent efforts by a state should be directed toward correlating and eliminating the cause of the crime rather than punishing the individual for having committed it. **Beyond a reasonable doubt** is less than absolute certainty, but more than high probability.

Juveniles must be treated with consideration to build their respect for authority. Officers must be firm but fair, and they must show genuine interest. They must try to understand the juveniles' reasoning. In handling juveniles, if

---

REALITY CHECK
The Importance of the Initial Contact between Police and Juveniles

Unfortunately, many law enforcement officers view dealing with juveniles as a nuisance task, on par with babysitting, and place little value on the significance this interaction can have on the future trajectory of delinquents and the overall crime levels in their jurisdiction. Considering the malleability of youthful attitudes and behavior patterns, this negative officer approach can prove extremely detrimental to law enforcement's mission to reduce crime:

To [some] officers, the first-time arrest of a juvenile for a minor violation seems a mundane and unimportant policing activity that does not meet the big-arrest standard. . . .

When examining the potential long-term negative impact on the community, the first-time arrest of a juvenile offender is a big arrest that criminal justice professionals cannot afford to treat as trivial. The way law enforcement agencies handle first-time juvenile offenders can affect the juvenile and his or her inclination to continue to violate the law. When treated as an insignificant event by the police, the first arrest represents a missed opportunity at intervention that could lay the foundation for repeated delinquency and perhaps hundreds of criminal acts over a lifetime. When handled proactively and with the appropriate gravity, the first police encounter can be a foundational life experience capable of reversing a juvenile's downward slide into potentially chronic, serious, and violent delinquency, as well as a key opportunity to achieve significant, long-term crime reductions for the community.

SOURCE: Thomas J. Lemmer and Rachel M. Johnston. "Reducing Crime through Juvenile Delinquency Intervention." *The Police Chief*, May 2004, pp.24–28.

officers resort to vulgarity or profanity, lose their tempers, display prejudicial behavior or label juveniles as "liars" or "no good," this is counterproductive. Such actions are often followed by further disruptive conduct by the juvenile or by a lack of cooperation in any attempt to divert juvenile conduct.

If a youth is detained, the officers must remember that juveniles have the same constitutional rights as adults, including the right to remain silent, the right to counsel, the right to know the specific charge and the right to confront witnesses. Given the *parens patriae* philosophy underlying the juvenile justice system, it might be expected that the police would exercise extra care in dealing with youths.

According to the Federal Bureau of Investigation's (FBI's) annual *Crime in the United States* report, of the juvenile offenders taken into custody in 2007, nearly 70 percent were referred to juvenile court jurisdiction and slightly more than 9 percent were referred to adult criminal court. Approximately one-fifth (20 percent) were handled within the department and released—called **station adjustment** or **street justice**. The remaining handful of cases were referred to a welfare agency or other police agency. Table 8.1 shows the police dispositions of juvenile offenders taken into custody in 2007, broken down by the size of the jurisdiction and whether the custody occurred within a metropolitan or non-metropolitan county.

One problem of referral for juvenile authorities and the court, especially in a metropolitan area, is that it may be difficult to determine by appearance alone if a person is a juvenile. Youths may lie about or try to manipulate their age for practical reasons. For example, a youth detained on a status offense may claim to be over the age limit and, consequently, *not* an offender. Or youths taken into custody for minor offenses such as disorderly conduct or prostitution often claim to be over the age limit, reasoning that if treated as adults they will simply be forced to spend a night in jail, hear a lecture by a judge and accept whatever penalty is disposed. If they identify themselves as juveniles, their detention usually is extended, and interference with their freedom and liberty may well be more substantial.

The Juvenile Holdover

An Implementation Guide for Juvenile Holdover Programs (Mowatt and Chezem, 2001) cites the following scenario:

> It was early Saturday morning. David, a 15-year-old who lives in a small town with a population of about 1,500, was driving his father's car and was stopped by the only police officer on duty. The headlights on David's car were not turned on and he was driving erratically. The officer suspected that David had been drinking. When tested with the officer's preliminary breath tester, David blew a 0.07. His blood alcohol content (BAC) was below the legal level of 0.08 for driving under the influence (DUI) in this state, but it is a zero-tolerance jurisdiction, meaning that the presence of any alcohol in the system of a 15-year-old was a violation.
>
> In addition, David did not have a valid driver's license and he was out after curfew. He was cited for all three violations, the car was secured, and a tow was ordered. David, now seated in the rear of the squad car, told the

Table 8.1   Police Disposition of Juvenile Offenders Taken into Custody, 2007 [2007 estimated population]

Population Group	Total[1]	Handled within Department and Released	Referred to Juvenile Court Jurisdiction	Referred to Welfare Agency	Referred to Other Police Agency	Referred to Criminal or Adult Court	Number of Agencies	2007 Estimated Population
TOTAL AGENCIES								
Number	663,991	129,404	461,909	2,430	8,141	62,107	5,242	120,286,534
Percent[2]	100.0	19.5	69.6	0.4	1.2	9.4		
TOTAL CITIES								
Number	560,393	117,588	387,512	1,775	7,098	46,420	3,937	87,798,925
Percent[2]	100.0	21.0	69.2	0.3	1.3	8.3		
GROUP I (250,000 and over)								
Number	138,954	41,670	94,226	20	604	2,434	37	25,796,709
Percent[2]	100.0	30.0	67.8	*	0.4	1.8		
GROUP II (100,000 to 249,999)								
Number	82,959	18,009	58,590	378	2,274	3,708	80	12,018,629
Percent[2]	100.0	21.7	70.6	0.5	2.7	4.5		
GROUP III (50,000 to 99,999)								
Number	105,992	19,497	76,429	414	1,295	8,357	234	15,972,903
Percent[2]	100.0	18.4	72.1	0.4	1.2	7.9		
GROUP IV (25,000 to 49,999)								
Number	75,606	12,211	53,794	254	1,671	7,676	360	12,405,704
Percent[2]	100.0	16.2	71.2	0.3	2.2	10.2		
GROUP V (10,000 to 24,999)								
Number	85,504	13,001	59,213	461	688	12,141	793	12,642,471
Percent[2]	100.0	15.2	69.3	0.5	0.8	14.2		
GROUP VI (under 10,000)								
Number	71,378	13,200	45,260	248	566	12,104	2,433	8,962,509
Percent[2]	100.0	18.5	63.4	0.3	0.8	17.0		
METROPOLITAN COUNTIES								
Number	81,552	8,543	59,834	493	879	11,803	636	24,275,366
Percent[2]	100.0	10.5	73.4	0.6	1.1	14.5		
NONMETROPOLITAN COUNTIES								
Number	22,046	3,273	14,563	162	164	3,884	669	8,212,243
Percent[2]	100.0	14.8	66.1	0.7	0.7	17.6		
SUBURBAN AREA[3]								
Number	288,762	47,148	198,657	1,429	2,557	38,971	3,278	58,405,783
Percent[2]	100.0	16.3	68.8	0.5	0.9	13.5		

[1]Includes all offenses except traffic and neglect cases.
[2]Because of rounding, the percentages may not add to 100.0.
[3]Suburban area includes law enforcement agencies in cities with less than 50,000 inhabitants and county law enforcement agencies that are within a Metropolitan Statistical Area. Suburban area excludes all metropolitan agencies associated with a principal city. The agencies associated with suburban areas also appear in other groups within this table.
*Less than one-tenth of 1 percent.
SOURCE: FBI Uniform Crime Reports 2007, Table 68. http://www.fbi.gov/ucr/cius2007/data/table_68.html

officer that he had been at a party and acknowledged that he had been drinking beer. David revealed that he had been drinking a lot lately. He stated that his parents were out of town for the weekend and could not be reached by phone. He was to be alone at home until late Sunday night and had no other relatives living in this community.

The officer had no on-duty backup and there were five more hours left on his shift. There was no safe place to drop David off, and department policy prohibited having the youth ride in the squad car for the remainder of the shift. The nearest emergency shelter facility for youths would be a three-hour round trip. Driving there would take up most of the time left on the officer's shift. The only option was to return to police headquarters and wait with David until morning. Then, arrangements could be made to locate his parents or to find a place for David to stay for the rest of the weekend. It was Friday night and because of one juvenile who was drinking alcohol and driving while impaired police coverage was not available for the community for the rest of the night.

The *Implementation Guide* (Mowatt and Chezem, p.1) notes: "When viewed from a national perspective, juvenile holdover programs are multifaceted. In general, however, they are short-term, temporary holding programs for youths that can be located in either a secure, non-secure or a combination secure/non-secure setting." The guide (pp.7–8) describes key elements of a successful holdover program as being easily accessible, integrated into a network of services for youths, with a trained staff able to respond to a youth's immediate needs, able to provide comfortable facilities with minimum services for an overnight stay and able to respond to and de-escalate the immediate situation if necessary (crisis intervention). An effective holdover program also has screening and assessment capacity, referral expertise and is able to coordinate post-release services to the youth and family and evaluate its effectiveness.

Detention

In some instances, law enforcement officers may determine that the most appropriate disposition is detention. **Detention** is the period during which a youth is taken into custody by police and probation before a petition is filed. Detention is governed by two requirements of the JJDP Act: (1) removing all juveniles from adult jails and lockups and (2) separating juvenile and adult offenders. The act states:

> Provide that juveniles alleged to be or found to be delinquent and youths within the purview of paragraph (12) (i.e., status offenders and non-offenders) shall not be detained or confined in any institution in which they have regular contact with adult persons incarcerated because they have been convicted of a crime or are awaiting trial on criminal charges.

In addition state laws and department policies may affect who is detained and under what conditions. Most state statutes governing the detention of juveniles are quite general. Among the criteria used by states are:

- For the juvenile's or society's protection
- Lack of parental care available
- To ensure a juvenile's presence at a juvenile court hearing
- The seriousness of the offense and the juvenile's record

Release vs. Detention   Juvenile court statutes often require that once children have been taken into custody, they may be released only to their parents, guardians or custodians. Where such a law exists, a decision to detain automatically follows if the parents, guardians or custodians cannot be found. The child is placed in detention and must be referred to court. Thus the police are removed from the referral process.

In most states police may take a child into custody for the child's own protection until appropriate placement can be made. Standards to guide police personnel in the decision whether to release or detain may be formally prepared in written instructions by police administrators and court authorities. In some states *mandatory referral* to juvenile authorities or even directly to court may be required for all crimes of violence, felonies and serious misdemeanors. Similarly all juveniles on parole or probation may be referred. Some jurisdictions refer if the juvenile has had previous contact with the police.

During detention, police have a **window of opportunity** to be an agency for change for youngsters (see box on page 240 for the importance of first arrests). Drug testing can be used diagnostically to identify high-risk youths before they become established in the cycle of illicit drug use and crime. Such youths can be put into drug-treatment programs, hopefully averting the drug-crime-drug cycle. Secure detention while awaiting adjudication is discussed in Chapter 10.

Prosecution

When the prosecutor receives a recommendation for petition (trial), at least three options are available: dismiss the case, file the petition or determine that the charges are so serious that the case should be heard in adult court, waiving jurisdiction. If a petition is filed, this begins the formal adjudication process. Based on police reports, the county attorney may refer a juvenile to the screening unit of the juvenile court.

Police as Mentors to Troubled Youths

Police who are committed to a mentoring relationship have an enormous impact on youths who are at risk of becoming chronic offenders. Carefully selected and trained police personnel can be the conduit for restoring youthful lives to productive relationships with families, schools and the community.

Mentoring is especially effective in dealing with troubled youths at risk of becoming juvenile offenders because it strikes directly at the individual's alienated condition. The youth's isolation and sense of meaninglessness are often dissolved over time through a long-term relationship characterized by respect. The youth's sense of powerlessness is eroded through a relationship with someone who helps the youth to clarify choices and who empowers the youth to make responsible decisions.

Police mentoring is an effective means available for optimizing meaningful contact between society and alienated youth. As a youth begins to bond with a mentor, a new worldview crystallizes, opening up a new range of perceived choices that reflects the values of the mentor and the community. Mentoring remains the best hope for reclaiming our troubled youths, our families, communities and society as a whole. To a large extent, the success or failure of the juvenile justice system depends on its effectiveness in handling youthful offenders—ensuring that for the vast majority of juvenile offenders their first brush with the law is the last.

The Juvenile Mentoring Program (JUMP) of the OJJDP supports one-to-one mentoring projects for youths at risk of failing in school, dropping out of school or becoming involved in delinquent behavior, including gang activity and substance abuse. The OJJDP defines mentoring as a one-to-one supportive relationship between a responsible adult 18 or older (mentor) and an at-risk juvenile (mentee), which takes place on a regular basis, one to two hours per week for an average of at least one year. The three principal program goals for JUMP are (1) to reduce juvenile delinquency and gang participation by at-risk youths, (2) to improve academic performance of at-risk youths and (3) to reduce the school dropout rate for at-risk youths. The OJJDP awards dozens of JUMP grants to communities throughout the nation each year.

The Police Response to Juveniles with Guns

A major concern in today's society is that of armed youth. A handful of legislation has been passed at the federal level in an effort to keep guns out of the hand of juveniles. The Gun Control Act of 1968 made it illegal for federally licensed firearms dealers to sell handguns to anyone under age 21. The 1994 Youth Safety Handgun Act prohibits the possession of a handgun by anyone under age 18. Nonetheless, state laws vary widely in terms of the minimum age of unrestricted purchase and possession of firearms, with some states seemingly in violation of federal law by setting minimum age limits for purchases from licensed dealers below age 18 for long guns and under 21 for handguns. For example, Montana allows 14-year-olds to legally purchase long guns, and Vermont has set 16 as the minimum age for legally purchasing both long guns and hand guns (see Table 8.2) (*Regulating Guns in America*, 2008, p.83). Wyoming is the only state that does not restrict, through any legislation, access to firearms by juveniles (p.76). And while federal law does not restrict juvenile offenders from purchasing or possessing firearms, 27 states do have such legislative restrictions.

Despite the legal restrictions imposed on juvenile gun use, youths seem to have little difficulty getting their hands on firearms if they want to. According to the Youth Risk Behavior Survey (YRBS), a national survey conducted every two years by the Centers for Disease Control and Prevention (CDC), in 2007, 5.2 percent of youth respondents admitted having carried a gun at least one day during the 30 days preceding the survey. While some youths, particularly those living in rural areas, use guns for sport and have grown up in a family with a long-standing tradition of gun use for hunting, other youths report carrying a gun for protection. Youths, particularly males, who carry a firearm for protection have been found to be significantly more likely to be involved in delinquent activity, as shown in Table 8.3.

 Boys who own guns for protection are significantly and substantially more likely to be involved in delinquent behavior than either those who do not own guns or those who own guns for sport.

In some cases youths obtain weapons not by buying them but as gifts from parents or other relatives. Many think it is wholly inappropriate for parents or legal guardians to supply children with weapons and that such

Table 8.2 Minors: Restrictions Based on Age or Juvenile Offender Status, 2008

Minimum Age for All Firearm Possession/Purchases (from Licensed or Unlicensed Sellers)[a]			
Jurisdiction	Handgun	Long Gun	Juvenile Offenders Restricted[b]
Federal	21	18	N
Alabama	18	—	N
Alaska	16/18	16/18	Y
Arizona	18	18	Y
Arkansas	18	18	N
California	21	18	Y
Colorado	18	18	Y
Connecticut	21	18	Y
Delaware	21	18	Y
District of Columbia	21	21	N
Florida	18	18	Y
Georgia	18	—	Y
Hawaii	21	18/21	Y
Idaho	18	18	N
Illinois	21	21	Y
Indiana	18	18	Y (handguns only)
Iowa	21	18	Y
Kansas	18	—	Y
Kentucky	18	—	Y
Louisiana	18	18	N
Maine	18	16	Y
Maryland	21	18	Y ("regulated firearms" only)
Massachusetts	21	18	Y
Michigan	18	18	N
Minnesota	18	16/18	Y
Mississippi	18	18	N
Missouri	18	18	N
Montana	14	14	N
Nebraska	21	—	N
Nevada	18	18/—	N
New Hampshire	18	—	N
New Jersey	21	18	Y
New Mexico	19	—	N
New York	21	16	N
North Carolina	18	—	N
North Dakota	18	—	N
Ohio	21	18	Y
Oklahoma	18	18	Y
Oregon	18	18	Y
Pennsylvania	18	18	Y
Rhode Island	21	18	N
South Carolina	21	—	N
South Dakota	18	—	N
Tennessee	18	18	N
Texas	18	18	N
Utah	18	18	Y
Vermont	16	16	N
Virginia	18	18	Y
Washington	21	18	Y
West Virginia	18	18	N
Wisconsin	18	18	Y
Wyoming	—	—	N

[a]No restrictions on purchase or possession by or transfer to persons over this age.
[b]See state summaries for details of restrictions on purchase and possession.
SOURCE: *Regulating Guns in America*. Legal Community Against Violence, 2008.

Table 8.3 Percentage of Boys Involved in Delinquency by Gun Ownership Status

Type of Delinquency	Gun Ownership Status (%)		
	No Gun Owned (n = 548)	Gun Owned for Sport (n = 27)	Gun Owned for Protection (n = 40)
Gun carrying	3.2	11.1	70.0
Gun crime	1.3	3.7	30.0
Street crime	14.8	18.5	67.5
Gang membership	7.2	11.1	55.0
Drug selling	3.5	7.4	32.5

SOURCE: Alan Lizotte and David Sheppard. *Gun Use by Male Juveniles: Research and Prevention.* Washington, DC: OJJDP Juvenile Justice Bulletin, July 2001, p.2. (NCJ 188992)

adults should be held liable, under parental-responsibility laws, for any crimes youths commit with those weapons. Unfortunately, parental-responsibility law is a gray area. Child access prevention (CAP) laws may also hold adults accountable when youths are allowed access to guns. Such charges are harder to dismiss than parental-responsibility laws. Unlike parent-responsibility laws, CAP laws draw a direct causal relationship between adults and the crimes committed by juveniles. If a parent possesses a firearm and fails to keep the firearm away from the children, it is easier to connect that to a criminal act by a child using the firearm. Florida passed the first CAP law in 1989, and 19 other states have enacted similar legislation (Brady Campaign to Prevent Gun Violence, 2008).

Data analysis of juvenile crime trends over the past two decades shows an interesting and undeniable correlation between the rise in youth violence (most notably a spike in youths committing homicides against youth) and a spike in youth possession of guns. The changing nature of youth crime has caused a shift in the justice system to a more punitive, "get tough" approach to dealing with such violent offenders, with many police agencies across the country altering their practices in reaction to this increase in violent juvenile offending. Straub (2008, p.1) notes: "In response to the surge in violent crime and the public's demand for quick, impressive action, many police departments have moved away from community policing, relying instead on traditional law enforcement strategies to fight crime. Tactical enforcement teams, 'stop and frisk' initiatives, neighborhood sweeps, gang injunctions, and public housing 'bar out' (a 'no-trespass' policy used by public housing authorities to reduce drug activity and other crimes) have been used to target and reduce violent crime."

The Boston Gun Project, Operation Ceasefire

One technique found to be effective in reducing juvenile gun crime is the strategy used by the Boston Gun Project in Operation Ceasefire, a widely publicized and replicated initiative that demonstrates the value of problem-solving planning to reduce gun violence. The specific strategies applied include gun use reduction tactics employing new gun-tracing technologies to interrupt the flow of illegal firearms to youths and a deterrence approach to inform juveniles of the severe criminal consequences they would face if caught with an illegal firearm. As a result of these and other strategies, youth firearm-related homicides dropped 75 percent during 1990–1998.

Research by Watkins et al. (2008) has verified that gun behaviors among juveniles are largely driven by gang membership, although such a relationship has long been recognized by law enforcement. The Boston Police Department implemented Operation Ceasefire by applying the technique of **pulling levers**—a deterrence strategy in which targeted gang members are arrested for the slightest infraction, even jaywalking—in an effort to stop the violence perpetrated by the Vamp Hill Kings (Kennedy et al., 2001). The Kings were invited to a forum where the master of ceremonies addressed them:

> "This isn't a sting; everybody's going to be home for dinner, we just wanted you to know a few things. And this is nothing personal either; this is how we're going to be dealing with violence in the future, and you just happened to be first. So go home and tell your friends about what you hear today."
>
> The forum was dramatic. In essence, the Working Group's message to the Kings was that they and their activities were known, and although the group could not stop every instance of offending, violence would no longer be tolerated. . . .
>
> Many gang members in the audience smiled and scoffed. They stopped when the Assistant U.S. Attorney assigned to the group spoke:
>
> "This kind of street crime used to be a local matter. Not anymore. The Attorney General cares more about youth violence than almost anything else. . . . We can bring in the DEA, we can bring in the FBI, we can bring in the ATF; we can prosecute you federally, which means you go to Lompoc, not stateside, and there's no parole in the federal system any more. You serve your time."
>
> The room became more silent when the panel turned to Freddie Cardoza, who was featured on his own flyer used as a handout [See Figure 8.1.]. (pp.35–37)

A study of the effect of the pulling levers deterrence strategy, in which criminal justice and social service attention was focused on a small number of chronically offending gang members responsible for the bulk of urban gun violence problems, found that the strategy was associated with a statistically significant decrease in the monthly number of gun homicides and gun-associated assault incidents (Braga et al., 2008, p.132).

Youth Firearms Violence Initiative

Another approach to juvenile gun crime was the Youth Firearms Violence Initiative (YFVI) launched in 1995 by the U.S. Department of Justice's Office of Community Oriented Policing Services (COPS). COPS provided up to $1 million to police departments in 10 cities[1] to fund interventions directed at combating

---

[1]The ten cities in the YFVI were Baltimore, Maryland; Birmingham, Alabama; Bridgeport, Connecticut; Cleveland, Ohio; Inglewood, California; Milwaukee, Wisconsin; Richmond, Virginia; Salinas, California; San Antonio, Texas; and Seattle, Washington.

FREDDIE CARDOZA

PROBLEM: VIOLENT GANG MEMBER

"Given his extensive criminal record,
if there was a Federal law against
jaywalking we'd indict him for that."

—Don Stern, US Attorney

SOLUTION: ARMED CAREER
CRIMINAL CONVICTION

Arrested with one bullet
Sentence: 19 years, 7 months
No possibility of parole

ADDRESS:

OTISVILLE FEDERAL
CORRECTIONAL INSTITUTE

Maximum Security Facility, New York

Figure 8.1   Cardoza Flyer Created by the Gun Project Working Group

the rise of youth firearms violence. Among the key findings of this initiative, according to Dunworth (2000, pp.1–2), were:

- A dedicated unit may exert a greater effect on gun-related crime than a unit that applies traditional tactics and uses patrol officers on a rotating basis.
- When employed as part of YFVI, traditional enforcement tactics did not produce significant changes in firearms violence levels.
- Cooperating with other law enforcement agencies and community organizations and representatives was a key factor in effective implementation of firearms violence control and prevention strategies.
- Proactive arrest policies focused on gun-related offenses were shown to have a consistent measurable association with subsequent gun-related crime.
- Most of the participating departments returned to traditional policing approaches when federal funding ended.

Table 8.4 summarizes the strategies and tactics used at five of the sites. It is of interest that only Baltimore implemented school-based activities.

Table 8.4   Police Department Strategies and Tactics of the Youth Firearms Violence Initiative (YFVI)

Site	Total Budget and Configuration	Street-Based Activities	School-Based Activities	Community-Based Activities	GIS*/Crime Analysis
Baltimore	$999,906 ▪ Cherry Hill: 9 officers ▪ Park Heights: 15 officers	▪ Juvenile Violent Crime Flex Team: surveillance, intelligence gathering and targeted enforcement ▪ Curfew Enforcement Team: focused on chronically truant students	▪ In Park Heights, two city police officers worked with middle and high schools ▪ Supported the Magnet School for Law Enforcement, a criminal justice curriculum for high school students ▪ Three officers implemented the Straight Talk About Risk (STAR) Program	▪ Community resource centers (Kobans) in schools provided a police presence and liaison with community groups ▪ Curfew enforcement officers provided information, counseling and housing to truant students and families	▪ Department had GIS capability prior to YFVI
Cleveland	$685,342 ▪ 27 officers, 2 sergeants	▪ Residential Area Policing Program (RAPP) Houses in neighborhoods with high violence, staffed around the clock for 90 days	None	▪ RAPP House officers coordinated cleanup and youth activities ▪ RAPP House used for neighborhood meetings	▪ Department had GIS capability prior to YFVI
Inglewood	$787,201 ▪ Strategy Against Gang Environments (SAGE) Gang Enforcement Task Force: 1 sergeant, 6 officers ▪ Strengthened the Street Terrorist Enforcement and Prevention (STEP) Task Force: 6 officers, 1 probation officer, 1 district attorney	▪ SAGE program: civil remedies against gang members; task force focused on weapons violations ▪ STEP: act with criminal sanctions against street gangs and a task force that conducted street enforcement ▪ Probation officer targeted gang members on probation	None	▪ Rites-of-Passage Mentoring Program used police officers, firefighters and community leaders to teach youths civic values, self-esteem and conflict mediation ▪ Gun and Weapons Buy-Back Program ▪ KIDSAFE campaign taught parents about the dangers of handgun use and possession ▪ Media and poster campaign addressed youth firearm violence prevention	▪ Juvenile records computerized for YFVI ▪ Internally developed a GIS system (with minimal YFVI funding)
Salinas	$999,524 ▪ Violence Suppression Unit (VSU): 1 lieutenant, 2 sergeants, 16 officers	▪ VSU: dedicated to work full time on suppressing youth handgun violence ▪ Crime tip hotline ▪ Intensified efforts to locate firearms and track down their origins	None	None	▪ An outside contractor implemented ArcView/ArcInfo system
San Antonio	$999,963 ▪ Rotation: 9 officers deployed nightly	▪ Weapons Recovery and Tracking Team ▪ Street Crime Arrest Team	None	None	▪ Research the youth firearm violence problem ▪ Computer linkup with trauma centers throughout the city

*Geographic information systems.
SOURCE: Terence Dunworth. *National Evaluation of the Youth Firearms Violence Initiative.* Washington, DC: National Institute of Justice Research in Brief, November 2000, p.5. (NCJ 184482)

Project Safe Neighborhoods

Another gun reduction initiative is Project Safe Neighborhoods (PSN), a nation-wide commitment to reduce gun crime by networking existing local programs that target gun crime and providing those programs with additional tools necessary to be successful. The goal is to take a hard line against gun criminals through every available means to create safer neighborhoods. Project Safe Neighborhoods seeks to achieve heightened coordination among federal, state and local law enforcement, with an emphasis on tactical intelligence gathering, more aggressive prosecutions and enhanced accountability through performance measures. The philosophy of PSN as applied to youth is based on the previously mentioned corresponding spikes in juvenile violent crime and juvenile gun possession, with the anticipation that a reduction in youths carrying firearms would also result in a reduction in violent juvenile crime. The Project Safe Neighborhoods Web site is http://www.psn.gov.

Of special concern to law enforcement are youths who carry guns in our schools. Although the 1994 Gun Free Schools Act requires schools receiving federal education funds to have a policy mandating the expulsion of students who bring firearms to school, some youths still manage to bring guns onto school property, as discussed shortly.

The Police Response to Youth Crime and Violence in Our Schools

Property crimes are nothing new for schools. A favorite target of youth out to commit vandalism has often been their local school, with such offenses ranging from spray-painted walls and broken windows to complete destruction of interior classrooms and other school property. Particularly when the offense is perceived as minor, such as graffiti or a few stolen items from a science classroom, these acts are unlikely to be reported to the police, making dealing with the problem that much more difficult (Petrocelli, 2007, p.32).

What has become of increasing concern to educational institutions and law enforcement agencies across the country is the prevalence of violent crime in our nation's schools. Many youths are demonstrating an increased capacity for violence, which has crept into the schools and made students fearful of victimization by their classmates. Metal detectors, surveillance cameras and drug- and weapons-detector dogs are a growing presence on school campuses nationwide. When the final bell rings and the class day is over, the violence carries over to extracurricular activities and athletic fields, where students often are taught to compete and win at all costs. Aggression is rewarded and even modeled by the parents who, in front of their own children, shamelessly hurl more than words at coaches, umps and parents of the opposing team.

Noonan and Vavra (2007) highlight the critical importance in understanding the dynamics of criminal acts in educational settings to allow law enforcement, school administrators, policymakers and the public to construct adequate, effective responses: "Schools and colleges are valued institutions that help build upon the nation's foundations and serve as an arena where the growth and stability of future generations begin. Crime in schools and colleges is therefore one of the most troublesome social problems in the Nation today. Not only does it affect those involved in the criminal incident, but it also hinders societal growth and stability."

In their five-year study, Noonan and Vavra found that 3.3 percent of all incidents reported via the National Incident-Based Reporting System (NIBRS) involved school locations. Offense records indicate that such incidents were most likely to include the use of personal weapons (the offender's hands, fists, feet, etc.), while reports of the offender's use of alcohol, computers and/or drugs were minimal. Reported offenders of crime in schools were most likely to be 13- to 15-year-old White males who were known to the victims; however, there was nearly an equally large number of 16- to 18-year-old reported offenders. More than half of the arrestees associated with crime at school locations were arrested for simple assault or drug/narcotic violations. Arrestees had similar characteristics to the reported offenders, most likely being reported as 13- to 15-year-old White non-Hispanic males who were residents of the community of the school location where the incident was reported. Interestingly, across all five years of the study, the highest number of offenses reported consistently occurred during October each year.

Dinkes et al. (2007) reports the following key findings related to indicators of school crime and safety:

- Overall victimization at school is down by half over the past decade.
- One out of 25 students are victims of crime at school—mostly thefts.
- Reports of gang presence at schools are up.
- Incidents of fighting at and away from school have increased slightly between 2003 and 2005.
- Incidents of weapon carrying at and away from school have remained steady over the past several years.
- Students report less fear of attacks at and on the way to school, but recent trends show increases in these indicators.
- Violent deaths at school remain rare.
- Twenty-eight percent of students ages 12–18 reported being bullied at school during the previous six months.

Several states have passed laws requiring school officials to report certain types of offenses to local police. Illinois school principals, for example, must report acts of intimidation and attacks on school personnel in addition to other crimes committed by students. In many states failure to report violent incidents to a law enforcement agency is a criminal offense—usually a misdemeanor.

Educators commonly detect and report incidents of suspected child abuse or family violence. Educators may also, however, be firsthand witnesses to and, on occasion, victims of violence, as the aggression experienced at home by some children finds its way onto school grounds. A variety of elements may lead police in a certain jurisdiction to respond to incidents of school violence.

A trend, particularly among smaller departments, in tailoring a more effective response to school violence is to provide more cross-training and pooling of resources. A comprehensive, step-by-step discussion of police response to school violence is beyond the scope of this text; however, several publications focus entirely on this subject. A particularly useful document addressing school violence is the *Guide for Preventing and Responding to School Violence* published by the International Association of Chiefs of Police (IACP). It is based on the input of more than 500 experts and 15 focus groups with a diverse range of disciplines.

The School Resource Officer (SRO) Program

A much publicized delinquency prevention plan, the police-school liaison program, was developed in 1958 in Flint, Michigan, with the cooperation of school authorities, parents, social agencies, juvenile court officials, businesses and the police department. The foundation for the police-school liaison program established a workable relationship with the police department and the public school system. This program gradually evolved into what is today the **school resource officer (SRO)** program.

Part Q of Title I of the Omnibus Crime Control and Safe Streets Act of 1968 defines the SRO as "a career law enforcement officer, with sworn authority, deployed in community-oriented policing, and assigned by the employing police department or agency to work in collaboration with school and community-based organizations." According to the National Association of School Resource Officers, school-based policing is the fastest growing area of law enforcement.

School resource officers do not enforce school regulations, which are left to the school superintendent and staff. Instead the officers work with students, parents and school authorities to apply preventive techniques to problems created by antisocial youths who have not or will not conform to the community's laws and ordinances. The techniques used by school resource officers involve counseling children and their parents, referring them to social agencies to treat the root problems, referring them to drug and alcohol abuse agencies and being in daily contact in the school to check their progress. Often school resource officers deal with predelinquent and early delinquent youths with whom law enforcement would not have been involved under traditional programs.

SROs frequently patrol the elementary school areas until school starts in the morning, and also during the noon hour and after school. They watch for any suspicious people or automobiles and for infractions of safety rules regarding routes to and from school. They also check the middle-school areas for anyone loitering around the building or grounds trying to pick up students in the area. Appendix B provides a detailed job description for an SRO.

Many aspects of the school resource officer program benefit students, the school and the community. The communication developed between the law enforcement agency and school personnel provides information to guide young people. Respect for law enforcement agencies is built up in the minds of the youths. The SRO becomes their friend. The effective preventive work of the school resource officer program may be a considerable part of the answer to the problem of juvenile antisocial behavior.

Goals of School Resource Officer Programs The goals of the school resource officer program fall into two general categories: preventing juvenile delinquency and improving community relations.

PERSPECTIVES FROM THE NATIONAL CONFERENCE ON JUVENILE JUSTICE (NCJJ)

The federal Safe Schools/Healthy Students (SS/HS) Initiative is based on the fundamental premise that a safe learning environment is critical to the success of the academic mission. The SS/HS Initiative is a collaborative effort between three federal agencies—the U.S. Department of Education, the U.S. Department of Justice and the U.S. Department of Health and Human Services—to apply evidence-based strategies to enhance the safety and, thus, the learning experience of our nation's students.

As discussed in a session at the 34th National Conference on Juvenile Justice, a key to success in the law enforcement/juvenile justice/school triumvirate is the proper selection of the SRO: "You don't just put anybody in this job. . . . Make sure you have an officer who likes kids. The kids want someone who cares for them." While this may seem obvious, many jurisdictions do not handpick their SROs for qualities that work in schools but rather have such a position as part of a regular rotation.

Another important facet of this partnership is sharing information using multiple agency agreements and knowing the state laws that apply to such information sharing when it involves adjudicated youths. Part of the benefit of involving law enforcement in the effort to keep schools safe is that they generally have a pulse on the community and can share relevant information on the dynamics of certain neighborhoods and families that feed into the schools. As one SRO states: "With a lot of the kids I deal with, I've also dealt with their parents."

SOURCE: Rosiak, John; Hampton, Craig; and Sanchez, Art. "The Role of Law Enforcement in Safe Schools." San Diego, CA: Seminar B-3 presented at the 34th National Conference on Juvenile Justice, March 5, 2007.

© Joel Gordon/Joel Gordon Photography

School resource officers (SROs) are a visible reminder of the need for law and order. They stress positive interactions with students who do not misbehave as well as dealing with those who are delinquent.

Preventing Delinquency In seeking to prevent delinquency, officers focus on both preventive actions and the official investigation of criminal activity, apprehension and court referral. Officers assigned to schools approach delinquency prevention through a variety of activities:

- *Acting as instructors* for various school groups and classes.
- *Acting as counselors* to students, separately or with school personnel.
- *Maintaining contacts with parents or guardians* of students who exhibit antisocial behavior.
- *Making public appearances.*
- *Maintaining files* of information on students contacted.
- *Investigating complaints of criminal activity* occurring within the school complex and the surrounding area.
- *Maintaining close contact with other police agencies.*

Improving Community Relations The second general goal of SRO programs focuses on community relations, projecting and maintaining an image of the police as serving the community, rather than simply enforcing laws. Enhancing community relations is accomplished in several ways.

Public appearances are a key technique. Officers speak and present films or slide programs to many types of groups, such as PTAs, service groups, church fellowships, civic gatherings, youth clubs and civil rights groups. There usually is an interplay of ideas at such gatherings, and the officers sell the idea of community service.

Another focus is *parent contacts*. Behavioral problems are often apparent in the school before they develop into more serious delinquent activity. Officers in the school know about such problems and can contact parents, working together with them to avoid any progression into serious delinquent behavior.

Possibly the most effective community relations technique at officers' disposal is *individual contact*. Officers have contact with many young people of all ages. In projecting an image of the "good guys," they influence the attitudes not only of those students counseled but also of their friends and families. Many popular myths about laws and law enforcement officers are dispelled through this type of interaction.

Another important area is *liaison work with other interested agencies,* including juvenile courts, social agencies, mental health agencies, other schools and private organizations. Officers gain operational knowledge of each and learn to coordinate their efforts with these other agencies to better treat children.

Displaying interest indicates to these agencies that police are concerned with more than simply apprehension and detention in dealing with delinquency. Undoubtedly teachers have a definite effect on their students' attitudes. Officers who help teachers with problem students improve teachers' image of the police. This, along with personally knowing a police officer, does much in long-range police-community relations and, as any preventive program must be, this preventive program is long range.

Finally, *recreational participation* is a type of interaction with youths that breaks down many walls of resentment. Officers who participate in organized athletics with youngsters build a rapport that is carried over into their other contacts with those youths.

SROs have traditionally served to educate students about topics such as pedestrian safety and the dangers of substance abuse. That role has broadened as local law enforcement agencies attempt to defuse potentially violent student situations. Among such situations is bullying.

Bullying

It has been said that bullying is suicide's quiet little secret, as some victims of bullying suffer such humiliation and loss of self-esteem they become violent toward themselves. Estimates based on suicide statistics compiled by the CDC place the number of suicides by children under age 19 that are bully-related in the triple digits.

Garrett (2006, p.8) notes: "Technology has made brutality—particularly the emotional kind—much easier to inflict. Through e-mails, blogs, Internet bulletin boards and Instant Messaging, cyber bullies can cast their wrath instantly—and anonymously. These tactics have far-reaching impacts on the juvenile community."

A leading researcher on bullying is Olweus (pronounced Ol-VEY-us), whose Bullying Prevention Program was developed in Norway and has since been replicated in the United States. According to the U.S. Web site for the Olweus Bullying Prevention Program (2008), this comprehensive, school-wide program is designed for use in elementary, middle or junior high schools and attempts

IN THE HEADLINES

In September 2006, 13-year-old Megan Meier met a boy—16-year-old Josh Evans—online through MySpace and they began to chat. A friendship developed and daily messages were exchanged. In mid-October, things took an abrupt turn when Josh suddenly wrote one day that he didn't want to be friends with Megan anymore because he'd heard she wasn't very nice to her friends. Upset by this, Megan immediately wrote back asking for answers. An online fight ensued and before long, bulletins (surveys) were being posted on MySpace saying "Megan Meier is a slut." "Megan Meier is fat." The final post from Josh that day—one the FBI has never been able to retrieve but that Megan's father recalls reading—said something to the effect of, "You are a horrible person and the world would be a better place without you." That evening Megan hung herself in her bedroom closet.

The investigation that followed revealed Josh Evans didn't exist. He was a hoax, a fictitious identity invented by Lori Drew, the mother of an ex-friend of Megan's, who wanted to find out what Megan was saying online about her daughter. In November 2008, Drew was convicted on three misdemeanor charges and faces up to three years in prison and a $300,000 fine for violating MySpace's terms of service (ToS) by misrepresenting her identity on the Web site.

The ploy that evolved into the most notorious case of cyber-bullying to date and which led to a girl's suicide has caused a shock wave throughout the country and reinforced the message that cyberspace can be a dangerous place for children. But it has also revealed dangerous gaps in legislation regarding online harassment and what charges, if any, can be brought against those who use the computer to bully others. As the direct result of this case, many jurisdictions have drafted laws making it a felony for adults who use online technology to harass children. Many, however, fear that a dangerous precedent has been set that could impede the freedom of speech we currently enjoy in the various ways we choose to communicate, including online messaging. And legal scholars and criminal justice experts around the country are voicing concern. Andrew Grossman, a senior legal policy analyst at the Heritage Foundation, told *The New York Times*, "If this verdict stands, it means that every site on the Internet gets to define the criminal law. That's a radical change." Sameer Hinduja, a professor of criminology and criminal justice at Florida Atlantic University, also stated to *The New York Times*, "It will be interesting to see if issues of safety and security will eventually trump the hallmark ideology of free, largely anonymous or pseudonymous participation in cyberspace."

In terms of juvenile justice and the welfare of children, this case is an eye-opener. Risks abound, not only from "traditional" criminals but from parents who show incredible lack of good judgment and, unfortunately, pass their distorted morals and manners of human interaction on to their own children. And that is perhaps what incenses people the most about this case—that a grown woman, a mother, would devise and participate in such bullying.

to restructure the existing school environment to reduce opportunities and rewards for bullying. The program has proven highly successful in Norway, and has demonstrated similarly positive results in the United States:

- In the 1990s in South Carolina, after one year of implementation, researchers found large, significant decreases in boys' and girls' reports of bullying others; large, significant decreases in boys' reports of being bullied; and decreases in boys' reports of social isolation.
- An evaluation of the program in 12 elementary schools in the Philadelphia area found significant reductions in self-reported bullying and victimization and significant decreases in adults' observations of bullying in the cafeteria and on the playground.
- The Chula Vista (California) Police Department implemented the program in 2003 in collaboration with local schools and found 17 percent less name-calling, 19 percent less exclusion from groups, 18 percent less hitting and kicking, 13 percent fewer false rumors, 21 percent fewer threats and 12 percent less racial name-calling. In addition bullying was reduced 23 percent in bathrooms, 27 percent in gym classes and 11 percent in the lunch room. Additionally, 12 percent more students were willing to intervene if they witnessed bullying and 82 percent of parents agreed that the school was treating bullying more seriously.

Although intervention against bullies is desirable from the standpoint of the victims, it is also beneficial to the aggressive students, who are much more likely than other students to increase their antisocial behaviors.

Being bullied can also lead its victims to turn their anger and frustration outward. Consider the following excerpt from a 15-year-old boy's journal: "I hate being laughed at. But they won't laugh after they're scraping parts of their parents, sisters, brothers and friends from the wall of my hate." These are the words of Kip Kinkel, who later killed his parents and then went on a shooting spree in his high school in Springfield, Oregon, killing two students and wounding two dozen more. According to the Center for the Study and Prevention of Violence, in 2006 guns caused nearly 80 percent of all violent deaths in schools.

School Shootings

It ranks as one of the worst nightmares a parent can imagine—the shooting of their child by another child while at school. Such shootings, although rare, capture intense media coverage, which can lead the public to believe these events are more pervasive than they actually are. Table 8.5 summarizes school shootings throughout the United States since 1996.

The School Shooter   Following traditional law enforcement protocol, many have tried to profile the shooters and victims involved in school violence, searching for a pattern that may help predict or prevent similar events in the future. To date, none have succeeded, and several experts contend this is a good thing. Mary Ellen O'Toole, a senior profiler with the FBI, cautions against relying on profiles or checklists of danger signs to identify the next youth likely to bring lethal violence to a school, stating simply: "Those things do not exist" (O'Toole, 2000, p.1).

PROGRAMS IN PRACTICE: THE SOUTH EUCLID (OHIO) SCHOOL BULLYING PROJECT

Following is a detailed description of how the South Euclid (Ohio) Police Department addressed bullying in their schools using the SARA (Survey, Analysis, Response and Assessment) model. The South Euclid School Bullying Project is a 2001 Herman Goldstein Award winner for excellence in problem-oriented policing.

Scanning Unchecked disorderly behavior of students led the school resource officer (SRO) to review school data regarding referrals to the principal's office. He found that the high school reported thousands of referrals a year for bullying, and the junior high school had recently experienced a 30 percent increase in referrals for bullying. Police data showed that juvenile complaints about disturbances, bullying and assaults after school hours had increased 90 percent in the past 10 years.

Analysis All junior high and high school students were surveyed. Interviews and focus groups were also conducted with students—identified as victims or offenders—teachers and guidance counselors. Finally, the South Euclid Police Department purchased a Geographic Information System to complete crime and incident mapping of hotspots within the schools. The main findings pointed to four principal areas of concern: the environmental design of school areas, teachers' knowledge of and response to the problem, parents' attitudes and responses, and students' perspectives and behaviors.

Environmental design findings revealed that locations in the school with less supervision or denser population (primarily the hallways, cafeteria and gymnasium) were more likely to have higher rates of bullying; students avoided certain places at school for fear of being bullied (e.g., hallways near lockers of students who were not their friends or who were not in their classes); and a vast majority of students reported witnessing bullying or being bullied during class.

Teacher issues revealed that although bullying occurred frequently, teachers and students infrequently intervened. And when students were asked what would happen if they told a teacher about an incident of bullying, more than 30 percent said "nothing." Finally, students said they wouldn't tell teachers about bullying because they were afraid of retaliation, expected the teacher to "do nothing" or were afraid the teacher wouldn't believe or support them, especially if the bully was popular or well liked by the teacher.

Parent issues revealed that students who reported being physically disciplined at home were more likely to report that they had been bullied. More than one-third of parents who had talked to their children about bullying had instructed them to fight back. Students said they would not tell a parent if they were bullied because they believed their parents would overreact.

Student issues revealed that students reporting they engaged in bullying typically perceived their own behavior as playful or a normal part of growing up. They said everyone gets picked on but some "don't know how to take it," "take things too seriously" or "just don't know how to fight back." Victims of bullying did not perceive this behavior as fun or normal, yet victims viewed bullies as popular. Students were more likely to seek adult help for someone else who was bullied than for themselves. Students with lower grade point averages were significantly more likely to physically hurt someone else. Students who were secure in a peer group were more likely to intervene in bullying and less fearful of retaliation. Students suggested that involvement in school activities helped them to form a niche where they felt safe, supported and free from victimization.

Response The SRO, collaborating with a social worker and university researchers, coordinated a Response Planning Team to respond to each of the areas identified in the analysis. Environmental changes involved modifying the school bell times and increasing teacher supervision of hotspot areas. Counselors and social workers conducted teacher training courses in conflict resolution and bullying prevention. Parent education included mailings with information about bullying, an explanation of the new school policy and discussion about what they could do at home to address the problems. Finally, student education focused on classroom discussions with homeroom teachers and students, and assemblies conducted by the SRO. The Ohio Department of Education also contributed by opening a new training center for at-risk students to provide a nontraditional setting for specialized help.

Assessment The results from the various responses were dramatic. School suspensions decreased 40 percent. Bullying incidents dropped 60 percent in the hallways and 80 percent in the gym area. Follow-up surveys indicated positive attitudinal changes among students about bullying and more students felt confident teachers would take action. The overall results suggested that not only were the school environments safer, but that early intervention also was helping at-risk students succeed in school.

SOURCE: Adapted from "The South Euclid School Bullying Project." In *Excellence in Problem-Oriented Policing: The 2001 Herman Goldstein Award Winners.* Washington, DC: National Institute of Justice, Community Oriented Policing Services and the Police Executive Research Forum, 2001, pp.55–62.

Table 8.5 A Summary of School Shootings

Date	Location and Estimated Population	Number Killed	Number Wounded	Shooter(s)
February 2, 1996	Moses Lake, WA (16,300)	2 students, 1 teacher	1	Barry Loukaitis, 14
February 19, 1997	Bethel, AK (6,500)	1 student, principal	2	Evan Ramsey, 16
October 1, 1997	Pearl, MS (23,600)	2 students	7	Luke Woodham, 16
December 1, 1997	West Paducah, KY (25,800)	3 students	5	Michael Carneal, 14
December 15, 1997	Stamps, AR (2,400)	0	2	Colt Todd, 14
March 24, 1998	Jonesboro, AK (52,500)	4 students, 1 teacher	10	Mitchell Johnson, 13 Andrew Golden, 11
April 24, 1998	Edinboro, PA (6,800)	1 teacher	2 students	Andrew Wurst, 14
May 19, 1998	Fayetteville, TN (7,500)	1	0	Jacob Davis, 18
May 21, 1998	Springfield, OR (50,700)	2 students	22	Kip Kinkel, 15
June 15, 1998	Richmond, VA (199,300)	0	1 teacher, 1 guidance counselor	Male, 14
April 20, 1999	Littleton, CO (41,300)	14 students (including 2 shooters), 1 teacher	23	Eric Harris, 18 Dylan Klebold, 17
May 20, 1999	Conyers, GA (8,500)	0	6	Thomas Solomon, 15
November 19, 1999	Deming, NM (14,900)	1 student	0	Victor Cordova, Jr., 12
December 6, 1999	Fort Gibson, OK (3,800)	0	4 students	Seth Trickey, 13
February 29, 2000	Mt. Morris, MI (3,100)	1 (6-year-old)	0	Male, 6
May 26, 2000	Lake Worth, FL (29,000)	1 teacher	13	Nathaniel Brazil, 13
March 5, 2001	Santee, CA (53,900)	2	13	Charles Williams, 15
March 7, 2001	Williamsport, PA (29,900)	0	1	Elizabeth Bush, 14
March 22, 2001	El Cajon, CA (90,200)	0	5	Jason Hoffman, 18
September 24, 2003	Cold Spring, MN (3,000)	2 students	0	Jason McLaughlin, 15
March 21, 2005	Red Lake, MN (1,430)	6 students (including shooter), 1 teacher, 1 security guard	7	Jeff Weise, 16
October 2, 2006	Nickel Mines, PA (unknown)	5 students, shooter	5	Charles Carl Roberts IV, 32
April 16, 2007	Blacksburg, VA (Virginia Tech student enrollment approx. 30,700)	33 (including shooter)	23	Seung-Hui Cho, 23
February 12, 2008	Oxnard, CA (193,000)	1	0	Brandon McInerney, 14

SOURCE: Adapted from Borgna Brunner, editor. *The Time Almanac*, 2002, p.362. Population data from the U.S. Bureau of the Census. Events post-2001 updated by authors.

The absence of a school shooter profile is actually beneficial because profiles tend to foster a blind reliance on a certain laundry list of traits or behaviors rather than encouraging an awareness of individual signals that may indicate a potential shooting incident (Caster, 2008, p.77). All school personnel, including SROs, should be trained to look for disturbing writings,

Playgrounds are a common location for bullying to occur. They should be carefully supervised.

comments and postings on Web sites. Most school shooters are not drug abusers and do not have an extensive juvenile record. They may, however, know a lot about firearms and may use high-quality weapons and train frequently (Caster, p.79).

Early Warning Signs　School violence almost never occurs without warning. Although use of profiles and checklists is strongly discouraged, early warning signs of violent behavior have been recognized which, when presented in combination, might aid in identifying and referring children who may need help. Among these are low tolerance for frustration, poor coping skills, signs of depression, alienation, lack of empathy, an exaggerated sense of entitlement, an attitude of superiority, anger management problems, intolerance, lack of trust, rigid and opinionated, and negative role models (O'Toole, 2000, pp.18–21).

Threat Assessment　O'Toole (2000, p.5) notes: "All threats are NOT created equal." Some herald a clear and present danger; others represent little danger.

 Threats may be classified as direct, indirect, veiled or conditional.

A **direct threat** identifies a specific act against a specific target and is delivered in a straightforward manner, clearly and explicitly; for example, "I am going to put a bomb in a locker." An **indirect threat** is vague and ambiguous; for example, "If I wanted to, I could blow up this school." A **veiled threat** strongly implies but does not explicitly threaten violence; for example, "We would be better off if this school were destroyed." A **conditional threat** warns that a violent act will occur unless certain demands are met; for example, "If you don't pay me $100,000, I will blow up this school."

O'Toole (pp.10–24) describes a four-pronged assessment approach to determine the likelihood of a student becoming a school shooter based on the "totality of the circumstances" known about a student.

 The four-pronged threat assessment approach examines the student's personality, family dynamics, school dynamics and the student's role in those dynamics, and social dynamics.

This model provides a framework to evaluate a student to determine whether he or she has the motivation, means and intent to carry out a threat.

The Police Response to School Shooters   Scanlon (2008, p.43) explains that in 1999, after the catastrophe at Columbine, law enforcement responded to school shooters by calling in highly trained and heavily armed SWAT teams. However, this is no longer the recommended tactic. When dealing with an active school shooter: "First responders no longer hold and contain, waiting for SWAT teams to arrive. Instead, they run to the gunfire and attempt to force surrender" (Scanlon, p.43).

 The role of the first responder in a school shooting situation is to pursue and engage the shooter.

In light of this change in philosophy, Caster (2008, p.79) stresses that active shooter training cannot be limited to situations where three or four more officers respond and form a team: "Good, solid training must be given to the officer inside the school so an adequate response can be successfully completed without waiting for more officers."

In Search of Safer Schools

A common measure to reduce school violence is automatic suspensions for weapons violations. The problem with school suspensions is that not only might the suspended student fall behind in assignments but the student might also commit crimes while on suspension. Other common measures include revising disciplinary codes, designating schools as drug-free zones and conducting conflict resolution and mediation programs.

 An effective approach to school security should include crisis planning, security technology and school/law enforcement/community partnerships.

Crisis Planning   Every agency and institution affected or involved during an episode of school violence must decide in advance how they plan to respond, knowing that no two situations will be exactly the same and even the best-laid plans will require on-the-spot, last-minute adjustments. For police, the first step is generally to obtain blueprints or floor plans and to conduct walk-throughs of local schools. Law enforcement should know the layouts of every school in its jurisdiction.

Some departments stage mock disasters to test their emergency preparedness for acts of school violence and to identify areas that need improving. Such drills frequently highlight the importance of collaboration and communication with other agencies for an effective response.

Schools must also necessarily participate in crisis planning. Most, if not all, schools have preparedness plans for emergencies such as fires, tornados, hurricanes or earthquakes. Many, however, have neglected to devise a response plan for school violence, thus remaining unsecure and unprepared for such crises. Some school systems in the United States have adopted a lockdown procedure as a standard response to the threat of an active shooter.

Security Technology   A second requirement to achieve safer schools involves implementing security technology, such as weapons screening programs, entry control systems and video cameras. Recognizing that a significant proportion of school violence is perpetrated by those who neither attend nor work at the school, many districts are implementing entry control systems, such as photo ID cards, to make it easier to spot outsiders.

Video cameras are also being installed as a way to curb school violence. Most cameras are not actively monitored but, rather, tape on a continuous loop and are reviewed only when an incident is reported. When a high school in Washington state became beset by bullying problems, they gathered as much data as they could using surveillance, police incident reports and student surveys. The lunchroom was identified as the center of bullying and harassment.

Sanchez (2007, p.110) describes how the city of Hollywood, Florida, uses digital surveillance technology for school security. The first school selected for the new technology was South Broward High School, which implemented wireless remote surveillance technology with 60 security cameras controlled from a single access point inside the camera room. School administrators and SROs have welcomed the ability to view footage from the cameras from their office computers or laptops.

While many other schools have found positive benefits in using video cameras and other security devices, technology cannot replace personnel. Technology works best when balanced with human resources.

Partnerships   Partnerships are a vital component in an effective response to school violence. While partnerships to address the issue of school violence can take many forms and involve numerous entities, one of the most effective approaches has been to station officers directly on school campuses as SROs.

Demand for SROs has increased dramatically, which can be understood by looking at the School Safety Pyramid developed by the Center for the Prevention of School Violence. Illustrated in Figure 8.2, the pyramid reflects the importance of the community policing concept in school safety, discussed shortly.

The community sits at the pyramid's base because the school environment often mirrors what is happening in the community. Community problems can disrupt the school environment and contribute to crime and violence in that environment. The school resource officer rests on the pyramid's next level because the SRO is an integral connection between the school and the community.

Many schools take a break during the summer months, a period that can be used for law enforcement personnel and school administrators to address some safety and security issues. Garrett (2008, p.6) suggests that police and school staff take advantage of this time to:

- Discuss the law enforcement–school partnership. A memorandum of agreement should be in place defining the roles and responsibilities of both and should be reviewed annually.

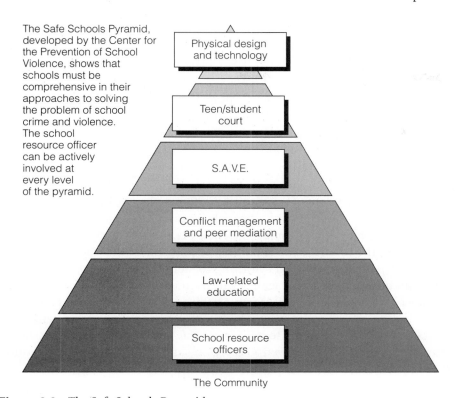

The Safe Schools Pyramid, developed by the Center for the Prevention of School Violence, shows that schools must be comprehensive in their approaches to solving the problem of school crime and violence. The school resource officer can be actively involved at every level of the pyramid.

Physical design and technology

Teen/student court

S.A.V.E.

Conflict management and peer mediation

Law-related education

School resource officers

The Community

Figure 8.2   The Safe Schools Pyramid

SOURCE: Ronnie L. Paynter. "Policing the Schools." *Law Enforcement Technology*, October 1999, p.35. Reprinted by permission of the Center for the Prevention of School Violence.

- Evaluate the school's physical security. Are the grounds, particularly near entrances, well lit? Do the entrances lock securely? Does vegetation obscure windows or hide doors? Are surveillance cameras operating as they should?
- Fine-tune crisis plans considering natural disasters, bus accidents, bomb threats, hostage situations, suicide and school shootings.
- Train for trouble.

Webb (2008) recommends a school walk-through, not only for SROs, but for every officer assigned to the beats in which schools are located, to familiarize themselves with the layout. Hard-copy maps or blueprints of every school in the district should also be stored and available to the on-duty supervisor.

The South Euclid School Bullying Project using problem solving was discussed earlier in the chapter. *School-Based Partnerships: A Problem Solving Strategy* (Uchida et al., n.d.) describes the SARA model in action in several schools/police departments. This report stresses: "Students provided excellent input regarding the problems and they tended to be more successful at retrieving information. School administrators and faculty assisted in policy change, provided program support and organized programs beneficial to the problem-solving effort. School support personnel (i.e., security staff, cafeteria workers, and the like) were key sources of information concerning problem identification such as locations, offenders and victims, and response development."

Other Efforts to Prevent School Violence

Some schools have supplemented their violence prevention efforts with programs, policies and procedures aimed at problematic student behavior. Intervention and behavior modification programs have proved successful in some jurisdictions. Increased staff presence in identified problem areas, such as the lunchroom, and a Big Brothers/Big Sisters mentoring program pairing high school and middle school students to help prevent bullying of freshmen have also proven to be effective.

Youth leadership programs can help thwart school violence when school-age students are provided with tools to assist authorities in the early detection of violence-prone students (Eckenrode, 2007, p.130). The desired outcome is a population of adolescents who, through acquired self-leadership skills, will reject violence and the use of illegal substances. Citing the old adage, "If you are not part of the solution, you're part of the problem," Eckenrode (p.144) contends: "If responsible parties try nothing to stem the tide of school violence, then no progress will be made against this frightening trend."

Many policies and procedures focus on the possession of weapons and other contraband on school property. And while it seems to make good sense that schools, in fulfilling their duty to maintain a safe learning environment, should restrict what students are allowed to carry on campus, policies and procedures aimed at achieving the goal of safety are not without controversy.

 Some schools have adopted controversial measures such as zero-tolerance policies or school security procedures known as lockdowns.

Zero-Tolerance Policies   Zero-tolerance policies mandating predetermined consequences or punishments, such as suspension or expulsion for specific offenses, have become a popular disciplinary choice. Critics of these policies caution school administrators to use them with discretion and common sense to avoid a net-widening effect.

Another controversial effort aimed at preventing school violence is the planned but unannounced lockdown.

AT ISSUE: DO ZERO-TOLERANCE POLICIES MAKE ZERO SENSE?

In May 2001, an 18-year-old high school honor student in Ft. Myers, Florida, was arrested and sent to jail on a felony charge of possession of a weapon on school property after a kitchen knife was seen on the floor of her car, which was parked in the school lot. Her explanation was that she had moved some possessions over the preceding weekend and had simply overlooked the knife, which had fallen out of its box. Despite this honest mistake and the student's academic standing, she was kept from attending her high school graduation ceremony and made to endure the humiliation of arrest and spending time behind bars.

Incidents such as this have led some authors and researchers to refer to "the dark side of zero tolerance"—the overzealous and often inappropriately strict punishments handed out under the pretense of keeping schools safe. But what are the costs to kids of these policies? In this case, did this zero-tolerance policy truly affect school safety? Should a student with no prior offenses, who offers an explanation such as the one described above, be treated the same as a student who knowingly brings a weapon into a school and keeps it, for example, in a locker? Should the type of weapon matter—for example, a kitchen knife versus a firearm? What about "weapons" made from items commonly found in school, such as rubber bands and paper clips?

Proactive Lockdowns Some schools use a **lockdown** not as a reactive response to a crisis, but rather as a proactive step to avoid a crisis. During a lockdown, high school students are held in classrooms while police and K-9s search the campus for contraband or any danger to a safe educational environment. Numerous legal issues must be considered if planning a lockdown, and collaboration with the district attorney's office is required (Guy, 2001, p.8).

While some criticize lockdowns as being frightening or intimidating to students, and some students complain they feel threatened when their day is interrupted by the police, this approach has not been challenged before school boards or in court. Furthermore, beyond curbing the possession of drugs and weapons in the public schools, these lockdowns emphasize the partnership between law enforcement and the school, providing visible evidence that government agencies are collaborating to prevent drug abuse and violence in schools and to provide a safe educational environment for students and teachers.

Although proactive lockdowns may be effective in locating and securing weapons that might be used in incidents of school violence, they are employed very infrequently in very few schools. Zero-tolerance policies fall dangerously short in their effectiveness if students believe any prohibited items they bring to school will go unnoticed. In fact, many weapons are discovered only after they have been used in a violent episode. Metal detectors, again, are used relatively infrequently, especially in smaller schools and in smaller communities, despite statistics showing these jurisdictions also are vulnerable to fatal school violence.

So even though these efforts are seen as luxuries for schools able to afford the fiscal and human resources needed to implement them, they cannot be relied on alone and are no substitute for the power of partnerships between students, teachers, officers, parents and other members of a community.

Partnerships and Community Policing

The need for cooperative efforts when dealing with juveniles cannot be stressed enough. Law enforcement must draw upon the expertise of psychologists, psychiatrists and social workers. They also need the assistance of parents, schools, churches, community organizations and businesses. Such collaboration is at the heart of community policing. The thrust of the *community policing* philosophy is toward proactive, problem-oriented policing, seeking causes to crime and allocating resources to attack those causes through partnerships.

Traditionally law enforcement has been *separate* from the community and *reactive*, responding to incidents as they occur. During the past few years, however, the emphasis has shifted to viewing law enforcement—indeed, the entire juvenile justice system—as part of the community, reliant upon collaborative efforts to deal with our nation's youths.

Besides police personnel, other participants vital in a community's effort to address school violence in particular and youth violence in general include parent group leaders, such as PTA officers; business leaders; violence prevention group representatives; youth workers and volunteers; family resource center staff; recreational and cultural organizations staff; mental health and child welfare personnel; physicians and nurses; media representatives; other criminal justice professionals, such as lawyers, judges and probation officers; clergy and other representatives from the faith community; and local officials, such as school board members.

Police officers need to be aware of the referral resources available in the community, including not only the names of the resource agencies but also addresses, phone numbers and contact persons. Among the possible referral resources for the juvenile justice system are the following:

- Child welfare and child protection services
- Church youth programs
- Crisis centers
- Detox centers
- Drop-in centers or shelters for youths
- Guardian *ad litem* programs
- Human services councils
- Juvenile probation services
- School resources, including chemical dependency counselors, general counselors, nurses, school psychologists and social workers
- Support groups such as Al-Anon, Emotions Anonymous and Suicide Help Line
- Victim/witness services
- YMCA or YWCA programs
- Youth Service Bureaus

Ideally law enforcement officers would serve on community boards and task forces that promote services for youths.

 SUMMARY

- Youths' attitudes toward law and law enforcement are tremendously influenced by personal contacts with law enforcement officers. Positive interactions are crucial to any delinquency prevention attempts.
- The primary responsibility of police officers assigned to child neglect or abuse cases is the immediate protection of the child.
- Challenges in investigating crimes against children include the need to protect the child from further harm, the possibility of parental involvement, the difficulty of interviewing children, credibility concerns and the need to collaborate with other agencies.
- The majority of police dispositions involve status offenses (violating curfew, truancy, loitering, underage smoking and drinking of alcoholic beverages, and running away).
- In the disposition of status offenders, how police resolve matters often depends on the officers' discretion, the specific offense and the backup available.
- Police officers have considerable discretionary power when dealing with juveniles.
- The most common procedure when confronting juveniles is to release the child, with or without a warning, but without making an official record or taking further action.

- The fundamental nature of the juvenile justice system is rehabilitative rather than punitive.
- Boys who own guns for protection are significantly and substantially more likely to be involved in delinquent behavior than either those who do not own guns or those who own guns for sport.
- When dealing with school violence it is important to recognize the threats that might be present. Threats may be direct, indirect, veiled or conditional.
- The four-pronged threat assessment approach examines the student's personality, family dynamics, school dynamics and the student's role in those dynamics, and social dynamics.
- The role of the first responder in a school shooting situation is to pursue and engage the shooter.
- An effective approach to school security includes crisis planning, security technology and school/law enforcement/community partnerships.
- Some schools have adopted controversial measures such as zero-tolerance policies or school security procedures known as lockdowns.

DISCUSSION QUESTIONS

1. What restrictions are placed on minors owning firearms in your state?
2. Do you believe police should make unofficial referrals, such as to community service agencies? What problems would police face when referring youths to community service agencies?
3. Do the police display a helping attitude toward youths when they make their referrals?
4. Do you believe the social standing, race and age of juveniles influence the referral procedure?
5. Which do you think is more effective, street justice by police or processing juveniles through the court system? Why?
6. Should the police be in the schools as a crime prevention method? Why or why not?
7. Joe, a 13-year-old White male, has been apprehended by a police officer for stealing a bicycle. Joe took the bicycle from the school grounds shortly after a program at the school by the police on "Bicycle Theft Prevention." Joe admits to taking the bicycle, but says he only intended to "go for a ride" and was going to return the bicycle later that day. Joe has no prior police contacts that the officer is aware of. The bicycle has been missing for only an hour and is unharmed. What should the officer do in handling the incident? Do you think the bicycle theft prevention program is worthwhile? Why or why not?
8. Have there been any instances of school shootings in your state?
9. Are there SROs in the schools in your city?
10. How important do you believe partnerships are in addressing school crime and violence?

REFERENCES

Brady Campaign to Prevent Gun Violence. Online: http://www.bradycampaign.org. Updated April 2008. Accessed December 12, 2008.

Braga, Anthony A.; Pierce, Glenn L.; McDevitt, Jack; Bond, Brenda J.; and Cronin, Shea. "The Strategic Prevention of Gun Violence among Gang-Involved Offenders." *Justice Quarterly*, March 2008, pp.132–162.

Caster, Richard. "Ten Things Police Chiefs Need to Know about School Shooting." *Law and Order*, April 2008, pp.77–80.

Dinkes, Rachel; Cataldi, Emily Forrest; Lin-Kelly, Wendy; and Snyder, Thomas D. *Indicators of School Crime and Safety: 2007.* Washington, DC: National Center for Education Statistics, December 2007.

Dunworth, Terence. *National Evaluation of the Youth Firearms Violence Initiative.* Washington, DC: National Institute of Justice Research in Brief, November 2000. (NCJ 184482)

Eckenrode, Lex T. "Can Youth Leadership Programs Thwart School Violence?" *The Police Chief*, October 2007, pp.130–146.

Garrett, Ronnie. "Internet 'Burn Books.'" *Law Enforcement Technology*, November 2006, p.8.

Garrett, Ronnie. "School's Out for Summer." *Law Enforcement Technology*, June 2008, p.6.

Guy, Joe D. "Lock Down." *Community Links*, September 2001, pp.7–8.

Kennedy, David M.; Braga, Anthony A.; and Piehl, Anne M. "Developing and Implementing Operation Ceasefire." *Reducing Gun Violence: The Boston Gun Project's Operation Ceasefire*, September 2001. (NCJ 188741)

Kyrik, Kelly. "Florida Department of Law Enforcement Crimes against Children Mobile Unit." *Police*, August 2007, pp.74–78.

Lemmer, Thomas J. and Johnston, Rachel M. "Reducing Crime through Juvenile Delinquency Intervention." *The Police Chief*, May 2004, pp.24–28.

Mowatt, Robert M. and Chezem, Linda. *An Implementation Guide for Juvenile Holdover Programs.* Washington, DC: National Highway Traffic Safety Administration, Office of Juvenile Justice and Delinquency Prevention and the American Probation and Parole Association, June 2001. (DOT HS 809260, NCJ 193986)

Noonan, James H and Vavra, Melissa C. *Crime in Schools and Colleges*, Washington DC: Federal Bureau of Investigation, October 2007.

Olweus Bullying Prevention Program. 2003, updated October 21, 2008. Online: http://www.clemson.edu/olweus/. Accessed December 30, 2008.

O'Toole, Mary Ellen. *The School Shooter: A Threat Assessment Perspective.* Washington, DC: Federal Bureau of Investigation, 2000. Online: www.fbi.gov/publications/school/school2.pdf

Petrocelli, Joseph. "School Vandalism." *Police*, October 2007, pp.32–35.

Regulating Guns in America: An Evaluation and Comparative Analysis of Federal, State and Selected Local Gun Laws, 2008 Edition. San Francisco, CA: Legal Community against Violence, February 2008.

Sanchez, Tomas. "School Watch Digital Surveillance Technology for School Safety." *The Police Chief*, August 2007, pp.110–112.

Scanlon, James. "Blueprint of a Bloodbath." *Law Enforcement Technology*, June 2008, pp.40–47.

Snyder, Howard N. and Sickmund, Melissa. *2006 Juvenile Offenders and Victims: 2006 National Report.* Washington, DC: U.S. Department of Justice, Office of Justice Programs, Office of Juvenile Justice and Delinquency Prevention.

Straub, Frank G. "Commissioner Frank Straub Testifies on Reducing Gang and Youth Violence." *Subject to Debate*, June 2008, pp.1, 4, 5.

Uchida, Craig D.; Solomon, Shellie; Katz, Charles M.; and Pappas, Cynthia E. *School-Based Partnerships.: A Problem-Solving Strategy.* Washington, DC: Office of Community Oriented Policing Services, no date.

Watkins, Adam M.; Huebner, Beth M.; and Decker, Scott H. "Patterns of Gun Acquisition Carrying and Use among Juvenile and Adult Arrestees: Evidence from a High-Crime City." *Justice Quarterly*, December 2008, pp.674–700.

Webb, David. "School Walk-Throughs." *Law and Order*, June 2008, pp.84–86.

Youth Risk Behavior Survey (NRBS). Centers for Disease Control and Prevention. Last reviewed October 16, 2008. Online: http://www.cdc.gov/vbrss.

Pretrial Services and Diversion

© AP/Wide World Photos

Youths who enter the juvenile justice system must proceed through various pretrial stages before their case has a chance of appearing before the court. In fact, for many juveniles, formal court processing never occurs, as they are diverted into various alternative programs based on their needs and offense history. Here, an 8-year-old boy accused of hitting his school principal with a wood pole appears with his attorney at a juvenile detention hearing in front of the court commissioner. The youth told police he brought the pole for protection from other students, but he did not explain why he attacked the principal.

DO YOU KNOW?

■ What two opposing philosophies about young people are?

■ What the dual role of the juvenile prosecutor is?

■ What the possible results of an intake hearing might be?

■ What four principles of effective intervention are?

■ What the results of effective diversion criteria should be?

■ What forms diversion from juvenile court may take?

■ What specialized courts are available for diverted youths?

■ What the two most common criteria for participating in drug court are?

■ What the four cornerstones of the Blueprint for Change are?

■ Who is eligible to participate in juvenile gun court?

■ What the three core principles of the balanced and restorative justice (BARJ) model are?

■ What the three main components of restorative justice are?

■ What the four models of restorative justice are?

CAN YOU DEFINE?

comorbidity	diversion	intake	petition
deep end strategy	dynamic risk factor	meta-analysis	public defender
detention hearing	family courts	net widening	static risk factor

CHAPTER OUTLINE

Introduction

Philosophies about Youth

Custody

Detention

Intake

Who Should Decide: The Juvenile Prosecutor or Intake Officer?

The Intake Hearing

Assessment

Principles of Effective Interventions

Diversion from Formal Juvenile Court

Diversion to Specialized Courts

Teen Court

Juvenile Drug Courts

Juvenile Mental Health Courts

Juvenile Gun Courts

Juvenile Traffic Court

Balanced and Restorative Justice

Victim-Offender Mediation

Community Reparative Boards

Family Group Conferencing

Circle Sentencing

Net Widening

Respite Care

The Importance of Timely Case Processing

Introduction

Having just examined in the previous chapter the role of the police in dealing with juveniles, it should come as no surprise that most young offenders enter the juvenile justice system through contact with a law enforcement officer. This chapter focuses on the decision points that occur *pretrial* in delinquency case processing, including custody, detention, intake and, very commonly, diversion. Figure 9.1 illustrates the stages a delinquency case typically passes through before it reaches the court for formal processing. Note that this figure is the first half of the flowchart that was presented in Chapter 1, and as was true with Figure 1.5,

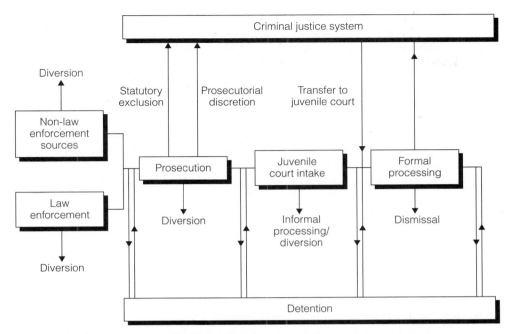

Figure 9.1 Pretrial Stages of Delinquency Case Processing

SOURCE: Adapted from Howard N. Snyder and Melissa Sickmund. *Juvenile Offenders and Victims 2006 National Report*. Washington, DC: U.S. Department of Justice, Office of Justice Programs, Office of Juvenile Justice and Delinquency Prevention, March 2006, p.105.

it must be noted that states and communities may vary somewhat in this generalized process. The organization of this chapter will roughly follow the flow outlined in Figure 9.1 and the steps that lead up to formal processing of a delinquent in juvenile court. However, before getting into the specifics of this chapter with the custody and detention of juvenile offenders, consider first how one's philosophy about young people can influence case processing and the decision to either divert an offender or process the offender formally through the courts.

Philosophies about Youth

Greene (2008, p.160) points out: "Kids with behavioral challenges are not attention-seeking, manipulative, limit-testing, coercive, or unmotivated. But they do lack the skills to behave appropriately. Adults can help by recognizing what causes their difficult behaviors and teaching kids the skills they need." Greene describes two opposing philosophies of child behavior.

 Two opposing philosophies of youths are: (1) kids do well if they want to, and (2) kids do well if they can.

Both philosophies have their advocates, but as Greene notes (p.161): "These two disparate philosophies have dramatically different ramifications for our assumptions about kids and how to proceed when they do not meet our expectations." As the various pretrial services are discussed, keep these two philosophies in mind.

Custody

As mentioned previously, most youth enter the juvenile justice system when they are taken into custody by police. Youths are considered to be in custody (arrested) when the police apprehend, stop or otherwise contact them and suspect them of having committed a status offense or a delinquent act. Children can be taken into custody by court order, under the laws of arrest or by a law enforcement officer if there are reasonable grounds to believe that the child is suffering from illness or injury, that the child is in immediate danger from the surroundings or that the child has run away. The Uniform Juvenile Court Act (UJCA) of 1968 notes: "The taking of a child into custody is not an arrest, except for the purpose of determining its validity under the constitution of this state or of the United States."

After children are taken into custody, law enforcement evaluates the situation by talking with the victim(s), the offender and the offender's parents or guardians and by reviewing any prior record the offender may have with the juvenile justice system. With this information, the officer decides on a course of action: release the juvenile to the parents, guardians or custodians; refer the juvenile to the prosecutor or intake division for processing into the system; or divert the juvenile to another agency such as a shelter care facility, or to a medical facility if needed. This decision is to be made "with all reasonable speed and without first taking the child elsewhere." Also, the parents, guardians or custodians and the court must promptly be given a written notice stating the reason the child was taken into custody.

Of all juvenile arrests made in 2003, 20 percent were handled within the police department and were resolved with juveniles being released to their parents or guardians, 70 percent were referred to juvenile court and the remaining 10 percent were referred for criminal prosecution or diverted to other agencies (Snyder and Sickmund, 2006, p.104).

Sometimes, however, a juvenile must be temporarily detained while a parent or guardian is located, or while other facets of a case are immediately tended to. In these situations, detention can be used. Note in Figure 9.1 (and also in Figure 1.5) that detention is always an option, at any stage of delinquency case processing.

Detention

One in five youths is detained between the referral to court and case disposition (Snyder and Sickmund, 2006, p.105). Section 14 of the UJCA deals with the detention of juveniles:

> A child taken into custody shall not be detained or placed in shelter care prior to the hearing on the petition unless his detention or care is required to protect the person or property of others or of the child or because the child may abscond or be removed from the jurisdiction of the court or because he has no parent, guardian, or custodian or other person able to provide supervision and care for him and return him to the court when required, or an order for his detention or shelter care has been made by the court pursuant to this Act.

The National Juvenile Detention Association (NJDA) provides the following definition: "Juvenile detention, as part of the juvenile justice continuum, is a process that includes the temporary and safe custody of juveniles whose alleged conduct is subject to court jurisdiction who require a restricted environment for their own and the community's protection while pending legal action. Juvenile detention may range from the least restrictive community-based supervision to the most restrictive form of secure care" (NJDA, 2007).

The UJCA provides in section 16 that a delinquent can be detained only in:

- A licensed foster home or a home approved by the court.
- A facility operated by a licensed child welfare agency.
- A detention home or center for delinquent children that is under the direction or supervision of the court or other public authority or of a private agency approved by the court.
- Any other suitable place or facility designated or operated by the court.

The final catch-all clause in this provision of the UJCA weakens the act's effectiveness.

Section 16 further specifies that delinquents may be kept in a jail or other adult detention facility only if one of the preceding is not available, the detention is in a room separate from adults and it appears that public safety and protection reasonably require detention. The act requires that the person in charge of a jail inform the court immediately if a person under age 18 is received at the jail. The act further stipulates that deprived or unruly children "shall not be detained in a jail or other facility intended or used for the detention of adults charged with criminal offenses or of children alleged to be delinquent." The intent of this section is to protect children from the harm of exposing them to criminals and the "degrading effect of jails, lockups and the like."

Austin et al. (2005, p.1) report: "Status offenders do not require secure detention to ensure their compliance with court orders or to protect public safety. However, recent data indicate that one-third of all youths held in juvenile detention centers are detained for status offenses and technical violations of probation. Detaining youths in facilities prior to adjudication should be an option of last resort only for serious, violent and chronic offenders and for those who repeatedly fail to appear for scheduled court dates."

Griffin and Torbet (2002, p.57) stress that detention is a process, not a place, and that those in charge of secure detention facilities understand how detention practices should be related to larger juvenile justice goals, and be guided by the following principles:

- Secure detention and detention alternatives are essential components of the juvenile justice system, integral to a complete continuum of local supervision and custody options for court-involved youth.
- Detention options must be short-term and appropriate to the level of risk posed by the youth.
- Detention services must be designed to safeguard the community and/or ensure the juvenile's appearance at subsequent hearings.
- Detention services must be consistent with the goals of the juvenile justice system—community protection, offender accountability and practical rehabilitation.

The NJDA (2007) lists the following critical components of juvenile detention:

- *Screening*—to ensure detention is the appropriate decision
- *Assessment*—to determine proper placement, supervision and custody level
- *Policies*—to promote the safety, security and well-being of juveniles and staff
- *Services*—to address the immediate educational, mental, physical, emotional and social needs of detained juveniles

Section 17 of the UJCA states that if a child is brought before the court or delivered to a detention or shelter care facility, an investigation must be made immediately as to whether detention is needed. If the child is not released, a petition must be filed promptly with the court. In addition an informal **detention hearing** should be held within a time period defined by state statute, typically ranging from 24 to 72 hours, to determine whether detention is required. A written notice of the time, place and purpose of the hearing is given to the child and, if possible, to the parents or guardians. Before the hearing begins, the court must inform the people involved of their right to counsel—court-appointed if they cannot afford to pay private counsel—and of the child's right to remain silent during the hearing.

Initial detention decisions are often made by either a prosecutor or an intake officer.

Intake

Intake is the initial phase of the juvenile court process. **Intake** is the stage at which someone must decide whether a referral merits a petition, that is, whether the matter described in the complaint against the juvenile should become the subject of formal court action. According to Griffin and Torbet (2002, p.34): "Intake may be the most crucial case processing point in the juvenile justice system because so much follows from that decision. Intake authority is entrusted to prosecutors in some jurisdictions—either in all cases or in those involving allegations of serious crimes—and to juvenile court intake or juvenile probation departments in others."

Who Should Decide: The Juvenile Prosecutor or Intake Officer?

Some debate has centered on which agency should have intake authority—the prosecutor's office or an intake officer in the juvenile probation department.

PERSPECTIVES FROM THE NATIONAL CONFERENCE ON JUVENILE JUSTICE (NCJJ)

The Vera Institute supports efforts to reform juvenile justice in New York state and has focused on detention for four important reasons. First, detention may have a detrimental impact when the place of detention is overcrowded and understaffed. Second, detention results in disproportionate minority confinement (DMC). For example, in New York, 95 percent of children in jail are children of color. Third, detention is expensive. In New York per diem of detention is very high, between $20 and $100 a day. Fourth, and perhaps most important, detention is seen as the gateway to deeper involvement in the juvenile justice system (Mogulescu et al., 2007).

This final point is important to keep in mind when weighing the long-term consequences to the juvenile of detention versus diversion.

The Juvenile Prosecutor   The dual role of the juvenile prosecutor is to protect the rights of the state and the safety of the community while at the same time keeping the best interest of the juvenile in mind (Abrahamson, 2007). The National District Attorneys Association (NDAA) Prosecution Standards—Juvenile Justice, standard 92.1(b) states:

 "The primary duty of the prosecutor is to seek justice while fully and faithfully representing the interests of the state."

The NDAA takes the stance that the prosecutor should have the exclusive right to make juvenile intake decisions and screen facts obtained from the police and other sources to determine whether those facts are legally sufficient for prosecution.

The Intake Officer   The intake officer decides whether a case should move ahead for court processing. This officer is usually a probation officer or designated court personnel, not a lawyer. The intake process of the juvenile justice system requires the development of employee screening practices, certification standards and caseload guidelines. Caseworkers should be certified to practice on the basis of education, training and experience.

In matters handled by intake, the biggest disparity from state to state is in how abused, neglected and dependent children are helped. Regarding juvenile offenders, the intake officer may release the youth to the parents with a warning or reprimand. Or the officer may release the youth on the condition that the youth enroll in a community diversion program or be placed on probation and be under the supervision of a juvenile court officer.

If the intake officer determines that the case should move ahead for court processing, the officer will recommend that a **petition** (charge) be filed and will refer the case to the juvenile court prosecutor. In addition, if a petition is recommended, the intake officer determines whether the youth should be detained pending further court action or be released to the custody of the parents pending the hearing. When juveniles are detained, this decision is reviewed by a judge or court administrator at a detention hearing.

PERSPECTIVES FROM THE NATIONAL CONFERENCE ON JUVENILE JUSTICE (NCJJ)

Abrahamson (2007) notes that decision to charge can be life changing. He provides the following scenario facing a juvenile prosecutor:

Delores Druggie has been charged with possession of methamphetamine. She is a hopeless addict and will probably kill herself with an overdose sometime in the near future. This time however she got hold of a substance that tested negative. The defense attorney is concerned about his client's welfare and tells you that if you charge a misdemeanor drug offense he will convince her to plead guilty so he can get her into drug rehab. He tells you that something has to be done or she will die. She won't respond to the advice of her parents or attorney.

Her parents tearfully plead with you not to drop the case because it was their only hope to save her. They ask that at the very least you should file and defer the prosecution conditioned on drug treatment.

Abrahamson then asks: "When as a prosecutor is it permissible to charge *in the interest of justice* when you have strong suspicion but less than probable cause? Your job is to do justice. Does that duty ever trump constitutional or legal guidelines? Does a prosecutor have a greater responsibility to protect the public from a clearly identified danger or conform to a standard dictated by the court or an administrative committee that could not possibly know what danger the public is facing?" He concludes: "Your role is to do what is right for all citizens under the guidelines established by your oath. With the special and most honorable role of also doing what is in the best interest of the juveniles you are called to prosecute while protecting the public."

The Intake Hearing

At the intake stage of the referral, the decision is made whether to adjust, settle or terminate the matter. Referrals are also made to other interests out of concern for the child's health, welfare and safety. This process in most states is called the intake hearing. The purpose of this proceeding is not to adjudicate the affirmation (guilty) or denial (not guilty) of juveniles in the matter, but to determine whether the matter requires the court's attention. Thus, the intake unit serves in an advisory capacity.

The person handling the juvenile offender at this stage—whether it is a prosecutor or an intake officer—must ask two basic questions:

1. From a review of the complaint and the evidence, is it clear that the complaint against the juvenile is *legally sufficient*? If not, the case should be dismissed.
2. If the complaint is legally sufficient, does a background investigation of legal and social factors—including interviews with the juvenile as well as parents, victims and others—indicate that the case should be formally processed? If not, diversion is the likely alternative.

 The intake hearing may result in dismissal, diversion, referral to juvenile court for adjudication or transfer to adult court.

Youths released at intake with no further processing should be followed up with after any referral to a community agency by either the police or the intake unit. Such follow-up promotes closer cooperation between the agencies involved and ensures that a youth does not "fall through the cracks," should the dismissal prove to have not been the most appropriate decision.

Another important function of the intake hearing is to provide an authoritarian setting in which a severe lecture or counsel may be administered to the youth so as to avoid future difficulties. Sometimes, a stern warning at this point is enough to put wayward youths back on track to lawful behavior.

Regardless of who performs the intake function, the decision-making process is roughly the same and covers the same points of assessment.

Assessment

One of the most important functions during intake is an accurate assessment of each youth. Young et al. (2006, p.135) studied implementation practices and dissemination of new assessment technologies in juvenile justice and concluded: "Assessment in juvenile justice exemplifies the 'science-practice gap' that has spurred a growing national interest in technology transfer." They describe the evolution of assessment instruments through four generations, beginning with the first generation that involved the professional judgment and intuition of the individual conducting the assessment. Second-generation assessments involved standardized assessments using actuarial methods, focusing on static risk factors such as age at first arrest and age of first alcohol or drug use. Third-generation assessments were more comprehensive, using static and dynamic risk and need factors. (Recall the definition of a risk factor from Chapter 4. A **static risk factor** is one that cannot be changed, such as an offender's delinquency record. A **dynamic risk factor**, in contrast, is one that can be changed, such as an offender's addiction to drugs.) The fourth generation of assessment involves a series of specialized instruments for particular needs.

Assessment instruments are of two basic types: generic (or generalized) and locally developed (or specialized). Miller and Lin (2007, p.552) studied the issues raised by applying a generic actuarial juvenile risk instrument (the Model Risk Assessment Instrument) to delinquency cases in New York City and found that a generic instrument is less predictive than a locally developed risk assessment tool and also performs less well than unassisted clinical judgment.

An example of a locally developed assessment tool is the PACT (Positive Achievement Change Tool), an evidence-based assessment tool linked to a case management system, developed by Florida's Department of Juvenile Justice. This innovative tool is designed to improve information gathering, standardize the risk classification process and more accurately determine the individualized risk and needs of young offenders (Olson, 2007, p.16). This Web-based, automated tool is synchronized with the department's existing information system, thereby alleviating paperwork overload. According to Olson (p.18), a key element of the new assessment tool is motivational interviewing (MI): "In recent years MI has gained increasing relevance in juvenile justice as the evidence piled up that behavioral change most frequently occurs when the motivation for change comes from within."

That motivation is important is emphasized by Murphy (2007, p.8) who presents 10 ways to motivate youths: (1) help make sure their basic needs are met; (2) build on their strengths; (3) be there! (4) provide external (tangible) rewards, not just for good results but for good effort; (5) recognize and support resiliency; (6) develop competencies; (7) ensure community support; (8) provide recognition (internal motivation); (9) involve them in goal setting; and (10) be motivated yourself—positive, enthusiastic, energetic. Assessment is the engine that drives good diversion decisions and good programs.

Some jurisdictions have developed juvenile assessment centers (JACs) to address service fragmentation among agencies providing services to youth involved with the juvenile justice system. A study by McReynolds et al. (2008, p.330) found that 30 percent of youths undergoing Orange County (Florida) JAC intake met criteria for one or another probable psychiatric disorder, with girls having higher rates of many disorders. Discussing the benefits of JACs, McReynolds et al. conclude: "This type of setting, where a range of assessments can be efficiently conducted, offers particular opportunities to determine service needs for young and first-time offenders at an early point in the juvenile justice intake process" (p.330).

However, because many jurisdictions lack the resources and expertise to develop their own locale-specific assessment instruments, many rely on generic instruments. Some of these are better assessment tools than others. One such tool gaining popularity and scientific acceptance is the Youthful Level of Service Inventory (Y-LSI), an assessment instrument that not only predicts risk of failure (risk classification) but also identifies specific areas of treatment needs, with the goal being to treat the criminogenic needs that place a juvenile at risk of offending, thus lowering recidivism. Administration of the Y-LSI involves a face-to-face interview during which 42 questions are asked to the juvenile offender, the items spanning eight risk domains: prior and current offenses/adjudications,

A CRITICAL NEED: ASSESSING MENTAL HEALTH ISSUES IN JUVENILE OFFENDERS

Shufelt and Cocozza (2006, p.2) compared mental health prevalence findings from recent juvenile justice studies and found a range of 67.2 percent to 72.6 percent with a positive diagnosis. Other studies have found even higher rates of mental health issues among juvenile detainees: "Nationally, research shows that up to 75 percent of youths in detention centers demonstrate diagnosable mental health disorders" (Hanger, 2008, p.36). Williams et al. (2008, p.25) explain: "Mental health screening is a brief process administered by nonclinical staff using a standardized tool. It is a triage process that is carried out with every youth soon after intake in pretrial detention during an initial probation intake interview or upon entrance into juvenile justice placement."

Clark (2008, p.8) reports on surveys completed by more than 500 juvenile detention administrators of 49 states, representing three-quarters of all juvenile detention facilities, which found that:

- Two-thirds of juvenile detention facilities hold youths who are waiting for community mental health treatment.
- Two-thirds of these juveniles have attempted suicide or attacked others.
- Juvenile detention facilities spend an estimated $100 million each year to house youths who are waiting for community mental health services.

The Northwestern Juvenile Project (Teplin et al., 2006), which involved a random sample of more than 1,800 juvenile detainees ages 10–18, studied psychiatric disorders of youths in detention by using a widely accepted and reliable measurement tool, the Diagnostic Interview Schedule for Children (DISC) Version 2.3. The longitudinal study looked at gender, race and ethnicity and age for six categories of disorders: (1) affective (major depressive episode, dysthymia, manic episode); (2) psychosis; (3) anxiety (panic, separation anxiety, over-anxious, generalized anxiety, obsessive-compulsive disorders); (4) attention deficit/hyperactivity disorder (ADHD); (5) disruptive behavior (oppositional-defiant and conduct disorders); and (6) substance abuse. The study found that nearly 66 percent of males and nearly 75 percent of females met the diagnostic criteria for one or more of the disorders identified (p.7).

Furthermore, many of the juveniles met the criteria for multiple disorders (known as **comorbidity**, when two or more diagnoses occur together in the same individual). Finally, the study revealed that a significant number of juvenile offenders—more than 20 percent of males and nearly 30 percent of females—who had any type of substance abuse disorder also had a major mental disorder (p.8).

Boesky (2007) provides a detailed explanation of the various types of psychological problems youths may have, many of which were previously discussed in Chapter 4 as risk factors for delinquency. A youth with *conduct disorder* violates the basic rights of others or of society through aggression, destruction and deceitfulness/theft. Such behaviors tend to be frequent, intense and chronic. *Attention deficit hyperactivity disorder* (ADHD) causes a youth to display inattention (e.g., losing things, being distractible and forgetful) and hyperactivity-impulsivity (e.g., fidgeting/squirming, being loud, always moving, excessive talking, blurting out answers and interrupting). *Mood disorders* include major depression and involve the following symptoms: irritability, diminished interest, changes in eating and/or sleeping, restlessness, fatigue, lack of concentration and suicidal behavior. *Dysthymia* occurs when a person has a depressed/irritable mood most of the day and more days than not, such as problems with appetite, sleep, fatigue, concentration and self-esteem. *Bipolar disorder* describes a period of abnormally and persistently elevated, expansive or irritable mood along with any three of the following: grandiosity, decreased sleep, rapid speech, flight of ideas, distractibility, increased activity, impulsive behavior. *Psychosis* may result in hallucinations, delusions and disorganized behavior/thinking/speech.

A mental health evaluation is a crucial step in assessing a juvenile offender and determining the most effective disposition for that individual, and it is a step that most often occurs while a youth is in detention.

SOURCE: Some of this information was obtained at the 34th National Conference on Juvenile Justice from Lisa Boesky, "Juvenile Offenders with Mental Health Disorders: What You NEED to Know." San Diego, CA: Seminar P-2 presented at the 34th National Conference on Juvenile Justice, March 4, 2007.

family circumstances and parenting, education and employment, peer relations, substance abuse, leisure and recreational activities, personality and behavior, and attitudes and orientations (Flores, Travis and Latessa, 2004, p.5). Evaluation of the Y-LSI shows this assessment tool can be significantly accurate in predicting case outcomes for both male and female juveniles, and across ethnicities, if the scores are normed for specific offender populations (Flores et al., p.5). Unfortunately, many departments fail to take this extra step and, thus, compromise the optimal capacity of this instrument.

As analysis of the Y-LSI and other assessment tools reveals that juvenile offender case outcomes benefit when assessment results are integrated with service provision. Tjaden and Martinez (2007, p.76) explain: "An integrated assessment (or client management) system refers to a relatively new concept in the classification and management of juvenile offender cases. In an integrated model, systematic assessment of a youth's criminogenic needs (or risk factors) provides the basis for all future client management activities including:

- Determining the level of risk and supervision needed.
- Developing a service plan and treatment interventions.
- Measuring the youth's progress.
- Adjusting the service plan to reflect changes in the youth's behavior or lack thereof."

Tjaden and Martinez suggest that such an integrated system keeps the focus on youth outcomes and provides clearer direction as to how one should intervene with at-risk youths: "Research provides ample evidence that certain interventions are more effective than others in addressing recidivism. Punitive sanctions, in and of themselves, are not particularly effective in changing a youth's behavior and, in some cases, may even increase recidivism. By the same token, not all forms of treatment are effective."

Principles of Effective Interventions

A growing body of research has provided evidence that certain features of interventions make them more effective than others at reducing juvenile recidivism. Awareness of these principles of effective intervention can help during the intake phase when assessing offenders and determining how best to process them. These principles are introduced briefly here, although they are equally relevant and pertinent at just about every stage between and including intake and corrections.

Any treatment or intervention used with juveniles should be evidence based, not merely a continuation of "this is how we've always done it." The "lowest" form of evidence is anecdotal, that derived from personal experience working in the field. Such evidence is not highly scientific but it makes us feel good because it holds a high degree of familiarity. In contrast, the "highest" form of evidence is empirical evidence gathered from controlled studies. Such evidence holds up to the rigors of statistical analysis but doesn't always make us feel good because it often suggests a change is needed in how an agency performs.

One way researchers determine which interventions are effective is by conducting a **meta-analysis**, or a "study of studies," to derive a quantitative review of a body of literature. Meta-analysis is now the favored approach by most criminal justice researchers. Latessa (2007) notes that not a single meta-analysis of the effects of official punishment alone (custody, mandatory arrests, increased surveillance, etc.) has found consistent evidence of reduced recidivism. He contends that psychopathic risk takers, those under the influence of a substance and those with a history of being punished appear to be resistant to punishment. In fact, the tougher the system gets on these young people, the tougher they get. The research he studied suggests that behavioral intervention is promising, as such intervention focuses on current *dynamic* risk factors such as friends, truancy and substance abuse, not on things that happened in the past (static risk factors). It is also action-oriented, not talk-oriented. Behavioral intervention teaches new skills and new ways to behave and uses good reinforcement techniques.

Meta-analysis has identified some major risk/need factors which, when assessed at intake, should influence how a delinquency case is processed (Latessa):

1. Antisocial/procriminal attitudes, values, beliefs and cognitive-emotional states (rage, anger, defiance and criminal identity)
2. Procriminal associates and isolation from prosocial others
3. Temperamental and antisocial personality pattern conducive to criminal activity including weak socialization, impulsivity, adventurous, pleasure seeking, restless, aggressive, egocentrism, below-average verbal intelligence, a taste for risk and weak problem-solving, lack of coping and self-regulation skills
4. A history of antisocial behavior evident from a young age, in a variety of settings and involving a number and variety of different acts—early onset is a powerful predictor. By age 12, up to 40 percent of later serious offenders have committed their first criminal act; by age 14, up to 85 percent have committed their first criminal act
5. Family factors that include criminality and a variety of psychological problems in the family of origin, including low levels of affection, caring and cohesiveness, poor parental supervision and discipline practices, and outright neglect and abuse
6. Low levels of personal educational, vocational or financial achievement
7. Low levels of involvement in prosocial leisure activities
8. Abuse of alcohol and/or drugs

These risk/need factors drive delinquent behavior and should be the focus of intervention options and measurement of progress (Latessa).

 Principles of effective intervention include:
- Risk Principle—target higher-risk offender (WHO)
- Need Principle—target criminogenic risk/need factors (WHAT)
- Treatment Principle—use behavioral approaches (HOW)
- Fidelity Principle—implement program as designed (HOW WELL)

Evidence shows that when these principles are adhered to, the outcome for delinquency cases is greatly improved. These principles are important to consider when making diversion decisions.

Diversion from Formal Juvenile Court

The juvenile court was established to prevent children from being treated as criminals and to let them "grow out of delinquency." This is the same rationale in the twenty-first century that considers diversion from the juvenile court as a viable option for some youths. **Diversion** is "the process of channeling a referred juvenile *from* formal juvenile court processing *to* an alternative forum for resolution of the matter and/or a community-based agency for help" (Griffin and Torbet, 2002, p.49). Table 9.1 contains the legal variables involved

Table 9.1   Test of Significance for Differences in Juvenile Court Practitioners'
Perceptions on the Effects of Legal Variables: Prior Record, Severity of Crime,
Severity of Injury/Damage and Premeditated Action

	County Attorneys (n = 48)		Court-Designated Workers (n = 52)		
	%	f	%	f	Chi-Square
Prior record[a]					
Important			3.8	2	4.31
Somewhat important	10.4	5	9.6	5	
Very important	89.6	43	88.3	45	
Severity of crime					
Not important	2.0	1	13.4	7	7.08*
Important	12.5	6	23.0	12	
Somewhat important	14.5	7	15.3	8	
Very important	70.8	34	48.0	25	
Severity of injury/damage					
Not important	2.0	1	9.6	5	5.81
Important	10.4	5	23.0	12	
Somewhat important	20.8	10	15.3	8	
Very important	66.6	32	51.9	27	
Premeditated action					
Not important	2.0	1	21.1	11	16.84**
Important	6.2	3	13.4	7	
Somewhat important	16.6	8	26.9	14	
Very important	75.0	36	38.4	20	

[a]The specific question asked was: "How important is prior record in making diversion decision? Not
important, important, somewhat important or very important?"
*$p < .05$. **$p < .001$.
SOURCE: Roberto Hugh Potter and Suman Kakar. "The Diversion Decision-Making Process from the Juvenile
Court Practitioners' Perspective." *Journal of Contemporary Criminal Justice*, February 2002, p.31. Reprinted by
permission.

in the diversion decision-making process from the perspectives of both county
attorneys and court-designated workers. The similarities and differences between the two groups are interesting. Prior record was the only legal variable
that was very important to both groups.

Table 9.2 presents the extra-legal variables influencing the diversion
decision-making process. County attorneys found the child's attitude toward the
offense and toward treatment as more important than did court-designated workers. Neither indicated that the local political environment was very important.
Diversion serves several purposes, including avoiding stigma of being labeled delinquent, involving the community and the victim and reducing court loads.

Although criteria for diversion vary from jurisdiction to jurisdiction, they
should all be based on specific guidelines. Furthermore, every diversion arrangement should be stated in a clear, complete, written agreement and have a
definite, limited duration (Griffin and Torbet, p.50).

Table 9.2 Test of Significance for Differences in Juvenile Court Practitioners' Perceptions on the Effects of Extra-Legal Variables: Child's Appearance, Child's Attitude toward Offense and Treatment and Local Political Environment

	County Attorneys (n = 48)		Court-Designated Workers (n = 52)		
	%	f	%	f	Chi-Square
Child's appearance[a]					
Not important	58.3	28	67.3	35	3.97
Important	27.0	13	15.3	8	
Somewhat important	14.5	7	9.6	5	
Very important			7.6	4	
Child's attitude toward offense[b]					
Not important	4.1	2	13.4	8	21.41**
Important	12.5	6	40.3	21	
Somewhat important	16.6	8	11.5	6	
Very important	66.6	32	32.6	17	
Child's attitude toward treatment[c]					
Not important			13.4	8	16.74**
Important	14.5	7	32.6	17	
Somewhat important	22.9	11	5.7	3	
Very important	58.3	28	46.1	24	
Local political environment[d]					
Not important	81.2	39	82.6	43	2.74
Important	8.3	4	7.6	4	
Somewhat important	10.4	5	4.0	2	
Very important			7.6	3	

[a]The specific question asked was: "How important is the child's appearance in making diversion decision? Not important, important, somewhat important or very important?"
[b]The specific question asked was: "How important is the child's attitude toward offense in making diversion decision? Not important, important, somewhat important or very important?"
[c]The specific question asked was: "How important is the child's attitude toward treatment in making diversion decision? Not important, important, somewhat important or very important?"
[d]The specific question asked was: "How important is the local political environment in making diversion decision? Not important, important, somewhat important or very important?"
SOURCE: Roberto Hugh Potter and Suman Kakar. "The Diversion Decision-Making Process from the Juvenile Court Practitioners' Perspective." *Journal of Contemporary Criminal Justice*, February 2002, p.32. Reprinted by permission.

Effective diversion criteria should result in the diversion of most minor offenders who have no serious prior involvement with the court and who, along with their families, accept services and sanctions voluntarily.

One of the most common forms of diversion is being ordered to do community service. Degelman et al. (2006) have developed a guide to making community service more meaningful: *Giving Back: Introducing Community Service Learning—Improving Mandated Community Service for Juveniles.* The "Preface" of this guide states:

Educators have long known the value of community service. Beyond its value to the community, they know that school-based community service can provide young people with the knowledge, skills and attitudes they need to assume the most important role in our society—that of active citizens.

Community service, as mandated by the courts, plays a prominent role in our juvenile justice system as well. Today, many juvenile justice professionals regard it as an opportunity for rehabilitation. They believe that mandated community service can help juvenile justice respondents understand the impact of their actions on others; give back to the communities they have harmed; learn critical-thinking, citizenship and problem solving skills; develop a personal stake in the well-being of their communities; and raise awareness of their own self worth.

Perhaps most important, many juvenile justice professionals, particularly in youth courts, have seen a possible correlation between effective community service, heightened civic awareness and reduced recidivism rates. (p.3)

 Diversion may include community service, restitution, letters of apology, participation in prosocial activities, mentoring or tutoring programs, work programs, educational programs, skill-development programs, counseling programs or referral to a specialized court to meet individual needs.

An in-depth description of these various options is beyond the scope of this text. However, the growing popularity of specialized courts does merit brief discussion.

Diversion to Specialized Courts

Amidst the burgeoning caseload crisis faced by courts—both juvenile and criminal—throughout the county, and the growing recognition that many youths who come in contact with the juvenile justice system face challenges better addressed outside the formal court system (e.g., drug abuse, mental health issues, etc.), many jurisdictions have developed specialized courts to handle cases with mitigating circumstances that lend themselves to an option shy of full, formal court processing. The stipulation set forth in these courts, however, is that if youth do not abide by the conditions set forth in specialized court rulings, their cases will be referred to the more stringent and formal juvenile court. Thus, these specialized courts offer youth an opportunity to avoid formal processing.

 Specialized courts include teen courts, drug courts, mental health courts, traffic courts and gun courts.

Teen Court

An innovative alternative to the traditional juvenile court is the teen court, also called peer, student or youth court: "Youth court is an intervention program and not a court within the judicial branch of government" (Fisher, 2006, p.1). Teen courts are juvenile diversion programs used primarily for first-time offenders in misdemeanor, nonviolent cases. Cases handled in teen court may include shoplifting/theft, alcohol possession, criminal mischief, vandalism/property damage and traffic offenses. Teen courts are also used for school disciplinary

A male bailiff swears in a female defendant in teen court in Miami, Florida. Teen courts are diversion programs, not formal courts within the judicial branch of government. As such, the processes and procedures they follow are substantially less formal, although their sanctions are generally deemed valid by the court.

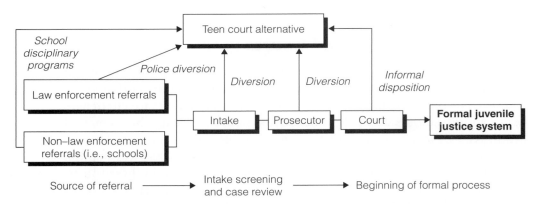

Figure 9.2   Points at Which Juvenile Offenders Can Be Diverted to Teen Court
SOURCE: The Urban Institute. Evaluation of Teen Courts Project. Reprinted by permission.

issues. Figure 9.2 shows the points at which juvenile offenders can be diverted to teen court.

The courtroom models used in teen courts are generally divided into four types: adult judge, youth judge, youth tribunal and peer jury. Youth volunteer roles in teen court hearings commonly include the defense attorney (youth advocate), prosecuting attorney (community advocate), clerk, bailiff, juror and sometimes judge. Table 9.3 presents courtroom models used by teen and youth courts in the United States.

Teen courts are voluntary and most require youth to admit to the charge and plead guilty, although a few are structured to determine guilt or innocence. In

Table 9.3   Courtroom Models Used by U.S. Teen and Youth Courts

	Adult Judge Model	Youth Judge Model	Tribunal Model	Peer Jury Model
Who performs the role of judge in the courtroom?	Adult	Youth	3 Youth	Adult (sometimes no judge)
Are teen attorneys included in the process?	Yes	Yes	Yes	No
What is the role of the teen jury during court?	Listen to attorney presentations, recommend sentence to judge	Listen to attorney presentations, recommend sentence to judge	Usually no jury	Question defendant, recommend or order sentence

SOURCE: Jeffrey A. Butts et al. *The Impact of Teen Court on Young Offenders*. Washington, DC: Urban Institute Justice Policy Center, April 2002, p.7. Reprinted by permission.

addition, parental consent is generally required for participation (Green, 2007). Teen courts are intervention programs, not courts within the judicial branch of government; therefore, their processes and procedures are significantly less formal and not held to the traditional due process requirements of regular courtrooms. However, their sanctions are recognized as valid by the court; therefore, youths who fail to abide by sanctions imposed by teen courts may face formal charges in juvenile court. The typical teen court process is shown in Figure 9.3. Figure 9.4 illustrates sanctions imposed by teen courts.

Teen courts provide an effective intervention in jurisdictions where the enforcement of misdemeanor charges is given low priority due to heavy caseloads of more serious offenses. In a collaborative report by the U.S. Department of Justice (DOJ) and the American Bar Association (ABA) titled *Youth Cases for Youth Court: Desktop Guide* (Fisher), it is noted that youth courts turn peer pressure into a positive tool by letting offenders know, through other teens, that their behavior was wrong.

Teen courts have spread rapidly across the nation in the past decade: "From rather humble beginnings, current data indicates that 1,128 teen court programs are present in 49 states and the District of Columbia" (Heward, 2006, p.1). The growth and acceptance of teen courts are exemplified by the establishment of the National Association of Youth Courts in 2007.

Youth Courts: An Empirical Update and Analysis of Future Organizational and Research Needs (2008) reports that in 2008 some 1,250 youth courts were in operation across the country, with the average court handling about 100 cases per year. An estimated 86 percent of the youth accepted into teen court successfully completed their sentence. The average youth court reported over 1,730 hours of completed community service. Furthermore, the typical youth court serving 100 offenders per year operated on a budget of less than $30,000.

The National Youth Court Center has set forth guidelines for communities considering implementing teen courts in *Youth Court: A Community Solution for Embracing At-Risk Youth* (Pearson and Jurich, 2005). Some teen courts address young people with substance abuse problems. In other jurisdictions separate juvenile drug courts have been established.

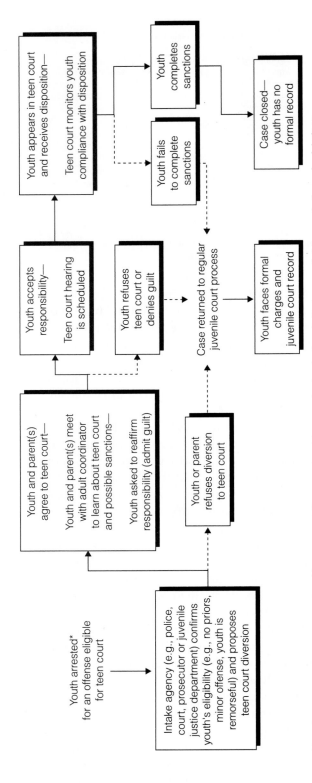

Figure 9.3 Typical Teen Court Process

Not all teen court cases are prompted by an arrest. Some teen courts accept school referrals for truancy, fighting and other rule violations. Others accept traffic violations. This report primarily addresses teen courts that handle delinquencies or violations of the criminal law.

SOURCE: Jeffrey A. Butts et al. *The Impact of Teen Court on Young Offenders*. Washington, DC: Urban Institute Justice Policy Center, April 2002, p.5. Reprinted by permission.

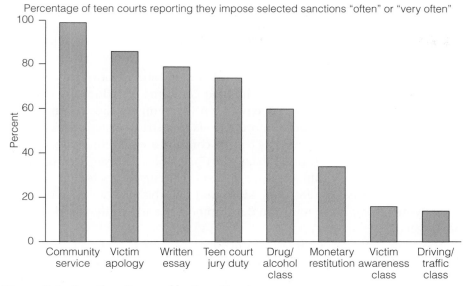

Percentage of teen courts reporting they impose selected sanctions "often" or "very often"

Figure 9.4 Sanctions Imposed by Teen Courts

SOURCE: Jeffrey A. Butts and Janeen Buck. *Teen Courts: A Focus on Research.* Washington, DC: OJJDP Juvenile Justice Research Bulletin, October 2000, p.6.

PROGRAMS IN PRACTICE: TEEN COURTS

The San Diego (California) Teen Court   This teen court is intended to empower youths to make positive choices and prevent juvenile crime by holding offenders accountable and repairing harm to communities. Eligible offenses for teen court include assault, battery, fighting, shoplifting and other thefts, possession (alcohol, tobacco, marijuana), disorderly conduct, trespassing, weapons on campus, curfew, daytime loitering and vandalism. Its primary model is an adult judge, a teen jury and student attorneys. Since its inception in 2001, the teen court has trained over 5,500 students.

Each year this court serves more than 100 offenders and their families and teaches more than 1,000 students about the juvenile justice system. Between 2001 and 2006 the court served 470 youth offenders and had only 33 reoffend, a 7 percent recidivism rate. Ninety-eight percent of offenders and their parents felt participation in the teen court changed the offenders' behavior in a positive way (Brown, 2007).

The Placer County (California) Peer Court   Placer County Peer Court's mission is "Diversion and prevention through accountability and education." Cases are referred to the court from juvenile probation, school site police officers, the juvenile court or local police agencies. Juveniles must be first-time offenders and must admit guilt to participate. This court also uses the adult judge, peer jury and attorney model. The peer jury decides the appropriate sentence. In addition each defendant must serve a minimum of two times on Peer Court juries and perform a minimum of ten hours of community service.

The court has separate panels that address specific problems. *Peer Court Tobacco Panels* hear all tobacco offenses referred by law enforcement agencies. A common element of tobacco panel sentences is community service, where defendants can see the effects of tobacco use on patients. Cessation classes, essays and fines may also be imposed. *Peer Court Truancy Panels*, comprised of three to five students who previously had truancy problems of their own and who have resolved those issues, hear attendance violations by student defendants (Green).

SOURCE: Information on both of these teen courts was presented at the 34th National Conference on Juvenile Justice in San Diego, California, on March 6, 2007.

Juvenile Drug Courts

"Reclaiming Futures" (2007, p.5) reports that the majority of youths in the juvenile justice system were under the influence at the time of their offense. Consequently, the juvenile justice system has become the default agency for providing drug and alcohol treatment services. As the juvenile courts have become increasingly overwhelmed with complex and difficult caseloads and diminishing resources, one approach that has emerged as a solution to the crowded court dockets is the drug court.

The first drug court was established in 1989 in Miami, Florida, to deal with adult drug offenders and had the dual expectations of reducing substance abuse and the related criminal behavior while freeing up the criminal court and corrections to handle other more serious non-drug-related cases (Myers, 2007, p.89). The popularity of drug courts, combined with promising research results, led to the application of drug court principles in juvenile drug cases. The philosophy behind the creation of juvenile drug courts is that children and adolescents are different from adults and that the root causes of drug use among young people are found in developmental and family-based risk factors (Myers).

According to the National Drug Control Strategy, 840,000 fewer young people were using illicit drugs in 2006 than in 2001. In spite of this positive report, the overall level of drug use is still unacceptably high, and the use of some substances such as prescription drugs is increasing ("White House Releases 2007 National Drug Control Strategy," 2007, p.3).

A typical juvenile drug court offers delinquents who meet certain eligibility criteria the option of participating in the drug court rather than in a traditional case processing.

 The two most common criteria for participating in a drug court are having a substance abuse problem and not having committed a violent offense.

Juvenile Drug Courts: Strategies in Practice (2003) lists 16 strategies that can be used in a juvenile drug court, summarized in Table 9.4. Participants who successfully complete a drug court program may be rewarded by dismissed charges, shortened sentences or reduced penalties.

Myers (p.90) reports that only 10 to 20 percent of juveniles enrolled in drug courts have used anything other than alcohol or marijuana, leading researchers to suggest that drug courts need to better distinguish adolescents who are substance abusers, or are likely to become drug dependent, from the larger majority of youths who have experimented with alcohol or other drugs but will not develop long-term problems as a result.

Frequently youths who have a substance abuse problem also have mental health issues.

Juvenile Mental Health Courts

Skowyra and Cocozza (2006, p.1) contend: "It is now well established that the majority of youths involved with the juvenile justice system have mental health disorders." Recall how some studies have found that up to three-fourths of all juvenile detainees have some type of diagnosable mental health issue. Indeed, it appears that many youth are placed into the juvenile justice system specifically as a way to access mental health services that would otherwise be unavailable to them in the community (Skowyra and Powell, 2006). These are among the major reasons behind the development of mental health courts.

Table 9.4   The Strategies Used in Juvenile Drug Courts

1. **Collaborative Planning**—Engage all stakeholders in creating an interdisciplinary, coordinated and systemic approach to working with youth and their families.

2. **Teamwork**—Develop and maintain an interdisciplinary, nonadversarial work team.

3. **Clearly Defined Target Population and Eligibility Criteria**—Define a target population and eligibility criteria that are aligned with the program's goals and objectives.

4. **Judicial Involvement and Supervision**—Schedule frequent judicial reviews and be sensitive to the effect that court proceedings can have on youth and their families.

5. **Monitoring and Evaluation**—Establish a system for program monitoring and evaluation to maintain quality of service, assess program impact and contribute to knowledge in the field.

6. **Community Partnerships**—Build partnerships with community organizations to expand the range of opportunities available to youth and their families.

7. **Comprehensive Treatment Planning**—Tailor interventions to the complex and varied needs of youth and their families.

8. **Developmentally Appropriate Services**—Tailor treatment to the developmental needs of adolescents.

9. **Gender-Appropriate Services**—Design treatment to address the unique needs of each gender.

10. **Cultural Competence**—Create policies and procedures that are responsive to cultural differences and train personnel to be culturally competent.

11. **Focus on Strengths**—Maintain a focus on the strengths of youth and their families during program planning and in every interaction between the court and those it serves.

12. **Family Engagement**—Recognize and engage the family as a valued partner in all components of the program.

13. **Educational Linkages**—Coordinate with the school system to ensure that each participant enrolls in and attends an educational program that is appropriate to his or her needs.

14. **Drug Testing**—Design drug testing to be frequent, random and observed. Document testing policies and procedures in writing.

15. **Goal-Oriented Incentives and Sanctions**—Respond to compliance and noncompliance with incentives and sanctions that are designed to reinforce or modify the behavior of youth and their families.

16. **Confidentiality**—Establish a confidentiality policy and procedures that guard the privacy of the youth while allowing the drug court team to access key information.

SOURCE: *Juvenile Drug Courts: Strategies in Practice.* Washington, DC: Bureau of Justice Assistance, March 2003, p.10. (NCJ 197866)

Diversion to such courts of juveniles with mental health needs holds many benefits for the youths themselves, the justice system and the community at large, including:

- Reducing recidivism.
- Providing more effective and appropriate treatment.
- Decreasing overcrowded detention facilities.
- Facilitating the further development of community-based mental health services. (Skowyra and Powell)

Cocozza and Shufelt describe mental health courts as "specialized courts that utilize a separate docket, coupled with a team approach and regular judicial supervision, to respond to individuals with mental illnesses who come in contact with the justice system." They note that the first adult mental health court opened in 1997 in Broward County, Florida, and recently expanded to address the mental health needs of juvenile offenders as well. The first juvenile mental health court opened in 2001 in Santa Clara County, California. The Court for the Individualized Treatment of Adolescents (CITA) accepts youths who were under age 14 at the time of their offense and have a serious mental illness, including brain disorders (schizophrenia, severe anxiety, bipolar disorder and severe ADHA) or severe head injury that has contributed to their offending. The court also accepts youths with certain developmental disabilities such as mental retardation and autism.

Skowyra and Cocozza (2006) propose a Blueprint for Change, providing a conceptual and practical framework for juvenile justice and mental health systems to use when developing strategies and policies aimed at improving mental health services for youths involved with the juvenile justice system. The model is based on four cornerstones that reflect those areas where the most critical improvements are necessary to enhance the delivery of mental health services to youths involved with the juvenile justice system.

 The four cornerstones of the Blueprint for Change model are collaboration, identification, diversion and treatment.

Juvenile Gun Courts

Throughout the nation, juvenile and **family courts** (courts with broad jurisdiction over family matters) have been criticized for not providing appropriate sanctions and program services for young offenders involved in gun crimes. Some states have instituted juvenile gun courts and targeted interventions that expose youths charged with gun offenses to the ramifications of such acts.

Gun courts are short-term, early intervention programs with an intensive education focus including a wide range of court personnel and law enforcement officials—judges, probation officers, prosecutors, defense counsel and police—working with community members. A major goal of gun court is to effectively deliver to juveniles the message that gun violence hurts victims, families and entire communities; guns cannot protect juveniles; being involved in gun violence will negatively affect their entire lives; and there are adults who can and will help them find nonviolent ways to solve problems. As Sheppard and Kelly (2002, p.8) note: "Before the gun court was implemented, police officers usually did not arrest youths for gun possession; they released the youth to a parent without filing any charges. Now that the court is in place, however, police can arrest youths for all gun-related offenses."

 First-time, nonviolent gun offenders age 17 and younger are sometimes eligible to participate in juvenile gun court programs.

A gun court is a type of problem-solving court that intervenes with youths who have committed gun offenses that have not resulted in serious physical injury. Most gun courts include several principal elements including

1. Early intervention.
2. Shorter, intensive programming (often a single two- to four-hour session).

3. An intensive educational focus to show youths the harm that can come from unlawful gun use and the immediate response that will result when youths are involved with guns.
4. The inclusion of a wide range of court personnel and law enforcement officials working together with community members. ("Gun Court," 2007)

Juvenile Traffic Court

Minors charged with traffic offenses may appear in juvenile traffic court with a parent or guardian. The juvenile is entitled to a trial if the citation is contested. If a minor admits the citation or is found by the judge or hearing officer to have committed the violation, the minor can be ordered to pay a fine, have driving privileges suspended or restricted, be required to do a certain number of hours of community service or be placed on probation (*Juvenile Justice Handbook*, 2008, p.7).

In addition to specialized courts, diversion can also be provided through various models of restorative justice, often through some form of conferencing.

Balanced and Restorative Justice

Bringing Balance to Juvenile Justice (2002, pp.1–2) notes:

> Since its inception in the late 1800s, the juvenile justice system has been an amalgam of contradictions and competing concerns. On some level, society believes that crime should result in punishment and that children must experience swift, certain and negative consequences for their crimes to deter them from future delinquency. Society also wants rehabilitation of wayward youths, but it wants to be protected from them while the rehabilitation takes place. The needs of crime victims must be central to the justice system. They need compensation for damages, contrition from offenders and a sense of justice restored. . . .
>
> [If the punishment model and the therapeutic intervention model] coexist in a jurisdiction, they are in constant conflict. If either one exists by itself, it fails to serve all stakeholders in the system.
>
> There is a better approach. Balanced consideration of community protection, offender accountability and competency development brings clarity and reason to juvenile justice issues. This comprehensive philosophy speaks to every aspect of delinquency, punishment, treatment and prevention. These three principles, fully implemented, create a juvenile justice system that truly operates in the best interest of the child and the community.

 "Ensuring community safety, insisting on offender accountability to victims, and equipping offenders in the system with skills so they are able to pursue non-criminal paths after release are the core principles of the Balanced and Restorative Justice (BARJ) model" (*Bringing Balance to Juvenile Justice*, p.2).

As Bazemore and Umbreit (2001, p.1) explain: "Restorative justice is a framework for juvenile justice reform that seeks to engage victims, offenders and their families, other citizens and community groups both as clients of juvenile justice services and as resources in an effective response to youth crime. . . . Reconciling the needs of victims and offenders with the needs of the community is the underlying goal of restorative justice. Unlike retributive justice, which is primarily concerned with punishing crime, restorative justice focuses on repairing the injury that crime inflicts."

 The three main components of restorative justice are the offender, the victim and the community, including juvenile justice professionals.

In the balanced and restorative justice format offenders, victims, community members and juvenile justice professionals have new roles as they seek to sanction offenders through accountability, rehabilitate them through competency development and enhance community safety. These new roles are briefly summarized in Table 9.5.

Table 9.5   New Roles in the Balanced and Restorative Justice Model

	Sanctioning through Accountability	*Rehabilitation through Competency Development*	*Enhancement of Community Safety*
Juvenile Offender	Must accept responsibility for behavior and actively work to restore loss to victims (if victims wish) and the community and face victims or victim representatives (if victims wish) and community members	Actively participates as a resource in service roles that improve quality of life in the community and provide new experiences, skills and self-esteem as a productive resource for positive action	Becomes involved in constructive competency building and restorative activities in a balanced program while under adult supervision, develops internal controls and new peer and organizational commitments, and helps others escape offending patterns of behavior
Victim	Actively participates in all stages of the restorative process (if victim wishes and is able), documents psychological and financial impact of crime, participates in mediation voluntarily and helps determine sanctions for juvenile offender	Provides input into the rehabilitative process, suggests community service options for juvenile offenders and participates in victim panels or victim-awareness training for staff and juvenile offenders (if victim wishes)	Provides input regarding continuing safety concerns, fear and needed controls on juvenile offenders and encourages protective support for other victims
Community Member	Participates as volunteer mediator/facilitator and community panel member, develops community service and compensated work opportunities for juvenile offenders with reparative obligations and assists victims and supports juvenile offenders in completing obligations	Develops new opportunities for youth to make productive contributions, build competency and establish a sense of belonging	Provides guardianship of juvenile offenders, mentoring and input to juvenile justice systems regarding safety concerns; addresses underlying community problems that contribute to delinquency; and provides "natural surveillance"
Juvenile Justice Professional	Facilitates mediation, ensures that restoration occurs (by providing ways for juvenile offenders to earn funds for restitution), develops creative/restorative community service options, engages community members in the process and educates community on its role	Develops new roles for young offenders that allow them to practice and demonstrate competency, assesses and builds on youth and community strengths and develops community partnerships	Develops range of incentives and consequences to ensure juvenile offender compliance with supervision objectives, assists school and family in their efforts to control and maintain juvenile offenders in the community and develops prevention capacity of local organizations

Adapted from Bazemore and Washington. "Charting the Future for the Juvenile Justice System: Reinventing Mission and Management. *Spectrum*." *Journal of State Government*, 1995, pp.51–66.
SOURCE: *Guide for Implementing the Balanced and Restorative Justice Model*. Washington, DC: Office of Juvenile Justice and Delinquency Prevention, December 1998, p.41.

Four models of restorative justice may also be a means of diversion: victim-offender mediation, community reparative boards, family group conferencing and circle sentencing.

Victim-Offender Mediation

Victim-offender mediation originated in the mid-1970s. Eligibility varies, but it is primarily used with first-time property offenders. Referrals are made by the court, the police and other entities. A mediator, victim and offender meet in a neutral setting such as a church or community center. Parents also may be involved. The primary outcome sought is to allow the victim to relay the impact of the crime to the offender, expressing feelings and needs while at the same time the offender has increased awareness of the harm of the offense, gains empathy with the victim and agrees on a reparative plan. For example:

> The victim was a middle-aged woman. The offender, a 14-year-old neighbor of the victim, had broken into the victim's home and stolen a VCR. The mediation session took place in the basement of the victim's church.
>
> In the presence of a mediator, the victim and offender talked for two hours. At times, their conversation was heated and emotional. When they finished, the mediator felt that they had heard each other's stories and learned something important about the impact of the crime and about each other.
>
> The participants agreed that the offender would pay $200 in restitution to cover the cost of damages to the victim's home resulting from the break-in and would also reimburse the victim for the cost of the stolen VCR (estimated at $150). They also worked out a payment schedule.
>
> During the session, the offender made several apologies to the victim and agreed to complete community service hours working in a food bank sponsored by the victim's church. The victim said that she felt less angry and fearful after learning more about the offender and the details of the crime. (Bazemore and Umbreit, 2001, p.9)

Community Reparative Boards

Reparative boards typically consist of a small group of citizens who have received intensive training and who then conduct public, face-to-face meetings with offenders ordered by the court to participate in the process. The target group is nonviolent offenders assigned to the board. During the board meeting, board members discuss with the offender the offense and its negative consequences. The board then develops a set of proposed sanctions that they discuss with the offender. The board also monitors compliance and submits a compliance report to the court. Following is an example of a community reparative board session:

> The reparative board convened to consider the case of a 17-year-old who had been caught driving with an open can of beer in his father's pickup truck. The youth had been sentenced by a judge to reparative probation, and it was the board's responsibility to decide what form the probation should take. For about 30 minutes, the citizen members of the board asked the youth several

simple, straightforward questions. The board members then went to another room to deliberate on an appropriate sanction for the youth. The youth awaited the board's decision nervously, because he did not know whether to expect something tougher or much easier than regular probation.

When the board returned, the chairperson explained the four conditions of the offender's probation contract: (1) begin work to pay off his traffic tickets, (2) complete a state police defensive driving course, (3) undergo an alcohol assessment and (4) write a three-page paper on how alcohol had negatively affected his life. The youth signed the contract, and the chairperson adjourned the meeting. (Bazemore and Umbreit, 2001, p.4)

Family Group Conferencing

Family group conferencing originated in New Zealand. Referrals are usually by police and school officials. Family group conferencing involves those most affected by a youth's crime, usually the victim, offender and family, friends and key supporters of the victim and offender. These individuals are brought together by a trained facilitator to discuss how they and others have been harmed by the offense and how that harm might be repaired. Such conferences typically take place in a social welfare office, school, community building or police facility. The primary outcomes sought are to clarify the facts of a case and to denounce crime while affirming and supporting the offender and restoring the victim's loss.

Eligibility criteria for such a conference usually include being no older than age 14 and being a first-time offender committing a nonviolent offence with no pending charges and admitting guilt. Consider the following example of a family group conferencing session:

> A family conferencing group convened in a local school to consider a case in which a student had injured a teacher and broken the teacher's glasses in an altercation. Group members included the offender, his mother and grandfather, the victim, the police officer who made the arrest and about 10 other interested parties, including two of the offender's teachers and two friends of the victim.
>
> The conferencing process began with comments by the offender, his mother and grandfather, the victim and the arresting officer. Each spoke about the offense and its impact. The youth justice coordinator next asked for input from the other group members and then asked all participants what they thought the offender should do to pay back the victim and the community for the damage caused by his crime. In the remaining 30 minutes of the hour-long conference, the group suggested that the offender should make restitution to the victim for his medical expenses and the cost of new glasses and that the offender should also perform community service work on the school grounds. (Bazemore and Umbreit, 2001, p.5)

Circle Sentencing

Circle sentencing is a modernized version of the traditional sanctioning and healing practices of aboriginal peoples in Canada and American Indians in the

United States. According to Bazemore and Umbreit (2001, p.6): "Circle sentencing is a holistic reintegrative strategy designed not only to address the criminal and delinquent behavior of offenders but also to consider the needs of victims, families and communities." The circle usually includes victims, offenders, family and friends of both, justice and social service personnel and interested community residents.

The target group is offenders who admit guilt and express willingness to change. The primary outcomes sought are to increase community strength and capacity to resolve disputes and prevent crime, develop reparative and rehabilitative plans, address victim concerns and public safety issues, assign victim and offender support group responsibilities and identify resources. Bazemore and Umbreit (p.7) provide the following example of a circle sentencing session:

> The victim was a middle-aged man whose parked car had been badly damaged when the offender, a 16-year-old, crashed into it while joyriding in another vehicle. The offender had also damaged a police vehicle.
>
> In the circle, the victim talked about the emotional shock of seeing what had happened to his car and his costs to repair it (he was uninsured). Then, an elder leader of the First Nations community where the circle sentencing session was being held (and an uncle of the offender) expressed his disappointment and anger with the boy. The elder observed that this incident, along with several prior offenses by the boy, had brought shame to his family. The elder also noted that in the old days, the boy would have been required to pay the victim's family substantial compensation as a result of such behavior. After the elder finished, a feather (the "talking piece") was passed to the next person in the circle, a young man who spoke about the contributions the offender had made to the community, the kindness he had shown toward elders and his willingness to help others with home repairs.
>
> Having heard all this, the judge asked the Crown Council (Canadian prosecutor) and the **public defender** [lawyer who works for the defense of indigent offenders] who were also sitting in the circle to make statements and then asked if anyone else in the circle wanted to speak. The Royal Canadian Mounted Police officer, whose vehicle had also been damaged, then took the feather and spoke on the offender's behalf. The officer proposed to the judge that in lieu of statutorily required jail time for the offense, the offender be allowed to meet with him on a regular basis for counseling and community service. After asking the victim and the prosecutor if either had any objections, the judge accepted this proposal. The judge also ordered restitution to the victim and asked the young adult who had spoken on the offender's behalf to serve as a mentor for the offender.

Considerations When Using a Restorative Justice Approach   Bazemore and Umbreit (2001) studied the four models of restorative justice just discussed and found that each model had strengths and weakness, concluding that different approaches will work best in difference situations (p.16). Griffin and Torbet (2002, p.51) recommend that when using diversion programs such as those just discussed, the programs will be more successful if they have a participatory rather

Table 9.6 Types of Alternative Dispute Resolution Programs

Adjudicatory	*Participatory*
Intent is to assert a moral or legal message and impose a solution	Intent is to preserve and enhance ongoing relationships
Facilitator/panel makes and imposes all decisions	Parties arrive at mutually acceptable agreement with aid of facilitator
Facilitator/panel assesses facts and culpability in determining appropriate remedy	Less fact-finding; parties define issues, engage in search for solutions
Focus is on the immediate conflict and the issues raised in the complaint	Focus is ongoing relationships among neighbors, family members, etc.
Teaches accountability for offenses	Teaches conflict-resolution and problem-solving techniques
The more formal the process and the more serious the problem presented, the more formal the resulting agreement	The more participatory and inclusive the process, the less formal the resulting agreement

Adapted from National Council of Juvenile and Family Court Judges, *Court-Appointed Alternative Dispute Resolution: A Better Way to Resolve Minor Delinquency, Status Offense and Abuse/Neglect Cases.* (1989) NCJFCJ: Reno, NV.
SOURCE: Patrick Griffin and Patricia Torbet, editors. *Desktop Guide to Good Juvenile Probation Practice.* Pittsburgh, PA: National Center for Juvenile Justice, June 2002, p.51. Reprinted by permission.

than an adjudicatory focus. The differences between these two approaches are summarized in Table 9.6. Furthermore, in many instances success is also more likely using a strength-based approach as opposed to a problem-centered approach. The features of these two approaches are summarized in Table 9.7.

Whatever form of pretrial service and diversion is used, juvenile justice officials must be careful not to "widen the net" for those entering the juvenile justice system.

Net Widening

Jamison (n.d., p.1) explains that **net widening** refers to involving youths in a diversion program who, without such opportunities, probably would not be involved in any type of intervention: "The process results in diversion of resources from youths most in need of intervention to youths who may require no intervention. This process depletes the system's resources and impairs its ability to properly intervene with appropriate youths. Instead of improving public safety, these early intervention and prevention strategies promote net widening by shifting resources from youths most in need to youths least in need."

Jamison (p.4) notes: "For the past 40 years criminal justice research repeatedly shows that almost 70 percent of youths who are arrested once are never arrested again. In other words, by doing nothing the state can achieve a 70 percent success rate—meaning no subsequent arrests—with first-time offenders. . . . By reducing net widening, research shows that systems can improve their effectiveness and better promote public safety. To shorten the net and improve public safety, juvenile justice systems and affiliated community-based agencies need to adopt a deep end strategy." A **deep end strategy** would target youths with the highest likelihood of continuing their delinquent careers without comprehensive interventions. Jamison suggests: "The current favored approach

Table 9.7   Problem-Centered Approach versus Strength-Based Approach

Problem-centered Approach	Strength-based Approach
Approaches clients with attention to their failure, dysfunction and deficits with an eye to fixing their flaws.	Approaches clients with a greater concern for their strengths, competencies and possibilities, seeking not only to fix what is wrong but to nurture what is best.
Assumes an "expert" role in naming clients' problems and then instructing clients how to fix them.	Assumes clients to be competent and "expert" on their life and situation. Helps clients discover how strengths and resources can be applied to negotiate third-party concerns and mandates while also furthering their wants and concerns as well.
Sanction-focused: client "takes the punishment" without taking responsibility or earning redemption.	Incentive-focused: holds youth accountable while furthering their prosocial interests, skills or passions.
Route to solution: fix the problem.	Route to solution: strengthen connection to clients' competencies, past successes, positive interests and wants.
Goals are obedience and compliance.	Initial goals are obedience and compliance; final goals are behavior change and growth.
No direct strategies are used for building motivation. Relies on coercion and "pushing from without."	Employs specific principles and strategies for building client motivation to change. Uses sanctions to stabilize out-of-control behavior but works to raise motivation that comes from within.
Court has nonnegotiable mandates, and probation officer determines both the goals and the means for reaching those goals.	Court has nonnegotiable mandates but beyond these, clients are partners in the process of setting personalized goals. Probation officer helps them focus on what they want to change, maintains the focus and works to increase positive options.

SOURCE: Patrick Griffin and Patricia Torbet, editors. *Desktop Guide to Good Juvenile Probation Practice.* Pittsburgh, PA: National Center for Juvenile Justice, 2002, p.97. Reprinted by permission.

of intervention with first-time offenders is counter to this strategy and a likely waste of the system's limited resources." One effort to reduce net widening is having available respite care.

Respite Care

Quraishi et al. (n.d.) explain that respite care is designed to give family members a needed break from one another, using trained counselors to help them get to the root of their problems and reunify them quickly: "Respite programs provide a viable alternative to non-secure detention and other 'custodial placement' for status offenders and can prevent future contact with the juvenile justice and child welfare systems." They suggest that respite care programs can be provided as voluntary walk-in or police drop-off centers for runaways, as court diversion programs for status offenders and as an alternative to nonsecure detention for status offenders already involved in family court. The programs are designed to give families in crisis the immediate assistance they need.

The Importance of Timely Case Processing

Whether the decision at intake is to use diversion or to refer to juvenile court, timely case processing is critical. Siegel and Halemba (2006, p.1) contend: "Timely intervention (informal or formal) is critical in attempting to disrupt the development of a youth's delinquent 'career' before her/his behavior becomes more engrained and chorionic. It also makes considerable intuitive sense to try to intervene before a youth is again referred on a subsequent law violation." They further assert: "There is little question that unnecessary delays in case processing may increase the likelihood of a juvenile's subsequent involvement with the court as well as the likelihood that the juvenile's law-violating behavior will continue to escalate." Siegel and Halemba (p.7) suggest the following time standards for processing informal/diverted cases:

- Filing of police report/referral: 75 percent of cases completed in 7 days; 98 percent in 10 days
- Intake screening: 75 percent completed in 7 days; 98 percent in 15 days
- Develop diversion plan: 75 percent in 3 days; 98 percent in 10 days
- Initiate diversion plan: 75 percent in 4 days; 98 percent in 25 days
- Total days to implementation: 75 percent in 21 days; 98 percent in 60 days

Ideally these times would be even shorter.

 SUMMARY

- Two opposing philosophies of kids are: (1) kids do well if they want to, and (2) kids do well if they can.
- "The primary duty of the prosecutor is to seek justice while fully and faithfully representing the interests of the state."
- The intake hearing may result in dismissal, diversion, referral to juvenile court for adjudication or transfer to adult court.
- Principles of effective intervention include:
  - Risk Principle—target higher-risk offender (WHO)
  - Need Principle—target criminogenic risk/need factors (WHAT)
  - Treatment Principle—use behavioral approaches (HOW)
  - Fidelity Principle—implement program as designed (HOW WELL)
- Effective diversion criteria should result in the diversion of most minor offenders who have no serious prior involvement with the court and who, along with their families, accept services and sanctions voluntarily.
- Diversion may include community service, restitution, letters of apology, participation in prosocial activities, mentoring or tutoring programs, work programs, educational programs, skill-development programs, counseling programs or referral to a specialized court to meet individual needs.
- Specialized courts include teen courts, drug courts, mental health courts, traffic courts and gun courts.
- The two most common criteria for participating in a drug court are having a substance abuse problem and not having committed a violent offense.
- The four cornerstones of the Blueprint for Change model are collaboration, identification, diversion and treatment.
- First-time, nonviolent gun offenders 17 and younger are sometimes eligible to participate in juvenile gun court programs.

- Ensuring community safety, insisting on offender accountability to victims and equipping offenders in the system with skills so they are able to pursue noncriminal paths after release are the core principles of the balanced and restorative justice (BARJ) model.
- The three main components of restorative justice are the offender, victim and community, including juvenile justice professionals.
- Four models of restorative justice may also be a means of diversion: victim-offender mediation, community reparative boards, family group conferencing and circle sentencing.

DISCUSSION QUESTIONS

1. Should there be a separate justice system for juveniles, or should all juveniles be dealt with in the adult system?
2. Is diversion being too soft on youths who commit status offenses?
3. Is restorative justice compatible with the juvenile justice system?
4. What form of restorative justice do you find most appealing?
5. Which philosophy of children do you believe is better?
6. How can the juvenile prosecutor fulfill both the role of protecting society and acting in the best interest of the child?
7. Have you seen any instances of net widening in your community?
8. What alternatives for diversion are available in your community?
9. Which of the pretrial services do you believe are most important?
10. Why can juveniles be detained before they have a trial?

REFERENCES

Abrahamson, Larry R. *Role and Purpose of the Juvenile Prosecutor.* San Diego, CA: Seminar B-4 presented at the 34th National Conference on Juvenile Justice, March 5, 2007.

Austin, James; Johnson, Dedel; and Weitzer, Ronald. *Alternatives to the Secure Detention and Confinement of Juvenile Offenders.* Washington, DC: Office of Juvenile Justice and Delinquency Prevention, September 2005.

Bazemore, Gordon and Umbreit, Mark. *A Comparison of Four Restorative Conferencing Models.* Washington, DC: OJJDP Juvenile Justice Bulletin, February 2001. (NCJ 184738)

Boesky, Lisa. "Juvenile Offenders with Mental Health Disorders: What You NEED to Know." San Diego, CA: Seminar P-2 presented at the 34th National Conference on Juvenile Justice, March 4, 2007.

Bringing Balance to Juvenile Justice. Alexandria, VA: American Prosecutors Research Institute, 2002.

Brown, Nicole. *Youth Courts: The Local, State and National Youth Justice Movement Continues.* San Diego, CA: Seminar D-4 presented at the 34th National Conference on Juvenile Justice, March 6, 2007.

Clark, Pam. "Juvenile Justice Faces Mental Health Issues." *Corrections Today*, February 2008, pp.8–13.

Cocozza, Joseph J. and Shufelt, Jennie L. *Juvenile Mental Health Courts: An Emerging Strategy.* Research and Program Brief. Delmar, NY: National Center for Mental Health and Juvenile Justice, June 2006.

Degelman, Charles; Doggett, Keri; and Medina, Gregorio. *Giving Back: Introducing Community Service Learning—Improving Mandated Community Service for Juvenile Offenders.* Chicago, IL: Constitutional Rights Foundation, 2006.

Fisher, Margaret E. *Youth Cases for Youth Courts: Desktop Guide.* Chicago, IL: American Bar Association, 2006.

Flores, Anthony W.; Travis, Lawrence F., III; and Latessa, Edward J. *Case Classification for Juvenile Corrections: An Assessment of the Youth Level of Service/Case Management Inventory (YLS/CMI), Final Report.* Unpublished report, funded by the U.S. Department of Justice. Document 204005, Award # 98-JB-VX-0108, February 2004. Made available online by the National Criminal Justice Reference Service (NCJRS) at http://www.ncjrs.gov/pdffiles1/nij/grants/204005.pdf.

Green, Karen. *Youth Courts: The Local, State and National Youth Justice Movement Continues.* San Diego, CA: Seminar D-4 presented at the 34th National Conference on Juvenile Justice, March 6, 2007.

Greene, Ross. "Kids Do Well If They Can." *Phi Delta Kappan*, November 2008, pp.160–167.

Griffin, Patrick and Torbet, Patricia. *Desktop Guide to Good Juvenile Probation Practice.* Pittsburg, PA: National Center for Juvenile Justice, June 2002.

"Gun Court." Washington, DC: OJJDP Model Programs Guide, 2007.

Hanger, JauNae M. "Indiana Addresses Mental Health in Juvenile Detention Centers." *Corrections Today*, February 2008, pp.36–38.

Heward, Michelle E. "An Update on Teen Court Legislation." Washington, DC: Office of Juvenile Justice and Delinquency Prevention, September 2006.

Jamison, Ross. *Widening the Net in Juvenile Justice and the Dangers of Prevention and Early Intervention*. San Francisco, CA: Center on Juvenile and Criminal Justice, no date. Online: http://207.158.206.242/pubs/net/netwid.html

Juvenile Drug Courts: Strategies in Practice. Washington, DC: Bureau of Justice Assistance, March 2003. (NCJ 197866)

Juvenile Justice Handbook 2008. Newcastle, CA: Placer County Peer Court Board of Directors, 2008.

Latessa, Edward J. *What Works and What Doesn't in Reducing Recidivism: The Principles of Effective Intervention*. San Diego, CA: Seminar P-5 presented at the 34th National Conference on Juvenile Justice, March 4, 2007.

McReynolds, Larkin S.; Wasserman, Gail A.; DeComo, Robert E.; John, Reni; Keating, Joseph M.; and Nolen, Scott. "Psychiatric Disorder in a Juvenile Assessment Center." *Crime & Delinquency*, April 2008, pp.313–334.

Miller, Joel and Lin, Jeffrey. "Applying a Generic Juvenile Risk Assessment Instrument to a Local Context." *Crime & Delinquency*, October 2007, pp.552–580.

Mogulescu; Sara; Salsich, Annie; and Townsend, Sharon. *Approaching System Change: The Vera Institute's Efforts to Support Juvenile Justice Reform in New York*. San Diego, CA: Seminar F-7 presented at the 34th National Conference on Juvenile Justice, March 6, 2007.

Murphy, Vivian L. "Motivating Youth." *Juvenile and Family Justice Today*, 2007, p.8

Myers, David L. "Assessing the Implementation and Effectiveness of Juvenile Drug Courts." *Criminal Justice Research Reports*, July/August, 2007.

National Juvenile Detention Association (NJDA). "Definition of Juvenile Detention." Richmond, KY: National Partnership for Juvenile Services, 2007.

Olson, Darryl. "Florida Makes PACT with State's Youthful Offenders." *Juvenile and Family Justice Today*, Winter 2007, pp.16–19.

Pearson, Sarah S. and Jurich, Sonia. *Youth Court: A Community Solution for Embracing At-Risk Youth*. Washington, DC: American Youth Policy Forum, 2005.

Quraishi, Fiza; Segal, Heiki J.; and Trone, Jennifer. *Youth Justice Program* New York: Vera Institute of Justice, no date.

"Reclaiming Futures Initiative Seeks to Improve Delivery of Services to Juvenile Delinquents." *Juvenile Justice Update*, June/July 2007, pp.9–10.

Sheppard, David and Kelly, Patricia. *Juvenile Gun Courts: Promoting Accountability and Providing Treatment*. Washington, DC: Office of Juvenile Justice and Delinquency Prevention, JAIBG Bulletin, May 2002. (NCJ 187078)

Shufelt, Jennie L. and Cocozza, Joseph J. *Youth with Mental Health Disorders in the Juvenile Justice System: Results from a Multi-State Prevalence Study*. Delmar, NY: National Center for Mental Health and Juvenile Justice, June 2006.

Siegel, Gene and Halemba, Gregg. *The Importance of Timely Case Processing in Non-Detained Juvenile Delinquency Cases*. Washington, DC: National Center for Juvenile Justice, July 2006.

Skowyra, Kathleen and Cocozza, Joseph J. *A Blueprint for Change: Improving the System Response to Youth with Mental Health Needs Involved with the Juvenile Justice System*. Research Program and Brief. Delmar, NY: National Center for Mental Health and Juvenile Justice, June 2006.

Skowyra, Kathleen and Powell, Susan Davidson. *Juvenile Diversion: Programs for Justice-Involved Youth with Mental Health Disorders*. Research and Program Brief. Delmar, NY: National Center for Mental Health and Juvenile Justice, June 2006.

Snyder, Howard N. and Sickmund, Melissa. *2006 Juvenile Offenders and Victims: 2006 National Report*. Washington, DC: U.S. Department of Justice, Office of Justice Programs, Office of Juvenile Justice and Delinquency Prevention, March 2006.

Teplin, Linda A.; Abram, Karen M.; McClelland, Gary M.; Mericle, Amy A.; Dulcan, Mina K.; and Washburn, Jason J. *Psychiatric Disorders of Youth in Detention*. Juvenile Justice Bulletin, April 2006.

Tjaden, Claus D. and Martinez, Orlando L. "Integrating Assessment Results with Service Provision." *Corrections Today*, February 2007, pp.76–78.

"White House Releases 2007 National Drug Control Strategy." *Juvenile Justice Update*, April/May 2007, pp.3, 12.

Williams, Valerli; Grisso, Thomas; Valentine, Melissa; and Remsburg, Nicole. "Mental Health Screening: Pennsylvania's Experience in Juvenile Detention." *Corrections Today*, February 2008, pp.24–27.

Young, Douglas; Moline, Karl; Farrell, Jill; and Bierie, David. "Best Implementation Practices: Disseminating New Assessment Technologies in a Juvenile Justice Agency." *Crime & Delinquency*, January 2006, pp.135–158.

Youth Courts: An Empirical Update and Analysis of Future Organizational and Research Needs. Washington, DC: Hamilton Fish Institute on School and Community Violence, 2008.

CHAPTER 10

The Juvenile Court

THE FIRST IDEA THAT SHOULD BE GRASPED CONCERNING THE JUVENILE
COURT IS THAT IT CAME INTO THE WORLD TO PREVENT CHILDREN FROM BEING
TREATED AS CRIMINALS.

—MIRIAM VAN WATERS

© Joel Gordon/Joel Gordon Photography

The juvenile court as an American institution has existed for more than 100 years, the original aim of which was to offer youthful offenders individualized justice and treatment rather than punishment. States today vary considerably in how they define the purposes of their juvenile courts, with some continuing to adhere to the traditional child welfare philosophy while others have shifted to a more punitive, "get tough" approach. Here a handcuffed teen stands before a juvenile judge at a preliminary hearing.

DO YOU KNOW?

- Whether the juvenile court has traditionally been primarily civil or criminal?
- What most state courts' purpose statement contains?
- What three classifications of children are under juvenile court jurisdiction?
- What two factors determine whether the juvenile court has jurisdiction?
- What the possible bases for the declaration of wardship are?
- What the three types of juvenile courts are?
- Who is part of the juvenile courtroom work group?
- What two actions juvenile courts may take on behalf of children in need?
- What two kinds of intervention for abused children are available?
- What the juvenile court process typically involves?
- How juveniles may be transferred to criminal court?
- Who can certify a juvenile as an adult?
- What a major concern when transferring a juvenile to criminal court is?
- What the results of transferring a juvenile to adult court may be?

CAN YOU DEFINE?

adjudicated
bifurcated hearing
blended sentence
certification
coercive intervention
civil law

competent
concurrent
  jurisdiction
decertification
guardian ad litem
  (GAL)

jurisdiction
justice model
juvenile court
reverse certification
statutory exclusion

therapeutic
  intervention
venue
waiver
welfare model

CHAPTER OUTLINE

Introduction
Basic Philosophy and Purpose
  of Juvenile Court
Differences in Purpose Clauses
The Welfare Model versus the
  Justice Model
Jurisdiction of the Juvenile
  Court
Factors Determining Jurisdiction
Other Cases within Juvenile
  Court Jurisdiction
Offenses Excluded from Juvenile
  Court Jurisdiction
Venue and Transfer

Types of Juvenile Courts
Characteristics of the Juvenile
  Court
Juvenile Court Personnel
Court Actions for Neglected
  and Abused Children
The Juvenile Court Process for
  Delinquency Cases
The Petition
The Detention Hearing
The Adjudication Hearing
The Dispositional Hearing
Transferring Juveniles to
  Criminal Court

Three Primary Transfer
  Mechanisms
Reverse Certification or
  Decertification
The Issues of Competency and
  Culpability
Consequences of Transferring
  Juveniles to Adult Court
Juveniles and Capital
  Punishment
Juvenile Delinquency
  Guidelines for Improving
  Juvenile Court Practices

Introduction

In the United States, justice for juveniles is administered by a separate system with its own juvenile court. The **juvenile court** has jurisdiction over minors (those below the age of majority) alleged to be delinquent, status offenders and dependents or those in need of decisions by the court. The juvenile justice court system enforces and administers a blend of civil and criminal law, but theoretically the system is a civil system. **Civil law** refers to all law that is not criminal, for example, contract law. A civil system was adopted by early juvenile courts to avoid inflicting the stigma of a criminal conviction on youths processed by the courts.

 The juvenile justice system has historically been a civil system.

Many of the concepts and terms provided in this chapter were briefly introduced in Chapter 1. A review of that chapter will provide an overview of the juvenile court and place it within the context of the juvenile justice system.

Basic Philosophy and Purpose of Juvenile Court

A philosophy underlying the juvenile court is that of *parens patriae*, a concept previously discussed. The aim of the first juvenile court was to offer youthful offenders individualized justice and treatment rather than punishment. Recall, however, that today there exists not one, but at least 51 different juvenile justice systems. According to the National Center for Juvenile Justice (Snyder and Sickmund, 2006, p.97), there is considerable variation in the way the states define the purposes of their juvenile courts—not just in their assumptions and underlying philosophies, but also in the approaches they take to the task. Some continue to adhere to the traditional child welfare philosophy while others have been heavily influenced by shifts occurring in the broader criminal justice community to "get tough" on offenders.

Differences in Purpose Clauses

Many juvenile court purpose clauses have been substantially and repeatedly amended over the years, reflecting philosophical or rhetorical changes in how states approach juvenile delinquency. Most state juvenile court purpose clauses fall into one or more of five thematic categories (Snyder and Sickmund, 2006, p.98).

 Most state juvenile court purpose statements contain (1) balanced and restorative justice (BARJ) clauses; (2) Standard Juvenile Court Act clauses; (3) legislative guide clauses; (4) clauses that emphasize punishment, deterrence, accountability and/or public safety; or (5) clauses with traditional child welfare emphasis.

At least 16 state purpose clauses incorporate the language of the balanced and restorative justice (BARJ) movement, which advocates that juvenile courts give balanced attention to three primary interests: public safety, individual offender accountability to victims and the community, and skill development to help offenders live law-abiding and productive lives. The restorative justice approach was discussed in Chapter 1.

Seventeen states have purpose clauses modeled after the Standard Juvenile Court Act, first issued in 1925 and revised many times. The declared purpose of the Standard Act is that "each child coming within the jurisdiction of the court shall receive . . . the care, guidance and control that will conduce to his welfare and the best interest of the state, and that when he is removed from the control of his parents the court shall secure for him care as nearly as possible equivalent to that which they should have given him."

Twelve states use all or most of a more elaborate, multipart purpose clause contained in the *Legislative Guide for Drafting Family and Juvenile Court Acts*, a publication issued by the Children's Bureau in the late 1960s. This guide states four purposes: (1) "to provide for the care, protection and wholesome mental and physical development of children" involved with the juvenile court; (2) "to remove from children committing delinquent acts the consequences of criminal behavior and to substitute therefore a program of supervision, care and rehabilitation"; (3) to remove a child from the home "only when necessary for his welfare or in the interests of public safety"; and (4) to assure all parties "their constitutional and other legal rights."

At least six states' purpose clauses can be loosely characterized as "tough" in that they veer away from the traditional rehabilitative slant to stress community protection, offender accountability and crime reduction through deterrence or outright punishment, either predominantly or exclusively. This is often a matter of interpretation, however. Texas and Wyoming, for example, have primarily adopted the multipurpose language of the *Legislative Guide* but have inserted two additional purpose points—the "protection of the public and public safety" and the promotion of "the concept of punishment for criminal acts"—into their list, giving their purpose clauses a decidedly more punitive edge.

At least four states, including the District of Columbia, have statutory language emphasizing the promotion of the welfare and best interests of the juvenile as the sole or primary purpose of the juvenile court system. For example, one state says only that accused juveniles should be "treated, not as criminals, but as children in need of aid, encouragement and guidance." Another declares that it intends to institute "all reasonable means and methods that can be established by a humane and enlightened state, solicitous of the welfare of its children, for the prevention of delinquency and for the care and rehabilitation of juvenile delinquents."

The Welfare Model versus the Justice Model

Traditionally, juvenile courts followed the **welfare model** with its underlying *parens patriae* philosophy that focuses on the "best interests of the child," as discussed in Chapter 1. As states experienced the wave of increasing juvenile violence during the late 1950s and early 1960s, many responded by viewing juveniles not as having problems, but as being problems. These states called for a **justice model** whereby youths would be held accountable and, in some instances, punished. The call for an increasingly punitive juvenile justice system was pushed further still during the 1980s and 1990s, as a new wave of juvenile violence swept through the country. Today, the tone of juvenile justice as a whole is decidedly more harsh than it was when the concept of a juvenile court was first developed.

AT ISSUE: WHAT IS THE MISSION OF THE JUVENILE COURT?

Juvenile justice in the United States is at a crossroads of sorts, adrift without a clear sense of purpose or mission. Many are calling for a return to the basics, when the juvenile court was first established, with a clear focus on rehabilitating children and giving youthful offenders a second chance. Others, however, argue that the "get tough" approach that has permeated the juvenile justice system over the past several decades and increasingly blurred the lines between the juvenile and criminal justice systems has been responsible for reversing the trend of rising juvenile violence and needs to be continued for the protection of society.

The *Federal Advisory Committee on Juvenile Justice Annual Recommendations Report to the President and Congress of the United States* (2007, p.3) has an opinion on what the mission of the juvenile court should be:

> Since the Juvenile Justice and Delinquency Prevention (JJDP) Act as was first enacted more than 30 yeas ago, the juvenile justice landscape has changed considerably. The basic premises of the original act remain—to

support state and local programs that prevent juvenile delinquent behavior, to offer core protections to youths in the juvenile justice system and to protect the safety of the community. . . .

One of the first questions that needs to be answered is, "What is the mission of the juvenile justice system? Should it focus on rehabilitation with a goal of reducing future criminal behavior in youths?" There are some who perceive the rehabilitative approach as too soft because it does not provide punitive consequences believed to reduce criminal behavior. However, research by criminologists over the past several years has shown that punitive consequences do not, in fact, reduce criminal behavior and in some cases actually increase it.

Herein lies the challenge to juvenile court: How does the court hold youth accountable for their criminal actions and *punish* them while at the same time maintaining a core belief that adolescents can change their ways and be *rehabilitated*?

Although this position is contrary to the social welfare philosophy of the traditional juvenile court, it is not necessarily contrary to the way that juvenile court judges have traditionally handled delinquent cases. Treating and caring for youthful criminals, rather than punishing them, is too contrary to our experience and too counterintuitive to be accepted by judges or the general public. A philosophy that denies moral guilt and punishment and views criminals as innocent, hapless victims of bad social environments may be written into law, but this does not mean that it will be followed in practice. Law violators, young and old, should be punished for their crimes. Children understand punishment, and they understand fairness.

Jurisdiction of the Juvenile Court

The **jurisdiction** of the juvenile court refers to the types of cases it is empowered to hear. In almost every state, the juvenile court's jurisdiction extends to three classifications of children: (1) those who are neglected, dependent or abused because those charged with their custody and control mistreat them or fail to provide proper care; (2) those who are incorrigible, ungovernable or status offenders and (3) those who violate laws, ordinances and codes classified as penal or criminal.

 The jurisdiction of the juvenile court includes children who are in poverty, neglected or abused; who are unruly or commit status offenses; and who are charged with committing serious crimes.

The juvenile court system has been criticized for its "one-pot" jurisdictional approach, in which deprived children, status offenders and youths who commit serious crimes are put into the same "pot." Historically, all three kinds of children were thought to be the products or victims of bad family and social environments. As a result, it was thought, they should be subject, as wards of the court, to the same kind of solicitous, helpful care. The common declaration of status was that of wardship.

The importance of differentiating between criminal and noncriminal conduct committed by juveniles and the limitation on the state's power under *parens patriae* were established more than 100 years ago in *People ex rel. O'Connell v. Turner* (1870). In this case Daniel O'Connell was committed to the Chicago Reform School by an Illinois law that permitted the confinement of "misfortunate youngsters." The Illinois Supreme Court's decision was that the state's power of *parens patriae* could not exceed that of the parents except to punish crime. The court ordered Daniel to be released from the reform school.

Factors Determining Jurisdiction

State statutes define who is under the juvenile court's jurisdiction. In most states two factors determine the jurisdiction of the court.

 Jurisdiction of the juvenile court is determined by the offender's age and conduct.

The limit for the exercise of the juvenile court's jurisdiction is determined by establishing a maximum age below which children are deemed subject to the improvement process of the court. A *child* is generally defined as a person under the maximum age that establishes the court's jurisdiction. Age 17 is accepted in two-thirds of the states and in the District of Columbia (see Table 1.1 in Chapter 1). Many states have lowered their juvenile court age cap in response to acts of violence committed by children younger than the established jurisdictional age. For example, a bill was passed in Texas to reduce from 14 to 10 the age at which youths can be tried in adult criminal court. The bill was motivated by the school shooting in Jonesboro, Arkansas, in which four students and a teacher were killed by two boys, ages 11 and 13.

Sixteen states have established a minimum age below which the court does not have jurisdiction, as shown in Table 10.1. States not listed in the table rely on case law or common law in determining the youngest age at which children come under the jurisdiction of the juvenile court. The rationale behind setting such a minimum age is that very young children are presumed to be incapable of criminal intent and, as such, should not be subject to prosecution and punishment the way older, more culpable individuals are. For instance, hitting (assault) and taking things that don't belong to them (theft) are very common behaviors among toddlers, but our system of justice does not attach any criminal intent to these acts given the extremely young age of the actors, and most would consider it ridiculous to bring such cases before a court. At some point, however, society seeks to begin holding children accountable for their actions, and their crimes.

Table 10.1 Lowest Age for Original Juvenile Court Jurisdiction in Delinquency Matters as of the End of the 2005 Legislative Session (Updated: March 30, 2006)

Age 6	Age 7	Age 8	Age 10	
North Carolina	Maryland	Arizona	Arkansas	Pennsylvania
	Massachusetts		Colorado	South Dakota
	New York		Kansas	Texas
			Louisiana	Vermont
			Minnesota	Wisconsin
			Mississippi	

No Specified Lowest Age				
Alabama	Georgia	Maine	New Jersey	South Carolina
Alaska	Hawaii	Michigan	New Mexico	Tennessee
California	Idaho	Missouri	N. Dakota	Utah
Connecticut	Illinois	Montana	Ohio	Virginia
Delaware	Indiana	Nebraska	Oklahoma	Washington
DC	Iowa	Nevada	Oregon	West Virginia
Florida	Kentucky	N. Hampshire	Rhode Island	Wyoming

© 2006 National Center for Juvenile Justice
SOURCE: Melanie King and Linda Szymanski. "National Overviews." *State Juvenile Justice Profiles*. Pittsburgh, PA: National Center for Juvenile Justice. Online: http://www.ncjj.org/stateprofiles/. Reprinted by permission.

Several states have moved to raise the upper limit of jurisdictional age to 18, an expansion in juvenile court jurisdiction driven by recent research that shows the human brain is not fully developed until the early to mid-20s. The last part of the brain to develop, the prefrontal cortex (PFC), is that region responsible for higher-order "executive-level" thinking, such as planning and future orientation, assessing and managing risk and reward, and controlling impulses. Indeed, these new studies merely confirm what parents of teenagers have always known—that adolescents often act first and think later.

Extended jurisdiction mechanisms allow the juvenile court to maintain authority even after a youth has aged beyond the upper age of original jurisdiction, if it is determined the continued provision of sanctions and services is in the best interests of the juvenile and the public. As of the end of the 2004 legislative session, 34 state statutes extended juvenile court jurisdiction in delinquency cases until the offender's 21st birthday (Snyder and Sickmund, 2006, p.103).

The issue of jurisdiction and age was first questioned in 1905 by the Pennsylvania Supreme Court. Frank Fisher was **adjudicated** (judged) a delinquent in the Philadelphia Juvenile Court. On appeal his lawyer challenged the constitutionality of the legislation establishing the court, urging in particular that Fisher was denied due process in the manner in which he was taken into custody and that he was denied his constitutional right to a jury trial for a felony. The Pennsylvania Supreme Court upheld a lower court's sanction. The court found that due process, or lack of it, simply was not at issue, since its guarantee applied only to criminal cases. The state could, on the other hand, place a child within its protection without any process at all if it saw fit to do so. Recall that in *Commonwealth v. Fisher* (1905) the court stated: "To save a child . . . the legislature surely may provide for the salvation of such a child . . . by bringing it into the courts of the state without any process at all, for the purpose of subjecting it to the state's guardianship and protection." The court further stated: "The natural parent needs no process to temporarily deprive his child of its liberty by confining it to his own home, to save it and to shield it from the consequences of persistence in a career of waywardness; nor is the state, when compelled as *parens patriae*, to take the place of the father for the same purpose, required to adopt any process as a means of placing its hands upon a child to lead it into one of its courts."

Similarly, the court argued, a jury trial could hardly be necessary to determine whether a child deserved to be saved. In addition to the jurisdictional age, *conduct* determines the juvenile court's jurisdiction. Although the definition of delinquency varies from state to state, the violation of a state law or local ordinance (an act that would be a crime if committed by an adult) is the main category. Youths who violate federal laws or laws from other states, who are wayward, incorrigible or habitually truant, who commit status offenses or who associate with immoral people are all considered delinquent and subject to juvenile court jurisdiction.

In *Roper v. Simmons* (2005) the Supreme Court articulated three reasons for a separate juvenile court for youths under age 18:

> First, as any parent knows and as the scientific and sociological studies tend to confirm, a lack of maturity and an underdeveloped sense of responsibility are found in youths more often than in adults and are more understandable among the youth. . . . Almost every state prohibits those under 18 years of age from voting, serving on juries or marrying without parental consent.
>
> Second, juveniles are more vulnerable or susceptible to negative influences and outside pressures, including peer pressure.
>
> Third, the character of a juvenile is not as well formed as that of an adult. The personality traits of juveniles are more transitory, less fixed.

Roper v. Simmons will be discussed again later in the chapter in the section dealing with juveniles and the death penalty.

Other Cases within Juvenile Court Jurisdiction

In addition to having jurisdiction over children who are in need of protection, who commit status offenses or who commit serious crimes, some juvenile courts have authority to handle other issues, such as adoptions, matters of paternity and guardianship. The court's jurisdiction is further extended by provisions in many states that it may exercise its authority over adults in certain cases involving children. Thus in many states the juvenile court may require a parent to contribute to child support, or it may charge and try adults with contributing to the delinquency, neglect, abuse or dependency of a child.

The state is the "higher" or "ultimate parent" of all children within its borders. The child's own parents' rights are always subject to state control when in

IN THE NEWS

The state's authority to take children from their families when it deems such measures to be in the best interest of the children is an awesome power. One of the largest child custody cases to date occurred in Texas in April 2008, when the state removed more than 400 children from the Yearning for Zion Ranch, a settlement of the Fundamentalist Church of Jesus Christ of Latter Day Saints (FLDS), in Eldorado, Texas, under allegations the polygamist sect was allowing physical and sexual abuse of the children and, specifically, sanctioning marriages for underage girls. The Texas Supreme Court later ruled that the categorical removal from the ranch and placement into foster care of all of the children by child protective services (CPS) was an overreach of state authority, since the state was unable to demonstrate evidence that more than several girls may, in fact, have been abused. The CPS investigation that followed confirmed 12 girls as victims of sexual abuse and neglect based on evidence these girls had been married at ages ranging from 12 to 15.

SOURCE: From *Eldorado Investigation*. A Report from the Texas Department of Family and Protective Services, December 22, 2008.

the court's opinion the best interests of the child demand it. If the state has to intervene in the case of any child, it exercises its power of guardianship over the child and provides him or her with the protection, care and guidance needed.

Although the substantive justice system for juveniles is administered by a specialized court, a great deal of variation exists in juvenile law between different jurisdictions. Before a court with juvenile jurisdiction may declare a youth a ward of the state, it must be convinced that a basis for that wardship exists.

 The possible bases for a declaration of wardship include demonstrating that the child is abused or neglected, or has committed a status offense or a criminal act.

Offenses Excluded from Juvenile Court Jurisdiction

Not all offenses committed by young people are within juvenile court jurisdiction. There are no firm assurances that a case will be heard in the juvenile court. The juvenile judge is given discretion to waive jurisdiction in a case and to transfer it to a criminal court if the circumstances and conduct dictate, as will be discussed later.

In some states delinquency is not exclusively within the scope of the juvenile court. Jurisdiction in juvenile court may be concurrent with criminal court jurisdiction—that is, it happens at the same time or may occur in either. Often this concurrent jurisdiction is limited by law to cases being handled by either court. Furthermore, certain offenses, such as murder, manslaughter or rape, may be entirely excluded from juvenile court jurisdiction. In states with such laws, children charged with these offenses are automatically tried in criminal court.

Several states have excluded specified offenses from juvenile court jurisdiction. Colorado statutes, for example, state:

> Juvenile court does not have jurisdiction over: children 14 or older charged with crimes of violence classified as Class 1 felonies; children 16 or older who within the previous two years have been adjudicated delinquent for commission of a felony and are now charged with a Class 2 or Class 3 felony or any nonclassified felony punishable by death or life imprisonment.

Several other states exclude youths who have had previous problems with the law.

Venue and Transfer

The geographic location of a trial, called its **venue**, is established by constitutional or statutory provisions. Usually proceedings take place in the county where the juvenile lives. If a proceeding involving a juvenile begins in a different county, the court may ask that the proceedings be transferred to the county where the juvenile lives. Likewise transfer can be made if the child's residence changes before proceedings begin.

Types of Juvenile Courts

The term *juvenile court* is somewhat of a misnomer. Only in isolated cases have completely separate courts for juveniles been established. Where they have been, it has been primarily in larger cities. Boston, for example, has a specialized court for handling juvenile matters, but its jurisdiction is less than city-wide. Elsewhere throughout the country, juvenile court jurisdiction resides in a variety of courts: municipal, county, district, superior or probate. Some are multiple-judge courts; others are served by a single judge.

 Juvenile courts are separated into three types: independent and separate courts, part of a family court and a unit within a trial court.

Independent and separate courts are those whose administration is entirely divorced from that of other courts. Such courts are found in Connecticut, Rhode Island and Utah. Many separate and independent courts are presided over by judges from other courts, however, so their separateness and independence is more in name than in reality. A second type of organization has juvenile court as part of *family court*. In addition to such matters as child custody and support, family courts often have jurisdiction over matters concerning delinquency, status offenses and child-victim cases. The third typical organization has juvenile court as a unit of the *trial court*.

Characteristics of the Juvenile Court

The juvenile court has had an uneven development and has manifested a great diversity in its methods and procedures. However, as early as 1920, Evelina Belden of the U.S. Children's Bureau listed the following as the essential characteristics of the juvenile court:

- Separate hearings for children's cases
- Informal or chancery procedure
- Regular probation service
- Separate detention of children
- Special court and probation records
- Provisions for mental and physical examinations

Unfortunately many juvenile courts lack these characteristics. Critics argue that such courts cannot claim to be juvenile courts.

In the United States, juvenile courts vary from one jurisdiction to another, manifesting all stages of the system's complex development. Its philosophy, structure and functions are still evolving. Rarely is the court distinct and highly specialized. In rural counties, juvenile court is largely rudimentary. Usually it is part of a court with more jurisdiction. In Minnesota, for example, it is a part of the probate court. Judges hold sessions for juveniles at irregular intervals or when the hearings can be held in clusters. Since there is great diversity, no simple description of U.S. juvenile courts can be given.

Juvenile Court Personnel

As with the criminal court, various participants are essential to the workings of the juvenile courtroom.

 The juvenile courtroom work group consists of judges, hearing officers, prosecutors, defense attorneys and probation officers.

The *judge* is the central authority in the juvenile court system. However, in many jurisdictions, assignment to the juvenile court is not a highly sought after position, with many judges viewing it as a dead-end assignment. Even judges fully committed to the welfare of juveniles may seek rotation to another assignment to further their careers.

A *hearing officer*, also called a *referee* or *commissioner*, may assist the judge. The hearing officer enters findings and recommendations the judge must confirm to make an order.

In most jurisdictions, the *prosecutor* is the dominant figure in intake processing and is typically responsible for negotiating the disposition of all but the most serious juvenile delinquency cases (Neubauer, 2008, p.433). Similar to the commonly perceived status of juvenile judges, appointment to be a juvenile prosecutor is not a highly desirable position. Usually juvenile prosecutors are assistant district attorneys right out of law school who hope to be promoted to felony court where they can practice "real law" and convict "real criminals" (Neubauer).

Defense attorneys have a very secondary role in juvenile court due to the court's informality. Many juveniles have no representation because juvenile prosecutors have heavy caseloads and tend to prosecute only the most serious cases. In some cases the juvenile court judge appoints a **guardian ad litem (GAL)** to represent youths and their best interests. Although most often an attorney, the GAL can be anyone who is concerned about the youths' best interests.

Probation officers have been a key part of juvenile court since its beginning. They are involved from the early stages of the process on. The probation officer, rather than a judge or prosecutor, usually is the first court official to have contact with the child. In addition, it is often the probation officer who recommends an informal disposition; and in more serious cases, the probation officer's recommendations, along with those of social workers, most often become the court's order.

Court Actions for Neglected and Abused Children

Two distinct kinds of court action may result for neglected or abused children.

 Court action on behalf of neglected and abused children may be noncriminal or criminal.

Court action on behalf of neglected, abused or dependent children may be *noncriminal*. It seeks to identify whether the child is in danger and, if so, what is needed for the child's protection. The parents may lose custody of the child, be required to pay child support or be ordered to make adjustments in care, custody and control. This type of action does not permit punitive sanctions against the parents, however.

A second option is *criminal* prosecution of the parents on charges that they have committed a harmful act against the child or have failed to discharge their responsibility, thus placing the child in active danger. This action does not involve the child's status. The scope of the court's position in these referrals is based on the juvenile court's responsibility for the child's welfare under the philosophy of *in loco parentis*.

Jones (2006b) explains that cases of neglect or abuse begin with filing an initial pleading with a court by a child protective services (CPS) caseworker and supervisor, often after consulting with the agency's lawyer. Most states allow only CPS to initiate child protection proceedings, but some states allow other public officials and even private citizens to do so. The petition is usually captioned "*In re* John Doe," meaning it is brought regarding him. The state or county is the petitioner and the parents, caretakers or child may be referred to as respondents, not defendants. The petition does not charge them with maltreatment.

The first event following the filing of a petition is the initial hearing, also known as a preliminary protective hearing, detention hearing, emergency removal hearing or temporary custody hearing. This hearing is the most critical state in the court process (Jones). At this hearing, the judge determines if reasonable efforts have been made to ensure the child's safety, assesses the child's safety and makes a placement decision. The hearing should establish a supportive atmosphere, treating parents with respect and focusing on understanding the problems the case presents and solving them as quickly as possible so the family can be safely reunited.

Some courts use pretrial conferences, also called settlement conferences, in child maltreatment cases. These conferences allow parents, their attorneys and the child's advocates to come to an agreement before the scheduled adjudication, often saving time and money. Many states are using mediation as a way to settle cases. If a conference is not settled by agreement or through mediation, it goes to adjudication, also called a fact-finding hearing. CPS has the burden of proving the maltreatment alleged in the petition. At the conclusion of adjudication, if the finding is in favor of CPS, the judge enters an ordering stating specific problems that must be resolved before the child can return home. At the disposition hearing the court decides whether the child needs the court's help and, if so, what services should be provided. Placement is the most important decision made at the dispositional hearing: left with or returned to the parents (under CPA supervision), kept in an existing placement or moved to a new placement. A case plan is also developed.

The next stage is usually a review hearing to evaluate the progress made in completing the case plan. The review hearing report by CPS should state whether the case plan is on target; whether the child's physical, emotional and mental health needs are being met; whether progress has been made toward achieving the case plan's objectives; what reasonable efforts have been made to achieve reunification; whether the child should be returned home and why or why not; what remains to be accomplished before reunification can be offered; what timetable has been established for returning the child home; and whether and how the case plan should be modified.

The final stage of the process is the permanency hearing, which should be held no later than 12 months after a placement other than with the family has occurred. Options include returning the child home, returning the child by a specific date (no longer than 3 months after the permanency hearing), terminating parental rights, granting legal guardianship or permanently placing the child with a relative, foster parent or other nonrelative (Jones). The following are commonly considered grounds for termination of parental rights:

- A child of any age has been in foster care for 15 of the most recent 22 months unless exceptions apply.
- The child is an abandoned infant.
- The parent has committed, aided or attempted the murder or voluntary manslaughter of a sibling of the child.
- The parent has committed a felony assault resulting in serious bodily injury to the child or a sibling of the child.

 The National Committee for Prevention of Child Abuse describes two kinds of intervention for deprived children: coercive and therapeutic.

Coercive intervention is out-of-home placement, detainment or mandated therapy or counseling. **Therapeutic intervention** is a recommendation of an appropriate treatment program. Coercive intervention should be used with children only when necessary, either to protect society or to impose an effective treatment plan for the children. Policy recommendations include the following:

- *Therapeutic intervention for all abused children who come to the attention of the court exhibiting problem behavior, regardless of the disposition of the case.* The present drift toward stricter delinquency statutes in some states, in which community protection is foremost and the best interest of the child standard is secondary, is based on an erroneous assumption. Protection of the community and rehabilitation of the child are not conflicting goals. Among this group of abused children are two subgroups particularly in need of attention: the child exhibiting violent behavior and the sexually abused child.
- *Specific and different treatment within the correctional system of the young person who was abused.* Much of our nation's delinquent population is in a debilitated condition—physically (neurologically), developmentally and psychologically. We know, for instance, that treatment for the abused child will have to take place over a long term. We know that corporal punishment, physical coercion and violent or belittling language are inappropriate therapeutic tools; they add institutional abuse to the existing familial abuse.
- *Early intervention.* The optimal point of intervention with an abused delinquent would be before the abuse has occurred. The earliest treatment intervention we can offer the young abused child would be aimed at keeping him or her from becoming a delinquent as a later reaction to the earlier abuse. The next opportunity for early intervention occurs when the young person comes to the attention of the court, before he or she becomes delinquent.

Youths who enter the court as minors in need of supervision could be recognized as the abused children they often are and helped in such a way as to preclude further delinquent activity.

- *Attractive, benign, broad-based intervention styles and services.* Services are needed that do not identify the clients as abusive, abused or delinquent. Efforts to strengthen families, particularly the development and provision of services that could be called parent education, are recommended.

If neglected and abused children are referred to juvenile court, these recommendations should be kept in mind. In some states juvenile court is referred to as dependency court. Krinsky (2006, p.16) states: "Decisions made in our nation's dependency courts play a critical role in the lives of more than half a million children currently in foster care, often profoundly altering their future." Noting that one in four foster youths reported never attending their own court hearing, Krinsky critically contends: "Courts should be organized to enable children and families to participate in a meaningful way in their own court proceedings." The reason: "Youths are in the best position to provide accurate and compelling insights into their wishes, needs and progress. Putting a human face to the discussion of these issues and experiences forces all concerned to see the system through their eyes." The National Council of Juvenile and Family Court Judges (NCJFCJ Staff Report, 2006, p.17) echoes: "Ensuring that children are both seen *and* heard in courtrooms is a fundamental of the NCJFCJ's Victims Act Model Court Project."

Badeau and Freundlich (2006, p.19) stress that *all* children, particularly the very young and those with disabilities, should be heard in court, should have effective representation and should have the timely input of those who care about them, noting: "Preschoolers may benefit from seeing the courtroom and being told what will happen there or from meeting the judge and then being present during some portion of the proceeding. Children with physical, communication, developmental or mental health/behavioral health challenges may also be able to participate with appropriate accommodations."

Finally, Jones (2006a, p.20) notes: "Children under the abuse and neglect jurisdiction of the juvenile court have great needs and face daunting challenges.... Foster youths need and deserve the opportunity to participate as partners with the court in making decisions that have enormous impact on their lives." However, he notes that many judges have well-intentioned concerns about youth participation in court proceedings, believing that the court process is too complex for them to effectively participate. Another concern is that children will miss valuable school time. An additional concern is that information discussed in court may be disturbing and upsetting to children. Jones suggests the following techniques judges can use for creating a child-friendly court:

- Help children understand, in simple terms, the purpose of the hearing, what issues might be discussed, what type of information might be helpful for them to share and what issues are appropriate to raise in court.
- Review the court report with the youth for any inaccuracies, clarifications or additions.
- Explain your role as a judge and the issues you can address. Also educate youths about their rights.

Table 10.2 Supreme Court Decisions Affecting Juvenile Court

Case	Year	Holding
Kent v. United States	1966	Established that juvenile transfers to adult court must consider due process and fair play, the child must be represented by an attorney and the attorney must have access to the juvenile records of child.
In re Gault	1967	Required that the due process clause of the Fourteenth Amendment apply to proceedings in state juvenile courts, including the right of notice, the right to counsel, the right against self-incrimination and the right to confront witnesses.
In re Winship	1970	Established proof beyond a reasonable doubt as the standard for juvenile adjudication proceedings, eliminating lesser standards such as a preponderance of the evidence, clear and convincing proof and reasonable proof.
McKeiver v. Pennsylvania	1971	Established that a jury trial is not a required part of due process in the adjudication of a youth as a delinquent by a juvenile court.
Breed v. Jones	1975	Established that a juvenile cannot be adjudicated in juvenile court and then tried for the same offense in an adult court (double jeopardy).
Oklahoma Publishing Co. v. District Court	1977	The press may report juvenile court proceedings under certain circumstances.
Smith v. Daily Mail Publishing Co.	1979	The press may report juvenile court proceedings under certain circumstances.
Eddings v. Oklahoma	1982	Defendant's youthful age should be considered a mitigating factor in deciding whether to apply the death penalty.
Schall v. Martin	1984	Established that preventive detention fulfills a legitimate state interest of protecting society and juveniles by detaining those who might be dangerous to society or to themselves.
Thompson v. Oklahoma	1988	Minimum age for death penalty is set at 16.
Stanford v. Kentucky	1989	Minimum age for death penalty is set at 16.
Roper v. Simmons	2005	Minimum age for death penalty is set at 18.

- Provide information on how children can advocate for themselves if they have concerns about the legal or social services they are receiving.
- Provide a list of legal terms and definitions that may be used in the hearing.
- Describe the roles of adults who take part in the hearing, including attorneys and family members. Explain what these individuals say or do at the hearing.
- Discuss how long the hearing will last and the time frames for future hearings.
- Ensure that youths have therapeutic and relational support both before and after the hearing to deal in healthy ways with any strong reactions or emotions that surface as the result of the hearing.

Youths who are status offenders, delinquents and serious, violent offenders also have the right to be heard during any of the stages in the juvenile justice process. Other very important Supreme Court cases presented in Chapter 2 have a direct bearing on juvenile court proceedings, as shown in Table 10.2, and should be kept in mind when looking at the juvenile court and how it differs from criminal court.

The Juvenile Court Process for Delinquency Cases

Changes in the juvenile court interrelate with such factors as industrialization, urbanization, population shifts, the use of natural resources, the rapid development of technology and the acceleration of transportation and communication.

All have influenced the family and neighborhood, forcing communities to find new or additional sources of social control. This has given considerable impetus to taking a broader look at the juvenile court process, another version of which is illustrated in Figure 10.1.

Custody, detention and intake were discussed in previous chapters. As noted, the juvenile court process is most often initiated by law enforcement, with police agencies referring roughly two-thirds of all arrested youths to a court with juvenile justice jurisdiction and diverting the other one-third. The court, in turn, may also choose to divert some juveniles out of the formal justice system to receive treatment or services from other agencies. Prosecutors, likewise, may file some juvenile cases—usually those involving serious, violent crimes or juveniles with extensive criminal histories—directly to criminal court. The use of formal processing for delinquents has become more likely in the past decade, with the petitioned caseload increasing 80 percent from 1985 to 2002 (Snyder and Sickmund, 2006, p.171). In 2005 juvenile courts processed nearly 1.7 million delinquency cases that involved juveniles charged with criminal law violations (Table 10.3).

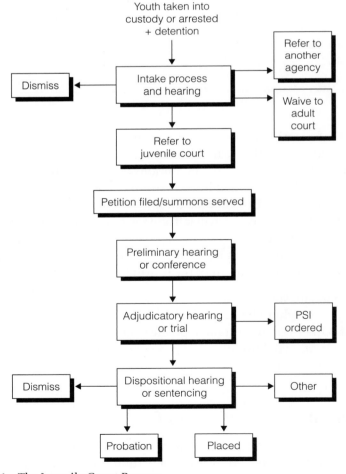

Figure 10.1 The Juvenile Court Process

Table 10.3 National Estimates of Juvenile Court Processing for Delinquency Cases

	1985	2005
TOTAL delinquency cases processed by juvenile court	1,161,500	1,697,900
Not petitioned	632,300	748,500
Petitioned		
Nonadjudicated (probation, other, dismissed)	184,900	318,500
Adjudicated	337,100	623,900
Waived to criminal court	7,200	6,900
Youth Age		
12 and under	133,600	144,600
13–15	565,600	820,200
16	260,300	400,800
17 and older	202,000	332,200
Gender		
Male	937,700	1,233,200
Female	223,800	464,700
Race		
White	846,400	1,090,200
Non-White	315,100	607,700

SOURCE: Adapted from C. Puzzanchera and W. Kang *Juvenile Court Statistics Databook*. Pittsburgh, PA: National Center for Juvenile Justice, September 12, 2008.

It is worth noting at this point that research has found that first-time court appearance during high school increases the chances of dropping out of high school independent of involvement in delinquency (Sweeten, 2006, p.462). Furthermore, the effect of court appearance is particularly detrimental to less delinquent youths, leading to two broad conclusions: "First, first-time court appearance during high school is more detrimental for education outcomes than first-time arrest without a court appearance . . . consistent with formal labeling theory. Second, the effect of court appearance is contingent on prior delinquency, but does not differ based on structural location [being disadvantaged]. The effect of court appearance does vary by prior delinquency involvement. Court appearance is less relevant for youths who are highly involved in delinquency; it is more detrimental to youths who are less involved in delinquency" (Sweeten, p.477). Such research offers beneficial insight on how best to process first-time offenders and cautions against a "get tough" response that brings the full weight of juvenile processing to bear on low-risk offenders.

 The juvenile court process usually involves the filing of a petition, a detention hearing, an adjudication hearing and a disposition hearing.

The Petition

If the decision is made to file charges against a juvenile, the district attorney files a petition, stating the name, age and address of the minor; what parts of the code sections the minor broke; if the charges are misdemeanors or felonies; the names and address of the parents or guardians; a short statement that says what happened; and if the minor is in custody or has been released.

The Detention Hearing

After the petition is filed, a detention hearing is held to decide if the minor should be placed in secure custody, as described in Chapter 9. The juvenile can contest the detention decision if the court determines the juvenile should be confined. Valid reasons for detaining a juvenile include that the minor disobeyed a court order, poses a high risk of running away if the court releases the juvenile, needs protection because the home is not a safe environment or the youth has mental or physical problems that warrant the system keeping the juvenile in detention. Approximately 20 percent of all delinquency cases involve detaining a youth between referral to court and the case disposition (Snyder and Sickmund, 2006, p.168).

Care must be taken when placing a juvenile in detention, and well-constructed policies must be implemented to specify where to detain youths. Inappropriate detention environments can pose significant risks to juveniles. According to one study, "Youth are 19 times more likely to commit suicide in jail than youth in the general population and 36 times more likely to commit suicide in an adult jail than in a juvenile detention facility" ("New Study Details the Dangers of Holding Youth in Adult Jails," 2008, p.11). The study also documented evidence that such youths are also more likely to be physically and sexually assaulted.

Although many well-intentioned policies aim to keep youth under age 18 physically separated from adult prisoners, and rightfully so, this sometimes results in the youth being placed in segregation or isolation, leading to exacerbated problems related to depression, anxiety and other mental disorders as well as increasing the risk of suicide. In addition, many detention facilities do not provide any educational services, which, for youths detained for any substantial length of time, can place them at even greater disadvantages for later success.

Timely Processing of Nondetained Juveniles   Just as timely processing of informal/diverted cases is important, so too is timely processing of formal/nondetained cases. Recall from Chapter 9 the statement by Siegel and Halemba (2006, p.1): "There is little question that unnecessary delays in case processing may increase the likelihood of a juvenile's subsequent involvement with the court as well as the likelihood that the juvenile's law-violating behavior will continue to escalate." Siegel and Halemba (p.12) give as an example of timely disposition of juvenile cases the expedited docket used in Tulsa, Oklahoma:

> The Tulsa County Juvenile Court established its special Arraignment Docket in March 2006 to reduce the number of non-detained juveniles who "fall through the cracks." Historically in Tulsa, as in many other places, there have been difficulties with tracking juveniles who are arrested for crimes but not detained. Before the creation of the Arraignment Docket, juveniles arrested and released were not given specific dates for their initial court hearings. . . . Referred juveniles and their parents would often wait months due to unavailable court dockets and time taken by the District Attorney's office to make filing decisions.
>
> [Now] when a juvenile is arrested and a decision is made to not detain the youth, the police officer provides notice to the juvenile and parents of an

initial semi-formal hearing date. The Arraignment Docket for non-detained juveniles begins at 9am Mondays through Thursdays. If a juvenile is arrested on a weekday, the arresting officer selects a court date that is one week from the day of arrest. If a juvenile is arrested on a weekend, the court date is set the second Tuesday after the arrest date. The seven to eleven day period from point of arrest to the arraignment hearing allows juvenile bureau staff to complete necessary background work to determine if the case should be diverted or otherwise handled informally or to forward the case to the District Attorney's Office for petition filing consideration.

The Adjudication Hearing

At the adjudication hearing (comparable to the trial in the adult system), the youth is questioned about the offense described in the petition. The juvenile's lawyer can cross-examine witnesses, object to evidence, present witnesses

Being adjudicated a delinquent is comparable to being convicted in criminal court. It is a formal legal finding of responsibility. Here a female delinquent stands with her attorney before the juvenile judge during an adjudication hearing.

and evidence, and argue the case to the court. If the evidence is insufficient, the judge may dismiss the case. If enough evidence exists that the child is delinquent, a court date is set for the disposition hearing. Being adjudicated a delinquent is comparable to being convicted in criminal court. It is a formal legal finding of responsibility. From 1985 to 2002, the number of cases in which the youth was adjudicated delinquent rose 85 percent (Snyder and Sickmund, 2006, p.173).

Most juvenile justice professionals recommend a **bifurcated hearing**, which is keeping the adjudication hearing separate from the dispositional hearing.

The Dispositional Hearing

At the dispositional hearing, the judge has to balance how to protect the community, how to fix the harm done and what is in the best interest of the minor. Juvenile courts commonly rely on the juvenile assessment contained in the investigative report and accompanying dispositional recommendations provided by probation officers, with judges following these recommendations more than 90 percent of the time. Griffin and Torbet (2002, p.68) suggest the following disposition recommendations checklist:

- What risks does the juvenile pose to the community?
- What is the juvenile's attitude toward the victim and the offense?
- What factors and circumstances contributed to the juvenile's offending?
- What skills does the juvenile need to acquire?
- What are the juvenile's (and the juvenile's family's) strengths, resources and receptiveness to intervention?

Based on the investigative report, the judge may place the youth on probation or in a foster home, release the child to the parents, commit the child to an institution, make the child a ward of the court or order one of the diversionary options discussed in Chapter 9. Serious juvenile offenders may be committed to mental institutions, reformatories, prisons, and county and state schools for delinquents.

Judicial discretion has been demonstrated to play a significant role in detention decisions of many cases. For example, Rodriguez (2007, p.651) studied the effects of race, ethnicity and community characteristics on detention decisions and found that the effect of race and ethnicity varies across communities and that economic and community-level data significantly affect detention decisions.

Most Common Juvenile Dispositions   The most common sentence given to juvenile offenders is probation. Of all youths adjudicated delinquent in 2004, 67 percent were placed on formal probation, 22 percent were placed in residential facilities and 15 percent received other dispositions, such as community service, restitution or referral to an outside agency (Stahl, 2008, p.2). Specific correctional sanctions are the topic of Chapter 11.

Blended Sentencing   A **blended sentence** contains both a juvenile and an adult sentence. Minnesota was the first state to use a blended sentence for youth who committed violent, but not extremely violent or murderous, crimes.

In Minnesota, if youths comply with the juvenile sentence, which usually includes longer, more intense supervision than a typical juvenile sentence, the criminal (adult) portion of the sentence is suspended and the youth will be released after serving the juvenile sentence without the stigma of a criminal record. If, however, the youth does not successfully adhere to the terms of the juvenile disposition, the criminal (adult) portion of the sanction is invoked. This format of sentencing is called *inclusive blend;* as of the end of the 2004 legislative session, 11 states were using this sentencing structure (Snyder and Sickmund, 2006, p.115).

Another arrangement is *contiguous blend,* which allows a judge to order a sentence that extends beyond the juvenile court's age of extended jurisdiction, effectively allowing the juvenile system to maintain authority and control over an offender even after the offender has "aged up" into the jurisdiction of the criminal court. Three states currently use this structure. The third type of blended sentence, used only by New Mexico, is *exclusive blend,* in which the juvenile court is simply allowed discretion to impose a criminal sanction on a youthful offender instead of a juvenile disposition (Snyder and Sickmund, p.115).

Critics of blended sentencing contend that this is a return to "getting soft" on juvenile crime. In reality, however, blended sentencing exposes youthful offenders to the possibility of receiving harsh criminal penalties and, in this regard, bears many similarities to provisions allowing the transfer of juveniles to criminal court, a process discussed shortly. Consequently, juveniles facing a court that uses blended sentencing are given the same due process protections afforded adult criminal defendants, including the right to be tried by a jury (Snyder and Sickmund, p.115).

Transferring Juveniles to Criminal Court

Every state has a provision of some sort allowing juveniles who meet specific criteria to be tried in criminal court and face adult sanctions. The rising rate of juvenile violent crime, a trend that began during the mid-1980s and peaked in 1994, fed a public fear and the demand that legislators "do something" to get tough on youthful predators. As a result, during the mid-1990s, 46 states passed legislation making it easier to transfer juvenile offenders to adult court. Most often the criteria for such transfers include the seriousness of the offense and the offender's prior criminal history, with repeat offenders and those charged with serious violent crimes being most likely to be waived to criminal court. The age of the offender can also play a role in the judge's or prosecutor's decision to transfer a case, with older juveniles (those approaching the age of majority, such as 17-year-olds) facing an increased likelihood of transfer.

Despite the allowance of such transfers, analysis of delinquency case processing data shows that a relatively small percentage of all juveniles arrested and formally placed into the justice system are transferred to adult criminal court. Of the estimated 1.66 million delinquency cases brought before the juvenile court in 2004, only 9,400 (0.57 percent) were waived to criminal court (Stahl, 2008, p.2).

Three Primary Transfer Mechanisms

The mechanisms used to transfer youth to adult criminal court fall into three broad categories.

 Juveniles may be transferred to criminal court via three basic mechanisms: judicial waiver, concurrent jurisdiction and statutory exclusion.

Table 10.4 summarizes the mechanisms states use to transfer juveniles to criminal court.

Judicial Waiver   Judicial waiver is the most common transfer provision, with 45 states allowing for this transfer mechanism as of the end of the 2004 legislative session (Snyder and Sickmund, 2006, p.112). **Waiver** is a transfer mechanism whereby the juvenile court judge is allowed the discretion to make an individual determination about whether a juvenile who meets statutory criteria should be tried in juvenile court or, instead, be waived to criminal court. Some states call this process **certification**, with a juvenile being *certified* as an adult and, as such, eligible to face the same criminal consequences as someone of legal age. Besides judicial waiver and certification, this transfer provision is alternately known as *remanding* or *binding over for criminal prosecution*.

Judicial waiver may be discretionary, presumptive or mandatory; the prevalence of their use is given in Table 10.4. In some states the waiver decision falls to the prosecutor.

 In some states the court makes the decision to certify a juvenile as an adult. In other states this is done by the prosecutor.

Waiver or certification is of paramount importance, since it may result in far more severe consequences to the juvenile than would have occurred had the youth remained under juvenile court jurisdiction. Furthermore, when waiver occurs certain procedural guidelines apply. For example, no statements made by the child before the transfer may be used against him or her in the criminal proceedings after the transfer. In this regard, such delinquency cases are handled in basically the same way as those involving adult offenders.

Five criteria generally guide the court's or prosecutor's decision on whether to try a minor as an adult: (1) the youth's age and criminal sophistication, (2) whether the youth can be adequately treated or rehabilitated before the juvenile court's jurisdiction's expires, (3) the youth's previous delinquency history, (4) the success of the court's previous attempts to rehabilitate the youth and (5) the severity of the alleged offense and amount of harm caused. Table 10.5 describes the characteristics of waived cases and the changes between 1990 and 1999.

Concurrent Jurisdiction   In some states, original jurisdiction over certain offenses resides with both juvenile and criminal courts, and it is left to the prosecutor to decide in which court to file a case. This transfer mechanism is known as **concurrent jurisdiction**, and it is used by relatively few states—15 as of the end of the 2004 legislative session (Snyder and Sickmund, 2006, p.113). This transfer provision is known variously among different jurisdictions as *prosecutorial discretion*, *prosecutorial waiver* or *direct file*.

Table 10.4   Mechanisms Used to Transfer Juveniles to Adult Court

Most States Have Multiple Ways to Impose Adult Sanctions on Juveniles

Statutes at the End of the 1999 Legislative Session

State	Judicial Waiver — Discretionary	Judicial Waiver — Presumptive	Judicial Waiver — Mandatory	Concurrent Jurisdiction	Statutory Exclusion	Reverse Waiver	Once an Adult, Always an Adult	Blended Sentencing
Total States	46	16	15	15	29	24	34	22
Alabama	■				■		■	
Alaska	■	■			■			■
Arizona	■	■		■		■	■	
Arkansas	■			■		■		■
California	■	■			■		■	■
Colorado	■	■		■		■		■
Connecticut			■			■		■
Delaware	■		■		■		■	
Dist. of Columbia	■			■			■	
Florida	■			■	■		■	■
Georgia	■		■	■	■		■	
Hawaii	■						■	
Idaho	■				■		■	■
Illinois	■	■	■		■		■	■
Indiana	■		■		■		■	
Iowa	■				■		■	■
Kansas	■	■					■	
Kentucky	■		■			■		
Louisiana	■		■	■	■			
Maine	■	■					■	
Maryland	■				■	■		
Massachusetts				■	■			■
Michigan	■			■			■	■
Minnesota	■	■			■		■	■
Mississippi	■				■	■	■	
Missouri	■				■		■	■
Montana	■			■	■	■		
Nebraska				■		■		
Nevada	■	■			■	■	■	
New Hampshire	■	■			■			
New Jersey	■	■	■					
New Mexico					■			■
New York					■	■		
North Carolina	■		■				■	
North Dakota	■	■	■				■	
Ohio	■		■				■	
Oklahoma	■			■	■	■		■
Oregon	■				■	■		
Pennsylvania	■	■			■	■		
Rhode Island	■	■	■		■		■	■
South Carolina	■		■	■	■	■	■	■
South Dakota	■				■	■		
Tennessee	■					■	■	
Texas	■						■	
Utah	■	■			■		■	
Vermont	■		■	■		■		■
Virginia	■			■		■	■	■
Washington	■				■		■	
West Virginia			■					■
Wisconsin	■				■	■	■	
Wyoming	■			■		■		

■ In states with a combination of provisions for transferring juveniles to criminal court, the exclusion, mandatory waiver or concurrent jurisdiction provisions generally target the oldest juveniles and/or those charged with the most serious offenses, while those charged with relatively less serious offenses and/or younger juveniles may be eligible for discretionary waiver.

SOURCE: Melissa Sickmund, *Juveniles in Court.* Washington, DC: Juvenile Offenders and Victims National Report Series Bulletin, June 2003, p.6.

Table 10.5 Characteristics of Delinquency Cases Waived (1990, 1994 and 1999)

	1990	1994	1999
Total Cases Waived	8,300	12,100	7,500
Most Serious Offense			
Person	32%	44%	34%
Property	45	37	40
Drugs	15	11	16
Public order	8	8	11
Gender			
Male	96%	95%	94%
Female	4	5	6
Age at Time of Referral			
15 or younger	10%	13%	14%
16 or older	90	87	86
Race/Ethnicity			
White	45%	51%	54%
Black	53	46	44
Other	2	4	2
Predisposition Dentention			
Detained	57%	55%	35%
Not detained	43	45	65

Note: Detail may not add to 100% because of rounding.
SOURCE: Charles M. Puzzanchera. *Characteristics of Delinquency Cases Waived 1990, 1994 and 1999.* Washington, DC: OJJDP Fact Sheet #04, September 2003, p.2. (FS 200304)

Statutory Exclusion   Another common way juveniles are transferred to criminal court is through **statutory exclusion**, a mechanism that describes instances where a state has passed legislation specifically banning certain youthful offenders from being tried in juvenile court. In fact, the largest number of juvenile transfers to criminal court results from statutory exclusion provisions, which currently exist in 29 states.

Statutory exclusion laws allow politicians, not judges, to decide which violent juveniles should be prosecuted by the criminal court. Some states have mandatory criminal court requirements for 14-, 15- and 16-year-olds for certain serious, violent offenses, such as murder and rape. These policies effectively tie judges' hands and remove all judicial discretion in determining whether a young offender would be better handled in the juvenile system.

Reverse Certification or Decertification

In some states the criminal court has exclusive jurisdiction over juveniles who commit specified serious crimes, such as murder, but the court may transfer the case to juvenile court by a process known as **reverse certification** or **decertification**. For example, New York statutes specify that juvenile court jurisdiction:

> Excludes children 13 or older charged with second degree murder and children 14 or older charged with second degree murder, felony murder, kidnapping in the first degree, arson in the first or second degree, assault in the first degree, manslaughter in the first degree, rape in the first degree, sodomy in the first degree, aggravated sexual abuse, burglary in the first or

second degree, robbery in the first or second degree, attempted murder, or attempted kidnapping in the first degree, unless such case is transferred to the juvenile court from the criminal court.

To decertify a case, the burden of proof is usually on the juvenile and defense council to show that there are mitigating circumstances and that the case is more appropriate for juvenile court processing. However, this process is rarely invoked. Older juveniles and those with a great number of risk factors are more likely to remain in the adult criminal justice system.

The Issues of Competency and Culpability

Two issues that are receiving increased attention of late are those concerning juvenile competency and culpability, two distinctly different constructs that are commonly confused, even by those supposedly well versed in criminal law: "Adjudicative competence refers to the ability of an individual to function effectively as a defendant in a criminal or delinquency proceeding. In contrast, determinations of culpability focus on the defendant's blameworthiness in engaging in the criminal conduct and on whether and to what extent he will be held responsible" (Scott and Steinberg, 2008, p.152).

As previously mentioned, emerging brain research has revealed that the parts of the human brain responsible for "executive functions" such as risk and consequence analysis, future planning and impulse control—behaviors all heavily connected to delinquency and criminal conduct—are still developing well into a person's early 20s. These findings have led many juvenile justice scholars to argue that young law violators, by virtue of their inherent developmental immaturity, simply lack the same degree of blameworthiness, or culpability, that adult offenders do. This is not to say that juveniles should not be held responsible for their actions, but it does call into question the practice of transferring youth to an adult system and holding them to the same standards of criminal blameworthiness that it does offenders in their 20s, 30s and beyond.

While transfer to criminal court is relatively infrequent, when it does occur, juveniles go through the same procedures and have the same constitutional rights as adults tried in a criminal court. This also means being held to the same competency standards as adults. However, a criminal proceeding meets due process requirements *only* when the defendant is **competent** to stand trial, including the ability to assist counsel and to participate in the process and make decisions about his or her rights. Under law a person's competence is conceptualized as a specific functional ability. The word *competent* is usually followed by the phrase "to . . ." rather than presented as a general attribute of a person. An adult who is deemed incompetent to stand trial for a specific offense may still be presumed competent to function as a custodial parent or to manage financial affairs. For the adult, specific incompetence must be proved case by case.

Conversely minors are presumed incompetent for most purposes, without any concern for whether they have the capacity to make required decisions in a practical sense. Juveniles who are deemed legally competent for one purpose are often considered generally incompetent in other decision-making contexts. For example, persons under legal age are generally prohibited from executing contracts, consenting to most medical treatment and procedures, marrying, voting, and so on. In many states, persons under age 16 are not allowed to drive. Youths under age 18 are ineligible to join the military. Persons under age 21 are not allowed to drink alcohol legally. Yet some states are willing to transfer to criminal court and try as adults 14-year-olds charged with serious violent crimes. Thus the concept of competency for such youthful offenders necessarily becomes an issue.

In general, there has been little recognition that youths in criminal court may be incompetent due to developmental immaturity. In addition, until now, little meaningful data have been available regarding the capacities of adolescents relevant for adjudicative competence. However, basic research on cognitive and psychosocial development suggests that some youths will manifest deficits in legally relevant abilities similar to deficits seen in adults with mental disability, but for reasons of immaturity rather than mental disorder. In addition, many youths involved in the criminal justice system are of below-average intelligence and are also more likely to comply with requests by authority figures.

 A major concern when transferring a juvenile to criminal court is that the juvenile may not be competent to stand trial there.

Consequences of Transferring Juveniles to Adult Court

Without a doubt, there are some juveniles who need to be treated as adults and transferred to the criminal courts for handling. However, many jurisdictions are now seriously reconsidering their transfer policies in the wake of mounting evidence that such practices are falling short of their intended effects (Steiner et al., 2006, p.49). In fact, the Centers for Disease Control and Prevention (CDC) has taken an official stance in recommending juveniles not be transferred to criminal court (Shepherd, 2007, p.7).

Applegate et al. (2009, p.71) report: "Recent research has shown that transfer may result in higher rates of conviction and a greater likelihood of incarceration. Furthermore, compared with their juvenile court counterparts, juveniles whose cases are transferred to the adult court are less likely to have rehabilitative programming available and are at greater risk of being victimized, but they are no more likely to be deterred or to deter others."

Numerous studies on the deterrent effect of juvenile transfer laws have found that transferred juveniles face increased rates of both recidivism and rearrest: "Juveniles with the highest recidivism rates were those who were incarcerated after being tried in the criminal court. . . . [O]verall, youth adjudicated in juvenile court had a 29-percent lower risk of rearrest than those tried in criminal court" (Redding, 2008, p.4).

 Evidence shows that transferring juveniles to adult court results in higher rates of conviction, greater likelihood of incarceration and greater risk of the youths being victimized. Furthermore, transfer to criminal court has been found to have little deterrent effect on youthful offenders and has been shown to actually increase juvenile recidivism.

Some studies have focused on how transfers negatively impact the maturation process of juveniles in mid- to late adolescence and interfere with their abilities to accomplish vital developmental tasks, thereby heightening their risk of failure once released from the justice system:

During this period (and into early adulthood), individuals normally make substantial progress in acquiring and coordinating skills in several areas that are essential to making the transition to the conventional roles that are part of self-sufficient adulthood. First, they acquire basic educational and vocational skills that enable them to function in the workplace as productive members of society. They also acquire the social skills necessary to establish stable intimate relationships and cooperate in groups. Finally, they begin to learn to behave responsibly without external supervision and to set meaningful personal goals for themselves (Scott and Steinberg, 2008, p.58).

The adult criminal justice system, which takes a decidedly more punitive stance than the juvenile system, is not designed to address the educational and vocational needs of youth, nor is it concerned with fostering the necessary prosocial relationships required between the juvenile and positive adult role models. The most enduring education a juvenile will likely receive while incarcerated in the adult system is how to become a better criminal.

In summary, not only do adult sanctions cause developmental damage to youth by interrupting and interfering with the social bonding and relationship structures necessary for adolescents to mature into integrated, law-abiding members of adult society, but the imposition of criminal sanctions has been found to actually increase the tendency of youth to recidivate, is considerably more expensive and resource-depleting that those occurring within the juvenile justice system and support structures, and yields very little benefit in terms of increased public safety, which begs the question: Are taxpayers and society at large best served by indiscriminately harsh treatment of juvenile offenders?

The *Federal Advisory Committee on Juvenile Justice (FACJJ) Annual Recommendations Report to the President and Congress of the United States* (p.5) states: "FACJJ believes that the majority of juvenile offenders should be handled by the juvenile justice system, not the criminal justice system. This belief supports a recommendation by the National Council of Juvenile and Family Court Judges that the decision about whether to transfer a juvenile charged with a serious crime to criminal court should be made by a juvenile delinquency court judge after an individual hearing with a youth who is represented by qualified council."

A study of how the public views juvenile transfers to criminal court found that public support of such policies rests on several factors, including offense and offender characteristics, views on the appropriate aims of juvenile sentencing, perceptions of juvenile maturity and expectations about the results of transferring juvenile cases to the adult criminal justice system (Applegate et al.). The study concluded that citizens want juvenile transfer used sparingly and selectively, and that support is greatest when the public believes that the adult system can provide effective rehabilitation as well as punishment.

Juveniles and Capital Punishment

The death penalty has always been one of the most contentious issues in discussions about American justice. Capital punishment as applied to youthful offenders has, until recently, been handled in very different ways by the individual states, with some states allowing the execution of persons who were as young as 16 at the time of their offense, and other states banning the death penalty for any offender, regardless of age.

The American Bar Association took an official stance against executing juveniles when it adopted the following policy statement in August 1983: "BE IT RESOLVED, That the American Bar Association opposes, in principle, the imposition of capital punishment upon any person for any offense committed while under the age of eighteen (18)." Nonetheless, more than 200 juvenile death sentences were handed down between 1973 and 2005, with the last execution for an offense committed as a juvenile occurring in 2003, when Oklahoma put to death 32-year-old Scott Allen Hain, who was 17 at the time of his crime. Previous editions of this text discussed the minimum ages authorized by the various states in which capital sentencing was used and presented data on how many juveniles were currently on death row. This has changed, however, in the wake of *Roper v. Simmons* (2005).

Prior to this case, the Supreme Court had upheld the constitutionality of capital punishment for juvenile defendants age 16 and older at the time of their crime. In *Thompson v. Oklahoma* (1988), the Court ruled that our society's standards of decency did *not* permit the execution of any offender under the age of 16 at the time of the crime. Yet, in *Stanford v. Kentucky* (1989), the Court held that execution for crimes committed at ages 16 and older did not necessarily violate the Eighth Amendment prohibition against "cruel and unusual punishment." For fifteen years following *Stanford*, 19 states permitted the sentencing to death of defendants convicted of capital crimes committed while they were 16 or 17 years old. Five states allowed capital punishment for defendants aged 17 or older, and fourteen states set age 16 as the minimum age for death penalty eligibility. The remaining 21 death penalty jurisdictions had expressly set a minimum age of 18 for imposition of the capital sentences.

Then came *Roper*, which effectively made moot the issue of the juvenile death penalty. For while some still advocate the appropriateness of this sanction, the Court has determined the practice of sentencing juveniles to death to be unconstitutional. This case began in 1993 when 17-year-old Christopher Simmons, a white boy with no prior criminal record or history of violence, kidnapped neighbor Shirley Crook during a burglary at her Missouri home, hogtied her and then pushed her off a bridge into the river below. The coroner ruled she died by drowning. According to reports, Simmons had bragged to friends that he could get away with the murder because of his age. The trial jury, however, disagreed and sentenced Simmons to death.

On appeal, Simmons's new lawyer argued that the jury, at sentencing, should have been informed of the numerous mitigating circumstances involving his client—that Simmons had a long family history of abuse, had a below-average IQ, suffered from alcohol and drug abuse, and had been diagnosed with a personality disorder—which, when considered collectively, would most likely have led the jury to choose a sentence of life in prison without parole (LWOP) instead of the death penalty.

After several appeals, the case had worked its way before the Supreme Court. In 2005 a tightly divided Court ruled 5-4 to overturn the capital sentence, declaring the execution of those who committed crimes as juveniles to be in violation of the Eighth and Fourteenth Amendments and an affront to society's evolving standards of decency. In reaching their decision, the Court cited public opinion polls that showed a steady decline in support for capital punishment for juvenile offenders and also made note of the fact that even in those states that allowed capital punishment of juveniles, very few actually imposed this ultimate punishment. In a lengthy opinion, Justice Kennedy, writing for the majority, stated in part:

> Capital punishment must be limited to those offenders who commit "a narrow category of the most serious crimes" and whose extreme culpability makes them "the most deserving of execution." . . . In any capital case a defendant has wide latitude to raise as a mitigating factor "any aspect of [his or her] character or record and any of the circumstances of the offense that the defendant proffers as a basis for a sentence less than death." . . .
>
> The death penalty may not be imposed on certain classes of offenders, such as juveniles under 16, the insane, and the mentally retarded, no matter how heinous the crime. . . .
>
> The reality that juveniles still struggle to define their identity means it is less supportable to conclude that even a heinous crime committed by a juvenile is evidence of irretrievably depraved character. From a moral standpoint it would be misguided to equate the failings of a minor with those of an adult, for a greater possibility exists that a minor's character deficiencies will be reformed. Indeed, "[t]he relevance of youth as a mitigating factor derives from the fact that the signature qualities of youth are transient; as individuals mature, the impetuousness and recklessness that may dominate in younger years can subside." . . .
>
> Once the diminished culpability of juveniles is recognized, it is evident that the penological justifications for the death penalty apply to them with lesser force than to adults. . . .
>
> When a juvenile offender commits a heinous crime, the state can exact forfeiture of some of the most basic liberties, but the state cannot extinguish his life and his potential to attain a mature understanding of his own humanity.
>
> Drawing the line at 18 years of age is subject, of course, to the objections always raised against categorical rules. The qualities that distinguish juveniles from adults do not disappear when an individual turns 18. By the same token, some under 18 have already attained a level of maturity some adults will never reach. For the reasons we have discussed, however, a line must be drawn. The plurality opinion in *Thompson* drew the line at 16. In the intervening years the *Thompson* plurality's conclusion that offenders under 16 may not be executed has not been challenged. The logic of *Thompson* extends to those who are under 18. The age of 18 is the point where society draws the line for many purposes between childhood and adulthood. It is, we conclude, the age at which the line for death eligibility ought to rest. (*Roper v. Simmons*, 543 U.S. 551, 2005).

The Court's ruling in *Roper v. Simmons* took 72 offenders off death row, converting their sentences to LWOP, and dashed prosecutors' hopes of seeking the death penalty for teen sniper Lee Boyd Malvo in those states where he had yet to stand trial for his involvement in the DC-area Beltway murders. Malvo is currently serving multiple LWOP sentences.

A DEBATE: JUVENILES AND THE DEATH PENALTY

Roper v. Simmons categorically prohibits capital punishment for offenders who commit crimes before age 18. This decision has caused an avalanche of debate. Consider both sides of the argument and the pros and cons associated with such a categorical ruling.

"It is difficult even for expert psychologists to differentiate between the juvenile offender whose crime reflects unfortunate yet transient immaturity, and the rare juvenile offender whose crime reflects irreparable corruption. . . . As we understand it, this difficulty underlies the rule forbidding psychiatrists from diagnosing any patient under 18 as having antisocial personality disorder, a disorder also referred to as psychopathy or sociopathy, and which is characterized by callousness, cynicism, and contempt for the feelings, rights, and suffering of others. . . . If trained psychiatrists with the advantage of clinical testing and observation refrain, despite diagnostic expertise, from assessing any juvenile under 18 as having antisocial personality disorder, we conclude that States should refrain from asking jurors to issue a far graver condemnation—that a juvenile offender merits the death penalty" (Justice Kennedy, excerpt from the opinion written for *Roper v. Simmons*, 2005).

"Some victim advocacy groups [wonder] what's so magical about a person's 18th birthday to make them eligible for a death sentence while killers just months younger are not. 'The idea that a male who is 17 years and 364 days old doesn't know better than a male who is 18 years old is absurd,' said . . . a Texas lawyer who filed a brief with the high court on behalf of the victims rights group Justice For All. 'Taking a human life is a bit more than voting or consuming alcohol or going to X-rated movies'" (Tisch, 2005).

Proponents of the juvenile death penalty argue:

- The death penalty provides a much-needed deterrent to violent youth in our society.
- Setting any one age as the "cutoff" for exclusion from execution is too artificial, considering the wide variety of individual offender differences on both sides of that line.

- The culpability of juvenile offenders should be determined on a case-by-case basis, factoring in the nature of the crime and the developmental maturity level of the individual juvenile.
- Lawmakers in each state, not the federal judiciary, should determine whether or not juveniles should be executed for capital crimes.

Those who oppose the juvenile death penalty, and who support the Court's decision in *Roper v. Simmons*, point to:

- A growing body of scientific research supporting the conclusion that juveniles are developmentally immature, particularly in regard to brain development and the ability to control impulses and plan appropriately for consequences of actions, and that, therefore youthful offenders should not be held to the same culpability standards as adult offenders.
- Data indicating a vast majority of juveniles on death row have histories of being abused, suffer from a host of mental illnesses and were addicted to drugs at the time of their offense.
- International opposition to the practice, with the execution of juveniles expressly forbidden in the United Nations Convention on the Rights of the Child, the Geneva Convention Relative to the Protection of Civilian Persons in Time of War, the International Covenant on Civil and Political Rights, and the American Convention on Human Rights.
- The company we keep—Iran, Pakistan, the Democratic Republic of Congo (DRC) and China are the only other countries to have allowed execution of juveniles since 2000. While Pakistan and China have since officially abolished the practice, Iran executed at least seven juvenile offenders during 2008. And with the exception of Somalia, the United States is the only other member of the United Nations that has not ratified the U.N. Convention on the Rights of the Child.

Juvenile Delinquency Guidelines for Improving Juvenile Court Practices

The National Council of Juvenile and Family Court Judges (NCJFCJ) has developed guidelines with the dual goals of improving both delinquency case processing and outcomes (*Juvenile Delinquency Guidelines: Improving Court Practice in Juvenile Delinquency Cases*, 2005). The guidelines identify preferred practices from intake to case closure and articulate 16 key principles that should frame the entire court process:

1. Juvenile delinquency court judges should engage in judicial leadership and encourage system collaboration.

2. Juvenile delinquency systems must have adequate staff, facilities and program resources.
3. Juvenile delinquency courts and juvenile abuse and neglect courts should have integrated one family–one judge case assignments.
4. Juvenile delinquency court judges should have the same status as the highest level of trial court in the state and should have multiple-year or permanent assignments.
5. All members of the juvenile delinquency court shall treat youths, families, crime victims, witnesses and others with respect, dignity, courtesy and cultural understanding.
6. Juvenile delinquency court judges should ensure their systems divert cases to alternative systems whenever possible and appropriate.
7. Youths charged in the formal juvenile delinquency court must have qualified and adequately compensated legal representation.
8. Juvenile delinquency court judges should ensure crime victims have access to all phases of the juvenile delinquency court process and receive all services to which they are entitled by law.
9. Juvenile delinquency courts should render timely and just decisions, and trials should conclude without continuances.
10. Juvenile delinquency system staff should engage parents and families at all stages of the juvenile delinquency court process to encourage family members to participate fully in the development and implementation of the youth's intervention plan.
11. The juvenile delinquency court should engage the school and other community support systems as stakeholders in each individual youth's case.
12. Juvenile delinquency court judges should ensure court dispositions are individualized and include graduated responses, both sanctions and incentives (discussed in Chapter 11).
13. Juvenile delinquency court judges should ensure effective post-disposition review is provided to each delinquent youth as long as the youth is involved in any component of the juvenile justice system.
14. Juvenile delinquency court judges should hold their systems and the systems of other juvenile delinquency court stakeholders accountable.
15. Juvenile delinquency court judges should ensure the court has an information system that can generate the data necessary to evaluate performance, facilitate information sharing with appropriate agencies and manage operations information.
16. The juvenile delinquency court judge is responsible to ensure that the judiciary, court staff and all system participants are both individually trained and trained across systems and roles.

The Annie E. Casey Foundation's *2008 KIDS COUNT Data Book* also makes recommendations for ensuring that the juvenile court system is effective, including reducing reliance on secure confinement, keeping youths out of the system, reducing racial disparities, increasing reliance on effective community-based services and implementing developmentally appropriate policies and interventions. This final recommendation is intended as harsh criticism of current policies and practices that push juveniles into the criminal justice system, particularly in light of growing research evidence that shows juveniles tried and punished as adults have higher recidivism rates than do youths retained in the juvenile justice system (p.15).

 ## SUMMARY

- The juvenile justice system is basically a civil system.
- Most state juvenile court purpose statements contain (1) balanced and restorative justice (BARJ) clauses; (2) Standard Juvenile Court Act clauses; (3) legislative guide clauses; (4) clauses that emphasize punishment, deterrence, accountability and/or public safety clauses; or (5) clauses with traditional child welfare emphasis.
- Juvenile court jurisdiction includes children who are in poverty, neglected or abused, who are unruly or commit status offenses and who are charged with committing serious crimes.
- Juvenile court jurisdiction is determined by the offender's age and conduct.
- The possible bases for a declaration of wardship include demonstrating that the child is abused or neglected or has committed a status offense or a criminal act.
- Juvenile courts are separated into three types: independent and separate courts, part of a family court and a unit within a trial court.
- The juvenile courtroom work group consists of judges, hearing officers, prosecutors, defense attorneys and probation officers.
- Court action on behalf of neglected, abused or dependent children may be non-criminal or criminal.
- The National Committee for Prevention of Child Abuse describes two kinds of intervention for deprived children: coercive and therapeutic.
- The juvenile court process usually involves the filing of a petition, a detention hearing, an adjudication hearing and a disposition hearing.
- Juveniles may be transferred to criminal court via three basic mechanisms: judicial waiver, concurrent jurisdiction and statutory exclusion.
- In some states the court makes the decision to certify a juvenile as an adult. In other states this is done by the prosecutor.
- A major concern when transferring a juvenile to criminal court is that the juvenile may not be competent to stand trial there.
- Evidence shows that transferring juveniles to adult court results in higher rates of conviction, greater likelihood of incarceration and greater risk of the youth being victimized. Furthermore, transfer to criminal court has been found to have little deterrent effect on youthful offenders and has been shown to actually increase juvenile recidivism.

DISCUSSION QUESTIONS

1. Should the juvenile court have two separate courts for civil and criminal matters?
2. Should there be a separate justice system for juveniles, or should all juveniles be dealt with in the adult system?
3. What is the purpose statement of the juvenile court in your area?
4. What criteria are used in decisions to waive juvenile court jurisdiction?
5. Who can certify a juvenile as an adult in your state?
6. Should juveniles be subject to the death penalty?
7. Do you think most juveniles are competent to stand trial in criminal court?

8. Does your state have the death penalty? If so, can juveniles under age 18 be executed?

9. Who has jurisdiction over maltreated youths in your community?

10. What are the major differences between juvenile court and adult criminal court?

REFERENCES

Applegate, Brandon K.; Davis, Robin King; and Cullen, Francis T. "Reconsidering Child Saving: The Extent and Correlates of Public Support for Excluding Youths from the Juvenile Court." *Crime & Delinquency*, January 2009, pp.51–77.

Badeau, Sue and Freundlich, Madelyn. "Hearing the Voices of Young Children with Disabilities in Court." *Juvenile and Family Justice Today*, Fall 2006, p.19.

Federal Advisory Committee on Juvenile Justice Annual Recommendations Report to the President and Congress of the United States. August 2007.

Griffin, Patrick and Torbet, Patricia. *Desktop Guide to Good Juvenile Probation Practice*. Pittsburg, PA: National Center for Juvenile Justice, June 2002.

Jones, William G. "Making Youth a Meaningful Part of the Court Process." *Juvenile and Family Justice Today*, Fall 2006a, p.20.

Jones, William G. *Working with the Courts in Child Protection*. User Manual Series. Washington, DC: Child Welfare Information Gateway, 2006b.

Juvenile Delinquency Guidelines: Improving Court Practice in Juvenile Delinquency Cases. Reno, NV: National Council of Juvenile and Family Court Judges, Summer 2005.

Krinsky, Miriam Aroni. "The Effect of Youth Presence in Dependency Court Proceedings." *Juvenile and Family Justice Today*, Fall 2006, pp.16–17.

National Council of Juvenile and Family Court Judges Staff Report. "NCJFCJ Model Courts Advocate Giving Children a Voice." *Juvenile Justice Today*, Fall 2006, p.17.

Neubauer, David W. *America's Courts and the Criminal Justice System*, 9th ed. Belmont, CA: Wadsworth Publishing Company, 2008.

"New Study Details the Dangers of Holding Youth in Adult Jails." *Juvenile Justice Update*, February/March 2008, pp.11–12.

Redding, Richard E. *Juvenile Transfer Laws: An Effective Deterrent to Delinquency?* Juvenile Justice Bulletin. Washington, DC: Office of Juvenile Justice and Delinquency Prevention, August 2008.

Rodriguez, Nancy. "Juvenile Court Context and Detention Decisions: Reconsidering the Role of Race, Ethnicity and Community Characteristics in Juvenile Court Processes." *Justice Quarterly*, December 2007, pp.629–656.

Scott, Elizabeth S. and Steinberg, Laurence. *Rethinking Juvenile Justice*. Cambridge, MA: Harvard University Press, 2008.

Shepherd, Robert E. "CDC Task Force Recommends against Transferring Juveniles to Adult Courts." *Juvenile Justice Update*, June/July 2007, pp.7–8.

Siegel, Gene and Halemba, Gregg. *The Importance of Timely Case Processing in Non-Detained Juvenile Delinquency Cases*. Pittsburgh, PA: National Center for Juvenile Justice (NCJJ), July 2006.

Snyder, Howard N. and Sickmund, Melissa. *Juvenile Offenders and Victims: 2006 National Report*. Washington, DC: U.S. Department of Justice, Office of Justice Programs, Office of Juvenile Justice and Delinquency Prevention, March 2006.

Stahl, Anne L. *Delinquency Cases in Juvenile Courts, 2004*. Washington, DC: U.S. Department of Justice, Office of Juvenile Justice and Delinquency Prevention, February 2008. (FS 200801)

Steiner, Benjamin; Hemmens, Craig; and Bell, Valerie. "Legislative Waiver Reconsidered: General Deterrent Effects of Statutory Exclusion Laws Enacted Post-1979." *Justice Quarterly*, March 2006, pp.34–59.

Sweeten, Gary. "Who Will Graduate? Disruption of High School Education by Arrest and Court Involvement." *Justice Quarterly*, December 2006, pp.462–480.

Tisch, Chris. "18 Is Threshold for Death Penalty." *St. Petersburg Times*, March 2, 2005.

2008 KIDS COUNT Data Book. Baltimore, MD: The Annie E. Casey Foundation, 2008.

CASES CITED

Commonwealth v. Fisher, 213 Pa. 48, 62 A. 198, 199, 200 (1905)

People ex rel. O'Connell v. Turner, 55 Ill. 280, 8 Am. Rep. 645 (1870)

Roper v. Simmons, 543 U.S. 551 (2005)

Stanford v. Kentucky, 492 U.S. 361 (1989)

Thompson v. Oklahoma, 487 U.S. 815 (1988)

CHAPTER 11

Juvenile Corrections

> IT IS IN THE JUVENILE JUSTICE SYSTEM THAT WE WILL SUCCEED OR FAIL IN REDUCING CORRECTIONS POPULATIONS.... IF WE DO NOT ADDRESS JUVENILE CORRECTIONS FULLY, THESE CHILDREN WILL END UP AS TOMORROW'S CLIENTS IN THE ADULT SYSTEM.
>
> —JOHN J. WILSON

© Joel Gordon/Joel Gordon Photography

Juvenile corrections serves the dual function of holding youthful offenders accountable for their behavior and providing them with the educational, vocational, personal and social skills needed to successfully return to the community as productive, self-regulated, law-abiding adults. Sometimes public safety requires juvenile offenders be removed from the community and securely confined. Here two female offenders spend time in their cell during lockdown.

Do You Know?

- What four components are typically included in a modern, comprehensive graduated sanctions system?
- What the most common disposition from the juvenile court is?
- What the formal goals of probation are?
- What the two main functions of a probation officer traditionally have been?
- What the single greatest pressure on probation officers is?
- What common intermediate sanctions are?
- What effect isolating offenders from the community might have?
- How public and private correctional institutions differ?
- Whether juvenile institutions are similar to adult institutions in terms of social organization and culture?
- What the six performance-based standards goals for corrections are?
- What most effective youthful offender programs include?
- What the weakest element in the juvenile justice system process often is?
- What two key components of effective aftercare are?

Can You Define?

aftercare
boot camp
criminogenic need principle
cruel and unusual punishment

deterrence
graduated sanctions
intensive supervision probation (ISP)
intermediate sanctions

ombuds
parole
probation
re-entry
responsivity principle

risk principle
shock incarceration

Chapter Outline

Introduction
Conservative and Liberal Philosophies of Corrections
The Concept of Graduated Sanctions
Standard Probation
The Probation Officer
Challenges Facing Probation
School-Based Probation
Intermediate Sanctions
Intensive Supervision Probation (ISP)
Community Service
Nonsecure Juvenile Residential Facilities

Nonresidential Day Treatment Alternatives
Electronic Monitoring and Home Detention
Training Schools
Boot Camps
Institutionalization: Long-Term Secure Confinement
Public versus Private Institutions
Social Structure within Correctional Institutions
The Impact of Incarceration
Challenges Facing Juvenile Correctional Facilities

Improving Conditions of Confinement
Achieving Effective Correctional Programs for Youth
Juveniles Sentenced to Adult Institutions
Re-Entry
Planning for Re-Entry
Principles of Intensive Aftercare Programs (IAPs)
Promising Aftercare Programs

Introduction

Corrections serves several functions, one of the most obvious being to protect the public by removing juvenile offenders from the community (this is the functional process or goal known as *incapacitation*). Corrections has a dual function with youthful offenders: holding them accountable for their behavior and providing them with the educational, vocational, personal and social skills needed to successfully return to the community as productive, self-regulated, law-abiding adults. This commonly includes treatment components aimed at modifying behavior and impulse control mechanisms, improving interpersonal relationship dynamics and tending to addictions or mental health needs.

As with any other area of criminal or juvenile justice, differing viewpoints exist regarding how to best handle offenders once they enter the "corrections" stage of the process. Before examining specific practices and policies within juvenile corrections, briefly consider two general, divergent philosophies of corrections.

Conservative and Liberal Philosophies of Corrections

The conservative attitude is to "get tough," "stop babying these kids" and "get them off the streets." Such conservative philosophies accept retribution as grounds for punishment and believe in imprisonment to control crime and antisocial behavior. Rehabilitative programs may be provided during incarceration, but it is imprisonment itself, with its attendant deprivations, that must be primarily relied on to prevent crime, delinquency and recidivism. Correctional treatment is not necessary.

This "law and order" reaction typifies conservatism, a trend that first affected adult offenders and now extends into juvenile justice. In 2007, one out of eight violent crimes was committed by juveniles (Rutledge, 2008, p.60). Minors were responsible for 173,225 robberies, rapes, aggravated assaults and murders and for about 1.8 million burglaries, major thefts, auto thefts and arsons. In some communities youth gangs terrorize neighborhoods and turn schools into combat zones. Rutledge points out that although the juvenile justice system was developed to deal with these often "hardened and vicious teenaged and preteen offenders who prey on modern society," some juvenile offenders get off too easy: "Notwithstanding the explosion of youth criminality, the court has largely continued to treat juvenile offenders in a more lenient and paternalistic fashion than adults" (p.61).

At the opposite end of the spectrum from the conservative philosophy is the liberal view of juvenile justice, whose proponents sharply censure the "get tough" approach and all its trappings, such as the need to build more prisons to hold the rising number of incarcerated youths. The liberal philosophy of juvenile justice advocates treatment, not punishment, for youths who become involved with the juvenile justice system. Those who advocate for a more liberal correctional approach point to our country's laws that prohibit juveniles to drink alcohol, vote, engage in legal contracts and marry because juveniles are still developing mentally and emotionally.

Rehabilitating Juvenile Offenders (2008, p.1) reports on two new surveys funded by the MacArthur Foundation showing strong public backing for the rehabilitation of youthful offenders and a greater willingness of taxpayers to pay for rehabilitating them: "More than 70 percent of the public agree that incarcerating youthful offenders without rehabilitation is the same as giving up on them. Nine out of 10 people surveyed believe that almost all youths who commit crimes have the potential to change." According to the president of the foundation: "Momentum is gathering across the nation to replace harsh, ineffective measures with programs that address the welfare of young people while preserving safe communities."

Morrell (2007, p.87) notes: "Rehabilitation is the ideological juxtaposition to retribution. It is positive, progressive and actually attempts to address offenders' needs.... Recent evidence demonstrates that these efforts are cost-effective and long lasting."

The Concept of Graduated Sanctions

Promising Sanctioning Programs in a Graduated System (2003, p.1) explains: "A graduated sanctions system is a set of integrated intervention strategies designed to operate in unison to enhance accountability, ensure public safety and reduce recidivism by preventing future delinquent behavior. The term **graduated sanctions** [emphasis added] implies that the penalties for delinquent activity should move from limited interventions to more restrictive (i.e. graduated) penalties according to the severity and nature of the delinquent act. In other words, youths who commit serious and violent offenses should receive more severe sentences than youth who commit less serious offenses." A graduated continuum of increasingly severe sanctions adheres to an underlying philosophy that youths should be dealt with in the least restrictive environment necessary to achieve the desired goals. While the administration of sanctions that "match" an offense in terms of severity appears to be common sense, some jurisdictions have not always handled juvenile offenders so rationally.

The basic premise underlying a graduated system is **deterrence**. Deterrence theory states that the decision to commit a crime is based on a cost-benefit calculation. If a person believes the legal costs of committing a crime are greater than the benefits, crime will be deterred. When a person believes the benefits outweigh the costs, a crime will be committed. Deterrence theory suggests that sanctions be tailored to be just severe enough to exceed the gain offered by crime. Overly severe sanctions are unjust; sanctions that are not severe enough will not deter.

Griffin and Torbet (2002, p.77) list the essential features of a good graduated sanctions system:

- *Certainty*: It responds to every infraction.
- *Speed*: The response is swift.
- *Consistency*: Similar infractions receive similar responses.
- *Economy*: The response chosen is the minimum likely to produce the desired result.
- *Proportionality*: The level of response should equal the level of the offense.

- *Progressiveness*: Continued noncompliance results in increasingly severe responses.
- *Neutrality*: Responses are an objective, impartial reaction to the offense.

Griffin and Torbet also contend: "Incentives—rewards for compliance—may be an even more useful tool for changing behavior than sanctions. Incentives for compliance should be delivered with the same consistency, immediacy and certainty as sanctions for noncompliance."

According to *Promising Sanctioning Programs in a Graduated System* (2003, p.2): "A modern comprehensive juvenile justice system must include programs less restrictive than confinement but more intensive than probation. But such a system should not simply be a hodgepodge of alternative programs. It must embody a correctional philosophy that can deal with youths who commit serious and violent offenses, 'one time and you're out youths,' and everyone in between." In other words, a juvenile justice system that offers a continuum of care must include a wide range of sanctions designed to increase offender accountability so a sanction can be matched to the seriousness of the offense.

 A modern, comprehensive graduated sanctions continuum set includes four components for targeted populations: (1) immediate sanctions within the community for first-time, nonviolent offenders, (2) intermediate sanctions (including probation) within the community for more serious offenders, (3) secure confinement programs for the most violent offenders and (4) re-entry/aftercare programs that provide high levels of social control and treatment services.

Immediate sanctions are usually diversion mechanisms that hold youths accountable for their behavior by avoiding formal court processing. They are typically appropriate for most first-time offenders, status offenders and some minor repeat offenders. Such sanctions usually follow restorative justice principles and include community service, informal hearings, family group conferences, mediation, mentoring, special courts and restitution. Diversion programs were discussed in Chapter 9. This chapter focuses on the other three components of graduated sanctions: probation and intermediate sanctions, secure confinement, and aftercare/re-entry.

Standard Probation

Probation has been called the "workhorse of the juvenile justice system" and falls at the least restrictive end of the continuum of intermediate sanctions. After the dispositional hearing, if the court orders that a youngster be placed on probation, certain procedures and commitments must be satisfied. An order must give the probation officer authority for controlled supervision of the youth within the community. The terms of the probation are described in the order. **Probation** allows youths adjudicated delinquent to serve their sentences in the community under correctional supervision.

An important responsibility of the probation officer is helping the court to establish the conditions for probation. Two kinds of probationary conditions are usually established: mandatory and discretionary. Most mandatory conditions specify that probationers (1) may not commit a new delinquent act, (2) must report as directed to their probation officer and (3) must obey all court orders. The discretionary conditions are more extensive, as illustrated by the discretionary conditions set forth in New Jersey Juvenile Statutes: pay a fine; make restitution; perform community service; participate in a work program; participate in programs emphasizing self-reliance, such as intensive outdoor programs that teach survival skills, including but not limited to camping, hiking and other appropriate activities; participate in a program of academic or vocational education or counseling, which may require attendance after school, evenings and weekends; be placed in a suitable residential or nonresidential program for the treatment of alcohol or narcotic abuse; be placed in a nonresidential program operated by a public or private agency that provides intensive services to juveniles for specified hours, which may include education, counseling to the juvenile and the juvenile's family if appropriate, vocational counseling, work or other services; or be placed with any private group home with which the Department of Corrections has entered into a purchase of service contract.

The New Jersey statute also allows the court to set conditions for the probationer's parents and to revoke the juvenile's driver's license as a condition of probation. Conditions may include such matters as cooperating with the program of supervision, meeting family responsibilities, maintaining steady employment or engaging in or refraining from engaging in a specific employment or occupation, pursuing prescribed educational or vocational training, undergoing medical or psychiatric treatment, maintaining residence in a prescribed area or in a prescribed facility, refraining from consorting with certain types of people or frequenting certain types of places, making restitution or reparation, paying fines, submitting to search and seizure or submitting to drug tests.

Several constraints govern the setting of probation conditions. The conditions must be do-able, must not unreasonably restrict constitutional rights, must be consistent with law and public policy and must be specific and understandable. If the conditions are *not* met, probation can be revoked. This is normally accomplished by the probation officer reporting the violation of conditions to the juvenile court. A violation of probation starts the judicial process over, beginning with a revocation hearing, where evidence and supportive information are presented to a juvenile judge. (Such hearings are also called *surrender hearings* or *violation hearings*.) If the court decides to revoke the probation, the youth can be institutionalized.

Probation originated with John Augustus (1784–1859), a prosperous Boston shoemaker and the first probation officer. He was the first to use the word *probation* in its modern sense, from Latin meaning a period of proving or trial (Griffin and Torbet, 2002). Several aspects of the system used by Augustus remain a basic part of modern probation. He thoroughly investigated each person he considered helping. He considered the person's character, age and likely future influences. Augustus not only supervised each defendant but also kept careful case records which he submitted to the court.

 Probation is the most common disposition of the juvenile or family court.

The number of cases adjudicated delinquent that resulted in probation increased 108 percent between 1985 and 2000 (Puzzanchera et al., 2004).

In 2002, of all the cases adjudicated delinquent, 385,400 received probation. Of those not adjudicated delinquent, 22,900 received probation; and of those not petitioned, 210,300 received probation, for a total of 618,600 juveniles on probation in 2002 (Snyder and Sickmund, 2006).

According to Griffin and Torbet (p.1): "We envision the role of juvenile probation as that of a catalyst for developing safe communities and healthy youths and families. We believe we can fulfill this role by:

- Holding offenders accountable.
- Building and maintaining community-based partnerships.
- Implementing results-based and outcome-driven services and practices.
- Advocating for and addressing the needs of victims, offenders, families and communities.
- Obtaining and sustaining sufficient resources.
- Promoting growth and development of all juvenile probation professionals."

The researchers reject the "closed, passive, negative and unsystematic approach that has too often characterized traditional juvenile probation practices." They (p.2) emphasize that protecting the public is a primary responsibility of juvenile probation. In addition, probation is a guidance program to help juveniles overcome problems that may lead to further delinquency and to supervise them. It functions as an alternative to a correctional facility and operates much like adult probation.

 The formal goals of probation are to protect the public, to hold juveniles accountable for their actions and to improve the delinquents' behavior—in short, rehabilitation.

Probation's goal of rehabilitation is sometimes short-circuited by the public's preoccupation with *control*. Probation may reflect public demands that the court "do something" about recurrent misconduct. It may be organized to keep the delinquent in line, to prevent any further trouble, and so the ultimate goal of reforming the delinquent's personality and conduct becomes subordinated to the exigencies of maintaining immediate control. Probationary supervision, consequently, takes on a decidedly short-term and negative character. Probation becomes a disciplinary regime to inhibit troublesome conduct.

Often, by the time a juvenile is placed on probation, he or she has a record of previous run-ins with the juvenile justice system, usually the police. The police regard probation as something juveniles "get away with" or "get off with." Many juveniles who receive probation instead of being sentenced to a correctional facility view it the same way, as a sort of paper tiger: "I never see my P.O. [probation officer]. It's a joke! Don't ask me to tell you what he looks like, I can't remember." The application of intensive supervision probation, which will be discussed shortly, is an effort to put more teeth into probation and eliminate some of the slack commonly associated with it.

The Probation Officer

Probation officers are in the unique position of serving both the court and the correctional areas of juvenile justice. While technically considered a correctional employee, a probation officer is an officer of the court first and foremost.

In many states probation officers determine whether the juvenile court has jurisdiction, especially at the intake stage. The probation representative also determines, to some degree, whether a formal or an informal hearing is called for. Informal hearings have critics, because informal processing requires an explicit or tacit admission of guilt. The substantial advantages that accrue from this admission (the avoidance of court action) also act as an incentive to confess. This casts doubt on the voluntary nature and truthfulness of admissions of guilt. The process results in informal probation.

Informal probation can be a crucial time in a juvenile's life. If it succeeds, the youngster may avoid further juvenile court processing and its potentially serious consequences. If informal probation efforts fail, the usual recourse is for the probation officer to request a petition be filed to make the case official. This could result in the youth being confined in a locked or controlled facility for disciplinary action.

Filing Petitions and Court Hearings   Recall from Chapter 10 the three phases of the juvenile court system that youths usually go through after a petition is filed. The probation officer may play an important role in each phase. During the first phase, the detention hearing, the judge may determine with the assistance of a probation officer whether a child's behavior is a threat to the public or to him- or herself. If so, the judge will order preventive detention of the youth. During the second phase, the adjudication hearing or trial, the judge will usually order a social investigation, presentence investigation (PSI) or predisposition report. The probation officer is responsible for investigating and assessing the child's home, school, physical and psychological situation. The *predisposition* or *presentence investigation report* has the objective of satisfying the goal of the juvenile court, which is to provide services.

Other Services   In addition to assessing the needs of probationers, devising a case plan or contract and supervising compliance with that contract, probation officers can also serve as mature role models. They can provide family counseling, crisis intervention and mediation. Mediation can be used to divert cases at intake, settle cases by community groups or by the probation officer and settle disputes between a juvenile and the school or family.

 The probation officer has traditionally been responsible for two key functions: (1) personally supervising and counseling youths on probation and (2) serving as a link to other community services.

While counseling skills are considered important, the role of probation officers has shifted to that of social service "brokers." In many jurisdictions, the probation officer links "clients" with available resources within the community, such as vocational rehabilitation centers, vocational schools, mental health centers, employment services, church groups and other community groups, such as Girl Scouts, Boy Scouts and Explorers. This broad use of community resources has some inherent risks. Linking youths to such groups may actually amplify a small problem into a much larger one. Over-attendance by a youth in one or more of these groups may become an attention-getting device. The over-prescription of community group participation may also reinforce the youth's or the community's perception of the problem as serious. In either case further delinquency may well result.

In 1987 the National Center for Juvenile Justice (NCJJ) established the Juvenile Probation Officer Initiative (JPOI) to increase professionalism in juvenile probation. The JPOI has developed *The Desktop Guide to Good Juvenile Probation Practice*, a reference book written by and for juvenile probation officers (Griffin and Torbet, 2002). The demanding, challenging, multifaceted role of the juvenile probation officer is illustrated in Table 11.1.

Challenges Facing Probation

Courts often attribute juveniles' troubles to something that is wrong with the youths or with their social milieu. The courts seldom recognize that a juvenile's problems may be the result of the juvenile justice system's ineffective delivery of guidance and control services. In many cases probation officers simply do not have the training, skills or resources to provide probationers with the kinds of assistance they might require. A problem commonly encountered at the dispositional stage is a lack of options to help or treat a youngster. Inexperienced or uninformed probation officers may recommend treatment that is simply not available. Often a youngster is placed on or continued on probation because of a lack of viable alternatives. Another inhibiting factor is time constraints brought about by unmanageably high caseloads. Even if probation officers possessed the skills necessary to offer psychotherapy, vocational guidance and school counseling with diverse types of youths, caseloads dictate that they would not have the time to exercise these skills.

 Excessive caseloads are probably the single greatest pressure on probation officers.

In most probation offices, especially in large urban areas, certain characteristics pervade the personality of the office. Juveniles are viewed by their records, in terms of the trouble they have caused or gotten into. Records are not regarded as formulations assembled by various people in the juvenile justice system. That is to say, a juvenile's record is treated as a set of relevant facts instead of as a social product created by an organization.

Problems such as illegal drug use, street gangs, school violence and abused, homeless and runaway youths have strained the resources of the juvenile justice system. Given that probation departments are the single largest component of juvenile corrections, these departments especially feel the strain. One proposed solution is privatization. Another solution is to implement school-based probation programs.

School-Based Probation

According to the Juvenile Sanctions Center (JSC), *School-Based Probation: An Approach Worth Considering* (2003), placing juvenile probation officers in schools rather than in central offices goes a long way toward increasing the contacts between officers and the youths they are monitoring, leading to more immediate and effective responses to problems: "School-based probation (SBP) changes the very nature of probation by physically moving probation officers from the 'fortress' of traditional central or district offices into middle, junior and high school buildings where youths on probation spend the majority of their day."

Table 11.1 The Multifaceted Role of the Juvenile Probation Officer

Role	Description
Cop	Enforces judge's orders
Prosecutor	Assists D.A., conducts revocations
Father confessor	Establishes helpful, trustful relationship with juvenile
Rat	Informs court of juvenile's behavior/circumstances
Teacher	Develops skills in juvenile
Friend	Develops positive relations with juvenile
Surrogate parent	Admonishes, scolds juvenile
Counselor	Addresses needs
Ambassador	Intervenes on behalf of juvenile
Problem solver	Helps juvenile deal with court and community issues
Crisis manager	Deals with juvenile's precipitated crises (usually at 2 A.M.)
Hand holder	Consoles juvenile
Public speaker	Educates public re: tasks
P.R. person	Wins friends, influences people on behalf of probation
Community resource specialist	Service broker
Transportation officer	Gets juvenile to where he or she has to go in a pinch
Recreational therapist	Gets juvenile to use leisure time well
Employment counselor	Gets youth a job
Judge's advisor	Court service officer
Financial advisor	Monitors payment, sets pay plan
Paper pusher	Fills out myriad forms
Sounding board	Listens to irate parents, youths, police, teachers, etc.
Punching bag	Person to blame when anything goes wrong, youth commits new crime
Expert clinician	Offers or refers to appropriate treatment
Family counselor/marriage therapist	Keeps peace in juvenile's family
Psychiatrist	Answers question: Why does the juvenile do it?
Banker	Juvenile needs cab fare money
Tracker	Finds youth
Truant officer	Gets youth to school
Lawyer	Tells defense lawyer/prosecutor what juvenile law says
Sex educator	Facts of life, AIDS and child support
Emergency foster parent	In a pinch
Family wrecker	Files petitions for abuse/neglect
Bureaucrat	Helps juvenile justice system function
Lobbyist	For juvenile, for department
Program developer	For youth, for department
Grant writer	For youth, for department
Board member	Serves on myriad committees
Agency liaison	With community groups
Trainer	For volunteer, students
Public information officer	"Tell me what you know about probation"
Court officer/bailiff	In a pinch
Custodian	Keeps office clean
Victim advocate	Deals with juvenile's victim

SOURCE: Adapted from Juvenile Probation Officer Initiative (JPOI) Working Group, *Desktop Guide to Good Juvenile Probation Practice.* Washington, DC: Office of Juvenile Justice and Delinquency Prevention, May 1993, pp.119–120.

According to the JSC document: "School-based probation represents an important shift in the delivery of probation services for in-school probations, and departments across the country are embracing this approach. More importantly, two evaluations of Pennsylvania's SBP program have documented several important benefits, including more contact, better monitoring, a focus on school success and a fit with balanced and restorative justice framework."

Intermediate Sanctions

Intermediate sanctions hold youths accountable for their actions through interventions that are more restrictive and intensive than standard probation yet which fall short of secure long-term incarceration. They provide swift, certain punishment while avoiding the expense and negative effects of institutionalization. Intermediate sanctions are appropriate for youths who fail to respond to immediate sanctions by reoffending and for some violent or drug-involved offenders who need supervision, structure and monitoring but not necessarily institutionalization.

 Common forms of intermediate sanctions are intensive supervision probation, community service, nonsecure juvenile residential facilities, nonresidential day treatment alternatives, electronic monitoring, house arrest, training schools and boot camps.

Sentencing alternatives at the more restrictive end of the intermediate sanctions continuum, such as training schools and boot camps, are often considered to be equivalent to incarceration in terms of harshness and severity of punishment. And while they are all considered secure conglomerate-care facilities, the training schools and boot camps are still alternatives to long-term confinement in a correctional institution. Thus, they are included in this discussion of intermediate sanctions.

Intensive Supervision Probation (ISP)

Intensive supervision probation (ISP) is highly structured probation intended to provide a higher level of control over an offender and, thus, increased public safety without the added cost incurred with residential placement or incarceration. Intensive supervision programs differ from routine or standard probation in that contact between the probation officer or caseworker and the juvenile offender is more frequent, caseloads are smaller and strict compliance is required. Furthermore, ISPs usually include:

- Greater reliance placed on unannounced spot checks; these may occur in a variety of settings including home, school, known hangouts and job sites.
- Considerable attention directed at increasing the number and kinds of collateral contacts made by corrections staff with family members, friends, staff from other agencies and concerned residents in the community.
- Greater use of curfew, including both more rigid enforcement and lowering the hour at which curfew goes into effect. Other measures for imposing control include home detention and electronic monitoring.
- Surveillance expanded to ensure 24/7 coverage.

Other components of intensive supervision are clear, graduated sanctions with immediate consequences for violations; restitution and community service; parent involvement; youth skill development; and individualized and offense-specific treatment.

To determine whether a probationer needs intensive supervision, the probation officer should have a classification procedure. Because intensive supervision is extremely time-consuming, it should be reserved for those probationers at greatest risk of violating their probation.

The National Institute of Corrections (NIC) Classification Project has been adopted by many juvenile court jurisdictions. NIC research suggests that an assessment of the following variables appears to be universally predictive of future delinquent behavior:

- Age at first adjudication
- Prior delinquent behavior (combined measure of number and severity of priors)
- Number of prior commitments to juvenile facilities
- Drug/chemical abuse
- Alcohol abuse
- Family relationships problems
- School problems
- Peer relationships problems

The NIC calls for a reassessment every six months. After the assessment is completed, a case plan must arrange services so the youth, the family and the community all are served. The National Council on Crime and Delinquency (NCCD) has a case planning strategy that involves two main components:

1. Analysis, including identification of problems, strengths and resources.
2. Problem prioritization based upon:
    - Strength—Is the problem an important force in the delinquent's behavior?
    - Alterability—Can the problem be modified or circumvented?
    - Speed—Can the changes be achieved rapidly?
    - Interdependence—Will solving the problem help resolve other problems?

This case plan is next reduced to a contract between the probation department, the juvenile offender and the family. The probation officer then presents this contract to the juvenile and the parents and reaches agreement on it, after which the probation officer monitors compliance with the contract.

Brank et al. (2008, p.193) studied the effects of using a team approach to service delivery in an ISP that focused on improving parent-child relationships and teaching youths how to choose better peers. The post-test showed that the experimental and control youths were not significantly different on key family or peer relationship measures. Yet, despite the null results, other valuable findings were gleaned from the research:

> First, intensive family interventions will take an enormous commitment of time and resources. A phasing in of different components will be useful in that the service providers and probation officers can become acclimated to each new component one at a time.

Second, general questions about family relationships may illicit false perceptions, or at least incomplete perceptions from the youths.

Third, legislators and policy makers should give careful consideration when implementing parental involvement programs in their statutes. The results from the current project imply that a simple inclusion of such language in the statutes (without the focused, intensive programs to back them up) will likely not result in the intended impact or any impact at all. (p.217)

Community Service

Community service is usually part of a graduated sanctions program and may be used alone or in combination with other sanctions, especially probation. It is an important component of most restorative justice approaches. In addition to performing work, community service sometimes requires offenders to speak to various community groups about their offenses and what such offending has cost them financially and emotionally.

Nonsecure Juvenile Residential Facilities

Court dispositions are often compromises among deterrence, incapacitation, retribution and rehabilitation. Community-based residential programs do not permit the freedom of dismissal or of suspended judgments, but neither do they isolate offenders from the community as institutions do. Community programs are sometimes perceived as being easy on youngsters and thus as not providing enough supervision to ensure deterrence, incapacitation and retribution. Nonetheless commitment to such programs represents a considerable degree of restriction and punishment when compared to dismissal, suspended judgment or

Youths assigned to community service or youths who volunteer may engage in graffiti removal projects.

informal processing out of the system at an early stage. In addition, community-based residential correctional programs, such as foster care and group homes, try to normalize social contacts, reduce the stigma of being institutionalized and provide opportunities for jobs and schooling. These environments, it is anticipated, will allow youths to continue maturing and developing prosocially while also attempting to treat or correct the deviant behavior that brought them into contact with the juvenile justice system.

 Isolating offenders from their normal social environments may encourage developing a delinquent orientation and, thus, further delinquent behavior.

The Juvenile Residential Facility Census (JRFC) collected data in 2002 from 3,534 juvenile facilities, 2,964 of which held a total of 102,388 offenders younger than 21 on the census date (570 facilities reported no juvenile offenders) (Sickmund, 2006). The five major categories of nonsecure residential programs are shelters, group homes, foster homes, foster group homes and other types of nonsecure facilities.

A *shelter* is a nonsecure residential facility where juveniles may be temporarily assigned, often in place of detention or returning home, after they are taken into custody or after adjudication while they await more permanent placement. Shelters usually house status offenders and are not intended for treatment or punishment.

A *group home* is a nonsecure facility with a professional corrections staff that provides counseling, education, job training and family-style living. The staff is small because the residence generally holds a maximum of 12 to 15 youths. Group home living provides support and some structure in a basically nonrestrictive setting, with the opportunity for close but controlled interaction with the staff. The youths in the home attend school in the community and participate in community activities. The objective is to facilitate reintegrating young offenders into society.

Group homes are used extensively in almost all states. Some are operated by private agencies under contract to the juvenile court. Others are operated directly by probation departments or some other governmental unit. Some, called boarding homes, deserve special mention. Since these homes often accommodate as few as three or four youths, they can be found in an apartment or flat in an urban setting. They are sometimes called "Mom and Pop" operations because the adults serve as parent substitutes. The adults are usually paraprofessionals whose strengths are personal warmth and an ability to relate to young people.

A *foster home* is intended to be family-like, as much as possible a substitute for a natural family setting. Small and nonsecure, foster homes are used at any of several stages in the juvenile justice process. In jurisdictions where a juvenile shelter is not available, foster homes may be used when law enforcement authorities take a juvenile into custody.

Foster care is used less for misbehaving and delinquent children than it is for children whose parents have neglected, abused or abandoned them. Social service agencies usually handle placement in and funding of foster care programs. The police and courts coordinate their efforts through these agencies.

PROGRAMS IN PRACTICE

The Colorado Boys Ranch (CBR) *Youth Connect* is a private, non-sectarian, nonprofit organization providing residential mental health services, education, and prevocational and vocational training for males 10–21 years old. Its mission is to achieve excellence in providing troubled youths with the means to become hopeful, productive citizens. All treatment is *customized* and designed to fit the unique mental health needs of each client. All treatment begins where the youth is cognitively and emotionally and proceeds at his pace (*empowerment*). Treatment offers the typical skills training (assertiveness, stress reduction, sensitivity, relationships training and the like), but CBR *Youth Connect* also provides "real-life" learning opportunities including banking programs, college credits, horsemanship programs, small animals therapy and horticulture.

Among *Youth Connect*'s most important components is its planned aftercare and discharge, a stage that is considered up-front at the time of admission. This individualized planning

incorporates a continuum of care based on individual needs and also focuses on the coordination of health care professionals and organizations, including the primary aftercare agency and persons providing or directing the services; the primary educational resources and recommendations; recommendations and arrangements for transition care and treatment; and appropriate prescribed medications, psychotherapy recommendations, and job training and community recreation. Aftercare and discharge plans are made collaboratively by youths, family, clinicians, referral sources, mental health centers and placement facilities. "We wrap a support system around the youth and family with the goal of restoring unity and giving them resources to move forward in life" (*CBR Youth Connect*).

SOURCE: *CBR Youth Connect*. 28071 Hwy 109, P.O. Box 681, La Junda, CO 81050. Online: http://www.cbryouthconnect.org.

A *foster group home* is a blend of group home and foster home. Foster group homes are run by single families, not professional staffs. They are nonsecure facilities usually acceptable to neighborhood environments that can give troubled youths a family-neighborhood type relationship. Foster group homes can be found in various parts of the United States.

Other nonsecure facilities include correctional farms, ranches and camps for youths, which are usually located in rural areas. These facilities are alternatives to confinement or regimented programs. The programs with an outdoor or rural setting encourage self-development, provide opportunities for reform and secure classification and placement of juveniles according to their capabilities. Close contact with staff and residents instills good work habits.

Nonresidential Day Treatment Alternatives

Many state and local governments are turning to nonresidential day treatment for delinquent juveniles because it appears to be effective and is less costly than residential care: "Day treatment facilities (also known as day reporting centers) are highly structured, community-based, post-adjudication, nonresidential programs for serious juvenile offenders. The goal of day treatment is to provide both intensive supervision to ensure community safety and a wide range of services to the offender to prevent future delinquent behavior" (*Promising Sanctioning Programs*, 2003, p.4).

Nonresidential day treatment corrections programs can take a variety of forms, such as community supervision, family crisis counseling, proctor programs and service-oriented programs, including recreational programs, counseling, alternative schools, employment training programs, and homemaking and financial planning classes. Other alternatives might include evening and weekend reporting centers, school programs and specialized treatment facilities.

Such programs can provide education, tutoring, counseling, community service, vocational training and social/recreational events.

Day treatment programs tend to succeed because they can focus on the family unit and the youth's behavior in the family and the community. They are also effective from a legal standpoint in states that require that youths be treated in the least restrictive environment possible.

Alternative Schools/Education   A variety of alternative education programs have been developed to serve vulnerable youths, including children with disabilities and those who drop out or are "pushed" out of traditional K–12 schools (or are at risk of either). The term alternative education refers to all educational programs that fall outside the traditional K–12 school system. The programs can be physically located in many different places, and sometimes the location is what makes the program "alternative" (e.g., in a juvenile justice center).

Alternative education program settings include (in order of distance from traditional classrooms in regular K–12 schools): resource rooms (separate room/teacher provides additional services like study skills, guidance, anger management, small group/individual instruction); a school-within-a-school; and, finally, pull-out programs, which can be run from a storefront, community center or former school and can include schools/programs within the juvenile justice system (detention, corrections, etc.) or a homeless services system (emergency and transitional shelters). These programs may be administered by any one of a variety of organizations including community-based organizations (CBOs), school districts, adult education divisions, state departments of juvenile justice, charter schools and, in the case of Job Corps, contractors to the U.S. Department of Labor.

Type and quality of alternative education programs vary. Most offer high school or General Educational Development (GED) diplomas. They can differ from traditional schools by having flexible hours and schedules, open admission and exit policies, and individualized instruction, often connected to employment. Alternative schools serve the dual purpose of reinforcing the message that students are accountable for their offenses and removing disruptive students from the mainstream.

Electronic Monitoring and Home Detention

Electronic monitoring (EM) requires offenders to wear bracelets or ankle cuffs that tell probation officers where the juveniles are. EM has been tried with some success in numerous jurisdictions and is sometimes a key component in intensive probation and parole programs. Electronic monitoring can be used to impose curfew, home detention (more restrictive than curfew, the offender must be home except when at work or at treatment) or home incarceration (the offender must be at home almost all the time).

Use of EM has grown considerably. Electronic monitoring is a supervision tool that can satisfy punishment, public safety and treatment objectives by providing cost-effective community supervision for offenders selected according to specific program criteria; promoting public safety through active surveillance; and increasing the confidence of legislative, judicial and releasing authorities in intensive supervision probation or parole program designs as a viable sentencing option.

Electronic monitoring is frequently used in conjunction with home incarceration (house arrest). Youths under such sentences are allowed to leave their homes for specific reasons, such as meeting with their probation officer, attending a treatment program or going to the doctor. The two general types of home confinement are pretrial and post-adjudication. Pretrial programs use home confinement as an alternative to detention to ensure that juveniles appear in court. Post-adjudication programs use home confinement as a more severe sanction than intensive supervision but less restrictive than incarceration.

Training Schools

Training schools exist in every state except Massachusetts, which abolished them in the 1970s. They vary greatly in size, staff, service programs, ages and types of residents. Some training schools resemble adult prisons, with the same distinguishing problems of gang-oriented activity, homosexual terrorism and victimization, which often lead to progressive difficulties or suicide.

Most legislation requires training schools to provide both safe custody and rehabilitative treatment. A 1983 federal court case, however, rejected the idea of a constitutional right to treatment and training: "We therefore agree . . . that, although rehabilitative training is no doubt desirable and sound as policy and perhaps of state law, plaintiffs have no constitutional right to rehabilitative training" (*Santana v. Collazo*, 1983). Treatment was discussed in Chapter 9.

Boot Camps

Juvenile boot camps are fundamentally the same as those for adults. Also known as **shock incarceration**, a **boot camp** stresses military discipline, physical fitness and strict obedience to orders, as well as educational and vocational training and drug treatment when appropriate. Most boot camps are designed for young, nonviolent, first-time offenders as a means of punishment and rehabilitation without long-term incarceration. Furthermore, offender consent is required for placement in shock incarceration.

Many offenders entering a boot camp lack basic life skills, are in poor physical condition, have quit school and have had frequent encounters with the justice system. Their self-esteem is low, and they are seen as losers. Young offenders' false sense of pride must be stripped away before positive changes can be made. This is a primary function of boot camps, just as it is in a military boot camp. The camps are intended to provide a foundation of discipline, responsibility and self-esteem to be built on.

More than a dozen states and the federal system currently operate at least one boot camp. Earlier editions of this text presented boot camps in a more promising light, for when they were first implemented in the early 1980s, there were high hopes that these "get tough" facilities could help turn delinquent kids around and put them on track for a more disciplined, law-abiding way of life. However, after several decades of implementation and numerous studies examining how boot camp graduates fared following release, a growing body

© Joel Stettenheim/CORBIS

Boot camp inmates display their utensils after eating. The Massachusetts "Boot Camp"
Facility is an alternative to incarceration for nonviolent offenders.

of contradictory evidence has accumulated. To date, results remain mixed, with some studies showing positive effects, others negative, and others nil.

Bottcher and Ezell (2005, p.309) examined long-term follow-up arrest patterns for juvenile boot camp participants and comparable youths who experience traditional incarceration. Juveniles committed to the California Youth Authority were randomly assigned to either a boot cap or to normal custody and parole. The findings indicated there were no significant differences in recidivism between the groups in terms of time to first rearrest or average rearrest frequency.

Research by Kurlychek and Kempinen (2007, p.42) found that adding a residential aftercare component for boot camp graduates improved the outcomes. Following graduation from Pennsylvania's Motivational Boot Camp, juveniles were required to complete a mandatory 90-day residential aftercare component: "One and two years after release, offenders who participated in aftercare had significantly lower recidivism rates than the control group. The two-year re-arrest rate for the boot camp graduates improved the outcomes. Two-year re-arrest rate for the experimental group was approximately equal to the one-year re-arrest rate for the control group. The results suggest that an aftercare program can ease the transition from the highly regimented boot camp environment to the community." Other studies have suggested that failure of boot camps to reduce recidivism might be a product of "low dosage effect," or the fact that the programs are too short in actual implementation, often only 90 days in duration, to have any significant long-term impacts.

Although no doubt exists that some programs are well structured and achieve success in reducing offender recidivism, more than a handful have been found to not only *not* reduce juvenile offending but to actually exacerbate

IN THE HEADLINES

"Boy, 14, Tells of Boot Camp Beatings."

A boy who says he witnessed the beating of Martin Lee Anderson recalled what he saw and heard at the Panama City boot camp.

By Marc Caputo, *Miami Herald*, February 26, 2006.

The screaming guards. The pressure points. The knee takedowns. The acrid ammonia stick shoved in the face of a rubber-legged 14-year-old named Martin Lee Anderson. Aaron Swartz can't forget any of it. Not because he saw it all the way most people did—in a grainy videotape of the guards and Martin before his death—but because Aaron was there, at Bay County Boot Camp, receiving much of the same violent treatment that still makes him shudder miles away from it all.

"They killed that boy. They didn't help him. They beat him,"' Aaron, also 14, told *The Miami Herald* in one of the first eyewitness—and earwitness—accounts of the dehumanizing experience of life at the Panama City lockup before, during and after Martin's arrival. Like every kid who's about to enter the Bay Boot Camp, Aaron said Martin lost his first name. From the moment he arrived Jan. 5, he was called "Offender Anderson," just like Aaron was "Offender Swartz." Actually, the names—and slurs and everything else—were screamed at them by "drill instructors," [or DIs], who slammed boys against concrete walls, shoved their thumbs in a painful pressure point behind their ears, and forced them to respond with a "Sir, yes sir!"

And just like every kid's hair, Martin's braids were shaved off aggressively by a mocking DI. It was there, as Martin sat in the barber chair, that Aaron first saw him. And Martin had the look: "scared, like everybody else," Aaron said. As Aaron tells it, time at the camp was measured in fear and pain, in increments of forced exercise, wall-slams, pressure points, knee takedowns and hammer-fist punches by DIs who video-taped it all. When the boys would go to bed, he said, they could hear the DIs watching the tapes in a nearby room, cheering on their greatest hits as if watching a sporting event.

And what atrocity had young Martin committed that gave DIs the authority to brutalize and demean him—treatments that would have landed any parent or caretaker behind bars—and that ultimately cost him his life? Martin was sent to the boot camp for violating probation, for stealing his grandmother's car and trespassing at school.

While not the first of such custodial deaths, Martin's case was the most recent to gain widespread publicity and focus harsh criticism toward the military structure of juvenile boot camps. In June 2006, Florida governor Jeb Bush signed into law the "Martin Lee Anderson Act," replacing the boot camp model used by five state facilities with STAR, a less-militaristic program that prohibits physical intervention against juvenile inmates.

---

delinquency and criminality in those who pass through them. Furthermore, investigations of several facilities have revealed how prevalent abuse of youth can be in these settings. In fact, the death of a 14-year-old at one of Florida's boot camps in 2006 led to a statewide moratorium on the use of such facilities.

Indeed, there has been a shift away from the militarized style of boot camps, toward a paradigm that emphasizes cognitive restructuring and greater attention to educational and vocational programming. Such a shift does seem to enhance the effectiveness of this correctional alternative for youthful offenders.

While boot camps, training schools and other residential facilities are certainly "custodial," in the sense offenders live there, if only briefly, and are not free to leave at will, these intermediate sanctions are generally used only for relatively short time periods (such as boot camps) and/or are nonsecure, meaning the offenders are not kept locked in (as with foster homes and the like). Recall that such intermediate sanctions are also typically reserved for first-time, nonviolent offenders. For a small percentage of juveniles, such intermediate sanctions are judged an inappropriate alternative for the severity of their offense or their extensive criminal history, and these youths are placed in long-term secure correctional institutions.

Institutionalization: Long-Term Secure Confinement

Juvenile offenders are placed in a variety of correctional institutions, often alongside adult offenders. Some of the most secure institutions are merely storage facilities for juvenile offenders. Here juvenile delinquents often simply "do their time," with release based on conditions of overcrowding and, amazingly, the system's inability to rehabilitate the offender. Such nonconstructive time, when juveniles should be developing their values and planning their futures, can be devastating. Although lockups may be needed for chronic, violent offenders, these facilities often serve as criminal training schools for juveniles. Table 11.2 summarizes respondents' views on what the emphasis should be, and is, in juvenile prisons.

Public versus Private Institutions

An investigation of the characteristics of inmates of public long-term juvenile institutions shows a pattern not unlike that of America's jails and prisons. The disadvantaged and the poor make up a large percentage of the population. In

Table 11.2 Respondents' Views on What Is and What Should Be the Main Emphasis in Juvenile Prisons and the Amount of Importance Placed on Each (in percentages)

A. Main Emphasis of Juvenile Prisons

Goals of Imprisonment	Is	Should Be
Rehabilitation: Do you think the main emphasis in juvenile prison is [should be] to try and rehabilitate the adolescent so that he might return to society as a productive citizen?	29.4	63.3
Punishment: Do you think the main emphasis in juvenile prison is [should be] to punish the adolescent convicted of a crime?	16.8	18.7
Protection: Do you think the main emphasis in juvenile prison is [should be] to protect society from future crime he might commit?	17.6	11.2
Not sure	36.1	6.7

B. Importance of Goals of Juvenile Institutions

Goals of Imprisonment	Very Important	Important	A Little Important	Not Very Important
Rehabilitation	64.5	30.0	4.3	1.1
Punishment	42.5	52.1	4.3	1.1
Protection	43.2	47.0	8.4	1.3

SOURCE: Melissa M. Moon, Jody L. Sundt, Francis T. Cullen and John Paul Wright. "Is Child Saving Dead? Public Support for Juvenile Rehabilitation." *Crime & Delinquency*, January 2000, p.26. Reprinted by permission of Sage Publications, Inc.

addition, disproportionate minority confinement (DMC) is common. Public facilities hold the majority of delinquent offenders and, thus, drive the trend for delinquency populations.

Private facilities, in contrast, drive the trend for status offender populations (Snyder and Sickmund, 2006, p.199). Whereas the private institutions of an earlier period were products of philanthropic or religious impulse, the newer ones result from a more economic, entrepreneurial drive. From the earliest days, private institutions attracted more youths from affluent backgrounds than did public institutions. Many newer private institutions have chosen to emphasize their mental health and drug treatment programs. In this way they can capitalize on young people from families who have medical insurance or who can pay their children's confinement and treatment costs. Private institutions may offer greater diversity in programs and structures than public institutions. They also may have very strict rules.

 Compared with public correctional institutions, private correctional institutions confine more Whites, more girls and more status offenders. The inmates are younger, and their stay is usually longer.

Social Structure within Correctional Institutions

Correctional institutions—whether high- or low-security, locked or unlocked, public or private, sexually integrated or segregated—often have an elaborate informal social organization and culture. The social organization includes a prestige hierarchy among inmates and a variety of inmate social roles. The inmate culture includes a complex of norms that indicate how inmates should relate to one another, to staff members and to the institutional regimen.

 The sociopolitical climate that exists in juvenile correctional institutions is the same as that found in adult institutions.

Despite the diverse ideologies and strategies pursued by correctional institutions, to a great extent they all generate an underlife that includes an informal social organization and an inmate code. While they are confined, youths are immersed in a culture that defines the institution, its staff and many of its programs in negative terms. This perspective does not lend itself to seeing the institution as benefiting the "best interests" of the youths.

The Impact of Incarceration

The negative effects of incarceration were introduced in Chapter 10. Numerous studies have found that the negative impacts of juvenile institutionalization commonly persist into adulthood. Results of one longitudinal study show that having been institutionalized as an adolescent significantly compromises multiple life domains in adulthood, especially for females (Lanctot et al., 2007).

Challenges Facing Juvenile Correctional Facilities

Major challenges in juvenile correctional facilities include overcrowding, violence, sexual assault, the problem of prison gangs and the specific needs of female offenders.

Overcrowding   Facility crowding affects a substantial proportion of youths in custody: "In 2002, 35 percent of facilities responding said that the number of residents they held on the census date put them at or over the capacity of their standard beds or that they relied on some makeshift beds. These facilities held more than 39,300 residents" (Snyder and Sickmund, 2006, p.223). *Conditions of Confinement* (n.d.) notes: "Crowding has an impact through a facility, making it difficult to provide adequate medical and mental health services, education and recreation. Crowding also raises the tension level between youths and staff and leads to increased use of isolation and restraints. It may also lead to increased violence and assaults."

Violence and Assaults   Confinement that subjects inmates to assaults and threats of violence is considered cruel and unusual punishment by some states. **Cruel and unusual punishment** is physical punishment or punishment far in excess of that given to a person under similar circumstances and, therefore, banned by the Eighth Amendment. Juveniles who are victims of assaults by other inmates may sue for violation of their right to be reasonably protected from violence in the facility.

Further, if juveniles are kept in isolation (segregation) to protect them from assault, they may nevertheless suffer sufficient sensory deprivation and psychological damage to violate their constitutional rights. Confinement in isolation often leads to the ultimate self-destruction—suicide.

Limited research suggests that younger inmates tend to assault others more than older inmates (Vivian et al., 2007, p.17). Such violence also tends to be more respected and even promoted by some staffs' failure to address or punish aggression by juvenile inmates. Some studies have found that inmates assault others to achieve higher status, reassure peers of their competence in the correctional environment and for defensive purposes. Most documented assaults in 2006 involved juveniles assaulting juveniles (46 percent), followed by mutually instigated fights (29 percent) and staff assaulted by juveniles (24 percent) (Vivian et al.). Actual assault cases tended to involve juveniles with higher numbers of referrals to separation, those who had two or more prior assault offenses and those with mental instabilities. Contextual factors that predicted escalation of an incident into an injury assault included placing youth in housing units that were either in the top quartile of separation rates or in the top quartile of assault rates (Vivian et al.).

Stickrath and Wallis (2007) describe the Ohio Department of Youth Services (DYS) plan for reducing aggression in juvenile facilities through a curriculum designed to build the skills needed to provide youths with behaviorally and emotionally appropriate alternatives to "fight or flight." The plan relies on in-service and preservice training of employees as well as multiple levels of staff in conflict resolution, defined as "a spectrum of processes that use communication skills and creative and analytic thinking to prevent, manage and peacefully resolve conflict." These conflict resolutions skills are then taught to youths, providing a common language for understanding conflict, expressing emotions (especially anger), interpreting nonverbal and verbal communication and engaging in problem solving to develop solutions.

Sexual Assault   In 2004, 2,821 sexual violence allegations were reported in juvenile correctional facilities, 30 percent of which were substantiated (Snyder and Sickmund, 2006, p.230). Local and private juvenile facilities reported more incidents than state-operated facilities. Such violence toward youth represents a gross failure of juvenile institutions to protect their wards. Roush (2008, p.32) suggests that three factors seem to play a role in all such occurrences: (1) an insufficient number of staff to provide adequate supervision, (2) an inadequate amount of relevant training to prepare workers to supervise competently and (3) the inability to screen out those adults who want to work with troubled and vulnerable youths for the wrong reasons.

Asbridge (2007, p.80) stresses: "Sexual assault—both youth-on-youth and staff-on-youth—in juvenile correctional settings is a problem that cannot be ignored." Asbridge (p.84) suggests the following strategies to address this situation: examine existing mechanisms for youths to report sexual assault by staff or other youths, talk frequently with staff and youths under their care, critically evaluate existing procedures for investigating juvenile complaints, ensure procedures are in place to provide the appropriate medical care for sexual assault victims, assess the supervision schemes used at the facility and ensure a strong network of policies and procedures built around best practices.

The dual relationships that staff in juvenile facilities have with youthful inmates, in which a professional relationship co-occurs with a social one, can be a highly troublesome issue (Roush, p.33). To prevent a dangerous interaction, agencies should strengthen appropriate formal structures such as good policies and procedures, and good recruitment, selection and orientation of new staff; zero-tolerance disciplinary procedures; and informal structures such as good, clear definitions of misconduct, training on expected practices and good supervision of staff (Roush). The institution might insist on uniforms, or at least a dress code, for staff; forbid profanity (staff may use the profane language of the streets to relate to offenders); and strengthen resident privacy. Two universal policies should be part of every institutional policy and procedure manual: (1) sexual contact between staff and youths is always forbidden and illegal, and anyone violating this policy will be fired and prosecuted; and (2) any person who fails to report known or suspected incidences of child sexual abuse will be fired and prosecuted (Roush).

The Prison Rape Elimination Act (PREA) of 2003 requires "the training of correctional staff sufficient to ensure that they understand and appreciate the significance of prison rape and the necessity of its eradication." PREA policies address the issue of prison rape from the perspective of staff and youths in custody, with a focus on raising staff awareness of "red flags" indicative of sexual misconduct, institutional culture and the importance of professionalism to create an atmosphere where youths feel comfortable reporting incidents of sexual misconduct to staff (Pihl-Buckley, 2008, p.44). It is vital for staff to recognize and understand that a professional dress code and appearance, as well as a use of respectful language, significantly affects their impact as role models for youths.

Prison Gangs   Prison gangs are quite different from the street gangs described in Chapter 7. Prison gangs rely on anonymity, whereas street gangs thrive on notoriety. Street gang members are usually undisciplined and not so-phisticated enough to fit into a prison gang until they have been through the entire juvenile justice system.

Although juvenile prison gangs are not a ubiquitous problem for every correctional facility, and some administrations have done an admirable job of separating gang members at intake and promptly quelling any type of inmate organization that suggests gang activity, for some institutions, gangs have a strong foothold and have proven extremely difficult to eradicate. In these facilities, gangs are responsible for causing numerous other problems, such as bullying, gambling, extortion of food and the imposition of other "taxes" on non-gang-affiliated inmates. Some youth report they fear leaving their cells for treatment and education programs because of intimidation or assault risks posed by gang members.

Juvenile Females in Corrections   Girls involved in the juvenile justice system bring unique challenges not as commonly found among the male offender population, such as higher rates of depression, lower self-esteem and a greater tendency to attempt suicide; more acute substance abuse treatment needs; and extraordinarily high levels of abuse and trauma (*Mental Health and Adolescent Girls in the Justice System*, 2003, pp.1–2): "Juvenile justice systems need to develop specific programs for girls that focus on building relationships and addressing victimization and improving self-esteem. Adolescent girls have multiple and unique programming needs, including health care, education, mental health treatment, mutual support and mentoring opportunities, prenatal care and parenting skills, substance abuse prevention and treatment, job training and family support-strengthening services."

Morton (2007, p.6) offers six guiding principles to ensure that correctional agencies provide gender-responsive management, supervision and treatment services for women and girls:

1. Acknowledge that being female makes a difference.
2. Create an environment based on safety, respect and dignity.
3. Develop policies, practices and programs incorporating the fact that women are relationship-oriented.
4. Address substance abuse, trauma and mental health issues in a comprehensive, integrated and culturally relevant manner.
5. Provide women an opportunity to improve their socioeconomic status.
6. Establish a system of community supervision and re-entry with comprehensive, collaborative services.

Many facilities were built with a "default" male population in mind, and even minor structural elements have been found to make a significant difference in how well female inmates cope in such environments. For example, modifications such as adding curtains to windows or, in bathrooms, additional toilet stalls, sinks, mirrors and outlets for blow dryers can go far toward lowering inmate stress, which can ultimately reduce violence levels or other incidents among adolescent females (Zavlek and Maniglia, 2007, p.59). Another consideration is the differing nutritional needs of adolescent girls versus boys. The food served to female inmates, which often is identical to that fed to their male counterparts—equal in calories, carbohydrates and sugars—might be altered. Simply adding a salad bar could have a significant positive impact (Zavlek and Maniglia, p.62).

Improving Conditions of Confinement

In 1980 Congress enacted the Civil Rights of Institutionalized Persons Act (CRIPA) to help eradicate unlawful conditions of confinement for juveniles held in correctional facilities. Through CRIPA the Department of Justice is authorized to bring action against state or local governments for violating the civil rights of any person institutionalized in a publicly operated facility.

Another way to improve confinement conditions and to protect the rights of youths in custody is to establish **ombuds** programs. Ombuds can monitor conditions, investigate complaints, report findings, propose changes, advocate for improvements, and help expose and reduce deficiencies in juvenile detention and correctional facilities.

Perhaps most important is setting standards, with particular emphasis on those performance-based standards with proven records of success or those otherwise identified as meeting "best practices" criteria.

 The performance-based standards goals for corrections cover security, order, safety, programming, justice and health/mental health.

- *Security:* To protect public safety and provide a safe environment for youths and staff. Security is essential for effective learning and treatment.
- *Order:* To establish clear expectations of behavior and an accompanying system of accountability for youths and staff that promotes mutual respect, self-discipline and order.
- *Safety:* To engage in management practices that promote the safety and well-being of staff and youths.
- *Programming:* To provide meaningful opportunities for youths to improve their educational and vocational competence, address underlying behavioral problems and prepare for responsible lives in the community.
- *Justice:* To operate the facility in a manner that is consistent with principles of fairness and that provides ways to ensure and protect the legal rights of youths and their families.
- *Health/Mental Health:* To identify and effectively respond to youths' physical and mental health problems and related behavioral problems throughout the course of confinement by using professionally appropriate diagnostic, treatment and prevention methods.

Achieving Effective Correctional Programs for Youth

Many youthful offender programs use a point system of rewards and consequences operating on four levels and in four areas: security, school, work and therapy. Positive behavioral interventions and support (PBIS) are long-term problem-solving strategies to reduce inappropriate behavior, teach more appropriate behavior and provide support. PBIS emerged in the early 1980s as an alternative to traditional behavioral approaches for students with severe disabilities who engaged in extreme forms of self-injury and aggression. Since then it has evolved into an approach used with a wide range of students, with and without disabilities.

 Most effective youthful offender programs include in-depth evaluation, screening and assessment; daily scheduling; point system discipline; positive behavioral support therapy; and education, including literacy, GED preparation and computer literacy.

Caldwell et al. (2006, p.148) examined the costs and benefits of an intensive treatment program for violent juvenile delinquent boys compared to the typical treatment provided in a secured juvenile corrections facility: "Outcome data indicated the initial costs of the intensive treatment program were more than offset by improved treatment progress and lowered recidivism. These results are consistent with those from other research that has found a beneficial impact from treating serious and violent offenders, and this study also illustrates the importance of considering longer-term outcomes in assessing the costs and benefits of treatment programs."

Their research found that the treatment group's total time incarcerated was significantly shorter and that youths in the matched comparison group averaged more than twice the number of total charged offenses in the follow-up period, and more than three times the number of violent offenses. Finally, although their study had a daily bed cost more than double that of the usual correctional program, the shorter treatment time and lowered recidivism rates resulted in criminal justice costs substantially lower than usual: "In total, the mean-per-youth cost for the comparison group was over $216,000, whereas the figure for the youths receiving the intensive treatment program was $173,000, meaning the net treatment group costs averaged 20 percent less than the comparison group."

A National Institute of Corrections (NIC) training program called *Youthful Offenders in Adult Corrections: A Systemic Approach Using Effective Interventions* is based on three primary principles that have emerged from research: risk, need and responsivity (Shomaker and Gornik, 2002, p.123): "The **risk principle** embodies the assumption that criminal behavior can be predicted for individual offenders on the basis of certain factors. Some factors, such as criminal history, are static and unchangeable. Others, such as substance abuse, anti-social attitudes and anti-social associates, are dynamic and changeable. With proper assessment of these factors, researchers and practitioners have demonstrated that it is possible to classify offenders according to their relative likelihood of committing new offenses with as much as 80 percent accuracy." Recall dynamic and static risk factors were introduced in Chapter 9 in the discussion on effective treatment interventions.

The **criminogenic need principle** is explained thusly: "Most offenders have myriad needs. However, certain needs are directly linked to crime. Criminogenic needs constitute dynamic risk factors or attributes that, when changed, influence the probability of recidivism. Non-criminogenic needs also may be dynamic and changeable, but they are not directly associated with new offense behavior" (Shomaker and Gornik). And thirdly, "The **responsivity principle** refers to the delivery of treatment programs in a manner that is consistent with the ability and learning style of an offender."

To summarize, the NIC's training program applies the risk principle to identify *who* should receive treatment, the criminogenic need principle to focus on *what* should be treated, and the responsivity principle to determine *how* treatment should be delivered.

In addition to intensive treatment for mental health issues, substance abuse problems and behavior problems, education is critically important within juvenile correctional facilities.

Education   Research evidence has shown that increased educational attainment plays a significant role in reducing juvenile recidivism: "The majority of students are at least two grade levels behind peers of the same age, and many have dramatic gaps between their chronological age and expected skills and knowledge" (Conlon et al., 2008, p.49). Individualized education programs (IEPs), as applied to youth in confinement facilities, are now governed by three pieces of federal legislation: the No Child Left Behind (NCLB) Act of 2001, the Individuals with Disabilities Education Improvement Act (IDEA) of 2004, and the Family Educational Rights and Privacy Act (FERPA). All personnel working in juvenile correctional facilities should know the provisions of these three pieces of legislation (Brooks, 2008, p.28).

Table 11.3 outlines characteristics of successful education programs in secure facilities.

Brooks (p.46) points out: "Confinement education programs are unique education programs—certainly different from the public school systems the lawmakers had in mind. This uniqueness requires innovative solutions and broad interpretations of the guiding principles of the legislation governing the delivery of educational services in confinement settings." However, given the many

Table 11.3   Characteristics of Successful Education Programs in Secure Facilities

- Administrators regard education as a vital part of the rehabilitation process.
- Programs help students develop competencies in basic reading, writing and math skills, along with thinking and decision-making skills and character development traits, such as responsibility and honesty.
- Student/teacher ratios reflect the needs of the students.
- Academic achievement is reinforced through incremental incentives.
- Teachers are competent, committed and trained in current research and teaching methods, rather than relying on old model drill and workbook exercises.
- Instruction involves multiple strategies appropriate to each learner's interests and needs.
- Youths are assessed for learning disabilities and provided with special education in full compliance with federal law.
- When appropriate, parents, community organizations and volunteers are involved in the academic program.
- Opportunities exist for on-the-job training, work experience and mentorships.
- Partnerships are developed with potential employers.
- Students are scheduled for jobs and further education prior to re-entry into the community.

SOURCE: *Abandoned in the Back Row: New Lessons in Education and Delinquency Prevention.* Washington, DC: Coalition for Juvenile Justice, 2001, pp.30–31.

educational and psychological challenges facing incarcerated students, retaining juvenile justice teachers is difficult: "Maintaining a qualified teacher work force is one of the most significant challenges in correctional education. One of the greatest frustrations of teachers in this situation is lack of resources, including out-dated textbooks and the need for more supplies and materials. In addition, they want to implement a sound, consistent behavior management system to reward students for good behavior and for making amends for unacceptable behavior, perhaps based on a point system. Finally, they want to be involved in the change process, wanting more input and involvement in the education program" (O'Rourke et al., pp.42–43).

Juveniles Sentenced to Adult Institutions

Meyer (2008, p.19) contends: "Our country's biggest law and order issue is not what is happening on the streets of our cities but, instead, what is not happening in our prisons. The counseling, educational and vocational services absent in many adult prisons are far more abundant in juvenile facilities." Research by Kupchik (2007, p.247) found that relative to adult facilities, juvenile facilities are generally smaller, have much lower inmate-to-staff ratios and place greater emphasis (in their official guidelines) on treatment, counseling, education and mentoring of inmates. Yet, every year, many juveniles are sentenced to serve time in adult facilities. Youth offenders housed in adult jails and prisons are more likely to commit suicide, to be sexually assaulted, to be beaten by staff and to be attacked with a weapon compared to youthful offenders housed in juvenile facilities.

Whether incarcerated in a juvenile or adult facility, most youths at some point are eligible for release, often through parole or, as it is now commonly called, re-entry or aftercare.

A DEBATE: HOUSING JUVENILES IN ADULT FACILITIES

A critical shortage of secure space for violent juvenile offenders has led to fervent debate between those who support and those who oppose housing juveniles in adult facilities. Advocates of juveniles in adult facilities believe we can no longer tolerate young people who commit violent crimes simply because of their age. Youths who choose to prey on other juveniles, senior citizens, businesspeople or homeowners must be held responsible. If that choice results in incarceration, perhaps youths who commit violent crimes will think twice before acting.

On the opposite side of the debate is the president and CEO of the Child Welfare League of America, Shay Bilchik (2003, p.21): "This country's laws recognize that juveniles are too young to drink alcohol, vote, engage in legal contracts and enter into marriage, all because they are still developing mentally and emotionally. Legislators created the juvenile justice system based on the belief that youths have much to learn, with the hope that early interventions might alter the path that youths pursue. . . . Too many communities are failing to determine which

offenders are beyond the reach of the juvenile justice system and failing to provide programs to hold those youths accountable in a timely manner, for the duration and intensity needed. As we increasingly transfer juveniles blindly, we are failing both our youths and our communities."

Confinement that subjects inmates to assaults and threats of violence is considered cruel and unusual punishment by some states. The impact of incarceration on juveniles often conflicts with the purpose of the juvenile justice system, which was created to remove children from the punitive forces of the criminal justice system. Exposing juveniles to coercive institutional conditions may jeopardize their emotional and physical well-being.

Recall that one provision of the JJDP Act was that status offenders and nonoffenders (youths who are abused or neglected) should be removed from juvenile detention and correctional facilities. It further mandated that when youths are detained in the same facilities as adults, they are to be completely segregated.

Re-Entry

Historically, the term **parole** has been used to describe the planned, supervised early release from institutionalization authorized by the correctional facility. Recently, **re-entry** has gained prominence in the field as the preferred term used to describe the process of transitioning youthful offenders from secure custody back into the community. Alternately, **aftercare**—the supervision of youths for a limited time after they are released from a correctional facility but while they are still under the control of the facility or the juvenile court—can also apply to this process previously called *parole*. All three terms are used interchangeably. However, the entities responsible for overseeing this process generally still go by the names *parole agencies* and *parole officers*.

Parole is unlike probation in both authority and concept. Probation can be granted only by the juvenile court and is subject to the court's stipulations. It provides the individual with freedom and continuity within the community. Parole, on the other hand, is a release from confinement issued by the correctional facility or a board on a recommendation by the correctional facility. Parole or re-entry follows some period of incarceration, whereas probation is an alternative to incarceration. Each state has its own procedures for parole, as do federal corrections. In Minnesota, for example, the Department of Corrections parole agents supervise juveniles sentenced to a correctional facility. The release of a juvenile from a correctional institution is the responsibility of a juvenile hearing officer, who uses a scale incorporating both the offense's severity and the delinquent's history.

After returning to the community, the youth is supervised by a parole officer or by a probation officer given that responsibility. The juvenile is required to abide by a set of rules, which, if violated, can return the youth to a locked or secure facility. The conditions under which a typical juvenile parole agreement is granted include obeying all federal, state and local laws and ordinances; obtaining approval before purchasing or using any motor vehicle, borrowing money, going into debt, doing any credit or installment buying, changing residence, changing employment, changing vocational or school programs or getting married; obtaining permission before leaving the state for any reason; keeping in close contact with the supervising agent; not possessing or using narcotics or other drugs except those prescribed by a physician; and not purchasing or otherwise obtaining any type of firearm or dangerous weapon.

The parole officer makes regular contacts and visits to the youth's residence, school or place of employment. One objective is to involve the family, school and community in helping the youth rehabilitate and integrate back into the community. This is also the goal of probation officers.

Unfortunately, the release and community return aspect of offender care is often poorly executed, with many jurisdictions failing to consider what will happen to these youth once they go back to the environments from which they came.

 Re-entry/aftercare is often the weakest element in the juvenile justice process.

Barriers to successful re-entry identified by researchers include lack of housing and educational options, limited interpersonal and life skills and education,

After offenders are released from a correctional facility, they continue to receive support and supervision from probation or parole officers. A crucial part of a re-entry plan is helping offenders find employment. Here a juvenile probation officer works with a client during a mock interview, as they discuss and prepare for the types of questions the youth is likely to encounter during a job interview.

substance abuse and/or mental health problems and lack of community support. The school is a crucial institution in aftercare for many offenders.

Planning for Re-Entry

The *Report of the Re-Entry Policy Council* (2005, pp.xxi–xxiii) sets forth specific details on promoting the safe, successful return of prisoners to the community. Although the report focuses on adults, it includes considerations for juveniles incarcerated in adult facilities, and the principles are equally applicable to juvenile correctional facilities. The basic premise is that planning for re-entry/aftercare should begin as soon as a person is incarcerated and continue through the person's release into the community. Indeed, "The role of correctional institutions in preparing for re-entry begins at intake when a case plan is built based on a validated assessment instrument in conjunction with parole" (Gibson and Duncan, 2008, p.58).

A significant element in the re-entry plan is the development of an individualized programming plan that details the specific treatment needs of the offender during incarceration, including physical and mental health care, substance abuse treatment, cognitive-behavioral therapy to develop positive behaviors and attitudes, education and vocational training and work experience. The plan also includes managing the key transition period including finding housing, providing continuity of care, creating employment opportunities and preparing family members, victims and the community. The report states that successful re-entry planning should ensure that community corrections officers have a range of options available to them to reinforce positive behavior and to address, swiftly and certainly, failure to comply with conditions of release (*Report of the Re-Entry Policy Council*).

Two key components of aftercare are that offenders receive both services and supervision and that offenders receive intensive intervention while they are incarcerated, during their transition to the community and when they are under community supervision (a continuity of treatment) (Gies, 2003, p.1).

 Two key components of aftercare are (1) services and supervision, and (2) intensive intervention while incarcerated, during transition into the community and while under community supervision.

Many juveniles being released from confinement and requiring aftercare come from dysfunctional or abusive homes and must be provided with alternative living arrangements. The types of aftercare that can help youths to transition back into the community include home visits prior to release, a continuation of the treatment program and services within the community, identification of community support systems, availability of 24-hour supervision and a gradual phasing-out of services and supervision based on the youth's response, not on a predetermined schedule. Unfortunately, in many jurisdictions, aftercare is an afterthought.

Table 11.4 summarizes the best and most promising transition practices for youths in custody.

Principles of Intensive Aftercare Programs (IAPs)

More than a decade ago, researchers Altschuler and Armstrong (1994) described an Intensive Aftercare Program (IAP) model designed to make the process of transitioning confined youth back into the community more successful. The IAP model is based on five underlying principles:

1. Preparing youth for progressively increased responsibility and freedom in the community
2. Facilitating youth-community interaction and involvement
3. Working with both the offender and community support systems on qualities needed for constructive interaction and the youth's successful return to the community
4. Developing new resources and supports where needed
5. Monitoring and testing the youth's and the community's ability to work productively together (*Intensive Aftercare Program (IAP)*, n.d.)

Table 11.4 Best and Promising Transition Practices for Youths in Custody

- Staff awareness of and familiarity with all county, state, local and private programs that receive and/or send youths to/from jail, detention centers or long-term correctional facilities.

- To the extent possible, individualized preplacement planning prior to the transfer of youths from jails or detention centers to the community or long-term correctional facilities.

- Immediate transfer of youth's educational records from public and private educational programs to detention centers or from other programs to detention or long-term correctional facilities.

- In short-term detention centers, an extensive diagnostic system for the educational, vocational and social, emotional and behavioral assessment of youths.

- In long-term correctional facilities, a range of specific educational programs (e.g., vocational and job-related skills, social skills, independent living skills and law-related education); support services (e.g., work experience and placement, alcohol and drug abuse counseling, anger management, vocational counseling, health education and training for parenthood); and external resources (e.g., speakers, tutors, mentors, vocational trainers and counselors, drug abuse counselors, employers and volunteers).

- Access to a resource center, which contains a variety of materials related to transition and support.

- Special funds earmarked for transition and support services.

- Regular interagency meetings, cooperative in-service training activities and crossover correctional and community school visits to ensure awareness of youths and agency transition needs.

- A process for the immediate identification, evaluation and placement of youths with disabilities.

- Individualized education program developed for each student with disabilities.

- Individual transition plan developed for all students, which includes the student's educational and vocational interests, abilities and preferences.

- A transition planning team formed immediately upon student entry into a long-term correctional facility to design and implement the individual transition plan.

- Community-based transition system for maintaining student placement and communication after release from a long-term correctional facility.

- Immediate transfer of youth's educational records from detention centers and long-term correctional facilities to community schools or other programs.

- Coordination with probation or parole to ensure a continuum of services and care is provided in the community.

- Coordination between educational program and justice system personnel to ensure that they advocate for youths with disabilities, cultivate family involvement, maintain communications with other agencies and place students in supportive classroom settings.

- A system for periodic evaluations of the transition program and all its components.

SOURCE: National Center on Education, Disability and Juvenile Justice, 2002, pp.179–180.

Recently, efforts have been made to adapt the traditional IAP model for use with girls in the juvenile justice system, incorporating the comprehensive, theoretically grounded approach to re-entry with compatible "best practices" for female juvenile offenders that emphasize individualized treatment plans and consistent relationships throughout the treatment process (Ryder, 2008, p.54). Gender-specific services for girls and young women should be designed to meet female offenders' unique needs, value the female perspective, celebrate the female experience and empower young women to reach their full potential.

Promising Aftercare Programs

Gies (2003, pp.8–24) describes six promising aftercare programs and compares the program characteristics as well as types of services and supervision options after release (see Table 11.5). Note that with one exception, all the programs facilitate transitional structure, use assessment and classification, develop individualized case planning, use rewards and sanctions, link to community services and combine intensive supervision and treatment.

Table 11.5 Comparison of Six Promising Aftercare Programs

	Intensive Aftercare Program	Thomas O'Farrell Youth Center	Bethesda Day Treatment Center	Florida Environmental Institute	Project CRAFT	GROWTH
General Program Information						
Location	Colorado/Nevada/ Virginia	Maryland	Pennsylvania	Florida	Florida/Maryland/ North Dakota/ Tennessee	Alabama
Funding	IAP grant, state funds	Maryland Department of Juvenile Services	Formula grant, private (nonprofit)	Florida Department of Juvenile Justice	CRAFT grant, state funds	Boys & Girls Clubs of South Alabama
Gender	Male	Male	Male/Female	Male	Male/Female	Female
Age	12–18	13–18	10–18	15–18	16–21	13–17
Risk of recidivism	High	High	High	High	High	High
Average length of program	*Colorado:* 10 months' incarceration, 8 months' aftercare *Nevada:* 8 months' incarceration, 8 months' aftercare *Virginia:* 7 months' incarceration, 6 months' aftercare	8 months' incarceration, 9 months' aftercare	6–12 months	9 months' incarceration, 9 months' aftercare	2–12 months	18 weeks' intensive treatment (residential or day treatment), minimum of 6 months' aftercare
Program Characteristics						
Facilitates transitional structure	Yes	Yes	Yes	Yes	Yes	Yes
Uses assessment and classification	Yes	Yes	Yes	No	Yes	Yes
Develops individualized case planning	Yes	No	Yes	Yes	Yes	Yes
Uses rewards and sanctions	Yes	Yes	Yes	Yes	No	Yes
Links to community treatment services	Yes	Yes	Yes	Yes	Yes	Yes
Combines intensive supervision and treatment	Yes	Yes	Yes	Yes	Yes	Yes

(continued)

Table 11.5 *(Continued)*

	Intensive Aftercare Program	Thomas O'Farrell Youth Center	Bethesda Day Treatment Center	Florida Environmental Institute	Project CRAFT	GROWTH
Types of Services and Supervision Options after Release						
Treatment services	■ Education ■ Employment ■ Vocational training ■ Mental health counseling ■ Life skills training ■ Drug/alcohol treatment	■ Education ■ Vocational counseling ■ Crisis intervention ■ Mentoring ■ Family services ■ Transportation	■ Individual, group and family counseling ■ Drug/alcohol treatment ■ Education ■ Life skills development	■ Education ■ Employment ■ Vocational skills ■ Family assistance	■ Employment ■ Drug/alcohol treatment ■ Housing services ■ Family services ■ Vocational training ■ Financial assistance	■ Female-specific life skills ■ Community service ■ Education ■ Functional Family Therapy ■ Adventure therapy ■ Trauma recovery ■ Substance abuse ■ Parenting teen
Supervision options	■ Staff contact (1–5/week) ■ Curfew ■ Urinalysis ■ House arrest ■ Electronic monitoring ■ Paging ■ Monthly court review ■ Day treatment (NV) ■ Furlough (NV) ■ Group home (VA)	■ Staff contact (12/month) ■ Coordination with probation staff ■ Surveillance	■ Intensive supervision program ■ Search and rescue ■ 24-hour crisis hotline ■ Treatment detention accountability	■ Staff contact (4/week) ■ Curfew ■ Required job attendance ■ Frequent calls	■ Coordination with parole and probation officers ■ Community work service ■ Traditional probation and parole	■ Staff contact (weekly empowerment meetings)

SOURCE: Steve V. Gies. *Aftercare Services.* Washington, DC: OJJDP Juvenile Justice Bulletin, September 2003, pp.23–24. (NCJ 201800)

 SUMMARY

■ A modern comprehensive graduated sanctions continuum set includes four components for targeted populations: (1) immediate sanctions within the community for first-time, nonviolent offenders, (2) intermediate sanctions (including probation) within the community for more serious offenders, (3) secure confinement programs for the most violent offenders and (4) re-entry/aftercare programs that provide high levels of social control and treatment services.

■ Probation is the most common disposition of the juvenile court.

■ The formal goals of probation are to protect the public, to hold juveniles accountable for their actions and to improve the delinquents' behavior—in short, rehabilitation.

■ The probation officer has traditionally been responsible for two key functions: (1) personally counseling youths who are on probation and (2) serving as a link to other community services.

- Excessive caseloads are probably the single greatest pressure on probation officers.
- Common forms of intermediate sanctions are intensive supervision probation, community service, nonsecure juvenile residential facilities, nonresidential day treatment alternatives, electronic monitoring, house arrest, training schools and boot camps.
- Isolating offenders from their normal social environments may encourage developing a delinquent orientation and, thus, further delinquent behavior.
- Compared with public correctional institutions, private correctional institutions confine more Whites, more girls and more status offenders. The inmates are younger, and their stays are usually much longer.
- The sociopolitical events that occur in correctional institutions for youths are the same as those found in adult institutions.
- The performance-based standards goals for corrections cover security, order, safety, programming, justice and health/mental health.
- Most effective youthful offender programs include in-depth evaluation, screening and assessment; daily scheduling; point system discipline; positive behavioral support therapy; and education, including literacy, GED preparation and computer literacy.
- Re-entry/aftercare is often the weakest element in the juvenile justice process.
- Two key components of aftercare are services and supervision, and intensive intervention while incarcerated, during transition into the community and while under community supervision.

DISCUSSION QUESTIONS

1. How effective is probation in juvenile justice? What, if any, changes should be made in the juvenile probation process?

2. Should parents, custodians or guardians of youths be actively involved in a youth's rehabilitation? Why or why not?

3. Is community corrections worthwhile? Does it work? What would you do to improve it?

4. Is there a difference in attitude between a youth who has been confined and one who has been directed by programs in community corrections? What makes the difference?

5. Do community corrections give judges more options in sentencing youths? Is this an advantage or disadvantage?

6. Should violent offenders be subject to community corrections or directed to a secure facility? Why?

7. What are some potential alternatives to secure detention? What problems may be involved in expanding alternative programs?

8. Do you support a conservative or a liberal approach to treating juveniles? Why? Why do you think society is inclined to a "get tough on juveniles" attitude?

9. What would constitute an effective re-entry/aftercare program in your community?

10. What resources are available while youths are under the control of the juvenile justice system and when they return to the community?

REFERENCES

Altschuler, D. M. and Armstrong, T. L. *Intensive After-care for High-Risk Juveniles: A Community Care Model.* Washington, DC: Office of Juvenile Justice and Delinquency Prevention, 1994.

Asbridge, Caleb S. "Sexual Assault in Juvenile Corrections: A Preventable Tragedy." *Corrections Today,* October 2007, pp.80–85.

Bilchik, Shay. "Sentencing Juveniles to Adult Facilities Fails Youths and Society." *Corrections Today*, April 2003, p.21.

Bottcher, Jean and Ezell, Michael E. "Examining the Effectiveness of Boot Camps: A Randomized Experiment with a Long-Term Follow Up." *Journal of Research in Crime and Delinquency*, 2005, p.309.

Brank, Eve; Lane, Jodi; Turner, Susan; Fain, Terry; and Sehgal, Amber. "An Experimental Juvenile Probation Program: Effects on Parent and Peer Relationships." *Crime & Delinquency*, April 2008, pp.193–224.

Brooks, Carol Cramer. "The Challenge of Following Education Legislation in Confinement Education Programs." *Corrections Today*, February 2008, pp.28–30, 46.

Caldwell, Michael F.; Vitacco, Michael; and Van Rybrock, Gregory J. *Journal of Research in Crime and Delinquency*, 2006, p.148.

CBR Youth Connect. 28071 Hwy 109, P.O. Box 681, La Junda, CO 81050. Online: http://www.cbryouth-connect.org

Conditions of Confinement. Building Blocks for Youth, no date.

Conlon, Bill; Harris, Scott; Nagel, Jeffrey; Hillman, Mike; and Hanson, Rick. "Education: Don't Leave Prison without It." *Corrections Today*, February 2008, pp.48–52.

Gibson, Steve and Duncan, Karen. "A Multifaceted Approach from Intake to Discharge." *Corrections Today*, February 2008, pp.58–59.

Gies, Steve V. *Aftercare Services.* Juvenile Justice Bulletin, Washington, DC: Office of Juvenile Justice and Delinquency Prevention, September 2003. (NCJ 201800)

Griffin, Patrick and Torbet, Patricia. *Desktop Guide to Good Juvenile Probation Practice.* Washington, DC: National Center for Juvenile Justice, June 2002.

Intensive Aftercare Program (IAP). Sacramento, CA: The Center for Delinquency & Crime Policy Studies (CDCPS), California State University, no date.

Kupchik, Aaron. "The Correctional Experiences of Youth in Adult and Juvenile Prisons." *Justice Quarterly*, June 2007, pp.247–270.

Kurlychek, Megan and Kempinen, Cynthia. "Beyond Boot Camp: The Impact of Aftercare on Offender Reentry." *Criminal Justice Research Reports*, January/February 2007, pp.42–43.

Lanctot, Nadine; Cernkovich, Stephen A.; and Giordano, Peggy C. "Delinquent Behavior, Official Delinquency and Gender: Consequences for Adulthood Functioning and Well-Being." *Criminology*, Vol. 45, No. 1, 2007, pp.131–157.

Mental Health and Adolescent Girls in the Justice System. Fact Sheet from the National Mental Health Association 2003. Online: http://www.nmha.org/children/justjuv/girlsjj.cfm

Meyer, Edward. "Get Tough on Crime, Not Kids." *Corrections Today*, February 2008, p.19.

Morrell, Barbara. "Rehabilitative Approaches to Corrections Bolstered by Knowledge of Effective Treatment Principles and Firm Public Support." *Criminal Justice Research Reports*, July/August 2007, pp.87–88.

Morton, Joann Brown. "Providing Gender-Responsive Services for Women and Girls." *Corrections Today*, August 2007, pp.6, 12.

O'Rourke, Tom; Catrett, Jack; and Houchins, David. "Teacher Retention in the Georgia DJJ: A Plan That Works." *Corrections Today*, February 2008, pp.40–43.

Pihl-Buckley, Heidi. "Tailoring the Prison Rape Elimination Act to a Juvenile Setting." *Corrections Today*, February 2008, pp.44–47.

Promising Sanctioning Programs in a Graduated System. Reno, NV: Juvenile Sanctioning Center, 2003.

Puzzanchera, Charles; Stahl, Anne L.; Finnegan, Terrence A.; Tierney, Nancy; and Snyder, Howard N. *Juvenile Court Statistics 2000.* National Center for Juvenile Justice, December 2004.

Rehabilitating Juvenile Offenders. Chicago, IL: MacArthur Foundation, 2005–2008.

Report of the Re-Entry Policy Council: Charting the Safe and Successful Return of Prisoners to the Community. New York: Council of State Governments, Reentry Policy Council, January 2005.

Roush, David W. "Sexual Misconduct in Juvenile Justice Facilities: Implications for Work Force Training." *Corrections Today*, February 2008, pp.32–35.

Rutledge, Devallis. "The Young and the Arrestless." *Police*, December 2008, pp.60–61.

Ryder, Judith. "Revamping the Altschuler and Armstrong Intensive Aftercare Program for Use with Girls in the Juvenile Justice System." *Criminal Justice Research Review*, March/April 2008, pp.54–57.

School-Based Probation: An Approach Worth Considering. Reno, NV: National Council of Juvenile and Family Court Judges, Juvenile Sanctions Center, 2003. Online: http://www.ncjfcj.org/content/view/513/331/

Shomaker, Nancy and Gornik, Mark. "Youthful Offenders in Adult Corrections: A Systemic Approach Using Effective Interventions." *Corrections Today*, October 2002, pp.112–123.

Sickmund, Melissa. *Juvenile Residential Facility Census, 2002: Selected Findings.* National Report Series. Washington, DC: Office of Juvenile Justice and Delinquency Prevention, June 2006.

Snyder, Howard N. and Sickmund, Melissa. *2006 Juvenile Offenders and Victims: 2006 National Report.* Washington, DC: U.S. Department of Justice, Office of Justice Programs, Office of Juvenile Justice and Delinquency Prevention.

Stickrath, Thomas J. and Wallis, Sarah. "Reducing Aggression in Juvenile Facilities: Ohio's Plan." *Corrections Today*, June 2007, pp.70–71.

Vivian, John P.; Grimes, Jennifer N.; and Vasquez, Stella. "Assaults in Juvenile Correctional Facilities: An Exploratory Study." *Journal of Crime and Justice*, 2007, p.17.

Zavlek, Shelley and Maniglia, Rebecca. "Developing Correctional Facilities for Female Juvenile Offenders: Design and Programmatic Considerations." *Corrections Today*, August 2007, pp.58–63.

CASE CITED

Santana v. Collazo, 714 F.2d 1172, 1177 (1st Cir. 1983)

CHAPTER 12

Preventing Delinquency and Recidivism

THE TRUISM THAT AN OUNCE OF PREVENTION IS WORTH A POUND OF CURE SURELY APPLIES TO DELINQUENCY. IF WE ARE TO CHECK . . . VIOLENT CRIME BY JUVENILES, WE MUST GO BEYOND TREATING SYMPTOMS, HOWEVER DILIGENTLY, TO EXAMINE CAUSES. NOR MUST WE BE SO PREOCCUPIED WITH WHAT IS WRONG WITH A MINORITY OF OUR YOUTH THAT OUR TUNNEL VISION BLINDS US TO WHAT IS RIGHT WITH THE MAJORITY.

—OJJDP

© Bob Daemmrich/PhotoEdit

Positive interactions between officers and youths can go a long way toward preventing delinquency and recidivism. It is vital that juveniles perceive authority figures as caring advocates, as opposed to heavy-handed adversaries, which can often be a challenging task.

Do You Know?

■ What approach to the delinquency problem emerged during the late 1960s?

■ What three approaches to juvenile crime prevention are?

■ What the three general levels of prevention are?

■ What an effective prevention approach must address?

■ How the numerator and denominator approaches to prevention differ?

■ What the two-pronged public health model for prevention consists of?

■ What the Blueprints for Violence Prevention Initiative is?

■ What two strategies have proved effective in reducing gun violence? What strategy has proved ineffective?

■ What antigang programs can be implemented?

■ What the purpose of drug testing in the school is?

Can You Define?

corrective prevention	mechanical	primary prevention	risk factors
denominator	prevention	protective factors	secondary
approach	numerator approach	punitive prevention	prevention
gateway drugs	polydrug use	recidivism	tertiary prevention

Chapter Outline

Introduction

Prevention Defined

Classifying Prevention Approaches

Prevention versus Control

Three Levels of Delinquency Prevention

Prevention as an Attack on Causes

Which Youth to Target: The Numerator and Denominator Approaches

Prevention and the Public Health Model

What Works in Preventing Delinquency and Violence?

Blueprints for Violence Prevention Initiative

Midwestern Prevention Project (MPP)

Big Brothers Big Sisters of America (BBBS)

Functional Family Therapy (FFT)

LifeSkills® Training (LST)

Multisystemic Therapy (MST)

Nurse-Family Partnership (NFP)

Multidimensional Treatment Foster Care (MTFC)

Olweus Bullying Prevention Program (OBPP)

Promoting Alternative THinking Strategies (PATHS)

The Incredible Years (IYS)

Project Toward No Drug Abuse (Project TND)

Truancy and Dropout Prevention

Communities In Schools (CIS)

Alternative to Suspension Program (ASP)

Alternative Schools

Safe Schools/Healthy Students (SSHS) Program

Project H.E.L.P.: High Expectations Learning Program

Preventing Delinquency through Improved Child Protection Services (CPS)

Violence Prevention

Reducing Gun Violence

Gang Prevention

Drug Use Prevention Programs

DARE

The National Commission on Drug-Free Schools

Parents: The Anti-Drug

A Reality-Based Approach to Drug Education

Drug Testing in Schools

Mentoring

Teens, Crime and the Community (TCC)

A Caution Regarding Net Widening in Prevention Efforts

Introduction

Common sense says it is better to prevent a problem than to react to it once it arises. The medical and health care fields have embraced this preventive approach by advocating it is better to prevent disease and other health issues before they occur than to try and treat or cure them after the fact. This same philosophy is true for juvenile delinquency as well as for child neglect and abuse. Traditionally our society's approach to youthful offending has been reactive, and juvenile courts and diversion programs have responded with a wide range of services focused on punishment, control or rehabilitation. However, "Attempting to reduce crime by focusing only on law enforcement and corrections is like providing expensive ambulances at the bottom of a cliff to pick up the youngster who falls off, rather than building a fence at the top of the cliff to keep them from falling in the first place" (Mendel, 2000).

In 1967 the President's Commission on Law Enforcement and the Administration of Justice advocated: "In the last analysis, the most promising and so the most important method of dealing with crime is by preventing it—by ameliorating the conditions of life that drive people to commit crime and that undermine the restraining rules and institutions erected by society against antisocial conduct." Subsequently this prevention emphasis was written into federal law in the Juvenile Delinquency Prevention Acts of 1972 and 1974 and the Juvenile Justice Amendments of 1977.

 During the late 1960s a new approach for dealing with delinquency emerged— a focus on the prevention of crime.

Each municipality, county and state is unique in its particular crime problems. Each is also unique in how it approaches crime and how it disposes of those who commit crime. What constitutes delinquency is subject to varied interpretations across places, times and social groupings. A youth's behavior may be viewed as "delinquent" by police, as "acting out" by mental health professionals, as "sin" by members of the clergy and as "just plain mischief" by those who view some misbehavior as a normal part of growing up. The National Crime Prevention Council (NCPC) Web site states:

> Many adults do not think well of teenagers. In individual teenagers, they see rebellion, mood swings and tempers. In groups of young people, they see threats (even when none are made), malice (even when they're just talking outside the local convenience store) and gangs (even in kids just walking around the mall). But the great majority of teens are sources of strength, not trouble, to their communities. They are, by and large, intensely interested in the adult world and eager to help. Even among those who get into trouble, the first brush with the juvenile justice system is usually the last.

In dealing with youth, it is critical to remember that adolescence is a developmental period often characterized by risk-taking, acting before thinking, impulsivity, defiance and challenging of adult authority. These are *normative* behaviors for teens in their search for self and separation from parents. Even "good" kids will likely experience some, if not all, of these behaviors during adolescence. For those in juvenile justice, it is crucial to know the difference between a youth who is on a path to delinquency and crime and one who is simply on the path to normal adulthood, with all of its "fits and starts."

Prevention Defined

Recall from the first chapter that there exists not one, but at least 51 different juvenile justice systems in this country. In fact, at a recent conference, a juvenile court judge from Pennsylvania noted that there are 60 counties in her state and, thus, 60 juvenile justice systems in that state. Juvenile justice is truly a local process, and with this extent of individualization comes inevitable variation in language and definitions. For example, an online search of various state statutes and juvenile justice departments revealed the following definitions of delinquency prevention:

- "Prevention" [is] the creation of conditions, opportunities and experiences that encourage and develop healthy, self-sufficient children and that occur before the onset of problems (Arizona State Senate, 2002).
- Prevention: Efforts that help prevent a youth from entering the juvenile justice system as a delinquent (Florida Department of Juvenile Justice, 2008).
- Delinquency Prevention. Programs to prevent or reduce the incidence of delinquent acts and directed to youth at risk of becoming delinquent to prevent them from entering the juvenile justice system or to intervene with first-time and nonserious offenders to keep them out of the juvenile justice system. This program area excludes programs targeted at youth already adjudicated delinquent, on probation, in corrections, and those programs designed specifically to prevent gang-related or substance abuse activities undertaken as part of other program areas (Illinois Department of Human Services, n.d.).
- *Prevention* is a process of intervention designed to alter the circumstances associated with problem behaviors. Effective prevention practices decrease problem behaviors and subsequent difficulties children and adolescents experience in school and in the community. Prevention includes a wide range of activities that address the needs of an equally wide range of children and youth (National Center on Education, Disability and Juvenile Justice, n.d.).

As these examples illustrate, *prevention* is a broadly defined term, open to wide interpretation. The common thread is that prevention encompasses any and all measures taken *before* delinquent behavior occurs.

Classifying Prevention Approaches

Several approaches to classifying prevention efforts have been set forth. Following are two ways to classify prevention efforts.

Prevention versus Control

Technically prevention is a measure taken *before* a delinquent act occurs to forestall the act; control is a measure taken *after* a delinquent act occurs. In this context, three kinds of prevention are relevant for juvenile justice.

Prevention can be corrective, punitive or mechanical.

- **Corrective prevention** focuses on eliminating conditions that lead to or cause criminal behavior.
- **Punitive prevention** relies on the threat of punishment to forestall criminal acts.
- **Mechanical prevention** is directed toward "target hardening," making it difficult or impossible to commit particular offenses. Locks on doors, bars on windows, alarms, security guards and many other options are available to protect possible targets of criminal acts.

Another way to classify prevention efforts is by level. These levels encompass the three methods just discussed.

Three Levels of Delinquency Prevention

The first line of defense against all forms of juvenile crime is prevention, whether *primary* (directed at the population as a whole), *secondary* (aimed at a specific at-risk population) or *tertiary* (targeted at an offending population to prevent repetition of the behaviors).

 Prevention may be primary, secondary or tertiary.

Primary Prevention   **Primary prevention** modifies and changes crime-causing conditions in the overall physical and social conditions that lead to crime. Corrective and mechanical prevention fit into this level. Primary prevention efforts are usually directed toward **risk factors**, those characteristics or variables that increase an individual's likelihood of committing delinquent acts, with no distinction made between those who have committed a crime and those who have not. Fitting into the primary prevention category are programs that provide after-school activities and mentoring, including boys and girls clubs, Big Brothers/Big Sisters and youth foundations.

An example of primary prevention is the community crime prevention program in Seattle, Washington. This program focused on preventing residential burglaries, specifically crimes of opportunity by juveniles who entered homes through unlocked doors and windows during the day when residents were away. Prevention efforts were aimed at contributing environmental factors. Certain neighborhoods and types of housing were identified as being vulnerable to burglaries using demographics, criminal incidents and physical characteristics statistics. The community then gave citizens home security checklists. Citizens in target areas used these checklists to protect their homes against relatively easy entry by burglars. This program was directed at making crime more difficult rather than at attacking individual motivations to commit crime. Such deterrence programs effectively increase the risks to potential burglars, thus decreasing the opportunities for burglary.

As noted by the American Psychological Association (APA) (n.d., pp.55–56) in its discussion of primary prevention programs: "Prevention programs directed early in life can reduce factors that increase risk for antisocial behavior and clinical dysfunction in childhood and adolescence." Among the most promising primary prevention programs are those that include family counseling for pregnant women and for new mothers in the home, with continued visits during the first few years of the child's life. The APA (p.55) reports that in a 20-year follow-up of one home visitor program, positive effects were seen for both the at-risk child and mother.

Preschool programs also hold promise if they include activities that develop intellectual, emotional and social skills and introduce children to responsible decision making. According to the APA (p.56):

> Primary prevention programs of the type that promote social and cognitive skills seem to have the greatest impact on attitudes about violent behavior among children and youth. Skills that aid children in learning alternatives to violent behaviors include social perspective-taking, alternative solution generation, self-esteem enhancement, peer negotiation skills, problem-solving skills training and anger management.

Secondary Prevention   **Secondary prevention** seeks early identification and intervention into the lives of individuals or groups found in crime-causing circumstances. It focuses on changing the behavior of those likely to become delinquent. Punitive prevention fits into this level. The APA (p.56) notes:

> Secondary prevention programs that focus on improving individual affective, cognitive and behavioral skills or on modifying the learning conditions for aggression offer promise of interrupting the path toward violence for high-risk or predelinquent youth. . . .
>
>   Programs that attempt to work with and modify the family system of a high-risk child have great potential to prevent development of aggressive and violent behavior.

Tertiary Prevention   **Tertiary prevention**, the third level, is aimed at preventing recidivism—that is, it focuses on preventing further delinquent acts by youths already identified as delinquent. Tertiary prevention is also called treatment or rehabilitation.

Prevention as an Attack on Causes

Of the three levels of prevention, primary and secondary prevention most closely approach the essence of *prevention*, in that they seek to preclude delinquent acts *before* they occur. Tertiary prevention is really remediation aimed at forestalling future acts after an initial act has been committed and detected.

Primary and secondary prevention activities are effective only if they address the underlying causes of delinquency. To prevent a behavior from occurring, those factors that stimulate the behavior must be removed or mitigated. Conditions that stimulate delinquent acts and those that lack constraints to inhibit those acts are both potential causes of delinquency.

 Effective prevention approaches must address both the conditions and the lack of constraints that cause delinquency.

Using a proactive approach to alter the environments that produce delinquency, an ecological analogy can be made, as stated by one police chief:

"We have to stop swatting at the mosquitoes and start looking to the swamps that produce them." With delinquents, as with mosquitoes, it is much harder to get rid of this year's swarm than to prevent next year's from hatching. This approach is consistent with the public health model introduced in Chapter 6.

Which Youth to Target: The Numerator and Denominator Approaches

The public health model focuses the scarce resources of the juvenile justice system on those at greatest risk—young Black males living in areas of poverty with high crime rates and drug dealing. Applying a mathematical analogy, consider the number of at-risk youths compared to the total number of youths in a population; the at-risk youths would be the *numerator* and the total number of youths would be the *denominator*.

Many crime and delinquency researchers suggest dealing with the denominator for best results. Focusing efforts only on juvenile offenders (i.e., taking a numerator approach) is unlikely to reduce youth crime, just as focusing only on those who are unemployed will not lower unemployment rates (because there is a vast pool of the "potentially unemployed"). The relative ineffectiveness of the numerator approach, and the contrasting effectiveness of the denominator approach, is seen in medicine. For example, a numerator approach in polio and tuberculosis would have had little impact on prevalence; but denominator approaches such as mass vaccination and screening have almost eradicated these diseases. Such an approach can also be effective in delinquency prevention.

 The **numerator approach** focuses on individuals and symptoms, whereas the **denominator approach** focuses on the entire group and causes.

One reason the denominator approach is ignored is because it tends to generate turf fights. It is also sometimes *easier* (albeit less effective) to act to improve an existing problem than to focus on a broader approach to prevent problems in the future. The denominator approach is consistent with the public health model.

Prevention and the Public Health Model

For more than a decade, juvenile justice has been shifting back toward a public health model in attempting to understand the causes of delinquency and tailor approaches to its prevention. Effective crime and delinquency prevention based on the public health model uses a two-pronged strategy involving risk and protective factors.

 The public health model's two-pronged juvenile crime prevention strategy reduces known risk factors and promotes protective factors.

Recall the discussion in Chapter 4 pertaining to risk and protective factors. As a brief review, risk factors are conditions, characteristics or variables that increase the likelihood that a child will become delinquent, whereas **protective factors** (which are often the opposite of corresponding risk factors) are strengths or assets that help reduce the negative impacts of risk factors by providing positive ways for an individual to respond to risks and avoid delinquency. Among the commonly identified protective factors are individual characteristics such as having a resilient temperament and positive social orientation; bonding with family and having positive relationships with other adults, teachers and peers; monitoring and supervision; positive discipline methods; and having healthy values and high standards. However, the OJJDP is very clear on one point: "It should be noted that risk and protective factors are neither causes nor cures. Rather, risk and protective factors are statistical predictors that . . . have a strong theoretical base."

What Works in Preventing Delinquency and Violence?

With many programs now having several decades of experience behind them, and the road ahead appearing more challenging than ever for those involved in handling juvenile delinquency and crime, the question has become: "What works?" The evidence, thus far, is mixed.

Research has begun to reveal that many popular anticrime programs simply do not work and that vast amounts of money continue to be spent on programs that, while they may enjoy widespread public and policy support, do not demonstrate any evidence of having positive impacts on juvenile delinquency and violence. A team of criminologists, led by Lawrence W. Sherman, reviewed more than 500 scientific evaluations of crime-prevention programs funded by the Justice Department, with a special focus on factors relating to juvenile crime and program effects on youth violence, and concluded that the following programs do *not* work (Sherman et al., 1998, p.7): gun buyback programs; military-style correctional boot camps; "scared straight" programs; shock probation/parole; residential programs for juvenile offenders using challenging experiences in rural settings; short-term nonresidential training for at-risk youth; summer jobs or subsidized work programs for at-risk youth; the DARE program; drug prevention classes focused on fear and other emotional appeals, including self-esteem; counseling and peer counseling of students in schools; home detention with electronic monitoring; and arrests of juveniles for minor offenses. Although this study was conducted over a decade ago, to date no new data have become available to refute or reverse these conclusions.

The news is not all bad, however. Programs that consistently demonstrate positive effects on youths at risk of developing delinquent behavior include those that strengthen the institutions of family and school in the youth's life, such as family therapy and parent training about delinquent and at-risk preadolescents; training or coaching in thinking skills for high-risk youth; clarifying and communicating norms about behavior through rules, reinforcement of positive behavior and school-wide initiatives (such as antibullying campaigns); providing social competency skills curriculums; providing frequent home visits to infants aged 0–2 in high-risk homes by trained nurses to help prevent child neglect and abuse; and rehabilitation programs for juvenile offenders that apply treatments appropriate to their risk factors (Sherman et al., pp.7–8).

In between the "what works" and "what doesn't work" categories are a multitude of programs that may hold promise but which have not yet produced enough evidence for researchers to know, one way or the other, if they are effective in preventing or reducing delinquency.

In considering strategies to prevent or reduce juvenile offending, one must necessarily look at the issue of **recidivism**, or repeat offending, and tertiary prevention efforts. It is hoped, presumably, that juvenile justice's handling of delinquency is effective to the degree that once children come into the system and receive some type of treatment, punishment or both, the response will be sufficient to turn the youths around and put them on a path of prosocial, law-abiding behavior, such that these individuals will never again cross paths with either the juvenile or criminal justice systems. The reality, however, is that some youths pass through the system only to go back to their old ways and offend again. In some cases, their experience in the justice system exacerbates their antisocial tendencies or other underlying issues, and these youth actually return to the streets worse than when they entered the system. As more programs have been evaluated and scientifically scrutinized for effectiveness in reducing recidivism, we have begun to see a clearer picture of what constitutes effective intervention. The principles of effective intervention, discussed in depth in Chapter 9, are worth considering again here in the context of tertiary prevention.

The current belief is that a dual approach—working to reduce risk factors while simultaneously building the skills and competencies that improve resiliency—holds the most promise for effective delinquency prevention

PERSPECTIVES FROM THE NCJJ
"What Works and What Doesn't in Reducing Recidivism: The Principles of Effective Intervention"

In trying to answer the question "what works," most research has led to the conclusion that punishment alone, in the absence of some form of human intervention or services, is unlikely to have much of an effect on recidivism. Evidence has also shown that while treatment is more effective than punishment in reducing recidivism, not all treatment programs are equally effective. Furthermore, what works for one offender might not work for another. The constellation of individual offender characteristics will drive treatment needs.

It is critical to target offenders with the highest probability of recidivism, and to provide the most intensive treatment to the highest-risk offenders. Interestingly, intensive treatment directed at low-risk offenders can actually increase recidivism.

Evidence has also shown that targeting for change criminogenic needs, as opposed to noncriminogenic needs, can have a much greater effect in reducing recidivism. This means programs that focus on changing antisocial attitudes, distancing offenders from antisocial friends, treating substance abuse and helping offenders control impulsive behavior are far more effective in preventing further offending than are those that try to build up an offenders' self-esteem, creative abilities (art therapy) or physical conditioning, all of which are noncriminogenic needs.

The most effective interventions are behavioral in nature: they focus on current factors that influence offender behavior;

they are action-oriented, and offender behavior is appropriately reinforced. Most effective behavioral interventions involve structured social learning where new skills and behaviors are modeled, cognitive-behavioral approaches that target criminogenic risk factors and family-based approaches that train family members on appropriate techniques. Two of the most effective programs are Functional Family Therapy (FFT) and Multisystemic Therapy (MST) (discussed shortly).

Cognitive-behavioral treatment (CBT) and intervention has been shown to be particularly effective in changing the behavior that drives delinquency. CBT is based on the principles that antisocial, distorted, unproductive, irrational thinking causes antisocial and unproductive behavior; that thinking can be influenced; and that we can change how we feel and behave by changing what we think. A meta-analysis of CBT found that, on average, this intervention reduced recidivism by 25 percent, but in those programs with the most effective configuration recidivism was reduced by more than 50 percent (Landenberger and Lipsey, 2005).

SOURCE: From a seminar presented by Edward J. Latessa, Ph.D., Professor, Division of Criminal Justice, University of Cincinnati, Cincinnati, OH, at the 34th National Conference on Juvenile Justice, San Diego, CA: Session P-5, Sunday, March 4, 2007.

(Federal Advisory Committee on Juvenile Justice, 2007, p.4). To this end, the OJJDP has, since 1996, actively sought and funded programs that show empirical evidence of effectively preventing youth crime and delinquency. This effort is known as the Blueprints for Violence Prevention Initiative.

Blueprints for Violence Prevention Initiative

Launched by the Center for the Study and Prevention of Violence (CSPV) at the University of Colorado at Boulder, the Blueprints initiative set out to identify effective violence prevention programs across the country so that communities could begin replicating successful programs locally.

 The Blueprints for Violence Prevention Initiative is the OJJDP's comprehensive effort to provide communities with a set of programs whose effectiveness has been scientifically demonstrated.

As of March 2008, more than 700 programs had been reviewed using rigorous selection criteria. Of these, 11 model programs, or Blueprints, were identified as being exemplary in their effects of reducing adolescent violent crime, aggression, delinquency, substance abuse, predelinquent childhood aggression and conduct disorders. Another 17 programs were identified as promising.

This section briefly discusses some of the programs that show the strongest empirical evidence of thwarting youthful offending, whether it is in keeping predelinquent behavior from evolving into actual delinquency or in serving as an intermediate intervention program to help reduce recidivism in youths who have already come into contact with the juvenile justice system. For a more complete description of these programs and the risk and protective factors each targets, access the search function on the OJJDP's Model Programs Guide (MPG) Web site from which the following section is adapted: http://ojjdp.ncjrs. org/programs/mpg.html (program descriptors created by Development Services Group: http://www.dsgonline.com/mpg2.5/prevention.htm).

Midwestern Prevention Project (MPP)

The Midwestern Prevention Project (MPP) is a comprehensive, community-based, multifaceted program for adolescent drug abuse prevention that targets the entire population of middle-school students, ages 10 to 12. The ultimate goal of MPP is to prevent or reduce the onset and prevalence of use of **gateway drugs** (alcohol, tobacco and marijuana) by (1) helping youths recognize the tremendous social pressures to use drugs and (2) providing skills in how to avoid drug use. MPP employs a system of well-coordinated, communitywide strategies, including mass media programming, a school program, continuing school boosters, a parent education and organization program, community organization and training and local policy change regarding tobacco, alcohol and other drugs. These components are introduced to the community in sequence at a rate of one a year, with the mass media component occurring throughout all the years.

The central component for the MPP drug prevention program is the school, where active social learning techniques are taught (modeling, role playing and discussion, with student peer leaders assisting teachers). The parental program consists of a parent–principal committee that reviews both school drug policy and parent–child communications training. The three other components—mass media coverage and programming, community organization and local health policy change—are used to send a consistent message supporting a norm of non–drug use. All components involve regular meetings of respective deliverers (e.g., community leaders for organization) to review and refine programs.

Big Brothers Big Sisters of America (BBBS)

Big Brothers Big Sisters (BBBS), an exemplary mentoring program, is a federation of more than 420 agencies that serve children and adolescents between the ages of 6 and 16, a significant number of whom are from disadvantaged single-parent households. The BBBS program seeks not to ameliorate specific problems but rather to provide a widespread foundation of support in all aspects of young people's lives through a professionally sustained one-on-one relationship between a youth and a caring adult.

In the community-based traditional program, the volunteer mentor commits substantial time to the youth, meeting for about 4 hours, two to four times a month, for at least 1 year. During this time together, the mentor and youth engage in developmentally appropriate activities such as walking; grocery shopping; watching television; visiting a library; washing the car; playing catch; attending a play, movie, school activity or sporting event; or just hanging out and sharing thoughts. BBBS has also added a school-based program in which volunteers meet with their Little Brother or Little Sister for an hour each week for such activities as playing educational games, working on homework or crafts, or just talking.

Although individual agencies occasionally customize their programs to fit specific needs, the integrity of the program is protected through a national infrastructure that oversees recruitment, screening, matching and supervision in a regulated process whereby adults who are most likely to be successful mentors are selected and matched to adolescents who share a common belief system. Staff supervision and support are critical to ensuring that mentor and mentee meet regularly to build positive relationships.

An 18-month study of eight BBBS affiliates found that when compared with a control group on a waiting list for a match, youths in the mentoring program were 46 percent less likely to start using drugs, 27 percent less likely to start drinking and 32 percent less likely to hit someone. Mentored youths skipped half as many days of school as control youths, had better attitudes toward and performance in school, and had improved peer and family relationships.

Functional Family Therapy (FFT)

Functional Family Therapy (FFT) is a family-based prevention and intervention program for dysfunctional youths ages 11 to 18 that has been applied successfully in a variety of multiethnic, multicultural contexts to treat a range of high-risk youths and their families. It integrates several elements (established clinical theory, empirically supported principles and extensive clinical experience) into a clear, comprehensive clinical model that allows for flexible, culturally sensitive and effective intervention across a variety of complex and multidimensional problems.

The specific phases of the FFT model are: engagement/motivation, behavior change and generalization. The engagement/motivation phase aims to reduce the intense negativity often characteristic of high-risk families. The goal of the behavior change phase is to reduce or eliminate problem behaviors and related family interaction dynamics by teaching skills such as effective family communication, proficient parenting, problem solving and conflict management. The generalization phase seeks to increase the family's capacity to access multisystemic community resources and proactively avoid relapse.

FFT ranges from an average of 8 to 12 one-hour sessions for mild cases to upward of 30 or more sessions of direct service for families in more difficult situations. Sessions are generally spread over a 3-month period and can be conducted in clinical settings as an outpatient therapy or as a home-based model. In addition to being a model Blueprint program, FFT is also endorsed by the National Institutes of Health panel of experts, the Substance Abuse and Mental Health Services Administration (SAMSHA) and the National Institute on Drug Abuse as being highly effective in reducing aggression, delinquency and substance abuse.

LifeSkills® Training (LST)

LifeSkills® Training (LST) is a classroom-based tobacco, alcohol and drug abuse prevention program for upper-elementary and junior high school students that targets individuals who have not yet initiated substance use. The program is designed to prevent the early stages of substance use by influencing risk factors associated with substance abuse, particularly occasional or experimental use. Recognizing that the most common approaches to substance abuse prevention for the past two decades have involved either presenting information about the dangers of drug use or using classroom discussion and classroom activities to enrich youths' personal and social development—approaches that have generally neglected to address the risk factors for substance abuse among youths and, therefore, have been largely ineffective—the LST curriculum is based on understanding the causes of tobacco, alcohol and drug use and targets the psychosocial factors associated with the onset of drug involvement.

The LST approach is based on the latest scientific evidence, teaching general personal and social skills in combination with drug resistance skills and normative education. Its prevention curriculum specifically provides students with the necessary skills to resist social pressures to drink alcohol, smoke cigarettes and use drugs; helps them develop greater self-esteem, self-mastery and self-confidence; increases knowledge of the immediate consequences of substance abuse; gives students tools to cope effectively with social anxiety; and enhances cognitive and behavioral competency to prevent and reduce a variety of health risk behaviors.

LST has been found to cut alcohol, tobacco and marijuana use among young adolescents by 44 percent. Long-term results of the program reveal a 66 percent reduction in regular (weekly) **polydrug use** (use of multiple types of drugs at once), a 25 percent reduction in pack-a-day smoking and a decrease in the use of inhalants, narcotics and hallucinogens. Long-term follow-up data reveal that reductions can last through twelfth grade.

Multisystemic Therapy (MST)

Multisystemic Therapy (MST) addresses the multiple aspects of serious antisocial behavior in adolescents across key settings within which youths live, work and play, and typically uses a home-based model of service delivery to reduce barriers that keep families from accessing services. Therapists have small caseloads of four to six families; work as a team; are available 24 hours a day, 7 days a week; and provide services at times convenient to the family. The average treatment involves about 60 hours of contact over a 4-month period.

MST therapists focus on empowering parents and improving parental effectiveness by identifying strengths and developing natural support systems (e.g., extended family, neighbors, friends, church members) and removing barriers (e.g., parental substance abuse, high stress, poor relationships between partners). Specific treatment techniques used to facilitate these gains are integrated from those therapies that have the most empirical support, including behavioral, cognitive-behavioral, and the pragmatic family therapies. In this family–therapist collaboration, the family takes the lead in setting treatment goals, with the therapist facilitating this effort.

Numerous studies of the MST approach with violent and chronic juvenile offenders showed this program produced 25 percent to 70 percent decreases in long-term rates of rearrest, and 47 percent to 64 percent decreases in long-term rates of days in out-of-home placements. A recent meta-analysis that included most of these studies (Curtis et al., 2004) indicated that the average MST effect size for both arrests and days incarcerated was 0.55, with efficacy studies having stronger effects than effectiveness studies.

In addition to being a model Blueprint program, MST is also endorsed by the National Institutes of Health panel of experts, the Substance Abuse and Mental Health Services Administration (SAMSHA) and the National Institute on Drug Abuse as being highly effective in reducing aggression, delinquency and substance abuse.

Nurse-Family Partnership (NFP)

The most serious and chronic offenders often show signs of antisocial behavior as early as the preschool years. Three risk factors associated with early development of antisocial behavior can be modified: (1) adverse maternal health-related behaviors during pregnancy, (2) child abuse and neglect and (3) troubled maternal life course. The Nurse-Family Partnership (NFP), already discussed in depth in Chapter 5, has been shown to have positive outcomes on obstetrical health, psychosocial functioning and other health-related behaviors of mothers, which ultimately benefits their children. The program also has reduced rates of child abuse and neglect by helping young parents learn effective parenting skills and deal with a range of issues such as depression, anger, impulsiveness and substance abuse. One study found that participating in the program was associated with a 79 percent reduction in state-verified cases of child abuse and neglect among mothers who were poor and unmarried. In their second year of life, nurse-visited children had 56 percent fewer visits to emergency rooms for injuries and ingestions than children who were not visited. Moreover, a 15-year follow-up study of one sample found that the program reduced arrests among the mothers, resulted in 54 percent fewer arrests and 69 percent fewer convictions among the 15-year-old adolescents, and resulted in 58 percent fewer sexual partners among the 15-year-olds.

When the program focuses on low-income women, program costs are recovered by the time the first child reaches age 4. The RAND Corporation estimated that once the child reaches age 15, cost savings are four times the original investment because of reductions in crime, welfare expenditures and health care costs and as a result of taxes paid by working parents.

Multidimensional Treatment Foster Care (MTFC)

Multidimensional Treatment Foster Care (MTFC) is a behavioral treatment alternative to residential placement for youth ages 11 to 18 who display chronic antisocial behavior or emotional disturbance or are delinquent. MTFC is a multifaceted intervention used across multiple settings and based on social learning theory, a model that describes the mechanisms by which individuals learn to behave in social contexts and the daily interactions that influence both prosocial and antisocial patterns of behavior. Intervention activities include:

- Behavioral parent training and support for MTFC foster parents.
- Family therapy for biological parents (or other aftercare resources).
- Skills training for youth.
- Supportive therapy for youth.
- School-based behavioral interventions and academic support.
- Psychiatric consultation and medication management, when needed.

Three components of the intervention work in unison to treat the youth: MTFC Parents, the Family and the Treatment Team. Evaluation results of MTFC are overwhelmingly positive and show that this program is not only feasible but is also, when compared with alternative residential treatment models, more cost-effective and leads to better outcomes for children and families.

Olweus Bullying Prevention Program (OBPP)

The Olweus Bullying Prevention Program (OBPP) was developed, refined and systematically evaluated in Bergen, Norway, after three young Norwegian boys committed suicide as a result of severe bullying by peers. The original project, which took place from 1983 to 1985, involved 2,500 youths in 42 schools throughout the city. Because bullying is such a prevalent problem, the program has been replicated throughout Norway and in other countries, including the United States.

OBPP is a universal intervention developed to promote the reduction and prevention of bullying behavior and victimization problems. The program, geared toward youths ages 6 to 14, is based on an ecological model and incorporates interventions aimed at a variety of levels within a child's environment: the individual children who are bullying and being bullied, the families, the teachers and students within the classroom, the school as a whole and the community. The principal venue for the program is the school; school staff have the primary responsibility for introducing and implementing the program and are provided ongoing support by OBPP project staff.

Adult awareness and behavior is crucial to the success of the OBPP, and two conditions must be met for the program to achieve its intended goals. First, the adults at school and, to some degree, at home must be made aware of the extent of bully–victim problems in the given school. Second, the adults must actively engage in changing the situation. Without adults' acknowledgment of schools' existing bully–victim problems and a clear commitment by a majority of the school staff to participate actively in the antibullying efforts, the program is likely to have limited, if any, success. These principles have been translated into numerous specific measures, or interventions, that are used at the school, class and individual levels.

The program has been implemented and assessed in a variety of cultures (e.g., Bergen, Norway; the southeastern United States; Sheffield, England; and Schleswig–Holstein, Germany) and school contexts (elementary and middle schools). The U.S. evaluation of the OBPP has produced somewhat modest but still positive findings. For example, a study of middle-school students revealed significant decreases in students' self-reports of bullying in the intervention schools, when compared with control schools. The program also appeared to slow the natural rate of increase in students' engagement in several other anti-social behaviors. There were, however, no effects on victimization, bullying of teachers, group delinquency, theft, substance abuse or attitudes toward bullying. And no program effects were found by year 2.

Promoting Alternative THinking Strategies (PATHS)

The Promoting Alternative THinking Strategies (PATHS) is a conflict resolution/interpersonal skills curriculum that promotes emotional and social competencies and reduces aggression and behavior problems in elementary school–aged children (ages 5–10), while simultaneously enhancing the educational process within the classroom. This school-based intervention, based on the ABCD (Affective-Behavioral-Cognitive-Dynamic) model of development, includes lessons in self-control, emotional understanding, self-esteem and interpersonal problem-solving skills. A basic premise of PATHS is that a child's coping mechanisms, as reflected in his or her behavior and internal regulation, are a function of emotional awareness, affective-cognitive control and behavioral skills, and social-cognitive understanding.

To this end, the PATHS curriculum contains numerous lessons that build protective factors by helping children identify and label feelings, express feelings, assess the intensity of feelings and manage feelings; understand the difference between feelings and behaviors; learn how to delay gratification and control impulses; reduce stress; read and interpret social cues; understand the perspectives of others; use steps for problem solving and decision making; achieve a positive attitude toward life; gain self-awareness; and learn effective verbal and nonverbal communication skills.

Although the curriculum is designed for use by educators and counselors and concentrates primarily on school and classroom settings, it also includes information and activities for use with parents. Ideally, the program should be initiated at the start of schooling and continued through sixth grade. Teachers generally receive training in a 2- to 3-day workshop and in biweekly meetings with the curriculum consultant.

Studies have compared classrooms receiving the intervention with matched controls using populations of normally adjusted students, behaviorally at-risk students and deaf students. Compared with the control groups, youths in the PATHS program have done significantly better in recognizing and understanding emotions, understanding social problems, developing effective alternative solutions and decreasing frequency of aggressive/violent solutions. Teachers reported significant improvements in children's self-control, emotional understanding, ability to tolerate frustration and use of conflict resolution strategies. Among special-needs youths, teachers reported decreases in internalized symptoms (sadness, anxiety and withdrawal) and externalized symptoms (aggressive and disruptive behavior).

The Incredible Years Series (IYS)

Youth on a trajectory of lifelong persistent antisocial behavior are often recognizable quite early in life. Young aggressive children may have already established a pattern of social difficulty in preschool that continues and becomes fairly stable by middle school. Many children with conduct problems (defined as high rates of aggression, defiance and oppositional and impulsive behaviors) have been asked to leave four or five schools by age 6, and by the time they enter middle school, their negative reputation and their rejection by peers and parents may be well established. Early intervention is crucial in reducing aggressive behavior and negative reputations before they develop into permanent, stable patterns.

The Incredible Years Series (IYS) targets children between the ages of 2 and 10 who exhibit or are at risk for conduct problems. The series, based on the social learning model, emphasizes the importance of the family and teachers in a child's socialization process and features three comprehensive, multifaceted and developmentally based curricula for parents, teachers and children. A basic premise of IYS is that negative reinforcement develops and maintains children's deviant behaviors and parents' and teachers' critical or coercive behaviors, sustaining a cycle of dysfunctional socialization that must be stopped. Therefore, the first step is to change parents' or teachers' behaviors so that the children's social interactions can be altered. If parents and teachers can learn to deal effectively with children's misbehavior and to model positive and appropriate problem-solving and discipline strategies, children can develop social competence and reduce aggressive behavior at home and at school. To achieve this goal, trained facilitators use interactive presentations, videotape modeling and role-playing techniques to encourage group discussion, problem solving and sharing of ideas.

In six randomized trials, the parent training component of IYS has been shown to reduce conduct problems and improve parenting interactions; these improvements have been sustained up to three years after the intervention. The cycle of aggression appears to have been halted for approximately two-thirds of families whose children have conduct disorders and who have been treated in clinics. In two randomized trials, the teacher training component has been shown to improve children's behavior in the classroom (improvements include less hyperactivity, antisocial behavior and aggression and more social and academic competence) and teachers' classroom management skills. The child training component resulted in significantly improved social skills and positive conflict management strategies with peers, in addition to reduced child behavior problems at home and school. Preliminary results of the classroom-based curriculum suggest it is effective in reducing overall classroom aggression and increasing children's social competence.

Project Toward No Drug Abuse (Project TND)

This school-based initiative is an interactive program designed to help high school youths (ages 14–19) resist substance use. The curriculum consists of twelve 40- to 50-minute lessons conducted over a 4-week period that include motivational activities, social skills training and decision-making components delivered through a variety of means, such as group discussions, role-playing exercises, videos, games and student worksheets. The program delivers detailed information to students about the social and health consequences of drug use, instruction on cognitive motivation enhancement activities to avoid drug use and correction of cognitive misperceptions. It addresses topics such as active listening skills, effective communication skills, stress management, coping skills, tobacco cessation techniques and self-control—all to counteract risk factors for drug abuse relevant to older teens. The program can be used in a self-instruction format or run by a health educator. Evaluation results show that TND can significantly reduce hard drug and alcohol use among high school students.

The preceding model programs all aim to prevent delinquency by reducing the negative impacts of risk factors while building up an arsenal of protective factors for youths to draw upon when navigating the often tumultuous waters of adolescence. Other exemplary and effective prevention programs can be found on the OJJDP Model Programs Guide Web site referenced earlier. Another area showing effective delinquency prevention benefits pertains to truancy and efforts to keep kids in school.

Truancy and Dropout Prevention

Truancy, as discussed in Chapter 4, is a risk factor for serious juvenile delinquency as well as a host of other complications in adult life. Truants are more likely to drop out of school, setting such individuals on a path of diminished opportunities for future employment and other economic challenges. Truancy has also been linked to increased risk of substance abuse and teen pregnancy. Thus the reasons to prevent truancy and keep kids in school are many.

An effective truancy prevention response requires a partnership approach, as illustrated in Figure 12.1.

It is no mystery that some youths are truant because they simply do not enjoy school or would rather hang out with their friends, and the communication between the school and the parents is lacking to the extent that the truancy is able to continue unchecked. Such administrative or system failures should be relatively easy to resolve once they are identified and made a priority by school officials. More challenging, from a practitioner's perspective, are those cases where the truancy stems from family or individual student factors, as these

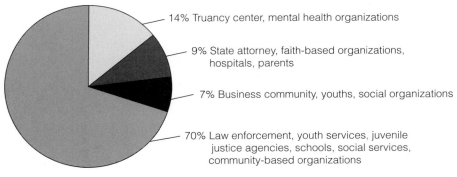

Note: *n* = 18 respondents.

Figure 12.1   Partners Identified as Necessary to Reduce Truancy

SOURCE: Myriam L. Baker, Jane Nady Sigmon and Elaine Nugent. *Truancy Reduction: Keeping Students in School.* Washington, DC: OJJDP Juvenile Justice Bulletin, September 2001, p.12. (NCJ 188947)

cases often require a therapeutic intervention above and beyond those needed to simply fix lax record-keeping or other supervisory loopholes. It is documented that some youths are absent from school because of personal mental health or substance abuse issues (sometimes in combination) or because family health or financial concerns put pressure on the student to either stay home to care for family members or go to a job to bring in essential funds to keep the family financially afloat.

The National Center for School Engagement (NCSE), a national leader in applying research to help communities prevent and reduce truancy, has worked with the OJJDP to evaluate various antitruancy programs across the country. Their *Toolkit for Creating Your Own Truancy Reduction Program* (available online: http://www.ncjrs.gov/pdffiles1/pr/217271.pdf) is a compendium of approaches taken by various jurisdictions. Their most recently available assessment of best practices in truancy prevention identified the following components of successful programs (Dimock, 2005):

- *Collaboration*—Truancy programs that include a broad-based collaborative as part of their approach are stronger and may last longer.
- *Family involvement*—Involving parents/guardians and other family members is critical and entails more than simply inviting their attendance at a school or court meeting. True participation means actively engaging the entire family, seeking their advice and experiences as "experts" in the lives of their children.
- *Comprehensive approach*—Effective programs focus simultaneously on both prevention and intervention and address the myriad reasons youth fail to attend school (personal, academic, school climate and family-related issues). An effective truancy program may need to help a family receive counseling, arrange for transportation solutions, negotiate schedules and extracurricular activities or advocate for families to receive financial aid to remove the pressure for children to choose work over school.
- *Use of meaningful sanctions and incentives*—Traditionally, sanctions for truancy have mirrored the punitive response given to other misbehavior: detention, suspension, petition to juvenile court, denial of privileges, and so on.

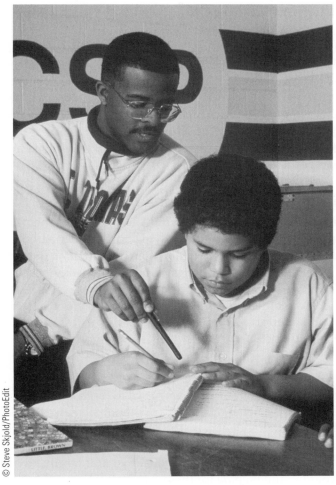

© Steve Skjold/PhotoEdit

Academic failure and low bonding with teachers are reasons why students may choose to drop out of school. For those youths struggling with coursework, tutoring can provide not only the necessary academic assistance but also a positive relationship with a caring adult.

Sanctions must be used judiciously, as these actions often are in direct conflict with the goal of keeping students in school (e.g., suspension). More effective is the use of meaningful incentives, which tend to be recognition-based but may also include special experiences (attending a sporting event or concert) or monetary rewards.

- *Supportive context*—This element is crucial to developing a sustainable and effective truancy program, for those that have support are much more likely to survive than those acting in isolation or fighting against a system that does not value its mission. A "context" can be an umbrella agency, a neighborhood, a collection of laws and policies or a political entity. Stakeholders to involve in this context, beyond the obvious educators, include law enforcement, mental health workers, mentors and social service providers,

- *Ongoing evaluation*—Programs must measure their impact in an effort to optimize delivery of services and identify where improvements or modifications are needed.

Communities In Schools (CIS)

The Communities In Schools (CIS) network is a web of local, state and national partnerships working together to bring at-risk youths four basics that every child needs and deserves: a personal one-on-one relationship with a caring adult, a safe place to learn and grow, a marketable skill to use upon graduation and a chance to give back to peers and community. CIS treats the student and his or her family in a holistic manner, bringing together in one place a support system of caring adults who ensure that the student has access to the resources that can help him or her build self-worth and the skills needed to embark on a more productive and constructive life.

Alternative to Suspension Program (ASP)

The Alternative to Suspension Program (ASP) addresses the problem of suspended students and how, instead of staying home under parental supervision during such suspensions, such students often tend to hang out at the mall, loiter at local convenience stores or engage in criminal activity such as breaking into homes and cars. To counter such unsupervised suspensions, many communities have implemented ASP, bringing together parents, schools and law enforcement in an effort to keep suspended students off the streets and away from criminal activity.

Alternative Schools

Alternative education programs are being used to reach at-risk youths. Such programs are based on the belief that failure in school increases the likelihood that youths will commit delinquent acts. The school is considered an appropriate vehicle to help children meet their early developmental needs in six major roles: learner, individual, producer, citizen, consumer and family member. Helping children recognize and prepare for these roles should prevent problems, including delinquency, in later life. Alternative schools commonly include such prevention programs as:

- *Job/career programs* that help youths define their career interests, provide vocational training and teach youths how to look for a job and other employment services.
- *Advocacy programs* in which youths, their families and school staff members monitor and pressure for needed changes in youth services.

Safe Schools/Healthy Students (SSHS) Program

The Safe Schools/Healthy Students (SSHS) program supports urban, rural, suburban and tribal school district efforts to link prevention activities with community-based services and thereby strengthen local approaches to violence prevention and child development. Plans are required to address six elements: (1) a safe school environment; (2) violence, alcohol and drug abuse prevention and early intervention programs; (3) school and community mental health prevention and treatment intervention services; (4) early childhood psychosocial and emotional development services; (5) education reform; and (6) safe school policies.

The U.S. Department of Housing and Urban Development (HUD) collaborates with the Office of Juvenile Justice and Delinquency Prevention (OJJDP) to create neighborhoods where community needs are met, and crime and drug abuse prevention efforts play a major role in community development efforts in public and Indian housing. Here, students attend a Step Up graduation ceremony at the Boys and Girls Club of Fullerton, California. Step Up, a job-training program for public housing residents, is a collaborative effort between HUD, the Department of Justice (DOJ) and the Department of Labor (DOL).

Project H.E.L.P.: High Expectations Learning Program

Project H.E.L.P.'s program mission is to ensure all students have the opportunities they need to work to their full academic and social potentials. This year-round educational program offers an extra 200 hours of supplemental classroom instruction per year to underachieving elementary school students. This supplemental instruction is offered within the context of a five-week summer term and a nine-month school year extension. To ensure a powerful transition into the regular school year, Project H.E.L.P. provides teacher continuity; the student's teacher during the summer term is also the student's teacher during the school year.

According to the program's Web site, "The key component in the success of Project H.E.L.P. has always been parental involvement. From the beginning, Project H.E.L.P. has set high standards for parent participation, and the prerequisite for enrollment in Project H.E.L.P. is a clear understanding of the role parents will need to play if they wish their children to be a part of the project." The parental performance standards include (1) attendance at weekly parent/teacher conferences during the summer term and monthly conferences during the school year extension, (2) setting aside time each evening to monitor homework and provide assistance and encouragement as needed, (3) attending parent seminars that offer encouragement, support and strategies to implement at home to enhance their child's prospects for academic programs and

(4) financial support through tuition, which typically covers 15 to 20 percent of program costs, with financial aid available to parents who demonstrate a need for tuition assistance.

Preventing Delinquency through Improved Child Protection Services (CPS)

One potentially powerful prevention effort, frequently overlooked, is to reduce the incidence of child neglect and abuse. Evidence clearly shows that a disproportionate number of neglected and abused children become delinquents, so preventing child neglect and abuse serves a dual function: "If the public remains silent about child neglect and abuse, then the supportive services these children need will not reach them. The children who survive may produce another generation to perpetuate the cycle of violence" (Ennis, 2000, p.95).

Although it is never recommended that a child be left in a family where abuse and neglect is actively occurring, there is a strong movement to preserve families and keep the custodial turnover of dependents to a minimum. What this means, of course, is that treatment and intervention services must be delivered efficiently and effectively to parents. In these cases, the need for collaborative efforts and the link between juvenile justice and child welfare are very clear.

For example, when a drug-dependent child is born and placed outside its biological family, the court must try to learn whether the mother is willing and able to undergo drug treatment, with the goal being eventual reunification of the family. If spousal abuse is the issue, and with recognition that child abuse often co-occurs in such environments, the system should act to get abuse treatment for the offending parent such that the child may safely stay with its family: "Child abuse is present in 30 to 70 percent of families in which there is spousal abuse, and the severity of the child abuse generally parallels the severity of the abuse to the spouse" (Graves, 2002, p.137).

Violence Prevention

The OJJDP identifies six principles for preventing delinquent conduct and reducing serious, violent and chronic delinquency:

1. Strengthen families to instill moral values and provide guidance and support to children
2. Support core social institutions such as schools, religious institutions and other community organizations to alleviate risk factors for youths
3. Promote delinquency prevention strategies that reduce the impact of risk factors and enhance the influence of protective factors for youths at the greatest risk of delinquency
4. Intervene immediately when delinquent behavior occurs
5. Institute a broad spectrum of graduated sanctions that provide accountability and a continuum of services to respond appropriately to the individual needs of an offender
6. Identify and control the small segment of serious, violent and chronic juvenile offenders

Many delinquency prevention efforts are unsuccessful because of their negative approach—attempting to keep juveniles from misbehaving. What has proved to work more effectively are positive approaches that emphasize opportunities for healthy social, physical and mental development. Table 12.1 presents several education, legal/regulatory change and environmental modification strategies to prevent youth violence.

In structuring violence prevention programs, communities and agencies must be mindful that different racial/ethnic groups experience different types of violence at different rates, and each calls for different prevention strategies.

Reducing Gun Violence

The political right resists any new gun-control legislation as unnecessary, suggesting more enforcement of existing laws. In opposition, the left advocates the policies of all other developed countries which have a virtual ban on handgun possession with tight registration and control over a limited number of long guns. Considering the strong pro-gun sentiment in this country, it seems unlikely that laws will be passed that take handguns out of the hands of citizens. As long as guns are a part of our society, they will invariably be used by some youths for violent purposes.

 Two programs known to work to reduce gun violence are uniformed police patrols in gun crime hot spots and background checks for criminal history to restrict gun sales in stores. Gun buyback programs do not appear to work.

Gang Prevention

Closely related to the general youth violence issue in this country is the concern over gangs. Preventing gangs and gang-related violence will undoubtedly have an impact on the overall level of juvenile violence. The National School Safety Center suggests several prevention and intervention strategies.

Behavior codes should be established and enforced firmly and consistently. Such behavior codes may include a dress code, a ban on the showing of gang

Table 12.1   Strategies to Prevent Youth Violence

Education	Legal/Regulatory Change	Environmental Modification
Adult mentoring	Regulate use of and access to weapons:	Modify the social environment:
Conflict resolution	Weaponless schools	Home visitation
Training in social skills	Control of concealed weapons	Preschool programs such as
Firearm safety	Restrictive licensing	Head Start
Parenting centers	Appropriate sale of guns	Therapeutic activities
Peer education		Recreational activities
Public information and education campaigns	Regulate use of and access to alcohol:	Work/academic experiences
	Appropriate sale of alcohol	
	Prohibition or control of alcohol	Modify the physical environment:
	sales at events.... Training of servers	Make risk areas visible
		Increase use of an area
	Other types of regulations:	Limit building entrances and exits
	Appropriate punishment in schools	
	Dress codes	

SOURCE: National Center for Injury Prevention and Control.

colors and a ban on using gang hand signals. Friendliness and cooperation should be promoted and rewarded.

Graffiti removal should be done immediately. Graffiti is not only unattractive, but it also allows gangs to advertise turf and authority. A Los Angeles school administrator suggests that graffiti be photographed before removal so the police can better investigate the vandalism. Evidence, such as paint cans and paint brushes, should be turned over to the police. In addition students might design and paint their own murals in locations where graffiti is likely to appear.

Conflict prevention strategies can also be effective. Teachers should be trained to recognize gang members and to deal with them in a nonconfrontational way. All gang members should be made known to staff. Teachers should try to build self-esteem and promote academic success for all students, including gang members. School-based programs can combine gang and drug prevention efforts.

Crisis management should be an integral part of the administration's plan for dealing with any gang activity that might occur. A working relationship should be established with the police department, and a plan for managing a crisis should be developed. The plan should include procedures for communicating with the authorities, parents and the public.

Community involvement can also be extremely effective in reducing or even preventing gang activity. Parents and the general public can be made aware of gangs operating in the community, as well as heavy metal and punk bands that promote violence or inappropriate behavior. They can be encouraged to apply pressure to radio and television stations and bookstores to ban material that promotes the use of alcohol or drugs, promiscuity or devil worship.

 Antigang programs include establishing behavior codes, removing graffiti, implementing conflict prevention strategies, developing a plan for crisis management and fostering community involvement.

The OJJDP's Gang Reduction Program (GRP) (*Best Practices to Address Community Gang Problems*, 2008, p.4) identifies two types of prevention in its integrated approach to targeting gangs:

- *Primary prevention*—targets the entire population in high-crime and high-risk communities. The key component is a One-Stop Resource Center that makes services accessible and visible to community members. Services include prenatal and infant care, after-school activities, truancy and dropout prevention, tutoring, mentoring and job programs. Other primary prevention initiatives include conducting workshops and training sessions to increase neighborhood and community awareness about gangs.
- *Secondary prevention*—identifies children ages 7–14 at high risk for joining gangs and, drawing on the resources of schools, community-based organizations and faith-based groups, intervenes with appropriate services before early problem behaviors turn into serious delinquency and gang involvement.

To optimize effectiveness, primary and secondary service providers must understand the gang culture and have experience working with at-risk youths and their families (*Best Practices*, p.26).

HIGHLIGHTS FROM THE FIELD—PREVENTION ACTIVITIES

Richmond, VA Through meetings with community representatives, project staff learned of a need for a number of programs that ultimately led to the funding of more than 50 programs. For example, community members identified the need for longer after-school hours and options for summer activities. The project expanded their partnership with Boys and Girls Clubs, and also entered into a partnership with the faith-based Richmond Outreach Center to provide additional activities and longer hours. A viable One-Stop Office has been a key part of integrating services to clients. The ability of the Office of the Attorney General to reach out to all partners and successfully communicate the overall goals of the project has contributed to successfully integrating services for clients.

Miami-Dade, FL The main prevention efforts were a direct response to a student survey that asked students what would keep them from getting involved in gang activities.

The response was "something to do or a job." The project designed an on-the-job training program that has been a main draw for students. The greatest success of the on-the-job training component of the project was the resulting level of pride and commitment that the youth showed while participating in the program. This component provides long-term effects and knowledge that the youth can use for career advancement and entrepreneurship.

Houston, TX Gang awareness presentations resulted in more calls from residents to report suspected gang-related crime according to reports from police.

SOURCE: Reprinted by permission from *Best Practices to Address Community Gang Problems: OJJDP's Comprehensive Gang Model*. Washington, DC: U.S. Department of Justice, Office of Juvenile Justice and Delinquency Prevention, June 2008, p.27. (NCJ 222799)

The National Crime Prevention Council's (NCPC's) *Effective Strategy: Provide Positive Alternative to Gang Activity* (2003) suggests: "By providing positive alternatives to violent gang activities and tracking interacting with gang members, community groups can combat gang violence successfully." A challenge to this approach is overcoming the fear of gang activity, which can make some individuals and groups reluctant to get involved. Another challenge is to gain the gang members' trust by listening to them and designing services that respond to their needs.

According to the NCPC, "Strategies to deter youth gang membership include education, counseling and alternative activities, such as recreation and job training." Respondents to surveys in several major cities with serious youth gang violence reported that providing positive alternatives for gang members was the most effective strategy, with community organization being next most effective. Suppression strategies were considered to be less effective except in conjunction with other approaches.

Drug Use Prevention Programs

Because of the known link between drug abuse and delinquency, many programs focus on drug abuse prevention. The Office of National Drug Control Policy (2009, p.7) states: "When it comes to alcohol and drugs, young people are especially vulnerable, in part because of the significant health and social consequences of early drug use and drug-using behavior. Consequently, youth should be provided with an array of prevention activities—from an evidence-based substance abuse prevention curriculum to random drug testing—to shield them from drug-related harms."

DARE

DARE is perhaps the best known and most recognized drug prevention program in the country. Although the program enjoys great popularity—schools love DARE, students and families love DARE, police departments love DARE—most of the research to date does not support the finding that DARE effectively reduces long-term drug use among students. Nonetheless, what the program has been able to do is forge positive relationships between youth and members of law enforcement, which supporters of the program advocate has a positive impact on juvenile behavior. The hope, although unsubstantiated through data at present, is that these prosocial bonds will serve as a protective factor for youth.

The National Commission on Drug-Free Schools

A comprehensive drug education and prevention program should have eight key elements:

1. Student survey, school needs assessment and resource identification
2. Leadership training of key school officials and staff with authority to develop policies and programs
3. School policies that are clear, consistent and fair, with responses to violations that include alternatives to suspension
4. Training for the entire staff on the school's alcohol and drug policies and policy implementation throughout
5. Assistance programs/support for students from preschool through grade 12, including tutoring, mentoring and other academic activities; support groups (e.g., Alcoholics Anonymous and Children of Alcoholics); peer counseling; extracurricular activities (e.g., sports, drama, journalism); vocational programs (e.g., work-study and apprenticeship); social activities (including drug-free proms and graduation activities); alternative programs (e.g., Upward Bound and Outward Bound); and community service projects
6. Training for parents, including the effects of drug use, abuse and dependency on users, their families and other people; ways to identify drug problems and refer people for treatment; available resources to diagnose and treat people with drug problems; laws and school policies on drugs, including alcohol and tobacco; the influence of parents' attitudes and behavior toward drugs including alcohol and tobacco, and of parents' expectations of graduation and academic performance of their children; the importance of establishing appropriate family rules, monitoring behavior of children, imposing appropriate punishments and reinforcing positive behavior; ways to improve skills in communication and conflict management; the importance of networking with other parents and knowing their children's friends and their families
7. Curriculum for preschool through grade 12, including information about all types of drugs, including medicines; the relationship of drugs to suicide, AIDS, drug-affected babies, pregnancy, violence and other health and safety issues; the social consequences of drug abuse; respect for the laws and values of society, including discussions of right and wrong; the importance of honesty, hard work, achievement, citizenship, compassion, patriotism and other civic and personal values; promotion of healthy, safe and responsible attitudes and behavior; ways to build resistance to influences that encourage drug use, such as peer pressure, advertising and other media appeals (refusal skills); ways to develop critical-thinking, problem-solving, decision-making,

persuasion and interpersonal skills; strategies to get parents, family members and the community involved in preventing drug use; and information on contacting responsible adults when young people need help and on intervention and referral services

8. Collaboration with community services to provide student assistance programs; employee assistance programs for school staff; latchkey child care; medical care, including treatment for alcohol and other drug abuse; nutrition information and counseling; mental health care; social welfare services; probation services; and continuing education for dropouts and pushouts

Curriculum should be developmentally oriented, age-appropriate, up-to-date and accurate. Individual components work best as part of a comprehensive curriculum program. When presented in isolation, components such as information about drugs can exacerbate the problem.

Parents: The Anti-Drug

The Office of National Drug Control Policy (ONDCP) through its National Youth Anti-Drug Media Campaign launched new national advertising targeting parents and other adult caregivers, reminding them that they are an important influence in their children's lives and that they can make a difference in their children's decision making. The campaign—called "Parents: The Anti-Drug"—focuses on five basic values: truth, love, honesty, communication and trust. The advertising sends consistent messages in all media—print, billboards, radio and television—to reassure parents that they can positively affect their children's decisions regarding drugs by spending time with them; listening to them genuinely; asking them what they think; giving them clear, consistent rules to follow; praising and rewarding them for good behavior; telling them they are loved; encouraging them to participate in extracurricular activities; and being involved in their lives. More information can be found online at http://www.theantidrug.com.

A Reality-Based Approach to Drug Education

It is reality that many teenagers experiment with drugs. Most conventional school-based drug education equates *any* use of illegal drugs with dangerous behavior when, in fact, experimenting with drugs seems to be a normal part of growing up for many youths. Drug use should not be equated with drug abuse. Students who experiment with drugs know others who have done so, with few ill effects and without becoming drug addicts. In fact, some suggest that taking an alarmist approach and overstating claims that any drug use sets a youth on an irrevocable course toward delinquency and a life of disadvantage can backfire and cause the source to lose credibility in the eyes of the juvenile, as youth often know of people who have experimented with drugs and then gone on to lead productive adult lives.

Drug Testing in Schools

In June 2002, the U.S. Supreme Court broadened the authority of public schools to test students for illegal drugs. Voting 5 to 4, the Court ruled to allow random drug tests for all middle- and high-school students participating in competitive extracurricular activities (*Board of Education of Independent School District No. 92 of*

Pottawatomie County et al. v. Earls et al., 2002). Justice Clarence Thomas commented: "We find that testing students who participate in extracurricular activities is a reasonably effective means of addressing the school district's legitimate concerns in preventing, deterring and detecting drug use. This ruling expands the scope of school drug testing, which previously was allowed only for student athletes."

 The purpose of drug testing is to prevent drug dependence and to help drug-dependent students become drug-free.

Mentoring

Mentoring is one of the oldest forms of prevention. The mentoring movement began at the end of the nineteenth century, when adults called the Friendly Visitors served as role models for poor children. During the 1970s, mentoring found its way into corporate America as a means for the ambitious employee to find success on the corporate ladder. Most recently mentoring has returned to its roots, focusing on disadvantaged youths and providing support and advocacy to children in need. Under the Juvenile Justice and Delinquency Prevention (JJDP) Act, the OJJDP is authorized to fund mentoring efforts.

Research has shown that youth who experience a mentoring relationship reap a variety of positive benefits, including better attendance and attitude toward school, diminished drug and alcohol use, improved social attitudes and relationships, more trusting relationships and better communication with parents, and a better chance of going on to higher education. The Big Brothers Big Sisters (BBBS) programs discussed earlier is one of the most effective mentoring programs currently in use throughout the country.

Teens, Crime and the Community (TCC)

The National Crime Prevention Council (NCPC) has consistently advocated for involving young people in bettering their communities. One program, Teens, Crime and the Community (TCC), is a nationwide effort sponsored by the NCPC and Street Law, Inc., and implemented at the local level to reduce the incidence of teen victimization and engage teens as crime prevention resources in their schools and communities. Participating teens tackle critical issues facing American society today, including violent crime, shoplifting, child abuse, rape, hate crime and substance abuse. More importantly, TCC empowers youths with the skills and knowledge to make a difference in addressing these problems.

A Caution Regarding Net Widening in Prevention Efforts

Net widening is a serious issue because it depletes system resources and impedes proper intervention with appropriate youths. Instead of improving public safety, some early intervention and prevention strategies promote net widening by shifting resources from youths most in need to youths least in need. Macallair and Roche (2001, pp.3–4) state:

> Many argue that the juvenile justice system should focus on first time or low level offenders who are more malleable to rehabilitation. Under this argument

net widening is a good thing because it allows the system to target youths early before they become serious delinquents. However, this argument is not supported by research.

For the past 40 years criminal justice research repeatedly shows that almost 70 percent of youth who are arrested once, are never arrested again. In other words, by doing nothing the state can achieve a 70 percent success rate—meaning no subsequent arrests—with first-time offenders.

Most youth who come in contact with the juvenile justice system are considered "low-risk" because the reality is most youth are not on a life course trajectory for persistent offending. By treating these first-time, low-risk offenders overly harshly, we not only waste precious resources that should be directed to the more serious and violent offenders, but we also risk criminalizing these youth and actually pushing them in a direction of delinquency instead of steering them away from it.

This realization is one of the new realities facing those in juvenile justice and serves as the part of the impetus for system reform, as will be discussed in the next and final chapter.

 ## SUMMARY

- During the late 1960s a new approach for dealing with delinquency emerged— a focus on the prevention of crime.
- Prevention can be corrective, punitive or mechanical.
- Prevention may be primary, secondary or tertiary.
- Effective prevention approaches must address both the conditions and the lack of constraints that cause delinquency.
- The numerator approach to prevention focuses on individuals and symptoms, whereas the denominator approach focuses on the entire group and causes.
- The public health model's two-pronged juvenile crime prevention strategy reduces known risk factors and promotes protective factors.
- The Blueprints for Violence Prevention Initiative is the OJJDP's comprehensive effort to provide communities with a set of programs whose effectiveness has been scientifically demonstrated.
- Two programs known to work to reduce gun violence are uniformed police patrols in gun crime hot spots and background checks for criminal history to restrict gun sales in stores. Gun buyback programs do not appear to work.
- Antigang programs include establishing behavior codes, removing graffiti, implementing conflict prevention strategies, developing a plan for crisis management and fostering community involvement.
- The purpose of drug testing is to prevent drug dependence and to help drug-dependent students become drug-free.

DISCUSSION QUESTIONS

1. Do you support the numerator or the denominator approach to juvenile crime prevention? Be prepared to defend your choice.
2. Do delinquency prevention programs succeed? Do the programs deter delinquency?

3. What prevention programs are available in your area? Is there a specific target area?
4. Are all three levels of delinquency prevention applied in your area? Which one best suits your area? Why?

5. If social responses treat youths' behavior as delinquent in prevention strategies, does this cause a labeling effect? How would you handle a program so that labeling was not a factor?

6. At what types of delinquency should programs be directed? Violent youths? Status offenders? Antisocial and criminal activity in general? Gang activity?

7. List the assumptions you think are basic to effective delinquency prevention programs. To what extent do you think each assumption is justified?

8. What are some contemporary attempts to prevent delinquency? Why are they effective or ineffective?

9. What programs exist in your area to prevent child neglect and abuse?

10. What programs to prevent child neglect and abuse do you think have the most promise?

REFERENCES

American Psychological Association. *Violence & Youth: Psychology's Response*, Vol. 1. Summary Report of the American Psychological Association Commission on Violence and Youth, no date.

Best Practices to Address Community Gang Problems: OJJDP's Comprehensive Gang Model. Washington, DC: U.S. Department of Justice, Office of Juvenile Justice and Delinquency Prevention, June 2008. (NCJ 222799)

Curtis, Nicola M.; Ronan, Kevin R.; and Borduin, Charles M. "Multisystemic Treatment: A Meta-Analysis of Outcome Studies." *Journal of Family Psychology*, Vol. 18, No. 3, 2004, pp.411–419.

Dimock, Kaki. *Truancy Prevention in Action: Best Practices and Model Truancy Programs*. Denver, CO: National Center for School Engagement, July 2005.

Effective Strategy: Provide Positive Alternatives to Gang Activity. Washington, DC: National Crime Prevention Council, 2003. Web site: http://www.ncpc.org

Ennis, Charles. "Twelve Clues That Could Save a Child." *Law and Order*, June 2000, pp.92–95.

Federal Advisory Committee on Juvenile Justice. *Annual Report 2007*. Washington, DC: U.S. Department of Justice, Office of Juvenile Justice and Delinquency Prevention, August 2007. (NCJ 219500)

Graves, Alexander. "Child Abuse and Domestic Violence." *Law and Order*, July 2002, pp.137–141.

Landenberger, Nana A. and Lipsey, Mark W. "The Positive Effects of Cognitive Behavioral Programs for Offenders: A Meta-Analysis of Factors Associated with Effective Treatment." *Journal of Experimental Criminology*, Vol. 1, No. 4, December 2005, pp.451–476.

Latessa, Edward J. "What Works and What Doesn't in Reducing Recidivism: The Principles of Effective Intervention." San Diego, CA: Seminar P-5 presented at the 34th National Conference on Juvenile Justice, March 5, 2007.

Macallair, Daniel and Roche, Tim. *Widening the Net in Juvenile Justice and the Dangers of Prevention and Early Intervention*. San Francisco, CA: The Justice Policy Institute, 2001. (NCJ 192131)

Mendel, Richard A. *Less Hype, More Help: Reducing Juvenile Crime, What Works and What Doesn't*. Washington, DC: American Policy Forum, 2000.

National Crime Prevention Council. Web site: http://www.ncpc.org

Office of Juvenile Justice and Delinquency Prevention. *Model Programs Guide, Version 2.5*. Washington, DC. Created under Cooperative Agreement #2004-JF-FX-K101. Available only online: http://www.dsgonline.com/mpg2.5/mpg_index.htm

Office of National Drug Control Policy. *National Drug Control Strategy: 2009 Annual Report*. Washington, DC: Office of National Drug Control Policy, The White House, 2009. (NCJ 225358)

Sherman, Lawrence W.; Gottfredson, Denise C.; MacKenzie, Doris L.; Eck, John; Reuter, Peter; and Bushway, Shawn D. *Preventing Crime: What Works, What Doesn't, What's Promising*. Washington, DC: U.S. Department of Justice, National Institute of Justice Research in Brief, July 1998. (NCJ 171676)

CASE CITED

Board of Education of Independent School District No. 92 of Pottawatomie County et al. v. Earls et al., 536 U.S. 822 (2002)

CHAPTER 13

Juvenile Justice at a Crossroads: The Accelerating Call for Reform

---

© Steve Liss/Time & Life Pictures/Getty Images

The unfortunate reality is that many youths are victims before they become victimizers—victims of abuse, neglect, prenatal drug exposure, dysfunctional families, poor parenting, poverty, lead exposure, intergenerational gang involvement, learning disabilities, mental illness—the list of risk factors is extensive. Juvenile justice is not just about working with the youths who have reached the stage of delinquency but is also about working with children before they make the transformation from victim to victimizer. The challenge today is getting involved with at-risk youth at the earliest stage possible.

DO YOU KNOW?

■ What factors encouraging policymakers to seek reform in the juvenile justice system are?

■ What the Federal Advisory Commission on Juvenile Justice has identified as key issues facing the juvenile justice system?

■ What nine tenets have been set forth by *A Blueprint for Juvenile Justice Reform*?

■ What key reform issues the Models for Change initiative has identified?

■ What the "hidden minority" problem in juvenile justice is and why it exists?

■ What the National Partnership for Juvenile Services (NPJS) is and what its focus is?

■ What work in the juvenile justice field offers and whether more practitioners are needed?

■ What trends indicate that America is moving toward reform in the juvenile justice system?

CHAPTER OUTLINE

Introduction

Federal Advisory Commission on Juvenile Justice

A Blueprint for Juvenile Justice Reform

Reduce Institutionalization

Reduce Racial Disparity

Ensure Access to Quality Counsel

Create a Range of Community-Based Alternatives

Recognize and Serve Youths with Specialized Needs

Create Smaller Rehabilitative Institutions

Improve Aftercare and Re-Entry

Maximize Youth, Family and Community Participation

Keep Youths Out of Adult Prisons

The Models for Change

Evidence-Based Practices to Overcome Language and Cultural Barriers

Public Attitudes toward Reforming the Juvenile Justice System

Champions for Change Award

The Future of Children

Measuring Performance

The National Partnership for Juvenile Services

A Career in Juvenile Justice

Ameliorating the Juvenile Justice Workforce Crisis

The Juvenile Justice Officer

The Role of Social Workers and Social Services

Where Juvenile Justice Stands Today

Introduction

More than 110 years have passed since the first juvenile court ushered in a separate justice system for juveniles, based on a belief that children were different from adults in crucial ways—biologically, emotionally, psychologically—and deserved a different, more rehabilitative-oriented approach to their wrongdoings. The stage for toughened juvenile sanctions began to be set during the 1970s, when the rehabilitative model came under attack, for both juvenile and adult offenders. Although we now understand that the collapse of this model was due, in large part, to poorly implemented programs and faulty research assessments, policymakers at the time (and the public as a whole) had lost faith in the concept of treatment and rehabilitation.

Then, in the late 1980s and early 1990s, when violent juvenile crimes rates were increasing at a fairly alarming rate, our policymakers decided, without any solid evidence upon which to base these decisions, to "get tough" on juvenile delinquency in the hopes that treating these kids more harshly would send a powerful message to youthful offenders and ultimately make us a safer nation.

This knee-jerk, reactionary response was spurred somewhat by criminal justice scholars who predicted (wrongly, in retrospect) that our country was on the brink of being overrun by juvenile "superpredators" unless we acted quickly and decisively to crack down on youthful offenders. John DiIulio, a well-respected and highly credible researcher, author and political scientist who is often credited with coining the term *juvenile superpredator*, has admitted that his prophecy never came to pass. Nonetheless, many in our juvenile justice system, and society as a whole, had accepted this shift toward a more punitive approach in dealing with juvenile delinquency as a way to ensure public safety. Even as statistics were beginning to show levels of violent juvenile crime were dropping in the latter part of the 1990s, the public still believed a generation of out-of-control youth posed an ever-present and growing threat of victimization. Tougher juvenile sentencing laws were passed, juvenile transfers to criminal court increased, and the general boundaries between the juvenile and adult system grew increasingly blurred.

Today, with the benefit of hindsight and several decades of research data, we are beginning to see more clearly the implications of this policy shift to get tough on delinquency. Many researchers and practitioners contend that the juvenile justice system is at a crossroads—does it stay the course of treating juveniles punitively or return to its original roots of being a distinctly separate system that seeks to treat and rehabilitate youthful offenders. Is there even a need for a separate juvenile justice system today? Should all offenders, regardless of age, be dealt with in one justice system? Or is there a valid reason to sustain a separate justice system for youth? Scott and Steinberg (2008b, p.282) contend:

> For a generation, there has been no clearly articulated rationale for maintaining a separate justice system for juvenile offenders or for dealing with them more leniently than adults. It is reasonable to assume that this conceptual void contributed to the seeming ease with which punitive reforms transformed the juvenile justice system in a relatively short period of time. . . . What is needed, and what this book [and a growing body of empirical evidence] begins to provide, is a new justification for policies that treat juveniles differently from adults and in so doing, protect the community and promote societal welfare.

Hopefully, as you have learned throughout this text, new data concerning human development, coupled with research on the impacts and effectiveness of various treatments and correctional interventions, provides the justification sought to maintain a distinctly separate system to handle youthful offenders and supports the contention that reform is needed and overdue in the juvenile justice system.

 Among the factors encouraging policymakers to seek reform are falling crime rates, state budget crises, new research on brain development in adolescents and evidence-based programs amenable to replication.

Mendel and Middaugh (2003) assert that the juvenile justice system has four crucial choices facing it in the twenty-first century:

- *Choice 1: Rhyme or Reason?* The simple rhyme "adult time for adult crime" turned America's juvenile justice debate on its head in the 1990s, leading

49 states and the District of Columbia to amend their laws such that increasing numbers of juveniles were transferred to and tried in adult courts.

■ *Choice 2: Confinement or Community?* Community-based treatment and intervention programs cost significantly less than secure confinement which, in these troubled economic times, can mean substantial savings to U.S. taxpayers. In addition, evidence has consistently shown that confinement is rarely the most effective or appropriate treatment for delinquency and that taxpayers get considerably more bang for their buck with community-based interventions.

■ *Choice 3: Rights or Wrongs?* Are we protecting the rights of court-involved youths? In 1967, in *In re Gault*, the Supreme Court clearly stated: "Under our Constitution, the condition of being a boy does not justify a kangaroo court." And what of the racial imbalance?

■ *Choice 4: Run-of-the-Mill or Research-Based Programming?* Juvenile justice needs to pay attention to what works and to researching what works. We can no longer justify throwing money into programs that have proven to be ineffective in reducing or preventing delinquency.

To help guide juvenile justice through this period of transition, numerous advisory committees, work groups and other initiatives have emerged, each with suggestions for reform. Although the various entities differ slightly in what they identify specifically for reform, considerable overlap also exists, as you will notice.

Federal Advisory Committee on Juvenile Justice

The Federal Advisory Committee on Juvenile Justice (FACJJ) is a consultative body established in 2004 by the Office of Juvenile Justice and Delinquency Prevention (OJJDP) to oversee the provision required by the Juvenile Justice and Delinquency Prevention (JJDP) Act. Composed of 56 appointed representatives of the nation's State Advisory Groups, the committee brings a breadth and wealth of experience, knowledge and leadership in the field in their mission to advise the President and Congress on matters related to juvenile justice, evaluate the progress and accomplishments of juvenile justice activities and projects, and advise the OJJDP administrator on the work of OJJDP.

According to the most recent *Annual Report* by the FACJJ (2008), states have identified five broad areas as the most critical issues confronting their juvenile justice systems:

1. The deinstitutionalization of status offenders (DSO)
2. Jail removal and sight and sound separation (detention reform)
3. Disproportionate minority contact
4. Effective assistance of counsel
5. Mental health, substance abuse and the juvenile justice system

 According to the Federal Advisory Committee on Juvenile Justice (FACJJ), the most critical issues confronting the nation's juvenile justice systems are the deinstitutionalization of status offenders, detention reform, disproportionate minority contact, effectiveness of legal counsel, and mental health assessment and substance abuse treatment.

The FACJJ's *Annual Report 2008*, a 65-page document, is a comprehensive assessment of what is working in various local jurisdictions and what some recommended steps are for improving the delivery and effectiveness of juvenile justice services in communities throughout the country. It is available online at: http://www.facjj.org/annualreports/ed_08-FACJJ%20Annual%20Report%2008.pdf. Another group actively working to address the reform needs of juvenile justice is the Youth Transition Funders Group (YTFG).

A Blueprint for Juvenile Justice Reform

The Juvenile Justice Work Group of the Youth Transition Funders Group (YTFG) consists of regional and national grant makers working across fields of justice, education, foster care and mental health to support policies and programs that treat youth like youth: "We aim to help governments and non-profits preserve public safety and improve young people's chances to become successful and productive adults" (Peterson, 2005). According to YFTG: "Today in America, more than three million young adults, ages 14 to 24, are neither in school nor employed. The [YTFG] is composed of foundations dedicated to improving the lives of these disconnected youths who are transiting out of foster care, entangled in the juvenile justice system or at risk of dropping out of school" (Peterson, p.15). The work group's *A Blueprint for Juvenile Justice Reform* sets forth nine basic tenets that lay the groundwork for juvenile justice reform across the nation.

 The nine tenets for juvenile justice reform set forth by *A Blueprint for Juvenile Justice Reform* are: reduce institutionalization; reduce racial disparity; ensure access to quality counsel; create a range of community-based alternatives; recognize and serve youths with specialized needs; create smaller rehabilitative institutions; improve aftercare and re-entry; maximize youth, family and community participation; and keep youths out of adult prisons.

Reduce Institutionalization

The best systems for reducing institutionalization are those that offer community-based alternatives using tools such as risk assessment and sentencing guidelines to distinguish between youths who pose risks to public safety and those who would be better served in less-restrictive settings. For example, the 12-year-old Annie E. Casey Foundation's Juvenile Detention Alternatives Initiative (JDAI) has decreased average daily populations in secure detention by 31–66 percent, while simultaneously improving indicators of public safety.

Reduce Racial Disparity

Young people of color are significantly over-represented in the justice and foster care systems and among struggling students. "In nearly every state, in every juvenile offense category—person, property, drugs and public order—youths of color received harsher sentences and fewer services than white youths who have committed the same category of offense" (Peterson, 2005, p.7). Some jurisdictions have significantly reduced racial disparity by analyzing data by race and ethnicity to detect disparate treatment, using objective screening instruments and coordinating with police to influence who comes into the juvenile justice system. They have also changed hiring practices so staff are more representative of youths in the system and have developed culturally competent programming and used mechanisms to divert those of color from secure confinement.

Ensure Access to Quality Counsel

Across the country, youths often face court hearings without the assistance of competent counsel—some appointed 5 minutes before the case is heard. Given their vulnerability, youths' access to competent counsel is essential. Suggested reforms include early assignment of counsel with specialized training on adolescent development, mental health and special education and cross-system representation if adolescents are involved in multiple systems. In addition, all jurisdictions must honor their constitutional obligation to provide counsel to indigent youths.

Create a Range of Community-Based Alternatives

Community-based programs include a range of approaches from probation to intensive supervision, home confinement, alternative education, family preservation, restitution, community service, and day and evening reporting centers with opportunities for recreation, education and counseling. According to *Blueprint* (Peterson, p.8):

> Three evidence-based programs are scientifically proven to prevent crime, even among youths with the highest risk of re-offending. Functional Family Therapy, Multidimensional Treatment Foster Care and Multi-Systemic Therapy (MST) all focus on the family. None involve incarceration. All deliver results. Evaluations of MST for serious juvenile offenders demonstrate reductions of 25 to 70 percent in long-term rates of re-arrest, reductions of 47 to 64 percent in out-of-home placements, improvements in family functioning and decreased mental health problems, all at a lower cost than other juvenile justice services.

Recognize and Serve Youths with Specialized Needs

All too often the juvenile justice system is a dumping ground for youth whose primary problems are serious emotional disturbances, developmental disabilities, substance abuse or some combination of these challenges. The problem of youths with mental illness was introduced in Chapter 9. Hunsicker (2007, p.60) points out: "The juvenile justice system is facing the trend experienced by the adult criminal justice system—the criminalization of mental illness. Youth facilities have become substitute mental health hospitals, while also facing the pressure of economic constraints, difficulties recruiting and retaining qualified staff and the possible shift in focus from a treatment and rehabilitation model to one of custody and control."

The majority of young people entering the juvenile justice system, up to 70 percent by some accounts, have a mental health disorder (Kennedy, 2007, p.24): "The number one priority in dealing with these juveniles should be to make sure that when they leave the justice system they will not be back." The three steps needed to make this priority a reality: (1) early screening and assessment,

(2) diverting young people from secure facilities into home- and community-based programs and (3) implementing evidence-based practices. Kennedy (p.26) stresses: "The child welfare system and the justice system should not serve as mental health service providers of last resort."

For juveniles with mental illness in the juvenile justice system, several alternatives for treatment are available in the community as well as within the juvenile justice system, including intermediate sanctions. Such youths need these alternatives, as formal placement within the juvenile justice system can be harmful to them. It is crucial that juvenile justice involvement is appropriate only when a youth's delinquency is the primary reason for confinement, not his or her disability.

Create Smaller Rehabilitative Institutions

Evidence supports treating youths like youths, not adults. This can be translated into smaller, more home-like facilities. Small rehabilitation centers can give youths the care and interaction needed to integrate back into society. Such facilities can be run by youth specialists to provide developmentally appropriate individual and group programming, with families participating in the rehabilitation to ensure youths successfully transition back into society.

The Missouri model provides an example. No facility contains more than 40 youths served by an ethnically diverse staff trained in youth development. The goal is to help youths transition into their communities as productive citizens. This model has proven "extremely successful." Seventy percent of youths released in 1999 avoided recommitment to any correctional program three years later, compared to a 45–75 percent re-arrest rate nationally. This model has been replicated in several jurisdictions.

Improve Aftercare and Re-Entry

This is closely related to the preceding discussion. Nearly 100,000 youths are released from institutions yearly. Critical to their success is having community agencies and schools ready to welcome them on their return. As noted in Chapter 11 and again here: "The best reentry programs begin while a youth is still confined. They require coordination between multiple government agencies and nonprofit providers, not only to develop new services, but to help youths better access existing services" (Peterson, 2005, p.9). When released, teenagers should enroll in school or have a job. Helping teens acquire job skills and earn money is highly motivational for many youths.

In 2004 the John D. and Catherine T. MacArthur Foundation selected Pennsylvania as the first site of its Model Systems Project, a multiyear, multimillion-dollar effort to produce replicable, system-wide juvenile justice reform. Pennsylvania's promising approach to aftercare, beginning when a youth is first sentenced and extending after release from confinement, has become a model program.

Maximize Youth, Family and Community Participation

True reform addresses not just the juvenile justice system, but engages those whom youths encounter daily. Reforming the juvenile justice system will take a total community effort, involving all stakeholders, including the youths

Visitors gather for an open house at the new Rogue Valley Youth Correctional Facility in Grants Pass, Oregon. The prison is one of five in Oregon to handle increasing numbers of young offenders.

themselves. Stark disparities between juvenile justice and education in spending prompted youth organizers, with support from the Surdna Foundation, to work with youths and staff inside locked facilities to improve the conditions under which youths are confined. A youth-made documentary moved advocates to call for alternate uses of their costly new juvenile justice facility, designed for 240 youths but housing only 65.

Keep Youths Out of Adult Prisons

This goal was a mainstay of the Juvenile Delinquency and Control Act of 1974. The hazards associated with incarcerating youths in adult prisons were discussed in Chapter 11. However, during the 1990s, 49 states changed their laws to increase the number of minors being tried as adults. *Blueprint* reports (Peterson, 2005, p.10) that about 210,000 minors nationwide are now being prosecuted in adult courts and sent to adult prisons each year despite studies showing that youths held in adult facilities are eight times more likely to commit suicide, five times more likely to report being a victim of rape, twice as likely to report being beaten by staff and 50 percent more likely to be attacked with a weapon. In addition, youths sent to adult court also return to crime at a higher rate.

The Models for Change

The National Center for Juvenile Justice (NCJJ), with funding from the Mac-Arthur Foundation, has implemented Models for Change, a movement advocating systems reform in juvenile justice: "Models for Change seeks to accelerate progress toward a more effective, fair, and developmentally sound juvenile justice system that holds young people accountable for their actions, provides for their rehabilitation, protects them from harm, increases their life chances, and manages the risk they pose to themselves and to the public" (Griffin, 2008, p.i). The report, *Models for Change 2008 Update: Gathering Force*, outlines specific achievements made in each of the four Model States (Illinois, Louisiana, Pennsylvania and Washington) and three Action Networks (DMC, Indigent Defense and Mental Health/Juvenile Justice) since December 2007.

Despite being funded by a different entity and administered by a different work group, the overlap between the key issues identified by *Models for Change*, the *Blueprint* tenets and the FACJJ's main reform concerns should be very apparent. *Models for Change* identifies seven key issues that should shape reform:

1. A model system includes effective *aftercare*. Juveniles returning to the community should be quickly connected with programs and services to help them adjust and succeed, and should begin school, job training or employment immediately.

2. The *mental health*, substance abuse and other specialized treatment they received while in care would continue, as would the strong support of family and other caring adults.

3. A model system includes *racial fairness*, that is, juveniles receive fair treatment regardless of their race or ethnicity. This requires that all hearings, decisions and services be bias-free and that the system routinely monitor compliance with fairness. If disparate treatment is found to exist, resources should be available to determine the causes and address them.

4. A model system includes *community-based alternatives* that are local and informal whenever possible.

5. It also includes *right-sizing jurisdictions*, featuring individualized and developmentally appropriate handling of young people accused of crime, acknowledging the fundamental developmental differences between young people and adults and not blurring the boundaries between the juvenile and criminal justice system without usurping the role of families, schools and communities.

6. A model system is also grounded on *evidence-based practices*, that is, programs, practices and services that are based on research and have demonstrated their effectiveness. It would also contribute to the ongoing development of a scientific base of support for its programs and services, continuously measuring the success of existing interventions and encouraging development and evaluation of innovative practices.

7. Finally, a model system provides for *juvenile indigent defense*, safeguarding the procedural and substantive right of all youths who come into conflict with the law. Competent legal counsel should be available as soon as possible after arrest and continue until the case is closed. Defense attorneys should have limited caseloads and adequate training and oversight, as well as access to investigators, experts, social workers and support staff.

 According to the Models for Change initiative, key issues in juvenile justice reform include effective aftercare, mental health treatment, racial fairness, community-based alternatives, right-sizing jurisdictions, evidence-based practices and juvenile indigent defense.

PERSPECTIVES FROM THE FIELD

At the 2nd Annual Models for Change National Conference held in Washington, DC, in December 2007, hundreds of participants—youth workers, researchers, judges, attorneys, educators, administrators and other juvenile justice advocates from across the nation—were welcomed to the national "movement to reform the juvenile justice system" by MacArthur Foundation President Jonathan Fanton with this opening remark:

> I use the word "movement" instead of "program" or "initiative" for a reason. Movements are based on values and animated by a vision of a more just and humane society. Movements arise from a broad base, starting locally, gathering force, and gaining national

momentum. And, most often, movements succeed in changing reality when the time is right and the public ready to embrace new ways of pursuing basic goals.

As Griffin (p.1) asserts: "Since Fanton spoke . . ., the sense of movement in the field of juvenile justice—of something fundamental changing and 'gathering force'—has grown stronger." This spirit of *movement* was palpable at the 36th National Conference on Juvenile Justice, held in Orlando, FL, in March 2009. A sea change is most certainly occurring in the way people in juvenile justice are approaching their mission, and this swinging of the pendulum is having a ripple effect on how policymakers and the public are perceiving the challenges we face today and in the future with regard to our youth.

Through Models for Change, the MacArthur Foundation has committed more than $100 million to juvenile justice research and reform, seeking not a single blueprint for change or a step-by-step guide for reform but, rather, to support the development of multiple models of comprehensive, home-grown systems reform. The movement began in Pennsylvania in 2004, and was then implemented in Illinois in 2005, Louisiana in 2006 and Washington state in 2007. Models for Change has also implemented action networks focusing on key issues in California, Colorado, Connecticut, Florida, Kansas, Maryland, Massachusetts, New Jersey, North Carolina, Ohio, Texas and Wisconsin.

In *Models for Change: Building Momentum for Juvenile Justice Reform*, Ziedenberg (2006, p.3) observes: "Juvenile justice policy in the United States has quietly passed a milestone. After a decade shaped by myths of juvenile 'superpredators' and the ascendency of punitive reforms, momentum for systemic reform is growing. . . . While some still beat the drum for harsher measures, a group of innovative state leaders from across the country are creating a new path toward fair, rational, effective, and developmentally appropriate models for juvenile justice reform."

This report cites (pp.4–5) a recent survey of policy changes indicating several trends, including large-scale institutional reform (Illinois, Louisiana and Mississippi); returning young people to juvenile court jurisdiction (Delaware, Illinois and Washington); strengthening aftercare services to help young people return to their communities (California, Indiana, Pennsylvania and Virginia); providing mental health treatment to young people who need it (Idaho, South Dakota, Virginia and Washington); investing in services rather than state confinement (Illinois, Louisiana, Maryland, Mississippi and Washington) and improving juvenile defense (Illinois, Michigan, Mississippi, Montana, Virginia and Wisconsin).

In partnership with its grantees, the MacArthur Foundation has developed a working framework for a model juvenile justice system grounded in eight principles reflecting widely shared and family-held values related to juvenile justice (Ziedenberg, p.7):

1. *Fundamental fairness.* All system participants—including youthful offenders, their victims and their families—deserve bias-free treatment.

2. *Recognition of juvenile-adult differences.* The system must take into account that juveniles are fundamentally and developmentally different from adults.

3. *Recognition of individual differences.* Juvenile justice decision makers must acknowledge and respond to individual differences in terms of young people's development, culture, gender, needs and strengths.

4. *Recognition of potential.* Young offenders have strengths and are capable of positive growth. Giving up on them is costly for society. Investing in them makes sense.

5. *Safety.* Communities and individuals deserve to be and to feel safe.

6. *Personal responsibility.* Young people must be encouraged to accept responsibility for their actions and the consequences of those actions.

7. *Community responsibility.* Communities have an obligation to safeguard the welfare of children and young people, to support them when in need and to help them grow into adults.

8. *System responsibility.* The juvenile justice system is a vital part of society's collective exercise of its responsibility toward young people. It must do its job effectively.[1]

Evidence-Based Practices to Overcome Language and Cultural Barriers

Traditional intake practices tend to divide most youths into "white" and "black" racial categories regardless of their ethnic origins, resulting in a "hidden minority" problem.

 Data collection practices have "lost" juveniles of Hispanic ethnicity, resulting in a "hidden minority" problem.

Torbet et al. (2006, p.6) notes that addressing disproportionate minority confinement (DMC) is a priority of the Pennsylvania Models for Change initiative, explaining that the federal minimum race categories are American Indian or Alaska Native, Asian, Black or African American, Native Hawaiian or other Pacific Islander and White. The Census 2000 race categories also exclude Hispanic, although there is also a category for some other race. Torbet et al.'s guidelines (p.4) for best practices for recording race and ethnicity recommend asking the following three questions, with the first two limited to fixed responses:

1. Hispanic/Latino? (Yes or no)
2. Race (5 categories): American Indian or Alaska Native, Asian, Black or African American, Native Hawaiian or other Pacific Islander, White
3. National origin, ancestry or tribal affiliation (optional)

One important initiative included in the Models for Change is that undertaken by the National Council of LaRaza (NCLR), the largest Hispanic civil rights and advocacy organization in the United States—working to improve conditions for Hispanic Americans. Their publication *Overcoming Language and Cultural Barriers Using Evidence-Based Practices* (2008, p.vii) notes that

---

[1]From the Justice Policy Institute, December 2006, Jason Ziedenberg, "Models for Change: Building Momentum for Juvenile Justice Reform."

although there are many evidence-based practices (EBPs) targeted at preventing delinquency, there is limited evidence of successful outcomes for Latinos: "This is due in part to insufficient documentation of the cultural and linguistic modifications and adaptations of EBPs. As a result, many Latino youth and families are inadequately treated and have limited access to such programs." Thus, one of their primary goals is to ensure that those programs and practices identified as effective (i.e., EBPs) be translated and adapted to meet the cultural and language needs of Hispanic youths. By extension, this principle would apply to other minority youths and families in contact with the juvenile justice system.

Public Attitudes toward Reforming the Juvenile Justice System

As part of the Models for Change initiative, the MacArthur Foundation commissioned the Center for Children's Law and Policy to determine the public's attitude toward reforming the juvenile justice system and found strong support for such reform (Soler, 2007, pp.1–2).

- "The public recognizes the potential of young people to change." The majority of respondents agreed that incarcerating juvenile offenders without rehabilitation is simply giving up on them.
- "The public supports redirecting government funds from incarceration to counseling, education and job training for young offenders" (8 out of 10).
- "The public views the provision of treatment and services as more effective ways of rehabilitating youths than incarceration." Fewer than 15 percent of those surveyed thought incarcerating juveniles was a "very effective" way to rehabilitate youths.
- "The public favors keeping nonviolent juveniles in small, residential facilities in their own communities rather than in large distant institutions" (75 percent of those surveyed).
- "The public believes the juvenile justice system treats low-income youth, African American youth and Hispanic youth unfairly. Almost two-thirds of respondents said that poor youth receive worse treatment than middle-class youth who get arrested for the same offense."

Champions for Change Award

Recognizing that true change usually depends on inspirational leadership, the Champions for Change Award is presented by the MacArthur Foundation to those who stand out among the many who are working hard to bring about the kind of reform resulting in better lives for so many young people in our country (*Champions for Change*, 2008). These individuals were chosen by colleagues in their own states.

James E. Anderson—Pennsylvania   Anderson is Executive Director of the Pennsylvania Juvenile Court Judges' Commission (JCJC) and has been central to some of the most important legislative actions affecting juveniles in Pennsylvania's juvenile justice system. The JCJC shepherded a bill through legislation promoting mental health services for delinquent youths by protecting them from self-incrimination for comments made during screening, assessment and evaluation. In addition, the JCJC and the Chief's Council engaged all 67 Pennsylvania counties in aftercare reform which will result in a closer alignment between juvenile probation and residential programs.

Elizabeth Clarke—Illinois   Clarke is founder and president of the Juvenile Justice Initiative (JJI) in Illinois. She has helped leverage MacArthur research to educate Illinois lawmakers about the latest findings around adolescent development and public attitudes about youths, race and crime while actively building a statewide coalition and enhancing public awareness of juvenile justice issues. The JJI spearheaded legislation representing the first rollback of automatic transfer laws in the country. In the first two years following the 2005 legislation, automatic transfers to adult court declined by almost two-thirds, affecting nearly 500 youths. In 2008 the JJI was instrumental in getting legislation passed requiring the early appointment of council and raising the age of juvenile court jurisdiction for all misdemeanors to age 18.

Paul Joseph Frick—Louisiana   Professor Frick is a research professor of psychology and chair of the Department of Psychology at the University of New Orleans. He has demonstrated that data is a powerful tool for change. Frick has developed a comprehensive mapping process of the juvenile justice system in each parish; formed and coordinated a state data group involving local universities, members of the National Resource Band and Lead Entity; created more than 35 data reports to aid the National Resource Band and local sites in selecting goals for their work and developed an Outcome Evaluation Plan to help evaluate effectiveness in reaching those goals.

Jacqueline van Wormer—Washington (state)   Van Wormer, a Benton and Franklin Counties Superior Court adjunct faculty member at Washington State University, has recruited two universities, dozens of faculty and countless graduate students into the juvenile justice reform arena. She has worked extensively in truancy reform as well as DMC issues. As one colleague states: "Jacque somehow unites the brain of a research worker, the heart of an advocate and the personal touch of a skilled team-builder."

The preceding award winners illustrate the diverse backgrounds and skills individuals can bring to the reform effort. Another influential publication is the Fall 2008 issue of *The Future of Children: Juvenile Justice*.

The Future of Children

In introducing *The Future of Children: Juvenile Justice*, Steinberg (2008, p.3) states: "American juvenile justice policy is in a period of transition. . . . State legislatures across the country have reconsidered punitive statutes they enacted with enthusiasm not so many years go. What we may be seeing now is a pendulum that has reached its apex and is slowly beginning to swing back toward more moderate policies, as politicians and the public come to regret the high economic costs and ineffectiveness of the punitive reforms and the harshness of the sanction." Indicators of this shift are noted in various ways—the Supreme Court abolishing the juvenile death penalty (*Roper v. Simmons*), several states having repealed or considering repealing statutes imposing sentences of life without parole (LWOP) on juvenile murderers, the scaling back of automatic juvenile transfer laws, a trend in states increasing the age to 18 for juvenile court jurisdiction and expanded procedural protection by authorizing findings of incompetence to stand trial on the basis of developmental immaturity.

Steinberg (p.4) asserts: "The scientific study of adolescent development has burgeoned in the past two decades, but its findings have not yet influenced juvenile justice policy nearly as much as they should." Indeed there exists a lag time of 10 to 15 years between the discovery and documentation of scientific evidence, such as that found by brain research, and the implementation of that data into public policy form (Culotta, 2009).

Steinberg (p.7) reminds us that most young offenders will desist from crime as they mature psychologically, merely in the course of normal development: "To protect society in the long run and to promote social welfare, the response to juveniles' antisocial behavior must not imperil their development into productive adulthood." Following are brief summaries of the articles in this issue of *The Future of Children: Juvenile Justice*, each of which nicely encapsulates a key issue in the big picture of juvenile justice reform.

Scott and Steinberg (2008a) emphasize the developmental perspective so vital to juvenile justice reform, noting that lawmakers and the public, until recently, have acted as if the differences between adolescents and adults were immaterial in matters dealing with youth crime policies. Fortunately, legislators and the public appear to be reconsidering the appropriateness, or rather inappropriateness, of a justice system that ignores age and immaturity when calculating criminal punishment: "A substantial body of new scientific knowledge about adolescence and about criminal activity during this important developmental period provides the building blocks for a new legal regime superior to today's policy. Under the developmental model, adolescent offenders constitute an intermediate legal category of persons who are neither children . . . nor adults" (p.16).

Mulvey and Iselin (2008) address the issue of improving professional judgment of risk and amenability in juvenile justice, noting that the juvenile justice system has been slow to adopt structured methods for assessing risk and amenability to treatment: "Juvenile justice professionals must make well-reasoned judgments about two key issues: the risk of future harm to the community posed by an adolescent and how likely the adolescent is to benefit from intervention" (p.37).

They point out that adolescents should be held responsible for antisocial acts but their responsibility mitigated by their diminished decision-making capacity, their susceptibility to peer influence and their unformed character. They conclude that most adolescent crime is the product of developmental immaturity, attested to by research showing that few adolescent offenders grow into adult criminals.

They (p.35) examine and recommend three ways to integrate structured judgment into the juvenile justice system: First, more reliance on actuarial methods of detention and intake would promote more efficient and equitable screening of cases for court involvement. Second, probation officers using structured decision making could provide more consistent and valid guidance for the court when formulating dispositions. Third, implementing structured data systems to chart adolescents' progress in placement could allow judges to oversee service providers more effectively.

Disproportionate minority contact (DMC) is addressed by Piquero (2008), who explains that the traditional research approach to DMC has been a comparative research endeavor to come up with an index figure. For example, if the youth population in a given jurisdiction was about 3 percent minority and 12 percent of juveniles in custody were minority, the index would be 4.0. States with an index greater than 1.0 were required to implement a plan to reduce this proportionality: "Asking how much minority overrepresentation in the juvenile justice system is due to differences in processing and how much to differences in offending no longer seems a helpful way to frame the discussion" (p.61). He says both processes contribute to the problem.

Piquero suggests that what started out as an issue of disproportionate minority *confinement* has broadened into disproportionate minority contact, affecting all points in the juvenile justice system. He recommends that researchers should move to other concerns, such as understanding the mechanisms that contribute both to differential involvement in crime and to differential treatment by decisions makers, and study the effect of various interventions to reduce disparities in both arenas and at different points in the process.

The controversy over whether juveniles should be processed in juvenile or adult court is discussed by Fagan, who suggests that between 20 and 26 percent of all juvenile offenders younger than 18 are prosecuted in adult court because their states' jurisdictional boundary is either 16 or 17: "Sending an adolescent offender to the criminal court is a serious and consequential step. It is an irreversible decision that exposes young lawbreakers to harsh and sometimes toxic forms of punishment that as the empirical evidence shows, have the perverse effect of increasing criminal activity" (2008, p.83). The impact of juvenile transfer to adult court was discussed in Chapter 10.

Grisso (2008) discusses the challenge of adolescent offenders with mental disorders and Chassin (2008) addresses the challenge of juvenile justice and substance abuse, both of which have been previously discussed.

Finally, Greenwood (2008) describes prevention and intervention programs for juvenile offenders: "Cost-effectiveness and cost-benefit studies make it possible to compare the efficiency of programs that produce similar results, allowing policymakers to achieve the largest possible crime-prevention effect for a given level of funding" (p.188). Greenwood (p.186) notes: "Fairly strong evidence now demonstrates the effectiveness of a dozen or so 'proven' delinquency-prevention program models and generalized strategies." Adding credibility to the argument is the fact that different reviews conducted by different groups of investigators have led to mostly the same five conclusions:

1. Family-based programs, such as functional family therapy, multisystemic therapy or multidimensional treatment foster care, are consistently more effective than programs focusing on treating individual juveniles alone.
2. In institutional settings, treatments that follow basic principles of cognitive-behavioral therapy are usually superior to other approaches.
3. Excessively harsh or punitive programs have either no effects or negative effects.
4. Incarceration is expensive and yields little benefit other than short-term incapacitation.
5. Even the best evidence-based programs must be implemented correctly to be effective.

This final point is critical. Most programs need to be adapted to fit the local jurisdiction, but the basic principles and processes should remain fairly intact. In addition, the impact of the intervention should be systematically assessed.

Measuring Performance

Historically the only measure of success of juvenile justice programs was the recidivism rate, which often gives an incomplete and ineffective assessment of a particular intervention, as it can preclude the possibility that other important goals may have been achieved despite the fact a youth committed another offense. Thomas (2006, p.2) suggests that all aspects of juvenile justice undertake performance measurement, which he defines as "assessing an organization's ability to do things, including measures of productivity (how much they do), effectiveness (how efficiently they do it), quality (how well they do it) and timeliness (how long it takes them to do it)." Measuring performance provides evidence of what works and what needs modification. The ultimate goal is to improve performance. Furthermore, a successful strategy must be replicable in a variety of places over an extended period of time. Thomas (p.5) suggests six essential features of such strategies:

1. Mission-based outcomes
2. Unambiguous unit of analysis (the individual case)
3. Consistent data collection instrument (simple and brief)
4. Reliable data collection agents
5. Clear strategy for entering and processing data
6. Regular and consistent dissemination of information generated by the data

Thomas (p.9) reports on five jurisdictions of a diverse array across the country, which illustrate it is possible, practical and useful to measure the performance of juvenile justice systems. The ultimate goal of this project on measuring performance is to produce a report card for the public and the local and state policymakers to see how well the juvenile justice system is fulfilling its missions. Such evaluations are effective in informing the public, celebrating successes, identifying weaknesses resource needs, preparing budgets and dealing with the media.

The National Partnership for Juvenile Services

Throughout this text the importance of partnerships and collaboration has been emphasized, as juveniles do not live in a vacuum. As poet John Donne wrote: "No man is an island. Do not ask for whom the bell tolls. It tolls for thee." These words ring true in the twenty-first century. Several juvenile justice organizations have realized they could accomplish more by working in partnership than by working alone or competing with one another for limited resources. The 9/11 shift in federal funding priorities prompted five nonprofit juveniles justice organizations to find an approach to minimize duplication and maximize resources, resulting in the creation of the National Partnership for Juvenile Services (NPJS) in the late 1990s. This coalition is made up of the National Juvenile Detention Association (NJDA), the National Association of Juvenile Correctional Agencies (NAJCA), the Juvenile Justice

Trainers Association, (JJTA), the Council for Educators of At-Risk and Delinquent Youth (CEARDY) and the National Association for Children of Incarcerated Parents (NACIP): "Each of the individual organizations represents different disciplines of the juvenile justice continuum; however, all of the organizations are formally united under one operational structure" (Jones, 2008, p.120).

 The National Partnership for Juvenile Services is a nonprofit collaboration of five juvenile justice advocacy groups committed to improving the nation's juvenile justice system by providing specific, results-oriented training and technical assistance.

Jones explains that collectively, each organization brings expertise and excellence in designing, developing and delivering:

- Best practices in staff training and professional development
- Community-based prevention and intervention programs
- Educational services for at-risk and delinquent youths
- Safe and humane treatment of confined youths
- Sound systemic approaches to operating an effective and efficient juvenile justice system while also ensuring the safety of the surrounding communities

Since it began, the NPJS has made significant contributions to the juvenile justice system by providing more than 300,000 hours of training and technical assistance nationwide (Jones, p.121). Such support should make a career in juvenile justice more appealing.

A Career in Juvenile Justice

For those who enjoy working with youths and families, the juvenile justice system can provide challenging and satisfying employment. With a growing priority placed on the high rates of juvenile delinquency and serious, violent offenses committed by youths, the juvenile justice system is expanding and should be a significant employer of personnel in the years ahead (Harr and Hess, 2010, p.34).

 Work in the juvenile justice field is very challenging and rewarding, and the need for juvenile justice practitioners is growing.

Howe et al. (2007, p.35) point out: "Juvenile justice workers fulfill a dual role: a public safety and accountability role, which involves the management of youths' behavior, and a rehabilitation and youth development role, which involves mentoring and coaching youths in pro-social skill development. This duality is a source of frustration as well as opportunity among the juvenile justice workers." They (p.34) also observe:

- The juvenile justice workforce comprises approximately 300,000 workers.
- Workers remain in the field because they enjoy working with children and families, and they want to help children achieve meaningful outcomes.
- Workers leave the field because of long hours, insufficient support from supervisors, low pay, lack of a career ladder and high stress.
- Workers perceive they are managing more high-need children than in the past, such as those with substance abuse or mental health disorders, and that they are not trained to manage this population.

A licensed social worker teaches a problem-solving seminar to youthful offenders in the revocation unit at Scioto Juvenile Correctional Facility in Colombus, Ohio

© AP/Wide World Photos

Howe et al. point out a "marketing crisis" in juvenile justice, citing data from a Brookings Institute survey in which 86 percent of students pursuing bachelor of arts and social work degrees said they were "not too seriously" or "not seriously at all" considering working in juvenile justice. When asked how informed they were about career opportunities in juvenile justice, 73 percent were "not too informed" or "not informed at all."

Ameliorating the Juvenile Justice Workforce Crisis

Howe et al. (2007, p.39) suggest the following to ameliorate the pending juvenile justice workforce crisis:

- Increase public perception of juvenile justice as a desirable career choice. Unless the field increases the visibility of the unique aspects of juvenile justice work and facilitates opportunities for education and training, other more visible fields will lure away qualified applicants.
- Increase the diversity of the workforce. Though juvenile justice is increasingly employing more women, individuals of color and bilingual/bicultural staff, much more must be done to align staff demographics with client demographics. Targeted recruitment of a more diverse workforce serves the dual purpose of increasing the available applicant pool while reflecting the diversity of the community and the client population.

The Juvenile Justice Officer

The juvenile officer must operate within a system that handles a broad range of offenders and victims. A significant challenge facing juvenile justice is that the system must deal effectively with a wide range of youth from extremely diverse circumstances—from children and youths who are abused and neglected, to those who commit status offenses and other minor offenses, to those who commit vicious, violent, predatory crimes.

In many departments, juvenile work is considered a promotion after three to five years as a patrol officer. In addition, increasing numbers of departments have school resource officers (SROs) who work within local schools. In the accepted school resource officer model, SROs engage in three types of activities: law enforcement, teaching and mentoring (Finn, 2006, p.1). The emphasis devoted to each duty varies considerably from school to school: "Interest has grown in placing sworn law enforcement personnel in schools to improve school safety and relations between officers and young people" (Finn, p.2). Finn's research found four main benefits of an SRO program: reducing the workload of patrol officers, improving the image of officers among juveniles, creating and maintaining better relationships with the schools and enhancing the agency's reputation in the community.

In addition to jobs with police agencies, careers in juvenile justice include group home child care workers and counselors, as well as intake officers and child care workers in juvenile detention facilities or correctional facilities, such as juvenile probation and so on. Those interested in working with juveniles might consider volunteering with a youth group to gain experience and to confirm that this is, indeed, an area of special interest. One initiative that has a place for everyone is the National Partnership for Juvenile Services.

The Role of Social Workers and Social Services

Social workers are involved in community supervision programs for troubled youths and their families, in juvenile court-sponsored, community-based diversion programs and in school-based counseling programs. Social work functions in all aspects of the juvenile justice system.

Usually a combination of approaches is most effective. Social work can provide a range of services that may include, but by no means be limited to, direct counseling with the juvenile. The broader role of social work within the context of juvenile facilities may include advocacy and brokerage on behalf of juveniles in their relations with family members, social agencies, school officials and potential employers. Social work tries by a variety of means to ease juveniles' passage through the most difficult stage of life and to prevent institutionalized youths from becoming brutal, embittered adults.

Where Juvenile Justice Stands Today

Juvenile justice stands at a crossroads, with those in the field and those about to enter it holding tremendous sway over the policies and practices that will shape how we deal with juvenile offenders—youths who either will be guided and encouraged to become productive, self-monitoring, law-abiding adults or who will become the next generation of criminals. For the vast majority of kids who have contact with the system, a positive outcome is entirely within reason. Collectively, the nation has begun to do all of the following:

America is beginning to act on the research; put the brakes on criminalization and turn away from failed approaches; recognize the limits of incarceration; and invest in proven alternatives (Griffin, 2008, pp.1–2).

What is important to acknowledge is that every juvenile in "the system" comes from somewhere—somewhere where things didn't work right. These youths are often victimized—abused, neglected, bullied, exposed to violence, unsupervised and left to raise themselves in an increasingly troubled and morally challenged society. They often come into the world with multiple strikes already against them—born to young, single and uneducated or undereducated mothers; exposed to a variety of drugs while still developing in the womb; stunted by a life of poverty and lack of early childhood stimulation. They may be trapped by intergenerational gang involvement or suffering from an undiagnosed mental illness. Every one of these circumstances and situations is an opportunity for "the system" to intervene and take notice of that child before the child makes the transition from *having* a problem to *being* a problem, before the child transforms from victim to victimizer. Juvenile justice is not just about working with the youths who have reached the stage of delinquency but is also about working with children *before* they make that transformation.

The challenge facing the juvenile justice system today is whether it will be a conductor or a custodian of the lives of the young people in its care: "Conductors just move juveniles through the system, but custodians guide, develop and take care of their juvenile charges" (Bayliss, 2007, p.106). "What this country needs is more people . . . who are interested in lighting candles, and fewer who blow them out" (Knight, 2008, p.63).

 ## SUMMARY

- Among the factors encouraging policymakers to seek reform are falling crime rates, state budget crises, new research on brain development in adolescents and evidence-based programs amenable to replication.
- According to the Federal Advisory Committee on Juvenile Justice (FACJJ), the most critical issues confronting the nation's juvenile justice systems are the deinstitutionalization of status offenders, detention reform, disproportionate minority contact, effectiveness of legal counsel, and mental health assessment and substance abuse treatment.
- *A Blueprint for Juvenile Justice Reform* sets forth nine basic tenets that lay the groundwork for juvenile justice reform across the nation: reduce institutionalization; reduce racial disparity; ensure access to quality counsel; create a range of community-based alternatives; recognize and serve youths with specialized needs; create smaller rehabilitative institutions; improve aftercare and re-entry; maximize youth, family and community participation; and keep youths out of adult prisons.
- According to the Models for Change initiative, key issues in juvenile justice reform include effective aftercare, mental health treatment, racial fairness, community-based alternatives, right-sizing jurisdictions, evidence-based practices and juvenile indigent defense.

■ Data collection practices have "lost" juveniles of Hispanic ethnicity, resulting in a "hidden minority" problem.

■ The National Partnership for Juvenile Services (NPJS) is a nonprofit collaboration of five juvenile justice advocacy groups committed to improving the nation's juvenile justice system by providing specific, results-oriented training and technical assistance.

■ Work in the juvenile justice field is very challenging and rewarding, and the need for juvenile practitioners is growing.

■ America is beginning to act on the research; put the brakes on criminalization and turn away from failed approaches; recognize the limits of incarceration; and invest in proven alternatives.

DISCUSSION QUESTIONS

1. Which aspect of the juvenile justice system do you think is most in need of reform?

2. What should the criteria for transferring violent juveniles to adult court be?

3. What are evidence-based programs and can you give an example?

4. What do you think are the major reasons for disproportionate minority contact?

5. Has your state made any reforms in their treatment of juveniles in the past few years?

6. What should be done about juveniles who were sentenced to adult criminal facilities before any reforms occurred?

7. Of the nine tenets of *A Blueprint for Juvenile Justice Reform*, which three do you think are most important?

8. How far should the pendulum swing between punitive and rehabilitative approaches to juvenile crime?

9. Should there be a bigger push for other aspects of services to juveniles or is the one-pot approach working?

10. Would you consider a career in the juvenile justice field? Why or why not?

REFERENCES

Bayliss, Bridget. "Juvenile Justice Professionals Discuss the Future of America's Youths." *Corrections Today*, April 2007, pp.106–107.

Champions for Change. Chicago IL: Models for Change, MacArthur Foundation, December 2008. Online: http://www.modelsforchange.net/reform-progress/Champions-for-Change.html

Chassin, Laurie. "Juvenile Justice and Substance Abuse." In *The Future of Children: Juvenile Justice*, Fall 2008, pp.165–184.

Culotta, Vincent. "Juvenile Waivers to Adult Court: New Issues, Growing Concerns and Potential Solutions." Orlando, FL: Seminar D-7 presented at the 36th National Conference on Juvenile Justice, March 13, 2009.

Fagan, Jeffrey. "Resolving Border Disputes." In *The Future of Children: Juvenile Justice*, Fall 2008, pp.81–118.

Federal Advisory Committee on Juvenile Justice (FACJJ). *Annual Report 2008*. Washington, DC: U.S. Department of Justice, Office of Juvenile Justice and Delinquency Prevention, November 2008. (NCJ 223723)

Finn, Peter. "School Resource Officer Programs: Finding the Funding, Reaping the Benefits." *FBI Law Enforcement Bulletin*, August 2006, pp.1–7.

Greenwood, Peter. "Prevention and Intervention for Juvenile Offenders." In *The Future of Children: Juvenile Justice*, Fall 2008, pp.185–210.

Griffin, Patrick. *Models for Change 2008 Update: Gathering Force*. Pittsburg, PA: National Center for Juvenile Justice, November 2008.

Grisso, Thomas. "Adolescent Offenders with Mental Disorders." In *The Future of Children: Juvenile Justice*, Fall 2008, pp.143–164.

Harr, J. Scott and Hess, Kären M. *Careers in Criminal Investigation and Related Fields: From Internships to Promotion*. Belmont, CA: Wadsworth Publishing Company, 2010.

Howe, Meghan; Clawson, Elyse; and Larivee, John. "The 21st Century Juvenile Justice Work Force." *Corrections Today*, February 2007, pp.34–39.

Hunsicker, Leslee. "Mental Illness among Juvenile Offenders—Identification and Treatment." *Corrections Today*, October 2007, pp.60, 61–63.

Jones, Michael A. "Welcome to the Path Less Traveled." *Corrections Today*, October 2008, pp.120–121.

Kennedy, Patrick J. "Mental Health Issues Burden the Juvenile Justice System." *Corrections Today*, December 2007.

Knight, Melissa. "Making Partnerships Work for the Benefit of Youths." *Corrections Today*, April 2008, pp.58–63.

Mendel, Dick and Middaugh, Susan. "A Matter of Choice: Forks in the Road for Juvenile Justice." *Advocacy*, Vol. 5, Issue 1, Spring 2003, pp.4–17. (NCJ 207825)

Mulvey, Edward P. and Iselin, Anne-Marie R. "Improving Professional Judgments of Risk and Amenability in Juvenile Justice." In *The Future of Children: Juvenile Justice*, Fall 2008, pp.35–58.

Overcoming Language and Cultural Barriers Using Evidence-Based Practices. Washington, DC: National Council of La Raza (NCLR), 2008.

Peterson, Julie. *A Blueprint for Juvenile Justice Reform.* Chicago IL: Youth Transition Funders Group, Spring 2005.

Piquero, Alex F. "Disproportionate Minority Contact." In *The Future of Children: Juvenile Justice*, Fall 2008, pp.59–80.

Scott, Elizabeth S. and Steinberg, Laurence. "Adolescent Development and the Regulation of Youth Crime." In *The Future of Children: Juvenile Justice*, Fall 2008a, pp.15–34.

Scott, Elizabeth S. and Steinberg, Laurence. *Rethinking Juvenile Justice.* Cambridge MA: Harvard University Press, 2008b.

Soler, Mark. *Potential for Change: Public Attitudes and Policy Preferences for Juvenile Justice Systems Reform.* Washington, DC: Center for Children's Law and Policy, November 2007.

Steinberg, Laurence. "Introducing the Issue." In *The Future of Children: Juvenile Justice*, Fall 2008, pp.3–14.

Thomas, Doug. *How Does the Juvenile Justice System Measure Up? Applying Performance Measures in Five Jurisdictions.* Washington, DC: National Center for Juvenile Justice, May 2006.

Torbet, Patricia; Hurst, Hunter, Jr.; and Soler, Mark. *Guidelines for Collecting and Recording the Race and Ethnicity of Juveniles in Conjunction with Juvenile Delinquency Disposition Reporting to the Juvenile Court Judges' Commission.* Pittsburg, PA: National Center for Juvenile Justice, October 2006.

Ziedenberg, Jason. *Models for Change: Building Momentum for Juvenile Justice Reform.* Justice Policy Institute, December 2006.

CASE CITED

Roper v. Simmons, 541 U.S. 1040 (2005)

Influences on Delinquency

Appendix A summarizes the influences on delinquency discussed throughout the book. The first column lists the various philosophies and theories set forth to explain delinquency and crime in general. The second column summarizes the general explanation of causes underlying these theories. The next six columns show how each philosophy or theory perceives specific influences on the basic causes, that is, how individual factors—the family, the community, the school, the social system and the criminal justice system—are related to and influence delinquency.

Philosophical Influences on Delinquency

Perspective	Causes of Delinquency	Individual	Family	Community	School	Social System	Criminal Justice System
Classical School of Criminality	People possess the ability to choose freely to do right or wrong—*free will*. They choose to do delinquent acts because the pleasure of the act outweighs the pain of punishment.	Free will is sole factor in considering delinquency and crime.	No influence	No influence	No influence	No influence	Purpose of punishment is *deterrence*; makes pain of punishment stronger than pleasure of act.
Positivist School of Criminality	A variety of factors influence or *cause* one to be delinquent. Since these factors *cause* delinquency, there is no free will. In most cases, the person has little or no control over the influence of these factors.	Biological and some psychological theories view the individual as the focal point. Causes of delinquency are within the individual or the environment acting on the person.	Control and learning theories recognize the *positive* influence of family on definitions of delinquency.	Learning and cultural deviance theories include or focus on the community, neighborhood or gang. They define the *subculture*.	Bonding and other control theories view school as one of the elements binding the person to the *correct* value system.	Culture sets goals and means of attaining the goals. *Strain* occurs if the means are not available.	System represents outer control. System is at fault because it labels delinquents who live up to the label.
Biological Early Theories	Criminals are *atavists* or biological throwbacks to a primitive state. Criminals are born, not developed.	Sole factor in causing delinquency is that individual is *biologically defective.*	*Criminal families* are evidence of inherited criminal behavior.	No influence	No influence	No influence	Delinquents should be quarantined.
Inherited Crime	Children inherit a *predisposition to* violence or a central nervous system that predisposes the person to crime.	Genetic predisposition of individual causes delinquency.	Chromosomal complement is inherited.	No influence	No influence	No influence	No influence

(continued)

Philosophical Influences on Delinquency (continued)

Perspective	Causes of Delinquency	Individual	Family	Community	School	Social System	Criminal Justice System
Psychological Psychoanalytical	Delinquents act out inner conflicts that result from pressure caused by failing to find appropriate releases. The psychic pressure is caused by poor or faulty child rearing.	Child did not develop properly through the infantile, latency and puberty periods.	Causes feelings of insecurity, rigidity, hostility or rebellion due to deficiencies in love, attention and child rearing.	[Not considered]	Fails to recognize and deal with problems and to develop appropriate releases of pressure.	[Not considered]	[Not considered]
Frustration-Aggression	Certain stimuli—weapons, pain, noise, temperature, odors—may cause aggression.	Influenced or acted upon by outside forces.	Failed to establish tolerance or controls to counterbalance frustrations.	Stimuli may be a function of community—overcrowding.	[Not considered]	Economic status of child/family may require that they live in certain areas where stimuli are more plentiful.	[Not considered]
Learning Theory	Based on models for youth behavior, they learn "appropriate" ways of reacting to situations. Delinquents learn that aggressive, violent, hostile reactions are successful, therefore appropriate.	The person is a blank slate, then learns the means of dealing with difficult, hostile and frustrating situations.	Serves as a strong model for behavior—bad and good.	Serves as a stronger model for behavior during adolescence.	Provides environment for modeling and reinforcing bad behavior.	[Not considered]	[Not considered]
Psychological/Environmental Factors (similar to Frustration-Aggression)	Urban crowding and ambient temperature cause irritability, frustration and violence.	Individual is unwittingly acted upon by environmental factors.	[Not considered]	Population density is a function of community.	[Not considered]	Social class restricts one's ability to live in less populated, more comfortable environments.	[Not considered]
Learning Theories	Crime is learned in interaction with others.	People are neither good nor bad but learn behavior that then directs them to certain acts or associates.	One of the primary social units where learning occurs.	Peers represent strong "significant others" from whom the person learns delinquency during adolescence and young adulthood.	Fails to reinforce definitions unfavorable to the violation of the law.	[Not considered]	[Not considered]

(continued)

Philosophical Influences on Delinquency *(continued)*

Perspective	Causes of Delinquency	Individual	Family	Community	School	Social System	Criminal Justice System
Differential Association	Criminal behavior is learned in interaction with those with whom delinquents associate and from whom they define law as favorable or unfavorable.	Learns behavior from others with whom the person differentially associates.	One of the intimate personal groups in which delinquent definitions are formed.	Fails to counter the delinquent associations and definitions; also, peers represent community.	Fails to counter the definitions and associations.	Defines the needs and values that give rise to criminal and noncriminal behavior.	[Not considered]
Social Learning Theory	Deviant behavior is learned and reinforced through social and nonsocial reinforcers.	Influenced through operant conditioning.	Provides rewards and punishments for behavior; therefore may reinforce delinquency.	Provides rewards and punishments for behavior; therefore may reinforce delinquency.	Helps or fails to reinforce conventional behavior.	[Not considered]	[Not considered]
Labeling Theory	Youths are viewed as delinquent; therefore they see themselves as delinquent and act according to this social- and self-concept.	Unwittingly labeled and then perpetuates the label.	May influence the labeling process.	May influence the labeling process.	May influence the labeling process.	Acts toward the youth based on the label.	Justice system discriminates and labels under-privileged youths as *delinquent*.
Conflict Theory	Social conflict, based on authority, power and economy, results in the weak suffering at the hands of the justice system, while the rich and powerful can violate the law with impunity.	Everyone conforms and everyone deviates, so it is unfair to categorize as good and bad. Categories are based on status, not behavior.	No influence except as an example of the power/authority dynamic.	No influence	No influence	A classed society with the poor discriminated against in every way.	Pawns of the powerful and tools of the state.

SOURCE: William V. Pelphrey. *Explanations of Delinquency: Fact or Fiction?* Washington, DC: U.S. Department of Justice, Serious Habitual Offender Comprehensive Action Program (SHOCAP), n.d.

Job Description: School Resource Officer (SRO)

- Is directly responsible to the Flint Police Division, Juvenile Bureau. However, is readily available to school administrators in time of need or emergency school-police matters.
- Patrols school area when called upon or as deemed necessary by the School Resource Officer.
- Contributes helpful information to the Regional Counseling Team.
- Assists Community School Director to mitigate antisocial behavior by investigating delinquent or criminal acts that take place during evening Community School Programs.
- Serves as a resource person or counselor for all youths, school administration and staff and members of the community with school-police related problems. Also is a resource person or counselor for those youths who have personal problems in their homes.
- Acts as resource person and serves on committees that provide services for youths.
- Gives presentations on police-related subjects to students in the classroom and to business and community organizations.
- Serves as a resource person to the Police School Cadet Program when called upon.
- Supervises and prepares necessary records and reports as requested by the Flint Police Division and Flint Community Schools.
- Assists with crowd control at school athletic events.
- Serves as a resource person for other police personnel.
- Refers youths into Probate Court or District Court when necessary.
- Performs other related duties as assigned or as appropriate.
- Suppresses by enforcement of the law any and all illegal threats, such as drugs and acts of violence, that endanger the children's educational program and improves community relations with police, schools and the general public.

SOURCE: Flint, Michigan, Police Department.

Summary of Program Characteristics

Program	Focus	Finding	Key Components
ABACUS and ASHS (New York, NY)	Prevocational training and GED preparation program for students with limited English proficiency	■ Increased English proficiency ■ Increased mathematics proficiency ■ Increased native language proficiency ■ Increased passing rates ■ Increased attendance rates ■ Increased SAT scores	■ English and native language instruction ■ Career preparation and guidance ■ Enrichment activities (field trips, guest speakers) ■ Individualized planning and tutoring ■ Flexible schedule (mornings, afternoons, evenings) ■ Focus on cultural heritage ■ Parent/guardian participation
Academy of Finance (New York, NY)	2 to 4 years of coursework in financial services with paid summer internship	■ 95% enrolled in post-secondary education ■ 33% (of 95%) post-secondary completion rates ■ 68% employed (half of these in financial services work) ■ 39% making $10 or more per hour	■ School-within-a-school ■ High standards (college preparatory courses) ■ Business-sponsored professional development and technical assistance ■ Curriculum continuously updated with the assistance of industry experts ■ Business tours/on-site workshops ■ Pertinent paid summer internships with workplace mentors
Academy of Travel and Tourism (New York, NY)	2 to 4 years of coursework in travel and tourism with paid summer internship	■ 90% enrolled in post-secondary education ■ 50% got at least a part-time job with their internship employer ■ 40% got travel or tourism jobs after graduation	■ School-within-a-school ■ High standards (college preparatory courses) ■ Financial support for college-level courses taught by college faculty ■ Professional development ■ Business tours/on-site workshops ■ Pertinent paid summer internship with workplace mentors
Alliance for Achievement (AL, FL, KY, MS, NC, SC)	Increase the rate of low-income students who attend college	■ Increased enrollment in college preparatory courses ■ Increased test scores in advanced math courses ■ Increased number of advanced courses ■ Elimination of tracking system	■ High expectations ■ Strength curricula with math and science course ■ Partnerships of middle schools, high schools and post-secondary institutions ■ Partnerships among schools, employers and community agencies ■ Regular adaptation to local needs ■ Holistic approach ■ Clear communication among partners

SOURCES: Donna Walker James (ed). *Some Things DO Make a Difference for Youth: A Compendium of Evaluations of Youth Programs and Practices.* Washington, DC: American Youth Policy Forum, 1997.

Donna Walker James (ed) with Sonia Jurich. *MORE Things That DO Make a Difference for Youth: A Compendium of Evaluation of Youth Programs and Practices, Volume II.* Washington, DC: American Youth Policy Forum, 1999, Reprinted by permission.

(continued)

(continued)

Program	Focus	Finding	Key Components
Alternative Schools (CA, CO, KS, MI, NJ, OH)	Small high schools focusing on "at-risk" youths designed to improve basic skills, graduation rates and college/employment prospects based on "High School Redirection" in Brooklyn, NY	Relative to a control group: ■ Improved attendance at 2 of 3 schools ■ Increased number of credits earned and high school graduation rates at 1 of 3 schools but: ■ No improvement in basic skills ■ Dropout rates from alternative schools in study were 40 to 80%	■ Small school (200–500+ students) ■ Small class sizes ■ Intensive remedial reading programs ■ Emphasis on basic skills instruction, giving students credit for small units of coursework ■ Close teacher-student relationships ■ Operational autonomy from school district
AmeriCorps (Hartford, CT)	Involve youths and young adults in community service activities in exchange for increased civic awareness, stipends and education awards	■ Provided needed services to communities ■ Increased interest in teaching and volunteerism among participants Children being tutored by AmeriCorps members: ■ Improved homework quality and quantity	■ Long-term training and support for volunteers ■ Tutoring and homework assistance for 400 elementary school children ■ Mentoring ■ Meaningful projects that address local needs ■ Clear goals/objectives guiding project implementation ■ Broad funding support to ensure sustainability of project
AmeriCorps (State/National)	Involve youths and young adults in community service activities in exchange for increased civic awareness, stipends and education awards	■ More than 9 million people served ■ Members showed gains in life skills ■ Gains were most significant for younger, low-skilled female members ■ Skill gains strongest for Hispanic members	■ Stipends and education awards for full-time participants ■ Education awards used to pay for college, graduate school and job training ■ Meaningful projects that address local needs
AVID (CA, CO, GA, IL, KY, MD, NC, NE, NJ, SC, TN, TX, VA)	Increase the rate of low-income, C-average students who enroll in demanding courses and pursue post-secondary education	Compared to non-AVID schools: ■ Increased enrollment and completion rates of college preparatory courses ■ Decreased school dropout rates Also showed: ■ Higher college enrollment and retention than the national average	■ Required enrollment in college preparatory classes ■ Integral part of the school day ■ Tutoring by college students ■ Enrichment activities ■ Classes on study skills ■ Team teaching ■ Professional development—teachers, tutors, others trained in AVID model ■ Emphasis on fidelity to AVID model ■ Parent/guardian and community involvement
Beacons (New York, NY)	Community centers in public school buildings offering a range of activities and services for participants of all ages	■ High level of participation ■ Long-term participation ■ Reduced risk behaviors among youths	■ Recreational activities ■ Adult education classes ■ On-site social and community services ■ Enrichment activities (homework help, reading group) ■ A safe place ■ Free, after-school child care ■ Experienced staff ■ Leadership development, youths as resources and community service ■ Parent/guardian and community involvement

(continued)

(continued)

Program	Focus	Finding	Key Components
Big Brothers, Big Sisters (AZ, KY, MN, NY, OH, PA, TX)	One-to-one match between young people (ages 5–18) and volunteer adult mentors	Relative to a control group: ■ 46% less likely to initiate drug use ■ 27% less likely to initiate alcohol abuse ■ 32% less likely to hit someone ■ Skipped fewer days of school and fewer classes ■ 37% less likely to lie to their parents	■ Stringent guidelines for screening volunteers ■ Orientation for volunteers ■ Matching process takes gender, race and proximity into account ■ Support for adult volunteers and youths through monthly phone contacts with the agency ■ Youths as resources (developmental rather than problem-oriented approach)
Boys and Girls Clubs of America (CA, FL, NY, OH, TX)	Provides after-school educational assistance and social activities for low-income children and youths in public housing	Relative to clubs without a special program and to sites with no clubs at all: ■ Reduced local drug and criminal activities ■ Decreased property destruction ■ Increased family involvement ■ Improved school attendance ■ Increased test scores in math, science, social studies and English ■ Increased average GPA	■ A safe place ■ Tutoring ■ Mentoring ■ Holistic approach (health and fitness, drug/pregnancy prevention) ■ Community service ■ Caring, knowledgeable adults ■ Parent/guardian participation ■ Structured weekly after-school schedule (reading, writing, required homework) ■ Trained staff and volunteers
California Conservation Corps	Improves youth employability through work in environmental conservation	Relative to a comparison group: ■ Generally had more earning power at the completion of the program	■ Educational experiences scheduled around work ■ GED, ESL and remedial classes as needed ■ Advanced educational opportunities
Career Academies (CA, DC, FL, MD, PA, TX)	Career-focused high school model to prepare youths for post-secondary education and employment	Relative to a comparison group: ■ Improved academic performance ■ Lower dropout rate ■ Graduates more likely to be working for academy sponsors (PA)	■ School-within-a-school model ■ Integration of academic and vocational curricula ■ Academic and vocational teachers working in teams ■ Low student-to-teacher ratio ■ Career theme determined by local employment involvement ■ Employer involvement ■ Financial and in-kind support from employer community
Career Academies (CA)	Career-focused high school model to prepare youths for post-secondary education and employment	Relative to a comparison group: ■ Increased graduation rates ■ Increased college enrollment ■ High scores on measures of preparedness for college	■ School-within-a-school model ■ Integration of academic and vocational curricula ■ Project-based learning ■ High standards ■ Career-centered theme ■ Employer involvement ■ Paid summer internships
Career Academies: JROTC (West Coast; Midwest)	A career-focused high school model integrated with a Junior Reserve Officer Training Corps program (JROTC)	Relative to a comparison group: ■ Increased GPA ■ Lower absenteeism rates ■ Lower dropout rates ■ Increased number of credits earned	■ School-within-a-school model ■ Rigorous academic core ■ Curriculum centered on a career theme ■ Employer involvement ■ Paid summer internships ■ One-hour weekly course on civic values, responsibility, leadership ■ Enrichment activities (drill team exercises, summer camp)

(continued)

(continued)

Program	Focus	Finding	Key Components
Career Beginnings (CA, FL, IN, NY, OH)	A high school program aimed at helping low-income, average-grade students to pursue post-secondary education	Relative to a control group: ■ Improved college attendance by 9.7%	■ Collaboration among local colleges, public secondary schools and the business community ■ Workshops and counseling on careers and college ■ Paid summer internships ■ Mentoring
CET (San Jose, CA and 25 other sites) See also JOBSTART and MFSPD	Long-term, non-residential training and employment program for low-income youths ages 17 to 21 who had dropped out of school	■ Increased earnings up to 30 months post-program and 60 months post-program for non-high-school dropouts ■ More participation in education and training, but equal GED attainment rates ■ Little reduction in welfare receipt	■ Basic skills instruction integrated with job-specific learning ■ Access to job-specific training right away, to participants without high school training or GEDs, with no upfront assessment of basic skills ■ Open-entry, open-exit ■ Intensive services concentrated in a short time period ■ Training in in-demand occupations, focused directly on researched needs of local labor market combined with strong job placement efforts
College Bound (FL, MA, MD, OH, PA)	Help disadvantaged students graduate from high school and go on to college through "last-dollar" scholarships and a four-year support structure	Relative to a comparison group: ■ Lower college drop-out rate ■ Higher persistence rate in college ■ Improved odds of attending a four-year school	■ Intensive, individualized counseling ■ 9th and 10th graders in-class presentation motivating them to consider college ■ 11th graders counseling on college application, financial aid, SAT and other tests ■ Financial aid package pays the difference between college financial aid award and full tuition
Communities in School (AR, AZ, CA, CO, FL, GA, IL, NC, NY, PA, SC, TX, VA, WA)	A dropout prevention program for "at-risk" youths providing social and health services in the schools	■ Improved attendance ■ Improved GPAs ■ Dropout rate of 7% per year vs. 12% per year nationally for low-income families ■ Improved graduation rates ■ Improvements were more significant for children most at-risk	■ Needs assessment ■ Case management services ■ Individual or group counseling ■ Mentoring ■ After-school or in-school programs ■ Holistic approach (e.g., conflict resolution, teen parenting, substance abuse prevention) ■ Emergency advice/referrals and programs for nonmembers ■ Ongoing staff and volunteer training
Community Schools (New York, NY)	A full-service school model combining academics with comprehensive services for youths and families	■ Improved attendance rates ■ Foster parent/guardian involvement ■ Full health coverage for students ■ Positive environment	■ Open extended hours and weekends year-round ■ Holistic approach (medical, dental, eye care and mental health services on site) ■ Child care and parenting training classes ■ Career development ■ Mentoring ■ College transfer courses ■ Parent/guardian participation ■ Community needs assessment ■ Community involvement

(continued)

(continued)

Program	Focus	Finding	Key Components
CS² (MA)	Promote school reform by mobilizing community resources to generate and support locally adopted ideas	Preliminary results show: ■ Increased student participation in internships, integrated academic/vocational coursework, curriculum designed with employer assistance, other supports ■ Increased test scores at one school and increased homework grades at another	■ Career development ■ Basic academic skills instruction ■ Support for students (e.g., tutoring liaison with community agencies) ■ Community-based approach using an intermediary organization and community "change agents" to work with community leaders ■ Staff development for teacher and change agents ■ Local governing boards or advisory committees
Dropout Demonstration Assistance Program (CA, FL, MD, MI, ND, OK, OR, SC)	Evaluation of 16 dropout prevention programs, K–12, services in school or alternative school settings	■ Higher grades ■ Fewer absences ■ Lower dropout rate ■ Perception of more caring teachers ■ More counseling and attention from guidance counselors	Programs were most successful when they: ■ Did not pull children out of class ■ Provided access to paid work for high school students ■ Provided flexible class schedules ■ Used a holistic approach ■ Provided tutoring, counseling and many caring adults ■ Offered staff training and support
Dropout Prevention and Re-Entry Projcts (CA, FL, MD, MI, ND, OK, OR, SC)	Demonstration projects focusing on vocational education components as effective dropout prevention methods	Out of 12 schools: ■ 10 increased GPAs ■ 7 reduced number of failed courses ■ 7 increased feeling of safety in schools ■ 5 produced more credits earned ■ 5 reduced absenteeism ■ 4 reduced dropout rates	■ Small class sizes ■ Highly structured, nurturing environment ■ Integration of academic and vocational curricula ■ Career development ■ Counseling ■ Caring, knowledgeable adults ■ Student entrepreneurial activities ■ Intense monitoring of student progress
¡Espanol Aumeñtativo! (Houston, TX)	One-year transitional program for Hispanic students at risk of dropping out of school	■ Increased test scores ■ Improved English literacy ■ Increased attendance rates	■ English and Spanish instruction ■ Bilingual instruction in content areas ■ Computer and Internet training ■ Parent/guardian participation (including home visits) ■ Professional development ■ Native Spanish-speaking teachers used innovative instructional strategies
4-H (Kansas City, MO)	An urban 4-H program, held after school for youths living in public housing	■ Increased school attendance ■ Increased grade point average ■ Improved classroom behavior ■ Improved home behavior ■ Reduced illegal activities in the community	■ Employment of local residents as site directors ■ Mentoring ■ Professional development ■ Parent/guardian, school and community involvement ■ Customized curriculum ■ Enrichment activities ■ Project-based learning ■ Recognition for school attendance, academic performance and behavior ■ Caring, knowledgeable adults ■ Holistic approach

(continued)

(continued)

Program	Focus	Finding	Key Components
Futures 2000 (KS, MA, NM)	Promote middle-school changes to improve transition to high school, career and college for low-income underachieving students	■ Improved attendance ■ Increased classroom participation ■ More enthusiasm by students and teachers ■ Students identified more career choices to explore ■ Greater parental/guardian involvement	■ Teacher-designed curriculum enhancers ■ Project-based learning ■ Teachers as coaches and facilitators ■ School/community partnership ■ Professional development
Gateway to Higher Education (New York, NY)	Comprehensive four-year secondary-school program, prepares students for higher education and for careers in science, medicine and technology	Relative to national data and comparison groups: ■ Increased enrollment in math and science courses ■ Increased number of students taking Regents, SAT and AP exams ■ Higher SAT scores than national averages, but lower achievement test scores ■ Improved high school grades, and graduation rates ■ 92% attended college	■ High standards (extended school day with double period of math and science; extended school year; summer program for juniors and seniors at universities and research institutes; advanced placement courses for all students) ■ Caring, knowledgeable adults ■ Enrichment activities (meet science professionals, museum, theater, opera and symphony field trips) ■ After-school experiential internships
Girls, Inc. (DE, NE, TN, TX)	Help young women to make informed decisions related to sexual behavior	Compared to a nonparticipating peer group: ■ Postponed sexual intercourse ■ Increased use of preventive measures	■ Age-specific programs with early intervention (from 9 to 18 years old) ■ Workshops for parents and daughters to improve communication ■ Assertiveness training, education and career planning ■ Linkage to community-based services ■ Parent/guardian and teacher involvement
Head Start (Nationwide)	Provide low-income children aged 3 to 5 with health and educational supports	Compared to nonparticipating siblings: ■ Improved vocabulary test scores ■ Improved passing rates ■ Improved immunization rates ■ African American student gains were not sustained over time	■ Programs tailored to local needs ■ Intellectual and social stimulation ■ Physical, mental health and nutrition services ■ Parent/guardian participation (including home visits)
High Schools That Work (Nationwide)	Full-school reform focused on raising the achievement level of career-bound high school students	For seven "most-improved" schools: ■ Improved math, reading and science scores ■ Increased number of students taking 4 or more courses in math ■ Increased average total credits earned ■ Improved quality of vocational courses ■ Greater involvement of families and teachers in students' educational progress	■ High expectations for all students (all students required to take 3 math and 3 science courses) ■ Elimination of general track ■ Integration of academic and vocational curricula ■ Functional and applied instructional strategies ■ Vocational/academic team teaching ■ Work-based learning ■ Guidance and counseling including parent involvement ■ Extra help and time when needed ■ Continual student assessment and evaluation of program

(continued)

(continued)

Program	Focus	Finding	Key Components
High/Scope Perry Preschool (Ypsilanti, MI)	27-year follow-up of an educational enrichment program for low-income minority children 3 to 4 years of age	Relative to control group: ■ Higher monthly earnings ■ Higher home ownership ■ Higher level of schooling ■ Less dependency on social services ■ Lower arrest rates	■ Structured and intensive program ■ Age-appropriate activities, child-initiated activities and individualized attention ■ Language, literacy, social development, music and arts ■ Low child-to-teacher ratio (10:1) ■ Parent/guardian participation (including home visits) ■ Professional development
Higher Ground (CA, CT, IL, IN)	Help low-income and minority students stay in college and graduate	Relative to a comparison group: ■ Increased college retention rate by 15% during first two years of college	■ Summer activities (orientation, academic enrichment, internships) ■ Career development (career planning and exploration, part-time employment, community-career connections) ■ Mentoring ■ Caring, knowledgeable adults ■ Coalition building to implement programs geared toward at-risk undergraduates ■ Holistic approach (developmental, flexible) ■ Professional development
Hoke County High School (Hoke County, NC)	High school educational reform using *High Schools That Work* principles (see High Schools That Work)	Relative to previous classes: ■ Increased number of students taking algebra, geometry and biology ■ Increased completion rate of recommended academic core ■ Increased SAT scores	■ High expectations ■ Replacement of low-level by high-level courses ■ Block schedule with more time for lab work ■ Strengthened vocational courses ■ Work-based learning ■ Employer involvement ■ Teacher visits to worksites ■ Professional development ■ Extra help for students to meet high standards
Home Visitation by Nurses (Elmira, NY)	Nurses conduct home visits from pregnancy through the first two years of baby's life to encourage young women to complete their education, obtain training, find jobs and improve parenting skills	Relative to comparison groups, participants in Elmira, NY: ■ Increased hours of work for young mothers ■ Reduced dependency on public assistance ■ Reduced number of subsequent pregnancies ■ Improved overall health habits of young mothers ■ Improved health of babies Memphis, TN: ■ Reduced number of subsequent pregnancies ■ Greater household incomes	■ Parent education (nutrition, health habits, prenatal care, infant development, use of the health care system) ■ Encourage parents to complete their education ■ Assist in making child care arrangements ■ Job skills development ■ Engage family in helping support woman and child and link family to formal health care services ■ Encourage women to keep prenatal visits ■ Interagency support and cooperation

(continued)

(continued)

Program	Focus	Finding	Key Components
I Have a Dream (Washington, DC)	An individual or group of sponsors guarantees college tuition to a group of 60 sixth or seventh graders from a pool of eligible disadvantaged youths to encourage school completion and college enrollment	■ "Dreamers" are more likely to remain in school ■ Improved academic performance and behavior ■ Increased peer support among participants	■ Guaranteed college tuition funding ■ Enrichment activities (tutoring, summer programs and field trips) ■ Caring, knowledgeable adults ■ Long-term follow-up (from 6th to 12th grade and beyond) ■ Mentoring ■ Case management
I Have a Dream (Chicago, IL)	An individual or group of sponsors guarantees college tuition to a group of 60 sixth or seventh graders from a pool of eligible disadvantaged youths to encourage school completion and college enrollment	Relative to a comparison group: ■ Increased high school graduation rates ■ Increased college enrollment rates, particularly in four-year colleges	■ High expectations ■ Enrichment activities (museums, field trips) ■ Tutoring ■ Mentoring ■ Support in job search and placement ■ Long-term support ■ Focus on peer support to build and maintain prosocial behavior ■ Working with families and linkage to existing community services ■ Financial support for college
Jobs for America's Graduates (Nationwide)	Aims to provide employability skills to students at risk of dropping out of high school, through nine months of in-school services and nine months of follow-up	■ High graduation rates ■ High likelihood of employment	■ Low student-to-specialist ratio ■ Strict accountability of specialists for student progress ■ Reduce barriers to employment ■ Classroom instruction in 37 employment competencies ■ Employer involvement ■ Work-based learning ■ Long-term (9 months) follow-up
Job Corps (Nationwide)	Residential training and employment program for low-income youth ages 16 to 24	Averaged over four years post-program, relative to a comparison group, Job Corps participants: ■ Were five times more likely to earn a high school diploma or GED ■ Had higher school attendance ■ Had 15% higher earnings ■ Missed fewer days of work ■ Were less involved in serious criminal activity ■ Were less dependent on public assistance	■ Diagnostic testing at entrance ■ Holistic approach (basic education, health education, parenting skills, social skills, cultural awareness, recreation) ■ Competency-based vocational education ■ Work-based learning ■ Career development ■ Zero tolerance for drugs and violence ■ Regular student progress reviews ■ Counseling/support services ■ Youths as resources (student government, leaderships and community service) ■ Incentive-based allowances ■ Post-program placement and support

(continued)

(continued)

Program	Focus	Finding	Key Components
JOBSTART/CET (AZ, CA, CO, CT, GA, IL, NY, PA, TX) See also CET and MFSPD	Long-term, nonresidential training and employment program for low-income youths ages 17 to 21 who had dropped out of school	Relative to a control group: ■ More likely to earn a high school diploma or GED ■ Less involvement in criminal activity Also: ■ Variable earnings (CET program in San Jose, CA showed highest earnings gains) ■ Earnings impact strongest for those less likely to be employed in the absence of the program, especially men with a prior arrest and custodial mothers	■ Self-paced basic education ■ Occupation skills training ■ Support services (child care, transportation, counseling) ■ Job placement assistance ■ Some life skills training and stipends tied to program performance ■ Longer-term services than traditional employment and training programs, including after job placement ■ Holistic approach (emotional development, safety, housing and health care)
KAPOW (IL, MI, NE, NY)	Employee volunteers provide information on work-related skills and careers to elementary school children	Compared to students in other schools: ■ Increased awareness about different careers ■ Increased awareness about the relationship between school and careers	■ Annual visits to worksites with hands-on projects ■ Monthly classroom visits by volunteer employees ■ Hands-on instructional methods ■ Employer involvement ■ Professional development ■ Flexible implementation and curriculum
LEAP (OH)	Welfare-reform program to encourage pregnant and parenting teens to remain in or return to school	Relative to a control group, girls still in school and/or under 18 years old were: ■ More likely to earn high school diploma or GED ■ More likely to be working ■ More likely to leave welfare rolls Not beneficial for girls over 18 years old who dropped out of school	■ Case management ■ Increases or reductions in welfare payments tied to school attendance ■ Programs adapted to local needs ■ Some reimbursement for child care and transportation Based on results at the best performing site, evaluators suggest that LEAP is more effective combined with a comprehensive school-reform strategy
Learn and Serve America (CA, NC, NM, NY, OH, PA, TX, WI)	Involve school-aged youths in community service and structured learning experiences	Relative to a comparison group: ■ Higher test scores in math and science ■ Higher grade point average Also: ■ Reduced likelihood of arrest and pregnancy (for middle-school students) ■ Provided needed services to community	■ Meaningful services that respond to community needs ■ Strong academic curriculum ■ Structured time to reflect on experience ■ Well-designed initiatives ■ Mutual benefits for participants and recipients ■ Cost-effective
Learn and Serve America, Higher Education (Nationwide)	Encourage post-secondary students to participate in community service while improving their academic and life skills	Relative to nonparticipants: ■ More likely to help others in trouble ■ More likely to prepare for graduate school ■ More likely to do extra work in academic courses ■ Improved leadership ability ■ Higher level of diversity awareness and acceptance	■ Community services in education, human needs, public safety or environmental needs ■ Integration of service experiences with academic courses ■ Structured time for reflection

(continued)

(continued)

Program	Focus	Finding	Key Components
Learn and Serve America, School and Community (CA, FL, NC, NM, NY, OH, PA, TX, WI)	Involve middle- and high-school age students in community service through service-learning	Relative to a comparison group: ■ Increased GPAs ■ Some increase on measures of personal and social responsibility, cultural diversity and "service leadership"	■ Meaningful services that respond to community needs ■ Integration of service experiences with academic courses ■ Regular reflection and writing to process the service experience ■ Significant amount of direct service hours ■ Group and individual service assignments
Manufacturing Technology Partnership Program (Genesee Co., MI)	School-to-work program between area vocational school and General Motors	Relative to a comparison group: ■ 90% go into post-secondary education ■ More likely to become employed after graduation ■ Higher wages upon graduation ■ High average GPAs ■ Higher levels of vocational credits ■ More math and science credits	■ High standards ■ Integration of academic and vocational curricula ■ Vocational teachers with industry experience ■ After-school and summer paid internships ■ Mentoring ■ Employers, academic and vocational teachers develop curriculum, adapt curriculum to employer needs ■ Post-secondary connection
Maryland's Tomorrow (MD)	Statewide dropout prevention program beginning in summer 9th grade	Relative to a comparison group: ■ Lower dropout rate ■ Higher GPAs ■ Higher test scores ■ Higher graduation rates	■ Individual case management and counseling ■ Intensive academic instruction each summer and during school year ■ Career development ■ Summer activities (subsidized part-time jobs, camps, etc.) ■ Personal and skills development ■ Peer support ■ Mentoring
Minority Female Single Parent Demonstration (CA, DC, GA, RI) See also CET and JOBSTART	Study of four foundation-funded employment and training programs for minority single mothers. Summary focuses on CET in San Jose, CA	Relative to a control group: ■ Increased earnings up to 30 months post-program, and 60 months post-program for non–high school dropouts ■ More participation in education and training, but equal GED attainment rates ■ Little reduction in welfare receipt	■ Concurrent and integrated basic skills instruction and job-specific training ■ Access to job-specific training right away, to participants without high school training or GEDs, with no upfront assessment of basic skills ■ Open-entry, open-exit ■ Intensive services concentrated in a short time period ■ Training in in-demand occupations, focused directly on researched needs of local labor market combined with strong job placement efforts
Multisystemic Therapy (MO, SC, TN)	Community-based treatment for youth offenders, their families and communities	Relative to a control group: ■ Fewer arrests Also: ■ Increased family cohesion ■ Decreased peer aggression	■ Intensive individualized treatment plan ■ Home-based and school-based interventions ■ Low staff-to-client ratio ■ Cost-effective
National Guard Youth Challenge Program (27 states)	Provide dropout youths with values, life skills, education and self-discipline	■ Increased reading and math levels ■ High retention rate ■ Reduced likelihood of arrest ■ Increased number of youths completing the GED	■ Five-month residential phase ■ Focus on academic and vocational education ■ Leadership development ■ Assistance with job placement/school applications ■ Long-term support ■ Mentoring

(continued)

(continued)

Program	Focus	Finding	Key Components
New American Schools (Nationwide)	Promote school reforms through new whole-school designs	■ Increased attendance rates ■ Increased academic performance ■ Decreased disciplinary infractions	■ High standards ■ Emphasis on hands-on methods ■ Careful design and implementation ■ Professional development ■ Works best with consistent, stable leadership
New Chance (CA, CO, FL, IL, KY, MI, MN, NY, OR, PA)	Improve employment and education prospects of young mothers	Relative to a control group: ■ More likely to earn GED Also: ■ Showed little other significant improvements ■ Need intensive family planning component ■ Need stronger emphasis on employment	■ Education (GED preparation, adult basic education) ■ Employment-related services ■ Health and personal development ■ Holistic approach (parenting education, child care, pediatric health care services) ■ Care management
New Futures (AR, CT, GA, MA, OH, PA)	Aimed at changing the prospects for at-risk youths	■ Improved reading scores ■ Decreased dropout rates ■ Postponed start of sexual activity	■ After-school programs ■ Remedial academic courses ■ Teams of students and teachers ■ Teen health centers ■ Career education centers
Project CRAFT (FL, MD, ND, TN, TX)	Promote reintegration of juvenile offenders into the community	■ Decreased recidivism rates ■ High program completion rates ■ High employment rates ■ High hourly wages	■ Intensive academic and work-based learning ■ Industry-validated preapprenticeship certificate ■ Job placement assistance; follow-up ■ Connect participant needs to community needs ■ Youths-as-resources philosophy ■ Case management/referral to community services ■ Partnership with business associations
Project PRISM (New York, NY)	Math/science and pre-engineering program for Chinese students with limited English proficiency	■ Improved English and native language proficiency ■ Increased grades in math and science tests ■ Increased attendance rates ■ Increased college enrollment rates ■ Low dropout rate	■ English and Mandarin classes ■ Bilingual education in content areas ■ Enrichment activities (tutoring, extracurricular and cultural activities) ■ Parent/guardian participation (e.g., home visits English classes, workshops) ■ Community participation (e.g., community newspaper, cultural activities) ■ Profession development
Project Redirection (AZ, CA, MA, NY)	Enhance educational, job-related and parenting skills of pregnant or parenting teenage girls	At the 5-year point, relative to a comparison group: ■ Increased likelihood of being employed ■ Increased hours worked ■ Higher average earnings ■ Children more likely to be enrolled in Head Start programs ■ Decreased dependency on welfare benefits	■ Employment of community members as mentors ■ Caring, knowledgeable adults ■ Individual counseling ■ Peer group sessions ■ On-site life management and employability components ■ Holistic approach (health care and education referrals)

(continued)

(continued)

Program	Focus	Finding	Key Components
ProTech (Boston, MA)	Connect high school students in career-pathways programs to paid internships	Relative to non-ProTech graduates: ■ More likely to go to college ■ More likely to find employment ■ Higher hourly wages ■ Increased certificate or degree completion	■ High standards ■ Clustering of student in rigorous math and science courses ■ Career development ■ Several weeks of rotations in workplace (juniors) ■ Part-time/full-time internships (juniors and seniors)
Quantum Opportunities (MI, OK, PA, TX, WI)	In-school or after-school program that provided comprehensive services for low-income, urban youths	Relative to a control group: ■ More likely to graduate from high school ■ Less likely to drop out of school ■ More likely to attend college ■ Less likely to become a teen parent ■ More likely to volunteer ■ Effects increased over time	■ Small stipends tied to program participation ■ Savings account for future college and training ■ Caring, knowledgeable adults (teachers and mentors) ■ Small staff-to-student ratio ■ Holistic approach (cultural activities, social services, basic skills training) ■ Financial resources to ensure continuity of the program ■ Quality staff
REAL (23 states)	Entrepreneurial education for youths geared toward rural economic development	■ Improved business skills In North Carolina: ■ At follow-up, 30% of graduates had started businesses and had average monthly sales of $3,622 ■ Graduates who already had businesses when they entered the program had average monthly sales of $17,608 at follow-up	■ Emphasis on business concepts and entrepreneurial skills ■ Courses range from planning to managing a business ■ Loans for business start-ups ■ Community support teams act as mentors/advisors ■ Professional development ■ Applied learning techniques
Safe Havens: B & GCAs, Girls, Inc. and YMCAs (Nationwide)	Promote healthier life styles for youths through experiences that serve as building blocks for a balanced adult life	■ Promoted social support ■ Engaged youths in healthy and challenging activities ■ Provided youths with safe environment ■ Significant percentage participated every day and over time	■ Holistic approach (educational activities, homework help, health and life skills education) ■ Leadership activities and a role for youths in decision making ■ Community service ■ Responds to local needs ■ Caring, knowledgeable adults ■ Youths-as-resources philosophy ■ Challenging and interesting activities ■ Sense of belonging and safety ■ Low staff-to-youth ratio
School-to-Work (National)	Improve the transition from school to post-secondary education and/or productive careers for all students	■ Increased student and employer participation ■ Expanded programs ■ Diversified and expanded work-based opportunities	■ Work-based learning ■ Integrated academic and vocational curriculum ■ Connect schools to community ■ Build partnerships between schools, business and labor ■ Employer involvement ■ Incremental implementation ■ Professional development

(continued)

(continued)

Program	Focus	Finding	Key Components
School-to-Work (New York state)	School-to-work initiatives in New York State	• STW students took more advanced math and sciences courses • Better attendance rates for STW students • Higher-quality work experience than that of non-STW students	• K–12 implementation of STW concepts • High expectations and standards • Close relationships with state Tech-Prep program • Collaboration between secondary and post-secondary faculties • Employer involvement
School-to-Work/Youth Apprenticeship Demonstration (Nationwide)	School-to-work demonstration project funded by the Department of Labor	• High rate of enrollment in post-secondary education and training • Increased number of students served over time • Strong ties with employers	• High standards • Career development • Integration of vocational and academic skills • Work-based learning (including job shadowing and paid work) • Mentoring • College-level courses taken in high school • College credit earned for work experience
School Transitional Environment Program (Large urban areas)	Prevention program designed to help at-risk students during school transition times	Relative to a comparison group: • Higher grades and better attendance rates in the first two years • Lower dropout rate (21 vs. 43%) • More positive perception of school environment	• School-within-a-school • Homeroom teachers are primary links among students, parents and the school • STEP teachers meet once a week to discuss students who may need additional assistance • Individual student counseling sessions approximately once a month • Professional development
Serve-America (CO, MA, OH, SC)	Service learning program for school-aged youths	Relative to a comparison group: • Fewer school absences • Increased time dedicated to homework • More likely to volunteer after the program ended • More hours of community service	• School-based and community-based programs • Flexible programs adapted to local needs • 40% tied services to academic courses (English or mathematics) • Careful implementation
Sponsor a Scholar (Philadelphia, PA)	Matches at-risk urban youths with mentors to improve chances of graduating from school and pursuing post-secondary education	Relative to a comparison group: • Three times more likely to go to college • Higher GPAs • Higher participation in college preparatory activities Also: • The more time spent with mentors, the better the outcomes	• Long term support • Mentoring • Limited financial support in college • Class coordinator • Academic support coordinator • Enrichment activities (jobs, study skills workshops, SAT) • Mentors and students attend cultural and sporting events • Training and oversight for mentors
STEP (CA, MA, OR, WI)	Stem summer learning loss for educationally and economically disadvantaged youths aged 14–15	Relative to a control group Short-term: • Improved math and reading score at the end of summer • Some improvement in risky behavior Long term: • Little change in teen pregnancy rate, educational or employment measures	• Remediation • Life skills development • Paid part-time work experience • Paid for summer class hours • School-year support (counseling/advocacy) • Focus on preventing teen pregnancy

(continued)

(continued)

Program	Focus	Finding	Key Components
STRIVE (FL, IL, NY, PA)	Provide tools to low-income youths and young adults to successfully enter the job market	■ Low job turnover for participants ■ Employers reported positive attitude and good qualifications	■ Three-week workshop on positive workplace behaviors; some training ■ Attitudinal training takes precedence over skills training ■ Job development assessment, consultation, resume writing and interviewing skills practice ■ Follow-up services up to two years
Student Support Services (Nationwide)	Academic counseling and peer tutoring to help disadvantaged kids stay in college	Relative to a comparison group: ■ Increased GPAs ■ Increased credits earned ■ More likely to stay at same post-secondary institution Also: ■ Improvements increased with increased participation	■ Peer tutoring ■ Counseling/academic advising ■ Special cultural events ■ Workshops and courses specific to the program ■ Holistic approach (addresses academic and nonacademic needs) ■ Build sense of community
Success for All/ Exito part Todos (AZ, CA, PA, TX)	Prevention and early intervention in potential reading problems for elementary-school students	■ Increased reading levels for participant students independent of level and native language	■ One-to-one reading tutors ■ Reading groups according to performance level ■ Coordination between ESL and regular teachers ■ Holistic approach (linkage to comprehensive services including health, mental health and nutrition) ■ Parent/guardian participation (family support teams) ■ Full-time program facilitator
Summer Youth Employment and Training Program (Nationwide)	Provides disadvantaged youths with summer work experience	■ Acquisition or improvement of work-related skills ■ Improved reading and math scores ■ Project-based learning most effective	■ Work experience (clerical, construction and recreation) ■ Basic academic skills ■ Vocational exploration and training ■ Minimum-wage summer jobs ■ Holistic approach (academic, vocational, support services) ■ In-school and out-of-school training ■ Technical assistance ■ Individualized attention ■ Caring, knowledgeable adults ■ Committed worksite supervisors ■ Employer involvement
Tech-Prep (National)	Improve career and post-secondary opportunities for youths	From 1993–1995: ■ Tech-Prep programs expanded nationwide ■ Number of Tech-Prep students holding paid jobs increased ■ Number of Tech-Prep students going to post-secondary education increased	■ Articulation agreements between schools and two-year colleges ■ Challenging high school courses tied to post-secondary programs ■ Integrated academic and work-based learning ■ Hands-on instruction ■ Collaboration between secondary and post-secondary, academic and vocational faculty
Tech-Prep (Texas, statewide)	Tech-Prep initiatives in Texas	■ Increased pass rates on Texas Assessment of Academic Skills ■ Decreased dropout rate compared to nonvocational students ■ Higher graduation rate than the nonvocational or other vocational students	■ Preparatory and supporting services ■ Employer and labor involvement ■ Career development ■ Work-based learning

(continued)

(continued)

Program	Focus	Finding	Key Components
Teen Outreach Programs (Nationwide)	Prevent teen pregnancy and improve academic performance	Relative to a comparison group: ■ Lower course failure rate ■ Lower suspension rate ■ Lower pregnancy rate	■ Service-learning component ■ Classroom component ■ Discussions connecting service-learning, classroom and life experiences ■ Positive peer and adult relationships ■ Holistic approach
Teenage Parent Demonstration (IL, NJ)	Improve the economic self-sufficiency of teen parents depending on welfare	Relative to control group: ■ Higher employment rates ■ Higher monthly earnings ■ Lower AFDC/food stamps payments No significant differences in the long term	■ Thirty hours/week of education, training and employment ■ Workshops in personal and employment-related skills ■ Career development ■ Referral to community agencies (job training and placements) ■ Child care assistance ■ Financial assistance for transportation and related expenses
Turner Technical High School (Miami, FL)	Provide disadvantaged youths with high academic and technical skills	Relative to the Miami-Dade County high schools: ■ Higher attendance rates ■ Higher scores on state tests ■ Increased percentage of academic scholarships ■ Lower dropout rates	■ Career academy model ■ High expectations and standards ■ "Two for one" (high school and industry certification) diploma ■ Teamwork (teachers and students work in teams) ■ Work-based learning ■ Integration of academic and vocational curriculum ■ Teacher participation in decision making ■ Employer involvement
Union City School District (NJ)	District-wide educational reform and technological enhancement	Overall: ■ Increased school retention ■ Increased standardized test scores for elementary- and middle-school students At Pilot Tech program: ■ Better communication among participants ■ Better student performance overall, particularly in writing	■ Comprehensive curriculum reform ■ Infusion of technology with electronic connection between schools and homes ■ Cooperative learning and team teaching ■ Employer involvement ■ Financial support from employers and school district ■ Collaboration among students, teachers, parents and community ■ Training of teachers, students and parents ■ Parent/guardian involvement ■ Block scheduling
Upward Bound (Nationwide)	Increase opportunities for low-income youths to attend college	Relative to a control group: ■ Earned more college preparatory credits in high school ■ Earned more vocational education credits ■ High attrition rate (37%) ■ Retention higher when work experience component included	■ Weekly and intensive summer activities usually hosted by colleges ■ High academic standards ■ Support services (counseling, financial aid and career planning, cultural awareness, tutoring, stipends) ■ Work component (some)

(continued)

(continued)

Program	Focus	Finding	Key Components
WAVE in Schools (CA, DC, IL, NJ, NY, OH, TN, TX)	School-based dropout prevention program	■ Increased GPAs ■ Improved feelings of self-esteem ■ Improved feelings of control over life	■ Four-year long sequence of courses ■ Focus on developing interpersonal, communication, study, leadership, employability and life skills ■ Employer involvement ■ Partnerships ■ Professional development ■ Technical assistance
WAY Scholarship (NY)	Long-term job training and support for youths in residential treatment center	■ Higher school/GED completion rates than other NYC at-risk students ■ 51% college enrollment rate ■ 65–89% work participation rate	■ High expectations for all youths ■ Long-term counseling and supports with follow-up ■ Emphasis on connection between school and work success ■ Positive peer culture ■ Life skills training ■ Caring, knowledgeable adults ■ Matched savings plan for after graduation
WI Youth Apprenticeship (WI)	Combine instruction in printing technologies with work-based training and experience	Compared to nonparticipants: ■ Increased likelihood of employment ■ Better jobs (higher earnings, full-time status, high skills) after graduation ■ Low absenteeism rate at school Also: ■ 75% hired by apprenticeship employer	■ Competency-based curriculum and assessment ■ Two-year part-time on-site training and work experience ■ Work-based learning ■ Mentoring ■ Technical college instruction in printing and academic courses ■ Integrated academic and vocational instruction ■ Collaborative school and industry oversight ■ Employer involvement ■ Caring, knowledgeable adults
YOU and Youth Fair Chance (YFC) (16 states)	Two related youth demonstration projects to improve opportunities for youths in high-poverty areas	■ Reduced school dropout rates ■ Reduced risk behaviors (teenage pregnancy, criminal activities)	■ Youths as resources (emphasized positive youth development) ■ Holistic approach (education, work training, life skills, social services) ■ Open to all youths in the target areas (15–19 in YOU; 14–30 in YFC) ■ Technical assistance (YFC) ■ Community-based learning center ■ Caring, knowledgeable adults ■ Flexible class schedules ■ Case management (YFC) ■ Community involvement ■ School-to-work approach (YFC)
Youth Build (CA, FL, IN, MA, OH)	Long-term (10 to 14 months) program that teaches out-of-school youths basic life and job skills through construction work	Relative to comparable programs: ■ Good attendance ■ Long average stay ■ High GED completion rates ■ Produced "job-ready" workers ■ High rate of employment in construction industry (66%) ■ Improved job-related behaviors	■ Remediation, including GED preparation ■ On-site work training and experience ■ Focused on needed community services ■ Mentoring ■ Positive peer support ■ Leadership development and civic education ■ Employer involvement ■ Support after graduation ■ Professional development ■ Youths-as-resources philosophy ■ Caring, knowledgeable adults

(continued)

(continued)

Program	Focus	Finding	Key Components
Youth Corps (CA, FL, MA, MD, NJ, NY, WA, WI)	Instill sense of work ethic and public service among low-income, out-of-school youths through paid community service projects	Relative to control group: ■ More likely to have paid work ■ Worked more hours ■ Lower arrest rates ■ Good and valued services provided to the community	■ Full-time paid work above the minimum wage ■ Addressed community needs
Youth as Resources (IN)	Empower youths to prevent crime and build safe and caring communities	■ Improved youth attitude ■ Developed personal and work-related skills ■ Provided needed services to communities	■ Youths as board members and decision makers ■ Provision of small grants for projects designed and implemented by youth ■ A system to recognize and celebrate positive youth contributions ■ Site-based director with broad role ■ Caring knowledgeable adults
Youth River Watch (Austin, TX)	Dropout prevention program with a work based component	Relative to comparison group: ■ Higher GPAs ■ Lower dropout rate ■ Higher passing rate	■ Project-based learning ■ Community service with clearly identifiable results ■ Peer mentoring ■ Community involvement ■ Enrichment activities

Glossary

The number following the definition refers to the chapter(s) in which the term is defined.

adjudicated—having been the subject of completed criminal or juvenile proceedings and having been cleared or declared a delinquent, status offender or dependent. (1, 10)

adult supremacy—subordination of children to the absolute and arbitrary authority of parents and, in many instances, teachers. (4)

aftercare—supervision given children and youths for a limited time after they are released from confinement but are still under the control of the institution or of the juvenile court. (11)

anomie—normlessness. (3)

anomie theory—states that the motivations for crime do not result simply from the flaws, failures or free choices of individuals. The American Dream contributes to crime directly by encouraging people to use illegal means to achieve culturally approved goals. (3)

anticipated strain—an individual's expectation that current stresses will continue into the future or that new stresses will be experienced. (5)

antisocial personality disorder—exists in persons at least age 18 who show evidence of a conduct disorder before age 15 as well as a pattern of irresponsible and antisocial behavior since the age of 15. (4)

attention deficit hyperactivity disorder (ADHD)—a common childhood disruptive behavior disorder characterized by heightened motor activity, short attention span, distractibility, impulsiveness and lack of self-control. (4)

beyond a reasonable doubt—degree of proof required for guilt in a juvenile court proceeding. It is less than absolute certainty, but more than high probability. If there is doubt based on reason, the accused is entitled to the benefit of that doubt by acquittal. (8)

bifurcated hearings—the delinquent act charged is held separately from the hearing to determine the disposition. (10)

binge drinking—the consumption of large quantities of alcohol within a short period of time. A common amount used in the United States is five drinks for adult males and four drinks for adult females within a two- to three-hour time span. (6)

biotic balance—an ecological term describing what occurs when the relations between the different species of plants and their necessary conditions for survival (e.g., climate, soil condition) maintain an equilibrium. All the organisms are thus able to survive and prosper. (2)

blended sentence—combines both a juvenile sentence and an adult sentence. In some states if youths comply with the terms of the juvenile sentence—which includes longer and more intensive supervision than a typical juvenile sanction—they will be released without the stain of an adult criminal record. If youths fail to comply with the terms of the juvenile sentence, they will receive the sentence that would have been incurred in criminal court. (10)

boot camp—a correctional facility that stresses military discipline, physical fitness, strict obedience to orders, and education and vocational training; designed for young, nonviolent, first-time offenders. Also called *shock incarceration*. (11)

Bridewell—the first correctional institution, which confined both children and adults considered to be idle and disorderly. (2)

certification—a procedure whereby a juvenile court waives jurisdiction and transfers the case to the adult criminal court. Also called a *waiver*. (10)

child savers—groups who promoted the rights of minors in the late 1800s and helped create a separate juvenile court. Their motives have been questioned by modern writers, who see their efforts as a form of social and class control. (2)

chronic juvenile offender—a youth who has a record of five or more separate charges of delinquency, regardless of the gravity of the offenses. (6)

civil injunction—a legal tool for addressing the hold that entrenched gangs have on urban neighborhoods; a spatially based, neighborhood-level intervention intended to disrupt a gang's routine activities. (7)

civil law—all law that is not criminal, including torts (personal wrongs), contract law, property law, maritime law and commercial law. The juvenile court functions under a blend of civil and criminal law. (10)

classical view of criminality—holds that delinquents are responsible for their own behavior, as individuals with free will. (3)

coercive intervention—out-of-home placement, detainment or mandated therapy or counseling. (10)

collective maltreatment—attitudes held as a group in a society that impede the psychological and physical development of children. (5)

common law—law of custom and usage. (2)

comorbidity—multiple disorders (when two or more diagnoses occur together in the same individual). (9)

competent—properly qualified, adequate. (10)

concordance—a high degree of similarity, as in heredity studies where identical twins were more likely to both have criminal records than were fraternal twins. (3)

concurrent jurisdiction—something happens at the same time, or a case may be heard in either juvenile or adult court. (10)

conditional threat—warns that a violent act will occur unless certain demands are met; for example, "If you don't pay me $100,000, I will blow up this school." (6)

conduct disorder—a behavioral disorder characterized by prolonged antisocial behavior ranging from truancy to fistfights. (4)

conflict theory—suggests that laws are established to keep the dominant class in power. (3)

consensus theory—contends that individuals within a society agree on basic values, on what is inherently right and wrong. (3)

contagion—a way to explain the spread of violence, equating it with the spread of infectious diseases. (6)

corporal punishment—inflicting bodily harm. (2)

corrective prevention—a strategy that focuses on eliminating conditions that lead to or cause criminal behavior. Also called *primary prevention*. (12)

crew—a group of taggers. (7)

criminogenic need principle—certain needs are directly linked to crime; criminogenic needs constitute

dynamic risk factors or attributes that, when changed, influence the probability of recidivism. (11)

critical theory—combines the classical free will and positivist determinism views of crime, suggesting that humans are both self-determined and society-determined; assumes humans create the institutions and structures that ultimately dominate and constrain them; includes labeling theory, conflict theory and radical theory. (3)

cruel and unusual punishment—physical punishment or punishment far in excess of that given to a person under similar circumstances and, therefore, banned by the Eighth Amendment. (11)

dark figure of crime—the unknown true number of crimes, which may be substantially greater than official data indicate. (1)

decertification—the court may transfer a case from criminal court back to juvenile court. Also known as *reverse certification*. (10)

decriminalization—legislation to make status offenses noncriminal acts. (1)

deep end strategy—targets youths with the highest likelihood of continuing their delinquent careers without comprehensive interventions. (9)

delinquent—a youth who commits an act that would be a crime were it to be committed by an adult. The term is intended to avoid stigmatizing youth as criminals. (1)

denominator approach—placing the focus of efforts on the whole population of youths, not just on the delinquents. (12)

dependency—the legal status of children over whom a juvenile court has assumed jurisdiction because the court has found their care to fall short of legal standards of proper care by parents, guardians or custodians. (5)

deserts—punishment as a kind of justified revenge; the offending individual gets what is coming. (2)

detention—temporary care of a child alleged to be delinquent who is physically restricted pending court disposition, transfer to another jurisdiction or execution of a court order. (8)

detention hearing—a hearing in juvenile court to determine whether a child held in custody shall remain in custody for the best interests of the child and the public. (9)

determinism—a philosophy that maintains that human behavior is the product of a multitude of environmental and cultural influences. (3)

deterrence—punishment as a means to prevent future lawbreaking. (2, 3, 11)

developmental pathways—development of disruptive and delinquent behavior in youth that typically occurs in an orderly, progressive manner. (4)

deviance—behavior that departs from the social norm. (6)

differential association theory—states that a person becomes delinquent because of an excess of definitions favorable to violation of law over definitions unfavorable to violation of law. (2)

direct threat—a threat that identifies a specific act against a specific target and is delivered in a straightforward manner, clearly and explicitly; for example, "I am going to put a bomb in a locker." (8)

discrimination—refers to unfair, differential treatment of a particular group of youths, for example, Hispanics. (1)

disparity—refers to a difference, but not necessarily involving discrimination. (1)

distributive justice—providing an equal share of what is valued in a society to each member of that society. This includes power, prestige and possessions. Also called *social justice.* (1)

diversion—the official halting of formal juvenile proceedings against an alleged offender and the referral of the juvenile to a treatment or care program by a private or public service agency. (1, 9)

double jeopardy—being tried for the same offense twice. (2)

due process—a difficult-to-define term; the due process clause of the U.S. Constitution requires that no person shall be deprived of life, liberty or property without due process of law, *or* carrying out the course of formal legal proceedings regularly and in accordance with established rules and principles, as provided for by the Fourteenth Amendment, with the result that no person is deprived of life, liberty or property unjustly. (2)

dynamic risk factors—individual, social or situational factors that often change; for example, associates, attitudes and stress levels. Compare *static risk factors.* (9)

EBD—emotionally/behaviorally disturbed. Usually emotionally/behaviorally disturbed youths have one or more of the following behavior patterns: severely aggressive or impulsive behavior; severely withdrawn or anxious behaviors, pervasive unhappiness, depression or wide mood swings; or severely disordered thought processes that show up in unusual behavior patterns, atypical communication styles and distorted interpersonal relationships. Such children may have limited coping skills and may be easily traumatized. (4)

ecological model—a sociological model used to compare the growth of a city and its attendant crime problems to growth in nature. (3)

expressive violence—an acting out of extreme hostility. Compare *instrumental violence.* (6)

extrafamilial sexual abuse—sexual abuse of a child by a friend or stranger, a non-family member. (5)

family courts—courts with broad jurisdiction over family matters, such as neglect, delinquency, paternity, support and noncriminal matters and behavior. (9)

fetal alcohol syndrome (FAS)—a condition in which children exposed to excessive amounts of alcohol while in the womb may exhibit impulsivity and poor communication skills, be unable to predict consequences or use appropriate judgment in daily life; the leading cause of mental retardation in the Western world. (4)

funnel effect—the phenomenon that, at each point in the juvenile justice system, fewer and fewer youths pass through. (1)

gang—a group of youths who form an allegiance for a common purpose and engage in unlawful or criminal activity; any group gathered together on a continuing basis to commit antisocial behavior. (7)

gateway drugs—tobacco, alcohol and marijuana. (12)

graffiti—wall writing, indoors or outdoors. Outdoors it is sometimes referred to as the "newspaper of the street." (7)

guardian ad litem (GAL)—an individual appointed by the court to protect the best interests of a child or an incompetent during the juvenile justice process. In some states this can only be an attorney. The appointed individual is a surrogate parent, guardian or custodian and can be replaced in the best interests of the child at any point in a juvenile proceeding. (10)

horizontal prosecution—an organizational structure strategy whereby individual assistant prosecutors or a small group of assistant prosecutors are responsible for certain phases of the adjudication of criminal complaints. Compare *vertical prosecution.* (7)

incapacitation—making incapable by incarcerating. (3)

Index crimes—Part I and Part II crimes of the Uniform Crime Reports (UCR), including homicide, nonnegligent manslaughter, forcible rape, robbery, aggravated assault, burglary, larceny, arson and motor vehicle theft. (1)

indirect threat—a threat that is vague and ambiguous; for example, "If I wanted to, I could blow up this school." (8)

individual abuse—physical or emotional abuse by parents or others as individuals. (5)

institutional maltreatment—the approved use of force and violence against children in the schools and in the denial of children's due process rights in institutions. (5)

instrumental violence—violence used for some type of gain, such as robbery. Compare *expressive violence*. (6)

intake—the point in the juvenile justice process that reviews referrals to the juvenile court and decides the action to be taken based on the best interests of the child and the public good. (9)

intensive supervision—a highly structured form of observation provided by probation. (11)

intermediate sanctions probation (ISB)—holds youths accountable for their actions through more restrictive and intensive interventions short of secure care. (11)

intrafamilial sexual abuse—sexual abuse of a child by a parent or other family member. (5)

jurisdiction—the authority of courts and judicial officers to decide a case. (10)

just deserts—see *deserts*. (2)

justice model—the judicial process wherein young people who come into conflict with the law are held responsible and accountable for their behavior. (2, 10)

juvenile court—a court having jurisdiction over individuals defined as juveniles and alleged to be delinquents, status offenders, dependents or in need of decisions by the court regarding their health, safety or welfare. (10)

juvenile justice—a system that provides a legal setting in which youths can account for their wrongs or receive official protection. (1)

labeling theory—views society as creating deviance through a system of social control agencies that designate certain people as deviants. This stigmatizes people; they are made to feel unwanted in the normal social order. Eventually they begin to believe the label is accurate and begin to act to fit the label. (3)

lex talionis—a legal principle establishing the concept of retaliation, that is, an eye for an eye. (2)

lockdown—high school students are detained in classrooms while police and dogs scour the campus, searching for contraband or any danger to a safe educational environment. (8)

maltreatment—includes neglect, medical neglect, physical abuse, sexual abuse and psychological abuse. (5)

maximalist alarmist perspective—the view that the time has come to reject the reluctance of earlier generations to face the facts and to recognize the enormity of the developing crisis. Parents are abusing and neglecting their children in record numbers, and exploitive

adolescents, pedophiles (child molesters) and other abusers are preying on youngsters with impunity. (5)

mechanical prevention—prevention efforts directed toward "target hardening" to make it difficult or impossible to commit particular offenses. (12)

medical model—the view that offenders are victims of their environment and thus are curable. (2)

meta-analysis—provides a quantitative review of a body of literature—now the favored approach by most criminal justice researchers. (9)

minimalist skeptical perspective—the view that huge numbers of honestly mistaken and maliciously false allegations are mixed in with true disclosures, making the problem seem worse than it really is and fueling the impression that it is spiraling out of control. (5)

minors—persons under the age of legal consent. (2)

moniker—a name adopted by a gang member to be used in place of his or her given name. (7)

natural law—the rules of conduct that are the same everywhere because they are basic to human behavior. (3)

neglect—a child is adjudged to be neglected if the child is abandoned; without proper care; without education or health care because of the refusal of a parent, guardian or custodian to provide them; or in need of supervision as a result of the neglect. (5)

net widening—diverting youths to other programs and agencies rather than away from the system. (2, 9)

Norman Rockwell family—a working father, a housewife mother and two children of school age (6 percent of U.S. households in the 1990s). (4)

numerator approach—the view that the focus of prevention efforts should be on those youths who are at greatest risk. (12)

ombuds—a person whose role is to improve conditions of confinement for juveniles and protect the rights of youths in custody; responsibilities include monitoring conditions, servicing delivery systems, investigating complaints, reporting findings, proposing changes, advocating for improvements, accessing appropriate care and helping to expose and reduce unlawful deficiencies in juvenile detention and correctional facilities. (11)

one-pot approach—lumps children and youths who are abused and neglected, those who commit minor offenses and those who commit vicious, violent crimes into the same judicial "pot." (1)

osteogenesis imperfecta (OI)—a condition characterized by bones that break easily and can be mistaken for child abuse. (5)

parens patriae—literally "parent of the country." The legal provision through which the state may assume ultimate parental responsibility for the custody, care and protection of children within its jurisdiction. The right of the government to take care of minors and others who cannot legally take care of themselves. (1)

parental efficacy—examines how parental support and control are interrelated. (4)

parole—supervised early release from institutionalization. (11)

particular justice—that which is fair and equal. (1)

petition—the formal process for bringing a matter before the juvenile court; a document alleging that a juvenile is a delinquent, status offender or dependent, and asking the court to assume jurisdiction; the same as a formal complaint in the adult criminal process. (9)

petitioned—formally charged. (1)

polydrug use—tobacco, alcohol and marijuana. (12)

poor laws—established the appointment of overseers to indenture poor and neglected children into servitude. (2)

positivist view of criminality—the belief that delinquents are victims of society. (3)

preventive detention—the confinement of youths who might pose a danger to themselves or to others or who might not appear at their trial. (2)

primary deviance—the original act defined as deviant by others. (3)

primary prevention—seeks to change conditions that cause crime. Also called *corrective prevention*. (12)

probation—a sentence that entails the release of an individual into the community under the supervision of the court, subject to certain conditions for a specific time. Only the court can provide probation. (11)

protective factors—elements that reduce the impact of negative risk factors by providing positive ways for a person to respond to such risks. (4, 12)

psychopath—virtually lacking in conscience; does not know right from wrong. (4)

public defender—a lawyer who works for the defense of indigent offenders and is reimbursed for services by a public agency. (9)

pulling levers—a strategy involving arresting targeted gang members for the slightest infraction, even jaywalking. (8)

punitive prevention—relies on the threat of punishment to forestall criminal acts. (12)

radial concept—the view that growth and development do not occur in isolation but instead involve a complex interaction of family, school and community, with the family being the first and most vital influence. As children grow the school becomes a more important influence, and as youths approach adolescence, the influence of parents and teachers becomes less and that of peers more influential. All of this occurs within the broader community in which children live. (4)

radical theory—the belief that crime is a product of the political economy that, in capitalist societies, encourages an individualistic competition among and between wealthy people and poor people (the intra- and inter-class struggle) and the practice of taking advantage of other people (exploitation). (3)

Rave—an all-night party with loud techno music, dancing, drinking and doing drugs. (6)

recidivism—repetition of criminal behavior; habitual criminality. (12)

re-entry—the preferred term to describe transitioning youthful offenders from secure custody back into the community. (11)

representing—a manner of dressing that uses an imaginary line drawn vertically through the body and shows allegiance or opposition. (7)

responsivity principle—the delivery of treatment programs in a manner consistent with the offender's ability and learning style. (11)

restorative justice—the view that justice involves not two, but four parties: offender and victim, government and community—all are injured by the crime. (1)

retaliation—personal revenge; the accepted way to deal with members of the tribe who break the rules. (2)

retributive justice—justice served by some sort of punishment for wrongdoing (*lex talionis*). (1)

reverse certification—when the criminal court has exclusive jurisdiction, the transfer of a case to the juvenile court. Also known as *decertification*. (10)

risk factors—elements existing within the community, family, school and the individual that increase the probability a young person will exhibit certain adolescent problem behaviors, including violence. (4, 12)

risk principle—embodies the assumption that criminal behavior can be predicted for individual offenders on the basis of certain factors. (11)

routine activity theory—identifies three elements as critical contributors to crime: (1) a motivated offender, (2) a suitable target and (3) lack of a capable guardian. Set forth by Felson in 1979. (3)

runaway—a youth who commits the status offense of leaving the custody and home of parents, guardians or custodians without permission and fails to return within a reasonable time. (5)

school resource officer (SRO)—a law enforcement officer assigned by the employing police department to a school. (8)

secondary deviance—an act that results because society has labeled the offender a deviant. (3)

secondary prevention—focuses on changing the behavior of juveniles likely to become delinquent. Includes *punitive prevention*. (12)

serious child delinquent—youth between the ages of 7 and 12 who has committed one or more acts of homicide, aggravated assault, robbery, rape or serious arson. (6)

serious juvenile offender—a juvenile who has been convicted of a Part I offense as defined by the FBI Uniform Crime Reports, excluding auto theft or distribution of a controlled dangerous substance, and who was between 14 and 17 years of age at the time the offense was committed. (6)

shock incarceration—a correctional facility stressing military discipline, physical fitness, strict obedience to orders and education and vocational training; designed for young, nonviolent, first-time offenders. Also called *boot camp*. (11)

social contract—a philosophy that entails free, independent individuals agreeing to form a community and to give up a portion of their individual freedom to benefit the group's security. (3)

social disorganization theory—states that urban areas produce delinquency directly by weakening community controls and generating a subculture of delinquency passed on from one generation to the next. (3)

social ecology theory—states that ecological conditions predict delinquency and that gang membership is a normal response to social conditions. (3)

social justice—providing an equal share of what is valued in a society to each member of that society, including power, prestige and status. Also called *distributive justice*. (1)

socialized delinquency—youthful behavior that violates the expectations of society but conforms to the expectations of other youths. (7)

static risk factors—historical (e.g., early onset of violence) or dispositional factors that are unlikely to change over time. Compare *dynamic risk factors*. (9)

station adjustment—occurs when a juvenile offender is handled by the police within the department and released. (8)

status offense—an offense by a juvenile that would not be a crime if committed by an adult, for example, truancy, running away, curfew violation, incorrigibility or endangering health and morals. (1)

stereotypical kidnapping—occurs when a stranger or slight acquaintance perpetrates a nonfamily abduction in which the child is detained overnight, transported at least 50 miles, held for ransom, abducted with intent to keep the child permanently or killed (Sedlak et al., 2002, p.4). (5)

strain theory—see *anomie theory*. (3)

street gang—a group of individuals who meet over time, have identifiable leadership, claim control over a specific territory in the community and engage in criminal behavior. (7)

street justice—a decision by police to deal with a status offense in their own way, usually by ignoring it. (8)

tagging—a form of visual vandalism whose dominant impression includes words, as compared to graffiti, which leaves only a hint of words; often added to existing graffiti. (7)

take into custody—the physical apprehension by a police action of a child engaged in delinquency. (8)

temporary custody without hearing—usually for 48 hours. (8)

tertiary prevention—the third level of prevention, aimed at preventing recidivism; focuses on preventing further delinquent acts by youths already identified as delinquents. (12)

therapeutic intervention—recommendation of an appropriate treatment program. (10)

thrownaway—a child whose family has kicked him or her out. (5)

truancy—loosely defined as habitual unexcused absence from school, considered a status offense because, while compulsory attendance laws vary from state to state, every state requires children between certain ages to be in school during the academic year absent a valid excuse. (4)

turf—the area claimed by a gang. (7)

Uniform Crime Reports (UCR)—the FBI's annual statistical summary titled *Crime in the United States*. (1)

universal justice—that which is lawful. (1)

veiled threat—strongly implies but does not explicitly threaten violence; for example, "We would be better off if this school were destroyed." (8)

venue—the geographic location of a trial, established by constitutional or statutory provisions. (10)

vertical prosecution—one assistant prosecutor or small group of assistant prosecutors handling one criminal complaint from start to finish through the entire court process. Compare *horizontal prosecution.* (7)

vicarious strain—stress experienced by others around an individual experiencing stress. (5)

violent juvenile offender—a youth who has been convicted of a violent Part I offense, one against a person rather than property, and who has a prior adjudication of such an offense; a youth convicted of murder. (6)

waiver—a procedure whereby juvenile court waives jurisdiction and transfers the case to the adult criminal court. Also called *certification.* (10)

welfare model—the approach traditionally used by juvenile courts following its underlying *parens patriae* philosophy focusing on the "best interests of the child." (10)

window of opportunity—a time when treatment is especially needed (in crimes) or likely to make a difference (during transition periods). (8)

youth gang—a self-formed association of youths distinguished from other types of youth groups by their routine participation in illegal activities. (7)

youthful offenders—persons adjudicated in a criminal court who may be above the statutory age limit for juveniles but below a specified upper age limit for special correctional commitment. (2)

Index